Lecture Notes in Computer Science 11496

Commenced Publication in 1973
Founding and Former Series Editors:
Gerhard Goos, Juris Hartmanis, and Jan van Leeuwen

Maxim Bakaev · Flavius Frasincar ·
In-Young Ko (Eds.)

Web Engineering

19th International Conference, ICWE 2019
Daejeon, South Korea, June 11–14, 2019
Proceedings

 Springer

Editors
Maxim Bakaev (iD)
Novosibirsk State Technical University
Novosibirsk, Russia

Flavius Frasincar (iD)
Erasmus University Rotterdam
Rotterdam, The Netherlands

In-Young Ko (iD)
Korea Advanced Institute of Science
and Technology
Daejeon, Korea (Republic of)

ISSN 0302-9743   ISSN 1611-3349 (electronic)
Lecture Notes in Computer Science
ISBN 978-3-030-19273-0   ISBN 978-3-030-19274-7 (eBook)
https://doi.org/10.1007/978-3-030-19274-7

LNCS Sublibrary: SL3 – Information Systems and Applications, incl. Internet/Web, and HCI

This Springer imprint is published by the registered company Springer Nature Switzerland AG
The registered company address is: Gewerbestrasse 11, 6330 Cham, Switzerland

Foreword

Today we are experiencing the Fourth Industrial Revolution, i.e., the fourth major industrial period since the initial Industrial Revolution from the 18th century. The Web is an important player in this revolution as it contributes to the blurring of the frontier between the physical and digital world, providing connectivity not only to computers but also to physical devices and everyday objects. Web applications make increasing use of Artificial Intelligence (AI) algorithms to improve their efficiency and effectiveness, as well as to provide new functionality that was previously unimaginable, in an increasingly complex world. AI is successfully used for the design, development, and maintenance of Web applications, decreasing the reliance on the human factor for these processes. Web Engineering (WE) aims to address these new challenges by providing the next generation of Web methodologies, techniques, and tools.

This volume contains the full research papers, short research papers, posters, demonstrations, PhD symposium papers, tutorials, and extended abstracts for the keynotes of the 19th International Conference on Web Engineering (ICWE 2019), held during June 11–14, 2019 in Daejeon, South Korea.

ICWE is the flagship conference for the WE community. Previous editions of ICWE took place at Cáceres, Spain (2018), Rome, Italy (2017), Lugano, Switzerland (2016), Rotterdam, The Netherlands (2015), Toulouse, France (2014), Aalborg, Denmark (2013), Berlin, Germany (2012), Paphos, Cyprus (2011), Vienna, Austria (2010), San Sebastian, Spain (2009), Yorktown Heights, NY, USA (2008), Como, Italy (2007), Palo Alto, CA, USA (2006), Sydney, Australia (2005), Munich, Germany (2004), Oviedo, Spain (2003), Santa Fe, Argentina (2002), and Cáceres, Spain (2001). The 2019 edition of ICWE was centered on the theme of "AI and the Web," hereby highlighting the impact that AI has on WE research today.

ICWE 2019 had nine research themes, namely, Web Mining and Knowledge Extraction, Web Big Data and Web Data Analytics, Social Web Applications and Crowdsourcing, Web User Interfaces, Web Security and Privacy, Web Programming, Web Services and Computing, Semantic Web and Linked Open Data Applications, and Web Application Modeling and Engineering.

The ICWE 2019 edition received 106 submissions, out of which the Program Committee selected 26 full research papers (24% acceptance rate) and nine short research papers (33% acceptance rate). Additionally, the Program Committee accepted two demonstrations, four posters, and four contributions to the PhD symposium. Also accepted were five tutorials lecturing on the advanced topics of (1) Exploiting Side Information for Recommendation, (2) Deep Learning-Based Sequential Recommender Systems: Concepts, Algorithms, and Evaluations, (3) Architectural Styles for the Development of WoT Applications, (4) Powerful Data Analysis and Composition with the UNIX Shell, and (5) Non-monotonic Reasoning on the Web, as well as the following four workshops: (1) Second International Workshop on Maturity of Web Engineering Practices (MATWEP 2019), (2) Third International Joint Workshop on

Engineering the Web of Things (EnWoT 2019) and Liquid Multi-Device Software (LMDS 2019), (3) 5th International Workshop on Knowledge Discovery on the Web (KDWEB 2019), and (4) International Workshop on Data Science and Knowledge Graph (DSKG 2019).

The excellent program would not have been possible without the support of the many people who helped with the successful organization of this event. We would like to thank all the chairs of the tutorials, demonstrations and posters, workshops, PhD symposium, publicity, as well as the local chairs for their dedication and hard work. Our thanks also goes to Bing Liu (University of Illinois at Chicago), Sunghun Kim (NAVER Corp./Hong Kong University of Science and Technology), and Antti Oulasvirta (Aalto University), who accepted to be our keynote speakers. Florian Daniel and Martin Gaedke deserve special thanks for their continuous advice and encouragement in setting up ICWE 2019 in Daejeon. We would like to also thank Michael Krug and Martin Gaedke for hosting the conference website. We are grateful to Springer for publishing this volume. In addition, we thank the reviewers for their thorough work, which allowed us to select the best papers to be presented at ICWE 2019. Last, but not least, we would like to thank the authors who submitted their work to ICWE 2019 and all the participants who contributed to the success of this event.

June 2019

Maxim Bakaev
Flavius Frasincar
In-Young Ko

Organization

Technical Committee

General Chair

In-Young Ko — Korea Advanced Institute of Science and Technology, South Korea

Program Committee Chairs

Maxim Bakaev — Novosibirsk State Technical University, Russia
Flavius Frasincar — Erasmus University Rotterdam, The Netherlands

Tutorial Chairs

Alessandro Bozzon — Delft University of Technology, The Netherlands
Tommaso Di Noia — Polytechnic University of Bari, Italy
Jie Zhang — Nanyang Technological University, Singapore

Workshop Chairs

Marco Brambilla — Politecnico di Milano, Italy
Cinzia Cappiello — Politecnico di Milano, Italy
Siew Hock Ow — University of Malaya, Malaysia

Demonstration and Poster Chairs

Oscar Diaz — University of the Basque Country, Spain
Irene Garrigos — University of Alicante, Spain
Angel Jimenez-Molina — University of Chile, Chile

PhD Symposium Chairs

Cesare Pautasso — University of Lugano, Switzerland
Abhishek Srivastava — Indian Institute of Technology Indore, India
Marco Winckler — Université Nice Sophia Antipolis, France

Publicity Chairs

Haklae Kim — Chung-Ang University, South Korea
Kecheng Liu — University of Reading, UK
Tomoya Noro — Fujitsu Laboratories, Japan
Alice Oh — Korea Advanced Institute of Science and Technology, South Korea

Local Arrangements Chairs

Soo-Kyung Kim   Hanbat National University, South Korea
Young-Woo Kwon   Kyungpook National University, South Korea
Seongwook Youn   Korea National University of Transportation, South
                           Korea

Steering Committee Liaisons

Florian Daniel   Politecnico di Milano, Italy
Martin Gaedke   Chemnitz University of Technology, Germany

Program Committee

Research Program Committee

Silvia Abrahão   Universitat Politècnica de València, Spain
Witold Abramowicz   Poznan University of Economics, Poland
Ioannis Anagnostopoulos   University of Thessaly, Greece
Maurício Aniche   Delft University of Technology, The Netherlands
Myriam Arrue   University of the Basque Country, Spain
Sören Auer   TIB Leibniz Information Center Science
                           and Technology and University of Hannover,
                           Germany
Marcos Baez   University of Trento, Italy
Luciano Baresi   Politecnico di Milano, Italy
Hubert Baumeister   Technical University of Denmark, Denmark
Boualem Benatallah   The University of New South Wales, Australia
Devis Bianchini   University of Brescia, Italy
Maria Bielikova   Slovak University of Technology in Bratislava,
                           Slovakia
Matthias Book   University of Iceland, Iceland
Gabriela Bosetti   Universidad Nacional de La Plata, Argentina
Alessandro Bozzon   Delft University of Technology, The Netherlands
Giorgio Brajnik   University of Udine, Italy
Marco Brambilla   Politecnico di Milano, Italy
Christoph Bussler   Google, USA
Jordi Cabot   Open University of Catalonia, Spain
Carlos Canal   University of Málaga, Spain
Cinzia Cappiello   Politecnico di Milano, Italy
Sven Casteleyn   Universitat Jaume I de Castelló, Spain
Richard Chbeir   University of Pau and Pays de l'Adour, France
Dickson K. W. Chiu   The University of Hong Kong, SAR China
Philipp Cimiano   Bielefeld University, Germany
Pieter Colpaert   Ghent University, Belgium
Oscar Corcho   Universidad Politécnica de Madrid, Spain
Alexandra Cristea   Durham University, UK

Research Additional Reviewers

Ali Aydin
Pablo Becker
Robert Bill
Maxime Buron
Karam Bou Chaaya
Juri Di Rocco
Shirin Feiz Disfani
Genet Asefa Gesese
Israel Gonzalez-Carrasco
Cesar Gonzalez-Mora
Lara Kallab
David Klein

Simon Koch
Hae-Na Lee
Jose Luis Lopez Cuadrado
Elio Mansour
Robert Moro
Marius Musch
Alvaro E. Prieto
Karol Rástočný
Jakub Ševcech
Rekha Singal
Tabea Tietz
Rima Türker

Demonstrations and Posters Program Committee

Jongmoon Baik	Korea Advanced Institute of Science and Technology, South Korea
Devis Bianchini	University of Brescia, Italy
Marco Brambilla	Politecnico di Milano, Italy
Carlos Canal	University of Málaga, Spain
Javier Luis Canovas	Universitat Oberta de Catalunya, Spain
Cinzia Cappiello	Politecnico di Milano, Italy
Sven Casteleyn	Universitat Jaume I de Castelló, Spain
Nathalie Moreno	University of Málaga, Spain
Gustavo Rossi	Universidad Nacional de La Plata, Argentina
Wieland Schwinger	Johannes Kepler University Linz, Austria
Jocelyn Simmonds	University of Chile, Chile
Manuel Wimmer	Vienna University of Technology, Austria
Marco Winckler	Université Nice Sophia Antipolis, France

PhD Symposium Program Committee

Tanveer Ahmed	Bennett University, India
Marco Brambilla	Politecnico di Milano, Italy
Florian Daniel	Politecnico di Milano, Italy
Tommaso Di Noia	Politecnico di Bari, Italy
Swapna Gokhale	University of Connecticut, USA
Geert-Jan Houben	Delft University of Technology, The Netherlands
Ralf Klamma	RWTH Aachen University, Germany
Lionel Medini	Université Claude Bernard Lyon 1, France
Tommi Mikkonnen	University of Helsinki, Finland
Pankesh Patel	Fraunhofer, USA
Gustavo Rossi	Universidad Nacional de La Plata, Argentina
Eleni Stroulia	University of Alberta, Canada
Manuel Wimmer	Vienna University of Technology, Austria

Sponsors

Keynotes

Lifelong Learning and Application to Sentiment Analysis

Bing Liu

Department of Computer Science, University of Illinois at Chicago,
Chicago, USA
liub@uic.edu

Abstract. The classic machine learning (ML) paradigm works under the closed-world assumption. Given a dataset, a ML algorithm is executed on the data to produce a model. The algorithm does not consider any other information in model training and the trained model cannot handle any unexpected situations in testing or applications. Although this paradigm has been very successful, it requires a lot of training data, and is only suitable for well-defined, static and narrow domains. In contrast, we humans learn quite differently. We always learn with the help of our prior knowledge. We learn continuously, accumulate the knowledge learned in the past, and use it to help future learning and problem solving. When faced with an unfamiliar situation in an open environment, we adapt our knowledge to deal with the situation and learn from it. Lifelong learning aims to achieve this capability. In this talk, I will introduce lifelong learning and discuss some of its applications in sentiment analysis and beyond.

Keywords: Lifelong machine learning · Sentiment analysis · Opinion mining

1 Introduction

The current dominant machine learning (ML) paradigm is to run an ML algorithm on a given dataset to generate a model. The model is then applied in a real-life performance task. We call this paradigm *isolated learning* [2] because it does not consider any previously learned knowledge. The problem with isolated learning is that it does not retain and accumulate knowledge learned in the past and use it in future learning. This is in contrast to our human learning. We humans never learn in isolation or from scratch. We always retain the knowledge learned in the past and use it to help future learning and problem solving. Without the ability to accumulate and use the past knowledge, an ML algorithm typically needs a large number of training examples in order to learn effectively. The learning environments are typically static and closed [3]. For supervised learning, labeling of training data is often done manually, which is very labor-intensive and time-consuming. Since the world is too complex with too many possible tasks, it is almost impossible to label a large number of examples for every possible task for an ML algorithm to learn. To make matters worse, everything around us also changes constantly, and the labeling thus needs to be done continually, which is a daunting task for humans.

In contrast, we humans learn quite differently. We accumulate and maintain the knowledge learned from previous tasks and use it seamlessly in learning new tasks and solving new problems. That is why whenever we encounter a new situation or problem, we may notice that many aspects of it are not really new because we have seen them in the past in some other contexts. When faced with a new problem or a new environment, we can adapt our past knowledge to deal with the new situation and also learn from it [2]. Over time we learn more and more, and become more and more knowledgeable and more and more effective at learning. *Lifelong machine learning* or simply *lifelong learning* (LL) aims to imitate this human learning process and capability [2, 6]. This type of learning is natural because things around us are closely related and interconnected. Knowledge learned about some subjects can help us understand and learn some other subjects. For example, we humans do not need 1,000 positive online reviews and 1,000 negative online reviews of movies as an ML algorithm needs in order to build an accurate classifier to classify positive and negative reviews about a movie. In fact, for this task, without a single training example, we can already perform the classification task. This is because we have accumulated so much knowledge in the past about the language expressions that people use to praise or to criticize things, although none of those praises or criticisms may be in the form of online reviews. Interestingly, if we do not have such past knowledge, we humans are probably unable to manually build a good classifier even with 1,000 positive reviews and 1,000 negative training reviews without spending an enormous amount of time. For example, if you have no knowledge of Arabic and someone gives you 2,000 labeled training reviews in Arabic and asks you to build a classifier manually, most probably you will not be able to do it without using a translator [2].

My original motivation for studying LL stemmed from my extensive application experience in sentiment analysis (SA) [4, 5] in a start-up company. After working on many projects for clients, I realized that there is a significant amount of sharing of knowledge for both sentiment classification and sentiment target (product aspects or features) extraction across domains (different types of products). As I see reviews of more and more products, new things get fewer and fewer. This is exactly a scenario for lifelong learning. In this talk, I will introduce lifelong learning and discuss some applications in sentiment analysis and beyond [1, 2, 5].

References

1. Chen, Z., Liu, B.: Topic modeling using topics from many domains, lifelong learning and big data. In: Proceedings of the 31st International Conference on Machine Learning (ICML), vol. 32, pp. 703–711. JMLR.org (2014)
2. Chen, Z., Liu, B.: Lifelong Machine Learning. Morgan & Claypool Publishers (2016, 1st edn.) and (2018, 2nd edn.)
3. Fei, G., Liu, B.: Breaking the closed world assumption in text classification. In: Proceedings of NAACL-HLT, pp. 506–514. ACL (2016)
4. Hu, M., Liu, B.: Mining and summarizing customer reviews. In: Proceedings of SIGKDD Conference on Knowledge Discovery and Data Mining (KDD), pp. 168–177. ACM (2004)

5. Liu, B.: Sentiment Analysis and Opinion Mining. Morgan and Claypool Publishers (2012)
6. Thrun, S.: Lifelong learning algorithms. In: Thrun, S., Pratt, L. (eds.) Learning to Learn. Kluwer Academic Publishers (1998)

Managing Deep Learning Debt at Naver/LINE

Sunghun Kim

Naver Corp., HKUST
hunkim@cse.ust.hk

Abstract. Deep learning has shown amazing results in both academic and industry, yielding many practical services and products such as machine translation, personal assistant, image retrieval, video recommendation and photo enhancement. However, in industry, it is common to observe legacy products with deep learning debt—the tremendous cost in converting traditional machine learning systems to deep learning. In order to utilize deep learning and boost the performance of existing products, it is necessary to examine our systems and repay any deep learning dept. This talk will describe my experience at Naver/LINE on managing deep learning dept, including challenges and their potential solutions.

Keywords: Deep learning · Technical debt

1 Introduction

Deep learning has shown amazing results in many areas including image classification [10], object detection [12], pose estimation, machine translation [4], chatbots [5], sentiment analysis, recommendation [11] and speech recognition [9]. It even generates computer programs using abstract syntax trees (AST) [13] and natural language [6–8].

These amazing achievements are not limited in academia but are well transformed into industry and yield many practical products such as machine translation, personal assistant, image retrieval, video recommendation and photo enhancement [1]. They significantly improve existing services and user experience.

In industry, it is common to observe legacy products due to technical debt—"a concept in software development that reflects the implicd cost of additional rework caused by choosing an easy solution now instead of using a better approach that would take longer." [3]. Similarly, there is much deep learning debt—due to the tremendous cost in converting traditional machine learning systems to deep learning which typically requires big data, high performance computing hardware, high-level knowledge acquiring and intensive model tuning.

For example, statistical machine translation was dominant for decades, but Google successfully transformed it to deep learning based neural machine translation [2] and achieves state-of-the-art performance. With deep learning, many rule based or manual feature extraction procedures are transformed to automatic feature learning and achieve better performance. As another example, traditional image processing mainly relies on shallow features from open CV. But recently it has been changed to deep learning and yields near perfect performance. Similar cases are happening in natural language processing.

This talk will describe my experience at Naver/LINE on managing deep learning dept including challenges and their potential solutions such as technical research, AI incubation and product development. Several guidelines to decide when to repay deep learning debt in practice will also be discussed.

Acknowledgment. I thank Dr. Xiaodong Gu for his valuable discussion and work at Naver.

References

1. Deep Learning. https://en.wikipedia.org/wiki/Deep_learning
2. Neural Machine Translation. https://ai.google/research/pubs/pub45610
3. Technical Debt. https://en.wikipedia.org/wiki/Technical_debt
4. Cho, K., et al.: Learning phrase representations using RNN encoder-decoder for statistical machine translation. arXiv preprint arXiv:1406.1078 (2014)
5. Gu, X., Cho, K., Ha, J., Kim, S.: DialogWAE: multimodal response generation with conditional wasserstein auto-encoder. In: Proceedings of the 7th International Conference on Learning Representations (ICLR 2019) (2019)
6. Gu, X., Zhang, H., Kim, S.: Deep code search. In: Proceedings of the 2018 40th International Conference on Software Engineering (ICSE 2018). ACM (2018)
7. Gu, X., Zhang, H., Zhang, D., Kim, S.: Deep API learning. In: Proceedings of the 2016 24th ACM SIGSOFT International Symposium on Foundations of Software Engineering (FSE 2016) (2016)
8. Gu, X., Zhang, H., Zhang, D., Kim, S.: DeepAM: migrate APIs with multi-modal sequence to sequence learning. In: Proceedings of the 26th International Joint Conference on Artificial Intelligence, IJCAI 2017 (2017)
9. Hannun, A., et al.: Deep speech: scaling up end-to-end speech recognition. arXiv preprint arXiv:1412.5567 (2014)
10. Hu, J., Shen, L., Sun, G.: Squeeze-and-excitation networks. In: Proceedings of the IEEE Conference on Computer Vision and Pattern Recognition, pp. 7132–7141 (2018)
11. Kim, D., Park, C., Oh, J., Lee, S., Yu, H.: Convolutional matrix factorization for document context-aware recommendation. In: Proceedings of the 10th ACM Conference on Recommender Systems, pp. 233–240. ACM (2016)
12. Shen, Z., Liu, Z., Li, J., Jiang, Y.G., Chen, Y., Xue, X.: Dsod: learning deeply supervised object detectors from scratch. In: Proceedings of the IEEE International Conference on Computer Vision, pp. 1919–1927 (2017)
13. Yin, P., Neubig, G.: Tranx: A transition-based neural abstract syntax parser for semantic parsing and code generation. arXiv preprint arXiv:1810.02720 (2018)

A New Type of Intelligence for Intelligent User Interfaces

Antti Oulasvirta

Aalto University, School of Electrical Engineering,
Finnish Center for AI, Finland
antti.oulasvirta@aalto.fi

Abstract. This talk describes on-going work towards intelligent user interfaces that better understand users and can better adapt to them. I discuss a type of machine intelligence where causal, predictive models of human-computer interaction are used with probabilistic inference and optimization. Several examples are presented from graphical user interfaces to the web.

Keywords: Intelligent user interfaces · Machine intelligence · Computational modelling · Probabilistic inference · Combinatorial optimization

1 Motivation and Scope

Using the Web as an example, I start by discussing shortcomings of everyday user interfaces (UIs), and previous attempts to adapt them for improved usability and user experience. I continue by arguing that modeling is the key to understanding why this has been unsuccessful. From logic to regression and deep learning, all forms of computational interaction are underpinned by a *model* and *methods* for (1) selecting appropriate actions and (2) updating the model in the light of data collected on users [5]. These jointly determine the system's capability to understand users and take appropriate action. I review previous work from this perspective, pointing out critical limitations.

I then introduce *simulator-based machine intelligence* (MI). In a continuum from white-box to black-box methods (e.g., deep learning), the approach offers a middle path that could be called grey-box MI. What this approach loses in representational power to deep learning, it gains in interpretability and lower dependency on data.

2 Method

In this section, I review simulator-based MI. It combines (1) *causal models*, typically in the form of computational simulations, adapted from behavioral and social sciences, with (2) *combinatorial optimization* or *planning* methods for action selection and (3) *probabilistic inference* in order to facilitate interaction. The approach is motivated by recent criticism of deep learning by Lake et al. [3], where they point out that in order to think more like humans, MI must incorporate causal modelling, physical and psychological theories, and harness decompositionality. I illustrate each technical part with examples.

3 Applications

Predictive models have been previously used in HCI for evaluation of designs, such as in CogTool [7]. I review applications of simulator-based MI, where algorithms are used to optimize or infer, or both: (1) generative design [4], (2) creativity support in design tools [2], (3) inference of user behavior from data [1], (4) ability-based optimization [6], and (5) adaptive interfaces [8]. These build on the capability lent by the model, which is to predict human responses and "speculate" about the consequences of its actions. I review application examples spanning graphical user interfaces, menu systems, interactive visualizations, recommendation systems, and interactive agents. To conclude this part, I provide an example implementation in self-optimizing web services.

4 Discussion

The key element of this approach is causal modeling of human-computer interaction. Causal models offer designers visibility and control via understandable terms. Evaluation, sense-making, design, and adaptation all have a meaningful and unified interpretation within this framework. Causal models can also explicate rationale for design outcomes, a long-sought goal in interaction design and HCI. The predictions of the model can be tested and used to improve the model.

References

1. Kangasrääsiö, A., Athukorala, K., Howes, A., Corander, J., Kaski, S., Oulasvirta, A.: Inferring cognitive models from data using approximate bayesian computation. In: Proceedings of the 2017 CHI Conference on Human Factors in Computing Systems, pp. 1295–1306. ACM (2017)
2. Koch, J., Lucero, A., Hegemann, L., Oulasvirta, A.: May AI? design ideation with cooperative contextual bandits. In: Proceedings of the SIGCHI Conference on Human Factors in Computing Systems. ACM (2019)
3. Lake, B.M., Ullman, T.D., Tenenbaum, J.B., Gershman, S.J.: Building machines that learn and think like people. Behav. Brain Sci. 40 (2017)
4. Oulasvirta, A.: User interface design with combinatorial optimization. Computer 50(1), 40–47 (2017)
5. Oulasvirta, A., Bi, X., Howes, A., Kristensson, P.O.: Computational Interaction. Oxford University Press (2018)
6. Sarcar, S., Jokinen, J.P., Oulasvirta, A., Wang, Z., Silpasuwanchai, C., Ren, X.: Ability-based optimization of touchscreen interactions. IEEE Pervasive Comput. 17(1), 15–26 (2018)

7. Teo, L.H., John, B., Blackmon, M.: Cogtool-explorer: a model of goal-directed user explo- ration that considers information layout. In: Proceedings of the SIGCHI Conference on Human Factors in Computing Systems, pp. 2479–2488. ACM (2012)
8. Todi, K., Jokinen, J., Luyten, K., Oulasvirta, A.: Familiarisation: restructuring layouts with visual learning models. In: 23rd International Conference on Intelligent User Interfaces, pp. 547–558. ACM (2018)

Contents

xxvi   Contents

Tutorials

Web Mining and Knowledge Extraction

Web Page Structured Content Detection Using Supervised Machine Learning

Roberto Panerai Velloso$^{(\boxtimes)}$ and Carina F. Dorneles

Universidade Federal de Santa Catarina - UFSC, Florianopolis, SC, Brazil
rvelloso@gmail.com, dorneles@inf.ufsc.br

Abstract. In this paper we present a comparative study using several supervised machine learning techniques, including homogeneous and heterogeneous ensembles, to solve the problem of classifying content and noise in web pages. We specifically tackle the problem of detecting content in semi-structured data (e.g., e-commerce search results) under two different settings: a controlled environment with only structured content documents and; an open environment where the web page being processed may or may not have structured content. The features are automatically obtained from a preexisting and publicly available extraction technique that processes web pages as a sequence of tag paths, thus the features are extracted from these sequences instead of the DOM tree. Besides comparing the performance between different models we have also conducted extensive feature selection/combination experiments. We have achieved an average F-score of about 93% in a controlled setting and 91% in an open setting.

Keywords: Web mining · Content detection · Noise removal ·
Record extraction · Structure detection · Information retrieval

1 Introduction

The web is an invaluable source of data and information about virtually any subject we can think of. Some of this information is made available to the public in a structured fashion (e.g., shopping items, news, search engine results, etc.), providing some level of organization that can be exploited and leveraged: one can use it to detect/find structured content in a document. But there are other parts of a document, besides the main content, that can have some sort of organization (template and menus, for instance), this organized "non-content" information adds noise to the extraction process, decreasing precision. How can we distinguish between them? This is the problem we tackle in this paper.

Extracting structured information, by itself, is an important task, but we must also be able to identify content, distinguish it from noise, so we do not end up with an unusable, bloated database, full of unimportant information (i.e., noise). According to [5,16] between 40%–50% of a web document refers to noise (menus, template, ads), this amount is more than enough to completely

© Springer Nature Switzerland AG 2019
M. Bakaev et al. (Eds.): ICWE 2019, LNCS 11496, pp. 3–18, 2019.
https://doi.org/10.1007/978-3-030-19274-7_1

compromise extraction precision. Since structured data can exist in any kind of web document, whether main content is structured or not, we must be able to identify it correctly independently from its source, even when there is no structured content, i.e. we must be able to identify noise in a document whose main content is textual as well as in a document whose main content is structured. So, once we have extracted the structured content from a document, how can we classify it as content or noise? We could not find in the literature, nor did we reach a deterministic and closed form way of solving this problem (classify content and noise), for this reason we decided to characterize (create conjectures for the features) content and noise the best we could and try out machine learning models to approximate a solution. Our goal is to classify **structured data**, specifically, as content or noise, but without restricting ourselves just to **structured content** documents (i.e., we also want to detect structured noise in textual content documents). This is a desirable property in order to avoid manual intervention (selecting only certain types of documents for processing) for the web is completely heterogeneous in all aspects. But we also evaluated the models in a controlled setting, when the web pages are known beforehand to have structured content. This scenario is not unrealistic (e.g., a focused crawler that retrieves only search result records from e-commerce sites), although it does demands more manual intervention.

Previous attempts at this problem, such as [6,7,17,19], were targeted at textual content, their performance is measured in tasks such as clustering and classification of web pages, not in terms of records extracted. It is also not clear whether or not these approaches can be used with structured content, they might remove part of the content, believing it is noise, without affecting clustering, but this removal would most likely impair record extraction. Other attempts ([15,16]), targeted at structured content, can not be used in an open environment (i.e., an environment where we encounter any kind of content: textual, structured or hybrid), they assume only structured content will be processed. Although this is not completely unrealistic, it is also not as general, demanding more controlled environments of execution (i.e., more manual intervention needed).

In this paper, we analyze several possible supervised machine learning models for structured content detection. Our investigation considered eight machine learning techniques (Logistic Regression, Gaussian Naive Bayes, k Nearest Neighbours, Support Vector Machine, Extra Trees, Gradient Boosting, Voting and Stacking Ensembles) and all possible combinations of features within each approach to find the one that suited best in each case and at the same time investigate feature importance. For the extraction phase we choose the method proposed in [15] because of the good quality of the results, its feasibility in a production environment (it is unsupervised and computationally efficient compared to other state-of-the-art approaches) and also because its source code is freely available for download, allowing reproducibility of results. This extraction method uses a signal processing approach to detect repetitive structural patterns in the document by means of stability and spectral analysis. The web page is converted to a sequence (or signal) representation, prior to extraction, and it is from this sequence that we derive the features used in our work.

The features proposed here are generated during the extraction phase. We just normalize their values, adding no overhead to the pipeline (once we have the model trained). We have attained 93% F-Score in a dataset consisting of 266 different HTML documents from various domains with structured content and 91% F-Score in a dataset with 327 different HTML documents, some with unstructured content (same 266 structured documents, plus 61 unstructured documents mostly from blogs, news, etc.). The novelty presented here lies in the nature of the features. We are using an alternative representation for the web documents, to the best of our knowledge this representation was first introduced in [11], and until now we have not found any content/noise detection proposal using features derived from this representation. Moreover, these features are automatically extracted, meaning that, once we have a trained classifier, no more human intervention is needed. These automatically acquired features contrast with [8], where human intervention is needed for feature extraction. At last, our investigation showed these features can be used to solve this problem effectively and efficiently using a simple and direct ML approach.

The rest of this paper is organized as follows: in Sect. 2, we present a brief review of related works; in Sect. 3, we reproduce some concepts needed for the understanding of our work; in Sect. 4, we describe and illustrate each feature used in solving the problem of content detection; in Sect. 5, we detail and discuss the experiments conducted; in Sect. 6, we analyze the results achieved and; in Sect. 7, we present our conclusions.

2   Related Work

In our research we have encounter quite a few proposals for web page noise removal, dating as far back as 1999 [9]. Most early works focused in textual content, where main applications were web page clustering and classification.

In [3,6,7,17] the main content of a web page is assumed to be textual, they might be a fit for a web page with structured content, but that is unlikely and we have no results published using these techniques for this purpose, as far as we know.

On the other hand, if we assume content is structured ([15,16]) we loose generality and became confined in this setting. An approach biased toward structured content works great in a controlled environment but can not perform well in an open environment where we may encounter textual and hybrid content as well, precision would drop drastically. There is a cost (usually manual intervention and usually high) associated with maintaining such a well controlled environment.

We also found many proposals that do not assume content to be structured or textual ([2,4,8,19,20]), but each has some limitation we intend to overcome in our work. In [4,19,20] several samples from the same template are necessary to train the model, and it only works for that particular template; in [8] human intervention is needed to define a priori rules; and in [2] predefined knowledge bases are required.

Much has changed, since this area of research has started, new applications have arisen, web development culture has changed, among other things. Due to the web's ever changing nature, any proposal based on too specific assumptions (content form, predefined knowledge, template specific, static heuristics rules, etc.) is deemed to rapidly become outdated.

3 Preliminaries

Since we are proposing a way of identifying structured content and noise, we need to build our work on top of an extraction technique. We chose the approach reported in [15] for two reasons: (i) the results reported are equivalent to other state-of-the-art approaches and; (ii) the computational complexity is lower, especially when compared to rendering-based approaches. This extraction technique uses an alternative representation for the web documents, a **tag path sequence** (or TPS), and here we detail this representation. The understanding of this alternate representation is needed because the features we use to classify content and noise are derived from it. For a more thorough explanation we refer the reader to the work in [15].

Definition 1. *(Tag Path) is a string describing the path from the root node of the DOM tree to another node in the tree. For example: "html/body/table/tr/td/#text".*

Definition 2. *(Tag Path Code – TPCode) is a numeric ascending code assigned to every different tag path string encountered in the document tree, in order of appearance. If a given path has already occurred, it is assigned the same code as before. The paths are built in depth first order. Figure 1 shows an example of this definition.*

Definition 3. *(Tag Path Sequence – TPS) is a sequence of TPCodes in the same order as they were built from the DOM tree. Figure 1 shows the resulting TPS for an HTML snippet as well as the set of TPCodes used in that sequence. In this paper we also refer to TPS as simply "sequence".*

The translation process from DOM tree representation to tag path sequence is depicted in Fig. 1. The HTML code is converted to a DOM tree in Step 1; the DOM tree is converted to a sequence of tag paths in Step 2 and; in Step 3 the TPS is built by assigning TPCodes to each tag path.

Figure 2 illustrates a real web page converted to its sequence representation with its structured regions encircled and its main content region highlighted. We will use this specific sequence and its main content region throughout Sect. 4 to characterize the features. The sequence was constructed according to the definitions in this section. Every point in the sequence (Definition 3) corresponds to a specific node in the DOM tree and has a TPCode value (Definition 2) that encodes the node's Tag Path (Definition 1).

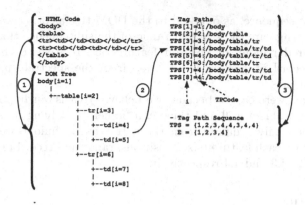

Fig. 1. Conversion of HTML snippet into a tag path sequence.

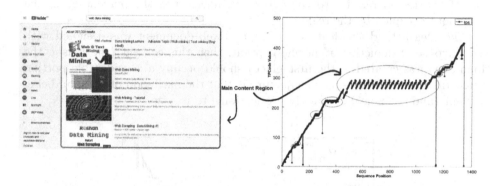

Fig. 2. Web page converted to sequence representation and its structured content.

Definition 4. *(Structured Region) is a region of the document that contains contiguous structured data (either content or noise) and, because of its structured nature, when converted to a TPS, exhibits a cyclic behaviour. This cyclic behaviour is a consequence of structure: the records are contiguous and have similar structure so the TPCs forming the structured region's TPS will repeat throughout the sequence, in cycles. This is illustrated in Fig. 2 where a document containing 20 SRRs (search result records) is converted to its TPS representation and we can see that each record becomes a cycle in the encircled main content region.*

4   Content Detection

In order to distinguish which structured regions are content and which are noise we consider six region features, extracted from the document sequence, such as: region **size**, **center** position, **horizontal** position, **vertical** position, region **range** and **record** proportion (record count vs record size). All features refer to the document sequence, as opposed to the DOM tree as other works do. The region size and range are the size and range of the subsequence that represents a given structured region; all position features are relative to the document sequence and record proportion is retrieved from the spectral analysis of the region's subsequence.

These features were chosen because we believe (that is our hypothesis) they characterize the problem well and thus, can be helpful solving it. As an extra, they can also be easily acquired from the extraction technique we are relying on. We will discuss each feature (size, positions, range and record proportion) in Subsects. 4.1, 4.2, 4.3 and 4.4 respectively.

4.1   Size Feature

The region size feature is a real number, between 0 and 1, that represents the size of the region relative to the entire document, i.e., the percentage of the document occupied by the region.

The idea behind this feature is that if a web document was designed with the purpose of depicting a specific content, then this content (the reason the document was created in the first place) should occupy a considerable portion of the document. That is, our conjecture is that the likelihood of a region being content (and not noise) is directly proportional to its size.

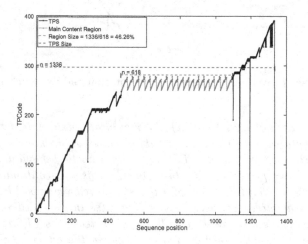

Fig. 3. Size feature example.

Figure 3 shows an example where the entire document sequence has size equal to 1,336 and the main content region subsequence has size 618. The size feature in this case, using Eq. 1, is equal to $\frac{618}{1,336} = 46.25\%$.

$$sizeFeat = \frac{regionSize}{sequenceSize} \tag{1}$$

4.2   Position Features

The region position features are actually comprised of three position features: center, horizontal and vertical positions. All three are real numbers between 0 and 1. The **center position** represents the distance from the center of the region to the center of the document; the **horizontal position** is the distance from the center of the region to the end of the document and; the **vertical position** is the distance from the vertical center of the region to the maximum value of the sequence.

With respect to the center position, the maximum possible distance is equal to half sequence size (e.g., when a region has size one and sits at the start/end of the document). The value of this feature is a percentage representing how close a region is from the center of the document (i.e., it is the distance complement). The rationale of our conjecture for this feature is similar to the size feature (Subsect. 4.1): the closer a region is to the center of the document, the higher the probability it refers to real content.

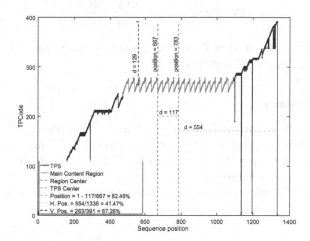

Fig. 4. Position feature example. (Color figure online)

Figure 4 shows an example where the document center (dark blue dashed line) is at position 667 (this is the maximum distance allowed) and main content region subsequence center (red dashed line) is at position 783, at a distance of 117 from document center (green dashed line). The value of this feature, using Eq. 2, is equal to $1 - \frac{117}{667} = 82.46\%$

$$centerPositionFeat = 1 - \frac{|regionCenter - sequenceCenter|}{sequenceCenter} \quad (2)$$

With respect to the vertical and horizontal position, we believe they are needed to provide a better indication of a region's position, **especially** when a document has no structured content (only structured noise), in this situation a noise region will be closer to the center of the sequence and further away from its extremes. If we were concerned only about documents with structured content, these two features would, probably, be of little value to us.

Figure 4 shows how the horizontal and vertical positions are calculated. The horizontal position is the distance from the center of the region to the end of the sequence (light blue dashed line). Using Eq. 4, the value of the horizontal position, in this example, is equal to $\frac{554}{1,336} = 41.47\%$.

$$horizPositionFeat = \frac{sequenceSize - regionCenter}{sequenceSize} \qquad (3)$$

The vertical position (black dashed line) is the distance from the vertical center of the region (i.e., its average value) to the vertical end of the sequence (i.e., its maximum value). Using Eq. 4, the value of the vertical position, in this example, is equal to $\frac{263}{391} = 67.26\%$.

$$vertPositionFeat = \frac{avg(region)}{max(sequence)} \qquad (4)$$

Throughout this paper we will refer to these three features simply as "center", "horizontal" and "vertical" features.

4.3   Range Feature

The range feature is a real number, between 0 and 1, that represents the percentage of the region range relative to the entire sequence. It is analogous to the Size Feature (Subsect. 4.1) only it is vertical instead of horizontal. The region range is simply the maximum value found in the sequence (or subsequence) minus the minimum value. The full sequence range is equivalent to its maximum value.

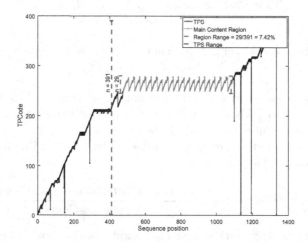

Fig. 5. Range feature example.

Figure 5 shows an example where region range is equal to 29 and document range is equal to 391. The value of this feature, using Eq. 5, is equal to $\frac{283-254}{391} = \frac{29}{391} = 7.42\%$ of document range.

$$rangeFeat = \frac{regionRange}{max(sequence)} \tag{5}$$

4.4   Record Feature

We use the ratio between the number of records and their average size as a feature to indicate if a region is content or noise. We hypothesize that the lack of proportion[1] between this two measures (record count and record size) indicates noise and, conversely, the closer they are from one another the more likely the region is content. We calculate this value as shown in Eq. 6.

$$recRatioFeat = \frac{min(numRecs, recCount)}{max(numRecs, recCount)} \tag{6}$$

The value of this feature is also a real number between 0 and 1, since the denominator in Eq. 6 is always greater or equal to the numerator.

This two measures are obtained as documented in [15], using the region's power spectrum density (PSD) [12]. Figure 6b shows the PSD of the main content region in Fig. 6a and its detected record count and average record size. The sequence in Fig. 6a is the extracted main content region from the sequence depicted in Fig. 2. In this example the number of records (represented by the red peak in Fig. 6b) detected is 20 and their average size is 31, therefore the value of the record feature, using Eq. 6, is equal do $\frac{20}{31} = 64.51\%$

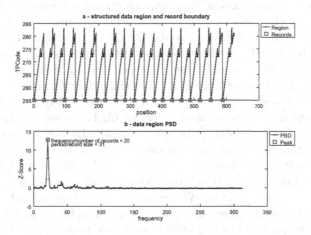

Fig. 6. Record count & size feature example.

Throughout this paper we will refer to this feature as "record" feature.

---

[1] i.e., a lot of small records or few large records.

5 Experiments

In this section we detail the experiments we conducted using supervised machine learning techniques with the features from Sect. 4. We also characterize the dataset used in the experiments, its statistical properties, features correlation, etc. The objectives of this experiments are to determine the parameters and the subset of features which are important in this classification problem and measure the classification performance in terms of precision, recall, accuracy and F-Score.

We have considered, in our study, the following machine learning techniques: Gaussian Naive Bayes (GNB), Logistic Regression (LR), k Nearest Neighbours (kNN), Gradient Boosting (GB), Extra-trees (EXT), Support Vector Machine (SVM), Voting Ensemble (VOT) and Stacking Ensemble (STCK). The voting and stacking ensembles are heterogeneous ensembles and are built from combinations of all the other models (GNB, LR, kNN, SVM, GB and EXT). These experiments were conducted using scikit-learn [13] framework. For the gradient boosting we used XGBoost [1] and for the ensembles we used MLxtend's [14] implementation.

We have conducted experiments to determine the best combination of parameters and features, within each approach, for solving the problem of distinguishing noise from content. To do so we ran a grid search for each algorithm with all feature combinations. We did so because the number of all possible combinations, for six features, is not prohibitive (only $2^6 - 1 = 63$ in total). After that we applied grid search, again, to select the best parameters for each algorithm. The feature set for each algorithm is documented in Table 8 (more details on that in Sect. 6).

For these experiments we have used a dataset consisting of 266 HTML documents with structured content from various domains (news, banking, hotels, car rental, tickets, electronics), plus 61 documents **without** structured content, totalizing 327 documents. The documents without structured content were added to the dataset to investigate the behaviour of the classifiers in the presence of this type of input. We use only one page per site to avoid introducing bias towards specific sites and/or templates[2]. These documents were processed using the technique proposed in [15], resulting in a total of 533 regions. We acknowledge that the size of our dataset is relatively small. The reason is that all regions, from every extracted document, have to be manually labeled as content or noise. To compensate this limitation we kept the dataset as diverse as possible: every document comes from a different web site, with different template and content. All documents were collected from production web sites of real-world companies (e.g., Booking, Google, Amazon, Wikipedia, etc.). We believe that this diversity contributes to the overall representativeness of our dataset, making this study relevant. Also, all pages were collected recently, to guarantee they are all using modern and up to date templates.

---

[2] This is possible because the extraction approach used also works with a single page input.

Table 1. Input dataset summary

# Content regions	254	47.65%
# Noise regions	279	52.35%
Total	533	100%
# Structured documents	266	81.35%
# Unstructured documents	61	18.65%
Total	327	100%

Table 2. Feature importance (vs class)

Feature	χ^2	ANOVA
Size	51.6426225	487.50116318
Center	25.8025951	260.93679423
Range	23.1719961	232.44608713
Record	4.71168623	26.59572956
Vertical	1.16942710	12.38250104
Horizontal	0.433793117	3.63505065

That is our input dataset[3] used for training and cross-validation and it is summarized in Table 1. Figure 7 shows a scatter plot of each feature, separately, with respect to the target class (content vs noise), it gives a rough idea of how content and noise are intertwined within each feature. Table 2 shows the features relative importance according to two different criteria (ANOVA and χ^2), both yielding the same results. Table 4 shows mean, coefficient of variation (CV), skewness and kurtosis for all features with respect to the target class. Table 3 shows the correlation between all features. We see that "size" vs "position", "size" vs "range" and "position" vs "range" have a stronger correlation compared to others, this fact reflected in feature selection for some models and these same three features (size, position and range), according to Table 2, are also the most important ones.

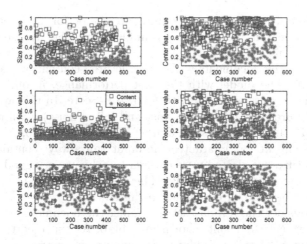

Fig. 7. Input dataset features: content vs noise.

---

[3] Our dataset is available at https://bit.ly/2D3lWFk.

Table 3. Feature correlation

	Size	Record	Range	Horiz.	Vert.
Content & Noise					
Center	**0.63**	0.08	0.45	−0.11	0.01
Size		0.08	**0.68**	−0.02	0.11
Record			0.08	0.04	0.03
Range				−0.01	0.08
Horizontal					**0.85**
Content					
Center	0.58	−0.11	0.21	−0.37	−0.07
Size		−0.10	0.53	−0.12	0.12
Record			−0.04	0.04	−0.04
Range				−0.03	0.08
Horizontal					0.65
Noise					
Center	0.25	−0.01	0.22	−0.15	−0.11
Size		−0.12	0.39	−0.15	−0.11
Record			−0.08	0.01	0.01
Range				−0.13	−0.09
Horizontal					0.89

Table 4. Feature statistics

Feature	Mean	CV	S kewness	Kurtosis
Content & Noise				
Size	0.27	0.87	0.92	2.90
Center	0.57	0.51	−0.18	1.71
Range	0.11	1.12	1.98	7.46
Record	0.40	0.68	0.52	2.15
Vertical	0.59	0.40	−0.49	2.42
Horizontal	0.55	0.47	−0.26	2.14
Content				
Size	0.44	0.49	0.28	2.47
Center	0.74	0.27	−0.81	2.95
Range	0.19	0.74	1.49	5.51
Record	0.46	0.61	0.22	1.89
Vertical	0.63	0.24	−0.80	3.58
Horizontal	0.57	0.26	−0.45	3.63
Noise				
Size	0.12	0.94	2.32	9.37
Center	0.41	0.65	0.58	2.16
Range	0.05	1.40	4.37	26.83
Record	0.34	0.74	0.81	2.74
Vertical	0.56	0.53	−0.15	1.69
Horizontal	0.53	0.61	−0.06	1.44

6   Results

We have used 5-fold cross-validation to evaluate the performance of each model with respect to precision, recall, accuracy and F-Score. The average result of 200 runs is shown in Tables 5 and 6.

When we omit the documents without structured content we get the results shown in Table 5. The model with the best performance, in our experiments, was the Logistic Regression (LR), with 93.57% F-Score. In this application we should prioritize precision (the web is vast and full of noise), with that in mind kNN performed a little better, with almost 94% precision. So, in a controlled environment, where we can guarantee the input will always contain structured content, the features we elected were enough to achieve very good results with relatively simple models (kNN and LR). There is, probably, no need to use more elaborate approaches and/or ensembles in this setting.

When we consider the full dataset, including the documents without structured content, we get the results shown in Table 6. As expected there is a drop in F-Score (column "Drop" in Table 6). The amount of unstructured documents corresponds, roughly, to 18% of the entire dataset (see Table 1) and yet we were able attain negative variations in F-Score lower than 1%, for this reason we consider this results to be very significant as they show it is possible, using the proposed approach, to identify noise no matter the content is structured or not.

Table 5. Results using dataset containing only structured content documents.

Model	Precision	Recall	Accuracy	F-Score
LR	93.30%	**93.85%**	**93.02%**	**93.57%**
GNB	91.97%	90.55%	90.62%	91.26%
kNN	**93.83%**	92.21%	92.59%	93.01%
SVM	93.60%	92.20%	92.37%	92.90%
EXT	91.88%	91.87%	91.23%	91.88%
GB	90.75%	90.14%	89.74%	90.44%
VOT	92.41%	92.20%	91.71%	92.31%
STCK	92.97%	92.20%	92.06%	92.59%

The most prominent drop, ironically, occurs with Logistic Regression (which performed best with only structured content documents). Gradient Boosting (GB), although not the best performing model in either setting, showed the lowest impact in F-Score. Another interesting result we see is that all ensembles (VOT, STCK and GB) have relatively low drop in F-Score (the lowest ones, in fact), with the exception of ExtraTrees (EXT) ensemble, which is the second largest. For this setting, where we have no guarantee that the documents have structured content (only that they may have structured noise), the best option would be the Voting heterogeneous ensemble with F-Score of 91.47% and largest precision (above 90%).

Table 6. Results using complete dataset (including unstructured documents).

Model	Precision	Recall	Accuracy	F-score	Drop
LR	87.97%	92.13%	89.45%	90.00%	−3.57%
GNB	89.69%	88.99%	89.47%	89.34%	−1.92%
kNN	89.72%	90.56%	90.02%	90.14%	−2.87%
SVM	89.51%	92.12%	90.77%	90.79%	−2.11%
EXT	88.80%	88.43%	88.71%	88.61%	−3.27%
GB	90.13%	88.97%	89.65%	89.55%	**−0.89%**
VOT	**90.45%**	**92.52%**	**91.33%**	**91.47%**	−1.38%
STCK	89.93%	91.81%	90.73%	90.86%	−1.73%

For the sake of precision score we have investigated the false positives and concluded that they are borderline cases, i.e., they are structured noise regions that we can not clearly classify, even when we visually inspect the document's TPS (without considering semantics, of course). These region's features are in a gray area, half way between content and noise. Fortunately, these cases seem to be a minority.

Table 7. Comparison w/other approaches

Algorit.	Prec.	Recall	F-Score	Acc.
BERyL [8]	n/d	n/d	90.00%	n/d
SIG [15]	92.02%	94.11%	93.05%	n/d
TPC [11]	90.40%	93.10%	91.73%	n/d
MDR [10]	59.80%	61.80%	60.78%	n/d
Our models				
LR	**95.45%**	95.45%	**95.45%**	94.80%
VOT	**93.02%**	90.91%	**91.95%**	90.91%

Table 8. Best set of features p/algorithm.

Model	Size	Center	Range	Record	Ver.	Hor.
LR	✓	✗	✓	✓	✗	✓
GNB	✓	✓	✓	✓	✓	✓
EXT	✓	✓	✓	✓	✓	✓
SVM	✓	✗	✓	✓	✓	✓
kNN	✓	✓	✓	✓	✓	✓
GB	✓	✓	✓	✓	✓	✓

In Table 7 we have compared our results with other, state-of-the-art, approaches found in the literature. We have compared the performance of our classifiers in both settings (Logistic Regression from Table 5, trained only with structured content, and Voting Ensemble from Table 6 trained with our full dataset) with the results published in [8,11,15], using their reference dataset (from [18]) as our test data, except for [8] for which the dataset is not publicly available, in this case we compare only against raw published results. The work in [11,15] deals specifically with structured content, no assessment was made in the presence of noise as we did in Table 6. We can see, in Table 7, that our work outperformed the other approaches (MDR [10] by a large margin). We've out-matched BERyL, TPC and MDR even in the presence of unstructured content documents. BERyL uses hand tailored rules to extract relevant features to train the classifiers and we have outperformed its results with automatically extracted features. With respect to the SIG [15] approach, we have achieve superior results in a controlled setting and better precision in an open environment.

We show in Table 8 the best performing features for each model, for the sake of documentation and reproducibility. Almost all models used all features, this shows that all features are relevant to the problem and somehow contribute to the solution. The exceptions are the Logistic Regression and Support Vector Machine. The Logistic Regression achieved the best results without "center" and "vertical" features, and SVM without "center" feature, that is probably due to the high correlation with other features as shown in Table 3: "center" feature has a considerable correlation with "size" and "vertical" feature with "horizontal".

7 Conclusion and Future Work

In our research, through observation, we have come up with the conjectures depicted here, for each feature and, through experimentation, we have confirmed these conjectures in two different situations: in a controlled setting (with 93.57% F-Score using Logistic Regression) and; in an open environment (with 91.47% F-Score using a heterogeneous voting ensemble). We believe these to be very good results, especially considering we are using only very basic information (size, position, etc.) to distinguish between content and noise and a direct ML approach.

We have also demonstrated the relevance of these features to the problem by testing every possible combination of features. Moreover, we have also shown that our proposal effectively solves the problem and is superior to other state-of-the-art approaches found in the literature.

Nonetheless, there is always room for improvements. Adding other features to the problem, perhaps using semantic features combined with the ones proposed here could yield some interesting results, especially when we consider borderline false positives where semantics could help improve precision even further. With an increased number of features though, testing all combinations becomes prohibitive, other approaches should then be employed (e.g., genetic algorithms) to find a good (maybe the best) combination of features. About the dataset size, more documents should be gathered, in the future, to improve confidence on our analysis and results, especially the relative performance of various models tested here.

References

1. Chen, T., Guestrin, C.: XGBoost: a scalable tree boosting system. In: Proceedings of the 22nd ACM SIGKDD (2016)
2. Cho, W.T., Lin, Y.M., Kao, H.Y.: Entropy-based visual tree evaluation on block extraction. In: Proceedings of the 2009 IEEE/WIC/ACM, pp. 580–583. IEEE Computer Society (2009)
3. Fernandes, et al.: Computing block importance for searching on web sites. In: CIKM, pp. 165–174. ACM (2007)
4. Fernandes, et al.: A site oriented method for segmenting web pages. In: SIGIR, pp. 215–224. ACM (2011)
5. Gibson, D., Punera, K., Tomkins, A.: The volume and evolution of web page templates. In: WWW, pp. 830–839. ACM (2005)
6. Kohlschütter, C., Fankhauser, P., Nejdl, W.: Boilerplate detection using shallow text features. In: WSDM, pp. 441–450. ACM (2010)
7. Kohlschütter, C., Nejdl, W.: A densitometric approach to web page segmentation. In: CIKM, pp. 1173–1182. ACM (2008)
8. Kravchenko, A., Fayzrakhmanov, R.R., Sallinger, E.: Web page representations and data extraction with BERyL. In: Pautasso, C., Sánchez-Figueroa, F., Systä, K., Murillo Rodríguez, J.M. (eds.) ICWE 2018. LNCS, vol. 11153, pp. 22–30. Springer, Cham (2018). https://doi.org/10.1007/978-3-030-03056-8_3
9. Kushmerick, N.: Learning to remove internet advertisements. In: Proceedings of the Third Annual Conference on Autonomous Agents, pp. 175–181. ACM (1999)
10. Liu, B., Grossman, R., Zhai, Y.: Mining data records in web pages. In: SIGKDD, pp. 601–606. ACM (2003)
11. Miao, G., Tatemura, J., Hsiung, W.P., Sawires, A., Moser, L.E.: Extracting data records from the web using tag path clustering. In: WWW, pp. 981–990. ACM (2009)
12. Oppenheim, A.V., et al.: Discrete-Time Signal Processing. Prentice Hall, Englewood Cliffs (1989)

13. Pedregosa, F., et al.: Scikit-learn: machine learning in Python. J. Mach. Learn. Res. **12**, 2825–2830 (2011)
14. Raschka, S.: Mlxtend: providing machine learning and data science utilities and extensions to Python's scientific computing stack. J. Open Source Softw. **3**(24), 638 (2018). https://doi.org/10.21105/joss.00638. http://joss.theoj.org/papers/10.21105/joss.00638
15. Velloso, R.P., Dorneles, C.F.: Extracting records from the web using a signal processing approach. In: CIKM 2017 (2017)
16. Velloso, R.P., Dorneles, C.F.: Automatic web page segmentation and noise removal for structured extraction using tag path sequences. JIDM **4**(3), 173 (2013)
17. Vieira, K., et al.: A fast and robust method for web page template detection and removal. In: CIKM, pp. 258–267. ACM (2006)
18. Yamada, Y., Craswell, N., Nakatoh, T., Hirokawa, S.: Testbed for information extraction from deep web. In: WWW, pp. 346–347. ACM (2004)
19. Yi, L., Liu, B., Li, X.: Eliminating noisy information in web pages for data mining. In: SIGKDD, pp. 296–305. ACM (2003)
20. Zheng, S., Song, R., Wen, J.R., Wu, D.: Joint optimization of wrapper generation and template detection. In: SIGKDD, pp. 894–902. ACM (2007)

Augmenting LOD-Based Recommender Systems Using Graph Centrality Measures

Bart van Rossum and Flavius Frasincar$^{(\boxtimes)}$ (iD)

Erasmus University Rotterdam, PO Box 1738, 3000 DR Rotterdam, The Netherlands
{vanrossum,frasincar}@ese.eur.nl

Abstract. In this paper we investigate the incorporation of graph-based features into LOD path-based recommender systems, an approach that so far has received little attention. More specifically, we propose two normalisation procedures that adjust user-item path counts by the degree centrality of the nodes connecting them. Evaluation on the MovieLens 1M dataset shows that the linear normalisation approach yields a significant increase in recommendation accuracy as compared to the default case, especially in settings where the most popular movies are omitted. These results serve as a fruitful base for further incorporation of graph measures into recommender systems, and might help in establishing the recommendation diversity that has recently gained much attention.

Keywords: Top-N recommendations · Linked Open Data · Information network schema · Random forest

1 Introduction

Recommender systems (RS) are algorithms aimed at presenting the user with items of which it is most likely that (s)he will enjoy them [11]. Over the past years, the rise of the Semantic Web has enabled a boost in their performance [12]. The structured knowledge representations available in the Linked Open Data (LOD) cloud allows for the construction of hybrid recommendation systems that leverage both user preferences as well as information on product features [4]. Combining the best of both worlds, these hybrid systems have been shown to consistently outperform other state-of-the-art recommendation systems [13].

One of the most promising ways of incorporating data from the LOD is by constructing a knowledge graph linking all users, items, and relevant semantic information, and including path-based features in hybrid recommendation systems. In other words, the number of connections in a knowledge graph between a user and an item determines the likelihood of this item being recommended to the user, an idea with strong intuitive appeal. This approach has been successfully employed in leveraging semantic information from the popular LOD dataset DBpedia [3] in the domain of books, films, and music [14,17].

© Springer Nature Switzerland AG 2019
M. Bakaev et al. (Eds.): ICWE 2019, LNCS 11496, pp. 19–31, 2019.
https://doi.org/10.1007/978-3-030-19274-7_2

While these semantic path-based features have greatly increased the accuracy of recommender systems, they do not nearly capture all relevant information embedded in a knowledge graph. One can imagine that the structure of this graph contains information that is potentially relevant to recommendation systems. The clustering of items and users or the relative importance of items within this graph, for example, are definitely factors of interest when recommending items to a user. To this day, however, this dimension of the knowledge graph has remained largely unexplored. While some authors have proposed including graph-based features in their RS, unifying graph-based features with the successful path-based ones remains an open challenge [13,16].

In this paper we propose a simple, yet effective way of unifying the previously mentioned two types of features. By normalising path-based features based on the centrality of the nodes along each path, we aim to improve the performance of hybrid recommendation systems. The rationale behind this proposal is as follows: paths between a user and an item along nodes with a high popularity in the network are unlikely to capture the unique preferences of this user, and should therefore contribute less to the score of this item. A user liking "The Matrix", for example, tells us more about the popularity of this movie then about the particular user. Since centrality measures offer a diverse set of ways of measuring the popularity of a node in a network, these are very much suited in performing this correction.

An additional benefit of this approach is its potential to diversify the set of items recommended to a user. The goal of diversification has been deemed more and more important recently, yet is usually in conflict with the goal of high recommendation accuracy [12,15]. The proposed use of normalised path-based features, however, can contribute to higher diversity whilst retaining or increasing accuracy, since items with a low centrality measure are more likely to be both recommended and unknown to the user.

This paper is structured as follows. Section 2 discusses related work, while Sect. 3 elaborates on the proposed methodology. Section 4 introduces the evaluation procedure and the obtained results, while Sect. 5 gives our conclusion and future work.

2   Related Work

The use of semantic path-based features in recommender systems is not novel, and has been successfully applied by the authors of [14]. In the book, film, and music domain, they leveraged data from DBpedia to train an ontology-based recommender system, enabling them to compare various learning-to-rank algorithms. This is where their approach differs from ours: since we are only interested in the added value of graph-based normalisation, we only employ random forests to train our recommender system. Moreover, since we are merely interested in the normalisation procedure, we limit the number of possible paths by defining a network schema in which only certain path types are allowed.

In this respect, our approach closely resembles the one used in [17], which pioneered the use of network schemas in path-based recommender systems. Moreover, the evaluation strategy employed by these authors is identical to the one we use. Whereas they also explore the benefits of feature selection, this aspect remains unexplored in this paper, due to our focus on normalisation.

An alternative approach that already captures more information about the graph structure is proposed by the authors of [16]. They propose `entity2rec`, a feature-construction algorithm that learns property-specific vector representations of users and items by simulating random walks through the knowledge graph. Subsequently they construct user-item relatedness scores based on these representations, feeding this into a recommender system. A downside of this approach is the need to tune several hyperparameters, and the extent to which it employs information from the graph is still very limited.

A second paper that utilizes graph-based features is [13], the authors of which construct item features that are directly based on graph centrality measures. Together with the aforementioned path-based measures, these are loaded into several types of recommender systems. Their results show that directly using centrality measures as input variables has little added value, since they mainly serve as an additional popularity measure and are not incorporated into the other features yet. Our approach differs from the one used in [13] as we aim to include graph centrality measures directly into the used path measures, thus exploiting the interaction effects between them.

In this paper we aim to use centrality measures by discounting popular node counts on the considered paths, thereby bridging the gap between path-based and graph-based features. As we exploit the structure of the information network to a further extent than has been done before, we hope this information will prove relevant to the recommender system and increase recommendation accuracy. Since it is unknown which type of normalisation is most suited for this purpose, we evaluate multiple procedures in various settings. In short, the main contribution of this paper is to build on the current semantic path-based recommender systems literature by controlling path-based features for graph-based measures. Similar to the aforementioned papers, we evaluate the effectiveness of this procedure on the MovieLens 1M dataset.

3   Methodology

In order to construct path-based features, we require a way of modeling the knowledge of the movie domain and user preferences. This is done in an information network, described in the following. Next, the definition of a meta path and the normalisation procedure are given, as well as the algorithm used to train the ranking function.

3.1   Information Network

An information network is defined as an undirected graph $G = (V, A)$, where V represents the set of vertices, or nodes, in the network, and A the set of edges between them. In our case, $V = I \cup U \cup E$, where I equals the set of items (movies), U the set of users, and E the set of entities. The latter set consists of all actors, directors, subjects, and entities otherwise linked to the movies. G is undirected as each edge $a \in A$ is assumed to be symmetric, reflecting the fact that we are mainly interested in the association between two nodes rather than any causal links between them. Moreover, we define the type function $t : A \to T$, representing that each edge a is of type $t(a) \in T$. Table 1 displays the elements of T, indicating that all edges link either items and users, or items and entities.

Table 1. Set of edge-types T

Connected sets	Type	k
I & U	likes	1
I & E	starring	2
I & E	director	3
I & E	cinematography	4
I & E	producer	5
I & E	editing	6
I & E	writer	7
I & E	musicComposer	8
I & E	narrator	9
I & E	basedOn	10
I & E	subject	11

In order to get an impression of what such a graph looks like, Fig. 1 shows a small example information network. Consisting of only 11 nodes and containing only the first three types of edges (likes, starring, and director), it is a heavily simplified version of the actual network we will work with. Nonetheless, it clearly displays the way in which the sets U, I, and E are linked. Moreover, it provides some intuition on how paths between items offer an indication of their similarity. We can infer Inception and The Prestige to be similar items, for example, since they are connected by multiple paths of different types.

3.2 Meta Paths and Path-Based Features

In order to assess the degree of similarity between items, we introduce the notion of a meta path. A meta path specifies the type of edges that connect nodes of a certain type. Using the notation introduced above, each meta path P of length l can be defined as:

$$P = V_1 \xrightarrow{t_1} V_2 \xrightarrow{t_2} \dots \xrightarrow{t_{l-1}} V_l \tag{1}$$

where $V_i \in V$, $i = 1, \dots, l$ and $t_i \in T$, $i = 1, \dots, l - 1$. In other words, a meta path specifies which type of semantic link exists between two types of

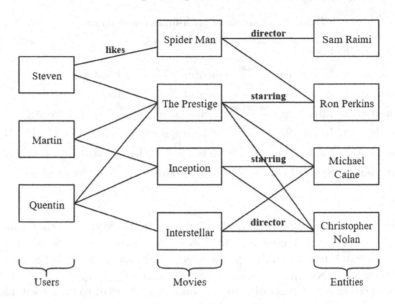

Fig. 1. Example information network

nodes. Note that there may exist multiple instances of each meta path in our information network G. Every instance p of P can be defined as a sequence of nodes and edges $(v_1, a_1, v_2, a_2, \ldots, a_{l-1}, v_l)$ where v_i is of type V_i, $i = 1, \ldots, l$ and $t(a_i) = t_i$, $i = 1, \ldots, l-1$.

In the following, we focus on symmetric meta paths of length $l = 3$ between items, i.e., all meta paths of the type $P = V_1 \xrightarrow{t} V_2 \xrightarrow{t} V_3$ for which $V_1, V_3 \in I$. These paths link all movies that have something in common, e.g., movies that are directed by the same director when we set $V_2 \in E$ and $t = \texttt{director}$. Note that this allows for $|T|$ different meta paths. In the following, we will refer to $P(k)$, $k = 1, \ldots, |T|$, as the meta path with t equal to the k-th element of T (as displayed in Table 1).

For each user-item pair $(u, i), u \in U, i \in I$, we can now construct a feature vector $\mathbf{x}_{u,i} \in \mathbb{R}^{|T|}$ as follows:

$$\mathbf{x}_{u,i}(k) = \sum_{j \in I_u^+} \#path_{i,j}(k), \quad k = 1, \ldots, |T| \tag{2}$$

where I_u^+ is the set of items liked by user u and $\#path_{i,j}(k)$ indicates the number of instances of $P(k)$ linking i and j. Intuitively, when elements in this vector are of larger magnitude, we expect the user u to be more interested in item i, as there exist more meta path instances linking it to items that he has previously liked.

To further clarify this procedure, we now demonstrate the feature construction for one of the users of Fig. 1. More specifically, we evaluate $\mathbf{x}_{u,i}$ for $u = $ Martin and $i \in \{$Interstellar, Spider Man$\}$. Since $I_{\text{Martin}}^+ = \{$The Prestige, Inception$\}$,

Table 2. Example of path-finding procedure

i	k	Path
Interstellar	1	Interstellar $\xrightarrow{\text{likedBy}}$ Quentin $\xrightarrow{\text{likes}}$ The Prestige
Interstellar	1	Interstellar $\xrightarrow{\text{likedBy}}$ Quentin $\xrightarrow{\text{likes}}$ Inception
Interstellar	2	Interstellar $\xrightarrow{\text{starring}}$ Michael Caine $\xrightarrow{\text{starringIn}}$ The Prestige
Interstellar	3	Interstellar $\xrightarrow{\text{directedBy}}$ Christopher Nolan $\xrightarrow{\text{directing}}$ The Prestige
Spider Man	1	Spider Man $\xrightarrow{\text{likedBy}}$ Steven $\xrightarrow{\text{likes}}$ The Prestige
Spider Man	2	Spider Man $\xrightarrow{\text{starring}}$ Ron Perkins $\xrightarrow{\text{starringIn}}$ The Prestige

this boils down to finding all the paths displayed in Table 2. Note that while the edge types are in fact symmetric, we have used asymmetric naming here for the sake of readability. Summing paths over each path type yields the following user-item features: $\mathbf{x}_{\text{Martin,Interstellar}} = \langle 2, 1, 1 \rangle$ and $\mathbf{x}_{\text{Martin,Spider Man}} = \langle 1, 1, 0 \rangle$. Based on these two features only, one would expect Martin to prefer Interstellar over Spider Man.

3.3   Centrality Measure and Normalisation Approaches

The features described in the previous section can be considered as the default case, path-based features which are not yet normalised in any way. In the following we describe a procedure that normalises the path count using the centrality of the nodes along the path. To this extent, we compute the degree centrality C_D of all nodes. As the normalisation is done separately for each meta path, i.e., for each element of the feature vector, we define this measure with respect to networks where only instances of a certain meta path are allowed. In other words, in computing this measure we only consider edges of one specific type, depending on the meta path of interest.

The degree centrality measures the number of nodes in the network a particular node is connected to. For any node $v \in V$ and meta path P it is defined as follows:

$$C_D(v, P) = deg(v, P) \tag{3}$$

where $deg(v, P)$ is the degree of node v in a network where only meta paths of type P are allowed. $C_D(i, P(1))$ with $i \in I$, for example, would measure the number of users that have liked item i, whereas $C_D(i, P(2))$ would reflect the number of actors starring in i.

Having introduced this centrality measure, we can define the actual normalisation procedure. In brief, every path between a user and an item is now inversely weighted by the relative degree centrality of the nodes along that path.

We propose two slightly different procedures, both of which will be evaluated. Firstly, one can consider a so-called 'compounding' procedure, which means that the normalised user-item feature $\mathbf{x}_{u,i}^c$ is now defined as follows:

$$\mathbf{x}_{u,i}(k) = \sum_{j \in I_u^+} \#path_{i,j}^*(k), \quad k = 1, \ldots, |T| \tag{4}$$

where

$$\#path_{i,j}^*(k) = \sum_{p \in P(k):i,s,j \in p} \frac{\overline{C}_D(i,p)}{C_D(i,p)} \times \frac{\overline{C}_D(s,p)}{C_D(s,p)} \times \frac{\overline{C}_D(j,p)}{C_D(j,p)} \tag{5}$$

in which $\overline{C}_D(i,P)$ is the average of C_D taken over all nodes of the same type as i. If $i \in I$, for example, this average is taken w.r.t. all movies in the network (not only on the considered paths, but only for the considered edges of type k). Note that i and j are necessarily of the same type, while s can be both from U or from E. From (6) it becomes clear that paths along nodes with relatively high centrality measures will now contribute less to the feature vector than in (2), since they are multiplied with a weighting factor that is below one.

Secondly, one can consider a normalisation procedure that still discounts popular nodes, yet is less sensitive to outliers. We will refer to it as the 'mean' procedure, which discounts using the arithmetic mean of the relative centrality measures along a path:

$$\#path_{i,j}^*(k) = \sum_{p \in P(k):i,s,j \in p} \frac{1}{3} \left(\frac{\overline{C}_D(i,p)}{C_D(i,p)} + \frac{\overline{C}_D(s,p)}{C_D(s,p)} + \frac{\overline{C}_D(j,p)}{C_D(j,p)} \right). \tag{6}$$

As before, we will demonstrate these procedures by considering their effect on two specific meta paths from Table 2 where $k = 2$, i.e., the paths Interstellar $\xrightarrow{\text{starring}}$ Michael Caine $\xrightarrow{\text{starringIn}}$ The Prestige and Spider Man $\xrightarrow{\text{starring}}$ Ron Perkins $\xrightarrow{\text{starringIn}}$ The Prestige. Table 3 displays the results of applying the two normalisation procedures to these specific paths, where the node degrees are computed based on Fig. 1 and the average node degrees are assumed to be 2 for all node types (for the considered edges of type k).

Table 3. Example of normalisation procedures

Node	C_D	$\overline{C}_D/C_D$	Node	C_D	$\overline{C}_D/C_D$
Interstellar	1	2	Spider Man	1	2
Michael Caine	3	2/3	Ron Perkins	2	1
The Prestige	2	1	The Prestige	2	1
Compound: $2 \times 2/3 \times 1 = 4/3$			Compound: $2 \times 1 \times 1 = 2$		
Mean: $1/3 \times (2 + 2/3 + 1) = 11/9$			Mean: $1/3 \times (2 + 1 + 1) = 4/3$		

Whereas in the example in Sect. 3.2 all paths contributed equally to the total, we see that the discounting creates variance in the path weights. First of all, both paths get a score above one due to the fact that (in this example) they star fewer actors than an average movie. Second, we find that the path via Ron Perkins receives a higher value than the one via the more popular actor Michael Caine. This clearly shows the rationale behind our procedure: when a user likes less-known entities, this gives us a clearer indication of his true preferences then when he likes more popular entities. Third, this example confirms our statement that the compounding procedure is more sensitive than the mean one: in both cases, it yields scores which in magnitude deviate most from one.

3.4   Training the Ranking Function

The aim of the recommender system is to recommend the most relevant items to a user, based on the knowledge present in G. This is done using a scoring function $f : \mathbb{R}^{|T|} \to \mathbb{R}$ which converts each user-item feature vector into a score indicating the expected relevance of the item to the user. More formally, for each item i rated $r_{u,i}$ by user u, we want that $f(\mathbf{x}_{u,i}) \approx r_{u,i}$. Note that we define $r_{u,i}$ to be 1 if u has liked i, and 0 otherwise. The function f will be learnt by training it on a training set $TS = \bigcup_{u \in U} \{\langle \mathbf{x}_{u,i}, r_{u,i} \rangle : i \in I_u^+ \cup I_u^- \}$, where once again I_u^+ is the set of items liked by user u and I_u^- is the set of items disliked by u.

Given such a function f, we can rank items based on their score and recommend the top-N to the user. As random forests have showed to perform well at such ranking tasks [6], this is what we will use to train f. Random forests are an ensemble technique that can be used for classification and regression, and aggregate the output of multiple decision trees to a single output variable [5]. Following [17], the random forest we will employ consists of 100 Classification and Regression Trees (CART), and each tree is trained on a subset of w randomly selected variables to prevent overfitting. In this setting we fix w to be $\sqrt{|T|}$.

4   Evaluation

The following describes the results evaluation protocol, starting with introducing the data used and the training of the random forest. Subsequently, the performance of the recommender system is analysed using an accuracy measure. Finally, the results are linked to the existing literature on accuracy versus diversity.

4.1   Data

The recommender system will be trained and evaluated using the MovieLens 1M dataset, containing 1,000,209 1-5-star ratings of 3,883 movies by 6,040 users [10]. The authors of [14] have attempted a mapping of each movie in the 1M dataset to a unique DBpedia URI, which we use here as well. This leaves us with 3,196 movies that together will form the set I. The set of users U is constructed by retaining only those users that have positively rated at least 15 items in I, to ensure there is sufficient information on each remaining user. We define a positive rating to be a 5-star one in order to remove any possible ambiguity w.r.t. liked movies. This way, a total of 3,854 users and 193,255 ratings remains. Using the aforementioned mapping, we query DBpedia for all RDF triples linking the movies to other entities. These can be triples from the Film domain, in which all information regarding a specific movie is stored, as well dcterms:subject triples, linking the movies to the Wikipedia categories they are part of. This way, the set of entities E and all the edges between I and E are retrieved. We refer the reader to [17] for more information on this querying procedure. A total of 13,649 unique entities is obtained.

Given these sets and the relations between them, we are able to construct the information network G. The implementation thereof is done in Neo4j[1], a graph database platform that allows for fast retrieval of meta paths between two items.

4.2 Evaluation Protocol

The procedure described above leaves us with a set of users that all have at least 15 positive ratings. For each user, we select 10 liked items that construct the test set for this user. For each positively rated item in this test set, we add 100 randomly selected items which the user did not like. Note that these can also be items that the user has not rated at all, for which we assume he does not like them. This leaves us with 10 batches of 101 items for each individual user.

The training set will contain the remaining positively rated movies of each user, up to a maximum of m items. We will evaluate two sizes of training profiles, $m = 5$ and $m = 50$. The training set per user is augmented with $2m$ randomly selected irrelevant items. The aggregate training set over all users is then used to train the random forest, as described in Sect. 3.4.

After the random forest has been trained, its accuracy is evaluated on the test set. The items within each batch are ranked based on their predictions from the ranking function. The top-N items are then recommended to the user, after which the recall@N measure is computed. This is defined as follows:

$$recall@N = \frac{\#relevant\ items\ recommended}{\#relevant\ items\ in\ batch}. \tag{7}$$

Since we assume there is only one relevant item per batch, this simplifies to:

$$recall@N = \mathbf{1}_{relevant\ item\ in\ top-N} \tag{8}$$

which can be seen as the probability of recommending a relevant item to a user when displaying the top-N results only. Note that this merely provides us with a lower bound on the actual accuracy of the system, as not all unliked items are indeed irrelevant to the user. This measure will be evaluated for multiple values of N, and subsequently averaged over the batches of all users.

---

[1] www.neo4j.com.

4.3   Results

Table 4 shows the recall@N measures for various levels of N and two profile sizes, i.e., two sizes of m. As expected, the accuracy is increasing in N, which follows directly from (8): as the set of top items is larger, the chances of finding a relevant item increase. The marginal effect is decreasing in N, however, indicating that the relevant item is unlikely to be positioned in the tail of the ranking. Comparing results for $m = 5$ with those of $m = 50$, we find that a bigger training set increases the accuracy of the recommender system. This is expected, since the random forest is better able to extract relevant patterns when trained on a bigger sample. Finally, we are able to compare the standard path count procedure with the normalised versions. The results indicate that the compounded measure never outperforms the standard one, while the mean-normalised approach scores similarly or higher than the standard procedure. This higher score is especially present in the smaller profile size.

Table 4. Recall@N for all movies

N	$m = 5$			$m = 50$		
	Standard	Compound	Mean	Standard	Compound	Mean
5	0.483	0.223	0.488	0.534	0.258	0.532
10	0.692	0.336	0.701	0.718	0.391	0.707
15	0.807	0.422	0.813	0.799	0.511	0.809
20	0.872	0.480	0.882	0.876	0.612	0.872
25	0.917	0.546	0.922	0.918	0.697	0.915

Whereas Table 4 displays the results based on the full set of items, it is also interesting to look at a setting in which the most popular items are out of consideration. These popular items are responsible for a relatively large share of the positive ratings, and therefore liked by most users. Omitting those from the sample tells us how well our recommender system performs at extracting the preferences that are actually unique to users. In order to filter the sample, we keep removing the most popular item from the set, until the removed items jointly account for 33% of the ratings, hereby following the approach proposed by [7]. After removing these items, the evaluation procedure is repeated.

Table 5 displays the results for the long tail only. A striking observation is the generally lower accuracy, which can be attributed to the omission of popular items. These items are liked by many users and therefore boost the accuracy of a recommender system. Only the results for the compounded path counts seem to benefit from this omission, most likely because the negative effect of the compounding procedure is diminished in this setting. The general patterns of Table 4 are observable here as well, except for the fact that the mean-weighting procedure now clearly outperforms the standard one. The potential explanation for the compounded results might hold here as well: the possible negative effect on accuracy due to recommending less popular items is diminished in a setting with fewer popular items. In contrast, the positive effect due to the normalisation procedure seems to dominate here, indicating that these normalised path count measures are indeed more meaningful.

Table 5. Recall@N for long tail only

N	$m = 5$			$m = 50$		
	Standard	Compound	Mean	Standard	Compound	Mean
5	0.387	0.257	0.436	0.449	0.329	0.510
10	0.619	0.390	0.647	0.667	0.505	0.728
15	0.766	0.499	0.787	0.795	0.638	0.848
20	0.857	0.595	0.876	0.860	0.741	0.915
25	0.911	0.675	0.921	0.915	0.819	0.953

4.4 Diversity and Popular Items

It is well-known that recommendation systems maximising accuracy usually recommend the most popular items, even though this is not always in accordance with user utility [18]. Rather than simply receiving a set of accurate recommendations, the user also wishes to be surprised by diverse and novel set of recommendations. Popular items alone rarely achieve this goal, yet shifting to less-popular items also implies a reduction in accuracy. All in all, this yields a trade-off between diversity and accuracy [19], the resolution to which has until now remained unclear.

Given the previously mentioned background, the main result from Sect. 4.3 is especially surprising. Despite the fact that our proposed procedure actively discounts popular items, we find that accuracy does not suffer, but even increases in certain settings. Moreover, the authors of [1] have shown that recommending fewer popular items increases the diversity of the recommendation set. This implies that graph-based normalisation alleviates the dilemma by maintaining or even increasing recommendation accuracy, whilst yielding an increase in diversity of the recommended items.

5 Conclusion

Path-based recommender systems usually rely on information networks, the structure of which contains a lot of knowledge relevant to the recommendations. Despite its potential, this graph structure has so far received little attention in literature. This paper proposes a novel method of unifying the path-based and graph-based features extracted from an information network. More specifically, we implement and test several normalisation procedures that discount path counts between users and items by the degree centrality measures of the nodes along this path. When evaluated on the MovieLens 1M dataset, the linear weighting procedure has been shown to significantly outperform the default approach. This effect is especially strong in the long tail of the dataset, where the normalisation procedure is not punished for recommending less popular movies. Next to a higher recommendation accuracy, this approach also yields the benefit of presenting more novel items to the user and increased diversity in the recommendation set.

Despite careful considerations, several limitations to this paper remain. First of all, since only the movie domain has been investigated, it remains an open question whether this method performs equally well in, e.g., the book and music domains. Second, there exist multiple other centrality measures and normalisation procedures, the performance of which might surpass that of the current set-up. Both of these provide relevant suggestions for future research.

Nonetheless, the implementation of graph-based measures in the context of recommender systems has proven to be fruitful, and constitutes a solid basis for future work. Potential benefit is to be gained especially in the area of diversity, which is recently gaining extra interest. Employing the structure of the information graph might be a promising way of accentuating less-known items and of recommending items that are as different from each other as possible, thereby increasing the diversity among recommendations. Incorporating diversity measures, as proposed by for example [12] and [15], into the current setting would give further insight into the feasibility of the proposed approach.

Next to the suggestions mentioned above, it is of much interest to investigate other methods of incorporating structural information on the information network into a RS. A user clustering approach as proposed by [2] and [9], for example, might benefit hugely from graph clustering algorithms (see [8] for an overview). This is especially likely to prove fruitful when information graphs containing both user- as well as content-based information like ours are considered, as compared to collaborative filtering approaches tried so far.

References

1. Adomavicius, G., Kwon, Y.: Improving aggregate recommendation diversity using ranking-based techniques. IEEE Trans. Knowl. Data Eng. **24**(5), 896–911 (2012)
2. Altingovde, I.S., Subakan, Ö.N., Ulusoy, Ö.: Cluster searching strategies for collaborative recommendation systems. Inf. Process. Manage. **49**(3), 688–697 (2013)
3. Auer, S., Bizer, C., Kobilarov, G., Lehmann, J., Cyganiak, R., Ives, Z.: DBpedia: a nucleus for a web of open data. In: Aberer, K., et al. (eds.) ASWC/ISWC-2007. LNCS, vol. 4825, pp. 722–735. Springer, Heidelberg (2007). https://doi.org/10.1007/978-3-540-76298-0_52
4. Bizer, C., Heath, T., Berners-Lee, T.: Linked data-the story so far. Int. J. Semantic Web Inf. Syst. **5**(2), 1–22 (2009)
5. Breiman, L.: Random forests. Mach. Learn. **45**(1), 5–32 (2001)
6. Chapelle, O., Chang, Y.: Yahoo! Learning to rank challenge overview. In: Proceedings of the Learning to Rank Challenge, pp. 1–24 (2011)

7. Cremonesi, P., Koren, Y., Turrin, R.: Performance of recommender algorithms on top-N recommendation tasks. In: Proceedings of the Fourth ACM Conference on Recommender Systems, pp. 39–46. ACM (2010)
8. Emmons, S., Kobourov, S., Gallant, M., Borner, K.: Analysis of network clustering algorithms and cluster quality metrics at scale. PloS One **11**(7), e0159161 (2016). https://journals.plos.org/plosone/article?id=10.1371/journal.pone.0159161
9. Gong, S.: A collaborative filtering recommendation algorithm based on user clustering and item clustering. J. Soc. Work **5**(7), 745–752 (2010)
10. Harper, F.M., Konstan, J.A.: The MovieLens datasets: history and context. ACM Trans. Intell. Syst. Technol. **5**(4), 19:1–19:19 (2015). https://dblp.uni-trier.de/rec/bibtex/journals/tiis/HarperK16
11. Jannach, D., Resnick, P., Tuzhilin, A., Zanker, M.: Recommender systems-beyond matrix completion. Commun. ACM **59**(11), 94–102 (2016)
12. Lops, P., de Gemmis, M., Semeraro, G.: Content-based recommender systems: state of the art and trends. In: Ricci, F., Rokach, L., Shapira, B., Kantor, P.B. (eds.) Recommender Systems Handbook, pp. 73–105. Springer, Boston (2011). https://doi.org/10.1007/978-0-387-85820-3_3
13. Musto, C., Lops, P., de Gemmis, M., Semeraro, G.: Semantics-aware recommender systems exploiting linked open data and graph-based features. Knowl.-Based Syst. **136**, 1–14 (2017)
14. Noia, T.D., Ostuni, V.C., Tomeo, P., Sciascio, E.D.: SPrank: semantic path-based ranking for top-N recommendations using linked open data. ACM Trans. Intell. Syst. Technol. **8**(1), 9:1–9:34 (2016)
15. Noia, T.D., Rosati, J., Tomeo, P., Sciascio, E.D.: Adaptive multi-attribute diversity for recommender systems. Inf. Sci. **382**, 234–253 (2017)
16. Palumbo, E., Rizzo, G., Troncy, R.: Learning user-item relatedness from knowledge graphs for top-N item recommendation. In: Proceedings of the Eleventh ACM Conference on Recommender Systems (RecSys 2017), pp. 32–36. ACM (2017)
17. Wever, T., Frasincar, F.: A linked open data schema-driven approach for Top-N recommendations. In: Proceedings of the Symposium on Applied Computing (SAC 2017), pp. 656–663. ACM (2017)
18. Zhang, M., Hurley, N.: Avoiding monotony: improving the diversity of recommendation lists. In: Proceedings of the 2008 ACM Conference on Recommender Systems (RecSys 2008), pp. 123–130. ACM (2008)
19. Zhou, T., Kuscsik, Z., Liu, J.G., Medo, M., Wakeling, J.R., Zhang, Y.C.: Solving the apparent diversity-accuracy dilemma of recommender systems. Proc. Nat. Acad. Sci. **107**(10), 4511–4515 (2010)

ST-Sem: A Multimodal Method for Points-of-Interest Classification Using Street-Level Imagery

Shahin Sharifi Noorian$^{(\boxtimes)}$ ⓘ, Achilleas Psyllidis ⓘ, and Alessandro Bozzon ⓘ

Delft University of Technology, Delft, The Netherlands
{s.sharifinoorian,a.psyllidis,a.bozzon}@tudelft.nl

Abstract. Street-level imagery contains a variety of visual information about the facades of Points of Interest (POIs). In addition to general morphological features, signs on the facades of, primarily, business-related POIs could be a valuable source of information about the type and identity of a POI. Recent advancements in computer vision could leverage visual information from street-level imagery, and contribute to the classification of POIs. However, there is currently a gap in existing literature regarding the use of visual labels contained in street-level imagery, where their value as indicators of POI categories is assessed. This paper presents *Scene-Text Semantics* (ST-Sem), a novel method that leverages visual labels (e.g., texts, logos) from street-level imagery as complementary information for the categorization of business-related POIs. Contrary to existing methods that fuse visual and textual information at a feature-level, we propose a late fusion approach that combines visual and textual cues after resolving issues of incorrect digitization and semantic ambiguity of the retrieved textual components. Experiments on two existing and a newly-created datasets show that ST-Sem can outperform visual-only approaches by 80% and related multimodal approaches by 4%.

Keywords: Points of Interest · Street-level imagery · Convolutional Neural Networks · Word embeddings · Semantic similarity

1 Introduction

An increasing amount of new data sources revolve around the concept of Point of Interest (POI) [2,3]. From a computational perspective, POIs represent real-world places as geometric point entities, in which people perform various activities. Online sources, such as geo-enabled social media and mapping applications, provide information about POI attributes (e.g. name, address, accessibility, provided facilities) and their functionality (e.g. opening hours, popularity, land use). A more recent addition to the spectrum of POI-related sources is street-level imagery. Unlike the well-established satellite imagery, this alternative source provides panoramic views of – primarily urban – environments at ground level.

M. Bakaev et al. (Eds.): ICWE 2019, LNCS 11496, pp. 32–46, 2019.
https://doi.org/10.1007/978-3-030-19274-7_3

A wealth of recent studies have used street-level imagery to analyze various aspects of urban environments [1,9,32]. Street-level imagery can be extracted from both proprietary (e.g. Google Street View) and public (e.g. Mapillary) online repositories. The information contained in street-level imagery is essentially visual. Thereby, POIs can be described based on morphological characteristics (e.g. height, color, materials, geometry) of their facades. A common feature which is found on several building facades, especially those of commercial stores and other business-related facilities, is *signs* or *visual labels*. These contain the name, logo, and other related information that help people identify businesses while navigating through physical space. Therefore, they could be a valuable source of information about the type and identity of a POI.

Advancements in computer vision, especially deep Convolutional Neural Networks (CNNs), have been successful in face detection, image segmentation, and scene recognition [22,30,31]. CNNs have also been used in the characterization of urban land uses [26,32], but several open challenges exist. Specific to the problem of POI classification, the performance of systems purely based on visual features is limited by issues of intra-class and inter-class differences in the appearance of store fronts across business categories [14]. Our hypothesis is that by incorporating semantically rich information from visual labels – e.g. the text from storefronts' signs – it is possible to substantially improve classification performance. The analysis and use of visual labels also present several challenges, e.g. their identification in street-level imagery, their transformation into textual information, and their disambiguation with regard to language and meaning.

This paper introduces a novel method, named *Scene-Text Semantics* (ST-Sem), that leverages visual labels from street-level imagery as complementary information for the classification of business storefronts. ST-Sem comprises three main components: (1) a *scene recognition* module classifies the POI type based on common visual characteristics of storefronts belonging to the same type; (2) a *scene-text semantic recognition* module detects textual information (e.g. labels, signs) in street-level imagery, transcribes it into a bag of words, and measures their semantic similarity against a reference corpus of business type descriptions; and (3) a *class rank module* which combines the prediction scores of the two aforementioned modules, and generates a final score for each candidate class. Contrary to existing approaches [13] that predominantly fuse visual and textual information at the feature level, ST-Sem combines visual and textual cues *after* resolving semantic ambiguities and incorrect digitization of the detected textual labels. Thanks to this late-fusion approach, ST-Sem can be more easily configured to work on different datasets (e.g. storefronts from different countries) with improved modularity and minimal visual models re-training.

Through extensive experiments, we show that ST-Sem is able to outperform state-of-the-art visual-only approaches for POI classification by 80%, and multimodal approaches by 4%. The experiments have been performed on the *Places* and *Con-text* datasets; and on a newly created dataset (that we contribute to the community) containing 1100 images from 22 classes of storefronts located in two countries. In addition to the quantitative comparison, we qualitatively analyze the performance of our method in an number of edge cases, to highlight limitations and suggest future directions of improvement.

The remainder of the paper is organized as follows: Sect. 2 discusses related work. In Sect. 3, we describe the ST-Sem method for POI classification from street-level imagery. Section 4 presents the experimental setup and discusses the obtained results. Finally, Sect. 5 summarizes the conclusions and discusses future lines of research.

2   Related Work

Capturing the semantics of POIs (e.g. bar or museum) is essential for facilitating location-based applications. While some location-based online social network services (e.g. Foursquare, Yelp) allow users to characterize the places they visit, the process is not automated and, instead, requires the users' help. In recent years, a considerable amount of methods are proposed by researchers for assigning semantic labels to unlabeled places [6,29]. Approaches on semantic place labeling mainly focus on user activity data to characterize POIs through their fine-grained visiting patterns.

Street-level imagery could be a useful data source in providing information about POI attributes (e.g. the type of POI) with higher spatial coverage. In recent years, researchers have demonstrated the feasibility of utilizing street-level imagery in mapping urban greenery [16], assessing physical changes in urban area [1], estimating city-level travel patterns [9], or in inferring subjective properties of urban areas such as safety, liveliness, and attractiveness [7]. Other works applied computer vision techniques to Google Street View images for finding morphological characteristics to distinguish European cities [5] or to infer the socioeconomic attributes of neighbourhood in US [8]. However, computer vision methods for POI types classification require large annotated datasets for training, which are currently available only for limited cities and countries.

Deep Convolutional Neural Networks (CNNs) have been successful in various vision-related tasks such as face detection, image segmentation, and scene recognition [22,31]. However, such breakthroughs in visual understanding do not imply that these models are suitable for fine-grained POI classification based on the visual appearance of store fronts from street-level imagery. This is due to the high degree of intra-class and the low degree of inter-class differences in the appearance of store fronts across business categories [14]. Yan et al. [28] take Spatial Context (i.e. nearby places) into account as complementary information to boost the performance of CNN models for classifying business places. Text in scene images, which frequently appears on the shop fronts, road signs, and billboards, usually conveys a large amount of valuable semantic information about the object or the scene in the same image. When it comes to the fine-grained classification of storefronts based on their business type, this textual information plays a crucial role in making more accurate predictions [21]. Most similar to our work, is that of Karaoglu et al. [13]. The latter proposed a multimodal approach that combines visual features and textual information from the imagery data in a single feature space as input for a SVM classifier. Our work differs from the existing literature in that we incorporate multilingual word embeddings trained on a large corpus to measure semantic relatedness between spotted textual information in street-level imagery and the candidate types of storefronts. Then, we propose a late fusion approach to leverage the obtained prediction scores of both modalities, and generate a final score for each candidate class. We compare ST-Sem against the approach of Karaoglu et al. [13] in Sect. 4, showing improved performance.

3 Methodology

This section presents ST-Sem, a novel multimodal approach for improving the fine-grained classification of business storefronts by leveraging visual and textual features in street-level imagery. The architecture of ST-Sem is depicted in Fig. 1. The image processing pipeline mainly consists of three components. First, the *Scene Recognition* module predicts the type of storefront at context level based on the common visual characteristics of each storefront type. Next, the *Scene-text Semantic Recognition* module detects textual data on the image and transcribes it into a bag of words and measures the semantic similarity between the bag of words, which usually represent the type of storefront, and each of the candidate types. Ultimately, the *Class Rank* module generates the final score for each candidate class by using a Linear Bimodal Fusion (LBF) method which combines the prediction scores from first and second modules. In the following paragraphs, we describe each component in detail.

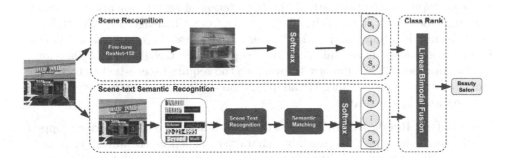

Fig. 1. Overview of the multimodal storefront image classification approach.

3.1 Scene Recognition

The scene recognition component is designed to classify images into one of the several candidate storefront types based on common morphological features. We use deep Convolutional Neural Networks (CNNs) which have been successful in several computer vision tasks [22,31].

Among a number of CNN models introduced for image classification tasks, we have employed the Residual Network (ResNet), which has shown superior performance on ImageNet classification [10].

We use the pre-trained `ResNet152-places365` model provided by [30], which includes the place categories[1]. *Places365* offers 365 classes, including some (e.g. `cliff` or `coral`) that do not qualify as POI type (e.g. `restaurant`) and, therefore, are not relevant in our setting. Without losing generality, we select 22 place types as our candidate class labels. Then, we fine-tune the pre-trained `ResNet152-places365` with a 22-way softmax classifier on the subset of the *Places* dataset. The last fully connected layer of the pre-trained network was removed and replaced by a new fully connected layer with 22 nodes to solve the storefront type classification problem. Then, the weights of the added fully connected layers were randomly generated from a Gaussian distribution with zero mean and standard deviation of 0.01.

3.2 Scene-Text Semantic Recognition

The scene-text extraction module is composed of three sub components. In the following paragraphs, we describe each sub-component in detail.

Scene-Text Detection. This sub-module aims at localizing and cropping text in images in the form of word boxes. Scene-text detection is challenging because scene texts have different sizes, width-height aspect ratios, font styles, lighting, perspective distortion, and orientation. In this work, we incorporate one of the state-of-the-art methods, named TextBoxes++ [17], which is an end-to-end trainable fast scene-text detector. The reason for choosing TextBoxes++ is that it outperforms state-of-the-art methods in terms of text localization accuracy and runtime issues of the *IC15* dataset [15] from Challenge 4 of the ICDAR 2015 Robust Reading Competition[2]. The *IC15* dataset is composed of 500 test images containing incidental scene text captured by Google Glass. Therefore, it is a good benchmark dataset to evaluate the required scene-text detector for storefront type classification. We adopt the pre-trained model parameters which are provided by the authors.

Scene-Text Recognition. The task of this sub-module is to transcribe cropped word images into machine-readable character sequences. However, it is considerably difficult to accurately recognize scene texts on street-level imagery because of the various shapes and distorted patterns of irregular texts. In order to tackle this problem, we adopt a multi-object rectified attention network (MORAN), proposed by [19]. MORAN consists of a multi-object rectification network (MORN) that rectifies images and an attention-based sequence recognition network (ASRN) that reads the text. In terms of reading rotated, scaled and stretched characters in different scene texts, this approach outperforms state-of-the-art methods on several standard text recognition benchmarks [19],

---

[1] https://github.com/CSAILVision/places365/.
[2] http://rrc.cvc.uab.es/?ch=4.

including the SVT-Perspective dataset [24] which contains 645 cropped images from Google Street View. In training the Scene-text recognition on the MJSynth dataset [11], which is dedicated for Natural Scene Text Recognition, we set the batch size to 64, the learning rate to 0.01 as suggested by the author. The model is trained for 10 epochs.

Semantic Matching. The semantic matching approach follows the assumption that textual information on the storefront indicates the type of business place. Given this assumption, the goal of the semantic matching module is to predict the type of storefront based on the semantic distance between the words extracted from the image and the standard name of each candidate storefront type, as defined in *ImageNet* synset[3], such as `cafe`, `bakery` etc. However, not all the words in street-level imagery should necessarily have semantic relations to the place type. Some words may have high similarity with one of the candidate classes, others may be completely irrelevant. For instance, words such as `hair`, `nail` or `beauty` on storefront images are likely to be related to a `Beauty Salon`. On the contrary, `OPEN/CLOSE` signs do not give any information about the type of storefront.

The text recognition module could result in some noisy texts, which need to be discarded. Before representing a word spotted by the word vector representation, we use a spell detection tool employing the Levenshtein Distance algorithm[4] to find permutations within an edit distance of 2 from the original word, and therefore remove noisy words. To further remove irrelevant words, we manually curated a blacklist of common – yet irrelevant – words, including verbs like `open`, `close`, `push`, `pull`, etc.

After reducing potential noise, we need to detect the language which the input word belongs to. In order to tackle this problem, we incorporate in our experiments the `polyglot` open source tool[5], which makes language prediction with a corresponding confidence score. If no language can be identified for the input word, English will be chosen as the default language.

Once the target language is determined, the recognized word must be transformed into a word vector representation. While there can be many implementations for capturing semantic relatedness [18], previous studies have shown that *word embeddings* [20,23] perform this task particularly well by measuring the cosine similarity of the word embedding vectors. These vector-based models represent words in a continuous vector space where semantically similar words are embedded close to one another. In our experiments, we adopt FastText [4] to transform recognized texts into a word vector representation. The main reason for incorporating FastText is its promising performance in overcoming the problem of out-of-vocabulary words, by representing each word as a bag of character n-grams. We use pre-trained word vectors for 2 languages (English and German), trained on Common Crawl and Wikipedia[6].

---

[3] http://www.image-net.org/synset.
[4] https://github.com/barrust/pyspellchecker.
[5] https://github.com/aboSamoor/polyglot.
[6] https://fasttext.cc/docs/en/crawl-vectors.html.

According to the detected language l, the corresponding pre-trained word vector V_l is selected; then, each recognized word is represented by the pre-trained 300-dimensional word vector as v_i. Finally, we use the method proposed by [25] to align the V_l in the same space as the English word vector for multilingual semantic matching. Similarly, each candidate class of storefront type C is represented by a word vector c_j with an English word embedding as reference. Then, we calculate the cosine similarity between each class label (c_j) and each spotted text (v_i) as follows:

$$\cos(\Theta_{ij}) = \frac{v_i^T c_j}{|v_i| \, |c_j|} \tag{1}$$

The probability scores P_i for each candidate storefront type is calculated by averaging similarity scores of all spotted words:

$$P_j = \frac{\sum_{i=1}^{K} \cos(\Theta_{ij})}{K} \tag{2}$$

Then, a softmax function is used to normalize the probability scores for each candidate storefront type by the sum of the N candidate ranking scores so that they sum up to 1. The softmax function can be formulated as follows:

$$\sigma(Z)_j = \frac{e^{Z_j}}{\sum_{n=1}^{N} e^{Z_n}} \tag{3}$$

where Z is a vector of probability scores, N is the number of candidate classes, $j = 1, 2, \ldots, N$ is the index of each probability score in the probability vector Z, and $i = 1, 2, \ldots, K$ is the index of each spotted text. Similar to the scene recognition module, the scene-text extraction module results in a probability score for each candidate storefront type which is between 0 and 1.

3.3   Class Rank

Inspired by search re-ranking algorithms in information retrieval, we use a Linear Bimodal Fusion (LBF) method (here essentially a 2-component convex combination), which linearly combines the ranking scores provided by the CNN model and the semantic similarity scores from the scene-text semantic recognition module, as shown in Eq. 4.

$$S_{mixed}(d) = w_v . S_v(d) + (1 - w_v) . S_t(d) \tag{4}$$

where S_{mixed}, $S_v(d)$, and $S_t(d)$ refer to the final ranking score, visual recognition score, and semantic similarity score for storefront type d respectively, w_v and w_t are the weights for the scene recognition component and scene-text extraction component, and $w_v + w_t = 1$. The weights are determined according to the relative performance of the individual components. Specifically, the weight for the scene recognition module is determined using the following equation:

$$w_v = \frac{acc_v}{acc_v + acc_t} \tag{5}$$

where acc_v and acc_t are the measured top@1 accuracy of scene recognition component and scene-text semantic recognition component, respectively.

4   Evaluation

This section reports on two experiments designed to assess the performance of our proposed approach in providing fine-grained classification of business storefronts using street-level imagery:

Comparison to Visual-Only Baselines. To show the utility and effectiveness of semantically rich textual information embedded in street-level imagery, we compare the classification performance of ST-Sem to two visual-only baselines, namely GoogLeNet [27] and ResNet152 [10].

Comparison with Multimodal Methods. We also compare ST-Sem with a state-of-the-art method for fine-grained classification of business places [13], to highlight the advantages of incorporating multilingual word embeddings for semantic matching between textual cues on the image and different types of storefronts. To the best of our knowledge, the work of [13] is currently the best performing method in literature.

4.1   Experimental Setup

Datasets. We performed the experiments on three datasets: *Storefront*, a manually created collection of storefront images; *Places* [30], and *Con-text* [13]. Images in the *Storefront* and *Con-text* contain textual information, while *Places* is a mixture of images with and without text.

The *Storefront* fills a gap in existing datasets for the evaluation of solutions based on street-level imagery. Unlike other datasets, all images in *Storefront* are taken from a street-side perspective with complex scenes and objects with less visual differences, thus making it more difficult to classify the type of storefronts. We populated the *Storefront* dataset using the Street View API[7] from Google. We have randomly collected storefront images from two countries: USA and Germany. Those images are used in the storefront business type classification. The dataset consists of 1100 images, equally distributed in 22 categories: Motel, Shoe Shop, Pharmacy, Jewelry, Candy Shop, Restaurant, Bakery, Cafe, Gift Shop, Pizzeria, Butcher, Bookstore, Icecream, Fastfood, Toy Shop, Auto Repair, Beauty Salon, Pet Shop, Supermarket, Bar, Clothing, and Hardware Store.

To further evaluate the model, we carry out two additional experiments on two benchmarks that are used for fine-grained classification of places, including the business places we are interested in: (1) The *Places* dataset, introduced by [30]. It contains more than 10 million images divided into 365 unique scene categories with 5000 to 30,000 images each, and 100 testing images per category. As not all 365 categories are relevant for our study, we have selected a subset of images based on the categories described above. And (2) the *Con-text* dataset [13]. It is a sub-class (i.e. building and business places)

---

[7] https://developers.google.com/streetview/.

of the *ImageNet* dataset which consists of 24,255 images divided into 28 categories: Steak House, Bistro, Pawn Shop, Cafe, Tavern, Tobacco, Dry Cleaner, Tea House, Country Store, Packing Store, Restaurant, Funeral, Repair Shop, Pharmacy, School, Computer Store, Medical Center, Diner, Pizzeria, Bakery, Hotspot, Massage Center, Pet Shop, Barber, Theatre, Bookstore. The properties of each dataset are described in Table 1.

Table 1. Dataset statistics: number of images and place types

Dataset	#Categories	Training	Testing
Storefront	22	-	1,100
Places	22	12,500	2,200
Con-text	28	24,255	2,800

Implementation Details. Our method is built upon several pre-trained models: ResNet152 [10] to extract image features, *TextBoxes++* [17] to localize texts in images, *MORAN* [19] to transform spotted texts into machine-readable character sequences, and 2 pre-trained word embeddings in two languages (English and German), trained on Common Crawl[8] and Wikipedia, to measure semantic relatedness between the transcribed words with the standard name of each candidate storefront type as defined in the *ImageNet* synset. A pre-trained *ResNet*152 model on *ImageNet*, is fine-tuned with a 28-way softmax classifier for the 28 candidate business types of the *Con-text* dataset. Similarly, a pre-trained *ResNet*152 model on the whole *Places* image database [30], is fine-tuned with a 22-way softmax classifier for *Places* and *Storefront*, which consist of 22 candidate types each. We used the same settings for fine-tuning the visual feature extractor on all datasets: the learning rate is set to 0.01 for the first 7K iterations, and then is divided by 10 every 10K iterations. The network is fine-tuned for 20 epochs. For the text representation, we only consider spotted words having more than 3 letters, under the assumption that words having less than 3 letters are not likely to provide relevant information for our classification task. The proposed method is implemented using the Caffe [12] deep learning framework. All the training and experiments are conducted on a NVIDIA Tesla P100 GPU. The source code of the pipeline, as well as the *Storefront* dataset, are available on GitHub[9].

Evaluation Metrics. Performance is evaluated using the following metrics: Average Precision (AP) of each category; and the mean of AP (mAP) over all

---

[8] http://commoncrawl.org/the-data/.
[9] https://github.com/shahinsharifi/ST-Sem.

categories. To calculate the Average Precision for each category, we use the formula used in [13,14] which is described as:

$$AP = \sum_{k=1}^{n} P(k)\Delta r(k) \qquad (6)$$

where k is the rank in the sequence of classified images, n is the number of images in the current category, $P(k)$ is the precision at cut-off k, and $\Delta r(k)$ is the change in recall from items $k-1$ to k in the sorted list.

4.2 Results

Comparison with Visual-Only Baselines. We conduct an experiment to compare the performance of the proposed method with two visual-only baselines. We fine-tune the pre-trained GoogLeNet with a 28-class softmax classifier on *Con-text* and a 22-class softmax classifier on *Places*. The fine-tuned models on *Places* are also used for the experiment on *Storefront* as both datasets consist of the same categories. Our goal is to show the influence of leveraging textual information from imagery on the classification of business-related places. Table 2 displays the quantitative comparisons between two visual-only baselines and ST-Sem on all three datasets described above. The experiment shows that leveraging textual information from imagery in addition to visual features significantly outperforms visual-only baselines on all three datasets. As shown in Table 2, improvement varies between datasets due to the different amount of images that contain text.

Table 2. Classification performance of visual-only baselines and the proposed ST-Sem method on three datasets.

Datasets	Method	mAP(%)
Storefront	GoogLeNet	39.4564
	ResNet152	42.1785
	ST-Sem	**70.0524**
Places	GoogLeNet	83.5912
	ResNet152	85.7122
	ST-Sem	**87.0775**
Con-text	GoogLeNet	60.2569
	ResNet152	63.2546
	ST-Sem	**78.0221**

We observe that both visual baselines have relatively weak performance on *Storefront*. We attribute the difference to the visual layout of images from the *Storefront* dataset, as they are all produced from a street-level imagery source that differs from the training data of the respective network.

This scenario clearly highlights the advantages of ST-Sem, where by reusing pre-trained classifiers it is possible to achieve remarkable classification performance (79% and 66% increase on GoogLeNet and ResNet152, respectively) even when abundant training data are not available. Notice that by exploiting textual information, ST-Sem we are able to improve the classification performance also on the *Places* and *Con-text* datasets, with a respective 2% and 20% increase on GoogLeNet and ResNet152.

Table 3 breaks down the results by business category on the *Storefront* dataset. For some categories such as Motel or Pharmacy, all methods show relatively good performance. We account this result to the morphological dissimilarity of these POIs when compared to other types of business-related places. On the contrary, as most of bakeries have quite similar facades compared to other types of storefronts, both visual baselines show lower performance. We also observe that both visual baselines have relatively equal performance across all classes, which points out that the effectiveness of visual similarity is generally limited when the training data differ from the scenes to be predicted. We assume that the cross-class variations in the performance of ST-Sem are mainly accountable to the semantic ambiguity of the text used in their storefronts (arguably, hotel signs are less ambiguous than bookstores or beauty salons). We leave such an analysis to future work.

Table 3. Classification performance in mAP (%) for visual baselines and the proposed model for top 10 business type on the storefront dataset. Legend: MO – Motel; SH – Shoe Shop; PH – Pharmacy; JW – Jewelry; CSH – Candy Shop; RE – Restaurant; BA – Bakery; BS – Beauty Salon; CA –Cafe; BS – Bookstore

Method	MO	SH	PH	JW	CSH	RE	BA	BS	CA	BS
GoogLeNet	75.7	18.3	71.6	40.2	67.6	38.5	11.5	10.0	39.9	21.7
ResNet152	74.2	23.0	75.6	33.7	69.1	40.9	9.6	9.3	44.7	23.7
ST-Sem	**94.5**	**72.5**	**87.3**	**66.2**	**88.6**	**87.0**	**72.7**	**74.0**	**91.5**	**61.6**

Comparison with Multimodal Methods. We compare ST-Sem with Karaoglu et al. [13], the best performing state-of-the-art method that addresses the problem of business type classification by leveraging textual information from images. We perform experiments on three datasets. The results of Karaoglu et al. [13] are replicated by using the source code provided by the author[10]. The CNN models which are used in both methods to extract visual features are fine-tuned on *Con-text* and *Places*, respectively. As shown in Table 4, ST-Sem outperforms the state-of-the-art results from 67.5% to 70.05% ($\sim$+4%) on the *Storefront* dataset. There is also a slightly better performance on *Context* ($\sim$+1%) and *Places* ($\sim$+2%).

---

[10] https://github.com/taotaoorange/words-matter-scene-text-for-image-classification.

The results show that, in addition to obvious advantages in terms of language independence and modularity, ST-Sem provides comparable or superior performance across a variety of datasets.

Table 4. Classification performance mAP (%) for ST-Sem and Karaoglu et al. [13]

Datasets	Method	mAP(%)
Storefront	Karaoglu et al.	67.55
	ST-Sem	**70.05**
Places	Karaoglu et al.	84.35
	ST-Sem	**86.08**
Con-text	Karaoglu et al.	70.7
	ST-Sem	**71.35**

Discussion. In this section we discuss examples of scenes where ST-Sem provides non-obvious correct (Fig. 2) and incorrect (Fig. 3) predictions. As shown in Fig. 2a and c, ST-Sem can recognize the type of storefront, even when there is no word having direct relation to their types (e.g. *book* or *clothes*); the proposed semantic matching module is able to infer that texts such as *Barnes & Noble* and *GAP* are, respectively, semantically close to *bookstore* and *clothing* in the vector space, thus enabling correct classification. As depicted in Fig. 2b, the proposed method is also capable of measuring the semantic similarity between different languages. More specifically, *Apotheke* is recognized as a German scene-text on the image and then, it is transformed into a multilingual word vector which is semantically similar to *Pharmacy*.

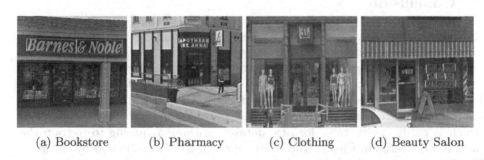

(a) Bookstore   (b) Pharmacy   (c) Clothing   (d) Beauty Salon

Fig. 2. Examples of correct classifications, with ground-truth label (GT) and probability score on the Storefront dataset. (a) GT: *Bookstore*, Predicted: *Bookstore - 0.71*; (b) GT: *Pharmacy*, Predicted: *Pharmacy - 0.83*; (c) GT: *Clothing*, Predicted: *Clothing - 0.75*, (d) GT: *Beauty Salon*, Predicted: *Beauty Salon - 0.67*

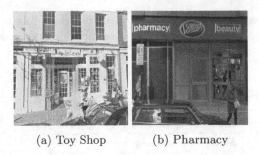

(a) Toy Shop   (b) Pharmacy

Fig. 3. Examples of incorrect classification results on the storefront dataset. (a) GT: *Toy Shop*, Predicted: *Bookstore - 0.58* (b) GT: *Pharmacy*, Predicted: *Beauty Salon - 0.42*

Figure 3 shows examples of incorrect prediction. As shown in Fig. 3a, the scene-text detector failed to detect textual information on the corresponding image due to the uncommon font used in the signs. Therefore, the classification is only based on the visual features. This failure shows an obvious limitation of our method, i.e. that the overall performance is highly dependent on the performance of the scene-text detection module. Without textual information, the system simply relies on visual features. Figure 3b shows that the scene-text recognition module recognized two informative words (`pharmacy` and `beauty`) on the image, but the storefront type is not correctly classified. The reason of failure is likely to be that the semantic similarity scores of `pharmacy` and `Beauty Salon` are almost equal for this particular storefront. Therefore, similarly to the previous failure case, classification was only based on the morphological features of the storefront, which can indeed be erroneous.

5   Conclusion

In this work, we have introduced `ST-Sem`, a multimodal method that integrates visual and text cues extracted from street-level imagery for fine-grained classification of POIs. `ST-Sem` is able to incorporate multilingual word embeddings that measure the semantic similarity between detected textual information in street-level imagery and the candidate types of POIs. Moreover, `ST-Sem`'s late-fusion approach improves the performance of fine-grained storefront type classification, which is easily configurable for new datasets without requiring to re-train the models from scratch. Clearly, the effectiveness of `ST-Sem` is limited by the quality of the scene-text detection and the semantic similarity components. However, `ST-Sem` can be easily extended to include more methods.

In future work, we plan to extend the `ST-Sem` pipeline by incorporating additional semantically-rich information in the classification process, such as contextual information and user reviews, where available. We also plan to extend the scope of our experiments to other cities and languages, to further demonstrate the generalizability of the approach.

References

1. Alcantarilla, P.F., Stent, S., Ros, G., Arroyo, R., Gherardi, R.: Street-view change detection with deconvolutional networks. Auton. Robots **42**(7), 1301–1322 (2018)
2. Balduini, M., Bozzon, A., Della Valle, E., Huang, Y., Houben, G.J.: Recommending venues using continuous predictive social media analytics. IEEE Internet Comput. **18**(5), 28–35 (2014)
3. Bocconi, S., Bozzon, A., Psyllidis, A., Titos Bolivar, C., Houben, G.J.: Social glass: a platform for urban analytics and decision-making through heterogeneous social data. In: Proceedings of the 24th International Conference on World Wide Web, pp. 175–178. WWW 2015 Companion. ACM, New York (2015)
4. Bojanowski, P., Grave, E., Joulin, A., Mikolov, T.: Enriching word vectors with subword information. Trans. Assoc. Comput. Linguist. **5**, 135–146 (2017)
5. Doersch, C., Singh, S., Gupta, A., Sivic, J., Efros, A.: What makes Paris look like Paris? ACM Trans. Graph. **31**(4) (2012)
6. Falcone, D., Mascolo, C., Comito, C., Talia, D., Crowcroft, J.: What is this place? inferring place categories through user patterns identification in geo-tagged tweets. In: 2014 6th International Conference on Mobile Computing, Applications and Services (MobiCASE), pp. 10–19. IEEE (2014)
7. Fu, K., Chen, Z., Lu, C.T.: Streetnet: preference learning with convolutional neural network on urban crime perception. In: Proceedings of the 26th ACM SIGSPATIAL International Conference on Advances in Geographic Information Systems, pp. 269–278. ACM (2018)
8. Gebru, T., Krause, J., Wang, Y., Chen, D., Deng, J., Aiden, E.L., Fei-Fei, L.: Using deep learning and google street view to estimate the demographic makeup of the us. arXiv preprint arXiv:1702.06683 (2017)
9. Goel, R., et al.: Estimating city-level travel patterns using street imagery: a case study of using Google street view in britain. PloS One **13**(5), e0196521 (2018)
10. He, K., Zhang, X., Ren, S., Sun, J.: Deep residual learning for image recognition. In: Proceedings of the IEEE Conference on Computer Vision and Pattern Recognition, pp. 770–778 (2016)
11. Jaderberg, M., Simonyan, K., Vedaldi, A., Zisserman, A.: Reading text in the wild with convolutional neural networks. Int. J. Comput. Vis. **116**(1), 1–20 (2016)
12. Jia, Y., et al.: Caffe: convolutional architecture for fast feature embedding. In: Proceedings of the 22nd ACM International Conference on Multimedia, pp. 675–678. ACM (2014)
13. Karaoglu, S., Tao, R., van Gemert, J.C., Gevers, T.: Con-text: text detection for fine-grained object classification. IEEE Trans. Image Proc. **26**(8), 3965–3980 (2017)
14. Karaoglu, S., Tao, R., Gevers, T., Smeulders, A.W.: Words matter: scene text for image classification and retrieval. IEEE Trans. Multimed. **19**(5), 1063–1076 (2017)
15. Karatzas, D., et al.: ICDAR 2015 competition on robust reading. In: 2015 13th International Conference on Document Analysis and Recognition (ICDAR), pp. 1156–1160. IEEE (2015)
16. Li, X., Ratti, C., Seiferling, I.: Mapping urban landscapes along streets using Google street view. In: Peterson, M.P. (ed.) ICACI 2017. LNGC, pp. 341–356. Springer, Cham (2017). https://doi.org/10.1007/978-3-319-57336-6_24
17. Liao, M., Shi, B., Bai, X.: Textboxes++: a single-shot oriented scene text detector. IEEE Trans. Image Proc. **27**(8), 3676–3690 (2018)
18. Lofi, C.: Measuring semantic similarity and relatedness with distributional and knowledge-based approaches. Inf. Media Technol. **10**(3), 493–501 (2015)

19. Luo, C., Jin, L., Sun, Z.: Moran: A multi-object rectified attention network for scene text recognition. Pattern Recognition (2019)
20. Mikolov, T., Sutskever, I., Chen, K., Corrado, G.S., Dean, J.: Distributed representations of words and phrases and their compositionality. In: Advances in Neural Information Processing Systems, pp. 3111–3119 (2013)
21. Movshovitz-Attias, Y., Yu, Q., Stumpe, M.C., Shet, V., Arnoud, S., Yatziv, L.: Ontological supervision for fine grained classification of street view storefronts. In: Proceedings of the IEEE Conference on Computer Vision and Pattern Recognition, pp. 1693–1702 (2015)
22. Parkhi, O.M., Vedaldi, A., Zisserman, A., et al.: Deep face recognition. In: BMVC, vol. 1, p. 6 (2015)
23. Pennington, J., Socher, R., Manning, C.: Glove: Global vectors for word representation. In: Proceedings of the 2014 Conference on Empirical Methods in Natural Language Processing (EMNLP), pp. 1532–1543 (2014)
24. Quy Phan, T., Shivakumara, P., Tian, S., Lim Tan, C.: Recognizing text with perspective distortion in natural scenes. In: Proceedings of the IEEE International Conference on Computer Vision, pp. 569–576 (2013)
25. Smith, S.L., Turban, D.H., Hamblin, S., Hammerla, N.Y.: Offline bilingual word vectors, orthogonal transformations and the inverted softmax. arXiv preprint arXiv:1702.03859 (2017)
26. Srivastava, S., Vargas Muñoz, J.E., Lobry, S., Tuia, D.: Fine-grained landuse characterization using ground-based pictures: a deep learning solution based on globally available data. Int. J. Geogr. Inf. Sci. 1–20 (2018)
27. Szegedy, C., et al.: Going deeper with convolutions. In: Proceedings of the IEEE Conference on Computer Vision and Pattern Recognition, pp. 1–9 (2015)
28. Yan, B., Janowicz, K., Mai, G., Zhu, R.: xnet+sc: Classifying places based on images by incorporating spatial contexts. In: 10th International Conference on Geographic Information Science (GIScience 2018). Schloss Dagstuhl-Leibniz-Zentrum fuer Informatik (2018)
29. Yang, D., Li, B., Cudré-Mauroux, P.: Poisketch: semantic place labeling over user activity streams. Technical Report, Université de Fribourg (2016)
30. Zhou, B., Lapedriza, A., Khosla, A., Oliva, A., Torralba, A.: Places: a 10 million image database for scene recognition. IEEE Trans. Pattern Anal. Mach. Intell. **40**(6), 1452–1464 (2018)
31. Zhou, B., Lapedriza, A., Xiao, J., Torralba, A., Oliva, A.: Learning deep features for scene recognition using places database. In: Advances in Neural Information Processing Systems, pp. 487–495 (2014)
32. Zhu, Y., Deng, X., Newsam, S.: Fine-grained land use classification at the city scale using ground-level images. IEEE Trans. Multimed. (2019)

Time and Location Recommendation
for Crime Prevention

Yihong Zhang[1]([✉]), Panote Siriaraya[2], Yukiko Kawai[2], and Adam Jatowt[1]

[1] Kyoto University, Kyoto, Japan
yhzhang7@gmail.com, adam@dl.kuis.kyoto-u.ac.jp
[2] Kyoto Sangyo University, Kyoto, Japan
spanote@gmail.com, kawai@cc.kyoto-su.ac.jp

Abstract. In recent years we have seen more and more open government and administrative data made available on the Web. Crime data, for example, allows civic organizations and ordinary citizens to obtain safety-related information on their surroundings. In this paper, we study crime prediction as a recommendation problem, using fine-grained open crime data. A common issue in current crime prediction methods is that, given fine-grained spatial temporal units, crime data would become very sparse, and prediction would not work properly. By modeling crime prediction as a recommendation problem, however, we can make use of the abundant selection of methods in recommendation systems that inherently consider data sparsity. We present our model and show how collaborative filtering and contextual-based recommendation methods can be applied. Focusing on two major types of crimes in the city of San Francisco, our empirical results show that recommendation methods can outperform traditional crime prediction methods, given small spatial and temporal granularity. Specifically, we show that by using recommendation methods, we can capture 70% of future thefts using only 20% man-hour, 13% more than traditional methods.

Keywords: Crime prediction · Web open data · Recommendation

1 Introduction

In recent years, we have seen more and more open government and administrative data made available on the Web. One particular example is crime data. Based on our recent investigation, five out of top ten largest U.S. cities now publish their crime data online, including New York City[1], Los Angeles[2], Chicago[3], and Philadelphia[4]. These crime data reveal information that was difficult to obtain before, and which is of particular interest to civic organizations and ordinary

---

[1] https://data.cityofnewyork.us/Public-Safety/NYPD-Complaint-Data-Historic/qgea-i56i.
[2] https://data.lacity.org/A-Safe-City/Crime-Data-from-2010-to-Present/y8tr-7khq/data.
[3] https://data.cityofchicago.org/Public-Safety/Crimes-2001-to-present/ijzp-q8t2.
[4] https://www.opendataphilly.org/dataset/crime-incidents.

© Springer Nature Switzerland AG 2019
M. Bakaev et al. (Eds.): ICWE 2019, LNCS 11496, pp. 47–62, 2019.
https://doi.org/10.1007/978-3-030-19274-7_4

citizens who are concerned about public safety. Researchers have then starting proposing crime prediction methods leveraging these data [8,20,23]. The outcome of crime prediction can be used in many scenarios. First, we can plan police patrols targeting the location and time for which the crimes are likely to happen. On the other hand, residents and tourists can avoid such locations and times when planning their outdoor activities.

In this paper, we consider crime prediction as a recommendation problem. Crime prediction deals with the problem of predicting the time and location where future crimes are likely to happen given past crime data [24]. We show that crime prediction can be properly modeled using existing recommendation system techniques that achieve accurate results. First we need to note that our work is not related to criminal profiling and series crime prediction, as studied in several works [6,12]. We consider, instead, the spatial and temporal factors hidden in past crime records. To the best of our knowledge, no previous work has positioned crime prediction as a recommendation problem.

We have seen in previous works that techniques such as kernel density estimation (KDE) can be used to map crime hotspots [8,9], considering that past crime records may indicate areas where crimes concentrate. While hotspot detection is effective for understanding geographical distribution of crimes, it does not consider their temporal aspects. We could simply assume no temporal effect and use hotspot map as our sole guidance, but previous study shows that incorporating temporal aspect can steadily increase the prediction accuracy [21]. There is a number of works that propose spatial temporal crime prediction methods that can output a probability that the crime will happen in a certain location on the next day [1,22,23]. However, this may not be so useful, as the police will need to patrol the location all day if it turned out that the probability is high. In our study, we would want to know not only the day, but also the hour, that a crime is likely to happen. This is necessary for effective planning of police patrols.

With finer spatial and temporal units, however, the problem emerges, which is the sparsity of data. Intuitively, given a limited number of crimes in the studied period, if the granularity is small, many of the spatial temporal units will have no crime records. Indeed, if we map 80 weeks of thefts in San Francisco[5] starting from January 1st, 2016, into 200 m × 200 m blocks, and $24 \times 7 = 168$ h in the week, about 87% of the spatial temporal units will have no criminal incidents. For the assault type of crime the corresponding number is 94%. Yet, it is intuitive that if a spatial temporal unit had no crime incident before, it does not mean it will have no crime in the future. According to *routine activity theory* [5], for a crime to occur, three elements should converge in time and space, namely, a motivated offender, a suitable target or victim, and the absence of a capable guardian. Based on this theory, crime occurrence in an area is mostly caused by the criminals in this area, who commit crimes when opportunity is noticed (if one neglects the guardians' aspect for simplicity). We can assume that crime occurring in a given area and at a given hour is influenced by two factors, criminals being present in that area, which is a property of the area, and people's

---

[5] Data obtained from DataSF: https://datasf.org/opendata/.

daily routine at that hour (e.g., commuting). We found that these two factors can be properly modeled as a recommendation problem.

In a typical recommendation system, there are three components, users, items, and user-item interactions. The user item interaction may be a review rating given by a user for an item, or a purchase record. Among various recommendation techniques, two main groups of methods are collaborative filtering and context-based rating prediction, both of which deal with sparse data [11,17]. It is not uncommon to have 99% sparsity in a product review dataset[6]. Methods in recommendation systems that mitigate sparsity are thus suitable for our fine-grained crime prediction case.

We will give a detailed explanation of our model in Sect. 3. In Sect. 4 we discuss context-based recommendation techniques which use Twitter data, and in Sect. 5 we present the experimental results. We focus on two common crime types, namely, theft and assault, in the city of San Francisco, though our approach can be easily extended to other crime types and cities. We summarize our contribution as follows:

- We model crime prediction as a recommendation problem. This modeling aims to solve the data sparsity issue when it is desirable to achieve fine-grained prediction. We also show that CF-type techniques and context-based rating prediction in recommender systems can be applied to crime prediction.
- We run extensive experiments on real-world crime data, comparing a number of recommendation approaches. We find that recommendation techniques are effective for predicting future crimes. For example, we show that with the prediction by recommendation methods, we can use 20% of man-hour to capture around 70% future thefts in San Francisco.

2   Related Works

Computational spatial-temporal analysis for crime has been studied extensively [24]. The types of temporal patterns studied include crime rate changes in long time periods (e.g., five years), seasonal and annually recurring patterns, and the sequential behavior of criminals [10]. Due to the lack of fine-grained crime records, however, hourly temporal patterns have been rarely studied. With a more general applicability, kernel density estimation (KDE) has been used to map crime hotspots [3]. The crime-based navigation system proposed by Galbrun et al. for example, maps a risk index to geographical points using KDE with past crime records [7]. Boni and Gerber propose to extend KDE with evolutionary optimization to improve crime prediction accuracy [1]. A problem with KDE mapping is that when the granularity is small, there will not be enough training data to properly learn a model [9]. Indeed, Boni and Gerber try to mitigate this problem by down-sampling the negative examples [1]. Another popular technique used for crime forecasting is ARIMA [4]. However, this technique does not consider the spatial factors hidden in the data.

---

[6] E.g., http://www.cs.cornell.edu/people/pabo/movie-review-data/.

Crime prediction using Web data as context has recently started attracting attention in research community following the availability of fine-grained spatial-temporal data. Wang *et al.* propose incorporating tweets into a crime prediction model [21]. They find that adding tweets into the prediction model improves prediction accuracy. However, their tweets are limited to a certain news account. Gerber later makes another study on incorporating tweets into crime prediction models [8]. Similarly, he transforms tweets using LDA and adds them to an existing model based on kernel density estimation (KDE). The experiments with 25 different crime types show that incorporating tweets improves prediction accuracy for 19 crimes types, but for a few other crime types the accuracy decreases. Wang *et al.* use\multiple data sources in a crime prediction model [20]. They use the total crime number provided by Chicago administration and divide the city by community areas as the unit of study. Zhao and Tang propose to incorporate crime complaint records, weather, Foursquare, and taxi flow data into a prediction model [23], targeting the city of New York. The unit of study is $2\,km \times 2\,km$ grid, and so, their method is difficult to be applied to a finer granularity because of data sparsity. Yang *et al.* build a crime prediction model, using both tweets and Foursquare data, as a binary classification problem [22], for which they divide the city into large grids and generate negative samples in even spaces.

A common problem in these studies is that, crime data will become very sparse if we study it based on finer granularity. For this reason, these works either have to treat days or weeks as atomic temporal units, and blocks of more than $1\,Km$ as the basic spatial unit, or need some down-sampling procedures to deal with the sparsity. In this paper, however, we approach crime prediction task based on hourly granularity of temporal units and a small spatial unit. We then show that existing recommendation techniques can operate on the condition of sparse data.

3   Crime Prediction as a Recommendation Problem

In this section, we discuss how crime prediction can be modeled as a recommendation problem. More specifically, we discuss how spatial temporal factors can be modeled as users and items. We also show that, with this modeling way, techniques used in recommendation systems can be applied for crime prediction.

3.1   Defining User and Item

Similar to a recommendation problem that has two latent factors, user and item, we argue that in crime prediction, we also have two latent factors, namely, time and location. Similar to the rating a user gives to an item which reflects the interaction between the user and the item, the number of crimes in a location at a given time also reflects the criminal interweaving between the location and time factors. Thus it is not difficult to consider time and location as user and item in a recommendation problem. Here we face a design choice, i.e., should we model time as the user or the item (and location as the other factor)? We propose to model time as the item and location as the user, instead of the other way around. We have two reasons. First, in a typical recommendation problem, the number of users is far more than the number of items. In our problem, we also find that, given a small granularity, the number of locations, typically thousands, is much higher than the number of time units, which in our study is $24 \times 7 = 168$ h in a week. Second, when we consider that crimes are mostly caused by the criminals living in the neighborhood, it is more appropriate to represent the human factor as the location, rather than as time. In this way, locations, like users, contain more inherent properties that are independent to each other, while time, like items, contains more relative properties that can be revealed by comparison.

As we mentioned, the advantage of modeling crime prediction as a recommendation problem, is that we can have a fine spatial temporal granularity, and use existing recommendation techniques that are effective for sparse data. Therefore in our work, we choose a spatial temporal granularity that are finer than most of the existing works. Specifically, we use 200×200 m blocks, and $24 \times 7 = 168$ h in a week. For the city we study, San Francisco, the spatial granularity will result in around 2,000 blocks that contain at least one theft or assault record. The total numbers of block-hour units are around 396k for theft and 324k for assault. The crime number and sparsity are shown in Table 1. The sparsity is calculated as the ratio of units that has 0 crime in all block-hour units. This level of sparsity is close to one in typical recommendation problems.

Table 1. Crime number and sparsity for crimes in SF.

	0	1	2	3	4	≥5	Sparsity
Theft	346,970	18,565	13,264	5,990	3,971	7,888	0.87
Assault	30,6278	76,56	5,446	2,055	1,421	1,720	0.94

We argue that a 0-crime block-hour unit does not mean that no crime will happen at that location and time. In product recommendation, even though the user rating for an item is absent, the user can still potentially buy and rate the item (thus the recommendation is needed). Similarly, even if no crime happened at a location and hour in past records, it is still possible for criminals to commit crime at that location and hour. We will need technique to infer this potential based on the sparse records. In the following section, we briefly review the *collaborative filtering* technique used in recommendation systems that can help us solve the problem.

3.2 Inferring Crime Potential

Collaborative filtering (CF) is a technique widely used in product recommendations. It is based on item or user similarities in the rating data, and accordingly, there are item-based CF and user-based CF. With item-based CF, items with similar ratings are ranked and recommended to the user. With user-based CF, user similarity is calculated based on the rating they give to items, and items from similar users are ranked and recommended to the user. Generally speaking, item-based CF provides better recommendation than user-based CF, because items are easier to be compared. In the following explanation, we assume item-based CF, but changing it to user-based CF is straightforward.

The first step of CF is to calculate the similarity matrix. Typically, given item i and j, and their rating vectors, $\vec{i}$ and $\vec{j}$, their similarity is calculated as the cosine similarity:

$$sim(i,j) = \cos(\vec{i}, \vec{j}) = \frac{\vec{i} \cdot \vec{j}}{\| \vec{i} \|_2 * \| \vec{j} \|_2}$$

Then, the prediction of the rating user u gives to item i can be calculated as the weighted sum:

$$P_{u,i} = \frac{\sum_{j=1}^{N} sim(i,j) * R_{u,j}}{\sum_{j=1}^{N} sim(i,j)}$$

where N is the number of items user u has given ratings, and $R_{u,j}$ is the rating user u has given to item j. By this calculation, the absent ratings for all remaining items can be inferred. In our crime prediction case, crime potential at a particular location and a time, for which no crime was recorded, can also be inferred in same way.

4   Incorporating Context Information

In addition to the user, item, and rating model, there is a group of works in recommendation systems that deal with another dimension of information, i.e., contextual information. For example, in an online shopping website, users will not only give a rating to the product they purchased, but also provide a detailed review in natural language texts explaining how the assessment was made. Such review is considered as the contextual information for the product, and has been extensively studied in recommendation [11,13,14]. Incorporating context information in recommendation often does not only improve the accuracy in rating prediction, but also reveals some insights about hidden factors behind the rating, for example, *why* two users agree on the same product but disagree on another product. In this section, we will discuss how crime prediction can be modeled into a context-based recommendation problem, and the techniques that can be applied.

4.1   Generating Context Information for Crime

In our model, which treats blocks as users, and hours as items, and crime number as ratings, we do not have contextual information like review texts in a shopping website. We need to find a second source that provides spatial-temporal text data. Nowadays microblogs like Twitter generate everyday millions of short texts that have geo-location attached. We can use such data to associate time and location to textual content. Indeed, unlike product reviews, which are mostly descriptions of the product that lead to the ratings, the tweets posted at a given time and location are usually not containing any descriptions of crimes. However, previous works show that tweet text is to some extend related to crime, and can be used to improve crime predictions [8,21]. For example, Gerber found that criminal damage is correlated with tweets of sports-oriented and museum-oriented topics [8]. In this paper, we also consider that tweets contain implicit information related to crime at certain hour and location, and can thus be used as the context information. We collect geo-tagged tweets and assign them with block indexes and hours based on their geo-locations and timestamps. Note that since we generalize temporal pattern to hours in a week, the tweets do not need to be collected in the same period as the crime.

4.2 Solutions for Context-Based Crime Prediction

Once we create context information for time and location, we can apply context-based recommendation methods. Here we demonstrate how two existing context-based methods can be applied to our crime prediction problems. First, we show a tensor decomposition-based technique, then we discuss a latent factor analysis technique.

Tensor Decomposition Analysis. Context information adds another dimension to the spatial temporal data. The simplest way to use the context information is to create a model for each of the spatial-temporal unit, where a bias parameter w indicates the effect of each of the k elements in context information:

$$f(\mathbf{x}_{ij}) = \mathbf{w}^T \cdot \mathbf{x}_{ij} = \sum_k w_k \cdot x_{ijk}$$

The parameter w can be learned using optimization techniques. However, this approach does not consider the spatial temporal effects. In content-based review rating prediction, Li $et\ al.$ proposed a model that incorporates the user and item effects, by creating a bias parameter w_{ij} that represents user item effects. In their model, the prediction function is defined as follows:

$$f(\mathbf{x}_{ij}) = (\mathbf{w}^0 + \mathbf{w}_{ij})^T \cdot \mathbf{x}_{ij}$$
$$= \sum_{k=1}^{K} (w^0 + w_{ijk}) \cdot x_{ijk}$$

A practical problem of using the above model is that given a large number of users and reviews, the number of parameters $\mathbf{w}_{ij}$ would increase drastically, making the model intractable. Also it would suffer data sparsity problems because a user usually only reviews a few of all items, and there would be no enough training data to learn the model. This is also true in our crime prediction problem, because most of time-location units would have no crime neither tweet data given fine granularity. To deal with the problem, Li *et al.* propose a tensor-decomposition-based technique [11]. First consider $\mathbf{w}_{ij}$ as a three dimensional tensor $\mathbf{W} \in \mathbb{R}^{M \times N \times K}$. This tensor can be decomposed into three low rank matrices, $\mathbf{U} \in \mathbb{R}^{M \times D}$, $\mathbf{V} \in \mathbb{R}^{N \times D}$, and $\mathbf{P} \in \mathbb{R}^{K \times D}$. $\mathbf{W}$ can then be computed by multiplying three matrices together:

$$\mathbf{W} = \mathbf{I} \times \mathbf{U} \times \mathbf{V} \times \mathbf{P}$$

where $\mathbf{I}$ is a identity tensor. In this model, the number of parameters becomes $D \times (M + N + K)$, which is significantly fewer than the full model, which has $M \times N \times K$ parameters. With this model, the objective function becomes:

$$f(\mathbf{x}_{ij}) = (\mathbf{w}^0 + \mathbf{w}_{ij})^T \cdot \mathbf{x}_{ij}$$
$$= \sum_{k=1}^{K} (w^0 + \sum_{f=1}^{D} u_{if} \cdot v_{jf} \cdot p_{kf}) \cdot x_{ijk}$$

After deriving the gradients of $\mathbf{U}$, $\mathbf{V}$, and $\mathbf{P}$, the model can be learned using gradient-descent-style optimization.

In [11], Bag-of-words (BOW) is used to represent review texts. We instead use word embedding as the text representation, which is a recent advancement in text processing, and is considered to be a better representation that captures semantics of the text [15]. More specifically, we use the GloVe word vectors that are trained on 2 billion tweets, and have 1.2 million word entries [16]. For tweets assigned to a block-hour unit, we first look up the GloVe vector for each word token, and then take the average of word vectors as the unit vector. This vector is then used as the context data $\mathbf{x}_{ij}$.

Latent Topic Analysis. In recent years, latent topic analysis for texts has been extensively studied. The commonly used model, Latent Dirichlet Allocation (LDA) [2], discovers a K-dimensional topic distribution θ_d for text documents, with words in the document d discussing topic k associated with probability $\theta_{d,k}$. At the same time, each topic k is also associated with a distribution ϕ_k, indicating the probability each word is used for the topic. Finally, θ_d is assumed to be drawn from a Dirichlet distribution.

Recently, it has been found that the latent topics in review text can be used together with the hidden factors in a user-item recommendation setting [13,14]. In the following we will give a quick review of a technique proposed by McAuley and Leskovec [14], called *hidden factor as topics* (HFT). First, the standard latent factor model predicts rating using offset parameter α, bias β_u and β_i, and K-dimension user item latent factors γ_u and γ_i.

$$rec(u, i) = \alpha + \beta_u + \beta_i + \gamma_u \cdot \gamma_i$$

The parameters are estimated typically by minimizing the Mean Squared Error (MSE):

$$\hat{\Theta} = \arg\min_{\Theta} \frac{1}{|\mathcal{T}|} \sum_{r_{u,i} \in \mathcal{T}} (rec(u,i) - r_{u,i})^2 - \lambda \Omega(\Theta)$$

where $\Omega(\Theta)$ is a regularizer that penalizes complex models.

The task of latent topic analysis in rating predicting is to find the correspondence between topics in review text and the ratings. In other words, it is desirable that a high rating, given by a high $\gamma_{i,k}$, will correspond to a high value in a particular topic $\theta_{i,k}$. However, the transformation is not straightforward, since θ_i represents probability, but γ_i can take any value in $\mathbb{R}^K$. McAuley and Leskovec propose the following formula for the transformation:

$$\theta_{i,k} = \frac{exp(\mathcal{K}\gamma_{i,k})}{\sum_{k'} exp(\mathcal{K}\gamma_{i,k'})}$$

where a parameter $\mathcal{K}$ is introduced to represent 'peakiness' of the transformation. A large $\mathcal{K}$ will push the calculation to consider only the most important topics. The parameters are estimated using objective function

$$f(\mathcal{T}|\Theta, \Phi, \mathcal{K}, z) = \sum_{r_{u,i} \in \mathcal{T}} (rec(u,i) - r_{u,i})^2 - \mu l(\mathcal{T}|\theta, \phi, z)$$

where corpus likelihood $l(\mathcal{T}|\theta, \phi, z)$ replaces the typical regularizer $\Omega(\Theta)$. Effectively, when there are few ratings for a product i, the corpus likelihood regularizer will push γ_i and γ_u to zero, causing the prediction rely on the review texts.

In our crime prediction, we apply the HFT technique on crime and context information. Tweet texts posted at an hour and a block are concatenated and used as the review text, and the method requires no further feature transformation. We use the implementation made available online by the authors in our evaluation[7]. For fitting the model, this implementation uses L-BFGS, a quasi-Newton method for non-linear optimization problems with many variables.

5   Evaluation

We conduct evaluation using various prediction methods, including recommendation and non-recommendation methods, on real-world crime datasets. In this section, we first present the experiment setup and then we discuss the results.

5.1   Experimental Dataset

In this paper, we focus on crimes in the city of San Francisco. We obtain crime data from the DataSF website[8], which contains crime records since 2003 until present. For the purpose of our study, we take a subset of 100 weeks since the

---

[7] https://cseweb.ucsd.edu/~jmcauley/.
[8] https://datasf.org/opendata/.

start of 2016 from this crime data. Out of 39 crime categories, we use the theft and assault, which are the most common property crime and violent crime. For the selected period, there are about 151k thefts and 42k assaults, compared to 313k of all other crime types. In the following experiments, we use the first 80 weeks as the training data and last 20 weeks as the testing data, except for the experiment on the effect of training size (for which the period of the training data is shorter). In areas with concentrated crimes, the crime numbers are abnormally high. In order to avoid distortion of predictions, we use a crime number of 5 for those units that have more than 5 crimes. In other words, the crime number for each particular block-hour is capped to a maximum of 5.

As the contextual data, we collect tweets posted in San Francisco area using the Twitter Filter API[9], between 2016 and 2017. Note that as we discussed, the contextual data need not to be in the same period as the crime data, as long as it can be organized into spatial temporal units[10]. There are some accounts that repeatedly sent tweets, most likely using automatic methods, that can have undesirable effect on predictions. To avoid these bots, we remove tweets from the top 1% most frequently posting users. As a result, we obtain about 371k tweets that have geo-coordinates and timestamps. We assign these tweets to block-hour units as described in Sect. 4.1.

5.2   Non-recommendation Methods

We will compare recommendation methods described in the previous sections, including item-based CF (CF-item), user-based CF (CF-user), tensor decomposition (TD), and Hidden Factor as Topics (HFT), with four non-recommendation baselines that are used in previous crime predictions, namely, historical sum, ARIMA, VAR, and KDE.

Historical Sum. A straightforward way to predict crime is to consider the same amount of crimes are likely to happen in the same location and the same hour in the future as in the past. Due to its simplicity and effectiveness, historical crime number has been used in practical systems, for example in [19]. With this approach, time and location of future crime is predicted to be the same as the time and location of crimes in the training data.

ARIMA. The *autoregressive integrated moving average* (ARIMA) is a common method used in time series forecasting, and has previously been used in crime prediction [4]. It consists of an autoregression model (AR) that captures lagged patterns, and a moving average model (MA) that captures long terms trends. Normally the parameters (p, d, q) need to be specified. In our experiments, we use the *auto.arima* function in R package *forecast* to automatically find the optimal parameters.

VAR. Vector autoregression (VAR) is a popular forecast method, particularly in econometrics [18]. It combines multiple signals together in an AR model for

---

[9] https://developer.twitter.com/en/docs/tweets/filter-realtime/overview.

[10] I.e., each tweet is assigned, based on its location and time stamp, to a particular spatial block among over 2,000 blocks and a particular hour out of 168 possible hours of a week.

forecasting, which means we can use it to incorporate contextual information. We use the GloVe-transformed tweets described in Sect. 4.2 as the contextual vector. We use the VAR function implemented in the R package *vars* to automatically find the optimal parameter and make predictions.

Kernel Density Estimation (KDE). KDE is a popular interpolation method to estimate crime in areas where there is lack of previous crime records, by considering geographical correlations. With pre-defined grids, the probability of crime to occur in one point is calculated based on its distance to grid points that have previous crime records:

$$f(p) = k(p, h) = \frac{1}{Ph} \sum_{j=1}^{P} K \left(\frac{||p - p_j||}{h} \right)$$

where p is the point where density is estimated, h is the bandwidth parameter that controls the smoothness of the estimation, P is the total number of crimes, K is the density function, $|| \cdot ||$ is the Euclidean distance between two points. Following [8], we use R package ks to estimate $k(p, h)$, with standard normal density function and the default band-width estimator Hpi. After estimating the density for each grid point, we transform the density into a probability function that indicates if a crime will occur in a spatial temporal unit:

$$Pr\left(occur = T | f(p)\right) = \frac{1}{1 + \exp^{-f(p)}}$$

Since KDE does not incorporate temporal effects, we calculate a KDE model for each hour.

5.3   Recommendation Performance

As a standard recommendation system evaluation metric, we measure *mean absolute error* (MAE) for recommendation and non-recommendation methods. MAE is calculated as the mean difference between the predicted and actual crime numbers in training data for block-hour units that have non-zero crimes. Since historical sum and CF methods preserve actual crime numbers in training data, thus have 0 MAE, they will not be measured here. Moreover, since the KDE method calculates the likelihood of future crime, and not the crime number, it is also not measured. MAE for the remaining methods are shown in Table 2.

Table 2. MAE of recommendation and non-recommendation methods

	ARIMA	VAR	TD	HFT
Theft	2.306	1.946	2.299	**1.408**
Assault	2.089	1.978	2.085	**1.645**

As we can see from Table 2, HFT achieves the best model fitting, by considering both the hidden factors and contextual data. VAR performs better than ARIMA, and shows that incorporating tweets as contextual information can effectively raise prediction accuracy.

5.4 Predicting Future Crimes

MAE calculated above indicates how a model fits the training data, but it does not tell the prediction of future crimes. Our next experiment studies the effectiveness of the methods for predicting future crimes. We follow [8] and use the *surveillance plot* as our measurement for future crime prediction effectiveness. A surveillance plot consists of a number of surveillance points. Each surveillance point tells the ratio of crime captured with the set of particular selected block-hour units. We can consider each block-hour unit corresponds to a man-hour. Thus we can easily interpret a surveillance point as the percentage of crimes captured given a certain amount of man-hour. To calculate the value for a surveillance point $sp(k)$, we first rank the block-hour units using the prediction, from high to low, then we take top $k\%$ units in the test data, and sum the amount of crime captured. The point value is thus calculated as

$$sp(k) = \frac{\sum_i^{k\% \times |U'|} u_i}{\sum_i^{|U'|} u_i}$$

where u_i is the number of crimes in unit i, and U' is the set of ranked units.

To draw a surveillance plot, we plot 100 surveillance points with their values. Surveillance plots for four selected methods, i.e., KDE, VAR, CF-item, and HFT, are shown in Fig. 1. As an overall evaluation, Area Under Curve (AUC) is calculated for each surveillance plot. Table 3 shows AUC for all presented methods, as well as surveillance levels at 20% and 50%, $sp(20)$ and $sp(50)$, which can be interpreted as the ratio of crime captured with 20% and 50% man-hour.

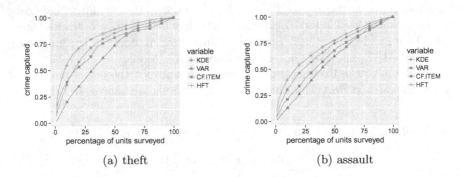

(a) theft   (b) assault

Fig. 1. Surveillance plots of selected prediction methods

Table 3. Future crime prediction accuracy with recommendation and non-recommendation methods

	Theft			Assault		
	AUC	surv 20%	surv 50%	AUC	surv 20%	surv 50%
Historical sum	0.705	0.202	0.735	0.588	0.352	0.598
KDE	0.766	0.579	0.856	0.681	0.463	0.744
ARIMA	0.633	0.263	0.734	0.563	0.241	0.621
VAR	0.653	0.347	0.734	0.578	0.261	0.621
CF Item	0.728	0.533	0.810	0.617	0.338	0.677
CF User	0.657	0.463	0.682	0.536	0.239	0.528
TD	0.812	0.698	0.885	0.703	0.498	0.767
HFT	0.824	0.709	0.886	0.725	0.539	0.773

According to Fig. 1 and Table 3, HFT achieves the highest accuracy among all the methods, followed closely by TD. This reveals the power to consider both spatial temporal hidden factors and context information. With HFT, 70% of thefts can be captured using 20% man-hour, and 88% with 50% man-hour. VAR performs only a little better than ARIMA, indicating the tweets are actually not a strong indicator for crimes. KDE, despite not considering temporal factors, achieves higher accuracy than CF methods, and the highest among non-recommendation methods. Nevertheless, it captures 13% fewer crimes than HFT with 20% man-hour. CF methods did not achieve very high accuracy, with item-based CF performing much better than user-based CF. This is likely due to that CF methods only consider one of two latent factors.

5.5 Effect of Training Data Size

Finally, we investigate the effect of training data size on prediction accuracy. Particularly, we aim to find out whether very small training data can still provide good prediction. We therefore create training datasets composed of 1, 3, 5, 10, and 20 weeks before the testing dataset. The testing dataset is the same as used in the previous experiment. We select the best performing recommendation and non-recommendation methods, i.e., HFT and KDE for comparison. The AUC results are shown in Fig. 2.

According to Fig. 2, HFT out-performs KDE steadily given the different training sizes. Both methods reach near-optimal performance compared to Table 3, with only one quarter (20 weeks) of training data. However, according to [14], HFT should perform much better when there is little training data, with prediction being driven by contextual information. We do not see it in our results. This is perhaps again due to tweets being weak predictor for crimes.

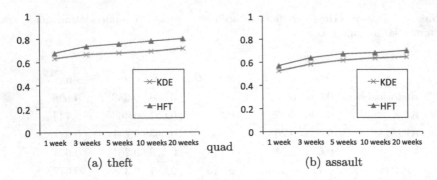

(a) theft   (b) assault

Fig. 2. for selected prediction methods with different training sizes

6   Conclusion

We have proposed to model crime prediction as a recommendation problem. By this modeling, we can have finer spatial temporal granularity, while using techniques in recommendation systems to mitigate the data sparsity problem. We present our method to model spatial and temporal factors as users and items, and discuss several recommendation techniques that can be applied. The techniques include collaborative filtering methods, as well as context-based rating prediction methods. Our extensive experiments with crime and contextual data collected for the city of San Francisco show that, recommendation methods such as HFT can outperform traditional crime prediction methods such as KDE. By using HFT, we can capture 70% thefts in San Francisco with 20% man-hours. We have also tested the effect of small training data size. In this work, we focus on thefts and assaults in San Francisco, while more crime types and cities can be studied in the future.

Acknowledgement. This research has been supported by JSPS KAKENHI Grant Numbers #17H01828, #18K19841 and by MIC/SCOPE #171507010.

References

1. Al Boni, M., Gerber, M.S.: Automatic optimization of localized kernel density estimation for hotspot policing. In: Proceedings of the 15th IEEE International Conference on Machine Learning and Applications (ICMLA), pp. 32–38. IEEE (2016)
2. Blei, D.M., Ng, A.Y., Jordan, M.I.: Latent Dirichlet allocation. J. Mach. Learn. Res. **3**(Jan), 993–1022 (2003)
3. Chainey, S., Tompson, L., Uhlig, S.: The utility of hotspot mapping for predicting spatial patterns of crime. Secur. J. **21**(1–2), 4–28 (2008)
4. Chen, P., Yuan, H., Shu, X.: Forecasting crime using the ARIMA model. In: Proceedings of the Fifth International Conference on Fuzzy Systems and Knowledge Discovery, FSKD 2008, vol. 5, pp. 627–630. IEEE (2008)

5. Cohen, L.E., Felson, M.: Social change and crime rate trends: a routine activity approach (1979). In: Classics in Environmental Criminology, pp. 203–232. CRC Press (2016)
6. Du, B., Liu, C., Zhou, W., Hou, Z., Xiong, H.: Catch me if you can: detecting pickpocket suspects from large-scale transit records. In: Proceedings of the 22nd ACM SIGKDD International Conference on Knowledge Discovery and Data Mining, pp. 87–96. ACM (2016)
7. Galbrun, E., Pelechrinis, K., Terzi, E.: Urban navigation beyond shortest route: the case of safe paths. Inf. Syst. **57**, 160–171 (2016)
8. Gerber, M.S.: Predicting crime using twitter and kernel density estimation. Decis. Support Syst. **61**, 115–125 (2014)
9. Hart, T., Zandbergen, P.: Kernel density estimation and hotspot mapping: examining the influence of interpolation method, grid cell size, and bandwidth on crime forecasting. Policing Int. J. Police Strat. Manage. **37**(2), 305–323 (2014)
10. Leong, K., Sung, A.: A review of spatio-temporal pattern analysis approaches on crime analysis. I. E-journal Crim. Sci. **9**, 1–33 (2015)
11. Li, F., Liu, N., Jin, H., Zhao, K., Yang, Q., Zhu, X.: Incorporating reviewer and product information for review rating prediction. In: IJCAI, vol. 11, pp. 1820–1825 (2011)
12. Liao, R., Wang, X., Li, L., Qin, Z.: A novel serial crime prediction model based on Bayesian learning theory. In: 2010 International Conference on Machine Learning and Cybernetics (ICMLC), vol. 4, pp. 1757–1762. IEEE (2010)
13. Ling, G., Lyu, M.R., King, I.: Ratings meet reviews, a combined approach to recommend. In: Proceedings of the 8th ACM Conference on Recommender systems, pp. 105–112. ACM (2014)
14. McAuley, J., Leskovec, J.: Hidden factors and hidden topics: understanding rating dimensions with review text. In: Proceedings of the 7th ACM Conference on Recommender Systems, pp. 165–172. ACM (2013)
15. Mikolov, T., Sutskever, I., Chen, K., Corrado, G.S., Dean, J.: Distributed representations of words and phrases and their compositionality. In: Advances in Neural Information Processing Systems, pp. 3111–3119 (2013)
16. Pennington, J., Socher, R., Manning, C.: GloVe: global vectors for word representation. In: Proceedings of the 2014 Conference on Empirical Methods in Natural Language Processing, pp. 1532–1543 (2014)
17. Sarwar, B., Karypis, G., Konstan, J., Riedl, J.: Item-based collaborative filtering recommendation algorithms. In: Proceedings of the 10th International Conference on World Wide Web, pp. 285–295. ACM (2001)
18. Toda, H.Y., Phillips, P.C.: Vector autoregression and causality: a theoretical overview and simulation study. Econometric Rev. **13**(2), 259–285 (1994)
19. Utamima, A., Djunaidy, A.: Be-safe travel, a web-based geographic application to explore safe-route in an area. In: AIP Conference Proceedings, vol. 1867, p. 020023. AIP Publishing (2017)
20. Wang, H., Kifer, D., Graif, C., Li, Z.: Crime rate inference with big data. In: Proceedings of the 22nd ACM SIGKDD International Conference on Knowledge Discovery and Data Mining, pp. 635–644. ACM (2016)
21. Wang, X., Brown, D.E., Gerber, M.S.: Spatio-temporal modeling of criminal incidents using geographic, demographic, and twitter-derived information. In: Proceedings of the IEEE International Conference on Intelligence and Security Informatics, pp. 36–41. IEEE (2012)

22. Yang, D., Heaney, T., Tonon, A., Wang, L., Cudré-Mauroux, P.: Crimetelescope: crime hotspot prediction based on urban and social media data fusion. World Wide Web **21**, 1–25 (2017)
23. Zhao, X., Tang, J.: Modeling temporal-spatial correlations for crime prediction. In: Proceedings of the 2017 ACM on Conference on Information and Knowledge Management, CIKM 2017, pp. 497–506 (2017)
24. Zhao, X., Tang, J.: Crime in urban areas: a data mining perspective. ACM SIGKDD Explor. Newsl. **20**(1), 1–12 (2018)

Incremental PARAFAC Decomposition for Three-Dimensional Tensors Using Apache Spark

Hye-Kyung Yang$^{(\boxtimes)}$ and Hwan-Seung Yong

Department of Computer Science and Engineering, Ewha Womans University,
Seoul, Korea
yang88710@ewhain.net, hsyong@ewha.ac.kr

Abstract. Recent studies have focused on the use of tensor analysis for
tensor decomposition because this method can identify more latent factor
and patterns, compared to the matrix factorization approach. The existing tensor decomposition studies used static dataset in their analyses.
However, in practice, data change and increase over time. Therefore, this
paper proposes an incremental Parallel Factor Analysis (PARAFAC) tensor decomposition algorithm for three-dimensional tensors. The method
of incremental tensor decomposition can reduce recalculation costs associated with the addition of new tensors. The proposed method is called
InParTen; it performs distributed incremental PARAFAC tensor decomposition based on the Apache Spark framework. The proposed method
decomposes only new tensors and then combines them with existing
results without recalculating the complete tensors. In this study, it was
assumed that the tensors grow with time as the majority of the dataset
is added over a period. In this paper, the performance of InParTen was
evaluated by comparing the obtained results for execution time and relative errors against existing tensor decomposition tools. Consequently, it
has been observed that the method can reduce the recalculation cost of
tensor decomposition.

Keywords: PARAFAC decomposition ·
Incremental tensor decomposition · Apache Spark

1 Introduction

Recent data analysis and recommender systems studies have focused on the use
of tensor analysis. A tensor generally consists of three-dimensional matrices [1]
and has more potential factors and patterns than a two-dimensional matrix. For
example, the Netflix tensor dataset constructed a three-dimensional tensor that
incorporates user indexing, contents indexing, time indexing, and ratings. We
can analyze and predict which user will select which content at what time. In
contrast, a two-dimensional matrix that consists of user and contents can analyze and predict which user will select which item, but without taking time into

© Springer Nature Switzerland AG 2019
M. Bakaev et al. (Eds.): ICWE 2019, LNCS 11496, pp. 63–71, 2019.
https://doi.org/10.1007/978-3-030-19274-7_5

account. Thus, tensor analysis can provide better recommendations than matrix analysis. However, it is difficult to analyze the tensor because it is sparse and large. Accordingly, most studies have approached tensor analysis using tensor decomposition algorithms, such as parallel factor analysis (PARAFAC) decomposition, Tucker decomposition, and high-order singular value decomposition (HOSVD). These algorithms are made for static tensor datasets. These algorithms should re-decompose a tensor to include new tensors. In other words, when a tensor is added (a streaming type of tensor), the previously decomposed algorithms should be re-decomposed as a whole tensor because a new tensor changes the existing results. Unfortunately, the recalculation costs of tensor decomposition methods are rather high because of repetitive operations. Therefore, we propose InParTen, which is a distributed incremental tensor decomposition algorithm for three-dimensional tensors based on Apache Spark[1]. Figure 1 shows an illustration of the incremental tensor decomposition method presented in this study. Incremental tensor decomposition is a method of reducing the recalculation cost when a new tensor is added. In this work, we assumed that the existing tensor increases with the time axis because most of the dataset is added over time. Because users and items slowly increase, unlike time, we considered time in this study.

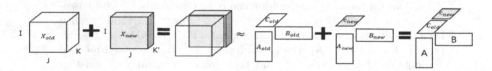

Fig. 1. Incremental PARAFAC decomposition of a three-dimensional tensor

In this study, we evaluated the performance of InParTen. We compared the execution time and relative errors with the existing tensor tools using various tensor datasets. The experimental results show that the proposed InParTen can handle large tensors and newly added tensors from the dataset. Furthermore, it can reduce the re-decomposition costs.

In Sects. 2 and 3, we describe the notation and operators for tensor decomposition and related work for tensor decomposition. Section 4 presents the InParTen algorithm, and Sect. 5 discusses the experimental results. Section 6 concludes the findings of this work and discusses future works.

2   Notation and Operators

PARAFAC decomposition is decomposed into a sum of rank-one tensors [1–6]. The three-dimensional PARAFAC decomposition can be expressed as

$$Tensor\ X \approx \sum_{r=1}^{R} \lambda_r a_r \circ b_r \circ c_r \tag{1}$$

---

[1] Apache Spark homepage, http://spark.apache.org.

To obtain the three factor matrices A, B, and C for the decomposed results, PARAFAC decomposition uses the alternating least square(ALS) algorithm. This approach fixes two factor matrices to solve another factor matrix; this process is repeated until either the maximum number of iterations is reached or convergence is achieved [1–3]. Naive PARAFAC-ALS algorithms are used for obtaining factor matrices as follows:

$$A = X_{(1)}(C \odot B)(C^\mathsf{T} C * B^\mathsf{T} B)^\dagger$$
$$B = X_{(2)}(C \odot A)(C^\mathsf{T} C * A^\mathsf{T} A)^\dagger \qquad (2)$$
$$C = X_{(3)}(B \odot A)(B^\mathsf{T} B * A^\mathsf{T} A)^\dagger$$

In this case, for the size of $I \times J \times K$ tensor X, the unfolding results are three matrices, $X_{(1)} \in \mathbb{R}^{I \times JK}$, $X_{(2)} \in \mathbb{R}^{J \times IK}$ and $X_{(3)} \in \mathbb{R}^{K \times IJ}$. In PARAFAC-ALS, the Khatri-Rao product ($\odot$) has intermediate data explosions. If two matrices, A of size 3×4 and B of size 5×4, undergo the Khatri-Rao product, the result size is 15×4. The Hadamard product ($*$) is the element-wise product; it must calculate two matrices of the same size.

3 Related Work

The naive PARAFAC-ALS algorithm cannot handle a large-scale tensor, because the Khatri-Rao product incurs an intermediate data explosion. The distributed PARAFAC decomposition studies have focused on avoiding the intermediate data explosion and handling large-scale tensors. In order to reduce the intermediate data explosion, GigaTensor [2], Haten2 [3], and BigTensor [4] suggest a PARAFAC algorithm to avoid the Khatri-Rao product; they use MapReduce to calculate only non-zero values using Hadoop. In addition, ParCube [5] realizes tensor decomposition by leveraging random sampling based on Hadoop. Furthermore, recent tensor studies that have used Apache Spark, which is a distributed in-memory big-data system, include S-PARAFAC [6] and DisTenC [7]. However, these algorithms must re-decompose the tensor when adding new tensors. More recently, studies on incremental tensor decomposition have been increasing. Zou et al. proposed an online CP that is an incremental CANDE-COMP/PARAFAC(CP) decomposition algorithm [8]. The author assumed that the tensor increases over time. Ma et al. proposed a randomized online CP decomposition algorithm called ROCP [9]. The ROCP algorithm, based on random sampling, suggests methods to avoid the Khatri-Rao product and to reduce memory usage. Gujral et al. [10] suggested SamBaTen, a sampling-based batch incremental CP tensor decomposition method. SamBaTen also assumes that the tensor increases over time. These tools are run only on a single machine because the tensor toolbox is based on MATLAB. Recently, SamBaTen was re-implemented in Apache Spark [12]. However, it cannot handle large datasets because it does not consider limited memory. Therefore, we consider an efficient memory process and reducing the re-decomposition cost using Apache Spark.

4   The Proposed InParTen Algorithm

We assume that the existing tensor is increased with time. Suppose that the existing tensor consists of (user, item, time) and its size is $I \times J \times K$, where I is the number of user indexes, J is the number of item indexes, and K is the number of time indexes. I and J have the same size in the added new tensor and the new value increases in the K-axis. When a new tensor X_{new} is added to the existing tensor X_{old}, the result of the new factor matrix obtained by decomposing the new tensor is added to the three factor matrices of the existing tensor. At that time, the existing A_{old} and B_{old} factor matrices have the same size as the A_{new} and B_{new} factor matrices. To update the A and B factor matrices, we add the A_{old} and A_{new} matrices as well as the B_{old} and B_{new}. In order to update the factor matrix of A, we calculate as follows:

$$P \leftarrow P + X_{new(1)}(C_{new} \odot B)$$
$$Q \leftarrow Q + (C_{new}^{\mathsf{T}} C_{new} * B^{\mathsf{T}}B) \qquad (3)$$
$$A = PQ^{\dagger}$$

Similarly, to update the factor matrix of B:

$$U \leftarrow U + X_{new(2)}(C_{new} \odot A)$$
$$V \leftarrow V + (C_{new}^{\mathsf{T}} (C_{new} * A^{\mathsf{T}}A) \qquad (4)$$
$$B = UV^{\dagger}$$

The initial values of P and U are set to $X_{old(1)}(C_{old} \odot B_{old})$ and $X_{old(2)}(C_{old} \odot A_{old})$ The initial values of Q and V are set to $(C_{old}^{\mathsf{T}}C_{old} * B_{old}^{\mathsf{T}}B_{old})$ and $(C_{old}^{\mathsf{T}}C_{old} * A_{old}^{\mathsf{T}}A_{old})$. However, the Khatri-Rao product is used to obtain the P, leading to the intermediate data explosion problem. We suggest obtaining the initial P and U without the Khatri-Rao product. We already solved the old factor matrices A, B, and C of the decomposed X_{old}. Therefore, we can obtain the initialized P as follows (5):

$$\begin{aligned} X_{old(1)}(C_{old} \odot A) &= A_{old}(C_{old} \odot B_{old})^{\mathsf{T}}(C_{old} \odot B_{old}) \\ &= A_{old}(C_{old}^{\mathsf{T}}C_{old} * B_{old}^{\mathsf{T}}B_{old}) \qquad (5) \\ &= A_{old}Q \end{aligned}$$

The U value can also be obtained by a similar method. However, it cannot solve the updated C factor matrix, unlike A and B, because the C_{old} and C_{new} matrices do not have the same size and are indexed differently. We should calculate the A and B factor matrices in a different way to solve the C factor matrix. In the C factor matrix case, the indexes of the C_{new} matrix are located in the bottom of the C_{old} matrix during the whole time owing to the increasing K-axis. To update the factor matrix of C, we can calculate as follows (6):

$$C = \begin{bmatrix} C_{old} \\ C_{new} \end{bmatrix} = \begin{bmatrix} C_{old} \\ X_{new(3)}(B \odot A)(B^{\mathsf{T}}B * A^{\mathsf{T}}A)^{\dagger} \end{bmatrix} \qquad (6)$$

Algorithm 1. Incremental PARAFAC-ALS algorithm

Input: New Tensor $X_{new} \in \mathbb{R}^{I \times J \times K_{new}}$,
factor Matrices A, B, C_{old}, rank R, max iteration T, λ_{old}
Output: factor Matrices A,B,C and λ
1: $Q = C_{old}^{\mathsf{T}} C_{old} * B^{\mathsf{T}} B$
2: $P = AQ$
3: $V = C_{old}^{\mathsf{T}} C_{old} * A^{\mathsf{T}} A$
4: $U = BQ$
5: **for** $t = 0 \cdots T$ **do**
6:    $C_{new} = SKhaP(X_{new(3)}, A, B)(B^{\mathsf{T}} B * A^{\mathsf{T}} A)^{\dagger}$
7:    normalization columns of C_{new} (storing norms in vector λ)
8:    $P = P + SKhaP(X_{new(1)}, C_{new}, B)$
9:    $Q = Q + (C_{new}^{\mathsf{T}} C_{new} * B^{\mathsf{T}} B)$
10:    $A = PQ^{\dagger}$
11:    normalization columns of A (storing norms in vector λ)
12:    $U = U + SKhaP(X_{new(2)}, C_{new}, A)$
13:    $V = V + (C_{new}^{\mathsf{T}} C_{new} * A^{\mathsf{T}} A)$
14:    $B = UV^{\dagger}$
15:    normalization columns of B (storing norms in vector λ)
16:    **if** convergence is met **then**
17:       **break** for loop; ;
18:    **end if**
19: **end for**
20: Update λ as the average previous λ_{old} and new λ
21: C can be added to the rows of C_{new}
$$C = \begin{bmatrix} C_{old} \\ C_{new} \end{bmatrix}$$
22: **return** A,B,C and λ

The incremental PARAFAC decomposition method is described in Algorithm 1. In lines 1 to 4, $P, Q, V,$ and U are calculated using the existing factor matrices through a decomposed tensor. Subsequently, we process the PARAFAC-ALS only with the added new tensors. We can solve C_{new} after the calculation of the A and B factor matrices. Eventually, we enable the update of A using the C_{new} and B factor matrices. Furthermore, we can solve the update of B using C_{new} and A factor matrices. In Algorithm 1, the $SKhaP$ function shown in lines 6, 8, and 12 can be calculated to avoid the Khatri-Rao product. In the $SKhaP$ function, we can calculate to avoid the intermediate data explosion as shown in

$$X_{new(1)}(C_{new} \odot B)_{(:,r)} = \sum_{y=1}^{JK_{new}} X_{new(1)(:,y)} C_{new}(\lceil \frac{y}{J} \rceil, r) B(y\%J, r) \quad (7)$$

When the iteration is completed, we can add a C_{new} matrix under the existing C matrix to update the C factor matrix. It is necessary to update the existing λ_{old} and the λ_{new} generated in decomposing the new tensor. The λ_{new} and the existing λ_{old} values are averaged and subsequently updated and stored.

5   Evaluation

5.1   Experimental Environment and Tensor Datasets

We evaluated the performance of InParTen on the basis of Apache Spark. We compared the execution time and relative errors with a decomposed complete tensor and the existing incremental tensor decomposition tool using various tensor datasets. The experimental environments used Hadoop v2.6 and Apache Spark v1.6.1. The experiments were conducted using a six-node worker, with a total of 48 GB memory.

Table 1. Tensor datasets

Data name	Data type	Tensor size	Non-zero
Sparse100	Synthetic data	$100 \times 100 \times 100$	312,969
Dense100	Synthetic data	$100 \times 100 \times 100$	10,000,000
Sparse500	Synthetic data	$500 \times 500 \times 500$	15,000
Dense500	Synthetic data	$500 \times 500 \times 500$	125,000,000
Yelp [4]	User,location, time	$70K \times 15K \times 108$	334,166
MovieLens [4]	User, moive, time	$71K \times 10K \times 157$	10,000,054
Neflix [12]	User,contents, time	$2M \times 17K \times 2182$	97,754,343

Table 1 lists the tensor datasets, which include both synthetic and real datasets. The synthetic tensor datasets used include Sparse100, Dense100, Sparse500, and Dense500. The real tensor datasets are Yelp, MovieLens, and Netflix. The Yelp, MovieLens and Netflix datasets consist of three indexes in the tensor and ratings from 1 to 5.

5.2   Experiment Method and Results

We compared the execution time and relative errors of the proposed method to those of existing tensor decomposition tools. The experiment was conducted with InParTen, several existing incremental tensor decomposition tools, and several non-incremental tensor decomposition tools. The incremental tensor decomposition tools used online CP based on MATLAB and two versions of SamBaTen, which are based on MATLAB and Apache Spark. The non-incremental tensor decomposition tools used S-PARAFAC and BigTensor. S-PARAFAC is based on Apache Spark, and BigTensor is Hadoop-based. In this work, we assumed that the existing data increased by a maximum 10% and we tested rank 10 and 10 iterations.

Table 2 compares the execution time of the existing tensor decomposition tools to that achieved by InParTen. Online CP and SamBaTen, based on MAT-LAB, cannot handle large datasets because they run on a single machine. Sam-BaTen (Spark-based) also cannot handle large datasets because of the excessive calculation overhead. However, InParTen can handle large tensor datasets as well as reduce the re-decomposition execution time.

Table 2. Comparison of execution time (min) between InParTen and the existing tensor decomposition tools

Data name	Big tensor	S-PARAFAC	Online CP	SamBaTen (MATLAB)	SamBaTen (Spark)	InParTen
Sparse100	14.40	2.29	0.10	0.51	2.72	1.47
Dense100	37.14	19.7	0.32	1.01	13.24	7.92
Sparse500	59.7	10.75	2.67	1.89	4.2	1.53
Dense500	N/A	402	N/A	N/A	N/A	8.5
Yelp	70.7	10.07	N/A	N/A	29	3.58
MovieLens	754.8	104	N/A	N/A	M/A	30.23
Neflix	N/A	1619	N/A	N/A	N/A	401

Table 3. Experimental values of relative error for different datasets

Data name	Big tensor	S-PARAFAC	Online CP	SamBaTen (MATLAB)	SamBaTen (Spark)	InParTen
Sparse100	0.43	0.42	0.41	0.48	0.43	0.42
Dense100	0.25	0.28	0.26	0.28	0.58	0.24
Sparse500	0.98	0.98	0.00	0.00	0.00	0.08
Dense500	N/A	0.31	N/A	N/A	N/A	0.31
Yelp	0.97	0.94	N/A	N/A	0.99	0.96
MovieLens	0.73	0.72	N/A	N/A	N/A	0.71
Neflix	N/A	0.72	N/A	N/A	N/A	0.69

Table 3 compares the relative errors results of InParTen and the existing tensor decomposition tools. It is an important point that InParTen can achieve relative errors similar to or better than existing tensor decomposition tools, because we have to re-decompose the whole tensor if the relative errors are relatively high compared to non-incremental tensor decomposition tools. We measured the similarity to the original tensor datasets by means of the relative error, which is defined as

$$RelativeError = \frac{\|X_{original} - \hat{X}\|_F^2}{\|X_{original}\|_F^2} \tag{8}$$

When the relative error is closer to zero, the error is smaller. At a result, the relative errors for the real datasets and sparse100 and sparse500 are high because they are sparse datasets. The error is increased because a value that is not in the original data is filled. InParTen was able to achieve similar relative errors to other tensor decomposition tools.

6   Conclusion and Future Work

In this paper, we propose InParTen, which is a distributed incremental PARAFAC decomposition algorithm. InParTen can reduce the re-calculation costs associated with the addition of new tensors. The proposed method decomposes new tensors and then combines them with existing results without complete re-calculation of the tensors. In this study, the performance of InParTen was evaluated by comparing the obtained results of execution time and relative error with existing tensor decomposition tools. Consequently, it was observed that the InParTen method can process large tensors and can reduce the re-calculation costs of tensor decomposition. In the future, we intend to study multi-incremental tensor decomposition.

Acknowledgement. This research was supported by Basic Science Research Program through the National Research Foundation of Korea (NRF) funded by the Ministry of Education (NRF-2016R1D1A1B03931529)

References

1. Kolda, T.G., Bader, B.W.: Tensor decompositions and applications. SIAM Rev. **51**(3), 455–500 (2009)
2. Kang, U., Papalexakis, E.E., Harpale, A., Faloutsos, C.: GigaTensor: scaling tensor analysis up by 100 times- algorithms and discoveries. In: Proceedings of the 18th ACM SIGKDD International Conference on Knowledge Discovery and Data Mining KDD 2012, pp. 316–324. ACM, Beijing, 12–16 August 2012
3. Jeon, I., Papalexakis, E.E., Kang, U., Faloutsos, C.: HaTen2: billion-scale tensor decompositions. In: Proceedings of the 31st IEEE International Conference on Data Engineering ICDE 2015, pp. 1047–1058. IEEE (2015)
4. Park, N., Jeon, B., Lee, J., Kang, U.: BIGtensor: mining billion-scale tensor made easy. In: Proceedings of the 25th ACM International on Conference on Information and Knowledge Management (CIKM 2016), pp. 2457–2460. ACM (2016)
5. Papalexakis, E.E., Faloutsos, C., Sidiropoulos, N.D.: ParCube: sparse parallelizable tensor decompositions. In: Flach, P.A., De Bie, T., Cristianini, N. (eds.) ECML PKDD 2012. LNCS (LNAI), vol. 7523, pp. 521–536. Springer, Heidelberg (2012). https://doi.org/10.1007/978-3-642-33460-3_39
6. Yang, H.K., Yong, H.S.: S-PARAFAC: distributed tensor decomposition using apache spark. J. Korean Inst. Inf. Sci. Eng. (KIISE) **45**(3), 280–287 (2018)
7. Ge, H., Zhang, K., Alfifi, M., Hu, X., Caverlee, J.: DisTenC: a distributed algorithm for scalable tensor completion on spark. In: Proceeding of the 34th IEEE International Conference on Data Engineering (ICDE 2018), pp. 137–148. IEEE (2018)

8. Zhou, S., Vinh, N.X., Bailey, J., Jia, Y., Davidson, I.: Accelerating online CP decompositions for higher order tensors. In: Proceedings of the 22nd ACM SIGKDD International Conference on Knowledge Discovery and Data Mining (KDD 2016), pp. 1375–1384. ACM (2016)
9. Ma, C., Yang, X., Wang, H.: Randomized online CP decomposition. In: Proceedings of the 2018 Tenth International Conference on Advanced Computational Intelligence (ICACI), pp. 414–419. IEEE (2018)
10. Gujral, E., Pasricha, R., Papalexkis, E.E.: SamBaTen: sampling-based batch incremental tensor decomposition. In: Proceedings of the 2018 SIAM International Conference on Data Mining (SDM2018), pp. 387–395. SIAM (2018)
11. SamBaTen based on Apache Spark Github. https://github.com/lucasjliu/SamBaTen-Spark. Accessed 18 Jan 2019
12. Bennett, J., Lanning, S.: The Netflix prize. In: Proceedings of KDD Cup and Workshop in Conjunction with KDD (2007)

Modeling Heterogeneous Influences for Point-of-Interest Recommendation in Location-Based Social Networks

Qing Guo[1]($\boxtimes$), Zhu Sun[2], Jie Zhang[1], and Yin-Leng Theng[1]

[1] Nanyang Technological University, 50 Nanyang Ave, Singapore 639798, Singapore
{qguo006,zhangj,tyltheng}@ntu.edu.sg
[2] Shopee, 2 Science Park Drive, Singapore 118222, Singapore
zhu.sun@shopee.com

Abstract. The huge amount of heterogeneous information in location-based social networks (LBSNs) creates great challenges for POI recommendation. User check-in behavior exhibits two properties, *diversity* and *imbalance*. To effectively model both properties, we propose an *Aspect-aware Geo-Social Matrix Factorization* (AGS-MF) approach to exploit various factors in a unified manner for more effective POI recommendation. Specifically, we first construct a novel knowledge graph (KG), named as *Aspect-aware Geo-Social Influence Graph* (AGS-IG), to unify multiple influential factors by integrating the heterogeneous information about users, POIs and aspects from reviews. We design an efficient meta-path based random walk to discover relevant neighbors of each user and POI based on multiple influential factors. The extracted neighbors are further incorporated into AGS-MF with automatically learned personalized weights for each user and POI. By doing so, both diversity and imbalance can be modeled for better capturing the characteristics of users and POIs. Experimental results on several real-world datasets demonstrate that AGS-MF outperforms state-of-the-art methods.

Keywords: Location-based social network · POI recommendation · Knowledge graph · Matrix factorization

1 Introduction

In location-based social networks (LBSNs), user check-in decision exhibits two critical properties: (1) *diversity*, a user's check-in is often jointly affected by multiple influential factors [3,11,13]; (2) *imbalance*, i.e., various influences carry different levels of importance for a check-in decision. Early studies often project the heterogeneous information to a homogeneous representation, which may cause information loss and disobey the check-in decision making process [9,11]. Recent studies thus explore heterogeneous representation such as knowledge graph (KG), to organize various types of information in a unified space, but fail to model the imbalance property [3,4,10,13,14].

© Springer Nature Switzerland AG 2019
M. Bakaev et al. (Eds.): ICWE 2019, LNCS 11496, pp. 72–80, 2019.
https://doi.org/10.1007/978-3-030-19274-7_6

Hence, to jointly capture the two properties of user check-in decision, we propose an *Aspect-aware Geo-Social Matrix Factorization* (AGS-MF) approach to leverage the capability of knowledge graph (KG) and matrix factorization (MF). AGS-MF is capable of unifying various influential factors as well as learning the saliences of them at the personalized level for each user and POI. In this paper, we employ geographical distance, social connection and user reviews to encode geographical, social and content influences, respectively. To accommodate various types of information in a unified representation space, we construct a novel knowledge graph – *Aspect-aware Geo-Social Influence Graph* (AGS-IG). Then, we design a meta-path based random walk process to efficiently discover reliable neighbors of each user and POI. The meta-paths are used to encode various influences. By assuming that neighbors should be closer to the given entity (either a user or POI) in the latent space, we incorporate regularizers into AGS-MF to constrain the distance of latent representations between them. To further capture the imbalance of various influential factors, personalized weights are further added to those regularizers, which represent the strength of neighbor relations regarding the corresponding meta-path. In this way, the latent representations of users and POIs can capture user preferences and POI characteristics, and preserve the heterogeneous information.

In summary, our major contribution lies in three folds: (1) We propose a novel knowledge graph (AGS-IG) to embed heterogeneous information of LBSNs in a unified space; (2) We propose AGS-MF to capture both diversity and imbalance properties of user check-in decision; (3) We conduct extensive experiments to evaluate our proposed approach on multiple real-world LBSN datasets, and empirical results demonstrate that our approach significantly outperforms state-of-the-art POI recommendation algorithms.

2   Aspect-Aware Geo-Social Influence Graph

Notations. Let U, L, C, A denote users, POIs, categories and aspects, respectively; u, l, c, a denote user, POI, category and aspect entities, respectively; the POIs visited by user u_i are defined as a preference vector $r_{u_i} = (r_{u_i,l_1}, r_{u_i,l_2} \cdots r_{u_i,l_j}, \cdots, r_{u_i,l_{|L|}})$, where r_{u_i,l_j} is the rating given by user u_i to POI l_j, and $|L|$ is the number of total POIs; each triple $< u_i, l_j, a_k >$ represents that user u_i has rated POI l_j with a review associated with aspect a_k.

AGS-IG Construction. We exploit social network, geographical distance and aspects from user reviews to build a knowledge graph to incorporate different types of information into a unified space, expressed by AGS-IG $= (U \cup L \cup A, E_{UU} \cup E_{UL} \cup E_{UA} \cup E_{LA} \cup E_{LL} \cup E_{AA})$. Specifically, E denotes the set of directed edges linking two entities; E_{UU} represents friendships; and E_{LL} represents POI-POI relations; E_{AA} denotes the semantic relations between aspects; E_{UL}, E_{UA} and E_{LA} are the sets of edges representing user-POI, user-aspect and POI-aspect relations, respectively. Figure 1 is a running example to depict the graph structure. Given AGS-IG, for a target user u_i, we can discover the relevant neighbors of each user and POI.

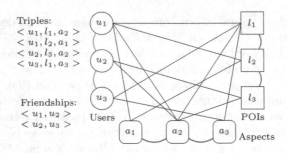

Fig. 1. A running example for AGS-IG structure

3   Meta-path Based Random Walk

Due to the large amount of entities involved in AGS-IG, we develop an effective meta-path based random walk process to retrieve semantically related neighbors. As a very useful concept to characterize the semantic patterns for a knowledge graph, meta-path [8] is used for capturing the semantic relations in AGS-IG. Given a meta-path $p = T_1 T_2 \cdots T_m \cdots$, where T_m is the type of the m-th entity, the transition probability between two linked entities is determined by the neighborhood size with constraint based by p, which is defined as follows:

$$\text{Prob}_{(v_m|v_{m-1},p)} = \begin{cases} \frac{1}{|\mathcal{N}_{T_m}(v_{m-1})|} & \text{if } T(v_m) = T_m \text{ and } T(v_{m-1}) = T_{m-1} \\ 0 & \text{otherwise} \end{cases} \quad (1)$$

where v_m is the m_{th} entity in p, $T(v_m)$ returns the type of v_m and $\mathcal{N}_{T_m}(v_{m-1})$ is the neighbor set of v_{m-1} in type T_m. By following p with the transition probability, the random walker can generate a path until it reaches the walk length. The process terminates if enough paths are created. Finally, we extract the neighbors from those paths for a given user or POI.

Note that as our goal is to find reliable neighbors for users and POIs, all meta-paths should start with U (L) and reach U (L) eventually. We select the following meta-paths: ULU, UU, $ULALU$ and UAU for users; LUL, LL and LAL for POIs. These meta-paths represent various influential factors that encode different semantic relations, e.g., UAU (LAL) can help discover neighbors sharing the same aspects while LL can find nearby POIs. Suppose we have two paths for u_1: $u_1 \rightarrow a_3 \rightarrow u_8$ and $u_1 \rightarrow a_7 \rightarrow u_2$, u_8 and u_2 are thus included in the neighbor set of u_1 regarding meta-path p, i.e., $\{u_2, u_8\} \subset \mathcal{N}_p(u_1)$.

4   Aspect-Aware Geo-Social Matrix Factorization

Matrix factorization (MF) [7] is an efficient method widely applied in recommender systems. It factorizes the user-POI rating matrix $R \in R^{|U| \times |L|}$ into low-rank user-latent matrix $\mathcal{U} \in R^{|U| \times d}$ and POI-latent matrix $\mathcal{V} \in R^{|V| \times d}$ (d is the dimension of latent vectors). The rating prediction of user u_i on a POI l_j, i.e.,

$\hat{r}_{i,j} = \mathcal{U}_i \mathcal{V}_j^\top$. Aspect-aware Geo-Social Matrix Factorization (AGS-MF) aims to incorporate the discovered neighbors that encode diverse influential factors into MF to better model users' preference and POIs' characteristics. By assuming that neighbors should be close to each other in the latent space, we integrate regularization terms into MF, so as to constrain the distance of latent feature vectors of the neighbors. Meanwhile, personalized meta-path weights for individual users are also incorporated to control the strength of regularization. Inspired by this idea, we also assign "personalized" weights of meta-paths for each POI. All the weights are jointly learned with user and POI latent feature vectors. By doing so, both diversity and imbalance properties of user check-in behavior can be effectively modeled in our unified framework. The objective function is thus defined as follows:

$$
\begin{aligned}
\mathcal{L} = \frac{1}{2} \sum_i I_{i,j}(r_{i,j} - g(\mathcal{U}_i \mathcal{V}_j^\top))^2 + \frac{\lambda_u}{2}||\mathcal{U}||_F^2 + \frac{\lambda_l}{2}||\mathcal{V}||_F^2 + \frac{\lambda_\Omega}{2}||\Omega||_F^2 + \frac{\lambda_\Theta}{2}||\Theta||_F^2 \\
+ \frac{\alpha_u}{2} \sum_{p \in \mathcal{M}_u} \sum_i ||\Omega_{i,p}(\mathcal{U}_i - \sum_{u_k \in \mathcal{N}_p(u_i)} s_{i,k}\mathcal{U}_k)||_F^2 \qquad (2) \\
+ \frac{\alpha_l}{2} \sum_{p \in \mathcal{M}_l} \sum_j ||\Theta_{j,p}(\mathcal{V}_j - \sum_{l_q \in \mathcal{N}_p(l_j)} s_{j,q}\mathcal{V}_q)||_F^2
\end{aligned}
$$

where $I_{i,j}$ is an indicator function that equals 1 if user u_i rated POI l_j and equals 0 otherwise; $r_{i,j} \in [0,1]$ is the rating of user u_i on POI l_j after min-max normalization; $g(x) = 1/(1 + exp(-x))$ is the logistic function that bounds the range of prediction into $[0,1]$; α_u and α_l are parameters to control the importance of user and item respectively; $\mathcal{M}_u$ and $\mathcal{M}_l$ represent the sets of meta-paths for users and POIs, i.e., $\mathcal{M}_u = \{ULU, UU, ULALU, UAU\}$ and $\mathcal{M}_l = \{LUL, LL, LAL\}$; $s_{i,k}$ represents the personalized PageRank value of k after normalization (i.e., $\sum_{k \in \mathcal{N}_p(i)} s_{i,k} = 1$); $\Omega_{i,p} \in \Omega$ and $\Theta_{j,p} \in \Theta$ represent the weights of meta-path p for u_i and l_j respectively, Ω and Θ are weight matrices for users and POIs respectively; $|| \cdot ||_F$ denotes the Frobenius norm; and λ_u, λ_l, λ_Ω, λ_Θ are regularization coefficient for easing over-fitting. We adopt the stochastic gradient descent approach [1] to optimize AGS-MF formulated by Eq. 2.

5 Experiments

5.1 Experiment Setup

Datasets. Yelp[1] dataset is utilized for evaluation. The toolbox developed in [15] is used for aspect extraction. Three cities are chosen for evaluation: Charlotte, Phoenix and Las Vegas. Table 1 summarizes the statistics of the three cities. Following the common preprocessing practice [4,13], users who visited more than 4 POIs are selected for evaluation. The earlier 80% check-ins of each user are selected as training set and the remaining 20% are testing set.

---

[1] https://www.yelp.com/dataset_challenge.

Evaluation Metrics. To evaluate the performance of all methods, we adopt several widely used metrics [2,12,13]: Precision, Recall and Mean Average Precision (denoted as $Pre@N$, $Rec@N$ and $MAP@N$) where N is the size of the Top-N recommended POI ranking list.

Table 1. Statistics of three cities

	Cities	CH	PH	LV
Dataset	Users	1,106	2,148	4,794
	POIs	2,724	2,603	4,274
	Aspects	1,355	1,952	4,180
	Reviews	33,966	61,596	150,080
	Categories	148	155	175
AGS-IG	User-POI	25,847	46,206	113,239
	User-Aspect	141,691	284,946	784,550
	User-User	5,803	23,766	46,407
	POI-Aspect	130,364	210,953	549,527
	POI-POI	79,530	112,248	405,310
	Aspect-Aspect	915,981	1,898,326	87,257,531
	Density	14.8%	11.5%	12.1%

Comparison Methods. (1) **UCF**: It is the user-based collaborative filtering; (2) **ICF**: It is the item-based collaborative filtering. (3) **MF** [7]: It is the basic matrix factorization; (4) **SRMF** [6]: It integrates social influence into MF; (5) **GeoMF** [5]: It is a state-of-the-art POI recommendation method, which incorporates geographical influence into MF; (6) **LFBCA** [9]: It is a state-of-the-art graph based approach via conducting personalized PageRank (PPR) over social network; (7) **TriRank** [4]: It is a state-of-the-art graph based method based on a tripartite graph with users, POIs and aspects; (8) **GeoSoCa** [13]: It is a state-of-the-art POI recommendation approach by integrating multiple influential factors into a unified linear framework; (9) **AGSRec** [3]: It is anther state-of-the-art algorithm, a graph-based ranking algorithm considering various factors by meta-paths.

Parameter Settings. We tune parameters to achieve the best results, or set parameters as suggested by original papers. For AGS-MF, $wn = 100$, $maxIter = 200$, $\gamma = 0.002$ for three datasets; for Charlotte, $d = 40$, λ_u, λ_l, λ_Ω, and λ_Θ are all set as 0.005, $\alpha_u = 0.08$ and $\alpha_l = 0.8$; for Phoenix and Las Vegas, $d = 30$, λ_u, λ_l, λ_Ω, and λ_Θ are all set as 0.001, $\alpha_u = 0.02$ and $\alpha_l = 0.8$.

5.2   Results and Analysis

Results of AGS-MF Variants. Figure 2 presents the experimental results of different AGS-MF variants. We cumulatively incorporate the selected meta-paths into AGS-MF and record the performance change accordingly[2].

Generally, it can be observed that the performance becomes better as more meta-paths are incorporated. Overall, the meta-paths starting with L deliver more significant enhancement than the ones starting with U. In particular, with the incorporation of meta-path LL which encodes geographical influence, the performance is enhanced significantly by 42.70%, 51.76% and 22.33% averagely in terms of precision, recall and MAP across different settings of N over three datasets. The great improvements by LL reinforce the effectiveness of geographical influence on user check-in behavior. Besides, the slight performance fluctuation reveals that certain meta-paths might be ineffective for some users, even cause some noises. This issue is eased by exploiting personalized weights for different meta-paths, i.e., AGS-MF can determine the saliency of each meta-path for each user and POI, implying it can well deal with noisy information. Thus, AGS-MF still consistently generates decent results with all meta-paths.

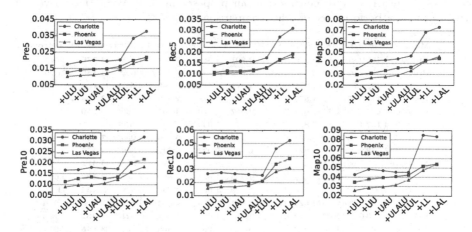

Fig. 2. Effect of meta-paths on the three datasets when meta-paths are gradually incorporated into AGS-MF.

Comparative Results. Table 2 provides the performance of all comparison methods on the three real-world datasets. Unsurprisingly, UCF, ICF and MF perform worse than other methods as they only consider user-POI interactions without any other auxiliary information. By considering relevant influential factors, the state-of-the-arts (e.g., LFBCA, TriRank, AGSRec, GeoSoCa) outperform all baseline methods.

---

[2] Due to space limitation, we only show the results with $N = 5, 10$ (N is the number of POI recommendations) and similar trends can be observed when $N = 20$.

Compared with state-of-the-art methods, our proposed approach performs better. This implies that recommendation performance can be further enhanced by appropriately considering the three influences. Our approach incorporates various influential factors in a non-trivial manner, i.e., leverages AGS-IG to unify them seamlessly, and learns the personalized weights of each user and POI. In particular, AGS-MF promotes the recommendation performance by a large margin, i.e., precision, recall and MAP are improved by 18.28%, 12.82% and 21.71% on average across different settings of N on the three datasets (with $p-value < 0.01$), compared with the best of other comparison approaches. Moreover, AGS-MF consistently outperforms other state-of-the-art methods with any setting of d. In particular, by learning personalized weights for different meta-paths, AGS-MF outperforms AGSRec in most cases by significant percentages. The precision, recall and MAP are averagely boosted by 13.36%, 8.94%, 16.89% across different settings of N on the three datasets, respectively (with $p - value < 0.01$). Especially, AGS-MF consistently outperforms AGSRec in

Table 2. Performance of comparison methods on the three real-world datasets. The best performance is highlighted in bold; the runner up is labeled with '*'; 'Improve' indicates the relative improvements that our proposed method AGS-MF achieves relative to the best performance of other comparison methods.

City	Metric	UCF	ICF	MF	SRMF	LFBCA	GeoMF	GeoSoCa	TriRank	AGSRec	AGS-MF	Improve(%)
Charlotte	Pre@5	1.483	0.976	1.817	2.586	2.007	2.901	2.586	2.821	3.018*	**3.776**	25.12
	Pre@10	1.456	0.922	1.798	2.134	1.881	2.562	2.134	2.532	2.633*	**3.186**	21.00
	Pre@20	1.433	0.945	1.581	1.917	1.939	2.372	1.917	2.360	**2.474**	2.411*	−2.54
	Rec@5	1.117	0.977	1.485	1.875	1.964	2.509	1.875	2.548	2.625*	**3.103**	18.21
	Rec@10	2.229	1.940	2.805	3.070	3.669	4.557	3.070	4.407	4.760*	**5.250**	9.87
	Rec@20	4.137	4.143	4.849	5.833	7.562	8.194	5.833	8.034	**8.558**	8.092*	−9.02
	MAP@5	3.086	2.039	3.659	5.328	4.188	5.702	5.328	5.586	6.033*	**7.323**	21.28
	MAP@10	3.788	2.566	4.369	5.922	4.939	6.807	5.922	6.747	6.949*	**8.345**	20.09
	MAP@20	4.255	3.061	4.751	6.281	5.589	7.528	6.281	7.203	7.946*	**8.441**	6.25
Phoenix	Pre@5	0.894	0.708	1.248	1.322	1.467	1.905	1.623	1.890	2.060*	**2.196**	6.60
	Pre@10	0.987	0.796	1.173	1.080	1.174	1.889	1.588	1.830	1.939*	**2.154**	11.09
	Pre@20	1.034	0.784	1.101	1.022	1.014	1.801	1.500	1.734	**1.869**	1.852*	−0.91
	Rec@5	0.693	0.771	1.028	1.022	1.536	1.723	1.600	1.751	1.821*	**1.932**	6.10
	Rec@10	1.604	1.742	1.880	1.628	3.592*	3.520	2.901	3.300	3.531	**3.845**	7.04
	Rec@20	3.370	3.489	3.603	3.092	6.130	5.850	5.700	6.126	**6.502**	6.163*	−5.21
	MAP@5	2.147	1.562	2.920	3.768	3.919	3.842	3.498	3.771	3.921*	**4.464**	13.85
	MAP@10	2.685	2.094	3.479	4.098	4.760	4.859	4.013	4.690	4.972*	**5.416**	8.93
	MAP@20	3.136	2.457	3.895	4.477	5.217	5.742	5.056	5.304	5.823*	**5.864**	0.70
Las Vegas	Pre@5	0.626	0.588	0.948	0.960	1.120	1.509	1.470	1.589	1.653*	**2.069**	25.17
	Pre@10	0.542	0.501	0.878	0.859	1.060	1.291	1.280	1.331	1.371*	**1.821**	32.82
	Pre@20	0.485	0.433	0.754	0.825	0.975	1.406	1.370	1.416	1.455*	**1.495**	2.75
	Rec@5	0.552	0.508	0.865	0.627	0.672	1.461	1.420	1.431	1.474*	**1.806**	22.52
	Rec@10	0.939	0.882	1.478	1.182	1.406	2.565	2.260	2.459	2.557*	**3.132**	22.49
	Rec@20	1.647	1.610	2.436	2.413	2.823	5.345	5.180	5.345	**5.502**	5.398*	−1.89
	MAP@5	1.340	1.310	2.191	1.714	2.222	3.428	3.250	3.306	3.571*	**4.644**	30.05
	MAP@10	1.612	1.586	2.530	2.074	2.685	3.860	3.820	3.882	4.154*	**5.385**	29.63
	MAP@20	1.819	1.613	2.251	2.393	3.063	4.282	4.100	4.349	4.883*	**5.580**	14.27

terms of MAP, indicating AGS-MF provides recommendations with better ranking quality by exploiting various influential factors via an integrate way.

6 Conclusion and Future Work

This paper focuses on exploiting the heterogeneous information in LBSNs to model both diversity and imbalance properties of user check-in behavior in a unified way. We first propose a novel knowledge graph (AGS-IG) by fusing social influence, geographical influence and aspects into a unified space, whereby we develop a novel POI recommendation approach – AGS-MF. It learns personalized weights of various influential factors in an automatic fashion. Empirical study on multiple real-world datasets demonstrates that our proposed method significantly outperforms state-of-the-art algorithms.

References

1. Bottou, L.: Large-scale machine learning with stochastic gradient descent. In: Lechevallier, Y., Saporta, G. (eds.) COMPSTAT 2010, pp. 177–186. Springer, Heidelberg (2010). https://doi.org/10.1007/978-3-7908-2604-3_16
2. Cheng, C., Yang, H., King, I., Lyu, M.R.: Fused matrix factorization with geographical and social influence in location-based social networks. In: AAAI, vol. 12, p. 1 (2012)
3. Guo, Q., Sun, Z., Zhang, J., Chen, Q., Theng, Y.L.: Aspect-aware point-of-interest recommendation with geo-social influence. In: UMAP, pp. 17–22. ACM (2017)
4. He, X., Chen, T., Kan, M.Y., Chen, X.: TriRank: review-aware explainable recommendation by modeling aspects. In: CIKM (2015)
5. Jamali, M., Ester, M.: A matrix factorization technique with trust propagation for recommendation in social networks. In: RecSys, pp. 135–142. ACM (2010)
6. Ma, H., Zhou, D., Liu, C., Lyu, M.R., King, I.: Recommender systems with social regularization. In: WSDM, pp. 287–296. ACM (2011)
7. Salakhutdinov, R., Mnih, A.: Probabilistic matrix factorization. In: NIPS, vol. 1, pp. 1–2 (2007)
8. Sun, Y., Han, J., Yan, X., Yu, P.S., Wu, T.: Pathsim: meta path-based top-k similarity search in heterogeneous information networks. VLDB Endow. 4(11), 992–1003 (2011)
9. Wang, H., Terrovitis, M., Mamoulis, N.: Location recommendation in location-based social networks using user check-in data. In: SIGSPATIAL (2013)
10. Xie, M., Yin, H., Wang, H., Xu, F., Chen, W., Wang, S.: Learning graph-based POI embedding for location-based recommendation. In: CIKM, pp. 15–24. ACM (2016)
11. Ye, M., Yin, P., Lee, W.C., Lee, D.L.: Exploiting geographical influence for collaborative point-of-interest recommendation. In: SIGIR, pp. 325–334. ACM (2011)
12. Yuan, Q., Cong, G., Sun, A.: Graph-based point-of-interest recommendation with geographical and temporal influences. In: CIKM, pp. 659–668. ACM (2014)
13. Zhang, J.D., Chow, C.Y.: Geosoca: Exploiting geographical, social and categorical correlations for point-of-interest recommendations. In: SIGIR, pp. 443–452. ACM (2015)

14. Zhang, J.D., Chow, C.Y., Zheng, Y.: ORec: an opinion-based point-of-interest recommendation framework. In: CIKM, pp. 1641–1650. ACM (2015)
15. Zhang, Y., Zhang, H., Zhang, M., Liu, Y., Ma, S.: Do users rate or review? Boost phrase-level sentiment labeling with review-level sentiment classification. In: SIGIR (2014)

Exploring Semantic Change of Chinese Word Using Crawled Web Data

Xiaofei Xu, Yukun Cao, and Li Li[✉]

College of Computer and Information Science, Southwest University,
Chongqing 400715, China
nakamura@email.swu.edu.cn, lily@swu.edu.cn

Abstract. Words changing their meanings over time reflects various shifts in socio-cultural attitudes and conceptual structures. Understanding semantic change of words over time is important in order to study models of language and cultural evolution. Word embeddings methods such as PPMI, SVD and word2vec have been evaluated in recent years. These kinds of representation methods, sometimes referring as semantic maps of words, are able to facilitate the whole process of language processing. Chinese language is no exception. The development of technology gradually influences people's communication and the language they are using. In the paper, a huge amount of data (300 GB) is provided by Sogou, a Chinese web search engine provider. After pre-processing, the Chinese language corpus is obtained. Three different word representation methods are extended to including temporal information. They are trained and tested based on the above dataset. A thorough analysis (both qualitative and quantitative analysis) is conducted with different thresholds to capture different semantic accuracy and alignment quality of the shifted words. A comparison between three methods is provided and possible reasons behind experiment results are discussed.

Keywords: Diachronic analysis · Word embedding ·
Web data mining · Chinese word evolution

1 Introduction

Using neural network for word embedding learning was first proposed as NNLM (Neural Network Language Model) [1]. Since then, word embedding methods have been proved to have excellent results in semantic analysis tasks [13]. It is evident that embedding is not only able to catch statistical information but syntactic information as well. Complex linguistic problems, such as exploring semantic change of words in discrete time periods [8] can thus be tackled properly. Moreover, embedding methods were used to detect large scale linguistic change-points [9] as well as to seek out regularities in acquiring language, such as related words tending to undergo parallel change over time [15].

© Springer Nature Switzerland AG 2019
M. Bakaev et al. (Eds.): ICWE 2019, LNCS 11496, pp. 81–88, 2019.
https://doi.org/10.1007/978-3-030-19274-7_7

Word2vec is typical low dimensional (usually from 50 to 300) word embedding method based on neural network, while SVD (Singular Value Decomposition) is a typical low dimensional word representation method based on matrix decomposition. These methods have achieved the state-of-the-art results in many diachronic analysis tasks [4,5,10] and diachronic-based applications [3,16]. However, due to the inconsistent context and the stochastic nature of the above embedding methods, words in different periods cannot be easily encoded into the same vector space [6]. Also, due to the absence of Chinese historical corpus [6], currently diachronic analysis on Chinese is not studied well. The previous work normally encoded words from different time periods into separate vector spaces first, and then aligned the learned low-dimensional embeddings [9]. The inherent uncertainty of embeddings will lead to high variability of a given word's closest neighbors [7]. The alignment approximates the relationship among vector spaces and forcibly consolidates inconsistent contexts onto a common context that will augment neighbor words' variability. Moreover, as the pair of word context fluctuates over time, the forcible consolidation will tamper word semantics undesirably.

The problem of alignment can be avoided by not encoding words to low-dimensional space [8]. Among them, the Positive Point-wise Mutual Information (PPMI) [14] outperforms a wide variety of other high-dimensional approaches [2]. PPMI naturally aligns word vectors by constructing a high-dimensional sparse matrix, with each row representing a unique word, and each column corresponding to it's context. Unfortunately, compared with low dimensional methods, PPMI introduces additional problems. In particular, building the PPMI matrix will consume a lot of computing resources in high-dimensional sparse environment. Though PPMI wards off alignment issues, it does not enjoy the advantages of low dimensional embeddings such as higher efficiency and better generalization.

In this paper, we first introduce three popular word representation methods, the PPMI, PPMI-based SVD and word2vec. Then we will introduce the experiment setup, including the data, data preprocessing and the evaluation metrics. Finally we will discuss the experiment results, the application of word diachronic analysis on Chinese and future works.

2   Related Work

Many contributions about word representation have been done by other researchers. In this paper, we mainly use three word representation methods. We choose PPMI as our sparse word representation method, which makes use of word co-occurrence information as its vector. We choose PPMI-based SVD and word2vec as our low-dimension word representation methods. The PPMI-based SVD can take the advantage of co-occurrence information and frequency information in the PPMI matrix. The word2vec can be considered as a neural network based word representation method which can take the advantage of the nonlinear expression ability of neural networks. We will introduce these three methods in detail in the following sections.

2.1   PPMI

In the PPMI, words are represented by constructing a high dimensional sparse matrix $M \in R^{|V_w| \times |V_c|}$ where each row denotes a word w, and each column represents a context c. The value of the matrix cell M_{ij} is the PPMI value that suggests the associated relationship between the word w_i and the context c_j, the value of matrix cell M_{ij} is obtained by:

$$M_{ij} = max \left\{ log \left(\frac{p(w_i, c_j)}{p(w_i)p(c_j)} \right), 0 \right\} \tag{1}$$

2.2   PPMI-Based SVD

SVD embeddings implement dimensionality reduction over a sparse high-dimensional matrix S, of which each row represents a word and each column corresponds to a potential feature of the word. More concretely, SVD decomposes the sparse matrix S into the product of three matrices, $S = U \cdot V \cdot T$, where both U and T are orthonormal, and V is a diagonal matrix of singular values ordered in the decent direction. In V, the top limited number of singular values retain most features of the word, that is, by keeping the top d singular values, we have $S_d = U_d \cdot V_d \cdot T_d$ which approximates S, then the word embedding $\overrightarrow{W}$ is approximated by:

$$\overrightarrow{W} \approx U_d \tag{2}$$

2.3   Word2vec

Bengio *et al.* [1] mentioned that language neural network model can be used in other ways to reduce the number of training parameters, such as recurrent neural networks. In order to quickly obtain a good word vector set, Mikolov *et al.* [12] invented a word vector training tool named word2vec[1]. It includes two models: the CBOW (Continuous Bag-Of-Word) model and the Skip-gram (continuous Skip-gram) model.

Both models are feed-forward neural network models, without the nonlinear hidden layer of the neural language model in [1]. This modification greatly simplified model structure and reduced training time.

In this paper, we use Skip-gram model as word2vec training model. Given an intermediate word w_t as the priori knowledge to predict the context of the other words, the training process of the Skip-gram model is implemented by maximizing the value of W_{t+j} in Eq. (4).

$$\frac{1}{|V|} \sum_{t=1}^{|V|} \sum_{-c \leqslant j \leqslant c, j \neq 0} log p(w_{t+j}|w_t) \tag{3}$$

where $|V|$ denotes the size of word dictionary obtained from the training corpus, c represents the number of context words before or after the middle word.

---

[1] http://word2vec.googlecode.com/svn/trunk/.

p(.) is a softmax regression function shown as Eq. (5):

$$p(w_o|w_i) = \frac{exp(v'_{w_o}{}^T v_{w_i})}{\sum_{w=1}^{|V|} exp(v'_{w_o}{}^T v_{w_i})} \tag{4}$$

where v_w and v'_w are the vector representations for the input layer and the output layer respectively.

In this paper, we use Skip-gram model with negative-sampling from word2vec (in this paper, we name it as SGNS), which is a fast and effective method to build a word representation.

2.4 Detect Diachronic Changes

We detect semantic change-point of the word by measuring the semantic similarity of its two profiles in respective time periods. The measure is as follows:

$$sim(w|x1, x2) = cos(\overrightarrow{W^{x1}}, \overrightarrow{W^{x2}}) \tag{5}$$

where $cos()$ calculates the cosine similarity of two vectors, which is between [0, 1]. w^{x1} and w^{x2} are profiles referring to exactly the same word w but appearing in periods of $x1$ and $x2$, respectively. Smaller value means more significant difference, that is, the meaning of word shifts greatly over time. We measure the semantic difference of a specific word at every two periods.

2.5 Alignment Method

In order to compare word vectors from different time-periods, we must align the vectors from different time-periods. The PPMI is naturally aligned, but PPMI-based SVD and word2vec is not naturally aligned, these two method may result in arbitrary orthogonal transformations. According to [6], we use orthogonal Procrustes to align the learned word representations. Suppose $W^{(t)} \in \mathbb{R}^{d \times |V|}$ as the matrix of word embeddings learned at year t. We align the embeddings by optimizing:

$$R(t) = \underset{Q^T Q = I}{\arg \min} ||W^{(t)}Q - W^{(t+1)}||_F \tag{6}$$

3 Experiment Results

3.1 Preprocessing

Dataset. In this paper, we use a large set of search engine crawled web pages provided by Sogou Lab [11]. Provided data is organized as XML style label texts. The data is raw XML labeled data and has no time tag in labels. After we analyzed the data, we found that the URL of every document may contain time information (this usually occurs in news sites). So, in this experiment, we use the URL provided time information.

To extract the time information from document data, we use regex to match time pattern like "YYYY-MM-DD" or "YYYY_MM_DD" in url, urls without this pattern will be deleted. Then we apply a filter that can clean all html labels and other useless symbols to build the final training corpus.

The word segmentation tool jieba[2] is applied for Chinese word segmentation (including the compound words).

After these preprocessing, we finally get about 52,324,791 lines of data consisting 467,826,233 words (225,182 unique words).

3.2   Number of Discovered Shift Words

The detection of linguistic change is shown by searching for semantically shifting words among time-periods and how many such kind of words are identified clearly in a given time slot. Two corpora, "Corpus 1998-2002" and "Corpus 2008-2012" are picked up because the two of 5-year range may exhibit the semantic shifting of the development process of Internet in China. We compare the semantic similarity of word vectors between two periods of time for each word. Moreover, in order to build a comprehensive understanding of the linguistic change, we identify shifting words with five different thresholds (the semantic similarities thresholds are set to 0.1, 0.2, 0.3, 0.4 and 0.5, respectively). The results are shown in Table 1. It is PPMI that detects the largest number of shifting words under the same conditions. From the Table 1. We can also find that the number of detected words of PPMI, SVD and SGNS are mainly distributed under 0.1, 0.4 and 0.5. This shows a interesting fact that the result of these three method have different distribution.

Table 1. Number of shifted words

Threshold	0.1	0.2	0.3	0.4	0.5
PPMI	12778	19157	19963	20146	20224
SVD	552	2371	6177	11048	15544
SGNS	9373	9382	9400	9604	11987

3.3   Visualizing Semantic Evolution of Words

We select some semantic changed words in the corpus generated by our methods, visualize them in three periods (1998–2002, 2003–2007 and 2008–2012). To draw the visualization for a given semantic-changed word, we extract words which are semantically similar neighbors in each period, placing them around the word at different distances according to the vector distance between the word and its neighbors. The visualization of semantic changed words are shown in Figs. 1 and 2. In Fig. 1, we can find that the meaning of "copy" in Chinese changes its mean at

---

[2] http://github.com/fxsjy/jieba.

about 2008–2012, moving towards "arena" in English. In Fig. 2, we can find that the meaning of "apple" in Chinese changes its mean at about 2003–2007, moving towards to "Apple Inc." in English.

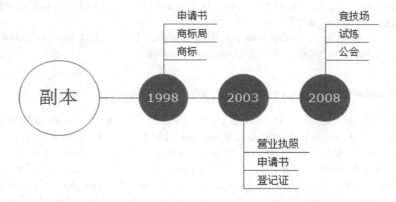

Fig. 1. Visualization of "copy" in Chinese

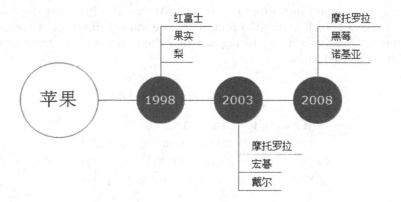

Fig. 2. Visualization of "apple" in Chinese

3.4 Discussions

Here we will discuss about three problems in our diachronic analysis result:

– How to find the representation of the semantically active words, given that they may change in meaning over time.
– How to judge a historical word embedding method is effective quantitatively.
– How to find a relationship between diachronic shift words, linguistic evolution and social changes.

As discussed in Sect. 1, words from different time periods cannot be easily projected into the same dense vector space. Suppose now they are directly represented in a single dense vector space, what would we do to trace their semantic change? Even though every word has a different profile in each corpus, together they have to be represented by one unique vector. That is, it remains unchanged in the varying time period and sensitive context of the word. Also, the word embeddings learn word representations in global which can also make polysemous words not stable. So it's still a problem need further study.

In this paper, we use different word distance thresholds to find the shifted words. As lack of ground truth data to reveal known word shifts, this may be a quantitative way to evaluate word embedding methods. But this kind of method is simple and inaccurate. A possible direction is to apply density analysis on word embedding results.

Also, as the result of our work, we can find the diachronic shift words, how to create a relationship between shift words, linguistic evolution and social changes is the next question. A possible direction is to design a global distance evaluation algorithm to embody the linguistic evolution, another possible direction is to use some social change event to analyze its relationship between shift words and social changes.

4 Conclusion and Future Work

Though low-dimensional method enjoy higher efficiency and better generalization, high-dimensional word representation methods still have its own advantages. In this paper, we use both high-dimensional and low-dimensional word representation method to build word vectors among time-periods. As current research have seldom work on Chinese corpus analysis, we use a large mount of data from Sogou search engine crawled pages to perform this analysis. After using three word representation method to train this Chinese corpus, we use different thresholds to get shifted words from the representation and visualize semantic evolution of words.

In the future, we mainly focus on research directions talked in discussion. The very next research topic is trying to reveal the relationship between word meaning shifts, linguistic evolution and social changes in Chinese corpus. We will also try to build a Chinese word shift ground truth data in order to achieve word shift evaluation quantitatively.

Acknowledgement. This work was supported by National Undergraduate Training Program for Innovation and Entrepreneurship (No. 201810635003), National Natural Science Foundation of China (No. 61877051) and CSTC funding (No. cstc2017zdcy-zdyf0366).

References

1. Bengio, Y., Ducharme, R., Vincent, P., Jauvin, C.: A neural probabilistic language model. J. Mach. Learn. Res. **3**, 1137–1155 (2003)
2. Bullinaria, J.A., Levy, J.P.: Extracting semantic representations from word co-occurrence statistics: a computational study. Behav. Res. Methods **39**(3), 510–526 (2007)
3. Garg, N., Schiebinger, L., Jurafsky, D., Zou, J.: Word embeddings quantify 100 years of gender and ethnic stereotypes. Proc. Nat. Acad. Sci. **115**(16), E3635–E3644 (2018)
4. Grayson, S., Mulvany, M., Wade, K., Meaney, G., Greene, D.: Exploring the role of gender in 19th century fiction through the lens of word embeddings. In: Gracia, J., Bond, F., McCrae, J.P., Buitelaar, P., Chiarcos, C., Hellmann, S. (eds.) LDK 2017. LNCS (LNAI), vol. 10318, pp. 358–364. Springer, Cham (2017). https://doi.org/10.1007/978-3-319-59888-8_30
5. Hamilton, W.L., Leskovec, J., Jurafsky, D.: Cultural shift or linguistic drift? Comparing two computational measures of semantic change. In: Proceedings of the Conference on Empirical Methods in Natural Language Processing, vol. 2016, p. 2116. NIH Public Access (2016)
6. Hamilton, W.L., Leskovec, J., Jurafsky, D.: Diachronic word embeddings reveal statistical laws of semantic change. arXiv preprint arXiv:1605.09096 (2016)
7. Hellrich, J., Hahn, U.: Bad company—neighborhoods in neural embedding spaces considered harmful. In: Proceedings of COLING 2016, the 26th International Conference on Computational Linguistics: Technical Papers, pp. 2785–2796 (2016)
8. Jatowt, A., Duh, K.: A framework for analyzing semantic change of words across time. In: IEEE/ACM Joint Conference on Digital Libraries (JCDL), pp. 229–238. IEEE (2014)
9. Kulkarni, V., Al-Rfou, R., Perozzi, B., Skiena, S.: Statistically significant detection of linguistic change. In: Proceedings of the 24th International Conference on World Wide Web, pp. 625–635. International World Wide Web Conferences Steering Committee (2015)
10. Levy, O., Goldberg, Y., Dagan, I.: Improving distributional similarity with lessons learned from word embeddings. Trans. Assoc. Computat. Linguist. **3**, 211–225 (2015)
11. Liu, Y., Chen, F., Kong, W., Yu, H., Zhang, M., Ma, S., Ru, L.: Identifying web spam with the wisdom of the crowds. ACM Trans. Web (TWEB) **6**(1), 2 (2012)
12. Mikolov, T., Chen, K., Corrado, G., Dean, J.: Efficient estimation of word representations in vector space. arXiv preprint arXiv:1301.3781 (2013)
13. Mikolov, T., Yih, W.t., Zweig, G.: Linguistic regularities in continuous space word representations. In: Proceedings of the 2013 Conference of the North American Chapter of the Association for Computational Linguistics: Human Language Technologies, pp. 746–751 (2013)
14. Turney, P.D., Pantel, P.: From frequency to meaning: vector space models of semantics. J. Artif. Intell. Res. **37**, 141–188 (2010)
15. Xu, Y., Kemp, C.: A computational evaluation of two laws of semantic change. In: CogSci (2015)
16. Yan, E., Zhu, Y.: Tracking word semantic change in biomedical literature. Int. J. Med. Informatics **109**, 76–86 (2018)

Web Big Data and Web Data Analytics

A Customisable Pipeline for Continuously Harvesting Socially-Minded Twitter Users

Flavio Primo[1] , Paolo Missier[1]([✉]) , Alexander Romanovsky[1] ,
Mickael Figueredo[2], and Nelio Cacho[2]

[1] School of Computing, Newcastle University, Science Central,
Newcastle upon Tyne, UK
{flavio.primo,paolo.missier,alexander.romanovsky}@ncl.ac.uk
[2] Universidade Federal do Rio Grande do Norte, Natal, RN, Brazil
neliocacho@dimap.ufrn.br

Abstract. On social media platforms and Twitter in particular, specific classes of users such as *influencers* have been given satisfactory operational definitions in terms of network and content metrics. Others, for instance *online activists*, are not less important but their characterisation still requires experimenting. We make the hypothesis that such interesting users can be found within temporally and spatially localised *contexts*, i.e., small but topical fragments of the network containing interactions about social events or campaigns with a significant footprint on Twitter. To explore this hypothesis, we have designed a continuous user profile discovery pipeline that produces an ever-growing dataset of user profiles by harvesting and analysing contexts from the Twitter stream. The profiles dataset includes key network and content-based users metrics, enabling experimentation with user-defined score functions that characterise specific classes of online users. The paper describes the design and implementation of the pipeline and its empirical evaluation on a case study consisting of healthcare-related campaigns in the UK, showing how it supports the operational definitions of online activism, by comparing three experimental ranking functions. The code is publicly available.

Keywords: Twitter analytics · Online user discovery ·
Online activists · Online influencers · Influence theories

1 Introduction

We present a customisable software framework for incrementally discovering and ranking individual profiles for classes of online users, through analysis of their social activity on Twitter. Practical motivation for this work comes from our ongoing effort to support health officers in tropical countries, specifically in Brazil, in their fight against airborne virus epidemics like Dengue and Zika. Help from community activists is badly needed to supplement the scarce public

© Springer Nature Switzerland AG 2019
M. Bakaev et al. (Eds.): ICWE 2019, LNCS 11496, pp. 91–106, 2019.
https://doi.org/10.1007/978-3-030-19274-7_8

resources deployed on the ground. Our past work has focused on identifying relevant content on Twitter that may point health authorities directly to mosquito breeding sites [22], as well as to users who have shown interest in those topics, i.e., by posting relevant content on Twitter [13].

The approach described in this paper generalises those past efforts, by attempting to discover users who demonstrate an inclination *to become engaged in social issues, regardless of the specific topic*. We refer to this class of users as *activists*. The rationale for this approach is that activists who manifest themselves online on a range of social initiatives, may be more sensitive to requests for help on specific issues than the average Twitter user. In the paper we experiment with healthcare-related online campaigns in the UK. Application of the approach to our initial motivating case study in ongoing as part of a long-term collaboration, and is not specifically discussed in the paper.

To be clear, this work is not about providing a robust definition of online activism, or to demonstrate that online activism translates into actual engagement in the "real world". Instead, we start by acknowledging that the notion of activist is not as well formalised in the literature as that of, for example, *influencers*, and we develop a generic content processing pipeline which can be customised to identify a variety of classes of users. The pipeline repeatedly searches for and ranks Twitter user profiles by collecting quantitative network- and content-based user metrics. Once targeted to a specific topic, it provides a tool for exploring operational definitions of user roles, including online activism, i.e., by combining the metrics into higher level, *engineered* user features to be used for ranking.

Although the user harvesting pipeline is generally applicable to the analysis of a variety of user profiles, our focus is on the search for a satisfactory operational definition of online activism. According to the Cambridge Dictionary, an *activist* is "A person who believes strongly in political or social change and takes part in activities such as public protests to try to make this happen". While activism is well-documented, e.g. in the social movement literature [5], and online activism is a well-known phenomenon [12], research has been limited to the study of its broad societal impact. In contrast, we are interested in the fine-grained discovery of activists at the level of the single individual, that is, we seek people who feel passionate about a cause or topic, and who take action for it. Searching for online activists is a realistic goal, as activists presence in social media is widely acknowledged, and it is also clear that social media facilitates activists communication and organization [17,23]. Specific traits that characterise activists include awareness of causes and social topic and the organization of social gatherings and activities, including in emergency situations, by helping organize support efforts and diffusion of useful information.

1.1 Challenges

The definition of online activism translates into technical challenges in systematically harvesting suitable candidate users. Firstly, the potentially more subdue nature of activists, relative to influencers, makes it particularly difficult to separate their online footprint from the background noise of general conversations. Also, interesting activists are by their nature associated to specific topics and manifest their nature in local contexts, for instance as organisers or participants to local events. Finally, we expect their personal engagement to be sustained over time and across multiple such contexts. These observations suggest that the models and algorithms developed for influencers are not immediately applicable, because they mostly operate on global networks, where less prominent users have less of a chance to emerge. Some topic-sensitive metrics and models have been proposed to measure social influence, for example, *alpha centrality* [6,15] and the *Information Diffusion* model [16]. Algorithms based on topic models have also been proposed to account for topic specificity [24]. However, these approaches are still aimed at measuring influence, not activism, and assume a one-shot discovery process, as opposed to a continuous, incremental approach.

1.2   Approach and Contributions

To address these challenges, the approach we propose involves a two-fold strategy. Firstly, we identify suitable contexts that are topic-specific and limited both in time and, optionally, also in space, i.e., regional initiatives, events, or campaigns. We then search for users only within these contexts, following the intuition that low key users who produce weak online signal have a better chance to be discovered when the search is localised and then repeated across multiple such contexts. By continuously discovering new contexts, we hope to incrementally build up a users' dataset where users who appear in multiple contexts are progressively more strongly characterised. Secondly, to allow experimenting with varying technical definitions of *activist*, we collect a number of network-based and content-based user profile features, mostly known from the literature, and make them available to experiment with a variety of user rankings.

The paper makes the following specific contributions. Firstly, we propose a data processing pipeline for harvesting Twitter content and user profiles, based on multiple limited contexts. The pipeline includes community detection and network analysis algorithms aimed at discovering users within such limited contexts.

Secondly, we have implemented a comprehensive set of content-based metrics that results into an ever-growing database of user profile features, which can then be used for mining purposes. User profiles are updated when they are repeatedly found in multiple contexts.

Lastly, for empirical evaluation of our implementation, we demonstrate an operational definition of the activist profile, defined in terms of the features available in the database. We collected about 3,500 users across 25 contexts in the domain of healthcare awareness campaigns in the UK during 2018, and demonstrated three separate ranking functions, showing that it is possible to identify individuals as opposed to well-known organisations. The application of the approach to the specific challenge of combating tropical disease epidemics in Brazil is currently in progress and is not reported in this paper.

1.3 Related Work

The closest body of research to this work is concerned with techniques for the discovery of online *influencers*. According to [11], influencers are *prominent individuals with special characteristics that enable them to affect a disproportionately large number of their peers with their actions*. A large number of metrics and techniques have been proposed to make this generic definition operational [19]. These metrics tend to favour high visibility users across global networks, regardless of their actual impact [8]. In contrast, activists are typically low-key, less prominent users who only emerge from the crowd by signalling high levels of engagement with one or more specific topics, as opposed to being thought-leaders. While such behaviour can be described using well-tested metrics [19], it should also be clear that new ways to combine those metrics are required. A method for creating Twitter user ontologies considering the content type of the tweets is proposed in [18]. This approach could be used to gain insights over a user, but fails to give a comprehensive description of the user activity as it is based only on recent user activity, also due to Twitter API limitations.

The algorithm proposed in [7] aims to identify influencers based on a single topic context, based on relevant social media conversations. Metrics include number of "likes", viewers per months, post frequency and number of comments per post, as well as the ratio of positive to negative posts. As some of these metrics are qualitative and difficult to acquire, however, this approach is not easy to automate. Another approach to ranking topic-specific influencers within specific events appears in [11], where network dynamics are accounted for in real-time. Once again however, the effect is to discover users who receive much attention, but do not necessarily create a real impact over users inside one topic.

Machine learning is used in [2] to analyse posted content and recognise when a user is able to influence another inside a conversation. This however requires substantial a priori ground truth, making this approach impracticable in our case. In addition, the need to create a classifier for each topic limits the scalability of the system.

A supervised regression approach is used in [14] to rank influence of Twitter users. It uses features that are not based on content, but the method performs poorly as it requires a huge training set to work effectively.

Unlike the majority of the influencer ranking algorithms, in [21] a topic-specific influencer ranking is proposed. First it harvests sequentially timed snapshots of the network of users related to a topic. Then it ranks the users based on the number of followers gained and lost in the considered snapshots.

Finally, [4] presents a model for identifying "prominent users" regarding a specific topic event in Twitter. Those are users who focus their attention and communication on the aforementioned topic event. Users are described by a feature vector, computed in real-time, which allows a separation between on-topic and off-topic users activity over Twitter. Similar to [2], problems of scalability and adaptability arise as two supervised learning methods are used, one to discriminate prominent users from the rest and the other to rank them.

2 Contexts and User Metrics

The aim of the pipeline is to repeatedly and efficiently discover user profiles from the Twitter post history within user-specified contexts and to use the process to grow a database of feature-rich user profiles that can be ranked according to user-defined relevance functions. The criteria used to define contexts, profile relevance functions, and associated user relevance thresholds can be configured for specific applications.

2.1 Contexts and Context Networks

A context C is a Twitter query defined by a set K of hashtags and/or keyword terms, a time interval $[t_1, t_2]$, and a geographical constraint s, such as a bounding box:

$$C = (K, [t_1, t_2], s) \tag{1}$$

Let $P(C)$ denote the query result, i.e., a set of posts by users. We only consider two Twitter user activities: an *original tweet*, or a *retweet*. Let $u(p)$ be the user who originated a tweet $p \in P(C)$. We say that both p and $u(p)$ are *within context C*. We also define the complement $\tilde{P}(C)$ of $P(C)$ as the set of posts found using the same spatio-temporal constraints, but which do not contain any of the terms in K. More precisely, given a context $C' = (s, [t_1, t_2], \emptyset)$ with no terms constraints, we define $\tilde{P}(C) = P(C') \setminus P(C)$. We refer to these posts, and their respective users, as "out of context C".

$P(C)$ induces a user-user social network graph $G_C = (V, E)$ where V is the set of all users who have authored any $p \in P(C)$: $V = \{u(p) | p \in P(C)\}$, and a weighted directed edge $e = \langle u_1, u_2, w \rangle$ is added to E for each pair of posts p_1, p_2 such that $u(p_1) = u_1, u(p_2) = u_2$ and either (i) p_2 is a retweet of p_1, or (ii) p_1 contains a mention of u_2. For any such edge, w is a count of such pairs of posts occurring in $P(C)$ for the same pair of users.

2.2 User Relevance Metrics

We support metrics that are generally accepted by the community as forming a core, from which many different social user roles are derived [19]. We distinguish amongst three types of features, which differ in the way they are computed from the raw Twitter feed:

Content-based metrics that rely solely on content and *not* on the user-user network. These metrics are defined relative to a topic of interest, i.e., a context;

Context-independent topological metrics that encode context-independent, long-lived relationships amongst users, i.e., follower/followee; and

Context-specific topological metrics that encode user relationships that occur specifically within a context.

All metrics are functions of a few core features that can be directly extracted from Twitter posts. Given a context C containing user u, we define:

$R1(u)$: Number of retweets by u, of tweets from other users in C;

$R2(u)$: Number of unique users in C, who have been retweeted by u;

$R3(u)$: Number of retweets of u's tweets;

$R4(u)$: Number of unique users in C who retweeted u's tweets;

$P1(u)$: Number of original posts by u within C;

$P2(u)$: Number of web links found in original posts by u within C;

$F1(u)$: Number of followers of u;

$F2(u)$: Number of followees of u

Note that, given C, we can evaluate some of the features above with respect to either $P(C)$ or $\tilde{P}(C)$ independently from each other, that is, we can consider an "on-context" and an "off-context" version of each feature, with the exception of $F1$ and $F2$ which are context-independent. For example, we are going to write $R1_{on}(u)$ to denote the number of context retweets and $R1_{off}(u)$ the number of out-of-context retweets by u, i.e., these are retweets that occur within C's spatio-temporal boundaries, but do not contain any of the hashtags or keywords that define C. We similarly qualify all other features. Using these core features, the framework currently supports the following metrics.

Content-based metrics:

$$\text{Topical Focus: [13]: } TF(u) = \frac{P1_{on}(u)}{P1_{off}(u) + 1} \tag{2}$$

$$\text{Topical Strength [3]: } TS(u) = \frac{P2_{on}(u) \cdot \log(P2_{on}(u) + R3_{on} + 1)}{P2_{off}(u) \cdot \log(P2_{off}(u) + R3_{off} + 1) + 1} \tag{3}$$

$$\text{Topical Attachment [4, 17]: } TA(u) - \frac{P1_{on}(u) + P2_{on}(u)}{P1_{off}(u) + P2_{off}(u) + 1} \tag{4}$$

The framework supports one **Context-independent topological metric** and one **Context-specific topological metric**, both commonly used, see e.g. [19]:

$$\text{Follower Rank: } FR(u) = \frac{F1(u)}{F1(u) + F2(u)} \tag{5}$$

$$\text{In-degree centrality: } IC(u) = \frac{indegree(u)}{N - 1} \tag{6}$$

where N is the number of nodes in the network induced by C. Note that the metrics we have selected are a superset of those indicated in recent studies on online activism, namely [12] and [17], and thus support our empirical evaluation, described in Sect. 4.

3   Incremental User Discovery

The content processing pipeline operates iteratively on a set of contexts within a given area of interest, for instance *2018 UK health campaigns*. This set is initialised at the start of the process and then updated at the end of each iteration, in a semi-automated way. The user discovery process is therefore potentially open-ended, as long as new contexts can be discovered. The new contexts are expected to be within the same topic area, but contexts that "drift" to new areas of interest are also acceptable. Each iteration takes a context C as input, and selects a subset of the users who participate in C, using the topical criteria described below, along with the set of their features and metrics. These users profiles are added to a database, where entries for repeat users are updated according to a user-defined function. The pipeline structure is described below, where the numbers are with reference to Fig. 1.

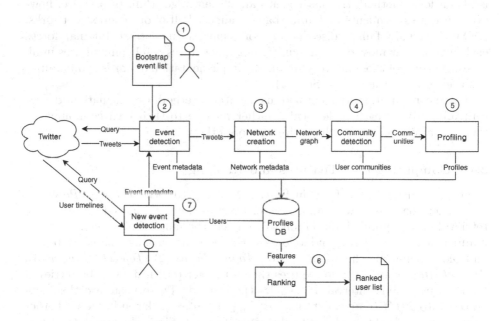

Fig. 1. Schematic diagram of the user discovery framework. Note that an initial list C of contexts (events) is provided to initialise the *event detection* step. The outputs from each of these steps are persisted into the Profiles DB.

Given C as in (2), all Twitter posts $P(C)$ that satisfy C are retrieved, using the Twitter Search APIs. Note that this step hits the API service limitations imposed by Twitter. For this reason, in our evaluation we have limited our retrieval to 200 tweets/context. This is sufficient, considering that repeated users appear consistently in our evaluation (Sect. 4). Twitter API limitations can be overcome by either extending the harvesting time, or by choosing more recent contexts, as the Twitter API is more tolerant with recents tweets.

The context network G_C is then generated (3), as defined in Sect. 2.1. The size of each network is largely determined by the nature of the context, and ranges between 140 and 400 users (avg 254, see Table 1).

Next, G_C is partitioned into communities of users (4). The goal of this partitioning is to further narrow the scope when computing in-degree centrality (6), to enable weak-signal users to emerge relative to other more globally dominant users. We have experimented with two of the many algorithms for discovering virtual communities in social networks, namely DEMON [9] and Infomap [20]. Both are available in our implementation, but based on our experimental comparison (Sect. 4) we recommend the latter.

DEMON is based on *ego networks* [1], and uses a label propagation algorithm to assign nodes to communities. Users may be assigned to multiple communities, an attractive feature when users are active in more than one community within the same context, i.e., a social event or a campaign. Label propagation is also a local method, translating into an efficient algorithm. In practice, however, in our experiments we found that for almost half of our context networks, DEMON actually fails to discover any communities. In contrast, Infomap forces each user into at most one community, but it generates valid communities in all cases. As some of those are very small, our implementation discards communities with fewer than 4 users (see Sect. 4).

Once communities are identified, using either method, we calculate in-degree centrality (6) for each node locally, either relative to their own community if they are available, and to the entire network otherwise.

3.1 Computing User Features and Ranking

Next, user metrics as defined in Sect. 2.2, along with the *Follower Rank* are computed from the network and the user features. This is achieved through bulk retrieval of user profile information (5), namely the number of tweets, retweets, number of followers $F1(u)$ and followees, $F2(u)$, along with user name, web link, and bio. Computing the other metrics: *Topical Focus* (2), *Topical Strength* (3), *Topical Attachment* (4) also requires the entire user post history to be retrieved for the entire time interval defined by the context. These posts are then separated into $P(C)$ (on-context) and $\tilde{P}(C)$ (off-context), depending on whether they contain a hashtag related to the context or not. Similarly, a post that contains a link is a *link on-topic* if it contains both a link and a hashtag related to the context, and a *link off-topic* otherwise. We also calculate the number of retweets for every post, i.e., $R1(u)$ and $R3(u)$, which are required to compute *Topical Strength*.

All of these features are persisted to a database which is made available for ranking purposes. User-defined functions can be specified to update the Rank of pre-existing users, e.g. by combining scores assigned at different times. The DB enables user-defined scoring functions, which result in user ranking lists (6). Examples of these are given later in Sect. 4. This framework approach is consistent with the experimental nature of our search for *activists*, which requires exploring a variety of ranking functions.

3.2   New Contexts Discovery

The final step within one iteration (7) aims to discover new contexts, so that the process can start again (2). Intuitively, once a score function has been applied and users have been ranked, we can hope to discover new interesting keywords and hashtags by exploring the timeline of the top-k users. Specifically, we consider each hashtag found in the timelines, which is related to the broader topic and not yet considered in past iterations. Each stored hashtag is then enriched with the information needed to perform a new iteration of the pipeline, namely (i) the temporal and spatial information of the context, and (ii) related hashtags. Currently this step is only semi-automated, as making a judgement on the relevance of the new terms requires human expertise. While automating this step is not straightforward, this is not a very time-consuming step, and one can imagine an approach where such task is crowdsourced.

While the process ends naturally when no new contexts are uncovered from the previous ones, the system continuously monitors the Twitter stream for recent contexts. These may typically include events that are temporally recurring, and use similar hashtags for each new edition. In this case, their relevance is assessed on the basis of their past history.

4   Empirical Evaluation

Existing methods to discover specific classes on online users are typically validated using a supervised approach, i.e., they rely on expert-generated ground truth. Such approaches, however, are vulnerable to the subjectivity of the experts, whereby the evaluation would be measuring the fit of the model to the specific experts' own assessment of user instances' relevance. In contrast, we follow an unsupervised approach with no a priori knowledge of user relevance. We aim to demonstrate the value of our pipeline in creating a database of online profiles that are ready to be mined, along with examples of candidate user ranking functions. In this approach, human expertise only comes into play to assess and validate the top-k user lists produced by these functions. We demonstrate the pipeline in action on a significant set of 25 initial contexts, and define three alternative ranking functions aimed at capturing the empirical notion of *online activists*. The pipeline is fully implemented in Python using Pandas and public libraries (NetworkX, Selenium) and is available on github[1]. All experiments are performed on a single Azure node with standard commodity configuration. Note that we do not focus on system performance as all components operate in near-real time. One exception is Twitter content harvesting, which is limited by the Twitter API and requires approximately 2 h per context.

4.1   Contexts and Networks

We have manually selected 25 contexts within the scope of health awareness campaigns in the UK, all occurring in 2018 and well-characterised using predefined

---

[1] https://github.com/flaprimo/twitter-network-analysis.

hashtags. Due to limitations imposed by Twitter on the number of posts that can be retrieved within a time interval, only 200 tweets were retrieved from each context. Table 1 lists the events along with key metrics for their corresponding user-user networks. To recall, *assortativity* measures how frequently nodes are likely to connect to other nodes with the same degree (> 0) or with a different degree (< 0). Negative figures (mean: -0.22, std dev: 0.17) are in line with what is observed on the broader Twitter network [10]. The very small figures for density, defined as $\frac{\#edges}{\#nodes \cdot (\#nodes-1)}$ (mean: 0.004, std dev: 0.002), suggest very few connections exist amongst users within a context. This makes it difficult to detect meaningful communities, as described below, thus for some contexts the topological metrics are measured on the entire network as opposed to within each community. This view is also supported by the average node degree (mean: 2.04, std dev: 0.46) and the ratio of strongly connected components to the number of nodes (mean: 0.98, std. dev. 0.02).

4.2 Communities

DEMON and Infomap produce significantly different communities in each network. DEMON identifies communities in only 48% of the networks, with an average of only 1.92 communities per network and a slightly negative (-0.28) average assortativity per community, in line with the average for their parent networks. Only the users who belong to one of those communities, about 6%, are added to the database. For the remaining 52% of networks where no communities are detected, users' in-degrees are calculated using the entire network, and all users are added to the database, for a total of 3,570 users being added to the database in our experiments using DEMON.

In contrast, Infomap provides meaningful communities for all networks. Those with fewer than 3 users are discarded, leaving 18.88 communities per network on average, with 8.5 users per community on average. When using Infomap, 3,567 users were added to the database (on average 253 users per network). The average assortativity across all communities is again slightly negative (-0.43). Table 2 compares the two approaches on the key metrics just discussed. On the basis of this comparison, we recommend using Infomap, which we have used for our evaluation.

4.3 Users Discovery

Repeat users who appear in multiple contexts are particularly interesting as they provide a stronger signal. Out of the total 3,567 users, 160 of those appear at least in two of the 25 contexts. After community detection, only 61 of these users are still seen as repeat users, while the remaining 99 are either removed altogether, or they only appear once. Of the 61, 57 appear twice, 2 appear three times, and 2 appear four times. Thus, only 1.6% of users appear more than once when communities with more than 3 users are considered, compared to the overall 4.5% of overall repeat users. Table 3 reports the top-10 repeat users

Table 1. List of contexts used in the experiments along with network metrics.

Context name	Period (2018)	Nodes	Edges	Density	Avg degree	Assortativity
16 days of action	11−25/12−10	396	349	0.002	1.8	−0.1
Elf day	12−03/12−12	365	436	0.003	2.4	−0.2
Dry january	01−01/01−31	235	234	0.004	2.0	−0.3
Cervical cancer prevention week	01−21/01−27	209	192	0.004	1.8	−0.1
Time to talk day	02−06/02−07	268	231	0.003	1.7	−0.2
Eating disorder awareness week	02−25/03−03	256	241	0.004	1.9	−0.2
Rare disease day	02−28/03−01	294	206	0.002	1.4	−0.2
Ovarian cancer awareness month	03−01/03−31	215	202	0.004	1.9	−0.4
Nutrition and hydration week	03−11/03−17	273	326	0.004	2.4	−0.3
Brain awareness week	03−11/03−17	307	281	0.003	1.8	−0.1
No smoking day	03−13/03−14	254	219	0.003	1.7	−0.3
Epilepsy awareness purple day	03−26/03−27	306	252	0.003	1.6	−0.2
Experience of care week	04−23/04−27	176	196	0.006	2.2	−0.1
Brain injury week	05−01/05−31	238	306	0.005	2.6	−0.1
Mental health awareness week	05−14/05−20	268	245	0.003	1.8	−0.5
Dementia action week	05−21/05−31	300	300	0.003	2.0	0.0
Mnd awareness month	06−01/06−30	141	234	0.012	3.3	−0.3
Wear purple for jia	06−01/06−30	165	245	0.009	3.0	−0.5
Carers week	06−11/06−17	270	277	0.004	2.1	0.0
National dementia carers	09−09/09−10	184	177	0.005	1.9	−0.2
Mens health week	06−11/06−17	264	214	0.003	1.6	−0.2
Stress awareness day	11−07/11−08	293	209	0.002	1.4	−0.2
National dyslexia week	10−01/10−07	229	235	0.004	2.1	−0.2
Ocd awareness week	10−07/10−13	202	193	0.005	1.9	−0.6
Jeans for genes day	09−21/09−22	246	325	0.005	2.6	−0.2

Table 2. Comparing DEMON to Infomap for community detection.

Metric	DEMON	Infomap
Fraction of networks with null communities	0.52	0.0
Number of communities per context (avg)	1.92	18.88
Fraction of network users added to the DB (avg)	0.06	0.59
Fraction of repeat users added to the DB across networks	0.28	0.37

along with their *Follower Rank*, and Fig. 2 shows the number of repeat users per context. As the table is sorted by number of occurrences then by *Follower Rank*, an indication of popularity, it is not surprising to find that top users include well-known names such as Mr. Hunt, who at the time of the events was Secretary of State for Health and Social Care in the UK, with $FR = 1$, and a number of associations and foundations active in the public healthcare space. More interesting are perhaps non-repeat users who emerge when ad hoc ranking is applied to the database, as we illustrate next.

Table 3. Top-10 repeat users, amongst those who belong to a community.

Username	Name	Follower rank	Participations
alzheimerssoc	Alzheimer's Society	0.99	4
dementiauk	Dementia UK	0.98	4
mentalhealth	Mental Health Fdn	0.97	3
colesmillerllp	Coles Miller LLP	0.65	3
jeremy_hunt	Jeremy Hunt	1.0	2
nhsengland	NHS England	0.99	2
carersuk	Carers UK	0.95	2
rdash_nhs	RDaSH NHS FT	0.88	2
alzsocseengland	Alzheimer's Society - South ...	0.64	2
mndassoc	MND Association	0.64	2

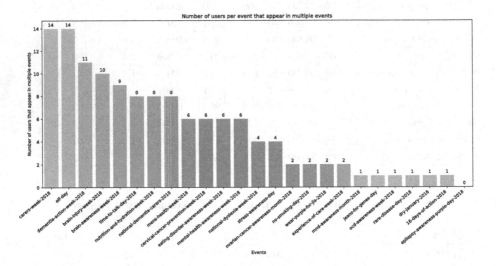

Fig. 2. Number of repeat users for each context

4.4 Users Ranking

To demonstrate the potential value of the database, albeit on a small scale, we have tested three user ranking functions. As mentioned, the aim of this exercise is to provide an objective grounding for engaging with experts on finding suitable operational definitions for specific user profiles. We consider good functions those that privilege individuals over organisations or business.

$$Ranking \; 1: R1(u) = \frac{1}{\sum_{u \in C} IC(u) + 1} \cdot \sum_{u \in C} TF(u) \tag{7}$$

$$Ranking \; 2: R2(u) = |FR(u) - 1| \cdot \left(\sum_{u \in C} TA(U) + \sum_{u \in C} IC(U) \right) \tag{8}$$

$$Ranking \; 3: R3(u) = |FR(u) - 1| \cdot \left(\sum_{u \in C} TA(U) + \frac{1}{\sum_{u \in C} IC(U) + 1} \right) \tag{9}$$

Function (7) is designed to promote users who are at the "fringe" of their community, while giving credit to generic on-topic activities during the contexts. To achieve this, *Topical Focus TF* is used as a positive contribution, while a large in-degree *IC* reduces the score. In contrast, function (8) penalises user popularity, i.e., by using the complement of *Follower Rank FR*, while rewarding prominence inside communities (in-degree *IC*) and information spreading by also considering shared links (*Topical Attachment TA*). Function (9) combines ideas from both (8) and (7).

The top-10 users for each ranking are reported in Table 4. To appreciate the effects of these functions, we have manually labelled the top-100 user profiles for each of the rankings, using a broad type classification as *individuals* as opposed to *institutional players* (associations, public bodies), or *professionals*. The fractions of on-topic users are 86%, 83%, and 38% for (7), (8), and (9) respectively.

Table 4. Top-10 ranked users for ranking functions (7), (8) and (9), with indication of whether the user is on-topic/off-topic and individual vs association/professional. Such categories are useful to evaluate the ranking functions.

	Ranking 1			Ranking 2			Ranking 3		
#	User	On-topic	Individual	User	On-topic	Individual	User	On-topic	Individual
1	homesnutrition	X		johnneustadt	X		johnneustadt	X	
2	ficajones	X	X	jo_millar27	X	X	solutions777	X	X
3	helenvweaver	X	X	hatchbrenner			kingste29344921	X	X
4	spriggsnutri	X		nchawkes	X	X	daisylu1964		X
5	critcarelthtr	X		moz0373runner	X	X	zakariamarsli	X	X
6	danielleroisin_	X	X	aimsonhealth	X	X	meowaaaaaa		X
7	mynameisandyj	X	X	wordsharkv5		X	vecta67		X
8	fionaliu92	X	X	fullcircle_play	X		cosfordfamily1	X	X
9	ldpartnership	X		qsprivatehealth	X		hayleycorriganx		X
10	milaestevam1		X	socialissp			jhbrasfie		X

Importantly, (9) identifies more individuals than institutions and professionals (96%) than (8) and (7), both at 33%p. Also, repeat users are rewarded in both rankings. Users with $FR(u) = 0$ and $min\_max(|Tweets(u)|) < 0.005$ are considered not active and have been assigned lowest score. Figure 3 shows the distribution of user types within the top-100 users for each of the three rankings, broken down into 10 users bins. We can see that individuals dominate in (9), and are fewer but emerge earlier in the ranks when (8) is used. We plan to conduct user studies to establish useful analytics to be incorporated into our framework.

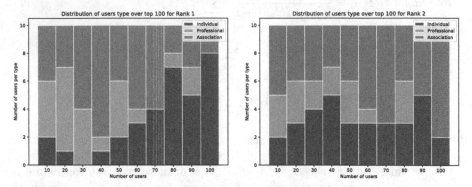

(a) Rank 1: 33 are individuals, 23 are professionals, 44 are associations

(b) Rank 2: 33 are individuals, 17 are professionals, 50 are associations

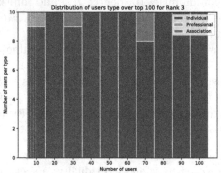

(c) Rank 3: 96 are individuals, 1 are professionals, 3 are associations

Fig. 3. Distribution of user types for top-100 users and for each ranking function.

5   Conclusions and Lessons Learnt

Motivated by the need to find an operational definition of "online activists" that is grounded in well-established network and user-activity metrics, we have designed a Twitter content processing pipeline for progressively harvesting Twitter users based on their engagement with online socially-minded events, or campaigns, which we have called *contexts*. The pipeline yields a growing database of user profiles along with their associated metrics, which can then be analysed to experiment with user-defined user ranking criteria. The pipeline is designed to select promising candidate profiles, but the approach is unsupervised, i.e., no manual classification of example users is provided. We have empirically evaluated the pipeline on a case study, along with experimental scoring functions to show the viability of the approach.

The design of the pipeline show that useful harvesting of interesting users can be accomplished within the limitations imposed by Twitter on its APIs. The next challenge is to automate the discovery of new contexts so that the pipeline may continuously add new and update users in the database. Only at this point will it be possible to validate the entire approach, hopefully with help from third party users, on a variety of new context topics.

Acknowledgments. The authors would like to thank Prof. Carlo Piccardi at Politecnico di Milano, Italy, for his useful suggestions and SmartMetropolis Project at Universidade Federal do Rio Grande do Norte, Brazil, for the support to the Brazilian team.

References

1. Arnaboldi, V., Conti, M., Passarella, A., Pezzoni, F.: Ego networks in twitter: an experimental analysis. In: 2013 Proceedings IEEE INFOCOM, pp. 3459–3464 (2013)
2. Biran, O., Rosenthal, S., Andreas, J., McKeown, K., Rambow, O.: Detecting influencers in written online conversations. In: Proceedings of the Second Workshop on Language in Social Media LSM 2012, pp. 37–45. Association for Computational Linguistics, Stroudsburg (2012)
3. Bizid, I., Nayef, N., Boursier, P., Doucet, A.: Detecting prominent microblog users over crisis events phases. Inf. Syst. **78**, 173–188 (2018)
4. Bizid, I., Nayef, N., Boursier, P., Faiz, S., Morcos, J.: Prominent users detection during specific events by learning on- and off-topic features of user activities. In: Proceedings of the 2015 IEEE/ACM International Conference on Advances in Social Networks Analysis and Mining 2015 ASONAM 2015, pp. 500–503. ACM, New York (2015)
5. Bobel, C.: "i'm not an activist, though i've done a lot of it": doing activism, being activist and the "perfect standard" in a contemporary movement. Soc. Mov. Stud. **6**(2), 147–159 (2007)
6. Bonacich, P., Lloyd, P.: Eigenvector-like measures of centrality for asymmetric relations. Soc. Netw. **23**(3), 191–201 (2001)
7. Booth, N., Matic, J.A.: Mapping and leveraging influencers in social media to shape corporate brand perceptions. Corp. Commun. Int. J. **16**, 184–191 (2011)
8. Cha, M., Haddadi, H., Benevenuto, F., Gummadi, K.P.: Measuring user influence in twitter: the million follower fallacy. In: ICWSM (2010)
9. Coscia, M., Rossetti, G., Giannotti, F., Pedreschi, D.: Demon: a local-first discovery method for overlapping communities. In: Proceedings of the 18th ACM SIGKDD International Conference on Knowledge Discovery and Data Mining KDD 2012, pp. 615–623. ACM, New York (2012)

10. Fisher, D.N., Silk, M.J., Franks, D.W.: The perceived assortativity of social networks: methodological problems and solutions. In: Missaoui, R., Abdessalem, T., Latapy, M. (eds.) Trends in Social Network Analysis. LNSN, pp. 1–19. Springer, Cham (2017). https://doi.org/10.1007/978-3-319-53420-6_1

11. Kardara, M., Papadakis, G., Papaoikonomou, A., Tserpes, K., Varvarigou, T.: Large-scale evaluation framework for local influence theories in twitter. Inf. Process. Manage. **51**(1), 226–252 (2015)

12. Lotan, G., Graeff, E., Ananny, M., Gaffney, D., Pearce, I., Boyd, D.: The Arab spring— the revolutions were tweeted: information flows during the 2011 Tunisian and Egyptian revolutions. Int. J. Commun. **5**, 31 (2011)

13. Missier, P., et al.: Recruiting from the network: discovering twitter users who can help combat zika epidemics. In: Cabot, J., De Virgilio, R., Torlone, R. (eds.) ICWE 2017. LNCS, vol. 10360, pp. 437–445. Springer, Cham (2017). https://doi.org/10.1007/978-3-319-60131-1_30

14. Nargundkar, A., Rao, Y.S.: Influencerank: a machine learning approach to measure influence of twitter users. In: 2016 International Conference on Recent Trends in Information Technology (ICRTIT), pp. 1–6, April 2016

15. Overbey, L.A., Greco, B., Paribello, C., Jackson, T.: Structure and prominence in twitter networks centered on contentious politics. Soc. Netw. Anal. Min. **3**(4), 1351–1378 (2013)

16. Pal, A., Counts, S.: Identifying topical authorities in microblogs. In: Proceedings of the Fourth ACM International Conference on Web Search and Data Mining - WSDM 2011 (2011)

17. Poell, T.: Social media and the transformation of activist communication: exploring the social media ecology of the 2010 Toronto G20 protests. Inf. Commun. Soc. **17**(6), 716–731 (2014)

18. Razis, G., Anagnostopoulos, I.: Semantifying twitter: the influence tracker ontology. In: 2014 9th International Workshop on Semantic and Social Media Adaptation and Personalization, pp. 98–103, November 2014

19. Riquelme, F., Gonzalez-Cantergiani, P.: Measuring user influence on twitter: a survey. Inf. Process. Manage. **52**(5), 949–975 (2016)

20. Rosvall, M., Bergstrom, C.T.: Maps of random walks on complex networks reveal community structure. Proc. Nat. Acad. Sci. U.S.A. **105**, 1118–1123 (2008)

21. Schenk, C.B., Sicker, D.C.: Finding event-specific influencers in dynamic social networks. In: 2011 IEEE Third International Conference on Privacy, Security, Risk and Trust and 2011 IEEE Third International Conference on Social Computing, pp. 501–504 (2011)

22. Sousa, L., et al.: Vazadengue: an information system for preventing and combating mosquito-borne diseases with social networks. Inf. Syst. **75**, 26–42 (2018)

23. Youmans, W.L., York, J.C.: Social media and the activist toolkit: user agreements, corporate interests, and the information infrastructure of modern social movements. J. Commun. **62**(2), 315–329 (2012)

24. Zhao, W.X., et al.: Comparing twitter and traditional media using topic models. In: Clough, P., et al. (eds.) ECIR 2011. LNCS, vol. 6611, pp. 338–349. Springer, Heidelberg (2011). https://doi.org/10.1007/978-3-642-20161-5_34

Predicting Graph Operator Output
over Multiple Graphs

Tasos Bakogiannis[1]([⊠]), Ioannis Giannakopoulos[1], Dimitrios Tsoumakos[2],
and Nectarios Koziris[1]

[1] CSLab, School of ECE, National Technical University of Athens, Athens, Greece
{abk,ggian,nkoziris}@cslab.ece.ntua.gr
[2] Department of Informatics, Ionian University, Corfu, Greece
dtsouma@ionio.gr

Abstract. A growing list of domains, in the forefront of which are Web
data and applications, are modeled by graph representations. In content-
driven graph analytics, knowledge must be extracted from large numbers
of available data graphs. As the number of datasets (a different type of
volume) can reach immense sizes, a thorough evaluation of each input
is prohibitively expensive. To date, there exists no efficient method to
quantify the impact of numerous available datasets over different graph
analytics tasks. To address this challenge, we propose an efficient graph
operator modeling methodology. Our novel, operator-agnostic approach
focuses on the inputs themselves, utilizing graph similarity to infer knowledge about them. An operator is executed for a small subset of the available inputs and its behavior is modeled for the rest of the graphs utilizing machine learning. We propose a family of similarity measures based
on the degree distribution that prove capable of producing high quality
models for many popular graph tasks, even compared to modern, state
of the art similarity functions. Our evaluation over both real-world and
synthetic graph datasets indicates that our method achieves extremely
accurate modeling of many commonly encountered operators, managing
massive speedups over a brute-force alternative.

Keywords: Graph analytics · Operator modeling · Graph similarity

1 Introduction

A huge amount of data originating from the Web can be naturally expressed
as graphs, e.g., product co-purchasing graphs [25], community graphs [28], etc.
Graph analytics is a common tool used to effectively tackle complex tasks such as
social community analysis, recommendations, fraud detection, etc. Many diverse
graph operators are available [12], with functionality including the computation
of centrality measures, clustering metrics or network statistics [8], all regularly
utilized in tasks such as classification, community detection and link prediction.

Yet, as Big Data technologies mature and evolve, emphasis is placed on areas
not solely related to data (i.e., graph) size. A different type of challenge steadily

© Springer Nature Switzerland AG 2019
M. Bakaev et al. (Eds.): ICWE 2019, LNCS 11496, pp. 107–122, 2019.
https://doi.org/10.1007/978-3-030-19274-7_9

shifts attention to the actual content. In content-based analytics [14], data is processed for sense-making. Similarly, in *content-sensitive* applications the quality of insights derived is mainly attributed to the input content. The plethora of available sources for content-sensitive analytics tasks now creates an issue: Data scientists have to decide which of the available datasets will be used for a given workflow, in order to maximize its impact. Yet, as modern analytics tasks have evolved into increasingly long and complex series of diverse operators, evaluating the utility of immense numbers of inputs is prohibitively expensive. This is notably true for graph operators, whose computational cost has led to extensive research on approximation algorithms (e.g., [11,30]).

As a motivating example, let us consider a dataset consisting of a very large number of citation graphs. We wish to identify those graphs that have the most well-connected citations and contain highly-cited papers. As a result, the clustering coefficient [8], a good measure of neighborhood connectivity, would have to be computed for all the graphs in the dataset in order to allow the identification of the top-k such graphs. To quantify the importance of each paper, we consider a centrality measure such as betweenness centrality [8]. Consequently, we would have to compute the maximum betweenness centrality score for each citation graph and combine the results with those obtained from the analysis based on the clustering coefficient. Yet, this could be a daunting task due to the operators' complexity and the size of the dataset.

The challenge this work tackles is thus the following: Given a graph analytics operator and a large number of input graphs, can we reliably predict operator output at low cost? In this work, we introduce a novel, *operator-agnostic* dataset profiling mechanism. Rather than executing the operator over each input graph, our work leverages the relationship between the dataset's graphs, expressed through a similarity measure, and infers knowledge about them. In our example, instead of exhaustively computing the clustering coefficient, we calculate a similarity matrix for our dataset, compute the clustering coefficient for a small subset of graphs and utilize the similarity matrix to estimate its value for the remaining graphs. We may then compute the maximum betweenness centrality for also a small subset of citation graphs and *reuse* the already calculated similarity matrix to estimate the scores for the rest of the graphs.

Our method is based on the intuition that, for a given graph operator, similar graphs produce similar outputs. This intuition is solidly supported by the existence of strong correlations between different graph operators ([7,20,22]). Hence, by assuming a similarity measure that correlates to a set of operators, we can use machine learning techniques to approximate their outcomes. Given a graph dataset and an operator to model, our method utilizes a similarity measure to compute the similarity matrix of the dataset, i.e., all-pairs similarity scores between the graphs of the dataset. The given operator is then run for a small subset of the dataset; using the similarity matrix and the available operator outputs, we are able to approximate the operator for the remaining graphs.

To the best of our knowledge, this is the first effort to predict graph operator output over large datasets. In summary, we make the following contributions:

- We propose a novel, similarity-based method to estimate graph operator output for large graph datasets. This method shifts the complexity of numerous graph computations to less expensive graph similarities. This choice offers two major advantages: First, our scheme is *operator-agnostic* since the computed similarity matrix can be reused. As a result, the similarity matrix computation is amortized and the cost of our method is ultimately dominated by the computation of that operator for a small subset of the dataset. Second, the method is agnostic to the similarity measure that is used. This property gives us the ability to utilize or arbitrarily combine different similarity measures.
- We introduce a family of similarity measures based on degree distribution with a gradual trade-off between detail and computational complexity. Despite their simplicity, they prove capable of producing highly accurate models, comparable or even surpassing other more costly, state-of-the-art similarity measures ([32, 35]).
- We offer an open-source implementation[1] of our method and perform an extensive experimental evaluation using both synthetic and real datasets. Our results indicate that we can accurately model a variety of popular graph operators, with errors that can be $< 1\%$, sampling a mere 5% of the graphs for execution. Amortizing the similarity cost over six operators, the process can produce up to $18\times$ speed-up. Our proposed similarity measures produce comparable or more accurate results to state-of-the-art similarity measures but run more than 5 orders of magnitude faster.

2 Methodology

In this section, we formulate the problem and describe the methodology along with different aspects of the proposed solution. We start off with some basic notation followed throughout the paper and a formal description of our method and its complexity.

Let a graph G be an ordered pair $G = (V, E)$ with V being the set of vertices and E the set of edges of G, respectively. The degree of a vertex $u \in V$, denoted by $d_G(u)$, is the number of edges of G incident to u. The degree distribution of a graph G, denoted by $P_G(k)$, expresses the probability that a randomly selected vertex of G has degree k. A dataset D is a set of N simple, undirected graphs $D = \{G_1, G_2, ..., G_N\}$. We define a graph operator to be a function $g \colon D \to \mathbb{R}$, mapping an element of D to a real number. In order to quantify the similarity between two graphs $G_a, G_b \in D$ we use a graph similarity function $s \colon D \times D \to \mathbb{R}$ with range within $[0, 1]$. For two graphs $G_a, G_b \in D$, a similarity of 1 implies that they are identical while a similarity of 0 the opposite.

Consequently, the problem we are addressing can be formally stated as follows: Given a dataset of graphs D and a graph operator g, without knowledge of the range of g given D, we wish to infer a function $\hat{g} \colon D \to \mathbb{R}$ that approximates

---

[1] https://github.com/giagiannis/data-profiler.

g. Additionally, we wish our approximation to be both accurate (i.e., $|g - \hat{g}| < \epsilon$, for some small ϵ) and efficient (i.e., $O(\hat{g}) < O(g)$). In this formulation, our goal is to provide an accurate approximation of g, while avoiding its exhaustive execution over the entire D. To achieve this goal, we utilize the similarity matrix R, an $N \times N$ matrix with $R[i, j] = s(G_i, G_j)$, where s is a given similarity measure. As a result, R contains all-pairs similarity scores between the graphs of D. R is symmetric, its elements are in $[0, 1]$ and the entries of its main diagonal equal 1.

Our method takes as input a dataset D and an operator g to model. It forms a pipeline that begins with the computation of the similarity matrix R based on s; calculates the actual values of g for a ratio $p \in (0, 1)$ of randomly selected graphs of D and, finally, estimates g for the remaining graphs of D by running a weighted version of the k-Nearest-Neighbors (kNN) algorithm [19]. The inferred function $\hat{g}$ is then given by the following equation:

$$\hat{g}(G_x) = \frac{\sum_{i \in \Gamma_k(x)} w_{xi} g(G_i)}{\sum_{i \in \Gamma_k(x)} w_{xi}} \tag{1}$$

Where $w_{xi} = R[x, i]$ is the similarity score for graphs G_x, G_i, i.e., $w_{xi} = s(G_x, G_i)$, $\Gamma_k(x)$ is the set of the k most similar graphs to G_x for which we have already calculated g and $g(G_i)$ the value of the operator for G_i. Our approach is formally described in Algorithm 1. The complexity of Algorithm 1 can be broken down to its three main components: (1) The calculation of the similarity matrix R in lines 3−4, for a given similarity measure s with complexity S. (2) The component which computes the operator g for pN graphs (lines 5−7), assuming that g has complexity M. And 3) the approximation of the operator for the remaining graphs (lines 8−10) using kNN. Thus, the overall complexity of our method is:

$$O(N^2 S + pNM + (N(1 - p))((pN)log(pN) + k)) \tag{2}$$

From Eq. 2, we deduce that the complexity of our method is dominated by its first two components. Consequently, the lower the computational cost of s, the more efficient our approach will be. Additionally, we expect our training set to be much smaller than our original dataset (i.e., $p \ll 1$).

Algorithm 1. Graph Operator Modeling

1: **procedure** APPROXIMATE($[G_1, G_2, ..., G_N], g, s, p, k$)
2:     $R \leftarrow [\,], T \leftarrow \{\,\}, A \leftarrow \{\,\}$
3:     **for** $(i, j) \leftarrow [1, N] \times [1, N]$ **do**
4:         $R[i, j] \leftarrow s(G_i, G_j)$
5:     **for** $i \leftarrow 1, p \cdot N$ **do**
6:         $r \leftarrow randint(1, N)$
7:         $T[G_r] \leftarrow g(G_r)$
8:     **for** $x \leftarrow [G_1, G_2, ..., G_N], x \notin keys(T)$ **do**
9:         $t \leftarrow findNeighbors(R, T, k, x)$
10:         $A[x] \leftarrow calcApproximation(R, t)$
11:     **return** A

It is important to note here that the $O(N^2 S)$ component corresponds to a calculation performed only *once*, whether modeling a single or multiple operators. Thus, given that the similarity matrix calculation happens once per dataset, its cost gets amortized over multiple graph operators, making the $O(pNM)$ factor the dominant one for our pipeline.

2.1 Similarity Measures

The similarity matrix is an essential tool in our effort to model graph operators under the hypothesis that similar graphs produce similar operator outputs. Relative to graph analytics operators, we propose a family of similarity measures based on graph degree distribution. Reinforced by the proven correlations between many diverse graph operators ([7,20,22]), we intend the proposed similarity measures to express graph similarity in a way that enables modeling of various operators.

▷ **Degree Distribution:** In order to quantify the similarity between two graphs we rely on comparing their degree distributions. We choose the Bhattacharyya coefficient BC [5] to perform this task. BC is considered a highly advantageous method for comparing distributions [1]. BC divides the output space of a function into m partitions and uses the cardinality of each partition to create an m-dimensional vector representing that space. As a measure of divergence between two distributions, the square of the angle between the two vectors is considered. In our case, the points of the output space are the degrees of the nodes of each graph. By dividing that space into partitions and considering the cardinalities of each partition, we effectively compare the degree distributions of those graphs. In our implementation, we use a k-d tree [4], a data structure used for space partitioning, to compute BC. We build a k-d tree once, based on a predefined percentage of vertex degrees from all the graphs in D. We then use the created space partitioning to compute degree distributions for each graph.

▷ **Degree Distribution + Levels:** As an extension of the degree distribution-based similarity measure, we consider a class of measures with increasing level of information. Intuitively, the degree of a vertex is a measure of its connectivity based on its immediate neighbors. Adding a level of indirection, we can consider the degree of a vertex at *level 1* as the degree of a super-node containing the vertex and all its immediate neighbors. Generalizing this idea to more than one levels gives us a measure of the indirect connectivity of a vertex. By combining the degrees of a vertex for multiple levels we obtain information up to *level* hops away. As an illustrative example, in Fig. 1 vertex u_0 has degree 4, when considering its direct neighbors, 1 when its neighborhood is expanded to *level* 1, and for *level* 2 it becomes 3. As a result, we quantify the similarity between graphs by calculating the degrees up to a certain level and use BC to compare the resulting degree distributions. A good property of this class of measures is that they provide us with a nice trade-off between accuracy and computational cost. Increasing the number of degree distribution levels involves additional computations but also incorporates more graph topological insights to it. In order to calculate the degrees for a given level, for each vertex we perform a depth-limited Depth First Search up to *level* hops away in order to mark the internal edges of the super-node. We then count the edges of the border vertices (vertices *level* hops away from the source) that do not connect to any internal vertices.

▷ **Degree Distribution + Vertex Count:** A second extension to our degree distribution-based similarity measure is based on the ability of our method to combine similarity matrices. Graph size (vertex count) is another graph attribute to measure similarity on. We formulate similarity in terms of vertex count as: $s(G_i, G_j) = \frac{min(|V_{G_i}|,|V_{G_j}|)}{max(|V_{G_i}|,|V_{G_j}|)}$. Intuitively, s approaches 1 when $|V_{G_i}| - |V_{G_j}|$ approaches 0, i.e., when G_i, G_j have similar vertex counts. To incorporate vertex count into the graph comparison, we can combine the similarity matrices computed with degree distributions and vertex counts using an arbitrary formula (e.g., linear composition).

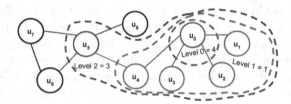

Fig. 1. Example of Degree Distribution + Levels

2.2 Discussion

In this section, we consider a series of issues that relate to the configuration and performance of our method as well as to the relation between modeled operators, similarity measure and input datasets.

▷ **Graph Operators:** This work focuses on graph analytics operators, namely centralities, clustering metrics, network statistics, etc. Research on this area has resulted in a large collection of operators, also referred to as *topology metrics* (e.g., [7,8,12,20]). Topology metrics can be loosely classified in three categories ([7,20,22]), those related to *distance*, *connectivity* and *spectrum*. In the first class, we find metrics like *diameter*, *average distance* or *betweenness centrality*. In the second, *average degree*, *degree distribution*, etc. Finally, the third class comes from the spectral analysis of a graph and contains the computation of *eigenvalues*, *eigenvectors* or other spectral-related metrics.

▷ **Combining Similarity Measures:** We can think of use cases where we want to quantify the similarity of graphs based on parameters unrelated to each other. For example, we might want to compare two graphs based on their degree distributions but also take under account their vertex count. This composition can be naturally implemented in our system by computing independent similarity matrices and "fuse" those matrices into one using a formula. This technique is presented in our evaluation and proves effective for a number of operators.

▷ **Regression Analysis:** Although there exist several approaches to statistical learning [19], we have opted for the kNN method. We choose kNN for its simplicity and because we do not have to calculate distances between points of our dataset (we already have that information from the similarity matrix). The kNN algorithm is also suitable for our use case since it is sensitive to localized data and insensitive to outliers. A desired property, since we expect similar graphs to have similar operator scores and should therefore be of influence in our estimations.

▷ **Scaling Similarity Computations:** Having to compute all-pairs similarity scores for a large collection of graphs can be prohibitively expensive. To this end, we introduce a preprocessing step which we argue that improves on the existing computational cost, reducing the number of similarity calculations performed. As, in order to approximate a graph operator, we employ kNN, we observe that, for each graph, we only require the similarity scores to its k most similar graphs for which we have the value of g, i.e., the weights in Eq. 1. Therefore we propose to run a clustering algorithm which will produce clusters of graphs with high similarity. Then for each cluster compute all-pairs similarity scores between its members, setting inter-cluster similarities to zero. By creating clusters of size much larger than k, we expect minimal loss in accuracy while avoiding a considerable number of similarity computations. As a clustering algorithm we use a simplified version of k-medoids in combination with k-means++, for the initial seed selection ([2,23]). For an extensive experimental evaluation of this technique we refer the reader to the extended version of our work in [34] which we have not included here due to space constraints.

3   Experimental Evaluation

▷ **Datasets:** For our experimental evaluation, we consider both real and synthetic datasets. The real datasets comprise a set of ego graphs from Twitter (TW) which consists of 973 user "circles" as well as a dataset containing 733 snapshots of the graph that is formed by considering the Autonomous Systems (AS) that comprise the Internet as nodes and adding links between those systems that communicate to each other. Both datasets are taken from the Stanford Large Network Dataset Collection [26].

We also experiment with a dataset of synthetic graphs (referred to as the BA dataset) generated using the SNAP library [27]. We use the `GenPrefAttach` generator to create random scale-free graphs with power-law degree distributions using the Barabasi-Albert model [3]. We keep the vertex count of the graphs constant to 4K. We introduce randomness to this dataset by having the *initial outdegree* of each vertex be a uniformly random number in the range $[1, 32]$. The Barabasi-Albert model constructs a graph by adding one vertex at a time. The *initial outdegree* of a vertex is the maximum number of vertices it connects to, the moment it is added to the graph. The graphs of the dataset are simple and undirected. Further details about the datasets can be found in Table 1.

▷ **Similarity Measures:** We evaluate all the similarity measures proposed in Sect. 2.1, namely *degree distribution + levels*, for levels $0, 1, 2$ and *degree distribution + vertex count*. When combining vertex count with degree, we use the following simple formula: $R = w_1 R_d + w_2 R_n$, with R_d, R_n the degree distribution and vertex count similarity matrices respectively. In our evaluation, $w_1 = w_2 = 0.5$. To investigate their strengths and limitations, we compare them against two measures functioning as our baselines. The first is a sophisticated similarity measure not based on degree but rather on distance distributions (from which the degree distribution can be deduced). *D-measure* [32] is based on the concept of network node dispersion (NND) which is a measure of the heterogeneity of a graph in terms of connectivity distances. It is a state-of-the-art graph similarity measure with very good experimental results for both real and synthetic graphs. Our second baseline comes from the extensively researched area of graph kernels. For the purposes of our evaluation, we opted for the geometric *Random Walk Kernel* (*rw-kernel*) [16] as a widely used representative of this class of similarity measures. In order to avoid the *halting* phenomenon due to the kernel's decay factor (λ^k) we set $\lambda = 0.1$ and the number of steps $k \leq 4$, values that are considered to be reasonable for the general case [33].

Table 1. Datasets overview

Name	Size (N)	$|V|$	$|E|$	Range $|V|$	Range $|E|$
TW	973	132	1,841	min: 6	min: 9
				max: 248	max: 12,387
AS	733	4,183	8,540	min: 103	min: 248
				max: 6,474	max: 13,895
BA	1,000	4,000	66,865	4,000	min: 3,999
					max: 127,472

▷ **Graph Operators:** In our evaluation, we model operators from all the categories mentioned in Sect. 2.2. As representatives of the distance class, we choose betweenness (**bc**), edge betweenness (**ebc**) and closeness centralities (**cc**) ([8, 29]), three metrics that express how central a vertex or edge is in a graph. From the spectrum class, we choose spectral radius (**sr**) and eigenvector centrality (**ec**). The first is associated with the robustness of a network against the spreading of a virus [21], while the second also expresses vertex centrality [6]. Finally, as a connectivity related metric we consider PageRank (**pr**), a centrality measure used for ranking web pages based on popularity [9].

All measures, except spectral radius, are centrality measures expressed at vertex level (edge level in the case of edge betweenness). Since we wish all our measures to be expressed at graph level, we will be using a method attributed to Freeman [13] to make that generalization. This is a general approach that can be applied to any centrality [8], and measures the average difference in centrality between the most central point and all others. All the graph operators are implemented in R. We use the R package of the `igraph` library [10] which contains implementations of all the algorithms mentioned.

▷ **kNN:** The only parameter we will have to specify for kNN is k. After extensive experimentation (omitted due to space constraints), we have observed that small values of k tend to perform better. As a result, all our experiments are performed with $k = 3$.

▷ **Error Metrics:** The modeling accuracy of our method is quantified using two widely used measures from the literature, the *Median Absolute Percentage Error* and the *Normalized Root Mean Squared Error*.

▷ **Setup:** All experiments are conducted on an Openstack VM with 16 Intel Xeon E312 processors at 2 GHz, 32 GB main memory running Ubuntu Server 16.04.3 LTS with Linux kernel 4.4.0. We implemented our prototype in Go language (v.1.7.6).

3.1   Experiments

▷ **Modeling Accuracy:** To evaluate the accuracy of our approximations, we calculate *MdAPE* and *nRMSE* for a randomized 20% of our dataset. We vary the sampling ratio p, i.e., the number of graphs for which we actually execute the operator, divided by the total number of graphs in the dataset. The results are displayed in Table 2. Each row represents a combination of a dataset and a graph operator with the corresponding error values for different values of p between 5% and 20%.

The results in Table 2 showcase that our method is capable of modeling different classes of graph operators with very good accuracy. Although our approach employs a degree distribution-based similarity measure, we observe that the generated similarity matrix is expressive enough to allow the accurate modeling of distance- and spectrum-related metrics as well, achieving errors well below 10% for most cases. In *AS* graphs, the *MdAPE* error is less than 3.2% for all the considered operators when only a mere 5% of the available graphs is examined. Operators such as closeness or eigenvector centralities display low *MdAPE* errors in the range of < 8% for all datasets. Through the use of more expressive or combined similarity measures, our method can improve on these results, as we show later in this Section. We also note that the approximation accuracy increases with the sampling ratio. This is expressed by the decrease of both *MdAPE* and *nRMSE* when we increase the size of our training set. These results verify that modeling such graph operators is not only possible, but it can also produce highly accurate models with marginal errors.

Specifically, in the case of the *AS* dataset, we observe that all the operators are modeled more accurately than in any other real or synthetic dataset.

Table 2. Modeling errors and execution speedup

		MdAPE (%)			nRMSE			Speedup ×			A. Speedup ×		
		5%	10%	20%	5%	10%	20%	5%	10%	20%	5%	10%	20%
AS	sr	1.3	1.1	0.9	0.05	0.03	0.02	6.4	3.8	3.3	18.0	9.5	4.9
	ec	0.1	0.1	0.0	0.01	0.00	0.00	5.7	4.5	3.1			
	bc	1.4	1.2	1.1	0.04	0.03	0.03	15.7	8.8	4.7			
	ebc	3.1	2.7	2.4	0.04	0.04	0.04	17.3	9.3	4.8			
	cc	0.4	0.4	0.3	0.01	0.01	0.01	14.0	8.2	4.5			
	pr	0.9	0.8	0.7	0.05	0.04	0.03	5.7	4.4	3.1			
TW	sr	16.3	15.3	14.7	0.10	0.10	0.10	13.3	8.0	4.4	14.8	8.5	4.6
	ec	8.0	7.7	7.7	0.14	0.14	0.13	13.1	7.9	4.4			
	bc	17.8	17.5	16.8	0.16	0.15	0.14	13.0	7.8	4.4			
	ebc	29.5	29.8	28.6	0.12	0.12	0.12	13.5	8.0	4.4			
	cc	3.3	3.0	2.9	0.10	0.10	0.09	13.0	7.9	4.4			
	pr	9.2	7.7	7.2	0.07	0.06	0.05	13.2	7.9	4.4			
BA	sr	3.3	1.8	0.9	0.04	0.03	0.03	5.6	4.4	3.0	16.3	9.0	4.7
	ec	0.4	0.3	0.3	0.01	0.01	0.01	3.7	3.1	2.4			
	bc	10.3	10.1	9.6	0.10	0.05	0.02	12.6	7.7	4.4			
	ebc	10.9	9.3	8.5	0.10	0.09	0.01	13.6	8.1	4.5			
	cc	2.4	2.2	2.1	0.04	0.04	0.03	9.9	6.6	4.0			
	pr	6.7	6.1	5.9	0.06	0.05	0.05	3.6	3.0	2.3			

This can be attributed to the topology of the *AS* graphs. These graphs display a linear relationship between vertex and edge counts. Their clustering coefficient displays very little variance, suggesting that as the graphs grow in size they keep the same topological structure. This gradual, uniform evolution of the *AS* graphs leads to easier modeling of the values of a given graph topology measure.

On the other hand, our approach has better accuracy for degree- than distance-related metrics in the cases of the *TW* and *BA* datasets. The similarity measure we use is based on the degree distribution that is only indirectly related to vertex distances. This can be seen, for example, in the case of *BA* if we compare the modeling error for the betweenness centrality (bc) and PageRank (pr) measures. Overall, we see that eigenvector and closeness centralities are the two most accurately approximated metrics across all datasets. Next up, we find PageRank, spectral radius, betweenness and edge betweenness centralities. Willing to further examine the connection between modeling accuracy and similarity measures, we have included *D-measure* and *rw-kernel* in our evaluation as well as the degree-level similarity measures and the similarity matrice combination technique.

▷ **Execution Speedup:** Next, we evaluate the gains our method can provide in execution time. The similarity matrix computation is a time-consuming step, yet an advantage of our scheme is that the matrix can be reused for different graph operators and thus its cost can be amortized. In order to provide a better insight, we calculate two types of speedups: One that considers the similarity matrix construction from scratch for each operator separately (provided in the *Speedup* column of Table 2) and one that expresses the average speedup for all six measures for each dataset, where the similarity matrix has been constructed once (provided in the *A. Speedup* column of Table 2).

The observed results highlight that our method is not only capable of providing models of high quality, but also does so in a time-efficient manner. A closer examination of the Speedup columns shows that our method is particularly efficient for complex metrics that require more computation time (as in the *ebc* and *cc* cases for all datasets). The upper bound of the theoretically anticipated speedup equals $\frac{1}{p}$, p being the sampling ratio. Interestingly, the *Amortized Speedup* column indicates that when the procedure of constructing the similarity matrix is amortized to the six operators under consideration, the achieved speedup is very close to the theoretical one. This is indeed the case for the *AS* and *BA* datasets that comprise the largest graphs, in terms of number of vertices: For all p values, the amortized speedup closely approximates $\frac{1}{p}$. In the case of the *TW* dataset which consists of much smaller graphs and, hence, the time dedicated to the similarity matrix estimation is relatively larger than the previous cases, we observe that the achieved speedup is also sizable. In any case, the capability of reusing the similarity matrix, which is calculated on a per-dataset rather than on a per-operator basis, enables our approach to scale and be more efficient as the number and complexity of graph operators increases.

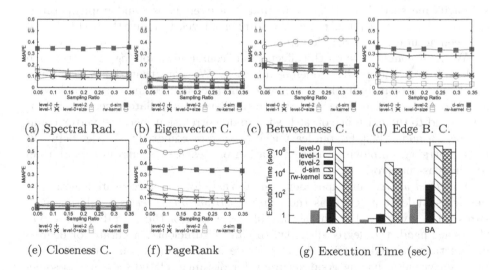

(a) Spectral Rad.   (b) Eigenvector C.   (c) Betweenness C.   (d) Edge B. C.

(e) Closeness C.   (f) PageRank   (g) Execution Time (sec)

Fig. 2. Similarity metrics comparison for *TW* dataset

▷ **Comparing Similarity Measures:** The results of the similarity measure comparisons, in the case of the TW dataset, are displayed in Fig. 2, where $MdAPE$ is used to express the modeling error. We compare six similarity measures: The *degree distribution + levels* measure (for levels equal from 0 to 2), a combination of *level-0* degree distribution with vertex count (denoted by *level-0 + size*), *D-measure* and the *Random Walk Kernel* based similarity measure (denoted by rw-kernel). The results indicate the impact that the choice of similarity measure has on modeling accuracy. A more suitable to the modeled operator and detailed similarity measure is more sensitive to topology differences and can lead to better operator modeling.

In all Figures, with the exception of PageRank, we observe that the *degree distribution + levels* similarity measure, for a number of levels, can model an operator more accurately than the simple degree distribution-based, effectively reducing the errors reported in Table 2. Indeed, the addition of more levels to the degree distribution incorporates more information about the connectivity of each vertex. This additional topological insights contribute positively to better estimate the similarity of two graphs. Examining the modeling quality, we observe that it increases but only up to a certain point, in relation to the topology of the graphs in the dataset. For example, since TW comprises of ego graphs, all the degrees of level > 2 are zero, since there exist no vertices with distance greater than 2; therefore, employing more levels does not contribute any additional information about the topology of the graphs when computing their similarity. Finally, we observe that, in specific cases, such as PageRank (Fig. 2f), enhancing the degree distribution with degrees of more levels introduces information that is interpreted as noise during modeling. PageRank is better modeled with the simple degree distribution as a similarity measure. As such, we argue that for a given dataset and graph operator, experimentation is required to find the number of levels that give the best trade-off between accuracy and execution time.

We next concentrate on the effect of the combination of degree distribution with vertex count in the modeling accuracy. We note that the vertex count contributes positively in the modeling of distance-related metrics while having a neutral or negative impact on degree- and spectrum-related metrics. This is attributed to the existence of, at least, a mild correlation, between vertex count and bc, ebc and cc [22]. For our least accurately approximated task, edge betweenness centrality, employing the combination of measures results in a more than 6× decrease in error.

For *D-measure*, our experiments show that, for distance-related metrics it performs at least as good as the *degree distribution + levels* similarity measures for a given level, with the notable exception of the PageRank case. On the other hand, the degree distribution can be sufficiently accurate for degree- or spectrum-related metrics. As *D-measure* is based on distance distributions between vertices, having good accuracy for distance-related measures is something to be expected. A good example of the effectiveness of *D-measure* is shown in the case of closeness centrality that involves all-pairs node distance information directly incorporated in *D-measure* as we have seen in Sect. 3. In

Fig. 2e we observe that by adding levels we get better results, vertex count contributes into even better modeling but *D-measure* gives better approximations. Yet, our methods' errors are already very small (less than 3%) in this case. Considering the *rw-kernel* similarity measure, we observe that it performs poorly for most of the operators. Although its modeling accuracy is comparable to *degree distribution + levels* for some operators, we find that for a certain level or in combination with vertex count a degree distribution-based measure has better accuracy. Notably, *rw-kernel* has low accuracy for degree and distance related operators while performing comparably in the case of spectrum operators.

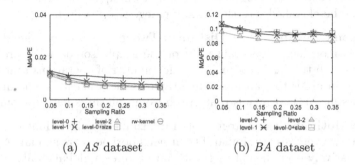

(a) *AS* dataset   (b) *BA* dataset

Fig. 3. Similarity Metric Comparison for Betweenness C.

Identifying betweenness centrality as one of the hardest operators to model accurately, we present $MdAPE$ approximation errors for AS and BA in Figs. 3a, 3b. These Figures do not include *D-measure*, since it was not possible to compute it because of its running time. We note that the approximation error is below 12% and that the *degree distribution + levels* measures further improve on it for both datasets. Compared to TW (Fig. 2), we observe that the *level-2* similarity measure provides better results for AS and BA but not TW, attributed to the ego graph structure with *level-2* degrees being zero. Finally, it is expected that *level-0 + size* for BA to be no different than plain *level-0*, since all the graphs in BA have the same vertex count by construction.

The aforementioned similarity measures have striking differences in their execution time. A comparison in computation time for different levels of the *degree distribution + levels* similarity measure is presented in Fig. 2g. In the case of *D-measure*, the actual execution time is presented for the TW dataset, since it was prohibitively slow to compute it for the other two datasets. For the remaining two datasets, we have computed *D-measure* on a random number of pairs of graphs and then projected the mean computation time to the number of comparisons performed by our method for each dataset.

Our results show that the overhead from *level-0* to *level-1* is comparable for all the datasets. However, that is not the case for *level-2*. The higher the level, the more influential the degree of the vertices becomes in the execution time. Specifically, while we find *level-0* to be 3.2× faster than *level-2* for TW, we observe that in the case of AS and BA it is 19× and 76× faster. The computation of the *D-measure* and the *rw-kernel*, on the other hand, are orders of magnitude slower. Given the difference in modeling quality between the presented similarity functions, we observe a clear trade-off between quality of results and execution time in the context of our method.

4   Related Work

Our work relates to the actively researched areas of graph similarity, graph analytics and machine learning. The available techniques for quantifying graph similarity can be classified into three main categories ([24, 36]):

▷ **Graph Isomorphism - Edit Distance:** Two graphs are considered similar if they are isomorphic. A generalization of the graph isomorphism problem is expressed through the *Edit Distance*, i.e., the number of operations that have to be performed in order to transform one graph to the other [31]. The drawback of approaches in this category is that graph isomorphism is hard to compute.

▷ **Iterative Methods:** This category of graph similarity algorithms is based on the idea that two vertices are similar if their neighborhoods are similar. Applying this idea iteratively over the entire graph can produce a global similarity score. Such algorithms compare graphs based on their topology, we choose to map graphs to feature vectors and compare those vectors instead.

▷ **Feature Vectors:** These approaches are based on the idea that similar graphs share common properties such as degree distribution, diameter, etc and therefore represent graphs as feature vectors. To assess the degree of similarity between graphs, statistical tools are used to compare their feature vectors instead. Such methods are not computationally demanding. Drawing from this category of measures, we base our graph similarity computations on comparing degree distributions.

▷ **Graph Kernels:** A different approach to graph similarity comes from the area of machine learning where kernel functions can be used to infer knowledge about samples. Graph kernels are kernel functions constructed on graphs or graph nodes for comparing graphs or nodes respectively. Extensive research on this area (e.g., [15,17]) has resulted in many kernels based on walks, paths, etc. While computationally more expensive they provide a good baseline for our modeling accuracy evaluation.

▷ **Graph Analytics and Machine Learning:** Although graph analytics is a very thoroughly researched area, there exist few cases where machine learning techniques are used. On the subject of graph summarization, a new approach is based on *node representations* that are learned automatically from the neighborhood of a vertex [18]. *Node representations* are also applicable in computing node or graph similarities as seen in [18]. However, we do not find works employing machine learning techniques in the field of graph mining through graph topology metric computations.

5   Conclusion

In this work we present an operator-agnostic modeling methodology which leverages similarity between graphs. This knowledge is used by a kNN classifier to model a given operator allowing scientists to predict operator output for any graph without having to actually execute the operator. We propose an intuitive, yet powerful class of similarity measures that efficiently capture graph relations. Our thorough evaluation indicates that modeling a variety of graph operators is not only possible, but it can also provide results of high quality at considerable speedups. Finally, our approach appears to present similar results to state-of-the-art similarity measures, such as *D-measure*, in terms of quality, but requires orders of magnitude less execution time.

References

1. Aherne, F.J., et al.: The bhattacharyya metric as an absolute similarity measure for frequency coded data. Kybernetika **34**(4), 363–368 (1998)
2. Arthur, D., Vassilvitskii, S.: k-means++: the advantages of careful seeding. In: Proceedings of the Eighteenth Annual ACM-SIAM Symposium on Discrete Algorithms, SODA 2007, New Orleans, Louisiana, USA, pp. 1027–10357-9 January 2007
3. Barabási, A.L., Albert, R.: Emergence of scaling in random networks. Science **286**(5439), 509–512 (1999)
4. Bentley, J.L.: Multidimensional binary search trees used for associative searching. Commun. ACM **18**(9), 509–517 (1975)
5. Bhattacharyya, A.: On a measure of divergence between two statistical populations defined by their probability distributions. Bull. Calcutta Math. Soc. **35**(1), 99–109 (1943)
6. Bonacich, P.: Power and centrality: a family of measures. Am. J. Sociol. **92**(5), 1170–1182 (1987)
7. Bounova, G., de Weck, O.: Overview of metrics and their correlation patterns for multiple-metric topology analysis on heterogeneous graph ensembles. Phys. Rev. E **85**, 016117 (2012)
8. Brandes, U., Erlebach, T.: Network Analysis: Methodological Foundations. Springer, New York (2005). https://doi.org/10.1007/b106453
9. Brin, S., Page, L.: The anatomy of a large-scale hypertextual web search engine. Comput. Netw. **30**(1–7), 107–117 (1998)
10. Csardi, G., Nepusz, T.: The Igraph software package for complex network research. Inter J. Complex Syst. **1695**, 1–9 (2006)
11. Eppstein, D., Wang, J.: Fast approximation of centrality. J. Graph Algorithms Appl. **8**, 39–45 (2004)
12. da, F., Costa, L., et al.: Characterization of complex networks: a survey of measurements. Adv. Phys. **56**(1), 167–242 (2007)
13. Freeman, L.C.: A set of measures of centrality based on betweenness. Sociometry **40**(1), 35–41 (1977)
14. Gandomi, et al.: Beyond the hype. Int. J. Inf. Manage. **35**(2), 137–144 (2015)
15. Gärtner, T.: A survey of kernels for structured data. SIGKDD **5**(1), 49–58 (2003)

16. Gärtner, T., Flach, P., Wrobel, S.: On graph kernels: hardness results and efficient alternatives. In: Schölkopf, B., Warmuth, M.K. (eds.) COLT-Kernel 2003. LNCS (LNAI), vol. 2777, pp. 129–143. Springer, Heidelberg (2003). https://doi.org/10.1007/978-3-540-45167-9_11

17. Ghosh, S., Das, N., Gonçalves, T., Quaresma, P., Kundu, M.: The journey of graph kernels through two decades. Comput. Sci. Rev. **27**, 88–111 (2018)

18. Grover, A., Leskovec, J.: node2vec: scalable feature learning for networks. In: SIGKDD, pp. 855–864. ACM (2016)

19. Hastie, T., Tibshirani, R., Friedman, J.: The Elements of Statistical Learning: Data Mining, Inference, and Prediction, 2nd edn. Springer, New York (2009). https://doi.org/10.1007/978-0-387-21606-5

20. Hernández, J.M., Mieghem, P.V.: Classification of graph metrics, pp. 1–20 (2011)

21. Jamakovic, A., et al.: Robustness of networks against viruses: the role of the spectral radius. In: Symposium on Communications and Vehicular Technology, pp. 35–38 (2006)

22. Jamakovic, A., Uhlig, S.: On the relationships between topological measures in real-world networks. NHM **3**(2), 345–359 (2008)

23. Kaufmann, L., Rousseeuw, P.: Clustering by means of medoids, pp. 405–416 (1987)

24. Koutra, D., Parikh, A., Ramdas, A., Xiang, J.: Algorithms for graph similarity and subgraph matching. Technical Report Carnegie-Mellon-University (2011). https://people.eecs.berkeley.edu/~aramdas/reports/DBreport.pdf

25. Leskovec, J., Adamic, L.A., Huberman, B.A.: The dynamics of viral marketing. TWEB **1**(1), 5 (2007)

26. Leskovec, J., Krevl, A.: SNAP Datasets: Stanford large network dataset collection, June 2014. http://snap.stanford.edu/data

27. Leskovec, J., Sosič, R.: Snap: a general-purpose network analysis and graph-mining library. ACM Trans. Intell. Syst. Technol. **8**(1), 1 (2016)

28. McAuley, J.J., Leskovec, J.: Learning to discover social circles in ego networks. In: Bartlett, P.L., Pereira, F.C.N., Burges, C.J.C., Bottou, L., Weinberger, K.Q. (eds.) Advances in Neural Information Processing Systems 25: 26th Annual Conference on Neural Information Processing Systems 2012. Proceedings of a meeting held December 3–6, 2012, Lake Tahoe, Nevada, United States, pp. 548–556 (2012)

29. Newman, M.E.J., Girvan, M.: Finding and evaluating community structure in networks. Phys. Rev. E **69**(2), 026113 (2004)

30. Riondato, M., Kornaropoulos, E.M.: Fast approximation of betweenness centrality through sampling. Data Min. Knowl. Discov. **30**(2), 438–475 (2016)

31. Sanfeliu, A., Fu, K.: A distance measure between attributed relational graphs for pattern recognition. IEEE Trans. Syst. Man Cybern. **13**(3), 353–362 (1983)

32. Schieber, T.A., et al.: Quantification of network structural dissimilarities. Nat. Commun. **8**, 13928 (2017)

33. Sugiyama, M., Borgwardt, K.M.: Halting in random walk kernels. In: Annual Conference on Neural Information Processing Systems, pp. 1639–1647 (2015)

34. Bakogiannis, T., Giannakopoulos, I., Tsoumakos, D., Koziris, N.: Graph operator modeling over large graph datasets. CoRR abs/1802.05536 (2018). http://arxiv.org/abs/1802.05536

35. Vishwanathan, S.V.N., Schraudolph, N.N., Kondor, R., Borgwardt, K.M.: Graph kernels. J. Mach. Learn. Res. **11**, 1201–1242 (2010)

36. Zager, L.A., Verghese, G.C.: Graph similarity scoring and matching. Appl. Math. Lett. **21**(1), 86–94 (2008)

Streaming Event Detection in Microblogs: Balancing Accuracy and Performance

Ozlem Ceren Sahin[1], Pinar Karagoz[1(✉)], and Nesime Tatbul[2]

[1] METU, Ankara, Turkey
{e1746668,karagoz}@ceng.metu.edu.tr
[2] Intel Labs and MIT, Cambridge, MA, USA
tatbul@csail.mit.edu

Abstract. In this work, we model the problem of online event detection in microblogs as a stateful stream processing problem and offer a novel solution that balances result accuracy and performance. Our new approach builds on two state of the art algorithms. The first algorithm is based on identifying bursty keywords inside blocks of blog messages. The second one involves clustering blog messages based on similarity of their contents. To combine the computational simplicity of the keyword-based algorithm with the semantic accuracy of the clustering-based algorithm, we propose a new hybrid algorithm. We then implement these algorithms in a streaming manner, on top of Apache Storm augmented with Apache Cassandra for state management. Experiments with a 12M tweet dataset from Twitter show that our hybrid approach provides a better accuracy-performance compromise than the previous approaches.

Keywords: Online event detection · Burst detection ·
Stream processing · Data stream management · Microblogging

1 Introduction

The emergence of microblogging services such as Twitter has caused a revolution in the way information is created and exchanged on the web [16]. Microblogs are user-generated short messages, typically in textual format. Twitter is the most popular microblogging service provider, with more than 300M monthly active users posting more than 500M tweets every day. As such, it constitutes a rich source of information for wide range of use, from market studies to real-time dissemination of breaking news. There has been a plethora of research in analyzing social media data, including microblogs posted on Twitter [3,5,17,27]. In this paper, we focus on one particular form of social media data analysis, that is, *event detection*. We consider an *event* as a happening that takes place at a certain time and place, causing a short window of sudden burst in attention from the microbloggers. The capability to accurately detect events as soon as they happen, i.e., in an *online* fashion, can be important in many ways, from

© Springer Nature Switzerland AG 2019
M. Bakaev et al. (Eds.): ICWE 2019, LNCS 11496, pp. 123–138, 2019.
https://doi.org/10.1007/978-3-030-19274-7_10

timely access to interesting news to tracking life-critical phenomena such as natural disasters [11, 20].

In this work, we hypothesize that online event detection is fundamentally a stream processing problem. Stream processing systems have been around for more than a decade, and today many mature, industrial-quality platforms are publicly available [1, 6]. These systems are highly tuned for low-latency/high-throughput processing over real-time data, making them ideal base platforms for building online event detection dataflows. Furthermore, we believe that capturing events accurately (i.e., no false positives or false negatives) is as equally important as detecting them with low latency. Unfortunately, while online event detection in social media has seen much attention from the research community [2, 5, 7, 22–24, 29], solutions that aim at addressing both accuracy and performance are limited to only a couple [13, 28].

In this paper, we explore the tradeoff between event detection accuracy and performance through stream-based design and implementation of two well-known algorithms from the literature, with opposite characteristics: a keyword-based algorithm and a clustering-based algorithm. The keyword-based algorithm is purely a syntactical approach in that, it is based on counting the occurrence of words, without paying attention to their meanings or relationships. The clustering-based algorithm, on the other hand, groups tweets by the similarity of their contents. While the former is simpler and faster, the latter is expected to produce more accurate results at the expense of taking a longer time to compute. As a novel contribution, we then propose a two-phase, hybrid algorithm, which first applies the keyword-based algorithm as an initial filtering phase, followed by the clustering-based algorithm as the final event detection phase. All of our techniques have been implemented on top of the Apache Storm distributed stream processing system augmented with the Apache Cassandra key-value store for state management, and have been experimentally tuned and evaluated based on a 12M tweet dataset that we collected from Twitter. We find that there is a clear accuracy-performance tradeoff between the keyword-based approach and the clustering-based approach. Moreover, the experiments verify our intuition that the hybrid approach can provide a good compromise between the two. More specifically, this work makes the following contributions:

- Parallel, stateful, stream-based design and implementations of two state of the art algorithms for online event detection,
- A new hybrid algorithm that combines the advantages of these two algorithms to balance event detection accuracy and performance,
- A detailed experimental evaluation based on Apache Storm and Apache Cassandra, using a real Twitter workload,
- Revealing of new research directions for improving both the algorithmic and the systems components of the problem space.

In the rest of this paper, we first present our event detection methods, their implementation, and experimental evaluation in Sects. 2, 3, and 4, respectively. We then summarize related work in Sect. 5, and conclude the paper with a discussion of future directions in Sect. 6.

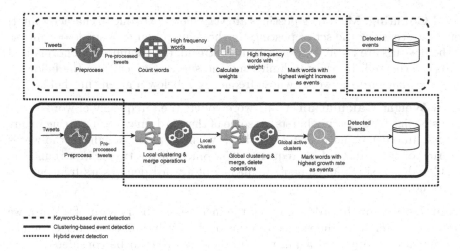

Fig. 1. Event detection methods

2 Event Detection Methods

In this section, we present three different event detection methods applied on streaming data. The first two are based on state of the art algorithms from the event detection literature, and the third is a hybrid extension of these that we newly propose in this paper. In all three methods, streaming posts are processed in windows of predefined time intervals, which are called *rounds*. In each round, the stream is processed as a chunk of tweets, resulting in a state. Hence, we can consider event detection as a state that is reached according to the change between two consecutive states.

For all three methods, first the following preprocessing step is applied: First, messages are tokenized and stemmed through an NLP parser[1]. Afterwards, stop words and geo-references including the phrase *"I am at"* are eliminated. Additionally, we normalize the words having characters that repeat more than two times (such as *"gooooaaaal!"*). Applying stemming and normalization are particularly important for aggregating the different occurrences of the same word.

2.1 Keyword-Based Event Detection Method

Our first method relies on detecting the unexpected increase in the occurrence or observation of the words with respect to a previous round. Then, such *bursty* words are considered to express an event. This method consists of three main steps that are applied in every round: *word counting, word weight calculation,* and *event detection* (see Fig. 1 for an overview). Hence, at the end of each round a set of event keywords are obtained.

---

[1] We use the Stanford NLP parser: https://nlp.stanford.edu/software/lex-parser.shtml.

Word Counting. Microblog postings are very short texts due to character limit. Hence, we consider the set of postings in the same round as a single document. As the postings are received from the input stream, the stemmed and normalized words are counted. In order to limit time and space complexity in the following steps, we eliminate the words whose frequency is below a given threshold.

Word Weight Calculation. Using word counts (i.e., frequency of words) may be misleading for detecting bursts, as some of the words may be appearing in any context. In order to normalize this effect, we measure the weight of the words in terms of *tf-idf*, instead of frequency [25]. Since all the tweets in a round are considered as a single document, frequency of a word denotes its frequency in the round.

Event Detection. In order to check the increase in observation of a word, we compare the weight of the words in terms of tf-idf values in consecutive rounds. The increase is compared against a threshold in order to be considered as an *event related word*.

2.2   Clustering-Based Event Detection Method

In the clustering-based method, the basic assumption is that a *cluster of tweets* with *high growth rate* corresponds to an event. As in the keyword-based method, each round is processed one by one and the resulting clusters are compared for event detection.

The method is composed of two basic steps: *cluster formation* and *event detection* (see Fig. 1 for an overview). In each round, these steps are applied in sequence.

Cluster Formation. We use four basic cluster operations: *creating a new cluster*, *updating a cluster*, *merging clusters*, and *deleting a cluster*. Each cluster has a representative term vector, which includes the frequent terms of the tweets in the cluster. Similarly, each tweet is represented by a term vector of stemmed words in the tweet. Hence, similarity of a tweet to an existing cluster is measured with cosine similarity between term vectors under a predefined threshold. As the tweets are received in a round, one of the cluster operations is applied.

- If the tweet content is not similar to any of the clusters, a *new cluster* is created.
- If the tweet content is similar to a cluster, then the *cluster is updated* by including the tweet in the cluster and updating the cluster's representative term vector.
- *Cluster merging* is applied in two stages. First, within each round, clusters are generated locally (i.e., only considering the tweets in the current round). Furthermore, at the end of a round, similar local clusters are merged. As the second stage of merging, the resulting local clusters are merged with the global clusters (i.e., the cumulative set of active clusters since the beginning of time) complying with the similarity threshold.

- In order to reduce the number of generated clusters, and hence improve execution time performance, *inactive clusters are deleted*. The condition for deletion is defined as follows: If a cluster is not active (i.e., not updated) for the last two rounds, then it is deleted.

Event Detection. In the clustering-based method, event detection is achieved through tracking the growth rate of clusters. The growth rate is calculated using the number of tweets that contribute to a cluster, as the ratio of the number of tweets added to the cluster to the total number of tweets in the cluster. To mark a cluster as an event, the *cluster growth rate* should be greater than a predefined threshold.

2.3 Hybrid Event Detection Method

The hybrid method combines the previous two methods in order to increase the efficiency of clustering by filtering tweets that do not include bursty keywords. First, bursty keywords are found by applying the steps used in the keyword-based event detection method, and then clustering is applied on tweets containing the bursty keywords. Finally, by using the cluster growth rates, this technique marks clusters as events (see Fig. 1 for an overview; notice how the tweets with bursty words found by the keyword-based method is fed as an input to the clustering-based method).

Tweet Filtering. As in the previous methods, words in a streaming tweet are tokenized and stemmed. Words are counted and those with low frequency are eliminated. By this elimination, we reduce the number of words to keep track of for burstiness. As in the first method, burstiness of a word is checked through the increase in its tf-idf value. The increase is compared against a predefined threshold in order to be considered as bursty keyword. Additionally, if the tf-idf value of a word is very high for only the last round, then we consider it as a bursty term as well.

Clustering. The hybrid method uses the same clustering technique as in the clustering-based method. Similarly, two-level clustering is applied, local and global. The basic difference here is that, in a round, instead of clustering all streaming tweets, only those that include any bursty term are fed into the clustering phase. By this way, time efficiency can be significantly improved.

Detecting Events Using Clusters. As the final step of the hybrid technique, event detection is performed by checking the growth rate of the cluster as applied in the clustering-based method.

3 Implementation

The three event detection methods studied in this work are implemented on the Apache Storm stream processing framework[2]. In Storm, an application is defined as a *topology*. A topology is an arbitrarily complex multi-stage stream

---

[2] http://storm.apache.org/.

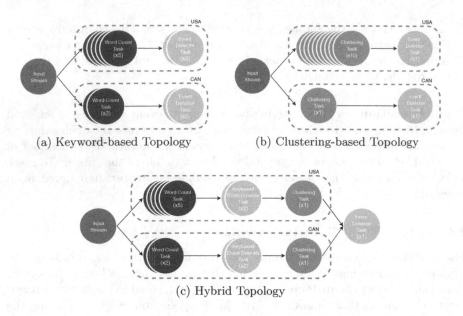

(a) Keyword-based Topology   (b) Clustering-based Topology

(c) Hybrid Topology

Fig. 2. Storm topologies

computation. It is a graph of spouts and bolts, such that a *spout* is a source of stream and a *bolt* is a stream processing task.

We use a single stream of tweets as our spout. In the experiments, we worked on the tweet stream filtered by geographical boundary. We limited the stream to the tweets posted in USA and Canada. Furthermore, we processed these two groups of tweets in parallel. Alternatively, it is possible to consider two groups of tweets as two separate streams, as well. We store the streamed data collection in the Apache Cassandra key-value store[3] to maintain each round of tweets for further processing in bolts. Within this spout, tokenization of the messages and stemming of the words are performed as well. The stream is emitted as a set of preprocessed words to the following bolt.

3.1   Keyword-Based Event Detection Topology

The structure of the keyword-based event detection topology is presented in Fig. 2a. The topology basically includes a single spout (denoted as *input stream*), and two types of bolts: word count bolt and event detector bolt. As described in Sect. 2, the tweet stream is processed in terms of rounds. We can consider the tweets in the same round as a single document. Word count bolt keeps track of the count of the words in the document of a round. When frequency counting is completed, event detector bolt calculates tf-idf values for the words, and compares the value with that of the previous round to determine *bursty keywords*.

---

[3] http://cassandra.apache.org/.

The topology given in Fig. 2a shows the parallelism and distribution applied in the experimental analysis. The upper path in the topology graph includes the bolts reserved for tweets from USA, whereas the lower path is for processing tweets from Canada. The figure shows the number of bolts allocated for each task, as well (the numbers given in parenthesis at the end of task label). The number of bolts to be allocated are determined empirically according to the work load on the task.

3.2   Clustering-Based Event Detection Topology

The structure of the clustering-based event detection topology is presented in Fig. 2b. As in the keyword-based approach, there is a single spout (denoted as *input stream*), and two types of bolts, but the tasks of the bolts are different than those in the previous topology.

Clustering bolt is responsible for clustering the incoming tweets on the basis of the similarity between the tweet and cluster representative vector. *Event detector bolt* keeps track of change in the size of the clusters to detect a burst in the size (hence to detect an event). As described in Sect. 2, various operations are applied on clusters. *New cluster construction*, and *cluster update* operations are performed in the *clustering bolt*, whereas *cluster deletion* is done as the last step in the *event detection bolt*. *Cluster merging* is applied in two stages. Within each round, clusters are generated locally. At the end of the round, similar local clusters are merged. As the second stage of merging, the resulting local clusters are merged with the global clusters complying with the similarity threshold.

Clustering in two stages, local and global, serves for two purposes. As the first one, storage access for updating the global clustering is more costly than doing so for the local clustering, due to the size of the clusters. Therefore, updating the clusters locally for processing the streaming tweets improves time performance. The second reason is due to the lack of transactional support in Storm's stream processing environment. When the streaming tweets are processed in a distributed way, different tweet processing nodes may access the same cluster for updating the cluster's term vector concurrently. This causes the loss of some of the updates and leads to incorrect clusters. While building the clusters locally, this problem is considerably reduced, since the local clusters are much smaller, and the tweets are processed in sequence within a bolt. This is an interesting technical problem that this work revealed, which we would like to study as part of our future work. For example, it would be interesting to explore the use of a transactional stream processing engine such as S-Store [15], as an alternative to Storm and Cassandra to handle both streaming and storage needs in a transactional manner. This could potentially improve both correctness and performance of our techniques.

As in the keyword-based topology, the clustering-based event detection topology given in Fig. 2b shows the parallel execution paths in the experiments for processing tweets from USA and Canada. Additionally, the number of bolts created for each task is shown as well. As presented in the figure, clustering task for the upper path has the highest requirement for distribution, due to high number of tweets and clusters.

3.3 Hybrid Event Detection Topology

The structure of the hybrid event detection topology is presented in Fig. 2c. As in the previous topologies, there is a single spout (denoted as *input stream*). However, the topology includes bolts for both detecting bursty keywords (the first two tasks in the topology) and clustering-based event detection (the last two tasks). The basic idea in this method is to filter the tweets such that only those tweets that contain some bursty keyword are clustered towards event detection. By this way, the load on the clustering tasks is reduced. The reduction in the load is obvious in the smaller number of bolts for the clustering task. As another result of the reduced load, just a single event detector node is allocated for both of the tweet processing paths.

In each of the three methods, it is important to create and manage state during execution. We realize this via batch-based stream processing. More specifically, we consider tweet blocks collected within 6-min rounds as batches. At the end of each round, *state* is generated and saved into a Cassandra store so that next round can use information resulting from the previous round. In the keyword-based method, tf of the words are stored as the state of the round in order to detect events through increment rate of tf-idf values. In the clustering-based method, clusters created/updated in each round constitute the state. Finally, for the hybrid method, both tf values and clusters created/updated in the round are stored as the state at the end of the round. Note that, event detection accuracy depends on correct state maintenance, as well as the event detection method employed.

4 Experimental Evaluation

In this section, we present an experimental evaluation of our event detection techniques in terms of accuracy and performance.

4.1 Setup

All experiments were run on a MacOS Version 10.13.3 machine with an Intel® Core™ i5 processor running at 3.2 GHz with 16 GB of memory.

We used a real Twitter dataset with nearly 12M tweets that we collected within a week, from May 31, 2016 to June 7, 2016. We filtered tweets by geographic location and worked with only the ones posted from USA and Canada. The complete dataset is stored in Cassandra and we replay it in a streaming fashion in our experiments in order to simulate a behavior similar to the real Twitter Firehose. In each of the experiments, we processed the tweets in *rounds* (i.e., time windows) of 6 min. We chose this window size so as to create a behavior that is as close to a realistic and stable system scenario as possible (i.e., tweet collection rate matches the processing rate, and the total latency of buffering and processing each tweet is not too high).

Our main evaluation metrics are the well-known Precision, Recall, and F1-measure for accuracy, and throughput (i.e., total number of input tweets processed per second) and total round processing latency for performance. The clustering-based event detection method (and therefore, the hybrid method which is also based on clustering) involves several parameters used as thresholds (such as cosine similarity threshold to merge clusters or the number of tweets in a local cluster). The optimal values for these parameters are obtained through validation experiments that are conducted on a smaller sample of the whole dataset.

4.2   Event Detection Accuracy and Performance

We now analyze the event detection accuracy of our methods against the *ground truth*. Furthermore, we report our findings on their computational performance.

Ground Truth Construction. We determined the set of events that constitute the ground truth through a user study involving three judges. The following process is applied by each of the judges independently: Given all clusters generated by the cluster-based and the hybrid event detection methods, the most frequent terms in representative term vectors of each cluster is examined in detail, making use of web search with the frequent terms in order to match the cluster with a real-world event that happened within the same time interval as the dataset collection. Some of the events were very clear and well-known events, such as *Death of Muhammad Ali*, which did not need detailed examination. On the other hand, some other events, such as *Offensive Foul by Kevin Love in NBA Finals Game I*, needed a more detailed web search. After the individual evaluation session by each judge, another session is conducted to compare their results. In this second session, the final set of events for the ground truth is determined under full consensus from all three judges. As a result, the ground truth includes 21 different events for the USA tweets and 4 different events for the Canada tweets, including events from the 2016 NBA Finals, the 2016 NHL Final, events about celebrities as well as first appearances of movie trailers and music videos, and the death of Muhammad Ali.

Accuracy Comparison. For accuracy evaluation, we used the well-known relevance metrics of *Precision, Recall,* and *F1-measure*. Since the output of the keyword-based method is a set of bursty keywords denoting events, precision is calculated as the ratio of the number of keywords matching some event to the number of keywords found. For the clustering-based and the hybrid methods, precision is calculated as the ratio of number of clusters matching some event to number of clusters found. Recall is calculated in the same way for all three

Table 1. Accuracy results for the keyword-based method

Method	Stream	Detected bursty keywords	Detected events	Undetected events	Precision	Recall	F1
Keyword	USA	220	14 (matching 135 keywords)	7	61%	67%	64%
	CAN	17	2 (matching 7 keywords)	2	41%	50%	45%
	All	237	16 (matching 142 keywords)	9	60%	64%	62%

Table 2. Accuracy results for the clustering-based and the hybrid methods

Method	Stream	Constructed clusters	Event clusters	Undetected events	Precision	Recall	F1
Clustering	USA	74	39	0	53%	100%	69%
	CAN	7	5	0	71%	100%	83%
	All	81	44	0	54%	100%	70%
Hybrid	USA	87	53	4	61%	80%	69%
	CAN	3	3	1	100%	75%	86%
	All	90	56	5	62%	79%	69%

Table 3. Clustering analysis for the clustering-based and the hybrid methods

Method	Stream	No. of clusters	Avg. SC	Min. SC	Max. SC	Std. dev.
Clustering	USA	74	0.855	0.15	1.0	0.276
Clustering	CAN	7	1.0	1.0	1.0	0.0
Hybrid	USA	87	0.62	0.0	1.0	0.41
Hybrid	CAN	3	1.0	1.0	1.0	0.0

methods, as the ratio of the number of detected events to the total number of events in the ground truth set. Finally, F1-measure is calculated conventionally, as the harmonic mean of precision and recall. Precision, Recall, and F1-measure values for the methods are shown in Tables 1 and 2. As seen in the results, the clustering-based method provides the highest recall, whereas the hybrid method performs better in terms of precision. This result is reflected in Table 3, as well. The clusters generated by the hybrid method for the USA tweets are all event clusters with high silhouette coefficient[4] values, whereas the clusters generated by the clustering-based method have lower average silhouette coefficient as well as a higher standard deviation. Keyword-based method has an intermediate-level performance, performing slightly better for recall than for precision.

Table 4. Performance results for all methods

Method	Number of tweets processed per sec.	Number of rounds processed per min.	Round processing time (Sec.)
Keyword	1200	9.3	6.5
Clustering	300	2.5	24
Hybrid	797	6.7251	8.96

Performance Comparison. In stream processing, processing time is an important metric to be able to cope with continuous data. Additionally, online event detection calls for timely processing to extract and present the events with the least possible delay. Since the streaming behavior is simulated in our experiments, the tweet arrival rates are set to the same level for each of the methods. For performance, we focus on measuring the throughput in terms of number of tweets processed per second, number of rounds processed per minute and round processing time. Table 4 summarizes our results. As expected, the most efficient method is the keyword-based event detection method with 1200 tweets per second and 6.5 s of round processing time on average. In contrast, since the clustering-based method performs many database accesses to maintain cluster state and it has to iterate over larger amounts of data, it incurs the lowest number of tweets processed per second and longest round execution time. The hybrid method shows a major improvement over the clustering-based method, bringing the round execution time down to 7.5 s. This proves that filtering tweets based on bursty keywords can be effective in reducing the cost of cluster computation.

4.3 Discussion

The key takeaways from our experimental study can be summarized as follows:

- The clustering-based method provides the highest recall value for USA events and overall. This is an expected result, since this method generates more number of clusters and performs a finer-grained analysis.

---

[4] The silhouette coefficient (SC) essentially measures how similar a given object is to its own cluster compared to the other clusters. Its value ranges between -1 and $+1$, where a higher value indicates higher clustering quality.

- On the other hand, the clustering-based method is also the least efficient method due to higher load of cluster processing and storing state. However, the idea of pre-filtering tweets using keyword counts is a promising way to improve the performance of the clustering-based method, as the performance results of our hybrid method indicate.
- The keyword-based method processes the tweet stream faster than the other two methods, and the bursty keywords provide good hints for detecting the events. However, the same keyword may be associated with several related yet different events. For example, the bursty keyword *game* appears in several clusters' representative vectors. Therefore, it is not easy to associate a keyword with an event precisely.
- Tweet filtering applied in the hybrid method brings considerable efficiency. It also provides a rise in precision per country, and in F1-measure for Canada events. However, there is a drop in recall, due to the filtering applied. Overall, clusters generated by the hybrid method strongly indicate the occurrence of relevant events from the ground truth dataset. The improvement in the time efficiency over clustering-based method brings an advantage for practical use as well.
- In the clustering-based method, we observed cases where multiple event clusters are generated in the same round corresponding to the same event, causing *fragmented clusters*. For example, for the event *Death of Muhammad Ali*, two clusters are generated in the same round, one of them containing frequent terms *champion, rest in peace*, whereas the other one containing *float, butterfly, sting*, referring to the famous quote *"Float like a butterfly, sting like a bee"*. Another advantage of the hybrid method we observed is that, it reduces the degree of this kind of fragmentation.
- In burst detection, processing the rounds separately and keeping the state is essential, yet this incurs a cost. Overall, this study shows that using a stream processing framework for online event detection is a viable idea and can facilitate implementation and scalability, while helping control accuracy. We note that the benefit of this approach could be further improved by providing stronger support for native storage of state and transactional processing to efficiently coordinate concurrent data accesses, which we plan to investigate in more depth as part of our future work.

5   Related Work

Event detection in social networks and microblogging platforms on the web has been a popular research topic for the past decade [5,17]. Like our work in this paper, a significant portion of previous research has focused on analyzing streams of Twitter posts [3,8]. Some of these focus on detecting specific types of events such as earthquakes [22,23] or crime and disasters [10], while others, like in our case, target detecting any type of event gaining interest among bloggers [7,21, 24]. In both cases, textual messages are first pre-processed to extract important features such as geo-location, followed by a clustering/classification step, where potential events are identified and selected.

Previous online event detection techniques follow various algorithmic approaches. Sayyadi et al. and Ozdikis et al. leverage keyword co-occurrence information to discover similar tweets [19,20,26], whereas Zhou and Chen focus on detecting composite social events based on a graphical model [32]. Petrovic et al. propose detecting new events from tweets based on locality-sensitive hashing (LSH) [21]. Systems like EvenTweet and Jasmine exploit location information from geo-referenced messages to detect local events more accurately [2,29], while Osborne et al. leverage Wikipedia for enhancing story detection on Twitter [18]. TwitterStand is a Twitter-based news processing system that focuses on the problem of noise removal from tweets [24]. TwitterNews+ proposes incremental clustering and inverted indexing methods for lowering the computational cost of event detection on Twitter [7]. Others also looked into the bursty topic detection problem [30,31]. Trend detection on Twitter is another related problem [4,12], where the emphasis is more on identifying longer term events. In [11], Liu et al., describe a system for removing noise in order to detect news events on Twitter. As the employed technique, they focus on first story detection, rather than burst detection.

Some of the studies use machine learning techniques for detecting events, thus they need a training set or several keywords. Medvet and Bartoli's study requires set of potentially related keywords to detect trending events with their sentiment polarity [14]. In [9], Illina et al. use textual messages and n-grams to classify the social media postings as event related and non-event related.

Our work differs from the above related work in that we take a stateful stream processing approach to accurate and efficient event detection. In this approach, we leverage a state-of-the-art system infrastructure based on a distributed stream processing system (Apache Storm) for low-latency event detection combined with a scalable key-value storage system (Apache Cassandra) for maintaining state. To our knowledge, there are two approaches that are the most closely related to ours: McCreadie et al.'s work on distributed event detection [13] and the RBEDS real-time bursty event detection system proposed by Wang et al. [28]. Like in our approach, both of these also implement online event detection solutions on top of Storm. However, they tackle different aspects of the problem. McCreadie et al. focus on scaling event detection to multiple nodes using a new distributed lexical key partitioning scheme as an extension to the LSH-based algorithm previously proposed by Petrovic et al. [21], while Wang et al. focus on applying the k-means clustering algorithm to the burst detection problem on Storm. Neither of these approaches pays attention to statefulness aspect of the problem and the need for balancing event detection accuracy and performance like we do. Thus, the three approaches are complementary.

6   Conclusion and Future Work

In this work, we model event detection problem as burst detection in frequency of keywords or in size of message clusters. We analyze the performance of three methods for event detection implemented on the Apache Storm distributed stream processing framework. These methods are evaluated on a real tweet dataset collected over a week and replayed as a stream. The experimental results show the applicability of our stream-based approach for online event detection. Among the compared methods, hybrid method provides a better balance between accuracy and processing time cost. It has lower recall value than clustering based method, but can detect event with higher precision.

This work uncovers several interesting problems that can be studied as future work. Semantic similarity based measurements can be utilized to prevent fragmentation of clusters related to the same event. On the other hand, fragmentation can be useful to detect events that may have different durations, which is an interesting direction for extending our work. In our stream simulations, we did not apply any normalization on the load of the rounds, but the topology is determined empirically to handle the average load. Automated adaptation of a topology for load balancing can be further studied. As another research direction, utilization of a transactional stream processing engine (instead of Storm and Cassandra) can be investigated and its effect on event detection accuracy and performance can be analyzed.

References

1. IEEE Data Engineering Bulletin: Special Issue on Next-Generation Stream Processing (2015)
2. Abdelhaq, H., et al.: EvenTweet: online localized event detection from Twitter. PVLDB **6**(12), 1326–1329 (2013)
3. Atefeh, F., Khreich, W.: A survey of techniques for event detection in Twitter. Comput. Intell. **31**(1), 132–164 (2015)
4. Becker, H., et al.: Beyond trending topics: real-world event identification on Twitter. In: International AAAI Conference on Weblogs and Social Media (ICWSM), pp. 438–441 (2011)
5. Cordeiro, M., Gama, J.: Online social networks event detection: a survey. In: Michaelis, S., Piatkowski, N., Stolpe, M. (eds.) Solving Large Scale Learning Tasks. Challenges and Algorithms. LNCS (LNAI), vol. 9580, pp. 1–41. Springer, Cham (2016). https://doi.org/10.1007/978-3-319-41706-6_1
6. González-Jiménez, M., de Lara, J.: Datalyzer: streaming data applications made easy. In: International Conference on Web Engineering (ICWE), pp. 420–429 (2018)
7. Hasan, M., Orgun, M.A., Schwitter, R.: TwitterNews+: a framework for real time event detection from the Twitter data stream. In: Spiro, E., Ahn, Y.-Y. (eds.) SocInfo 2016. LNCS, vol. 10046, pp. 224–239. Springer, Cham (2016). https://doi.org/10.1007/978-3-319-47880-7_14
8. Hromic, H., Prangnawarat, N., Hulpuș, I., Karnstedt, M., Hayes, C.: Graph-based methods for clustering topics of interest in Twitter. In: Cimiano, P., Frasincar, F., Houben, G.-J., Schwabe, D. (eds.) ICWE 2015. LNCS, vol. 9114, pp. 701–704. Springer, Cham (2015). https://doi.org/10.1007/978-3-319-19890-3_61
9. Ilina, E., Hauff, C., Celik, I., Abel, F., Houben, G.-J.: Social event detection on twitter. In: Brambilla, M., Tokuda, T., Tolksdorf, R. (eds.) ICWE 2012. LNCS, vol. 7387, pp. 169–176. Springer, Heidelberg (2012). https://doi.org/10.1007/978-3-642-31753-8_12

10. Li, R., et al.: TEDAS: a Twitter-based event detection and analysis system. In: IEEE International Conference on Data Engineering (ICDE), pp. 1273–1276 (2012)
11. Liu, X., et al.: Reuters tracer: a large scale system of detecting & verifying real-time news events from Twitter. In: ACM International on Conference on Information and Knowledge Management (CIKM), pp. 207–216 (2016)
12. Mathioudakis, M., Koudas, N.: TwitterMonitor: trend detection over the Twitter stream. In: ACM SIGMOD International Conference on Management of Data (SIGMOD), pp. 1155–1158 (2010)
13. McCreadie, R., et al.: Scalable distributed event detection for Twitter. In: IEEE International Conference on Big Data, pp. 543–549 (2013)
14. Medvet, E., Bartoli, A.: Brand-related events detection, classification and summarization on Twitter. In: IEEE/WIC/ACM International Joint Conferences on Web Intelligence and Intelligent Agent Technology (WI-IAT), pp. 297–302 (2012)
15. Meehan, J., et al.: S-store: streaming meets transaction processing. Proc. VLDB Endow. (PVLDB) **8**(13), 2134–2145 (2015)
16. Milstein, S., et al.: Twitter and the micro-messaging revolution: communication, connections, and immediacy - 140 characters at a time (An O'Reilly Radar Report) (2008). http://wcigcnd.com/files/teaching/haas/2009/readings/OReillyTwitterReport200811.pdf
17. Mokbel, M.F., Magdy, A.: Microblogs data management systems: querying, analysis, and visualization (tutorial). In: ACM SIGMOD International Conference on Management of Data (SIGMOD), pp. 2219–2222 (2016)
18. Osborne, M., et al.: Bieber no more: first story detection using Twitter and Wikipedia. In: SIGIR Workshop on Time-Aware Information Access (TAIA) (2012)
19. Ozdikis, O., et al.: Semantic expansion of tweet contents for enhanced event detection in Twitter. In: International Conference on Advances in Social Networks Analysis and Mining (ASONAM), pp. 20–24 (2012)
20. Ozdikis, O., et al.: Incremental clustering with vector expansion for online event detection in microblogs. Soc. Netw. Anal. Min. **7**(1), 56 (2017)
21. Petrovic, S., et al.: Streaming first story detection with application to Twitter. In: Human Language Technologies: Conference of the North American Chapter of the Association for Computational Linguistics (HLT-NAACL), pp. 181–189 (2010)
22. Sakaki, T., Okazaki, M., Matsuo, Y.: Earthquake shakes Twitter users: real-time event detection by social sensors. In: International Conference on World Wide Web (WWW), pp. 851–860 (2010)
23. Sakaki, T., et al.: Tweet analysis for real-time event detection and earthquake reporting system development. IEEE Trans. Knowl. Data Eng. (TKDE) **25**(4), 919–931 (2013)
24. Sankaranarayanan, J., et al.: TwitterStand: news in tweets. In: ACM SIGSPATIAL International Conference on Advances in Geographic Information Systems (GIS), pp. 42–51 (2009)
25. Sarma, A.D., et al.: Dynamic relationship and event discovery. In: ACM International Conference on Web Search and Data Mining (WSDM), pp. 207–216 (2011)
26. Sayyadi, H., et al.: Event detection and tracking in social streams. In: International Conference on Web and Social Media (ICWSM), pp. 311–314 (2009)
27. Sellam, T., Alonso, O.: Raimond: quantitative data extraction from Twitter to describe events. In: Cimiano, P., Frasincar, F., Houben, G.-J., Schwabe, D. (eds.) ICWE 2015. LNCS, vol. 9114, pp. 251–268. Springer, Cham (2015). https://doi.org/10.1007/978-3-319-19890-3_17

28. Wang, Y., Xu, R., Liu, B., Gui, L., Tang, B.: A storm-based real-time micro-blogging burst event detection system. In: Wang, X., Pedrycz, W., Chan, P., He, Q. (eds.) ICMLC 2014. CCIS, vol. 481, pp. 186–195. Springer, Heidelberg (2014). https://doi.org/10.1007/978-3-662-45652-1_20
29. Watanabe, K., et al.: Jasmine: a real-time local-event detection system based on geolocation information propagated to microblogs. In: ACM International Conference on Information and Knowledge Management (CIKM), pp. 2541–2544 (2011)
30. Xie, W., et al.: TopicSketch: real-time bursty topic detection from Twitter. IEEE Trans. Knowl. Data Eng. (TKDE) **28**(8), 2216–2229 (2016)
31. Zhang, T., Zhou, B., Huang, J., Jia, Y., Zhang, B., Li, Z.: A refined method for detecting interpretable and real-time bursty topic in microblog stream. In: Bouguettaya, A., et al. (eds.) WISE 2017. LNCS, vol. 10569, pp. 3–17. Springer, Cham (2017). https://doi.org/10.1007/978-3-319-68783-4_1
32. Zhou, X., Chen, L.: Event detection over Twitter social media streams. VLDB J. **23**(3), 381–400 (2014)

Supervised Group Embedding for Rumor Detection in Social Media

Yuwei Liu[1], Xingming Chen[1], Yanghui Rao[1(✉)], Haoran Xie[2], Qing Li[3],
Jun Zhang[4], Yingchao Zhao[5], and Fu Lee Wang[6]

[1] School of Data and Computer Science, Sun Yat-sen University, Guangzhou, China
{liuyw23,chenxm47}@mail2.sysu.edu.cn, raoyangh@mail.sysu.edu.cn
[2] Department of Mathematics and Information Technology,
The Education University of Hong Kong, Tai Po, Hong Kong
hrxie2@gmail.com
[3] Department of Computing, The Hong Kong Polytechnic University,
Hung Hom, Kowloon, Hong Kong
csqli@comp.polyu.edu.hk
[4] School of Computer Science and Engineering,
South China University of Technology, Guangzhou, China
junzhang@ieee.org
[5] School of Computing and Information Sciences,
Caritas Institute of Higher Education, Tseung Kwan O, Hong Kong
yczhao@cihe.edu.hk
[6] School of Science and Technology, The Open University of Hong Kong,
Kowloon, Hong Kong
pwang@ouhk.edu.hk

Abstract. To detect rumors automatically in social media, methods based on recurrent neural network and convolutional neural network have been proposed. These methods split a stream of posts related to an event into several groups along time, and represent each group using unsupervised methods such as paragraph vector. However, many posts in a group (e.g., retweeted posts) do not contribute much to rumor detection, which deteriorates the performance of rumor detection based on unsupervised group embedding. In this paper, we propose a Supervised Group Embedding based Rumor Detection (SGERD) model that considers both textual and temporal information. Particularly, SGERD exploits post-level textual information to generate group embeddings, and is able to identify salient posts for further analysis. Experimental results on two real-world datasets demonstrate the effectiveness of our proposed model.

Keywords: Rumor detection · Social media ·
Convolutional Neural Network

1 Introduction

A rumor is defined as a story or a statement whose truth-value is unverified or deliberately false [18]. Nowadays, with the rapid growth of social media, large amounts of rumors are easily spread across the Internet. This brings negative

© Springer Nature Switzerland AG 2019
M. Bakaev et al. (Eds.): ICWE 2019, LNCS 11496, pp. 139–153, 2019.
https://doi.org/10.1007/978-3-030-19274-7_11

effect (e.g., public panic) onto the society. For example, on April 23th of 2013, a rumor about "explosion" that injured Barack Obama in the White House spread through Twitter and wiped out $130 billion in stock value[1]. Therefore, it is crucial to detect rumors on social media effectively and as early as possible before they get spread widely.

In the previous studies, there have been several methods aiming to detect rumors for each post [18,25]. Individual posts typically contain limited context, and rumors may be depicted by the same truth-telling way as non-rumor ones. Besides, a single post does not reflect much about the temporal property of a claim spreading on social media. Therefore, current studies on rumor detection aim to classify the aggregation of posts by identifying an event as a rumor or not [8,11,27,28]. An event, which may possess true or false information, is defined as a set of posts (e.g., microblogs, tweets, and wechats) related to some specific claim [11]. Most previous approaches for rumor detection are based on applying conventional supervised learning algorithms with manually designed features. A wide variety of handcrafted features, such as content-based, user-based, and propagation-based features [1,8,12,25], have been incorporated. Some other rumor detection methods exploit complicated features, e.g., user's feedback [19], variation of features along event lifecycle [12], signals posts reflecting skepticism about factual claims [28] and conflict viewpoints [4]. Recently, Gated Recurrent Unit (GRU) and Convolutional Neural Network (CNN) based methods [11,27] have been shown to be competitive for rumor detection over events. These two methods both view an event as a series of posts, by splitting posts into groups along time. GRU is particularly suited for modeling sequential phenomena and capable of capturing the variation of contextual characteristic over rumor diffusion, and CNN can extract both local and global features through the convolution operation and reveal these high-level interactions [26]. However, there are some drawbacks in these models. Firstly, GRU is bias towards the latest groups [16] and CNN is not inherently equipped for a sense of time series [2]. Secondly, they identify rumors according to content features of groups represented by tf-idf or unsupervised paragraph vector [9]. We observe that posts on social media are full of redundant posts, and many posts about an event contribute less to rumor detection. Therefore, it is unsuitable to generate group embedding by tf-idf or unsupervised paragraph vector. Thirdly, since these models use group representations as the input, salient posts that contribute to rumor classification are arduous to get, yet are important for further analysis in real-world tasks, such as public opinion monitoring, where picking out salient posts is crucial for experts to verify conclusions drawn by automatic methods. Furthermore, the above-mentioned models only use the content information, while other useful features of groups (e.g., temporal information) are ignored. Recently, Liu et al. [10] incorporates attention mechanism to model content and dynamic information of individual post for rumor detection. However, without grouping the

---

[1] https://www.forbes.com/sites/kenrapoza/2017/02/26/can-fake-news-impact-the-stock-market/.

aggregated posts, it cannot utilize variation of features along an event's lifecycle while it is helpful for rumor detection [12]. In addition, the model may be very complex when an event consists of a large number of posts.

To address the issues mentioned above, we propose a model named Supervised Group Embedding based Rumor Detection (SGERD) in this paper. First, in order to make each group contain as many correlated posts as possible, we split posts of each event into several groups with equal time interval by following [27]. Our intuition is that the representation of groups using unsupervised methods is arduous to alleviate the negative effects of redundant posts in a group, thus we directly take the content of posts as the input to learn the task-oriented representation for each post, and extract the local features of nearby posts to generate group embeddings. Furthermore, considering that the influence of groups on different time windows is dissimilar, we model the temporal information of groups and equip SGERD with a sense of group order.

The main contributions of our work are as follows:

- We conduct rumor detection at the post-level by proposing a supervised method to learn group embeddings, which significantly improves the model performance. Moreover, we can conveniently pick out meaningful posts from each event.
- We incorporate temporal information besides textual features into neural networks, which is shown to be helpful for rumor detection.
- Experiments are conducted on two real-world datasets, and the results show that SGERD is effective and outperforms state-of-the-art methods.

The remainder of this paper is organized as follows. We review related work in Sect. 2, and present the SGERD for rumor detection in Sect. 3. We detail the dataset, experimental results, and discussion in Sect. 4. Finally, we present conclusions in Sect. 5.

2   Related Work

In recent years, the task of detecting rumors on the Internet has received considerable attention. As for research objectives, most studies attempted to detect rumors at the post level, i.e., classify a single post as rumor or not [18,25], or identify whether the aggregation of posts under an event is rumor [8,11,27,28]. Some other researches aimed to detect fake images [3] and identify hoax articles in WiKipedia [7]. With respect to rumor detection methods, many previous studies employed traditional classifiers using different sets of hand-crafted features. For instance, various features are extracted from the content, user characteristics, and the propagation pattern [1,8,12,25]. Moreover, some rumor detection methods exploited complicated features, such as user's feedback [19], variation of features along an event's lifecycle [12], signals posts reflecting skepticism about factual claims [28], and conflict viewpoints [4].

Recently, Gated Recurrent Unit (GRU) [11,14], Convolutional Neural Network (CNN) [27] and attention based method [10] have been proposed for rumor detection. Different from other prior works, they exploited the content of posts rather than typical features of events (e.g., the retweet number of an event and the information related to evaluate a user's credibility). Yu et al. [27] adopted a two-layer CNN model named CAMI to extract both local and global features of events. First, posts of an event are split into twenty groups according to an equal time interval. Then, the groups are embedded into representations with fixed sizes by paragraph vector [9]. Last, the model takes group embeddings of the event as input and detects whether the event is rumor. Liu et al. [10] proposed an attention-based approach called AIM to detect rumors using content and dynamic information. However, their approach does not utilize grouping method and the number of model parameters is proportional to the number of posts in each event. In this way, classification will be intractable when there are great numbers of posts in events. Ma et al. [14] regarded rumor detection and stance classification as highly relevant tasks. They associated them and proposed a model which utilizes a multi-task learning scheme to model features shared by two tasks. Some studies modeled the propagation structures of different events by exploiting tree-kernel [13] and recursive neural network [24] in order to capture the patterns of propagation trees.

In the above, methods integrating various hand-crafted features into traditional classifiers only rely on limited context and cannot capture high-level features, thus they fail to be adaptive to complicated occasions of social media. Methods based on GRU have a preference for the latest group of events, while the latest one may not play a key role in rumor detection [27]. Though CAMI using CNN achieves the state-of-the-art performance, it has the drawback of not being equipped with a sense of time series. AIM does not utilize the grouping method, thus it cannot model variation of features along an event's lifecycle, which is useful for rumor detection [12], and fails to be applied to events with a large number of posts.

3   Proposed Rumor Detection Model

3.1   Definitions

According to [11,27], an event is defined as a set of posts related to a specific claim, e.g., "Trump Campaign colluded with Russia during 2016 presidential election", and each post is associated with a timestamp. In this way, an event contains much more information than a single post. We denote an event instance as $e = (post_i, timestamp_i)$, consisting of ideally all relevant posts $post_i$ at $timestamp_i$, where $timestamp_i$ is in chronological order and $timestamp_1$ is the start time of e, i.e., timestamp of the first post of the corresponding event e. The total number of posts under e is denoted as $|e|$, and thus $i \in [1, |e|]$. Based on this definition, our task is to detect whether a sequence of relevant posts associated with an event is rumor. Following the previous work [27], we split posts of an event into n groups according to an equal time interval for each event and set n to twenty.

3.2   Model Structure

The overall model architecture is illustrated in Fig. 1, which contains four modules: split posts into n groups and learn task-oriented post embedding, construct group embedding G over a variable length of posts, learn temporal embedding T_{emb} to equip model with a sense of group order, and employ a series of convolution operations for classification.

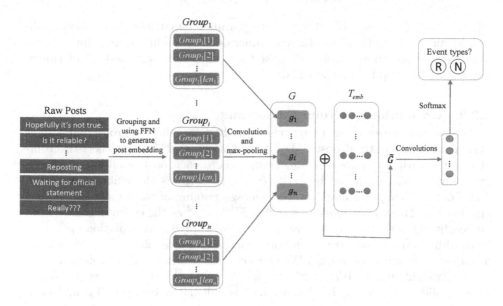

Fig. 1. The architecture of SGERD

3.2.1   Representation of Posts in Each Group

For an event instance e with n groups, our input consists of streams of posts, which can be interpreted as a time series where nearby posts are likely to be correlated. The work of Shen et al. [20] shown that a model only using simple operations (e.g., parameter-free pooling operation) on word embeddings may have comparable performance for some tasks. Inspired by their work, different from the procedure utilized in the literature [27] for rumor detection, we use average word embeddings to represent posts instead of paragraph vector [9] for a simpler procedure. Concretely, let $(v_1, v_2, ..., v_L)$ denote a sequence of words of a post, where each word v_i is represented by a d-dimensional word embedding trained by Word2Vec [15], and L is the number of words this specific post contains. We represent each post as the average word embeddings of this post: $\frac{1}{L}(\sum_{i=1}^{L} v_i)$. This operation can be viewed as average pooling and result in an embedding with the same dimension d as word embedding v_i.

However, post representation by average word embeddings is not task-oriented, i.e., it is represented by unsupervised method and thus not suitable for rumor detection. For the purpose of generating a representation of each post that fits for detecting rumor, we utilize a fully connected feed-forward network (FFN) [22] to apply to each post. It consists of two linear transformations with a hidden Rectified Linear Unit (ReLU) [17] nonlinearity in between as follows:

$$\text{FFN}(x) = \text{ReLU}(xW_1)W_2, \tag{1}$$

where $W_1 \in R^{d \times h}$ and $W_2 \in R^{h \times d}$ are parameter matrices. It uses trainable weight matrices to attend to different dimensions of the input, and thus we can obtain the representation of each post that more suits for the task of rumor detection after applied by the FFN.

3.2.2   Generation of Group Embedding

In this section we propose a supervised method to generate group embedding over a variable length of posts. We define $Group_i \in \mathbb{R}^{len_i \times d}$ as the i-th group of event e with a sequence of len_i posts, where each post is allocated by the grouping method proposed by [27], $Group_i[j] \in \mathbb{R}^d$ as the embedding of the j-th post in $Group_i$ obtained by the average pooling of word embeddings and applied Eq. (1), and $Group_i[j : j + len] \in \mathbb{R}^{(len+1) \times d}$ as the concatenation of the embeddings from post j up to post $j + len$. We apply the convolution operation to combine nearby posts from temporal windows of filter size, and extract local features for group embeddings. We denote a one-dimensional convolution filter F as a weight matrix $W_F \in \mathbb{R}^{ws \times d}$, where ws is the size of filter F. When F is applied to $Group_i$, the dot product is calculated between W_F and each possible windows of ws successive posts representations, then bias b_F is added and activation function f is applied. This results in a feature map $p \in \mathbb{R}^{len_i - ws + 1}$ with entry j as

$$p[j] = f(W_F \cdot Group_i[j : j + ws - 1] + b_F), \tag{2}$$

where $j \in [1, 1 + len_i - ws]$, $b_F \in \mathbb{R}$, f is a non-linear function such as ReLU. Note that the weights of convolutional kernels are shared across different groups. After the convolution operation, a sequence of local features of nearby posts is extracted, where each one is corresponding to posts of the same time window. Since many posts do not contribute to rumor detection, we want to restrain the non-salient local features and keep important features in the group embedding that are helpful for rumor detection. For this purpose, finally, we apply a max-over-time pooling operation [5] over the feature map p and take the maximum value as the salient feature. The general idea is to mine one significant feature with the highest value of each feature map corresponding to this specific filter, and meanwhile ignore some less important information. After the pooling operation, we aggregate the local features to obtain a global representation for groups, i.e., each group is represented by a fixed length vector $g_i \in \mathbb{R}^m$, whose size is equal to the number of filters.

To equip our SGERD with a sense of group order, as well as to model the influence of each group within different time windows, we incorporate temporal information $T = [t_1, t_2, ..., t_n]$ of e into the generated group embeddings, where each entry t_i is min-max normalized time interval of end time of the i-th group and start time of e, i.e. this time interval is the latest timestamp of post in the i-th group minus start time of e. This is similar to exploiting the information about the position of tokens in a sequence by position embeddings [2, 23]. In particular, we embed T by a weighted vector $V \in \mathbb{R}^n$ and a bias b_T, followed by a non-linear hyperbolic tangent (tanh), which results in T_{emb} with each row as:

$$T_{emb}[i] = \tanh(T \circ V^{\mathrm{T}} + b_T), \tag{3}$$

where $i \in [1, m]$, $b_T \in R$, and $\circ$ represents the element-wise multiplication.

Finally, both group embedding and temporal embedding are combined to obtain a temporal-aware group embedding: $\tilde{G} = G + T_{emb}$, where $G = [g_1, g_2, ..., g_n]$ and the columns of $\tilde{G}$ can be viewed as tuned group embeddings with the temporal information. Temporal embedding is useful in our architecture since they give our SGERD a sense of which parts of event it is currently dealing with and reflect different influence of each group (ref. Sect. 4.3).

3.2.3   Group Embedding-Based Rumor Detection

After constructing embedding for each group, we repeat the above convolution operation twice to extract low and high level group features from $\tilde{G}$, while these operations use different settings of filters. Then, a fully connected layer and the ultimate output $\hat{l}_e$ are obtained via softmax, where $\hat{l}_e$ is the predicted probability of event e being the category of rumor.

Our model is trained end-to-end by minimizing the following error over the training set D:

$$J = - \sum_{\forall e \in D} l_e \ln \hat{l}_e - \sum_{\forall e \in D} (1 - l_e) \ln (1 - \hat{l}_e) + \frac{\lambda}{2} \|\theta\|_2, \tag{4}$$

where l_e is the ground truth label of e, λ is the regularization term, and θ is the parameter set to be trained during learning. Training is done through stochastic gradient descent over shuffled mini-batches with Adam [6] update rule.

4   Experiment

In this section, we evaluate the performance of the proposed model for rumor detection. We have designed the experiments to achieve the following goals: (i) to compare the performance of different methods in detecting rumors, (ii) to evaluate the function of different components for learning group embedding, (iii) to evaluate the effectiveness of mainstream methods in early detection of rumors, and (iv) to validate the model performance by extracting salient posts which contribute more to detect rumors.

4.1 Dataset

Following previous works on rumor detection [12,27], we evaluate the effectiveness of our SGERD on two real-world datasets: Weibo and Twitter. There are 2,313 and 2,351 events belonging to rumor and non-rumor in Weibo, 498 and 494 events belonging to rumor and non-rumor in Twitter, respectively. As for temporal information, average time intervals of events are 2,460.7 h and 1,582.6 h for Weibo and Twitter, respectively. The above numbers of rumor events from Weibo were obtained from Sina community management center[2], and similar numbers of non-rumor events were gathered by crawling the posts of general threads that are not reported as rumors. For Twitter, rumor and non-rumor events were confirmed by Snopes[3]—an online rumor debunking service, and combined with some non-rumor events from two public datasets [1,8].

4.2 Experimental Settings

To demonstrate the effectiveness of our proposed SGERD on rumor detection, we have implemented the following baselines for comparison:

AIM is an attention-based method which utilizes both content and dynamic information of posts [10].

CAMI is based on two CNN hidden layers [27]. Input layer is content features of groups learned by paragraph vector [9], and groups have fixed number of twenty.

GRU-2 is based on two GRU hidden layers [11]. Input layer is content features represented by tf-idf, and time span of each group has variable length.

SVM-TS is a SVM classifier with linear kernel which uses time-series structures to model the variation of social context features [12]. These features are manually designed and based on contents, users and propagation patterns.

RFC is a Random Forest Classifier which aims to fit the temporal tweets volume curve with three parameters [8].

DT-Rank is a ranking model implemented by decision tree method to detect trending rumors, which ranks the clustered results by focusing on rumors with enquiry phrases and cluster disputed factual claims [28].

DTC is a Decision Tree Classifier, which models information credibility based on overall statistic handcrafted features [1].

SVM-RBF is a SVM-based Classifier adopting RBF kernel, which models information credibility based on overall statistic handcrafted features [25].

Note that although the method proposed by Ma et al. [14] can also detect rumor, jointly optimizing rumor detection and stance classification makes it unsuitable for comparison here. Methods that model propagation structures [13, 24] need propagation trees of posts for each event, thus they are not able to be compared for Weibo and Twitter. Following the setting of previous works [11,27], we select 10% of data for validation, and split the remaining 90% into training

---

[2] https://service.account.weibo.com/.
[3] https://www.snopes.com/.

and testing sets in a 3:1 ratio for both datasets. Note that validation, training and testing sets are stratified shuffled according to classes. We employ *Accuracy*, *Precision*, *Recall* and F_1 to evaluate the performance on rumor detection [27].

Our proposed SGERD is implemented based on Keras[4]. For each dataset, we set the regularization term λ to be 0.001, the dimensionality of word embedding d as 100, the inner layer dimensionality h of FFN as 50, and the filter size ws of each convolution layer as $(3, 3, 3)$. Finally, the corresponding filter numbers m for three layers are $(50, 20, 20)$ and $(50, 10, 10)$ for Weibo and Twitter, respectively. The above hyperparameters are tuned in the validation dataset.

4.3   Comparison with Baselines

Table 1 presents the performance of different methods in terms of *Accuracy*, *Precision*, *Recall*, and F_1. The accuracy on Twitter is generally much lower than on Weibo because Twitter is smaller than Weibo and has higher ratio of reposts. We can observe the performance ranking of these methods on rumor detection as follows: SGERD, CAMI, AIM, GRU-2, SVM-TS, RFC, DTC, SVM-RBF, and DT-Rank. All methods based on deep neural network (DNN) perform better than other conventional ones. The classical methods, i.e., SVM-TS, RFC, DTC, SVM-RBF, and DT-Rank, are mainly implemented by combining traditional classifiers with different sets of handcrafted features. They are not able to capture high-level features, thus fail to be effective in complicated scenarios of social media. In contrast, methods based on DNN, i.e., SGERD, CAMI, AIM, GRU-2, can dig out deep latent semantic features and tend to be adaptive to complicated scenarios. Furthermore, DT-Rank extracts organized expressions from posts with enquiry phrases, which is not common in the datasets we used. Thus relying on limited enquiry phrases, DT-Rank has rather restricted adaptability to different datasets. Compared to SVM-RBF and DTC, both SVM-TS and RFC achieve a better performance by integrating time-series structure, which confirms that temporal features are significant to rumor detection.

Among all DNN based methods, our proposed SGERD outperforms all previous published DNN based methods for rumor detection. All these methods can model high-level features and dig out deep latent semantic information of posts, and thus reach a high performance. However, these methods all have limitations. GRU-2 is capable of capturing the variation of contextual characteristic over rumor diffusion, but GRU-2 has bias towards the latest group which usually does not play a key role. CAMI has been proven as able to extract both local and global features through convolution operation and reveal those high-level interactions, but its major model structure is implemented based on simple CNN, which is not inherently equipped with a sense of group order. Both GRU-2 and CAMI use unsupervised methods to generate group embeddings, which do not consider the different importance of each post. AIM employs two kinds of attention mechanisms to help exploit dynamical information of each post, however, the potential interactions among nearby groups are discarded since grouping

---

[4] https://keras.io/.

Table 1. Rumor detection results (R: Rumor; N: Non-rumor)

Method	Class	Weibo				Twitter			
		Accuracy	Precision	Recall	F_1	Accuracy	Precision	Recall	F_1
AIM	R	0.911	0.930	0.887	0.908	0.767	0.759	0.786	0.772
	N		0.894	0.934	0.913		0.776	0.748	0.761
CAMI	R	0.926	0.922	**0.929**	0.925	0.771	**0.785**	0.750	0.767
	N		**0.930**	0.922	0.926		0.759	**0.793**	0.775
GRU-2	R	0.908	0.922	0.892	0.907	0.762	0.744	0.804	0.773
	N		0.894	0.923	0.908		0.784	0.721	0.751
SVM-TS	R	0.862	0.832	0.906	0.867	0.744	0.762	0.714	0.737
	N		0.897	0.819	0.856		0.729	0.775	0.751
RFC	R	0.847	0.802	0.919	0.857	0.731	0.724	0.750	0.737
	N		0.906	0.775	0.835		0.738	0.712	0.725
DT-Rank	R	0.737	0.691	0.852	0.763	0.682	0.678	0.696	0.687
	N		0.811	0.624	0.705		0.685	0.667	0.676
DTC	R	0.832	0.838	0.821	0.829	0.717	0.753	0.652	0.699
	N		0.827	0.843	0.835		0.690	0.784	0.734
SVM-RBF	R	0.820	0.827	0.806	0.816	0.722	0.740	0.688	0.713
	N		0.814	0.834	0.824		0.706	0.757	0.730
SGERD	R	**0.943**	**0.958**	0.925	**0.941**	**0.798**	0.782	**0.830**	**0.805**
	N		0.929	**0.960**	**0.944**		**0.817**	0.766	**0.791**

methods are not utilized. By overcoming these shortcomings, SGERD achieves a considerable performance improvement on rumor detection.

4.4   Ablation Experiments

To evaluate the function of different components for learning group embedding, we implement three variations of SGERD, denoted as SGERD - P, SGERD - G, SGERD - T_{emb}, respectively. Compared with SGERD, SGERD - P directly utilizes the unsupervised average word embeddings to generate group embedding, rather than learn the representation of each post with supervision. Similarly, SGERD - G is conducted by employing max-pooling operation over the supervised post embeddings to represent a group without convolution operation to learn local features for the group embedding. Note that these two variations of our model do not use temporal embedding. To investigate the functional performance of temporal embedding, SGERD - T_{emb} is implemented by removing temporal embedding from SGERD. The results of ablation experiments on rumor detection for each dataset are show in Table 2.

Compared to SGERD - T_{emb}, SGERD - P decreases its performance on both two datasets. SGERD - G decreases by 0.3% and 0.4% on Weibo and Twitter dataset, respectively. This shows that learning the representation of each post with supervision is helpful for the rumor detection task, because it can generate more task-oriented post embedding. Similarly, SGERD - G decreases by 0.5% and 0.9% on Weibo and Twitter dataset, respectively. This shows that

Table 2. Rumor detection results (R: Rumor; N: Non-rumor)

Method	Class	Weibo				Twitter			
		Accuracy	Precision	Recall	F_1	Accuracy	Precision	Recall	F_1
SGERD - P	R	0.934	0.928	0.940	0.934	0.785	**0.791**	0.777	0.784
	N		0.941	0.928	0.934		0.779	**0.793**	**0.786**
SGERD - G	R	0.932	**0.929**	0.935	0.932	0.780	0.756	**0.830**	0.791
	N		0.935	**0.930**	0.933		**0.810**	0.730	0.768
SGERD - T_{emb}	R	**0.937**	0.925	**0.950**	**0.937**	**0.789**	0.773	0.821	**0.797**
	N		**0.950**	0.924	**0.937**		0.808	0.757	0.781

the convolution operation for extracting local features of nearby posts is important to detect rumors. Furthermore, it is obvious that the decreased performance brought by SGERD - G is relatively significant when compared with SGERD - P. We assume that it is because the convolution operation can combine features of multiple posts in the same time windows, which may be discarded by directly employing max-pooling operation over the post embeddings. Compared to SGERD in Table 1, SGERD - T_{emb} decreases by 0.6% and 0.9% on Weibo and Twitter, respectively, which indicates that the temporal information of posts plays an important part on deciding whether or not an event is rumor, and our temporal embeddings successfully model the temporal features. Finally, all these variations without specific components still perform better than state-of-the-art methods, which indicates that it is better to model the post-level content using our supervised method than the unsupervised aggregation of groups.

4.5 Early Detection of Rumors

In practical occasion, rumor is usually requested to be detected as early as possible, and thus early detection of rumor is a crucial task. To investigate the performance of SGERD on early detection of rumors, we set several detection deadlines, posts after which are not considered in early detection. The mean official report time (ORT) of rumor given by the debunking services of Snopes and Sina community management center is taken as a reference. We conduct early detection experiments on AIM, CAMI, GRU-2 and SVM-TS for comparison, since these methods have the best performance among all mainstream methods. Although DT-Rank is mainly adopted in early detection task, its performance on rumor detection is much poorer than other baseline methods, and thus we do not take it into consideration.

Accuracy of different methods during different detection deadlines is presented in Fig. 2, from which we can observe that the accuracy curve of most methods will climb from a small value and gradually converge to a certain accuracy. During first several hours, the accuracy of SGERD climbs rapidly and tends to converge to a relatively high value at the earliest time, while other methods take longer time to converge and cannot reach such a high accuracy. The accuracy of SGERD will reach 91.4% for Weibo and 77.3% for Twitter within 12 h, which is much earlier than the official report time of rumor.

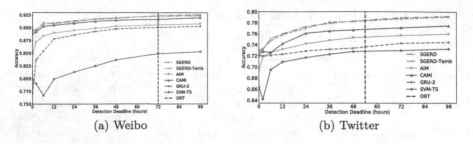

(a) Weibo   (b) Twitter

Fig. 2. Early detection performance of rumors

When discarding the temporal embedding, SGERD - T_{emb} achieves an accuracy curve nearly coinciding with that of SGERD, which indicates that temporal embedding has a rather limited impact on early detection. This is because the proposed temporal embedding is designed to model temporal information for sequences of posts, which requires the input sequence being long enough. However, for early detection of rumors, the detection deadlines are restricted in a certain range and the number of posts is limited, resulting in that the temporal features of posts cannot be captured and temporal embedding for early detection cannot be as effective as usual rumor detection. Similarly, SVM-TS and GRU-2 model time series information of the input sequences in a way which conflicts with the requirement of early detection. Therefore, SVM-TS and GRU-2 are unsuitable when the detection deadline is early, and the climbing rates of their accuracies curves are slow and the convergence accuracies are low. Without integrating the temporal information, CAMI can extract key features even with a short sequence of posts, and its accuracy curves therefore become steadier and keep in higher accuracy than GRU-2 and SVM-TS. However, CAMI does not consider the different importance of each post in the same group. AIM ignores the variation among the nearby groups as it does not group the posts. Therefore, their accuracy curves converge to lower levels when compared with SGERD. With the benefit of modeling from post level, our SGERD can mine useful posts and alleviate the negative effect of redundant posts, and it ranks the first for early detection in every stage.

4.6   Samples of the Salient Posts

Similar to the visualization work in information retrieval [21], we present samples of the salient posts extracted by SGERD. Firstly, for each post, we evaluate the output of CNN before the max-over-time pooling operation, i.e., picking out the largest output value p^* as in Eq. (2) among all the different filters to represent this post. Secondly, we sort all the posts according to their output value p^*, and trace back to posts that have large output value for each event. Finally, we get the salient posts making significant contribution to rumor detection. Figure 3 presents several events, from which we can visualize posts with large output values in blue that contribute more to rumor detection. Similarly, we illustrate trivial posts with small output values in green for comparison.

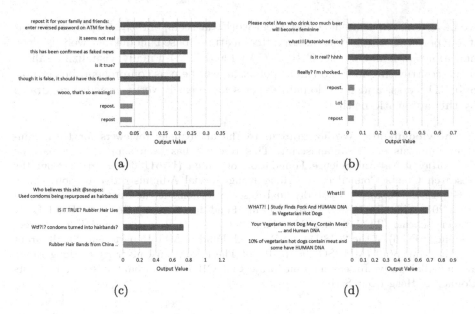

Fig. 3. Extracted salient and trivial posts in rumor events. Blue and green color represent posts with large and small output values, respectively. Note that the feature of a post is extracted from that post together with posts in the same window, but only the center post is selected here. (Color figure online)

Sample (a) is an identified rumor on Weibo about "Enter reversed password when robbers threaten you to take money from ATM and it will call the police for help secretly", sample (b) is an incorrect opinion of beer spreading on Weibo, which claims that beer causes male feminization, sample (c) is a false news of hairbands exported from China on Twitter, and sample (d) is a fabricated information on Twitter that vegetarian hot dog contains meat and human DNA. From above examples, we can observe that many posts express doubts and opposition to these events, such as "is it true?", have a relatively large output value, while the posts with small value are redundant (e.g., "repost") or just make a factual description. This step of visualization is especially useful for rumor detection because it provides explanatory information about how the model works, and helps understand better what is learned by SGERD.

5 Conclusions

In this paper, we have proposed a supervised group embedding based rumor detection model named SGERD. Our SGERD processes each event starting from posts and leverages the max-pooling operation to alleviate the effect of redundant posts, so it is able to pick out salient posts. Furthermore, SGERD incorporates temporal information to equip CNN with a sense of group order, and it models the influence of different groups. To demonstrate the effectiveness of our SGERD, we have done experiments on two real-world datasets, and the results show that it outperforms traditional handcrafted features based models as well as deep neural network models (i.e. GRU-2, CAMI and AIM). Finally, visualizing salient posts contributing more to rumor detection can help us comprehend better how SGERD works, and help domain experts more easily verify conclusions drawn by this automatic method.

Acknowledgments. We are grateful to the anonymous reviewers for their valuable comments on this manuscript. This research has been supported in part by the National Natural Science Foundation of China (U1611264), a grant from the Research Grants Council of the Hong Kong Special Administrative Region, China (UGC/FDS11/E03/16), the Individual Research Scheme of the Dean's Research Fund 2017–2018 (FLASS/DRF/IRS-8), Top-up Fund for General Research Fund/Early Career Scheme (TFG-3) and Seed Fund for General Research Fund/Early Career Scheme (SFG-6) of the 2018 Dean's Research Fund to MIT Department, Small Grant for Academic Staff (MIT/SGA05/18-19) of The Education University of Hong Kong, and a Collaborative Research Grant (project no. C1031-18G) from the Research Grants Council of Hong Kong SAR.

References

1. Castillo, C., Mendoza, M., Poblete, B.: Information credibility on Twitter. In: WWW, pp. 675–684 (2011)
2. Gehring, J., Auli, M., Grangier, D., Yarats, D., Dauphin, Y.N.: Convolutional sequence to sequence learning. In: ICML, pp. 1243–1252 (2017)
3. Gupta, A., Lamba, H., Kumaraguru, P., Joshi, A.: Faking sandy: characterizing and identifying fake images on Twitter during hurricane sandy. In: WWW, pp. 729–736 (2013)
4. Jin, Z., Cao, J., Zhang, Y., Luo, J.: News verification by exploiting conflicting social viewpoints in microblogs. In: AAAI, pp. 2972–2978 (2016)
5. Kim, Y.: Convolutional neural networks for sentence classification. In: EMNLP, pp. 1746–1751 (2014)
6. Kingma, D.P., Ba, J.: Adam: a method for stochastic optimization. CoRR abs/1412.6980 (2014)
7. Kumar, S., West, R., Leskovec, J.: Disinformation on the web: impact, characteristics, and detection of Wikipedia hoaxes. In: WWW, pp. 591–602 (2016)
8. Kwon, S., Cha, M., Jung, K., Chen, W., Wang, Y.: Prominent features of rumor propagation in online social media. In: ICDM, pp. 1103–1108 (2013)
9. Le, Q.V., Mikolov, T.: Distributed representations of sentences and documents. In: ICML, pp. 1188–1196 (2014)
10. Liu, Q., Yu, F., Wu, S., Wang, L.: Mining significant microblogs for misinformation identification: an attention-based approach. ACM Trans. Intell. Syst. Technol. **9**(5), 50:1–50:20 (2018)
11. Ma, J., et al.: Detecting rumors from microblogs with recurrent neural networks. In: IJCAI, pp. 3818–3824 (2016)
12. Ma, J., Gao, W., Wei, Z., Lu, Y., Wong, K.: Detect rumors using time series of social context information on microblogging websites. In: CIKM, pp. 1751–1754 (2015)

13. Ma, J., Gao, W., Wong, K.: Detect rumors in microblog posts using propagation structure via kernel learning. In: ACL, pp. 708–717 (2017)
14. Ma, J., Gao, W., Wong, K.: Detect rumor and stance jointly by neural multi-task learning. In: WWW Companion, pp. 585–593 (2018)
15. Mikolov, T., Chen, K., Corrado, G., Dean, J.: Efficient estimation of word representations in vector space. CoRR abs/1301.3781 (2013)
16. Mikolov, T., Kombrink, S., Burget, L., Cernocký, J., Khudanpur, S.: Extensions of recurrent neural network language model. In: ICASSP, pp. 5528–5531 (2011)
17. Nair, V., Hinton, G.E.: Rectified linear units improve restricted Boltzmann machines. In: ICML, pp. 807–814 (2010)
18. Qazvinian, V., Rosengren, E., Radev, D.R., Mei, Q.: Rumor has it: identifying misinformation in microblogs. In: EMNLP, pp. 1589–1599 (2011)
19. Rieh, S.Y., Jeon, G.Y., Yang, J.Y., Lampe, C.: Audience-aware credibility: from understanding audience to establishing credible blogs. In: ICWSM, pp. 436–445 (2014)
20. Shen, D., et al.: Baseline needs more love: on simple word-embedding-based models and associated pooling mechanisms. In: ACL, pp. 440–450 (2018)
21. Shen, Y., He, X., Gao, J., Deng, L., Mesnil, G.: A latent semantic model with convolutional-pooling structure for information retrieval. In: CIKM, pp. 101–110 (2014)
22. Tan, Z., Wang, M., Xie, J., Chen, Y., Shi, X.: Deep semantic role labeling with self-attention. In: AAAI, pp. 4929–4936 (2018)
23. Vaswani, A., et al.: Attention is all you need. In: NIPS, pp. 6000–6010 (2017)
24. Wong, K., Gao, W., Ma, J.: Rumor detection on twitter with tree-structured recursive neural networks. In: ACL, pp. 1980–1989 (2018)
25. Yang, F., Liu, Y., Yu, X., Yang, M.: Automatic detection of rumor on Sina Weibo. In: SIGKDD Workshop, pp. 13:1–13:7 (2012)
26. Yin, W., Schütze, H.: Convolutional neural network for paraphrase identification. In: HLT-NAACL, pp. 901–911 (2015)
27. Yu, F., Liu, Q., Wu, S., Wang, L., Tan, T.: A convolutional approach for misinformation identification. In: IJCAI, pp. 3901–3907 (2017)
28. Zhao, Z., Resnick, P., Mei, Q.: Enquiring minds: early detection of rumors in social media from enquiry posts. In: WWW, pp. 1395–1405 (2015)

Fast Incremental PageRank on Dynamic Networks

Zexing Zhan[1,2], Ruimin Hu[1,2(✉)], Xiyue Gao[1,2], and Nian Huai[1,2]

[1] National Engineering Research Center for Multimedia Software,
School of Computer Science, Wuhan University, Wuhan 430072, China
hrm@whu.edu.com
[2] Hubei Key Laboratory of Multimedia and Network Communication Engineering,
Wuhan University, Wuhan 430072, China

Abstract. Real-world networks are very large and are constantly changing. Computing PageRank values for such dynamic networks is an important challenge in network science. In this paper, we propose an efficient Monte Carlo based algorithm for PageRank tracking on dynamic networks. A revisit probability model is also presented to provide theoretical support for our algorithm. For a graph with n nodes, the proposed algorithm maintains only nR random walk segments (R random walks starting from each node) in memory. The time cost to update PageRank scores for each graph modification is proportional to $n/|E|$ (E is the edge set). Experiments on 5 real-world networks indicate that our algorithm is 1.3–30 times faster than state-of-the-art algorithms and does not accumulate any errors.

Keywords: PageRank tracking · Monte Carlo · Random walk · Incremental computing · Dynamic networks

1 Introduction

PageRank [6] was first used by Google in 1998 to provide better results in their search engine. It measures the popularity of a web page from the topological structure of the Web, independent of the page content. Over the last decades, PageRank has emerged as a very effective measure of reputation for both web graphs and online social networks, which was historically known as eigenvector centrality [5] or Katz centrality [11]. However, real-world networks are very large and are evolving rapidly. For example, there are 60T web pages in the Web, and it grows with more than 600K new pages every second. In this case, PageRank algorithms that work only for static networks are insufficient, especially when it is desirable to track PageRank values in real-time rather than to wait for a batched computation.

This work was supported by the National Natural Science Foundation of China [grant No. U1736206] and the National Key R&D Program of China [grant No. 2017YFC0803700].

A dynamic network is a sequence of graphs $\{G(t) : t = 0, 1, 2, ...\}$, so that $G(t + 1)$ is obtained by inserting an edge to or removing an edge from $G(t)$. To efficiently track PageRank scores on dynamic networks, incremental algorithms are necessary. Currently, there are two main categories of incremental PageRank algorithms: aggregation algorithms and Monte Carlo based algorithms. A detailed description of these algorithms is provided in Sects. 2 and 3. In this paper, we focus on Monte Carlo based algorithms. Existing Monte Carlo based algorithms have two main drawbacks. Firstly, they accumulate errors over lengthy evolution. Both [3] and [14] simply assume that a random walk would never revisit a node. This assumption however is not the truth, which makes the approximation error accumulate quickly on real-world networks. Also, since [14] does not save any random walk segments, its way to adjust previous random walk segments also brings error. Secondly, they are inefficient. For each graph modification, existing algorithms simulate too many unnecessary random walks to update PageRank values. Besides, [3] keeps a duplicate of a random walk segment for every node it is passing through, which makes it really a disaster to maintain them.

To address those two limitations mentioned above, we propose a novel Monte Carlo based algorithm for PageRank tracking on dynamic networks. Our method supposes each edge has its own revisit probability as is often the case in real-world networks. A revisit probability model is presented to provide theoretical support for our algorithm. Besides, our method saves only nR random walk segments (R random walks starting from each node) in memory. An efficient and well structure method is implemented to maintains these random walk segments. Experiments on several real-world networks show that our method is 1.3–30 times faster than state-of-the-art algorithms and does not accumulate any errors in long-term evolution. Our main contributions are as follows:

- Theory: we propose the revisit probability model for analyzing Monte Carlo based PageRank tracking problem.
- Algorithm: we propose an efficient algorithm that also improves the accuracy.
- Experiments: we report experiments on 5 real-world networks, and compare our algorithm to state-of-the-art methods.

The rest of the paper is structured as follows. Section 2 describes some preliminaries for Monte Carlo based algorithms; Sect. 3 surveys related works; Sect. 4 presents the revisit probability model and the proposed algorithm; Sect. 5 reports experimental results; Finally, Sect. 6 concludes this work.

2 Preliminaries

Before describing related work, we briefly describe some preliminaries for Monte Carlo based PageRank tracking algorithms.

2.1   PageRank

The basic idea of PageRank is that more important pages are likely to receive more links from other pages. That means, the importance of a page depends on the number and quality of links to the page. Hence, the PageRank value π_v of page v is computed by taking into account the set of pages $\boldsymbol{in}_v$ pointing to v. According to Brin and Page [6]:

$$\pi_v = \alpha \sum_{u \in in_v} \frac{\pi_u}{outdeg_u} + (1 - \alpha). \tag{1}$$

Here $\alpha \in (0, 1)$ is the teleport probability and $outdeg_u$ is the outdegree of page u, that is the number of hyperlinks coming out from u. When stacking all π_v into a vector $\boldsymbol{\pi}$, we get:

$$\boldsymbol{\pi} = \alpha \boldsymbol{P} \boldsymbol{\pi} + (1 - \alpha) \boldsymbol{1}. \tag{2}$$

where $\boldsymbol{1} = [1, ..., 1]$ and $\boldsymbol{P} = \{p_{v,u}\}$ is the transition matrix, such that $p_{v,u} = 1/outdeg_u$ if there is a hyperlink from u to v and $p_{v,u} = 0$, otherwise.

2.2   Approximating PageRank

The Monte Carlo method [2] approximates PageRank by simulating exactly R random walks starting from each node in a graph. Each of these random walks can be terminated at each step either with probability ϵ (here we call ϵ as the reset probability and $\epsilon = 1 - \alpha$), or when it reaches a dangling node. A dangling node is a node that does not contain any out edge. Assume for each node u, V_u is the total number of times that all simulated random walks visit v. Then, we approximate the PageRank of v, denoted by π_u, with:

$$\tilde{\pi}_u = \frac{V_u}{nR/\epsilon} \tag{3}$$

where n is the number of nodes in a graph.

2.3   Updating PageRank

By storing all simulated random walk segments, the original Monte Carlo method allows to perform continuous update of the PageRank as the structure of the graph changes. However, when an edge $e(u, w)$ is modified at time $t + 1$, it has to adjust all those random walk segments passing through node u at time t. Fortunately, [3] proved that a random walk segment needs to be adjusted only if it visits the node u and picks w as the next node. In expectation, the number of times a walk segment visits u is $\frac{\pi_u}{\epsilon}$. For each such visit, the probability for the walk to need a reroute is $\frac{1}{outdeg_u(t+1)}$. And there are a total of nR random walk segments. Define M_{t+1} to be the number of random walk segments that need to be adjusted at time $t + 1$. By union bound, we have:

$$E[M_{t+1}] \le \frac{nR}{\epsilon} E[\frac{\tilde{\pi}_u(t)}{outdeg_u(t+1)}]. \tag{4}$$

3   Related Work

In this section, we review some works for tracking PageRank on evolving networks. A simple way to keep the PageRank scores updated is to recompute the values using the simple power iteration method [6] for each change in the network. But, this can be very costly. For a network that has n nodes, with a reset probability of ϵ, it takes $\Omega(\frac{kn^2}{1/(1-\epsilon)})$ total time to recompute the PageRank values for k edge modifications. Similarly, the Monte Carlo method [2], working by simulating exactly R random walk starting from each node, results in a total $\Omega(\frac{knR}{\epsilon})$ work, which is also inefficient. Therefore, lots of incremental methods were proposed for updating the approximation of PageRank. Based on their core techniques, these methods can be categorized into two general categories:

- Aggregation Algorithms

The basic observation of methods in this category is that evolution of the graph is slow, with large parts of it remaining unchanged. Based on that, several aggregation algorithms were proposed in [7,8,10,19]. When an edge $e(u, w)$ is inserted to or removed from a network at time $t + 1$, these algorithms carefully find a small subset $S(t)$ of nodes around u and w whose PageRank values need to be updated. By contracting all other vertices $V \backslash S(t)$ to a single super node s, a small network $\bar{G}(t)$ is obtained. Then, these algorithms compute PageRank scores on the small network $\bar{G}(t)$ using static PageRank algorithms. The main disadvantage of these method is in accuracy. It depends largely on the choice of the subset $S(t)$. Although several methods for choosing $S(t)$ had been discussed in [13], but no theoretical guarantee was provided. Furthermore, even if the approximation error at time t is small, approximation errors can accumulate in long-term evolution [17].

- Monte Carlo based Algorithms

In order to explain the computational properties of PageRank, [16] shows that the general theory of Markov chains [18] can be applied to PageRank if the Web does not contain dangling nodes [4]. Under this hypothesis, [2] proposed and analyzed several Monte Carlo type methods for approximating PageRank, which allow to perform continuous update of the PageRank as the structure of the graph changes. These methods form the basis of Monte Carlo based algorithms for PageRank tracking. But they are very inefficient. Lately, [3] showed that a random walk segment needs to be adjusted only if it passes through the modified edge. However, denote M_{t+1} as the actual number of random walk segments needed to be adjusted, they provided only a upper bound of M_{t+1} in expectation for performance analysis as In Eq. (4), that can not be directly used in practice. This algorithm stores all random walk segments in a database, where each segment is stored at every node that it passes through, i.e., totally $\frac{nR}{\epsilon}$ random walk segments. For each node u, they also keep two counters: one, denoted by $W_u(t)$, keeping track of the number of random walk segments visiting u, and one, denoted by $outdeg_u(t)$, keeping track of the outdegree of u. Then, when an edge $e(u,w)$ is inserted or removed, with probability $1 - (\frac{outdeg_u(t)-1}{outdeg_u(t)})^{W_u(t)}$ it adjusts all random walk segments passing through node u. Interestingly, when a graph is build from scratch with k edges inserted, the time complexity is less than $\Omega(\frac{nR\ln k}{\epsilon})$ to keep PageRank scores updated all the time [3,15]. Another more efficient algorithm that stores no random walk segment was proposed in [14]. For each node u, this method keeps only a counter, denoted by $V_u(t)$, keeping track of the total times that all random walk segments visiting u. To adjust a random walk segment, we must first remove it, then simulate a new one. This method removes a previous random walk segment by simulating a new random walk and decrease $V_u(t)$ by 1 for every node u it is passing through. Although the random walk segment to be removed and the new simulated one follow the same distribution, they are actually different segments. Hence, its way to adjust random walk segments also brings error.

4   Proposed Method

Here, we present a novel method for tracking PageRank on evolving networks. The proposed method is an adaptation of the Monte Carlo method. We first present the revisit probability model, which provides theoretical support for our algorithm. Then we propose our algorithm.

4.1   The Revisit Probability Model

Previous works did not consider the situation that a random walk may revisit an edge or a node. However, this situation is so common that we can not ignore it. Let r_{uv} be the revisit probability of edge $e(u,v)$, we define it as following.

Definition 1 (edge revisit probability). *For a graph $G(t)$, $r_{uv}(t)$ is the probability that a random walk staring from node u and picking v as the next node (passing through edge $e(u,v)$) revisits the node u.*

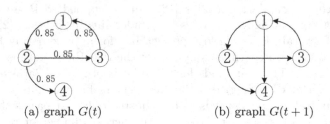

(a) graph $G(t)$ (b) graph $G(t+1)$

Fig. 1. Initial graph $G(t)$ and $G(t+1)$ with edge $e(1,4)$ inserted.

To get a better sense of $r_{uv}(t)$, we use Example 1 for explanation. It should be aware that r_{uv} is determined only by the reset probability ϵ and the graph structure. Before describe Example 1, we provide the definitions of random walk path and random walk segment here.

Definition 2 (random walk path). *A random walk path is an unique and finite sequence of nodes denoted as* $\{u_1, u_2, u_3, u_4, ..., u_n\}$, *where there is an edge from* u_{i-1} *to* u_i.

Definition 3 (random walk segment). *A random walk segment is an instance of a random walk path.*

Example 1. In this example, we calculate $r_{12}(t)$ on graph $G(t)$ in Fig. 1(a) with $\epsilon = 0.15$. We let a random walk terminate: with probability ϵ at each step; when it reaches a dangling node; when it revisits node ①. We list the probability of all random walk paths starting from edge $e(1, 2)$ in Table 1. Among all these random walk paths, only path 4 revisits node ①. Therefore, by Definition 1 we get $r_{12}(t) = 0.36125$, which is quite a high probability.

Table 1. The probability of all paths starting from $e(1, 2)$ in $G(t)$.

No.	Path x	$\mathbb{P}(X = x)$	
1.	① → ②	0.15	0.15
2.	① → ② → ④	$0.85 \times \frac{1}{2}$	0.425
3.	① → ② → ③	$0.85 \times \frac{1}{2} \times 0.15$	0.06375
4.	① → ② → ③ → ①	$0.85 \times \frac{1}{2} \times 0.85$	0.36125
Sum.			1

Then we define the probability that a random walk starting from node u revisits the node u at time t as

$$R_u(t) = \sum_{v \in out_u(t)} \frac{1 - \epsilon}{outdeg_u(t)} r_{uv}(t), \tag{5}$$

where $out_u(t)$ is the set of nodes that u pointing out to. Since any random walk can terminate at node u with probability ϵ, we should multiply it by $1 - \epsilon$.

Assume $W_u(t)$ is the number of random walk segments passing though u at time t, and $V_u(t)$ is the total times visited by those random walk segments. The relation between $V_u(t)$ and $W_u(t)$ can be express with $R_u(t)$ as the sum of a geometric series

$$V_u(t) = W_u(t)(1 + R_u^1(t) + R_u^2(t) + ...) = \frac{W_u(t)}{1 - R_u(t)}. \tag{6}$$

For a large and complex network, it is impossible to compute $R_u(t)$ directly as in Example 1. So, we use an estimation of $R_u(t)$ as

$$\widetilde{R}_u(t) = 1 - \frac{W_u(t)}{V_u(t)}. \tag{7}$$

We also find the following two observations when a graph changes, which make it possible for accurate PageRank tracking.

Observation 1. *When an edge $e(u, w)$ is modified at time $t + 1$, r_{uv} remains unchanged for any node $v \in \boldsymbol{out}_u(t)$ and $v \neq w$, where $\boldsymbol{out}_u(t)$ is the set of nodes that u pointing out to.*

Proof. r_{uv} is affected if and only if any random walk path starting from edge $e(u, v)$ visits the modified edge $e(u, w)$ before it revisits node u. However, if a path visits the modified edge $e(u, w)$, then it must first pass through node u. So we prove the proposition.

Similarly, we can prove that the following Observation 2 is also true.

Observation 2. *When an edge $e(u, w)$ is modified at time $t + 1$, walk count $W_u(t+1)$ remains unchanged but visit count $V_u(t+1)$ is affected, i.e., $W_u(t+1) = W_u(t)$ but $V_u(t + 1) \neq V_u(t)$.*

We already know that a random walk segment needs to be adjusted only if it visits the modified edge. Denote M_{t+1} as the actual number of random walk segments that need to be adjusted. With the revisit probability model, the core problem of PageRank tracking can be defined as

Definition 4 (core problem). *Given a graph $G(t)$ and the modified edge $e(u, w)$ at time $t + 1$, compute the value of M_{t+1} by using $W_u(t)$, $V_u(t)$ and $R_u(t)$.*

In the rest part of this section, we show how to solve this problem. We treat adding an edge and removing an edge separately, since they are different. When adding an edge $e(u, w)$ at time $t + 1$, no random walk segment really passes through the new edge $e(u, w)$ at time t, i.e., things have not happened yet. And when removing an edge $e(u, w)$ at time $t + 1$, some random walk segments did pass through the removing edge $e(u, w)$ at time t.

Adding an Edge. When adding an edge $e(u, w)$ to a graph $G(t)$, we get $outdeg_u(t + 1) = outdeg_u(t) + 1$. And from Eq. (5), we have

$$R_u(t + 1) = \frac{(1 - \epsilon)r_{uw} + outdeg_u(t)R_u(t)}{outdeg_u(t + 1)}. \tag{8}$$

We first prove the following proposition:

Proposition 1. *When adding an edge $e(u, w)$ to a graph $G(t)$ at time $t + 1$, M_{t+1} is given by:*

$$M_{t+1} = \frac{W_u(t)}{outdeg_u(t + 1) - outdeg_u(t)R_u(t)}. \tag{9}$$

Proof. When $W_u(t)$ random walks set off from node u at time $t + 1$, $\frac{outdeg_u(t)}{outdeg_u(t+1)}$ of them pick previous $outdeg_u(t)$ edges of u as the next step, and $\frac{1}{outdeg_u(t+1)}$ of them pick the new adding edge $e(u, w)$. Any random walk picking the new adding edge $e(u, w)$ will need to be adjusted. If we let the this part of them just terminate there, then all random walks will visit the new adding edge $e(u, w)$ no more than once. After several steps, $R_u(t)$ of those random walks picking previous $outdeg_u(t)$ edges return to the node u. These random walks set off from node u again. We repeat this process until no random walk return to the node u. Therefore, we could count the total times that all $W_u(t)$ random walks visit node u as

$$V_{all} = W_u(t)(1 + \frac{outdeg_u(t)R_u(t)}{outdeg_u(t+1)} + ...) = \frac{W_u(t)}{1 - \frac{outdeg_u(t)R_u(t)}{outdeg_u(t+1)}}. \qquad (10)$$

Since we let a random walk terminate when it visits the new adding edge $e(u, w)$, it is obvious that $M_{t+1} = \frac{V_{all}}{outdeg_u(t+1)}$. So we prove the proposition.

Removing an Edge. Removing an edge $e(u, w)$ from a graph $G(t)$ can be viewed as an inverse modification of adding an edge, so we have $outdeg_u(t) = outdeg_u(t+1) + 1$ and

$$R_u(t) = \frac{(1 - \epsilon)r_{uw} + outdeg_u(t+1)R_u(t+1)}{outdeg_u(t)}. \qquad (11)$$

Similarly to adding an edge, the following Proposition 2 also proves to be true.

Proposition 2. *When removing an edge $e(u, w)$ from a graph $G(t)$ at time $t+1$, M_{t+1} is given by:*

$$M_{t+1} = \frac{W_u(t)}{outdeg_u(t) - outdeg_u(t+1)R_u(t+1)}. \qquad (12)$$

However, we only know the estimation of $R_u(t)$ instead of $R_u(t+1)$. Remember that our method stores all nR random walk segments. So when removing an edge $e(u, w)$ from a graph, M_{t+1} is just the number of random walk segments passing through edge $e(u, w)$. This problem is also solved.

4.2 Algorithm for Tracking PageRank

For a graph with n nodes, our algorithm maintains only nR random walk segments (R random walks starting from each node) in memory. Each random walk segment is assigned an unique id, called segment id. We save all these random walk segments in a hash-table, so that they can be accessed in $O(1)$ time. For each node u, our method also keeps a counter and a set: the counter, denoted by $V_u(t)$, keeping track of the total times that all random walk segments visiting u at time t, the set, denoted by $S_u(t)$, keeping track of all random segments' id who pass through node u at time t. Then the number of random walk segments passing through u, denoted by $W_u(t)$ is equal to size of $S_u(t)$, i.e., $W_u(t) = |S_u(t)|$. Every time we add or remove a random walk segment, $V_u(t)$ and $S_u(t)$ are automatically updated in $O(1/\epsilon)$ time as in Algorithm 1.

Algorithm 1. Segment Management

Let $S_u(t)$ be a set, $V_u(t)$ be a value kept for node u and sid be the segment id.
1: **function** ADDSEGMENT($sid, newSeg$)
2:   **for** each u in $newSeg$ **do**
3:     $V_u(t)\ +=\ 1$
4:     Add sid to $S_u(t)$
5:   **end for**
6:   Add $newSeg$ to hash-table with key sid
7: **end function**
8:
9: **function** REMOVESEGMENT(sid)
10:   Get segment seg from hash-table with key sid
11:   **for** each u in seg **do**
12:     $V_u(t)\ -=\ 1$
13:     **if** sid in $S_u(t)$ **then**
14:       remove sid from $S_u(t)$
15:     **end if**
16:   **end for**
17:   Remove seg from hash-table
18: **end function**

Algorithm 2. Adding or removing node

Let u be the node added or removed.
1: **function** ADDNODE(u)
2:   **for** $i = 0 \rightarrow R$ **do**
3:     $sid, newSeg \leftarrow$ simulate a random walk starting from w
4:     Call AddSegment($sid, newSeg$)
5:   **end for**
6: **end function**
7:
8: **function** REMOVENODE(u)
9:   **for** each sid whose segment starts from u **do**
10:     Call RemoveSegment(sid)
11:   **end for**
12: **end function**

The original static Monte Carlo method in [2] is used as an initial solution for our method. When adding an edge $e(u,w)$ to a graph $G(t)$ at time $t+1$, for each random walk segment in $S_u(t)$, with probability $M_{t+1}/W_u(t)$ we redo it starting from the new edge $e(u,w)$. That means, we redo a random walk segment starting from where the first time it visits node u, and force it to pick node w as the next node. When removing an edge $e(u,w)$ from a graph $G(t)$ at time $t+1$, all random walk segments passing through edge $e(u,w)$ need to be adjust. For each random walk segment, we simply redo it starting from where the first time it visits node u.

Sometimes, when adding or removing an edge $e(u,w)$, nodes u and w are also added or removed. Remember that the original Monte Carlo method simulates exactly R random walks starting from each node in a graph. So, when a node u is added to a graph, we also simulate R random walks starting from u. And when a node u is removed from a graph, we also remove all random walk segments starting from u. The proposed method is summarized in Algorithms 2 and 3.

Algorithm 3. Adding or removing edge

Let $e(u, w)$ be the edge modified at time $t + 1$.
```
 1: function ADDEDGE(e(u, w))
 2:     Compute M_{t+1} as in Eq. (9)
 3:     Add e(u, w) to graph G(t)
 4:     for each sid in S_u(t) do
 5:         if random(0, 1) ≤ M_{t+1}/|S_u(t)| then
 6:             newSeg ← redo segment starting from the new edge e(u, w).
 7:             Call RemoveSegment(sid)
 8:             Call AddSegment(sid, newSeg)
 9:         end if
10:     end for
11:     if node u is new added then
12:         Call AddNode(u)
13:     end if
14:     if node w is new added then
15:         Call AddNode(w)
16:     end if
17: end function
18:
19: function REMOVEEDGE(e(u, w))
20:     Remove e(u, w) from graph G(t)
21:     for each sid whose segment passes through e(u, w) do
22:         newSeg ← redo segment starting from the first node u.
23:         Call RemoveSegment(sid)
24:         Call AddSegment(sid, newSeg)
25:     end for
26:     if node u is removed then
27:         Call RemoveNode(u)
28:     end if
29:     if node w is removed then
30:         Call RemoveNode(w)
31:     end if
32: end function
```

---

5 Experiments

In this section, we conducted experiments with real-world dynamic networks. The overview of our experiments is as follows:

- Experimental settings (Sect. 5.1): The platform and datasets we used in our experiments are present here. We also introduced the comparison methods and parameter settings.
- Accuracy (Sect. 5.2): We evaluated the accuracy of the proposed algorithm. We first verified that the proposed method does not accumulate errors in long term evolution. Then we compared our algorithm to existing methods.
- Efficiency and scalability (Sect. 5.3): We first investigated the average update time for a single edge modification. We observed that the proposed algorithm is 1.3–30 times faster than state-of-the-art algorithms. Then we showed that the proposed algorithm is also suitable for large networks.

5.1 Experimental Settings

We conducted the experiments on a desktop computer with 8 GB of RAM and AMD CPU R5-2400G@ 3.60 GHz running Windows 10. 5 real-world dynamic graphs with time-stamps, obtained from http://snap.stanford.edu/data/ and http://konect.cc/networks/, were used in our experiments, which are listed in Table 2.

Table 2. Dynamic networks that we experimented with.

Dataset	email-Enron	email-Eu-core	wiki-talk-ja	facebook-wosn	sx-askubuntu
Static nodes	3.6K	1K	0	52K	0
Dynamic nodes	75K	0	397K	11K	159K
Static edges	43K	25.6K	0	1.28M	0
Dynamic edges	3.0M	33.2K	1.0M	1.81M	964K

During our experiments, we compared our approach with the IMCPR algorithm proposed in [14], and the BahmaniPR algorithm proposed in [3]. The original static Monte Carlo based PageRank algorithm (MCPR) proposed in [2] was used as the ground-truth method. A detailed description of how these algorithms work could be found in Sects. 3 and 4.

There are two errors in the IMCPR method that make it perform very poor and unstable. Firstly, it computes M_{t+1} by $V_u(t)/(outdeg_u(t)-1)$ when removing an edge, which will cause a divide by zero error if $outdeg_u(t) = 1$. Secondly, it adds or removes an edge before it simulates a random walk to remove a previous random walk segment. The order is wrong, which causes the random walk segment to be removed and the new simulated one do not follow the same distribution. We fixed these two errors and named the new version IMCPR2, which is the actual algorithm we used for comparison.

All algorithms were implemented in Python 2.7, and ran with parameters $\epsilon = 0.15$ and $R = 16$.

5.2 Accuracy

We first evaluated the accuracy of the proposed method. The accuracy is measured by cosine similarity defined as

$$Accuracy = \cos(\widetilde{\pi}, \pi),$$

where π is the "ground-truth" PageRank vector by MCPR and $\widetilde{\pi}$ is the approximation by evaluated algorithms.

For adding edges, the initial network $G(0)$ was set as a network with all static edges, and an initial PageRank solution was also computed by the MCPR method. Then we inserted dynamic edges one-by-one in time order, which follows the preferential attachment model [1]. Similarly, for removing edges, we set the initial network $G(0)$ as the whole graph with both static edges and dynamic edges. We then sequentially removed dynamic edges from the current network in reverse time order. We traced the accuracy every time 4% percentages of dynamic edges were inserted or deleted. The results are shown in Fig. 2. These show that the proposed algorithm does not accumulate any errors in long-term evolution.

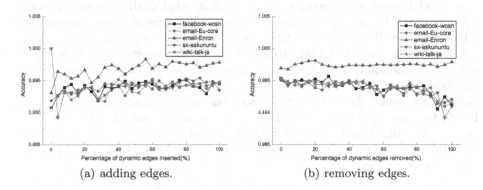

(a) adding edges.   (b) removing edges.

Fig. 2. PageRank tracking accuracy of this work on 5 real-world networks.

We also plotted the comparison results on email-Eu-core network in Fig. 3. Results show that the proposed method performs best both in adding and deleting edges. And IMCPR2 accumulates errors more faster than BahmaniPR in long-term evolution. The reasons are as follows:

- Both IMCPR2 and BahmaniPR lack theory supports, so the estimation of M_{t+1} or the probability they used for PageRank tacking are not accurate;
- IMCPR2 does not save any random walk segment, therefore its way to adjust random walk segments also brings error;
- IMCPR2 deals with an added or removed node u by setting $V_u(t) = R$ or 0, which is not correct.

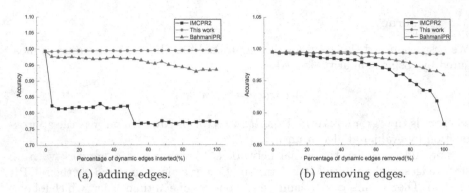

(a) adding edges.   (b) removing edges.

Fig. 3. Accuracy comparison of the algorithms on network email-Eu-core.

5.3 Efficiency and Scalability

Here, we investigated the efficiency and scalability of the proposed method. As in the previous accuracy evaluation, the network with only static edges was set as the initial network $G(0)$ for adding edges, and the whole graph with both static edges and dynamic edges was set as the initial network $G(0)$ for removing edges. We measured the average update time for a single edge insertion and deletion. The results are list in Table 3. These show that the proposed method is about 1.3 times faster than IMCPR2 algorithm and 30 times faster than BahmaniPR algorithm. BahmaniPR method is slow because it adjusts too many unnecessary random walk segments to update PageRank scores for a single edge modification. And since IMCPR2 method does not save any random walk segment, it has to simulate $2M_{t+1}$ random walks for each edge modification. However, our experiments show that simulating M_{t+1} random walks is much slower than updating M_{t+1} saved random walk segments in memory, especially for graphs with weighted edges.

Table 3. Average update time (ms) for inserting or deleting a single edge.

Dataset	email-Enron		email-Eu-core		wiki-talk-ja		facebook-wosn		sx-askubuntu	
	ins	del	ins	del	ins	del	ins	del	ins	del
This work	0.57	0.46	0.41	0.29	42.0	36.4	2.06	1.87	4.83	3.17
IMCPR2	0.89	0.65	0.73	0.64	65.8	49.2	3.43	2.56	8.01	5.19
BahmaniPR	20.6	17.4	16.5	13.2	–	–	50.3	46.2	74.1	59.8

We also verified that the proposed algorithm is scalable for large networks. For a graph with n nodes, the update time for a single edge modification is actually inversely proportional to the average outdegree $|E|/n$, where E is the edge set. To verify this claim, we plotted the relation between the average update

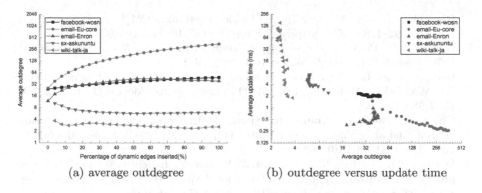

(a) average outdegree   (b) outdegree versus update time

Fig. 4. Scalability of the proposed method.

time and the average outdegree $|E|/n$ in Fig. 4(b). We measured the average outdegree and the average update time every time 4% percentages of dynamic edges were inserted. Results on real-world datasets show that the average update time of 4 networks except email-Enron are inversely proportional to their average outdegree. And the email-Eu-core network, which does not contain any added or removed nodes, perfectly supports our claim. Figure 4(a) also shows that the average outdegree of a graph keeps stable or increases when it grows larger. Therefore our algorithm is also suitable for large networks.

6   Conclusions

In this paper, we proposed an efficient PageRank tracking algorithm on dynamic networks, which does not accumulate errors in long term evolution. The proposed algorithm is practically 1.3–30 times faster than state-of-the-art algorithms. We also presented a revisit probability model, which overcomes existing limitations of state-of-the-art Monte Carlo algorithms for tracking PageRank in dynamic networks. In future work, we hope to extend our method to Personalized PageRank [9,12,20] as well.

References

1. Albert, R., Barabási, A.L.: Statistical mechanics of complex networks. Rev. Mod. Phys. **74**, 47–97 (2002). https://doi.org/10.1103/RevModPhys.74.47. https://link.aps.org/doi/10.1103/RevModPhys.74.47
2. Avrachenkov, K., Litvak, N., Nemirovsky, D., Osipova, N.: Monte Carlo methods in PageRank computation: when one iteration is sufficient. SIAM J. Numer. Anal. **45**(2), 890–904 (2007). https://doi.org/10.1137/050643799
3. Bahmani, B., Chowdhury, A., Goel, A.: Fast incremental and personalized PageRank. Very Large Data Bases **4**(3), 173–184 (2010). https://doi.org/10.14778/1929861.1929864

4. Bianchini, M., Gori, M., Scarselli, F.: Inside PageRank. ACM Trans. Internet Technol. **5**(1), 92–128 (2005). https://doi.org/10.1145/1052934.1052938
5. Bonacich, P.: Power and centrality: a family of measures. Am. J. Sociol. **92**(5), 1170–1182 (1987). https://doi.org/10.1086/228631
6. Brin, S., Page, L.: The anatomy of a large-scale hypertextual web search engine. Int. World Wide Web Conf. **30**, 107–117 (1998). https://doi.org/10.1016/S0169-7552(98)00110-X
7. Chien, S., Dwork, C., Kumar, R., Simon, D.R., Sivakumar, D.: Link evolution: analysis and algorithms. Internet Math. **1**(3), 277–304 (2004). https://doi.org/10.1080/15427951.2004.10129090
8. Desikan, P.K., Pathak, N., Srivastava, J., Kumar, V.: Incremental Page Rank computation on evolving graphs. In: International World Wide Web Conferences, pp. 1094–1095 (2005). https://doi.org/10.1145/1062745.1062885
9. Guo, W., Li, Y., Sha, M., Tan, K.L.: Parallel personalized PageRank on dynamic graphs. Proc. VLDB Endow. **11**(1), 93–106 (2017). https://doi.org/10.14778/3151113.3151121
10. Kamvar, S.D., Haveliwala, T.H., Manning, C.D., Golub, G.H.: Exploiting the block structure of the web for computing PageRank. Stanford University Technical Report (2003)
11. Katz, L.: A new status index derived from sociometric analysis. Psychometrika **18**(1), 39–43 (1953). https://doi.org/10.1007/BF02289026
12. Kloumann, I.M., Ugander, J., Kleinberg, J.: Block models and personalized PageRank. Proc. Natl. Acad. Sci. U. S. A. **114**(1), 33 (2017). https://doi.org/10.1073/pnas.1611275114
13. Langville, A.N., Meyer, C.D.: Updating markov chains with an eye on google's PageRank. SIAM J. Matrix Anal. Appl. **27**(4), 968–987 (2006). https://doi.org/10.1137/040619028
14. Liao, Q., Jiang, S.S., Yu, M., Yang, Y., Li, T.: Monte Carlo based incremental PageRank on evolving graphs. In: Kim, J., Shim, K., Cao, L., Lee, J.-G., Lin, X., Moon, Y.-S. (eds.) PAKDD 2017. LNCS (LNAI), vol. 10234, pp. 356–367. Springer, Cham (2017). https://doi.org/10.1007/978-3-319-57454-7_28
15. Lofgren, P.: On the complexity of the Monte Carlo method for incremental PageRank. Inf. Process. Lett. **114**(3), 104–106 (2014). https://doi.org/10.1016/j.ipl.2013.11.006
16. Ng, A.Y., Zheng, A.X., Jordan, M.I.: Stable algorithms for link analysis. In: International ACM SIGIR Conference on Research and Development in Information Retrieval, pp. 258–266 (2001). https://doi.org/10.1145/383952.384003
17. Ohsaka, N., Maehara, T., Kawarabayashi, K.I.: Efficient PageRank tracking in evolving networks. In: ACM SIGKDD International Conference on Knowledge Discovery and Data Mining, pp. 875–884 (2015). https://doi.org/10.1145/2783258.2783297
18. Seneta, E.: Non-negative matrices and Markov chains. Popul. Stud. J. Demogr. **37**(1), 476 (1981). https://doi.org/10.1007/0-387-32792-4
19. Tong, H., Papadimitriou, S., Yu, P.S., Faloutsos, C.: Proximity tracking on time-evolving bipartite graphs. In: SIAM International Conference on Data Mining, SDM 2008, Atlanta, Georgia, USA, 24–26 April 2008, pp. 704–715 (2008). https://doi.org/10.1137/1.9781611972788
20. Zhang, H., Lofgren, P., Goel, A.: Approximate personalized PageRank on dynamic graphs. In: ACM SIGKDD International Conference on Knowledge Discovery and Data Mining, pp. 1315–1324 (2016). https://doi.org/10.1145/2939672.2939804

Social Web Applications and Crowdsourcing

Crowdsourced Time-Sync Video Recommendation via Semantic-Aware Neural Collaborative Filtering

Zhanpeng Wu[1,2], Yan Zhou[1,2], Di Wu[1,2(✉)], Yipeng Zhou[3], and Jing Qin[4]

[1] School of Data and Computer Science, Sun Yat-sen University,
Guangzhou 510006, China
{wuzhp5,zhouy347}@mail2.sysu.edu.cn,
wudi27@mail.sysu.edu.cn
[2] Guangdong Key Laboratory of Big Data Analysis and Processing,
Guangzhou 510006, China
[3] Department of Computing, Faculty of Science and Engineering,
Macquarie University, Sydney, NSW 2109, Australia
yipeng.job@gmail.com
[4] School of Nursing, The Hong Kong Polytechnic University, Hong Kong, China
harry.qin@polyu.edu.hk

Abstract. As an emerging type of video comments, time-sync comments (TSCs) enable viewers to make comments on video shots in a real-time manner. Such comments well reflect user interests in the frame level, which can be utilized to further improve the accuracy of video recommendation. In this paper, we make the first attempt in this direction and propose a new video recommendation algorithm called SACF by exploiting temporal relationship between time-sync comments and video frames. Our algorithm can extract a rich set of semantic features from crowdsourced time-sync comments, and combine latent semantic representations of users and videos by neural collaborative filtering. We conduct extensive experiments using real TSC datasets, and our results show that our proposed algorithm can improve the recommendation performance by 9.73% in HR@10 and 5.72% in NDCG@10 compared with other baseline solutions.

Keywords: Recommender system · Time-synchronized comment · Collaborative filtering

1 Introduction

The past decade has witnessed a dramatic increase of online videos, including online TV episodes, online movies, user-generated contents, livecast, and etc. The traffic generated by world-leading online video websites (e.g., Youtube, Netflix, Tencent Video, Hulu) has dominated the whole Internet backbone. In our daily life, users watch online videos for learning, news, and funny stuff. Normally, users

© Springer Nature Switzerland AG 2019
M. Bakaev et al. (Eds.): ICWE 2019, LNCS 11496, pp. 171–186, 2019.
https://doi.org/10.1007/978-3-030-19274-7_13

tend to make comments on video after watching. In recent years, there emerges a new type of video comments, called Time-Sync Comments (or Danmu, bullet-screen comments), which allow a user to make comments on video shots in a real-time manner. Time-sync comments are flying across the screen and people who are watching the same video also see the flying comments. To date, the service of time-sync comments has been provided by quite a few online video websites, such as YouTube[1], Twitch[2], AcFun[3], BiliBili[4], NicoNico[5], and so on. In Fig. 1, we show an example of a video clip[6] with time-sync comments.

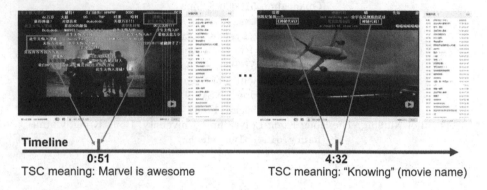

Fig. 1. Example of a crowdsourced time-sync video.

Different from conventional video comments, time-sync comments are syn-chronized with a video's playback time. It provides a possibility for viewers who are watching the same video to share their watching experience and interact with each other. Latent features can be extracted from time-sync comments to provide more detailed information on user interests. For instance, viewers who wrote comments in nearby playback time positions are likely to have some kinds of similarity or association (e.g., like or dislike a specific video shot). Intuitively, those viewers can be categorized into the same group with implicit similar prefer-ences. Moreover, a continuous bundle of time-sync comments can describe video contents to some extent. Such kind of information is useful for video recommen-dation to further improve user experience.

In this paper, we propose a new video recommendation algorithm for crowd-sourced time-sync videos, which is called *SACF (Semantic-Aware Collabora-tive Filtering)*. The basic idea of SACF is to exploit the temporal relationship between time-sync comments and video frames, and extract latent semantic

[1] https://www.youtube.com/.

[2] https://www.twitch.tv/.

[3] http://www.acfun.cn.

[4] https://www.bilibili.com.

[5] https://www.nicovideo.jp.

[6] Available at https://www.bilibili.com/video/av22135056.

representations of time-sync comments to provide more accurate video recommendation. Our proposed algorithm can model user preferences in the frame level. In summary, our main contributions in this paper can be listed as below:

- We propose a novel video recommendation algorithm called SACF to improve the performance of crowdsourced time-sync videos. Our algorithm extends traditional video recommendation algorithms by embedding latent semantic representations extracted from TSCs.
- To better utilize interaction patterns, we integrate all the representations with a multi-layer perceptron (MLP) model. By embedding extra semantic-aware information, our approach can easily achieve similar user and item interest filtering, and mitigate the cold-start problem.
- We also validate our proposed algorithm using a real TSC dataset obtained from the BiliBili video website. The experiment results show that our algorithm significantly outperforms other baselines by up to 9.73% in HR@10 and 5.72% in NDCG@10.

The rest of our paper is organized as follows: we first introduce the relevant work in Sect. 2. We describe the details of our algorithm in Sect. 3. The dataset and experiments are introduced in Sect. 4. Finally we conclude the whole paper and discuss our future work in Sect. 5.

2 Related Work

The topic of recommender systems has been extensively studied in the past years. He *et al.* [8], Koren *et al.* [13], Mnih and Salakhutdinov [19] have shown the excellent ability of matrix factorization model in the field of rating prediction problem. In addition to such classic research question, Top-K recommendation using implicit feedback are also worthy of attention. Hu *et al.* [9] and Rendle *et al.* [21] are the masterpieces of them. Moreover, in recent years, neural network models [29] have gained widespread attention because of their ability to easily fit multi-dimensional features and learn nonlinear relationships, which are concerned by Covington *et al.* [4] and He *et al.* [7].

With the development of this field, in order to improve the effectiveness in user preference modeling, the incorporation of contextual information has attracted major research interests, such as the work of Adomavicius and Tuzhilin [1] and Verbert *et al.* [25]. User review is one of the most effective contextual information to model user preference and these algorithms are receiving more and more research attention. Tang *et al.* [23] aims to incorporate user- and product-level information for document sentiment classification. Tang *et al.* [24] leverages the reviews for user modeling and predicts the rating of user review. In addition, lots of the review-based models focus on enhancing the effectiveness of rating prediction, like Ganu *et al.* [5], McAuley and Leskovec [17]. To achieve better overall recommendation performance, Liu *et al.* [15], Tan *et al.* [22], Wu and Ester [27] extract the user opinions from review text and combine these information into the conventional models for higher recommendation accuracy. Besides, Zhang *et al.* [30] integrates traditional matrix factorization technology with word2vec model proposed by Mikolov *et al.* [18] for precise modeling. Notably, these proposed models mainly focus on rating prediction problem, and learn knowledge from traditional reviews which are longer than time-sync comments and contain richer content and semantics.

Time-synchronized comment is first introduced by Wu *et al.* [26] for video shot tagging. Recently, as an emerging type of user-generated comment, TSC has many practical properties to describe a video in frame-level. As mentioned by He *et al.* [6], herding effect and multiple-burst phenomena make TSC significant different from the traditional reviews, and it also proves that TSCs have a great correlation with video frame content and user reactions. Thus this emerging comment type is worthy of being used for video highlight shot extraction and content annotation, presented by Xian *et al.* [28] and Ikeda *et al.* [10]. Besides, an increasing number of models are trying to label videos based on TSCs, such representative work as Lv *et al.* [16]. Chen *et al.* [3] and Ping [20] further leverages the TSCs to extract the features of video frames and applies it to key frame recommendation. However, these methods are clinging to the video shot itself and do not consider the co-occurrence among TSCs.

Compared with the aforementioned approaches, we conduct a semantic-aware collaborative filtering algorithm, which can efficiently extract latent representations from TSCs within the videos and achieve significantly performance improvement in Top-K recommendation task.

3   Design of Semantic-Aware Video Recommendation Algorithm

By fusing latent semantic representation from video TSCs and traditional interaction paradigm as a composite entity, we propose our semantic-aware collaborative filtering (SACF) video recommendation algorithm, which has flexibility and non-linearity profited by exploiting multi-layer perceptron as a fundamental framework. We will discuss the details of our algorithm in the following subsections.

3.1   Problem Definition

We first define the problem formally. Suppose there are N users $\boldsymbol{u} = \{u_1, u_2, \ldots, u_N\}$, M videos $\boldsymbol{i} = \{i_1, i_2, \ldots, i_M\}$ and T TSCs $\boldsymbol{c} = \{c_1, c_2, \ldots, c_T\}$. The TSC written by user u leaving in video i at video time t is defined as a 2-tuple $<u_i^t, c_i^t>$. Thereby, for each video $i \in \boldsymbol{i}$, we can obtain two different sequences, that is, TSC writer sequence $\boldsymbol{s}_i^{(u)} = (u_i^1, u_i^2, \ldots, u_i^{T_i})$ and TSC content sequence $\boldsymbol{s}_i^{(c)} = (c_i^1, c_i^2, \ldots, c_i^{T_i})$, where T_i is the amount of TSCs in video i and each element within the sequence is ranked by its video time.

Suppose the representation of user u is defined as $\boldsymbol{w}_u$, and the representation of video i is defined as $\boldsymbol{d}_i$. The user semantic representations $\boldsymbol{W} = \{\boldsymbol{w}_u | u \in \boldsymbol{u}\}$

Table 1. Notations used in SACF algorithm

Notation	Description
T_i	Total number of TSCs in video i
$\boldsymbol{u}$	The set of N users $\{u_1, u_2, \ldots, u_N\}$
$\boldsymbol{i}$	The set of M videos $\{i_i, i_2, \ldots, i_M\}$
$\boldsymbol{c}$	The set of T TSCs $\{c_i, c_2, \ldots, c_T\}$
u_i^t	User u writes a TSC in video i at time t
c_i^t	The TSC content c written in video i at time t
$\boldsymbol{s}_i^{(u)}$	The sequence of TSC users $(u_i^t)_{t=1}^{T_i}$ in video i
$\boldsymbol{s}_i^{(c)}$	The sequence of TSC content $(c_i^t)_{t=1}^{T_i}$ in video i
$\boldsymbol{w}_u$	Semantic representation of user u
$\boldsymbol{W}$	Semantic representations of $\boldsymbol{u}$
$\boldsymbol{d}_i$	Semantic representation of video i
$\boldsymbol{D}$	Semantic representations of $\boldsymbol{i}$
$\boldsymbol{P}$	Latent representations of $\boldsymbol{u}$
$\boldsymbol{Q}$	Latent representations of $\boldsymbol{i}$
$\boldsymbol{v}_u$	Index of user u
$\boldsymbol{v}_i$	Index of video i
f	Interaction function
Θ	Parameters of neural network
Φ_L	The activation function of Lth layer
$\boldsymbol{x}_L$	The hidden state of Lth layer
$\mathcal{O}$	The set of positive
$\mathcal{O}^-$	The set of sampled negative
$\mathcal{D}$	The set of training data

and video semantic representations $\boldsymbol{D} = \{\boldsymbol{d}_i | i \in \boldsymbol{i}\}$ are learned from the sequencing data $\boldsymbol{s}_i^{(u)}$ and $\boldsymbol{s}_i^{(c)}$, which exploit the improved word embedding technology.

Given all the historical user-video interaction data $\mathcal{D} = \{\mathcal{O}, \mathcal{O}^-\}$, where $\mathcal{O}$ and $\mathcal{O}^-$ denote the positive and negative instances, respectively. For a user u and a set of corresponding unseen videos, our goal is to find a interaction function $f(\cdot)$ to rank all the unseen videos based on how much s/he like the video. The top K most likely to watch videos are the final results recommended to user u. For reference, we list the notations used throughout the algorithm in Table 1.

3.2 Latent Semantic Representation

In this section, we explain the methods to capture latent semantic representation, which aim to extract the similarity lurked in users and videos. Before digging into the details, to better model the information of Internet slangs, we need to conduct a few data preprocessing work:

- Different character components within a TSC may indicate different meanings. Thus, we will split a complete TSC into multiple substrings, where each substring represents a series of consecutive characters of the same type and these substrings will be treated as part of the TSC set c as well. These character types can be English letter, pure number and Chinese character. For instance, TSC "awesome!!2333" will be treated as two TSCs, i.e. "awesome" and "2333" (laughter).
- Moreover, the excessive TSCs will obviously impair the performance of the algorithm. Thereby, those Chinese substrings that are too long will also be segmented (the threshold of segmentation in our experiments is more than five consecutive Chinese characters).

Inspired by [14,18], we propose the improved word embedding methods to learn representations. In this schema, each user is mapped to a unique latent vector $\boldsymbol{w}_u$ and each vector is represented as one column of the matrix $\boldsymbol{W}$ where $\boldsymbol{W}$ indicates the user semantic representation matrix. Given the sequence of user $\boldsymbol{s}_i^{(u)}$ from a finite user set $\boldsymbol{u}$, the objective function aiming at maximizing is formulated as follows,

$$\frac{1}{T_i} \sum_{t=k}^{T_i-k} \sum_{-k \leq j \leq k, j \neq 0} \log p(u_i^t | u_i^{t+j}) \tag{1}$$

where k is the context window size and $p(\cdot)$ is the softmax function,

$$p(u_i^t | u_i^{t+j}) = \frac{\exp(\boldsymbol{w}_{u_i^t}^T \cdot \boldsymbol{w}_{u_i^{t+j}})}{\sum_{u' \in u} \exp(\boldsymbol{w}_{u_i^{t+j}}^T \cdot \boldsymbol{w}_{u'})} \tag{2}$$

After the training converges, users who have the similar watching patterns will be projected to a similar position in the vector space. We leave these user semantic representations $\boldsymbol{W} = \{\boldsymbol{w}_u | u \in \boldsymbol{u}\}$ for later use. Likewise, TSC and video are mapped to a unique latent vector $\boldsymbol{w}_c$ and $\boldsymbol{d}_i$, respectively. Each vector is a column of their respective matrix, $\boldsymbol{W}_c$ and $\boldsymbol{D}$ where $\boldsymbol{D}$ indicates the video semantic representation matrix. We will further leverage the information within $\boldsymbol{W}$ and $\boldsymbol{D}$ in the next subsection. Given the sequence of $\boldsymbol{s}_i^{(c)}$ from a finite TSC set c, the objective function is defined as,

$$\frac{1}{T_i} \sum_{t=k}^{T_i-k} \sum_{-k \leq j \leq k, j \neq 0} \log p(c_i^t | c_i^{t+j}) \tag{3}$$

Similarly, the softmax function can be formulated as,

$$p(c_i^t | c_i^{t+j}) = \frac{\exp(\boldsymbol{z}_{c_i^t, i}^T \cdot \boldsymbol{z}_{c_i^{t+j}})}{\sum_{c' \in c \text{ and } i' \in i} \exp(\boldsymbol{z}_{c_i^{t+j}, i}^T \cdot \boldsymbol{z}_{c', i'})} \tag{4}$$

where the latent vector z is constructed from w_c and d_i. In particular, the vector z is the sum of w_c and d_i. Our ultimate goal is to obtain the video semantic representation set $D = \{d_i | i \in i\}$ for the next step.

3.3   Algorithm Design

We now elaborate the SACF algorithm in details. Our approach employs a deep neural network, which is empowered the capability to learn the non-linear interactions from input data and can be easily embedded with extra features. Therefore, in addition to treat the identify of a user and a video in pure collaborative filtering as basic input feature, SACF also transforms the video TSC corpus to two kinds of representations, which are generated from user and video latent semantic information. As shown in Fig. 2, on the top of the input layer, each user and video is mapped to two corresponding vectors, i.e. identification dense vector and latent semantic representation vector. The generation methods of latent semantic representation have been fully explained in Sect. 3.2. And then such a 4-tuple of embedding vectors is fed into a multi-layer neural network, where each layer is combined with fully connection. The final output layer represents a predictive probability $\hat{r}_{ui}$, which is trained by minimizing the binary cross-entropy loss between $\hat{r}_{ui}$ and its target value r_{ui}.

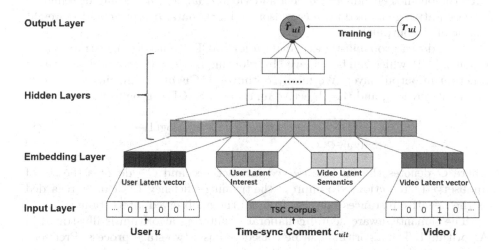

Fig. 2. SACF model structure for time-sync video recommendation.

Consequently, we can further formulate the SACF algorithm as,

$$\hat{r}_{ui} = f(P^T v_u, Q^T v_i, W^T v_u, D^T v_i, | P, Q, W, D, \Theta) \tag{5}$$

where P and Q denote the latent factor matrix for users and videos respectively. W is the user semantic representation matrix, and analogously, D is the video semantic representation matrix which extracts the latent features from the TSC corpus. v_u and v_i separately denote the index vector of user u and video i. Θ represents the parameters of the interaction function $f(\cdot)$.

As mentioned above, the function $f(\cdot)$ can be further defined as a multi-layer neural network,

$$f(P^T v_u, Q^T v_i, W^T v_u, D^T v_i)$$
$$= \sigma(\Phi_L(\Phi_{L-1}(\ldots\Phi_1(P^T v_u, Q^T v_i, W^T v_u, D^T v_i)\ldots))) \quad (6)$$

where σ is the mapping function of output layer and Φ_L denotes the Lth hidden layer in neural network. More specifically, we formulate each layer as follows,

$$x_1 = \Phi_1(p_u, q_i, w_u, d_i) = \begin{bmatrix} p_u & q_i & w_u & d_i \end{bmatrix}^T$$
$$x_2 = \Phi_2(x_1) = g_2(A_2^T x_1 + b_1)$$
$$\ldots \quad (7)$$
$$x_L = \Phi_L(x_{L-1}) = g_L(A_L^T x_{L-1} + b_L)$$
$$\hat{r}_{ui} = \sigma(h^T x_L)$$

where A_L, b_L and g_L respectively denote the weight matrix, bias vector and activation function of the Lth layer. p_u and q_i are the dense vector embedded with the one-hot encoding of user u and video i. w_u and d_i are latent semantic representation generated from crowdsourced TSC data. h represents the weight vector of the output layer.

To endow a probabilistic explanation for SACF, we need to constraint $\hat{r}_{ui}$ in range of $[0, 1]$, which can be achieved by adopting *Logit* or *Probit* as an activation function in output layer. We finally optimize SACF by minimizing the binary cross-entropy loss, and the objective function of SACF can be formulated as,

$$\mathcal{L} = -\sum_{(u,i)\in\mathcal{O}\cup\mathcal{O}^-} r_{ui} \log \hat{r}_{ui} + (1 - r_{ui}) \log(1 - \hat{r}_{ui}) \quad (8)$$

where $\mathcal{O}$ denotes the set of observed interactions, and $\mathcal{O}^-$ denotes the set of unobserved interactions. To improve the training efficiency, $\mathcal{O}^-$ can be regarded as the negative instances sampled from all the unobserved interactions.

The semantic-aware neural collaborative filtering algorithm is illustrated in Algorithm 1. The algorithm can be considered as a two-stage process. Precisely, we pretrain the semantic representation of users and items in the first stage and embed it with the user-video interaction data in the second stage to maintain a holistic recommendation task. The algorithm works when the video has a series of TSC data. These data contain meta information about users and videos, and thus even if the user rarely sends any TSC, the algorithm can still leverage the implicit information to get the probability of watching a video.

Algorithm 1. Semantic-Aware Neural Collaborative Filtering Algorithm

---

1: **procedure** SEMANTIC-AWARE NEURAL COLLABORATIVE FILTERING

    Input: User-item interaction set $\mathcal{D}$, TSC writer sequence set $\{s_1^{(u)}, s_2^{(u)}, \ldots, s_M^{(u)}\}$ and TSC content sequence $\{s_1^{(c)}, s_2^{(c)}, \ldots, s_M^{(c)}\}$ for M videos

    Output: Representations of P, Q, W, D and network parameters Θ

2:     initialize matrix W and D

3:     **for** $i = 1 \rightarrow M$ **do**

4:         $s_i^{(c)} \leftarrow SameTypeCharacterSegmentation(s_i^{(c)})$

5:         $s_i^{(c)} \leftarrow ExtraLongCharacterSegmentation(s_i^{(c)})$

6:         **for each** $u_i \in s_i^{(u)}$ and its contextual users $Context(u_i)$ **do**

7:             **for each** $u_i' \in Context(u_i)$ **do**

8:                 **update** W by optimizing $softmax(u_i|u_i')$

9:             **end for**

10:        **end for**

11:        **for each** $c_i \in s_i^{(c)}$ and its contextual TSCs $Context(c_i)$ **do**

12:           **for each** $c_i' \in Context(c_i)$ **do**

13:              **update** D by optimizing $softmax(c_i|c_i')$

14:           **end for**

15:        **end for**

16:     **end for**

17:     initialize matrix P and Q

18:     **for each** training epoch **do**

19:        **for each** paired index $(v_u, v_i) \in Loader(\mathcal{D})$ **do**   ▷ *Loader* will provide multiple iterators over the dataset

20:           **compute:**

21:              $\hat{r}_{ui} \leftarrow f(P^T v_u, Q^T v_i, W^T v_u, D^T v_i)$

22:              $loss \leftarrow criterion(\hat{r}_{ui}, r_{ui})$

23:           **update** P, Q and Θ by minimizing the $loss$

24:        **end for**

25:     **end for**

26:     **return** P, Q, W, D and Θ

27: **end procedure**

---

4   Performance Evaluation

To demonstrate the superiority of our method, a time-sync video dataset crawled from Bilibili website is utilized for performance evaluation. We will discuss an overview of the dataset and experiment settings before presenting the experimental results.

4.1   Dataset Overview

Bilibili is one of the most popular TSC video sharing websites in China, and leads a trend of video interaction via TSC. We collected the video meta information and its corresponding TSC data from Bilibili website till December 15th, 2018. Note that the video TSC data we collected is only a part of fully historical data, because the platform will periodically remove the stale TSC data from the TSC pool and remain the latest TSC data. For the sake of reflecting the experimental results more significantly, we mainly focus on the data of gaming category, which attracts the most traffic on Bilibili. Based on these premises, our collected dataset totally contains 57,294 users and 2,637 videos. All these videos include 836,806 TSCs and 3,483 user-generated tags. More detailed statistic analyses are presented in Table 2.

Table 2. Overall statistics of our time-sync comment dataset

# of videos	2,637
# of users	57,294
# of TSCs	836,806
# of user-generated tags	3,483
Avg # of TSCs per user	14.61
Avg # of TSCs per video	317.33
Avg # of user-generated tags per video	7.01
Max/Min # of TSCs for a user	731/5
Max/Min # of TSCs for a video	4393/1
Max/Min # of user-generated tags for a video	14/1
Max/Min # of TSCs for a user leaving in a video	299/1

4.2   Experiment Settings

Evaluation Metrics. To evaluate the performance of TSC video recommendation, we employ two widespread adopted metrics, that is, *Hit Ratio* (HR) and *Normalized Discounted Cumulative Gain* (NDCG) [11]. These two metrics can respectively measure the classification and ranking performance in recommendation problem.

Baselines. Besides SACF method, we also implement two other algorithms for comparison, which are described as below,

- **MLP** is proposed by [7]. It is a pure collaborative filtering method, which uses only the identifies of user and item as embedding features. Previous work has shown its strong generalization ability benefited from DNN model.
- **TCF** is a variant of SACF. In contrast to SACF, TCF embeds the user-generated video tag information instead of the TSC information in SACF. It is a highly competitive baseline for video recommendation that fuses with conventional content features.

Parameter Settings. For better generality and comparison, we chose the widely used *leave-one-out* [2, 7, 8] evaluation schema, which holds the latest interaction as a test case and use the rest as training set. All the algorithms are optimized by the cross-entropy function defined in Eq. (8), where we randomly sample 4 negative instances for each positive instance. We use *Adam* [12] as optimizer to train algorithms, and fix the batch-size and learning rate at 256 and 0.001. Besides, in fairness, the number of hidden layers is set to 4 in all the experiments.

4.3   Experiment Results

Experiment 1: Performance Comparison. Since the size of last hidden layer implies the learning capability in DNN models, we can evaluate the performance in different factor size to achieve comprehensive comparison. Figure 3 illustrates that SACF outperforms other two baselines with the factors of 8, 16, 32 and 64 in both metrics when embedding size (ES) is set to 64. And the overall performance trend is presented as MLP<TCF<SACF. Meanwhile, it is worth mentioning that all the curves have different degrees of decline when factors become larger, indicating that a large factor size may probably cause overfitting and degrade the overall performance.

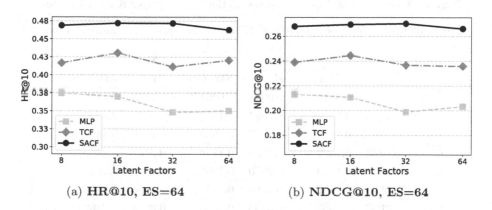

(a) **HR@10, ES=64**   (b) **NDCG@10, ES=64**

Fig. 3. Performance comparison in different size of latent factors.

Table 3 shows the precise results in different factor size. We notice that our proposed SACF algorithm exceeds MLP with a maximum performance improvement of 9.73% in HR@10 and 5.72% in NDCG@10. To the contrast of TCF, SACF also outperforms with 4.13% and 2.58% respectively.

We also evaluate the performance in Top-K recommendation. We fix embedding size (ES) to 64 and latent factor (LF) size to 8. The results presented in Fig. 4 show that, both HR@K and NDCG@K follow the same trend, i.e. MLP<TCF<SACF, where K ranges from 1 to 10. These findings further reveal that SACF has significantly performance advantages over the baselines.

Table 3. Performance of HR@10 and NDCG@10 in different size of latent factors.

Algorithm	LF = 8		LF = 16		LF = 32		LF = 64	
	HR@10	NDCG@10	HR@10	NDCG@10	HR@10	NDCG@10	HR@10	NDCG@10
MLP	0.3746	0.2131	0.3701	0.2107	0.3484	0.1987	0.3504	0.2033
TCF	0.4168	0.2390	0.4306	0.2445	0.4116	0.2367	0.4205	0.2359
SACF	0.4688	0.2680	0.4719	0.2696	0.4718	0.2703	0.4626	0.2662

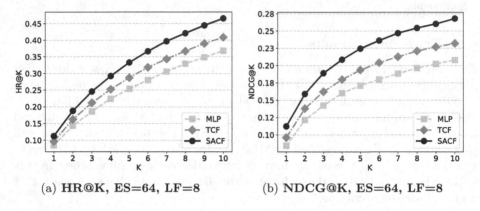

(a) **HR@K, ES=64, LF=8**   (b) **NDCG@K, ES=64, LF=8**

Fig. 4. Performance of Top-K recommendation where ranges K from 1 to 10.

Table 4. Performance of HR@10 and NDCG@10 in Top-K recommendation.

Top-K	MLP		TCF		SACF	
	HR@10	NDCG@10	HR@10	NDCG@10	HR@10	NDCG@10
K = 1	0.0846	0.0846	0.0961	0.0961	0.1123	0.1123
K = 2	0.1435	0.1216	0.1623	0.1380	0.1877	0.1590
K = 3	0.1858	0.1424	0.2117	0.1623	0.2456	0.1890
K = 4	0.2243	0.1602	0.2526	0.1798	0.2922	0.2085
K = 5	0.2538	0.1710	0.2870	0.1935	0.3328	0.2245
K = 6	0.2805	0.1800	0.3184	0.2042	0.3666	0.2362
K = 7	0.3057	0.1883	0.3433	0.2126	0.3968	0.2469
K = 8	0.3291	0.1962	0.3671	0.2209	0.4209	0.2544
K = 9	0.3483	0.2024	0.3900	0.2269	0.4443	0.2604
K = 10	0.3746	0.2131	0.4168	0.2390	0.4688	0.2680

The detailed performance data of Top-K recommendation is presented in Table 4. Normally, as the value of K increases, all the performance indicators are gradually improving. At the same time, the performance gap between SACF and the other two baselines is gradually expanding.

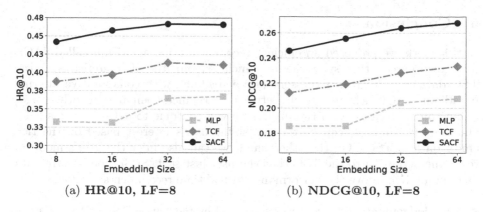

(a) HR@10, LF=8   (b) NDCG@10, LF=8

Fig. 5. Performance comparison in different size of embedding vector.

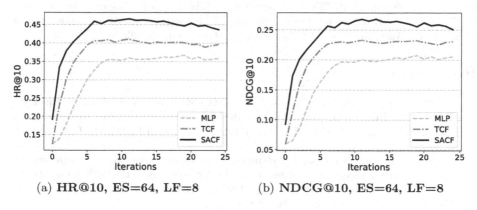

(a) HR@10, ES=64, LF=8   (b) NDCG@10, ES=64, LF=8

Fig. 6. Recommendation performance in different number of iterations.

Experiment 2: Impact of Embedding Size. The size of embedding vector determines the feature description ability especially when we embed various kinds of input data. Towards this end, we further investigate the impact of embedding size, which is summarized in Fig. 5. The latent factor (LF) size is set to 8. The empirical evidence shows that the performance curves rise first and then stabilize. We speculate that increasing the embedding size can partly alleviate recommendation efficiency, but as the dimension continues to rise, it also brings the risk of overfitting and harms the recommendation performance.

Experiment 3: Performance Changes with Iterations. As the number of iterations increases, the parameters in the neural network will be updated numerous times, and the fitting effect goes from underfitting to overfitting. Figure 6 shows the recommendation performance of the algorithms of each iteration on our dataset. We can see that with more iterations, the performance first rises rapidly and then decreases gradually in both two metrics, which indicates that the more iterations may lead to overfitting.

5   Conclusion

In this work, we proposed an efficient recommendation algorithm called SACF for crowdsourced time-sync videos, which exploits the characteristics of the TSC data. By integrating the semantic embedding with collaborative filtering paradigm, SACF achieves much better performance compared to other algorithms on real datasets. In the future, we will continue to delve into this field. On the one hand, we can better model the user's interest based on the rich emoji data in TSCs. On the other hand, we can also infer the user's mood in real time according to the TSC that the user just sent. Such mood-aware data can definitely improve the performance in real-time recommender systems.

Acknowledgement. This work was supported by the National Key R&D Program of China under Grant 2018YFB0204100, the National Natural Science Foundation of China under Grant 61572538, Guangdong Special Support Program under Grant 2017TX04X148, Hong Kong Innovation and Technology Commission under Grant ITS/319/17, Australia Research Council under Grant DE180100950.

References

1. Adomavicius, G., Tuzhilin, A.: Context-aware recommender systems. In: Ricci, F., Rokach, L., Shapira, B., Kantor, P.B. (eds.) Recommender Systems Handbook, pp. 217–253. Springer, Boston, MA (2011). https://doi.org/10.1007/978-0-387-85820-3_7
2. Bayer, I., He, X., Kanagal, B., Rendle, S.: A generic coordinate descent framework for learning from implicit feedback. In: Proceedings of the 26th International Conference on World Wide Web, pp. 1341–1350. International World Wide Web Conferences Steering Committee (2017)
3. Chen, X., Zhang, Y., Ai, Q., Xu, H., Yan, J., Qin, Z.: Personalized key frame recommendation. In: Proceedings of the 40th International ACM SIGIR Conference on Research and Development in Information Retrieval, pp. 315–324. ACM (2017)
4. Covington, P., Adams, J., Sargin, E.: Deep neural networks for youtube recommendations. In: Proceedings of the 10th ACM Conference on Recommender Systems, pp. 191–198. ACM (2016)
5. Ganu, G., Elhadad, N., Marian, A.: Beyond the stars: improving rating predictions using review text content. In: WebDB, vol. 9, pp. 1–6. Citeseer (2009)
6. He, M., Ge, Y., Chen, E., Liu, Q., Wang, X.: Exploring the emerging type of comment for online videos: Danmu. ACM Trans. Web (TWEB) **12**(1), 1 (2018)
7. He, X., Liao, L., Zhang, H., Nie, L., Hu, X., Chua, T.S.: Neural collaborative filtering. In: Proceedings of the 26th International Conference on World Wide Web, pp. 173–182. International World Wide Web Conferences Steering Committee (2017)
8. He, X., Zhang, H., Kan, M.Y., Chua, T.S.: Fast matrix factorization for online recommendation with implicit feedback. In: Proceedings of the 39th International ACM SIGIR Conference on Research and Development in Information Retrieval, pp. 549–558. ACM (2016)
9. Hu, Y., Koren, Y., Volinsky, C.: Collaborative filtering for implicit feedback datasets. In: Eighth IEEE International Conference on Data Mining, ICDM 2008, pp. 263–272. IEEE (2008)

10. Ikeda, A., Kobayashi, A., Sakaji, H., Masuyama, S.: Classification of comments on Nico Nico Douga for annotation based on referred contents. In: 2015 18th International Conference on Network-Based Information Systems (NBiS), pp. 673–678. IEEE (2015)
11. Järvelin, K., Kekäläinen, J.: Cumulated gain-based evaluation of IR techniques. ACM Trans. Inf. Syst. (TOIS) **20**(4), 422–446 (2002)
12. Kingma, D.P., Ba, J.: Adam: a method for stochastic optimization. arXiv preprint arXiv:1412.6980 (2014)
13. Koren, Y., Bell, R., Volinsky, C.: Matrix factorization techniques for recommender systems. Computer **8**, 30–37 (2009)
14. Le, Q., Mikolov, T.: Distributed representations of sentences and documents. In: International Conference on Machine Learning, pp. 1188–1196 (2014)
15. Liu, H., He, J., Wang, T., Song, W., Du, X.: Combining user preferences and user opinions for accurate recommendation. Electron. Commer. Res. Appl. **12**(1), 14–23 (2013)
16. Lv, G., Xu, T., Chen, E., Liu, Q., Zheng, Y.: Reading the videos: temporal labeling for crowdsourced time-sync videos based on semantic embedding. In: AAAI, pp. 3000–3006 (2016)
17. McAuley, J., Leskovec, J.: Hidden factors and hidden topics: understanding rating dimensions with review text. In: Proceedings of the 7th ACM Conference on Recommender Systems, pp. 165–172. ACM (2013)
18. Mikolov, T., Sutskever, I., Chen, K., Corrado, G.S., Dean, J.: Distributed representations of words and phrases and their compositionality. In: Advances in Neural Information Processing Systems, pp. 3111–3119 (2013)
19. Mnih, A., Salakhutdinov, R.R.: Probabilistic matrix factorization. In: Advances in Neural Information Processing Systems, pp. 1257–1264 (2008)
20. Ping, Q.: Video recommendation using crowdsourced time-sync comments. In: Proceedings of the 12th ACM Conference on Recommender Systems, pp. 568–572. ACM (2018)
21. Rendle, S., Freudenthaler, C., Gantner, Z., Schmidt-Thieme, L.: BPR: Bayesian personalized ranking from implicit feedback. In: Proceedings of the Twenty-fifth Conference on Uncertainty in Artificial Intelligence, pp. 452–461. AUAI Press (2009)
22. Tan, Y., Zhang, M., Liu, Y., Ma, S.: Rating-boosted latent topics: understanding users and items with ratings and reviews. In: IJCAI, pp. 2640–2646 (2016)
23. Tang, D., Qin, B., Liu, T.: Learning semantic representations of users and products for document level sentiment classification. In: Proceedings of the 53rd Annual Meeting of the Association for Computational Linguistics and the 7th International Joint Conference on Natural Language Processing (Volume 1: Long Papers), vol. 1, pp. 1014–1023 (2015)
24. Tang, D., Qin, B., Liu, T., Yang, Y.: User modeling with neural network for review rating prediction. In: IJCAI, pp. 1340–1346 (2015)
25. Verbert, K., et al.: Context-aware recommender systems for learning: a survey and future challenges. IEEE Trans. Learn. Technol. **5**(4), 318–335 (2012)
26. Wu, B., Zhong, E., Tan, B., Horner, A., Yang, Q.: Crowdsourced time-sync video tagging using temporal and personalized topic modeling. In: Proceedings of the 20th ACM SIGKDD International Conference on Knowledge Discovery and Data Mining, pp. 721–730. ACM (2014)
27. Wu, Y., Ester, M.: Flame: a probabilistic model combining aspect based opinion mining and collaborative filtering. In: Proceedings of the Eighth ACM International Conference on Web Search and Data Mining, pp. 199–208. ACM (2015)

28. Xian, Y., Li, J., Zhang, C., Liao, Z.: Video highlight shot extraction with time-sync comment. In: Proceedings of the 7th International Workshop on Hot Topics in Planet-Scale mObile Computing and Online Social neTworking, pp. 31–36. ACM (2015)
29. Zhang, S., Yao, L., Sun, A.: Deep learning based recommender system: a survey and new perspectives. arXiv preprint arXiv:1707.07435 (2017)
30. Zhang, W., Yuan, Q., Han, J., Wang, J.: Collaborative multi-level embedding learning from reviews for rating prediction. In: IJCAI, pp. 2986–2992 (2016)

On Twitter Bots Behaving Badly: Empirical Study of Code Patterns on GitHub

Andrea Millimaggi and Florian Daniel[(✉)]

Politecnico di Milano, Via Ponzio 34/5, 20133 Milan, Italy
andrea.millimaggi@mail.polimi.it, florian.daniel@polimi.it

Abstract. Bots, i.e., algorithmically driven entities that behave like humans in online communications, are increasingly infiltrating social conversations on the Web. If not properly prevented, this presence of bots may cause harm to the humans they interact with. This paper aims to understand which types of abuse may lead to harm and whether these can be considered intentional or not. We manually review a dataset of 60 Twitter bot code repositories on GitHub, derive a set of potentially abusive actions, characterize them using a taxonomy of abstract code patterns, and assess the potential abusiveness of the patterns. The study does not only reveal the existence of 31 communication-specific code patterns – which could be used to assess the harmfulness of bot code – but also their presence throughout all studied repositories.

Keywords: Bots · Harm · Abuse · Code patterns · GitHub · Twitter

1 Introduction

Social networks, microblogging or instant messaging services like Facebook, Twitter, Instagram, LinkedIn, WhatsApp, Telegram, and similar are the foundation of the Web 2.0, that is, the Web made of content and services provided by the users themselves. Over the last 15 years, these applications have enabled users all around the world to stay informed, share ideas and discuss opinions. In short, they revolutionized online communication to billions of humans.

In the recent years, a new phenomenon has arisen: *bots*, i.e., algorithmically driven entities that behave like humans in online communications and increasingly participate in conversations without the human participants necessarily being aware of communicating with a machine [8]. State-of-the-art artificial intelligence, speech technology and conversational technology enable the implementation of software agents whose communications are only hardly distinguishable from those by human agents. Combined with generally low transparency about the true nature of bot accounts, humans are easily fooled.

In [6], we have started asking ourselves whether the increasing presence of bots may lead to harmful human-bot interactions that may hurt the human participant in the conversation, and by searching for papers, news, blog posts, and

© Springer Nature Switzerland AG 2019
M. Bakaev et al. (Eds.): ICWE 2019, LNCS 11496, pp. 187–202, 2019.
https://doi.org/10.1007/978-3-030-19274-7_14

similar we found a variety of anecdotal evidence that this may indeed happen. Of course, bots are not harmful in general. But sometimes, intentionally or unintentionally, software-driven conversations may just break common conversational rules, etiquette, or even the law. It is important to acknowledge the problem, to be able to provide countermeasures and to prevent people from getting hurt.

As we show in our discussion of related works, most of the literature today focuses on the detection of bots and on telling bots and humans apart starting from the evidence (e.g., posts, comments, likes) that is observable and accessible online. There is very little information on assessing the harms caused by this presence of bots, even less so on the reasons that lead to harm. This paper studies this latter aspect and aims to identify how harm is caused by bots to understand the likely, underlying intentions. Doing so requires looking behind the curtain, away from the content shared online and into the actual code implementing the bots' communication logic. The contributions of this paper are:

- The construction of a *dataset* of social bot GitHub code repositories for Twitter; the analysis focuses on code written in Python and on project metadata.
- An *abuse-oriented classification* of bot code repositories according to how the developers themselves advertise their projects.
- A *qualitative, systematic code review* that identifies 31 potentially *abusive code patterns* that may lead to harmful interactions with human users and a discussion of the possible *intentions* underlying these patterns.
- A *qualitative analysis* of the potential harmfulness of each identified pattern.

Next, we elaborate on the background of the work, then in Sect. 3 we describe the dataset we use for our study and report on a preliminary analysis of the data. In Sect. 4, we detail the method underlying the analysis and describe the respective results: actions, patterns and possible consequences. After overviewing related works, we conclude the paper and outline future works.

2   Background

2.1   Harm and Abuse in Human-Bot Interactions

Harm occurs when someone suffers an injury or damage, but also when someone gets exposed to a potential adverse effect or danger. In prior work [6], we identified the following types of harm caused by bots:

- *Psychological harm*: it occurs when someone's psychological health or well-being gets endangered or injured. An example of a bot causing psychological harm is Boost Juice's Messenger bot that was meant as a funny channel to obtain discounts by mimicking a dating game with fruits but used language that was not appropriate for children (http://bit.ly/2zvNt0E).
- *Legal harm*: it occurs when someone becomes subject to law enforcement or prosecution. A good example is the case of Jeffry van der Goot, a Dutch developer who had to shut down his Twitter bot generating random posts, after it sent out death threats to other users (http://bit.ly/2Dfm71P).

- *Economic harm*: it occurs when someone incurs in monetary cost or loses time that could have been spent differently. For example, in 2014 the bot wise_shibe provided automated answers on Reddit and users rewarded the bot with tips in the digital currency Dogecoin, convinced they were tipping a real user (http://bit.ly/2zu2b6r).
- *Social harm* occurs when someone's image or standing in a community gets affected negatively. An example of a bot causing social harm was documented by Jason Slotkin whose Twitter identity was cloned by a bot, confusing friends and followers (http://bit.ly/2Dfq4DH).
- *Democratic harm* occurs when democratic rules and principles are undermined and society as a whole suffers negative consequences. Bessi and Ferrara [2], for instance, showed that bots were pervasively active in the on-line political discussion of the 2016 U.S. Presidential election.

These types of harm may happen while bots perform regular *actions*, such as posting a message or commenting a message by someone else, that are not harmful per se and that also human users would perform. What needs to happen in order to cause harm is the abusive implementation of these actions. *Abuses* we found are: *disclosing sensitive facts, denigrating, being grossly offensive, being indecent or obscene, being threatening, making false allegations, deceiving users, spamming, spreading misinformation, mimicking interest, cloning profiles*, and *invading spaces* that are not meant for bots. Some of these may be subject to legal prosecution (e.g., threatening people), others only breach moral, ethical or social norms, yet they still may be harmful to unprepared human users.

2.2 Platform Policies and Permissions

In order to properly assess the behavior of a bot, it is important to understand the position of the platforms targeted by bots in relation to automation through bots. For this purpose, we manually surveyed the *usage policies* of a selection of social networks (Facebook, Twitter, Thumblr), instant messaging platforms (Telegram, Whatsapp, Facebook Messenger), platforms for media sharing (Instagram, Pinterest), a professional network (LinkedIn) and Reddit.

All platforms provide developers with *programmable interfaces* (APIs) that can be used for the development of bots; Messenger and Telegram even come with APIs specifically tailored to bots, more specifically, chatbots. Whatsapp is the platform that is most restricted: its Business API allows the implementation of bots, but it seems limited to company use only; however, Android intents (https://bit.ly/2RwjScE) can be used locally on the mobile phone to interact with Whatsapp programmatically. Where an API is provided, it typically allows programmatic access to essentially *all functionalities* that would also be available to users via the platforms' user interfaces. Users of the APIs must *authenticate* with the platforms (the preferred protocol is OAuth) and obtain a *token* enabling programmatic access; only Telegram gives tokens without authentication. All of the studied APIs are *REST APIs*; Facebook and Twitter also provide access to *streaming, live data*. To ease development, some platforms (Facebook, Twitter,

Messenger, LinkedIn) are equipped with developer-oriented *software development kits* (SDKs), even in multiple programming languages. Others (Twitter, Instagram) provide more basic programming *libraries*.

As for the usage policies, almost all platforms impose some kind of *limitation*. For instance, "200 calls per hour per user" per app on Facebook. Twitter uses message-level limits, e.g., to prevent aggressive following practices. Only Messenger does not explicitly limit usage and instead even states "you can safely send 250 requests per second." Some platforms impose specific *requirements*, such as "keep your app's negative feedback below our threshold" (Facebook) or "automated bots must respond to any and all input from the user" (Messenger). An explicit *code review* is needed for Facebook, Instagram and Messenger. *Automation* is generally allowed, although commonly limited to actions the target users have explicitly granted permission to; Twitter, for instance, disallows "sending messages in an aggressive or discriminate manner." Most policies even include *content restrictions* like "don't create fake accounts" (Facebook) or "don't send tweets containing links that are misleading." All surveyed platforms explicitly state that they may *suspend* accounts or apps if they violate their policies.

3   Dataset: Twitter Bot Code Repositories

This paper follows a Data Science methodology [9] to extract new knowledge from data. We thus describe here the dataset underlying our study and provide a first analysis of how developers themselves describe their own bot projects.

3.1   Data Sources and Retrieval

In this paper, we specifically focus on Twitter (https://twitter.com) and bots written in Python. The former is an opportunistic choice, shared by most literature on the topic (see Sect. 5 for related works) and is motivated by the openness of Twitter compared to other platforms. The latter stems from the observation that Python is the most used language for Twitter bot implementations in GitHub (35.4% of the repositories we analyzed for Twitter use it). GitHub (https://github.com) is the code hosting service we use for data collection; the choice is again

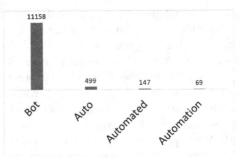

Fig. 1. Distribution of GitHub search results by searched keywords (includes all programming languages).

driven by adoption: with about 31M users and 100M projects (or "repositories"), GitHub is today's most used code hosting service (https://www.alexa.com/topsites/category/Computers/Open_Source/Project_Hosting).

In order to identify candidate repositories for our analysis, we used GitHub's search API with a combination of two terms, "Twitter" and any among "bot," "automation," "auto" and "automated." Fig. 1 shows the distribution of results obtained by the search considering still all programming languages. As the result of the query "Twitter bot" shows, the term "bot" is highly used for Twitter (we performed similar searches for all platforms mentioned in Sect. 2.2, and the results distributions do vary from platform to platform). The search represents the state of GitHub as of October 29, 2018, the date the search was performed. For each identified repository, we collected all code files included in the repository as well as a subset of the respective project metadata: URL, programming language, description (a short line of text), and fork/subscriber/watcher counts.

3.2 Preliminary Analysis

As the purpose of this paper is to understand how bots implement their interactions with humans, the analysis necessarily requires a manual inspection. This, in turn, requires a careful selection of repositories, in order to keep the size of the dataset manageable and the selected repositories meaningful. Before choosing which repositories to keep and which not, we thus run a simple analysis based on the textual descriptions of the projects in order to obtain a preliminary understanding of which actions the repositories implement.

The analysis followed a top-down approach: We took as starting point the actions identified in our previous work [6], i.e., *talk with user, redirect user, write post, comment post, forward post, like message, follow user,* and *create user,* and matched the retrieved repositories with these action labels. In order to match repositories with action labels, we manually inspected the descriptions of the first 100 items as returned in order of relevance by the GitHub search API and extracted textual keywords from the descriptions. Examples of keywords are: *send messages, reply to messages, chat, post, tweet, tag, poke,* and similar. Then we mapped all keywords to respective action labels, such as {*send messages, reply to messages, read messages, direct message, chat*} → *talk.*

The mapping exercise produced evidence for the existence in the dataset of all the actions above, plus the addition of 3 new action labels: some projects explicitly claimed to implement a *spam* functionality; others implemented a *poke user* and a *recommend user* functionality.

According to [6], spamming is actually an abuse of the actions *write post* or *forward post,* but we kept it as the descriptions explicitly use the keyword. Poking and recommending users are not functionalities of Twitter: the former is a specific action of Facebook and the latter of LinkedIn, but they appeared anyway in the classification. Very likely the two actions refer to bots that provide cross-platform functionalities, starting from Twitter, which are however out of the scope of this paper.

The goal of this inspection was to enable the automatic labeling of the repositories with action labels by analyzing the keywords found in their descriptions and the informed selection of repositories for manual inspection. The automation was achieved by transforming all keywords (and their variants) into regular expressions that could easily be searched for in the repository descriptions. The results of the classification of all retrieved Twitter repositories is shown in Fig. 2. It is evident that the most popular action labels are: *follow user*, *forward post*, *write post*, and *talk with user*. Interestingly, the label *like post* is not as important, while all other actions have very little support in the dataset.

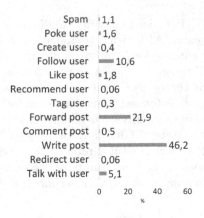

Fig. 2. Labels of repositories.

3.3   Final Dataset

With the goal of maximizing the likelihood of being able to identify recurrent patterns in the code while guaranteeing diversity in the dataset, we applied the following criteria for the selection of the code repositories to be included in the study:

- Selection of repositories that use as main programming language *Python*.
- Exclusion of all those repositories that, after manual inspection, were considered *out of scope*, e.g., because not implementing bots at all or because not implementing any direct communication with other platform users.
- For each of the four most used actions (according to the preliminary analysis), selection of 5 repositories randomly chosen from the respective *best* repositories, according to the ranking provided by GitHub. The respective scores account for the number of forks, clones, likes, and similar. This choice assures that there is a minimum number of popular projects in the dataset for which we can assume to find code patterns with reasonable support.
- For each of the four most used actions, random selection of 5 repositories from the *rest* of the respective retrieved repositories. This choice aims to include also examples that are less popular, while still useful for our analysis.
- Selection of 10 repositories randomly chosen from the *best* repositories we could *not classify* automatically in the preliminary analysis. This assures the presence of a-priori unknown but popular repositories.
- Selection of 10 repositories randomly chosen from the *rest* of the *not classified* repositories, again to assure a representative selection of generic, a-priori unknown repositories.

The final dataset selected for analysis in this paper is thus composed of 60 GitHub Twitter bot repositories whose main programming language is Python. In average, each repository comes with 3 files (standard deviation of 2.02) with an average number of lines of code of 192, an average size of 21.39 KBytes, an average number of subscribers of 3, and an average number of watchers of 13. The most popular repository (twitter-contest-bot, https://github.com/kurozael/twitter-contest-bot) has been forked 99 times, the least popular one (tweet-pix, https://github.com/mseri/tweetpix) 0 times, with an average of 5 forks per project across all projects included.

4   Identification and Analysis of Abusive Code Patterns

4.1   Method

To the best of our knowledge, this is the first study that aims to understand and categorize how state-of-the-art social bots implement their interactions with human actors and whether it is possible to identify explicit intentions for the behaviors the bots exhibit in their social communications; no results exist yet. Starting from the dataset described above, we thus perform a manual, systematic review [10] of the code retrieved from GitHub, in order to (i) identify which code passages implement *interactions* with humans, (ii) categorize the concrete *actions* the bots use in their interactions (similar to [6]), and (iii) identify different implementation *patterns* for each categorized action, along with respective *examples* (green field analysis). Actions and patterns were first categorized by one of the authors and then agreed on and integrated by both authors. The result is a conceptual framework composed of actions, patterns and code examples that may allow us to infer the intention behind possible abuses.

4.2   Actions: How Bots Participate in Communications

The preliminary analysis of our dataset in Sect. 3.2 has shown that Twitter bot developers promise almost all of the typical actions also human users can perform when using social networks. In order to understand which actions are really implemented in the repositories forming our dataset, and how, we reviewed all code files of the dataset manually looking for relevant code fragments. For a code fragment to qualify as *action* it either has to (i) implement some form of interaction by the bot with other users or (ii) implement application logic that manages content or user data fetched from the social network. An action thus represents a self-contained interaction of the bot with content and/or users.

The result of this iteration is summarized in Table 1, which describes the 9 actions that represent a consistent synthesis of all examples identified by this exercise. As expected, the bottom-up analysis brought up a set of typical *social network actions*, declined in Twitter terminology. Bots *follow* other users, *like* their tweets, *tweet* own content, *mention* other users in their tweets, or *retweet* tweets by others. Inside private chat rooms, they also *talk to* other users using instant messages. This result is in line with the actions identified in [6].

But there is more. Looking at the code of the bots further produced three *internal actions* that support their social network actions: bots heavily *search* Twitter for users or tweets, in order to harness accounts and content to work with; they intentionally *pause* or delay their interactions, in order to impersonate users; and they may *store* content they retrieve from the network for later use. These internal actions are observed only in the code of the bots and would not be identifiable by looking at the externally visible communications of the bots only, as done by most literature on the topic. Later in this paper, we will see that also internal actions that are not immediately visible to users may lead to abuses and harm.

Table 1. Synthesis of online communication actions implemented by Twitter bots

Action	Description
Search	Search users or tweets using names, keywords, hashtags, ids or similar or by navigating social network relationships (e.g., friends of friends, followers of friends, friends of followers, followers of followers)
Follow	Follow users to establish social relationships
Like	Like tweets by other users to endorse them
Tweet	Post a new tweet to communicate content
Mention	Mention other users in tweets using @ to attract attention
Retweet	Re-post tweets by other users to endorse them
Talk to	Send direct messages to users to converse with them
Pause	Pause the conversation flow of the bot
Store	Store content retrieved from the social network for later use

4.3   Code Patterns: How Bots Implement Their Actions

Focusing on the code fragments considered relevant as communication actions, a second iteration of the code review aimed at synthesizing all examples of action implementations into a taxonomy of recurrent code patterns that explains how actions are implemented in practice. For a code fragment to qualify as a *pattern*, two requirements must be met: (i) it must be possible to abstract the fragment and to associate it to at least one action, and (ii) it must recur at least two times in the dataset. A pattern thus represents the intended function of a set of instructions, not their syntactic manifestation in the code.

Even accounting for different names of identifiers in the code, without this type of semantic abstraction it would be necessary to perform a purely syntactic similarity search. However, given the diversity of the repositories and developers that characterize our dataset, only unlikely it would have been possible to spot two fragments that are syntactically equivalent.

Table 2. Taxonomy of code patterns used for the implementation of actions.

Action	Pattern	Description
Search	*User search*	Search user account by name, keyword, id or similar
	Tweet search	Search tweets by keyword or hashtag
	Trend search	Search trending topics or hashtags by location
Follow	*Indiscriminate follow*	Follow users without checking suitability of users, usernames or content shared
	Whitelist-based follow	Follow only users whose attributes or tweets match some element of a given whitelist
	Blacklist-based follow	Don't follow users whose attributes or tweets satisfy one or more criteria specified in a blacklist
	Phantom follow	Follow users and unfollow them as soon as a given condition is satisfied, e.g., a limit of friends reached or being followed back
Like	*Indiscriminate like*	Like tweets without checking suitability of content, user or username
	Whitelist-based like	Like only tweets by users whose attributes or content match some element of a whitelist
	Blacklist-based like	Don't like tweets whose attributes or users match an element of a blacklist
	Mass like	Aggressively like tweets of given users
Tweet	*Fixed-content tweet*	The content of the tweet is taken from a fixed, static collection of predefined messages
	AI-generated tweet	The text of the tweet is automatically generated using AI/NLP tools
	Trusted source tweet	The content of the tweet is taken from a source that can be considered trusted
	Tweet with opt-in	Tweets are sent only to people who ask to interact with the bot, sending it a message or mentioning it in a tweet
Mention	*Indiscriminate mention*	Mention other users without checking suitability of username or content shared
	Targeted mention	Classify users on the basis of their tweets and mention them in targeted messages
	Whitelist-based mention	Mention only users whose attributes match some element of a whitelist
	Blacklist-based mention	Don't mention users whose attributes match elements of a blacklist
Retweet	*Indiscriminate retweet*	Retweet tweets without checking content or username for suitability
	Whitelist-based retweet	Retweet content only from users whose attributes match some element of a whitelist
	Blacklist-based retweet	Don't retweet tweets whose attributes or users satisfy some condition expressed in a blacklist
	Mass retweet	Aggressively retweet multiple tweets by selected users
Talk to	*Indiscriminate talk*	Send direct, instant messages to users without checking their suitability
	Talk with opt-in	Reply only to messages sent to the bot (passive behavior)
	AI-generated talk	Generate messages using AI/NLP tools
	Fixed-content talk	Take message from a fixed list of predefined phrases
	Targeted talk	Classify users based on their tweets or attributes and target message accordingly
Pause	*Mimic human*	Use pauses in instant messages to deliver human-like conversation experience to other humans
	Satisfy API constraints	Use as short as possible pauses just to avoid being blocked by API usage limitations
Store	*Store persistently*	Store retrieved content or user information for later use

For instance, it is possible to interact with the Twitter API using direct, low-level HTTP requests, or one can use a dedicated API wrapper library, such as (in order of use in our dataset): tweepy (http://www.tweepy.org), Twitter libraries (https://bit.ly/2Gg3WJC), TwitterAPI (https://bit.ly/2UwSZri), Twython (https://bit.ly/2aOjCnT), or own, proprietary libraries. Similarly, there are different options for the automatic generation of text for tweets or instant messages, such as nltk (https://www.nltk.org/) or seq2seq (https://bit.ly/2Ry2FQt). Patterns abstract away from these implementation choices and aim to capture the essence of what the developer wanted to implement.

The result of this analysis is reported in Table 2, which names and summarizes the identified patterns. These 31 patterns concisely represent the different interpretations of the 9 actions as implemented in the approximately 140 code examples collected and analyzed.

Example 1. Let us inspect the following two lines of code to understand the logic of the proposed patterns:

```
for tweet in tweepy.Cursor(api.search, q=QUERY).items():
    tweet.user.follow()
```

The code uses the tweepy library to interact with Twitter and implements two actions: *search* and *follow*. The *search* action is reified by the *search user* pattern (which exact feature is used for the search is unknown as the content of QUERY is not visible). The *follow* action is reified by the *indiscriminate follow* pattern, as line 2 follows all users without applying any filter on the users.   ◁

Example 2. The following three lines of code show a concrete implementation of the *blacklist-based mention* pattern:

```
def mentions(count, max_seconds_ago, id_blacklist) :
    return [mention for mention in api.mentions_timeline(count=count)
        if not mention.id in id_blacklist ]
```

The code defines a function that returns all the ids of the users that have mentioned the bot in prior tweets (expressing some form of interest in the bot) and whose ids are not contained in the list of banned ids id_blacklist.   ◁

Incidentally, these examples are also representative of two recurrent types of patterns across multiple actions: for all those actions that somehow endorse a user or a tweet (follow, like, mention, retweet), the analysis identified patterns that do so *indiscriminately* or that do so by first checking if the involved user is *blacklisted* or not. Independently of these examples, the analysis also identified other recurrent types of patterns for these actions that endorse users only if they are *whitelisted*. Other notable patterns implement massively repeated actions like *mass like* and *mass retweet*, which aggressively endorse content by given users, or specially targeted actions like *targeted mention* and *targeted talk*, which instead carefully select the users to interact with (e.g., suicide candidates) and send them particularly tailored messages (e.g., to point to help and prevent suicide).

4.4 Effects of Actions: Assessing Potential Harmfulness

Considering again the indiscriminate, blacklist and whitelist patterns, it is important to acknowledge that they implement different levels of sensibility of risk as perceived by the developer. Indiscriminately retweeting content expresses either a high level of trust in the users who produce the retweeted content, or it expresses a lack of awareness of the risks that retweeting for example offensive, denigrating or obscene content may have on the reputation of the bot owner. Either way, it becomes evident that each pattern may have a different effect or impact on the users a bot interacts with.

In our prior work [6], we identified 12 major types of abuses bots have committed in the past (see the top-right list in Fig. 3) and that have produced harm (remember Sect. 2.1). The first half of these abuses are legally prosecutable in most democratic countries (see, for example, New Zealand's Harmful Digital Communications Act of 2015 [14]). The typical question that remains unanswered when harm occurs is *why* the respective abuse was committed.

Some bots intentionally create spam messages, e.g., to influence political elections [2], but then there are bots like Microsoft's AI-based chatbot Tay that got trained by multiple colluding users, e.g., to offend Jews (http://bit.ly/2DCdqM4). Evidently, the bot was not ready for orchestrated attacks. From the outside, it is generally not possible to tell why abuse happens. This paper provides a look inside the logic that drives bots, and attempts a technical explanation for some of the abuses. In fact, patterns may have the following *effects*:

- *Enable an abuse*, if they implement logic that by design performs an abuse. For example, the *phantom follow* pattern enables mimicking interest for opportunistic reasons, e.g., to be followed back by users, or the *mass retweet* pattern enables artificially boosting the visibility of a user.
- *Prevent an abuse*, if they implement logic that aims to prevent the bot from performing an abuse. The *blacklist-based follow* pattern, for instance, prevents interactions with unwanted users, while the *tweet with opt-in* pattern prevents spamming users not interested in the bot.
- *Be vulnerable to content abuse*, if they implement interactions with users and/or content that may be inappropriate. The *indiscriminate follow* pattern, for instance, causes the bot to follow users that may have inappropriate usernames or spread inappropriate content. The vulnerability may arise when endorsing content or users or when feeding user-provided content to AI algorithms without proper prior checks (see the example of Tay).
- *Be vulnerable to trust abuse*, if they forward, store or analyze content retrieved from users. The *store persistently* pattern is an example of this threat. A user sharing, for instance, sensitive information via personal messages is vulnerable if stored data are leaked to unintended audiences.

These four effects may translate into human users of the social network getting harmed or not. But harm in this context has two sides: if a user gets harmed through interaction with a bot, this may also affect and possibly harm the owner

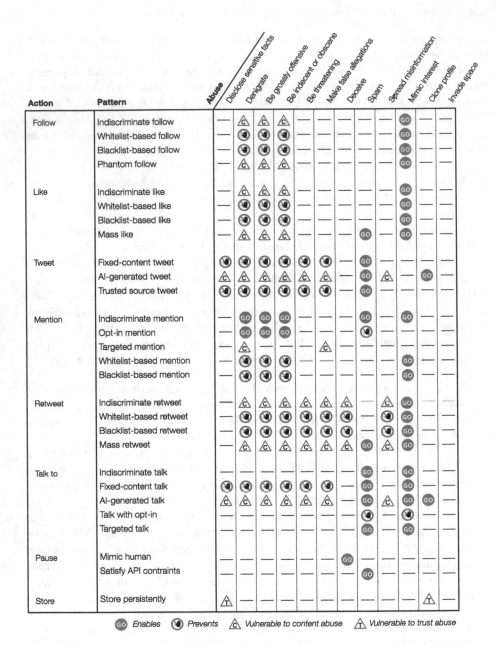

Fig. 3. Potential effects of actions and patterns on the users in online communications: patterns either enable, prevent or are vulnerable to abuses. For example, following an account with a denigrating or offending username may perpetuate and endorse the denigration or offense.

of the bot himself. If a bot threatens someone or discriminates people, the owner may become subject to legal prosecution. If it leaks private data, it may be suspended by the social network, as this violates the usage policies.

Figure 3 graphically summarizes for the patterns in Table 2 (except the *search* patterns without side-effects) which abuses they may enable, prevent or risk to commit. It is meant to create awareness in bot developers of the effects the code they write may have once their bot is deployed and interacting with people.

Coming back to the *why* question and the technical considerations on the possible abuses, it seems reasonable to conclude: (i) that bots that explicitly enable abuses *intentionally* try to do harm or at least accept the possibility to do so; (ii) bots that are vulnerable to content abuse by other users may *unintentionally* cause harm, while still being responsible for the content they endorse or spread; and (iii) bots that are vulnerable to trust abuse, if they leak data, may do so intentionally (e.g., it they sell data) or unintentionally (e.g., if intruders steel data). Regarding this last case, we did not find any hint for intentional leaks in our dataset.

It is important to note that the analyzed dataset features only a few bots that implement patterns that aim to prevent abuses, which testifies a generally low awareness of the problem and commitment to mitigate risk by developers. Specifically, only 5 repositories implement blacklist-based patterns, 2 control if the user is verified by a whitelist (implementing multiple patterns), 6 use opt-in verification, 4 use a trusted source for tweets, and 8 use fixed content instead. Finally, we did not find any indication of effects of the identified patterns on the abuse *invade space* (it refers to bots invading spaces, e.g., online discussion groups or social networks, that are not meant for bot participation), as Twitter is generally open to bots.

5 Related Works

As already hinted at in the introduction, the topic of social bots has so far been approached mostly from the perspective of telling humans and bots apart, that is, with the intention of *detecting* bots. The work that is most closely related to this aspect is Botometer, formerly known as BotOrNot [7, 8], an online tool that computes a bot-likelihood score for Twitter accounts and allows one to tell bots and genuine user accounts apart. The tool builds on more than 1000 features among network, user, friends, temporal, content and sentiment features, and uses a random forest classifier for each subset of features. The training data used is based on bot accounts collected in prior work by Lee et al. [11], who used Twitter honeypots to lure bots and collected about 36000 candidate bot accounts following or messaging their honeypot accounts.

Some works go further and turn their focus to *specific types* of social bots and, thereby, harms. For instance, Ratkiewicz et al. [13] studied the phenomenon of *astroturfing*, i.e., political campaigns that aim to fake social support from people for a cause, and showed that bots play a major role in astroturfing activities in Twitter. Cresci et al. [5] specifically focused on the problem of *fake followers*.

They constructed a dataset of human accounts (manually and by invitation of friends) and bought fake followers from online services like http://fastfollowerz. com. The work compares two types of automatic classifiers, classifiers based on expert-defined rules and feature-based classifiers (machine learning), and shows (i) that fake followers can indeed be spotted and (ii) that black-box, feature-based classifiers perform better than white-box, rule-based classifiers. In addition, the work also produced a publicly available, labeled dataset that can be used for research purposes. Varol et al. [15] propose a bottom-up approach to the identification of bots with similar online behavior. The classifier used is the one adopted by Botometer, while the dataset used also included a manually annotated collection of Twitter accounts. After classifying accounts into bot or not, the authors further clustered the bot accounts into three types of bots: *spammers*, *self promoters*, and accounts that *post content from applications*. Chu et al. [4] coined the term *cyborg* to refer to bot-assisted humans in social networks and used a manually labeled dataset of 6000 randomly sampled Twitter accounts and a random forest classifier plus entropy measures to classify accounts into bots, cyborgs and humans.

In terms of *datasets* analyzed for bot detection, Beskow and Carley [1] propose four tiers of data for the classification of Twitter accounts: single tweet text (tier 0), account + one tweet (1), account + full timeline (2), and account + timeline + friends timelines (3). The assumption is that bot detection is achieved using feature-based classification or AI algorithms. In fact, with their tool bot-hunter, the authors study different machine learning techniques for tier-1 datasets. Differently from these classification-based approaches, Cao et al. [3] describe SybilRank, a tool for the detection of sybil accounts (bots) in social networks by analyzing the social graph (of Facebook, in the specific study). The study in this paper focuses on a different type of dataset, i.e., code, to understand the internals of bots, not their externally visible behavior or traces.

Little or no work has been done so far on the analysis of *harms* and *abuses*, as proposed in this paper. Perhaps the work by Varol et al. [15] can be seen as an ethical alarm: it estimates that between 9% and 15% of all accounts in Twitter are likely automated accounts and shows that bots are able to apply sophisticated communication tactics, distinguishing between humans and bots.

6 Conclusion

This paper proposes an original perspective on bots for online communication: instead of looking at messages or network activity, which is the typical practice in literature, it analyzes the code that produces them. To the best of our knowledge, this is the first study of its kind in this area. The study contributes to the state of the art in a threefold fashion: It extracts *31 patterns* that implement different variants of 9 communication actions from a dataset of 60 GitHub Twitter bot repositories (approximately 75–80 h of manual code inspection). Then, it discusses the *effects* the patterns may have at runtime and provides a systematic mapping of patterns to potential abuses as a reference for developers.

Finally, it proposes a technical interpretation of why abuses may happen by linking the *intentionality* of abuses to the nature of the patterns, distinguishing between intentional and unintentional patterns. These ethical aspects are particularly relevant to web engineering if we consider that many understand bots as the apps of tomorrow. As a possible usage scenario, social network providers that host third-party bot code (e.g., Facebook) could use these patterns to implement early warning systems to prevent harm.

The findings of this paper are empirical and stem from a careful, manual systematic code review. They are limited by nature. As for the *internal validity*, the study suffers of course from the limited size of the dataset; perhaps more repositories would have allowed us to identify more patterns. Also, the open-source nature of the projects may provide a limited view on the possible patterns, as developers of intentionally malicious bots may not share their code. The focus on Python was needed to keep the dataset manageable. The careful, randomized selection of repositories aimed to increase internal validity. As for the *external validity*, different programming languages and communication platforms may behave differently. However, the core of the actions and patterns proposed in this paper are similar in other platforms and programming languages. These may differ in platform-specific functionalities (e.g., poking a user in Facebook), but the abstractions of this paper make the actions and patterns portable.

As for the next steps, we are already working on the implementation of a suitable, formal language for action patterns and a respective pattern search engine for the automated retrieval of patterns from large numbers of code repositories based on the approach proposed in [12]. Expanding the horizon of the investigation beyond Twitter and Python is planned next.

References

1. Beskow, D.M., Carley, K.M.: Bot-hunter: a tiered approach to detecting & characterizing automated activity on twitter. In: SBP-BRiMS 2018 (2018)
2. Bessi, A., Ferrara, E.: Social bots distort the 2016 US presidential election online discussion. First Monday **21**(11) (2016)
3. Cao, Q., Sirivianos, M., Yang, X., Pregueiro, T.: Aiding the detection of fake accounts in large scale social online services. In: Proceedings of the 9th USENIX conference on Networked Systems Design and Implementation, pp. 15–15 (2012)
4. Chu, Z., Gianvecchio, S., Wang, H., Jajodia, S.: Detecting automation of twitter accounts: are you a human, bot, or cyborg? IEEE Trans. Dependable Secure Comput. **9**(6), 811–824 (2012)
5. Cresci, S., Di Pietro, R., Petrocchi, M., Spognardi, A., Tesconi, M.: Fame for sale: efficient detection of fake Twitter followers. Decis. Support Syst. **80**, 56–71 (2015)
6. Daniel, F., Cappiello, C., Benatallah, B.: Bots acting like humans: understanding and preventing harm. IEEE Internet Comput. (2019, in print). https://ieeexplore.ieee.org/document/8611348
7. Davis, C.A., Varol, O., Ferrara, E., Flammini, A., Menczer, F.: BotOrNot: a system to evaluate social bots. In: WWW 2016, pp. 273–274 (2016)
8. Ferrara, E., Varol, O., Davis, C., Menczer, F., Flammini, A.: The rise of social bots. Commun. ACM **59**(7), 96–104 (2016)

9. Hey, T., Tansley, S., Tolle, K.M., et al.: The Fourth Paradigm: Data-intensive Scientific Discovery, vol. 1. Microsoft Research Redmond, WA (2009)
10. Kitchenham, B.: Procedures for performing systematic reviews. Keele University, Keele, UK **33**(2004), 1–26 (2004)
11. Lee, K., Eoff, B.D., Caverlee, J.: Seven months with the devils: a long-term study of content polluters on Twitter. In: ICWSM, pp. 185–192 (2011)
12. Paul, S., Prakash, A.: A framework for source code search using program patterns. IEEE Trans. Soft. Eng. **20**(6), 463–475 (1994)
13. Ratkiewicz, J., Conover, M., Meiss, M.R., Gonçalves, B., Flammini, A., Menczer, F.: Detecting and tracking political abuse in social media. In: ICWSM, pp. 297–304 (2011)
14. The Parliament of New Zealand: Harmful Digital Communications Act 2015. Public Act 2015 No 63 (2015). http://www.legislation.govt.nz/act/public/2015/0063/
15. Varol, O., Ferrara, E., Davis, C.A., Menczer, F., Flammini, A.: Online human-bot interactions: Detection, estimation, and characterization. arXiv preprint arXiv:1703.03107 (2017)

CrowDIY: How to Design and Adapt Collaborative Crowdsourcing Workflows Under Budget Constraints

Rong Chen$^{(\boxtimes)}$, Bo Li, Hu Xing, and Yijing Wang

Dalian Maritime University, Dalian 116026, China
rchen@dlmu.edu.cn

Abstract. Workflow quality is a key determinant of crowdsourcing complex work, but finding ways to task design and plan has proved illusive. Instead, we formulate it as an optimization problem with budget constraints and fewer decision variables to set. We propose a two-staged approach CrowDIY that can not only estimate task attributes based on previous tasks but also optimize them with budget constraints in order to publish tasks more wisely in a timely manner. Several experimental studies have been conducted, and the results show compelling evidence that, under different conditions, the proposed approach can effectively reduce the workload of workflow design and plan, while avoiding commonly encountered trial-and-error in crowdsourcing workflows and leading up to successful complex outcomes.

Keywords: Crowdsourcing workflow · Workflow design and plan · Task publishing · Optimization

1 Motivation and Background

The dominant infrastructure in human computation systems today is *workflow*, which typically splits a business process into multiple microtasks and asks distinct workers to carry them out in pre-specified steps on services like Amazon's Mechanical Turk (MTurk), CrowdFlower and CrowdSPRING [4]. There is little doubt that crowdsourcing workflows (CWs) are powerful because they build operational knowledge into software [2], allowing people around the world to work collaboratively and contribute meaningfully.

Though CW techniques pushed the boundary of crowsourcing [8], task requesters still need to program their own workflow or intervene continuously on the execution of their manmade workflow [9]. Task requesters need to make a variety of decisions regarding the task they want to submit [12]. To understand the complexity behind practical usage, we use the example of writing short essay about Dalian – a tourist city in China. Figure 1 shows the screenshot of a crowdsourcing workflow G_1 composed of eleven tasks with indexed numbers inside circles (denoted as $T_1, T_2, ..., T_{11}$). Tasks are of specified types: *question and answer* (QA), *choice, merge, notification*, AND- and OR-node. To design G_1 with a graphical web UI on CrowDIY (Crowdsourcing - Do It Yourselves), the requester decomposes essay writing into several steps: (1) Puts a

M. Bakaev et al. (Eds.): ICWE 2019, LNCS 11496, pp. 203–210, 2019.
https://doi.org/10.1007/978-3-030-19274-7_15

204   R. Chen et al.

question to crowd for suggesting aspects to describe Dalian via QA node T_1, (2) Chooses three hot aspects via majority voting (T_2), (3) Asks crowd to write about the selected aspects (later bound to culture (T_3) and architecture (T_4) and transportation (T_5) at runtime), and then asks others to read and give their rates $(T_6, T_7,$ and T_8 respectively), (4) Combine the content via a merge node T_9, (5) Makes his own decision via choice node T_{10}, and (6) T_{11} to notify the completion. Figure 1 also shows the execution status of G_1 that started from T_1, ran through task nodes (denoted in green), steps into T_9 for merging, and will end in T_{11} for notification.

T₁: Aspects to describe Dalian
T₂: Requester's choice
T₃: Dalian's cultrue
T₄: Dalian's architecture
T₅: Dalian's transportation
T₆: Reader's choice
T₇: Reader's choice
T₈: Reader's choice
T₉: Combine the contents
T₁₀: Requester's choice
T₁₁: Completion notification

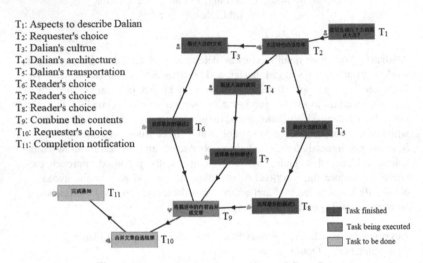

Fig. 1. The motivational example workflow G_1.

Provided with task decompositions (e.g. via a map-reduce paradigm [7], a divide-and-conquer strategy [6], and a customized policy [1]), the design and plan of workflows like G_1 are still not easy because at least information such as the task type and description, time effort, time allotted, the reward for which the worker actually booked the task, and the time it took from publishing to booking should be defined for each task at the design time. We address the problem of crowdsourcing workflow optimization (CWO), and propose a two-staged approach that can not only estimate attributes and parameters but also optimize them with budget constraints, and then publish tasks more wisely in a timely manner.

2 Proposed Approach

2.1 Problem Statement

A *workflow* can be characterized by a directed acyclic graph (DAG) G = (**T**, **E**) where the nodes **T** = $\{T_1, T_2, ..., T_n\}$ correspond to the tasks and the edges **E** indicate the data dependencies between tasks.

Definition 1 (Total Cost). The total cost of a workflow G = (**T**, **E**) is the sum of all task rewards, defined as:

$$Cost(G) = \sum_{\forall T_i \in T} r_i \tag{1}$$

Besides rewards, more attributes are associated with a task in a real crowdsourcing workflow; they are *type*, *level of difficulty*, *effort to complete* in terms of the number of time points, *time allotted*, *reward*, *latest booking time* for booking, *earliest publishing time* and *buffer time*. Concisely, each task T_i is characterized by T_i = (type$_i$, lod$_i$, etc$_i$, ta$_i$, r$_i$, lbt$_i$, ept$_i$, bt$_i$).

Definition 2 (Sequential and Parallel Execution). A sequential execution of a workflow G = (**T**, **E**) is a sequence of tasks $sp = [T_1, T_2, ..., T_n]$, such that T_1 is the initial task, T_n is the final task, and for every task T_i ($1 \leq i \leq n$):

- T_i is a direct successor of one of the tasks in *sp*.
- T_i is not a direct successor of any of the tasks in *sp*.
- There is no state T_j in *sp* such that T_j and T_i belong to two alternative branches of the workflow.
  A parallel execution of a workflow G is a set $pp(G) = \{sp_1, sp_2, ..., sp_m\}$ of sequential executions of G such that all the parallel branches of every AND-node in $sp_j = [T_1, T_2, ..., T_n]$ ($1 \leq j \leq m$) are executed when that AND-node is entered. Formally,
- If T_i is the initial task of one of the parallel regions of an AND-node, then, for every other parallel region C, one of the initial tasks of C belongs to the set $\{T_1, ..., T_{i-1}, T_{i+1}, ..., T_n\}$.

The second goal of the CW research is to manage business processes in terms of time, e.g. by controlling the *estimated total execution time*, which means the longest sequential execution path that covers all parallel regions.

Definition 3 (Estimated Total Execution Time) Let $sp = [T_1, T_2, ..., T_n] \in pp(G)$ be any sequential execution of a workflow G. The estimated total execution time of G, denoted by *ETime*(G), is the maximum of *ETime*(sp):

$$ETime(sp) = lbt_1 + \sum_{i=1}^{n} ta_i \tag{2}$$

$$ETime(G) = \max_{\forall sp \in pp(G)} ETime(sp) \tag{3}$$

The present research makes two extensions to the available CW studies: (1) A fewer task attributes (e.g. type$_i$ and lod$_i$) are mandatory while others are optional. The mandatory part are set manually while the optional part can be defined by functions that take mandatory lod$_i$ and historical task data as arguments. (2) We control the execution time by minimizing the overdue risk while ensuring the deadline and the cost budget. Next we offer an overview of our approach CrowDIY before formalizing them as the CWO problem.

2.2   CWO Formulation

Throughout this paper, time-related parameters and task attributes are supposed to be characterized in terms of time points t_0 (start time), t_1, t_2, ..., t_D (deadline time) such that each t_i defines a point in time that i time slices have elapsed.

Definition 4 (Overdue Risk). The overdue risk of any task T_i with respect to start time t and buffer time bt is defined as:

$$f(lod_i, t, bt) = lod_i \cdot [\alpha_2(t+bt)^2 + \alpha_1(t+bt) + \alpha_0] \tag{4}$$

with weights α_0, α_1 and $\alpha_2 \in [0..1]$.

A CWO problem is to find a solution of task attributes with minimized overdue risk while not exceeding the deadline and the cost budget. There exist two solution scenarios: *static assignment*, in which *lbt*s and *ta*s of all tasks are set while aggregating estimated execution time in design phase, and *dynamic assignment*, in which *ept*s and *bt*s are set for initial tasks to be published while aggregating the estimated execution time of tasks not yet run.

Definition 5 (Static CWO Assignment). Let G = (**T**, **E**) be a workflow under design, R_{max} be the budget in score points, and D_{max} be the deadline in time points. A static CWO assignment is to find: for each task T_i in $sp = [T_1, T_2, ..., T_n] \in pp(G)$ ($1 \leq i \leq n$), the lbt_i and the ta_i that, minimize

$$\sum\nolimits_{\forall T_i \in sp} f(lod_i, lbt_i, ta_i)$$

subject to

$$ta_i < lbt_i - lbt_{i-1}(i \geq 2) \tag{5}$$

$$Cost(G) \leq R_{max} \tag{6}$$

$$ETime(G) \leq t_{D_{max}} \tag{7}$$

Note that the real execution time of tasks may be different from what was estimated. Let $\mathbf{T}_C \subseteq \mathbf{T}$ be tasks that have already completed so far, and $\mathbf{E}_C = \{<T_1, T_2> \mid \forall T_1, T_2 \in \mathbf{T}_C, <T_1, T_2> \in \mathbf{E}\}$ be edges that have already been covered. We separate G into two subgraphs: the completed part $G_C = (\mathbf{T}_C, \mathbf{E}_C)$, and the part not completed $\overline{G}_C = (\mathbf{T}-\mathbf{T}_C, \mathbf{E}-\mathbf{E}_C)$.

Definition 6 (Dynamic CWO Assignment). Let $\mathbf{T}_C = \{T_1, T_2, ..., T_C\}$ be tasks G = (**T**, **E**) of that have already completed at time point t_C, and G = $G_C \cup \overline{G}_C$, and *In* $(\overline{G}_C) = \{T_i \mid T_i$ is the initial task of any sequential execution $sp \in pp(\overline{G}_C)\}$. Let R_{max} be the budget in terms of score points, and D_{max} be the deadline in terms of the number of time points. A dynamic CWO problem is to find: for each task $T_s \in In(\overline{G}_C)$, and for each task $T_i \in sp \in pp(\overline{G}_C)$ $(i \neq s)$, the ept_s, the bt_s, the lbt_i, and the ta_i that, minimize

$$\sum\nolimits_{\forall T_i \in sp} f(lod_i, lbt_i, ta_i) + \sum\nolimits_{\forall T_s} f(lod_s, ept_s, bt_s)$$

subject to

$$t_C \le ept_s < lbt_s (\forall T_s \in In(\overline{G}_C)) \tag{8}$$

$$ta_s \le bt_s (\forall T_s \in In(\overline{G}_C)) \tag{9}$$

$$ta_i < lbt_i - lbt_{i-1} (i \ge 2) \tag{10}$$

$$Cost(G) + Cost(\overline{G}_C) \le R_{max} \tag{11}$$

$$ETime(\overline{G}_C) \le t_{D_{max}} \tag{12}$$

2.3 Solution Algorithms

Algorithm 1 depicts the overall procedure of CrowDIY, which starts from *Task*, max reward R_{max}, max deadline D_{max} to perform workflow design and revise (Step 1), planning (Steps 2–4) and publishing (Steps 7–10) remained tasks to crowd workers until all tasks are finished or the Dynamic CWO has no solution.

Algorithm 1. Crowdiy(*Task*, R_{max}, D_{max})

1: G←Design(*Task*, R_{max}, D_{max}),
2: Set up G with Estimate(G);
3: CWO←Transform(t_0, G, R_{max}, D_{max});
4: < because it require, R_{min}, D_{min}>←Solve(CWO);
4: <*Task*, R_{min}, D_{min}>←Solve(CWO);
5: **if** $R_{max} < R_{min}$ or $D_{max} < D_{min}$ **then**
6:    **if** not terminate **then** goto Step 1;
7: $t_C \leftarrow t_1$;
8: **do** increase t_C;
9:    **if** a task is finished **then** Publish(G, T_C, R_{max}, D_{max});
10: **until** $In(\overline{G}_C)$ empty or no solution;

Algorithm 2. Publish(G, T_C, R_{max}, D_{max})

Input: Workflow G, tasks completed so far T_C, max reward R_{max}, max deadline D_{max}
Output: <*Task*, R_{min}, D_{min}>

1: Let G = $G_C \cup \overline{G}_C$;
2: Let $In(\overline{G}_C)=\{T_i \mid T_i$ is the initial task of any sequential execution $sp \in pp(\overline{G}_C)\}$;
3: CWO←Transform(t_C, $\overline{G}_C$, R_{max}, D_{max});
5: <*Task*, R_{min}, D_{min}>←Solve(CWO);
6: **if** non-empty *Task* **then** publish task $T_i \in In(\overline{G}_C)$;
7: return <*Task*, R_{min}, D_{min}>;

Design($Task$, R_{max}, D_{max}) means that the requester can design a CW via the Web UI in several steps: decompose complex tasks into small ones by calling divide(Task), place a choice node for selecting answers, manage task dependencies and structure (AND-node or OR-node), later combine the results into a coherent solution via merge node, and finalize with a notification node. Design can be extended recursively or revised repeatedly by Algorithm 1 (from step 1 to 6). As described by Algorithm 2, Transform(t_C, $\overline{G}_C$, R_{max}, D_{max}) instantiates constraints Eqs. (8)–(12) and the overdue risk function Eq. (4) for $\overline{G}_C$ at current time t_C.

3   Evaluation and Results

We implemented the solution method in a crowdsourcing workflow system CrowDIY in Python [5], running on the Django Web Framework with SQlite and other tools for solving the CWO problem and generating workflow. To solve the CWO problem, CrowDIY integrates Gurobi, Cplex and Choco through constraint programing in Java in order to find static and dynamic CWO assignments. We set weights of Eq. (4) with $\alpha_0 = 0.25$, $\alpha_1 = 0.4$, and $\alpha_2 = 0.5$.

Workflows were generated with JGraphT–a Java library of graph theory data structures and algorithms [10], and mandatory attributes such as node type and level of difficulty are generated uniformly in random. We vary the number of workflows from 1 to 500 while the number of tasks in every workflow is in [6..20]. We assumed that there were 3000 workers and task attributes were generated. For every task type, we generated other task attributes that are linearly dependent on task difficulty as we did in case studies. Also 300 workers were assigned the least time allotted to finish a task and the minimum acceptable reward, which were generated using the normal distribution based on the average reward, average allotted time and their allowable deviation parameters. So we prepared a large number of different workflows with randomizing workflow structures and diverse deadlines, and tasks in them have various allotted times and booking times.

The number (#W) of workflows ranges from 1 to 500, and each is compared with the reference case #W = 1. First, we guess the max deadline D_{max} for every workflow in every case. If the manmade D_{max} does not make sense, there is no solution to the CWO formulation of the workflow under consideration. So we can count the number of trial-and-error (#E) of CWO solving. If D_{max} makes sense, then we guess the max reward R_{max}. If the manmade R_{max} works, constraint solvers return the overdue risk and their execution time (#T) in seconds. In particular, #OR indicates the multiple of 329.7 or 722.1, namely the overdue risk of the reference case #W = 1. If R_{max} is implausible, "no solution" means that, at design time the workflow is found more likely to "fail" because it requires the deadline extension. So we compare the time extension (#X) in time points raised by failed workflows. The more time extension failed workflows require, the better solution the constraint solver can ensure. All metrics we used are reported on average for all the workflows we prepared.

The first experiment is to find the best solver for workflow plan (i.e. static CWO assignment). The comparison results were summarized in Table 1. It can be seen that as #W grows, their performance present the trend of linear growth under four metrics. Also we can see that the performance of Gurobi and Cplex are similar in #E, #OR, and #X. But Gurobi is much better than Cplex in terms of #T. So we choose Gurobi to conduct the rest experiments.

Table 1. Results from comparative constraint solvers.

	Gurobi				Cplex				Choco			
#W	#E	#OR 329.7	#T	#X	#E	#OR 329.7	#T	#X	#E	#OR 722.1	#T	#X
1	0	1	2.3	0	0	1	2.9	0	0	1	4.1	0
10	0	5.5	2.9	0	0	5.5	4.8	0	0	5.5	6.0	0
50	0	13.6	3.5	0	0	13.6	18.1	0	0	13.7	26.4	0
100	1	23.7	7.5	1	1	23.7	23.5	1	1	23.4	65.6	1
200	3	27.8	11.0	7	4	27.9	59.0	7	1	28.0	130.0	3
300	5	31.0	10.2	10	5	31.1	91.5	11	1	31.3	146.6	3
400	6	34.1	15.0	12	7	34.1	116.3	13	1	34.2	272.8	4
500	9	38.0	17.1	17	10	38.1	165.0	18	2	38.1	299.8	4

The second experiment is to verify whether buffer time influences the final outcome of all workflows in the task publishing algorithm with a linear dependence $bt_s = x \cdot ta_s$ ($x \in \{0.2, 0.5, 1, 2, 3, 4, 5, 6\}$). It can be seen from Fig. 4 that the optimal results have achieved the minimum value when buffer time is almost equal to its allotted time. In case of smaller buffer time, for example $x = 0.2$ and $x = 0.5$ (x-axis), more tasks were not booked on time, so the reward to workers should be raised. At the same time, lack of time also increase the possibility of missing deadlines. That is why three metrics (#OR, #X and #E) have higher values. If the buffer time is larger, for instance coefficient $x \in [2..6]$, the values of three metrics are higher than the optimal results, but still much lower than the buffer time. This is because tasks can be booked earlier by workers.

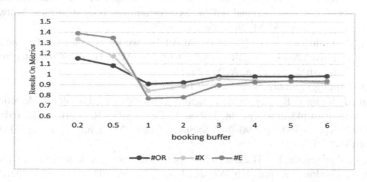

Fig. 4. Finding the most appropriate buffer time.

4 Conclusion and Future Work

The present approach eases the complexity behind collaborative crowdsourcing process, but dynamic approach to publishing cannot guarantee the time constraints because there is a lot of uncertainty in crowdsourcing, especially the anonymous people with uncertain skills and commitments. What merits future investigation includes advancing the training of Estimator and the control of workflow, and exploiting statistical sampling of people from the crowd after they contributed meaningfully in previous tasks [3, 11].

Acknowledgments. This work is supported by the National Natural Science Foundation of China (No. 61672122, No. 61602077), the Natural Science Foundation of Liaoning Province of China (No. 2015020023), the Educational Commission of Liaoning Province of China (No. L2015060) and the Fundamental Research Funds for the Central Universities (NO. 3132016348).

References

1. Bernaschina, C., Catallo I., Fraternali P., Martinenghi, D., Tagliasacchi, M.: Champagne: a web tool for the execution of crowdsourcing campaigns. In: International Conference on World Wide Web (Companion), pp. 171–174. ACM, New York (2015)
2. Bigham, J.P., Bernstein, M.S., Adar, E.: Human-computer interaction and collective intelligence. In: Handbook of Collective Intelligence, pp. 57–84. MIT Press (2015)
3. Chen, R., Chen, S.-F., Zhang, X.-Y.: A two-staged task assignment algorithm for worker recommendation in a crowdsourcing environment. In: International Conference on Industrial Engineering and Engineering Management, Singapore, pp. 2034–2038 (2017)
4. Doan, A., Ramakrishnan, R., Halevy, A.Y.: Crowdsourcing systems on the world-wide web. Commun. ACM **54**, 86–96 (2011)
5. Huang, Y.-T.: Design and implementation of a workflow system for crowdsourcing. Master thesis, Dalian Maritime University (2017). (in Chinese)
6. Kittur, A., Smus, B., Khamkar, S., Kraut, R.E.: CrowdForge: crowdsourcing complex work. In: Annual ACM Symposium on User Interface Software and Technology, pp. 43–52. ACM, New York (2011)
7. Kulkarni, A., Can, M., Hartmann, B.: Collaboratively crowdsourcing workflows with turkomatic. In: ACM Conference on Computer Supported Cooperative Work, pp. 1003–1012. ACM, New York (2012)
8. Little, G., Chilton, L.B., Goldman, M., Miller, R.C.: TurKit: human computation algorithms on mechanical turk. In: Annual ACM Symposium on User Interface Software and Technology, pp. 57–66. ACM, New York (2010)
9. Retelny, D., Bernstein, M.S., Valentine, M.A.: No workflow can ever be enough: how crowdsourcing workflows constrain complex work. In: ACM Human-Computer Interaction, CSCW, vol. 1, Article 89, 23 p. ACM (2017)
10. JGraphT. https://jgrapht.org. Accessed 10 Jan 2019
11. Gadiraju, U., Kawase, R.: Improving reliability of crowdsourced results by detecting crowd workers with multiple identities. In: Cabot, J., De Virgilio, R., Torlone, R. (eds.) ICWE 2017. LNCS, vol. 10360, pp. 190–205. Springer, Cham (2017). https://doi.org/10.1007/978-3-319-60131-1_11
12. Catallo, I., Martinenghi, D.: The dimensions of crowdsourcing task design. In: Cabot, J., De Virgilio, R., Torlone, R. (eds.) ICWE 2017. LNCS, vol. 10360, pp. 394–402. Springer, Cham (2017). https://doi.org/10.1007/978-3-319-60131-1_25

Finding Baby Mothers on Twitter

Yihong Zhang[1](✉), Adam Jatowt[1], and Yukiko Kawai[2]

[1] Kyoto University, Kyoto, Japan
yhzhang7@gmail.com, adam@dl.kuis.kyoto-u.ac.jp
[2] Kyoto Sangyo University, Kyoto, Japan
kawai@cc.kyoto-su.ac.jp

Abstract. In this paper, we study the task of detecting mothers of babies on Twitter. This could be beneficial for baby mother users to find friends, and for companies, organizations or experts to deliver accurately targeted information. Prior works have proposed supervised classification methods to detect generic latent attributes of Twitter users such as age, gender, and political orientation. However, methods and features for classifying generic attributes do not perform well for more specific attributes, such as whether a user is a mother of a young baby. We design feature sets based on followed accounts and profile pictures, which are largely overlooked in existing work. Comparing to three established feature sets, the experimental evaluation shows that our specifically-designed feature sets considerably improve classification accuracy.

Keywords: Twitter · Social media analysis · User discovery

1 Introduction

On a social media websites such as Twitter, there is a wide range of information associated with users, including profile description, profile picture, home location, past tweets, and follower-following connections[1]. However, such platform often does not explicitly provide user attributes such as gender, age, and various other user characteristics. Hence a number of existing works have proposed methods to predict these attributes [1,6,8]. Recently, detecting special minor groups of users has also attracted considerable attention. For example, dedicated approaches have been proposed to detect users who suffer depression or users who are in various phases of drug addition [2–4]. With regard to parenting, Morris investigates usage of social media such as Twitter and Facebook by mothers of young children [5], which provides findings related to our work.

In this paper, we present a solution for automatically detecting *mothers who have baby children* on Twitter. Similar to Morris' study, we define a baby as a child that is less than three years old [5]. As Morris's study shows, mothers with baby children tend to often actively seek information and advice from baby caring experts, facility providers, and other mothers in the same situation.

---

[1] https://dev.twitter.com/overview/api/users.

© Springer Nature Switzerland AG 2019
M. Bakaev et al. (Eds.): ICWE 2019, LNCS 11496, pp. 211–219, 2019.
https://doi.org/10.1007/978-3-030-19274-7_16

We can devise various applications in the face of such needs. For example, we can generate information on which streets are frequently used by other mothers with young babies by detecting baby mothers in social media, and this information can be then used for specialized route recommendation. The pilot interview we conducted with baby mothers within our research group revealed that, baby mothers are willing be provided with such applications. In general, our method for automatic detecting mothers having babies will be beneficial for mothers who wish to contact other mothers in similar situation, and for experts, as well as organizations who aim to provide targeted and on-time information.

In the existing works on Twitter users classification, the most often used information are users' past tweets [6,8,10]. However, as Morris has found in her study, baby mothers who use Twitter often do not share their baby information in tweets, except for profile pictures [5]. Based on our investigation, a Twitter user who is a mother to a baby would nevertheless seek baby-related information by following expert and consultant accounts. Therefore, instead of using information contained in users' tweets as in the prior works, we focus on the accounts a user follows. We devise a set of new features based on followed accounts and some other information. We manually select some baby mothers and non-baby mothers from real Twitter users for training and testing our prediction model. According to experimental results, the classification accuracy using our proposed features is higher than using the established feature sets.

2   Related Work

In recent years, discovering latent Twitter user attributes has become an important research topic. For instance, Rao et al. [8] propose a machine learning approach to discover gender, age, place of origin, and political orientation based on features extracted from users' past tweets. Pennacchiotti and Popescu [6] propose another machine learning approach to discover political affiliation, ethnicity, and to find Starbucks fans among Twitter users based on profile, tweet behavior, and tweet contents. Sharma et al. [9] introduce a method to infer keywords associated with the biographical information and expertise of a user. However, it is unclear whether these generic methods can be effective in our task of discovering baby mothers. We compare this generic method with our own approach in terms of classification accuracy.

Recently, detecting special groups of social media users who are in need also attracts researches. MacLean et al. study users with drug addition problems in a online forum [4]. Their focus is on detecting users in different phases of drug addition, including using, withdrawing, and recovering. De Choudhury et al. study Twitter users who suffer depression [3]. They propose a detection method based on several signals including tweet posting activities, social network graph, lexicon-based emotion analysis, linguistic style, and special words used by patients. Among several classifiers, they found that Support Vector Machine (SVM) provides best prediction results. The authors make a similar study of mothers who recently gave birth [2]. The features they used include engagement, network, emotion, and linguistic style. Their prediction mainly focuses on detecting changes occurring between the time of prepartum and postpartum, and it is unclear if it is effective for detecting baby mothers among different types of users. We also compare that method with our own approach. Nevertheless, to the best of our knowledge, our work is the first proposal of categorizing SNS users according to whether they are mothers to a baby.

3   Features for Finding Baby Mothers

We follow the approach for detecting latent attributes of social media users using machine learning, which include devising features, labeling examples, and testing models. Our main contribution is that we not only propose a novel task but also introduce specific novel features effective for detecting mothers with babies. In this section, we discuss the features we consider in our framework, which include existing and novel features. The data preparation and learning models will be discussed in the next section.

3.1   Existing Features

Bag-of-Words on Tweets (BOW). The simple presentation of users' text as term frequency has been a baseline method in several user classification works, including author profiling task in PAN competitions 2017 [7]. Following [7], we use BOW of 1,000 most frequent terms to represent a user's tweets.

Socio-Linguistic. We study a feature set for generic attribute detection. Proposed in [8], this feature set is used with SVM for detecting gender, age, regional origin and political orientation. The entire feature set is listed in Table 1. Most of these features are based on lexicons. Some lexicons are pre-defined, others are generated from the data (e.g., possessive bigrams). The feature value indicates the count of occurrences of the lexicon words in the user's tweets.

Postpartum. The second feature set we use is specialized for detecting behavior of new mothers. Proposed in [2], the feature set includes posting behavior, ego-network, and linguistic style. The complete feature set is listed in Table 2. Designed to distinguish standard and extreme behavior changes for new mothers, this is the closest feature set we find to our goal of detecting baby mothers. This feature set considers tweeting activities such as retweeting, mentioning, and linking, as well as simple social network features such as the number of followers and followees. The main part of the feature set, however, is writing style analysis based on LIWC[2] and ANEW[3] lexicon.

3.2   Novel Features

Interest Keywords. A baby mother will have a strong tendency to seek information about health advices, baby-related event news, and experiences of other mothers. We consider that it is not what the user tweets about but what she

---

[2] http://liwc.wpengine.com/.

[3] http://csea.phhp.ufl.edu/media/anewmessage.html.

Table 1. Socio-Linguistic features for generic user attribute detection

Feature name	Length	Description/example
SMILEYS	124	A list of emoticons compiled from the Wikipedia
OMG	1	Abbreviation for "Oh My God"
ELLIPSES	1	"...."
POSSESIVE BIGRAMS	by data	E.g. my XXX, our XXX
REPEATED ALPHABETS	1	E.g. niceeeeee, noooo waaaay
SELF	by data	E.g., I xxx, Im xxx
LAUGH	5	E.g. LOL, ROTFL, LMFAO, haha, hehe
SHOUT	1	Text in ALLCAPS
EXASPERATION	5	E.g. Ugh, mmmm, hmmm, ahh, grrr
AGREEMENT	3	E.g. yea, yeah, ohya
HONORIFICS	4	E.g. dude, man, bro, sir
AFFECTION	1	E.g. xoxo
EXCITEMENT	1	A string of exclamation symbols (!!!!!)
SINGLE EXCLAIM	1	A single exclamation at the end of the tweet
PUZZLED PUNCT	1	A combination of any number of ? and ! (!?!!??!)

wants to read that provides the hint on the user interest. In Twitter, a user will see most often the tweets posted from the accounts that they follow. So instead of the tweets a user posted, we are interested in the accounts a user chose to follow. Our first feature set is based on the descriptions of accounts followed by a user. Specifically, we generate *tf-idf* scores for the words used in the followed account descriptions. To use *tf-idf*, we first extract frequently used keywords from all account descriptions we have in the data, resulting in a list of m keywords. Then we concatenate descriptions of all accounts a user followed as one document. Last, we generate a *tf-idf* vector of length m. In our experiments, we set the frequency thresholds to 100, resulting in a keyword list of 1,370 words. We find that different threshold values produce similar classification results.

Mom-Words. We generate a list of words likely to be used by baby mothers, not necessarily baby-related. For this, we choose a popular online forum about parenting of baby children, and we collect messages posted in it. The forum we selected is *MomForum.com*, which is a dedicated sharing platform for discussing parenting and baby-related issues. We fetch 100 threads from one of the sub-forums that discusses parenting of 0–2 years old babies[4]. We then tokenize

---

[4] http://www.momforum.com/forumdisplay.php/76-Babies-amp-Toddlers-(0-2-years-old).

Table 2. Postpartum features for detecting postpartum behavior of new mothers

Feature name	Length	Description/example
Engagement	5	Average normalized number of posts per day
		Mean proportion of reply posts
		Fraction of retweets
		The proportion of links
		Fraction of question-centric posts
Ego-network	2	The number of followers
		The number of followees
Emotion	4	Positive emotion - fraction of positive emotion words in LIWC
		Negative affection - fraction of negative emotion, anger, anxiety, and sadness words in LIWC
		Mean of activation per post based on ANEW
		Mean of dominance per post based on ANEW
Linguistic style	22	Fraction of words from 22 selected LIWC linguistic styles

and generate a list of frequent keywords from these threads using a frequency threshold of 5 and removing stopwords. As the result, we obtain a lexicon of 299 words, including *child, feeding, dad*, etc. Based on this lexicon, we generate a *Mom-word* usage feature vector for each user, where the i-th element is the frequency of i-th word in the lexicon occurring in the user's tweets.

Pictures. We also deploy the latest image processing techniques to extract information from user profile pictures and generate a picture feature vector. We use a free online API[5] that has the capability to output the age and the gender of people shown in an image with relatively high accuracy. For the particular application of discovering baby mothers, we are most interested in whether the picture shows a baby. We generate a vector that includes four binary values, each indicating whether the profile picture contains a baby ($age \leq 3$), a young child ($3 < age \leq 6$), an adult woman ($20 < age \leq 50, gender = female$), and an adult man ($20 < age \leq 50, gender = male$). Note that there can be several people of different age and or gender present in a picture.

4   Experimental Analysis

We conduct an empirical study by testing our feature sets on a number of real Twitter user data. We aim to find out the effectiveness of our feature sets in comparison to the established user-classification feature sets. In this section, we present the experimental setup and discuss the results.

---

[5] https://www.angus.ai/.

4.1   Dataset Preparation

We collect from Twitter a number of user profiles, and manually label them according to whether they belong to baby mothers or not. Since the proportion of baby mothers is small among all Twitter users, instead of randomly collecting user accounts on Twitter, we use some heuristics to select candidates before labeling. First we find some *attraction* Twitter account based on several handpicked Web articles[6]. These accounts post mother-related information, and should contain a large portion of baby mothers in their followers. Using Twitter API for searching followers[7], we collect all followers from the picked accounts, including their account names, descriptions, and the numbers of followers and followees, resulting in the set of 18,536 users and their data. From these users, we first remove ones who have more than 200 followers. This considers both Twitter API limit[8] and the practicality of our solution, because celebrity users who have a large number of followers cannot be considered as typical users, and will distort the classification model.

We next extract a number of *very likely* candidates from remaining users whose profile description contains keyword "mother" or "mom". Note that this filtering does not bias the classification because features used for building classification models do not consider these profile descriptions. Then from the followers of the very likely candidates, we find a number of *less likely* candidates, for which we do not use any filtering. The intuition is that the followers of a baby mother might include other baby mothers, among family and friends. Finally, we manually label positive and negative examples from these very likely and less likely candidates, by looking at all available user information, including profile description, picture, and past tweets. For very likely candidates, we have 197 positives and 59 negatives, while for less likely candidates, we have 106 positives and 583 negatives. In total, we have 303 positives and 642 negatives.

4.2   Learning Model and Evaluation Matrix

Rao *et al.* finds that the Support Vector Machine (SVM) with linear kernel provides the best classification results with Socio-Linguist features [8], while De Choudhury *et al.* finds that SVM with radial kernel provides the best result with their postpartum features [2]. As such, in experiment results, we show SVM with linear kernel results, except for feature sets that include postpartum features, for which we use SVM with radial kernel results. We also investigate other machine learning models including *Naive Bayes, Random Forest, Linear Discriminant Analysis,* and *Logistic Regression,* and find that Random Forest (RF) generally

---

[6] For example, *17 Funny Moms on Twitter,* http://mashable.com/2013/05/10/funny-twitter-moms/. Particularly, we pick four accounts from this article: @jennawrites, @laneymg, @shriekhouse, and @MarinkaNYC. The selection considers the number of followers in these accounts and Twitter API limit for collecting followers.

[7] https://developer.twitter.com/en/docs/accounts-and-users/follow-search-get-users/api-reference/get-followers-list.

[8] Currently Twitter API allows searching 200 followers each minute.

provides the best results and performs better than SVM. Thus, we show the results for SVM and RF. We use the SVM and RF implementation in R package e1071[9] and randomForest[10].

We measure the *precision*, *recall*, and *f-value* for the positive prediction results for the classification accuracy. The f-value is calculated as $\frac{2 \times precision \times recall}{precision + recall}$. We apply three-fold cross-validation that uses two parts for training and one part for testing. For random forest, we run the experiment ten times and show the average results.

4.3 Results and Discussion

We first test the effectiveness of each individual set of the proposed features, namely, interest keywords, mom-word in tweets, and picture analysis. This result is shown in Table 3. We see that interest keyword provides the highest accuracy with random forest classifier, reaching f-value of 0.579. We also see that the Picture feature set achieves the highest precision with SVM, but has a very low recall. This is reasonable, because if the profile picture contains a baby child, the user would very likely be a baby mother. However, a large portion of baby mothers do not show their babies on profile pictures. Similarly, mom-word features reach a high precision but a low recall with random forest, because if a user uses special words she is likely to be a mother, but not all mothers make mother-related posts.

Table 3. Classification accuracy of individual sets of proposed features

	Interest		Mom-word		Picture	
	SVM	RF	SVM	RF	SVM	RF
precision	0.581	0.753	0.443	0.732	**0.773**	0.728
recall	**0.553**	0.474	0.471	0.354	0.121	0.095
f-value	0.556	**0.579**	0.456	0.477	0.209	0.167

Next we compare the proposed feature sets with baseline feature sets, namely BOW, socio-linguistic (SocLing) and postpartum behavior feature (Postpartum). The results are shown in Table 4. In this experiment, the proposed feature set is the combination of all three feature sets discussed above. As we can see from the results, with SVM, the proposed features reach f-value of 0.562, more than 7% higher than those reached by BOW, SocLing, and Postpartum. With random forest, the proposed features reach the highest precision of 0.785, and the highest f-value of 0.623, more than 15% higher compared to those reached by three baselines.

---

[9] https://cran.r-project.org/web/packages/e1071/e1071.pdf.

[10] https://cran.r-project.org/web/packages/randomForest/randomForest.pdf.

Table 4. Classification accuracy comparison of existing and proposed features

	BOW [7]		SocLing [8]		Postpartum [2]		Proposed	
	SVM	RF	SVM	RF	SVM*	RF	SVM	RF
precision	0.471	0.760	0.508	0.761	0.589	0.601	0.587	**0.785**
recall	0.516	0.343	0.418	0.341	0.228	0.302	**0.540**	0.519
f-value	0.490	0.472	0.458	0.469	0.326	0.402	0.562	**0.623**

*using radial kernel

Table 5. Effects of combining existing and proposed features

	BOW + Proposed		SocLing + Proposed		Postpartum + Proposed		All	
	SVM	RF	SVM*	RF	SVM	RF	SVM	RF
precision	0.584	0.790	0.550	0.797	0.786	0.792	0.562	**0.808**
recall	**0.521**	0.497	0.520	0.505	0.250	0.501	0.507	0.461
f-value	0.551	0.609	0.534	**0.617**	0.379	0.613	0.532	0.587

*using radial kernel

We are also interested in whether combining the proposed features with the established feature sets improves the accuracy. The results are shown in Table 5. Comparing this table to Table 4, we see that by adding the proposed features, all baseline features achieve higher accuracy. It improves f-value of BOW from 0.472 to 0.609, for SocLing from 0.469 to 0.617, and for Postpartum from 0.402 to 0.613. Combining all features together, we achieve a precision of 0.808, the highest among all cases we tested. However, the achieved f-value of 0.587 is lower than that achieved by using the proposed features alone.

5 Conclusion

In this paper, we study the problem of finding mothers with baby children on Twitter. Following a supervised machine learning approach, we propose novel features based on followed accounts, vocabulary used, and profile pictures. Experimental results with real Twitter user data show that the proposed features are highly effective for baby mother discovery, and achieve considerably higher classification accuracy compared to three baselines of established feature sets. In future we plan to extend our approach on other user groups such as people with disabilities or rare diseases.

Acknowledgement. This research has been supported by JSPS KAKENHI Grant Numbers #17H01828, #18K19841 and by MIC/SCOPE #171507010.

References

1. Barberá, P.: Birds of the same feather tweet together: Bayesian ideal point estimation using Twitter data. Political Anal. **23**(1), 76–91 (2015)
2. De Choudhury, M., Counts, S., Horvitz, E.: Predicting postpartum changes in emotion and behavior via social media. In: Proceedings of the SIGCHI Conference on Human Factors in Computing Systems, pp. 3267–3276. ACM (2013)
3. De Choudhury, M., Gamon, M., Counts, S., Horvitz, E.: Predicting depression via social media. In: Proceedings of the Seventh International Conference on Web and Social Media, vol. 13, pp. 1–10 (2013)
4. MacLean, D., Gupta, S., Lembke, A., Manning, C., Heer, J.: Forum77: an analysis of an online health forum dedicated to addiction recovery. In: Proceedings of the 18th ACM Conference on Computer Supported Cooperative Work & Social Computing, pp. 1511–1526. ACM (2015)
5. Morris, M.R.: Social networking site use by mothers of young children. In: Proceedings of the 17th ACM Conference on Computer Supported Cooperative Work & Social Computing, pp. 1272–1282. ACM (2014)
6. Pennacchiotti, M., Popescu, A.M.: A machine learning approach to Twitter user classification. In: Proceedings of the Fifth International Conference on Weblogs and Social Media, pp. 281–288 (2011)
7. Rangel, F., Rosso, P., Potthast, M., Stein, B.: Overview of the 5th author profiling task at pan 2017: gender and language variety identification in Twitter. In: Working Notes Papers of the CLEF (2017)
8. Rao, D., Yarowsky, D., Shreevats, A., Gupta, M.: Classifying latent user attributes in Twitter. In: Proceedings of the 2nd International Workshop on Search and Mining User-Generated Contents, pp. 37–44 (2010)
9. Sharma, N.K., Ghosh, S., Benevenuto, F., Ganguly, N., Gummadi, K.: Inferring who-is-who in the Twitter social network. ACM SIGCOMM Comput. Commun. Rev. **42**(4), 533–538 (2012)
10. Zhang, Y., Szabo, C., Sheng, Q.Z.: Improved object and event monitoring on Twitter through lexical analysis and user profiling. In: Proceedings of the 17th International Conference on Web Information System Engineering, pp. 19–34 (2016)

Web User Interfaces

An End-User Pipeline for Scraping and Visualizing Semi-Structured Data over the Web

Gabriela Bosetti[1]([✉]) [iD], Sergio Firmenich[1,2] [iD], Marco Winckler[3] [iD],
Gustavo Rossi[1,2] [iD], Ulises Cornejo Fandos[1] [iD], and Előd Egyed-Zsigmond[4] [iD]

[1] LIFIA, Facultad de Informática, UNLP, 50th St. and 120th St., La Plata, Argentina
{gabriela.bosetti,sergio.firmenich,gustavo.rossi,
ulisescornejo.fandos}@lifia.info.unlp.edu.ar
[2] CONICET, Buenos Aires, Argentina
[3] i3S, Université Nice Sophia Antipolis, 2000, route des Lucioles, bât. Euclide B,
BP 121, Sophia Antipolis, France
winckler@i3s.unice.fr
[4] Université de Lyon, LIRIS, INSA-Lyon, 7 Av. Jean Capelle, Villeurbanne, France
elod.egyed-zsigmond@insa-lyon.fr

Abstract. The Web is a vast source of semi-structured datasets that
are made readily available to support the construction of new knowledge.
Information visualization techniques have been demonstrated as a suitable
alternative for allowing users to analyze and understand a large amount
of data. However, the steps required for visualizing semi-structured data
obtained from the Web is not straightforward, and it requires proper treatment before information visualization techniques could be applied. In this
work, we present a visualization pipeline for describing the fundamental
operations required for visualizing semi-structured data over the Web. We
employ Web Scraping and Web Augmentation techniques for supporting
interactive visualizations and solving tasks without changing the context
of use of the data. Our approach is duly supported by a framework including scraping-, augmenting- and visualization-tools and it has been applied
to different kinds of websites to demonstrate its validity and feasibility. Our
ultimate goal is to expand the limits of our technology for improving the
user interaction with websites and creating new experiences for a better
understanding of large datasets.

Keywords: Infovis · Web augmentation · Web Scraping

1 Introduction

The Web is a massive source of public datasets. NetCraft[1] reported over
1.8 billion sites in the World at the beginning of 2017 and the NationalPost
predicts[2] that by 2020, the amount of data produced annually will increase

---

[1] https://news.netcraft.com/archives/2017/01/12/january-2017-web-server-survey.
html.
[2] https://nationalpost.com/news/big-data-and-analytics-taking-off-at-brocks-
goodman-school-of-business.

© Springer Nature Switzerland AG 2019
M. Bakaev et al. (Eds.): ICWE 2019, LNCS 11496, pp. 223–237, 2019.
https://doi.org/10.1007/978-3-030-19274-7_17

4,300%. The Web not only made easier access to raw data but also made it available to everyone. In a recent survey published by data.world[3], 63% of citizens explore and interact with data to achieve a broad spectrum of tasks. The Broadband Commission for Sustainable Development (set up by the ITU and the UNESCO) estimates that the number of Internet users will represent half of the world's population at the end of 2019 at least [1]. In the context of the increasing amount of data, information visualization might play a role in helping many users to understand data. Visualization is indeed an important aspect of data analysis that allows conveying information in a visual format highlighting patterns, trends, and correlations among data [2].

Information visualization techniques are powerful tools specifically designed to support the exploration and analysis of large datasets, helping users to deal with complex decision-making tasks [3,4]. Information visualization techniques might improve both users' cognitive abilities and users' performance with tasks by relieving the working memory and improving decision accuracy, even on elderly people [5]. Many visualization techniques are intended to be used by specialized users (such as system administrators Mahendiran et al. [6]) but more and more often information visualization techniques (such as CivilAnalysis [7]) are developed to larger audiences.

Currently, more and more Web sites embed information visualization techniques to present their data in context. Nonetheless, this practice is not widespread and most Web sites still only display semi-structured data. The operations required for visualizing semi-structured data obtained from the Web is not straightforward, and it requires proper treatment before information visualization techniques could be applied. While the questions related to the design are central to the development of information visualization techniques, this paper is interested in the process, the so-called visualization pipeline, that allows transforming semi-structured data into graphical representations.

This paper investigates problems and possible solutions to build visualizations for helping end-users to analyze datasets available over the web. Our ultimate goal is to develop a technology that allows end-users to collect and visualize semi-structured data directly over the web site that publish the datasets. As we shall see, the answer to this problem is intimately associated with the many operations along the visualization pipeline. Hereafter, we present an approach and a tool that combines Web Scraping, Web Augmentation, and Information Visualization techniques. Moreover, we evaluate the validity and feasibility of the tools by running them over different kinds of websites.

2 Background and Motivation

2.1 Information Visualization

Many aspects of a visualization design are driven by the type of data we are looking at. In order to become understandable by users, data sources are often transformed along a process (the visualization pipeline) that transforms raw

---

[3] https://data.world/data-science-by-the-numbers.

data into a graphical representation that fits on the user screen. This process is shown at Fig. 1 encompasses four operations: (i) **data acquisition**; (ii) **filtering**; (iii) **visual mapping**; and, (iv) **rendering**. It is worthy of notice that user interaction (shown as dashed lines) might affect all operations in the pipeline.

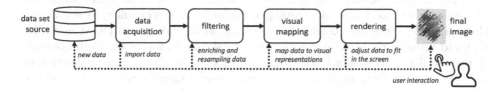

Fig. 1. Information visualization pipeline, adapted from Munzner (2014) [2].

Data acquisition is one of the most complex problems to be solved, mainly because the dataset might be available in various formats and most of visualizing techniques are specifically designed to handle a particular type of data (such as tables, clusters or lists). But there are exceptions such as Prefuse [8] which is an extensible user interface toolkit for crafting interactive visualizations that can handle both structured and unstructured data. And yet, the visualization process with Prefuse starts with abstract data represented in some canonical form (such as unstructured, graph, and tree data). In most cases, if the dataset is not on the format of the tool, it becomes tough to get benefits of the visualization technique.

When a dataset is loaded into the tool, it might contain information that is not relevant for solving the problem we are looking at. So that filtering operations come in place to remove noise, to fix attributes (ex. wrong character encoding), and to enrich the dataset (ex. add missing labels). An example of the use of filtering operation as a key feature of tools is illustrated by WebGIVI [9] which helps researchers to interpret large gene datasets by associating genes and informative terms (iTerm) that are obtained from the biomedical literature.

The visual mapping is at the core of the design of information visualization techniques. It allows the association of data attributes (such as gender and age) to visual variables (as form, color, size or texture). Mapping can be hard-coded or adjusted by the users. A good example is uVis Studio [10] which allows developers to compose visualizations by dragging-and-dropping building blocks, then binding controls to data and visualizing results with immediate feedback. Techniques such as dynamic bidding provide flexibility and interactivity for users to customize their views according to their needs.

The rendering operations define how the visualization techniques are displayed to the users. At this step, the tools might perform geometric transformations to make data to fit in the screen. The rendering also defines if the visualization is to be seen in a standard application or an element that can be integrated into another context of use. A flexible rendering is illustrated here by the framework Webcharts [11] which can adapt the rendering to three types of users: for developer who uses the framework for creating an application; for the visualization developer, who extends the framework with new visualizations; and for the end-user, who may dynamically change the visualization of the data in the application, with no need of waiting for an update of the application that incorporates the latest visualizations.

The pipeline, shown in Fig. 1, is part of all visualization tools regardless of the technology used for the implementation. As far as Web technology is a concern, there are many libraries based on JavaScript that manipulate DOM and CSS to build visualization techniques that can be displayed inside the Web browser. A very well-known library is D3 [4] [12] which already offers a huge collection of interactive visualizations. The very common use of these libraries is to feed the visualizations with data that comes from some API or fixed data specified by Website developers. In most cases, the creation and the use of visualization techniques still remain something very technical that requires programming skills.

Viégas et al. [13] were pioneers in the democratization of information visualization techniques over the Web; their Web site called ManyEyes allowed people to create visualizations based on a predefined set of techniques available. Data acquisition in ManyEyes was simplified at the most, requiring a simple cut and paste; but it was not possible to connect tools for automating the information extraction from the Web. In addition to that, the rendering of the visualizations created by ManyEyes is not flexible and they cannot be integrated into other contexts of use than the Web site.

2.2   Web Scraping and Web Augmentation

We suggest that information visualization of datasets over the Web can be enhanced with Web augmentation and Web scraping technology.

Web Scraping allows transforming unstructured data available on the Web, typically in HTML format, into structured data that can be analyzed and stored analyzed in a central local database. For example, MeatBrain [14] is a tool that extracts data from Web sites and, eventually, aggregates different data into a new Web page. It is also very common that scrappers let their users define which part of Web sites to extract, meanwhile others may do it automatically.

Web scrapers are often the base for other applications such as search engines, Web automation, Web testing, and Web augmentation tools. It is interesting to notice that, although not every Web augmentation tool employs Web scraping, most of them contain some scrapper functionality that is used to parse the Web pages' DOMs in order to materialize the augmentation. Web augmentation typically allows to adapt existing third-party Web sites in order to add new content or functionality [15] and we suggest that it can be a suitable alternative to integrate visualization techniques into Web sites that lack visualization features.

There are different alternatives to achieve Web Augmentation at client-, server- or proxy-side. Client-side scripting is the most common alternative that can be evaluated through browser weavers like Greasemonkey[5]) or browser extensions.

---

[4] https://d3js.org/.
[5] https://www.greasespot.net/.

Annotation [16] is a broadly used technique to configure these underlying Web scrappers following a manual or semi-automatic approach. Actually, some Web augmentation approaches based on annotations arose to improve information visualization. For instance, Reform [17] allows developers to define general purpose applications that require some information to work. In this sense, end-users are responsible for the web content annotation from where that information must be extracted.

Other Web augmentation approaches may work based on an automatic scraper because their augmentation effect is not variable. VizMe [18] is a tool supporting an approach for handling additional data and tasks through augmented browsing. It is intended to provide extra information to the user in the same context of use, therefore, avoiding the switching between Web pages. That work emphasizes the visualization of such further data into the browsed Web page; they deal with the problem of how additional information is communicated to the user. They propose visualizations at different levels: visual cues at micro-level for hypermedia items and additional layers at macro-level for Web pages. At the micro-level, they present time-referenced Google data in a time-plot when the user highlights some Web content. At macro-level, they offer a wide range of visualizations on a floating panel, as a tag cloud based on the important words from the text on a Web page, a search engine to Google extra information or an editor to merge content from different pages. Similarly, another approach (Enhanced Web Page Content Visualization with Firefox) use natural language processing and machine learning techniques to help users to get a better overview of the pages they read, presenting graph-based visualizations.

3   Augmenting Web Sites with Visualization Techniques

In this paper, Web Augmentation (WA) is used to allow end users to build on-demand visualizations of semi-structured data sources available over the Web without changing the user's context of use, which means that visualizations are embedded into the web site users are visiting. The data acquisition is simplified by allowing users to select raw data presented in the Web page and turn them into visualization. This solution has the advantage of refreshing the visualization automatically when the Web page is updated. We also propose to reuse the data in search-results or with documents sharing the same structure. It is also possible to track the changes for a concrete element in the DOM through time, in order to analyze its evolution through visual means.

Providing users with a means to visualize any third-party semi-structured Web content presents some challenges from the point of view of the Web Engineering, mainly at the beginning of the visualization pipeline, where the data acquisition happens. The different structures inherent to the data representation in a page (HTML elements) must be understood to automatically extract and interpret their content to create a dataset serving as the input for a visualization. Moreover, first, it is mandatory to understand which are the HTML structures that may represent a target dataset to be visualized in a new way.

In this context, we formulated an initial set of questions: how many such HTML structures do exist? Can users benefit from visualizing existing data spread over the Web through alternative visualizations? Are augmentation-based-visualizations useful to solve any general-purpose task? Or is it better to use domain-specific ones? Does the user feel in control by using visualizations through WA or does he want more expressiveness power? Is specialized domain-knowledge a requirement for applying a visualization into any Web page? This work is a first step towards answering those questions, and Web Augmentation is presented as a bridge for joining Web Scraping and the benefits of visualization techniques for solving tasks without changing the context of use where data appears. It is not just about expanding the limits of technology but also enhancing the user experience in any Web page –even third-party– by the addition of a new feature. We aim at covering the gap between the existing Web scraping and visualization tools and techniques. In this approach:

1. users –with no need for knowledge in low-level scraping– can abstract raw data on a Web page into a data model specification (DMS),
2. users choose and apply alternative visualizations for the DMS
3. a repository of infovis augmentations do exist
4. developers can extend the existing visualizations in case existing specific visualizations do not cover a concrete task or domain, so users can apply them on any existing and third-party Web page

4   Web Sites: A Perspective on Content, Structure and Time

A first step towards the visualization of third-party raw data in the Web is to analyze how much and how diverse are the HTML structures presenting homogeneous content on the Web. To do so, we choose to analyze a sample of sites that can match into a table dataset type [2]. In this sense, our target datasets may be referred to as tables, which have rows (members), columns (variables) and cell values (datums).

To avoid sample bias, we took the list of sites from the top 50 popular sites according to Alexa's ranking for Argentina[6] as the target sample. We considered all the sites with a collection of at least five homogeneous elements representing a dataset member with more than a single variable. Regarding the dataset variables, only those that are present in all occurrences of the dataset members were considered. Besides, HTML elements not containing textual raw-data were not taken into account (e.g. images with no alternative text, «like» or «share» action buttons). The target datasets were searched in a limited part of the site: the homepages of the sites. If there was no data to visualize in the homepage (e.g., Google's default page) we triggered a search using the search engine of the site, to check if their Search Engine Results Pages (SERP) may contain items that may represent a dataset. The remaining pages of the sites were not

---

[6] https://www.alexa.com/topsites/countries/AR Dec. 18th, 2018 at 22:00 h UTC-3.

analyzed. If more than one possible dataset was detected for a site, we studied
only the one with the most members and variables, respectively. The keywords
used in the case of searching were «facts» and «certificado», respectively. It is
worth mentioning that all the sites have been analyzed in a private-browsing
tab, except for the ones that require log-in (e.g., Facebook or Twitter). From the
50 sites, we kept only 42 sites for analysis; we discarded 3 sites not meeting the
requirement of content suitable for all audiences, 2 sites with the same domain,
2 sites that were offline at the time of analyzing and 1 site with a broken engine.

From the 42 sites, only 10 did not present any data with a heterogeneous
structure. This leaves us with 76% of sites with data that may be visualized
in an alternative way. These sites use different HTML elements to represent
the data: 2 of them do it through a table («table»), 3 through an ordered list
(«ol»), 5 through an unordered list («ul»), 6 through a set of article elements
(«article»), and 16 through a hierarchy of homogeneous divs («div»). As shown
in Table 1, we classified those cases in 3 categories: HTML tables, HTML lists
and HTML hierarchical containers. In this work, we propose at least 3 kinds of
dataset extractors.

Table 1. HTML structures

Dataset presentation	HTML Table	HTML list	HTML hierarchy
Dataset	table	ol/ul	div
Variables/columns	thead > tr	-	-
Members/rows	tbody > tr	li	div/article
Datum/cell	td > *	*	*
Occurrences in the sample	2	8	22

Regardless of such general HTML structure, different combinations of inner
elements were found to present the datasets datum or table's cell value, which
is the meaning of the «*» symbol in the Table 1. For instance, in YouTube's
site we considered two anchors presenting the video title and video category,
respectively, and two spans for the views and the date of publication. Since these
data are shared by all the analyzed instances, they represent a variable of the
dataset. The shared variables make it possible to claim that raw-data in existing
and popular Web sites is comparable, and that it may be the target of our
proposed visualizations. On average, the amount of dataset members analyzed
ranged from 5 to 74, with an average of 18.6 and a standard deviation of 14.8
occurrences. We also found an average of 3.4 variables of the members, ranging
from 2 to 6, and with a standard deviation of 1.2 variables.

We also observed that different mechanisms must be implemented for updating the visualization when it is required to include extra members from a dataset
presented in a different context (e.g., on the second page of a dynamic table, or
a SERP). Just 8 of the 32 sites with possible datasets had paginated members.

Therefore, in the 75% of the cases it was possible to retrieve extra members for the dataset through a user interaction: in 11 cases when the page is scrolled down, and in the remaining cases when a single link is clicked (10 cases, e.g., the «next» anchor), multiple links (2 cases, e.g. «page 1» or «page 2» anchors), or a button (1 case).

Obtaining such extra members (e.g., more videos appearing at the bottom of the page when the user scrolls down on the search engine of YouTube) or accessing a similar page which presents different data (e.g., two different pages of a YouTube video), allow reusing the same structure understanding. Such elements can be referenced by evaluating different Web locators [19], like XPath, CSS or JQuery selectors. We previously worked on the definition of user-defined scrappers capable of extracting similar elements loaded in different contexts [16]. So far, everything seems to be a question of how to map different HTML structures to the constitution of a dataset, and how to reuse the initial selectors to get more HTML elements to consider when the information is paginated. However, it is also a matter of time, since using the same selectors allows obtaining the same information at different times. Moreover, although a website may change over time (as you can check by using the Internet Archive [7]), Aldalur and Díaz [19] presented an approach for generating regenerative locators that use contingency data to evaluate alternative location strategies in case the DOM of a website changes. They validated their approach by taking a sample of a webpage from 8 websites every three months, and they find out that using their resilient locators, they were able to successfully regenerate the locators of the 73% of the samples. Therefore, using a locator over time for extracting elements and creating one or multiple datasets over time is plausible.

5   AlVis: An End-User Tool for Web Content Visualization

In the previous section, we presented the typical information visualization pipeline adapted to end-user activities in scenarios where they want to add alternative visualization to existing and third-party Web content. Moreover, we presented an analysis that we have made over several kinds of Web page's DOM structures in order to understand how to extract datasets from these semi-structured content. In this section, we present AlVis (ALternative VISualization through web augmentation), our end-user tool for visualizing Web content which is deployed as a Web extension [8]. We first present the use process of this tool, explaining the matching between interaction steps in the tool with the steps explained in the adapted pipeline. Later, we show the tool in action through some examples.

---

[7] https://archive.org/web/.

[8] AlVis prototype is publicly available https://github.com/gbosetti/alvis.

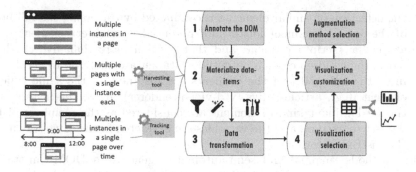

Fig. 2. AlVis use process for visualizing third-party raw-data in Web pages

The AlVis process (Fig. 2) requires six interaction steps by end-users:

1. DOM annotation (corresponds to the Data Acquisition step in the pipeline): define which part of the current Web site's DOM will be extracted. This step can be manual or semi-automatic. For a manual step, an annotation tool is required such as the one we have defined in previous work, called WOA (Web Objects Ambient) [16]. The semi-automatic way requires that users choose some semi-structured data automatically discovered by the AlVis extractors. For this regard, and based on the analysis presented in Sect. 4, we have defined the following extractors:

   - TableExtractor. Through this strategy, all the HTML tables present in the DOM are retrieved and analyzed. The extractor checks for the definition of the «thead» to identify the variables of the dataset, and the «tbody» to generate the output. In both cases, what is extracted are the children of such elements: a collection of «tr» elements. If multiple elements compose a «tr» element, these are split into new columns, in case the user needs to use them separately. The name of the column is the same but with the addition of an index.

   - ListExtractor. This strategy retrieves all the «ol» and «ul» elements from the current document. For each list, it takes all the «li» elements as possible members of the dataset. The variables are generated in a second round, by traversing all the possible members of the dataset and keeping just the leaf children elements that are present on all the members, based in its type. This means that if an «ol» has 5 «li», and only two of them have an element «anchor», then it is not considered as a variable. Under this strategy, the variables exist but their names are not representative: it is a combination of the name of the DOM element type concatenated with an index. The user will be able to redefine his name when manipulating the data after its extraction.

   - HierarchyExtractor. In this case, the variables are created in the same way as for the ListExtractor. What's different is the detection of similar elements representing the members of the dataset to be extracted (as the «li» elements inside a list for the ListExtractor). In this case, the detection of similar elements is conducted by traversing the full body of the page's document looking for potential «container» elements that are not a «script» element, and that contain more than five children. Then, the children of each potential container are analyzed to check that more than the 50% of the elements are instances of the same type of element (e.g., articles, divs, ytd-video-renderer). If so, the instances of the predominant kind of element are considered as the members of the dataset to extract, and the variables are extracted in the same way as for the ListExtractor.

Both methods (manual and semi-automatic) generate a DOM annotation template that is stored in the AlVis local storage, in this way AlVis can be aware of the desired data structure for a particular Web site when this is loaded again in the future.

2. Data-Items materialization (corresponds to the Data Acquisition step in the pipeline): materialization is the process by which a DOM extractor parse the Web page's DOM to extract the data and their underlying data model. For any of the extractors defined for AlVis, the output is always a JSON that would be used for the further steps in this process.

3. Data transformation (corresponds to the Filtering step in the pipeline): some data could require to be curated by end-users before going on into the visualization steps. For instance, if some value extracted must be passed through a transformation function, or even if the data model requires some refinement, such as adding or changing naming columns heads. Moreover, this interaction steps allows users to delete data that is not required for the visualization.

4. Visualization selection (corresponds to the Visual Mapping step in the pipeline): This step allows end-user to choose a kind of visualization from the currently available ones. Although the AlVis tool includes a framework for adding new kinds of visualizations, the current prototype already covers the most common ones. It is important to mention that for the same dataset, several visualizations can be used.

5. Visualization customization (corresponds to the Visual Mapping step in the pipeline): Once a visualization is chosen, the user may customize which values to use, and other several aspects related inherent to the visualization being configured.

6. Augmentation method selection (corresponds to the Rendering step in the pipeline): finally, the last interaction steps in AlVis let users define how the alternative visualization must be rendered. Visualization could be added in a pop-up window or can be woven in the original Web page's DOM with different insertion strategies.

To illustrate this process, we present an example. For the sake of space, the example is based on using a semi-automatic extraction. The process starts with the user navigating the Web and identifying a raw dataset. For instance, the Latest Human Development Ranking by the United Nations Development Programme [9]. A screenshot of the page without augmentations can be found

---

[9] http://hdr.undp.org/en/2018-update.

in Fig. 3. In such page there is a table reporting variables as «the expected years of schooling» and «the gross national income» by country. Consider that a user wants to take his customized ranking as the dataset to visually identify the countries with higher gross national income and their proportion concerning the countries with the lower values. In the same Figure, it can be observed that the page is presenting 25 results by page. The user may want to create a visualization just with such a number of members, or he may want to do it with all the paginated results in the HTML table. For a matter of space, we will explain the simplest case.

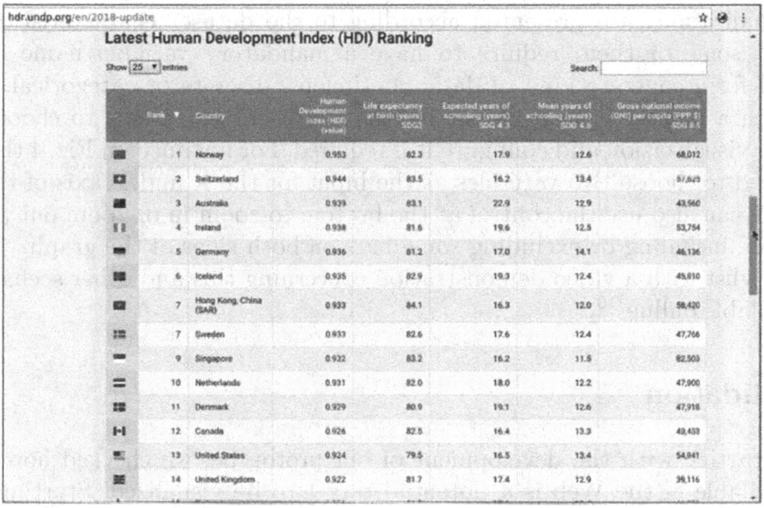

Fig. 3. A capture of the HTML table to extract data from

The first step is to extract the data to create the user's dataset of interest. It involves using one of three strategies, matching the structures mentioned in Table 1. All the extraction techniques generate the same output: a JSON with the variable names, and the members of the dataset. In case any element is not detected, it is defined as «undefined».

Under our approach, such extractors are evaluated when the user clicks the browser action of the AlVis extension (first step of Fig. 4); it is a button in the browser's toolbar that can be clicked to evaluate all the extractors with the content of the current page. From that moment on, an «extract» button is added at the bottom of all the DOM structures recognized by the extractors in the current webpage (step 2 of Fig. 4) without any extra user intervention, transparently performed.

When the user clicks the «extract» button, the extracted dataset is shown below in a new div under the HTML structure, which presents an editor to manipulate the dataset and use it through different visualization techniques.

This is the second step the user must carry out. For instance, she can change the variable names, remove variables or members, transpose the matrix, apply operators to the data. A screenshot of the extracted data presented through the editor is shown in the last step of Fig. 4.

The results of the two first steps are the transformation of raw data into a dataset. Both steps can be envisioned as part of what Card et al. [20] calls «Data Transformation» in their well-known model. What follows is the visualization selection and its customization.

Regarding visualization selection, our approach contemplates a framework where the visualizations represent an extension point. We provided a base of visualizations, like the ones listed at the top of Fig. 4, but these can be extended. The visualizations are presented according to the dataset characteristics. For instance, some of them require to have a mandatory variable name or are designed for a concrete kind of data: continuous, discrete or categorical. However, such a process is transparent for the end user, who needs to choose any available visualization and configure it if required. For instance, in Fig. 4 the user is required to choose two variables as the input for the X and Y axis of the bar chart. He can also use the control at the bottom to zoom in or zoom out part of the graph, including or excluding some bars on both sides of the graph.

A playlist with a video demonstration concerning this and other scenarios is also available online [10].

6 Validation

Before starting with the development of our prototype, we checked how much data available in the Web is a potential target to be visualized. Starting from the same sample described in Sect. 4, which was focused on the kinds of HTML structures, we also analyzed if such structures have data that makes sense to visualize without making data transformations. We discarded all the cases with no numerical variables and no repeated textual values or dates (e.g., a new's dataset with just two variables: «title» and «description»). The number of highlighted sites was 10, leaving 22 sites with data that could make sense for some user to visualize. In order to check the extractors, and for the sake of space, we took the two first sites from the sample matching each type of HTML structure (Table 1), and we used our described techniques to check if the proposed extraction techniques succeeded. The sites chosen were youtube.com, clarin.com.ar, wikipedia.org, twitter.com, blogger.com, and bna.com.ar. The extractors were successfully tested in the six sites, these were capable of extracting all the default members of the dataset and observed properties, with no exception.

---

[10] https://www.youtube.com/playlist?list=PLHuNJBFXxaLBFgtbBCZ7kOUUFd-Z3aaJK.

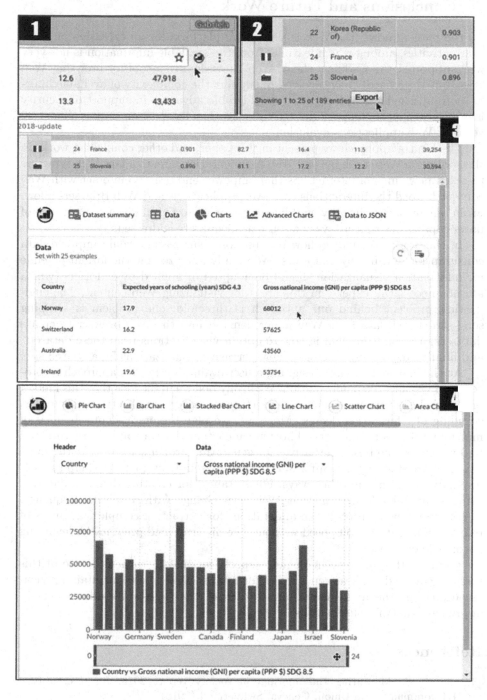

Fig. 4. Extracting and visualizing data from a page

7   Conclusions and Future Work

As the reader knows, the Web is a powerful platform for an extensive range of user activities, among which learning from the available information is not very well supported. As we know them, Web Browsers are a tool for browsing Web sites, but these hardly have evolved to support the complexity of available information, although there have been considerable advances in support of security issues as well as to support the technologies that have arisen during almost 30 years of Web applications evolution.

The kind of approach we present in this paper, and other compelling works in the context of Web mashups and Web Augmentation, aim to adapt Web browsers to reach new kinds of interactions that empower end-users to interact with Web content beyond the interactions that Web applications and Web Browsers allow. From our humble point of view, these approaches are vital given the advance of users capabilities that are very often not adequately addressed.

In this work, we analyze how information visualization would improve data consumption and use by end-users. We mainly analyze how the formal pipeline for information visualization should be adapted or applied by end-users (which are not necessarily experts in this area) for visualizing Web content. The engineering problem behind our approach is threefold: one problem is scraping semi-structured data from Web under demand into the Web browser to create datasets, a second problem is how to obtain visualizations from these datasets, and finally how to plug in-context new pervasive visualizations for any Web site.

At this moment, we are designing a user evaluation for our approach to process and visualize Web information. We firmly believe in the idea that this kind of browser's behavior would make the user's tasks faster and also the user's understanding of information deeper. Moreover, we plan a more in-depth analysis of multiple websites to understand how much content share a similar structure and find which are the best alternatives for generating proper selectors. At the same time, we are studying how information can be usefully extracted to help users in its analysis and use in other ways. For instance, for creating dynamic datasets using temporal information that Web sites change with a specific frequency. Furthermore, using user-driven annotations for extracting complex instances of information that are composed without a semi-structured presentation enabling automatic extraction.

Finally, other more technological aspects for making easier the use of this tools are devised, such as repositories for quickly sharing and maintaining visualizations and the implementation of a library that allows Web developers to apply this kind of visualizations internally.

References

1. Sanou, B.: Measuring the information society report 2018. In: International Telecommunication Union, Geneva, Switzerland (2018)
2. Munzner, T.: Visualization Analysis and Design. AK Peters/CRC Press, New York (2014)

3. Yi, J.S., ah Kang, Y., Stasko, J.: Toward a deeper understanding of the role of interaction in information visualization. IEEE Trans. Vis. Comput. Graph. **13**(6), 1224–1231 (2007)
4. Shneiderman, B.: The eyes have it: a task by data type taxonomy for information visualizations. Craft Inf. Vis., 364–371 (2003)
5. Price, M., Crumley-Branyon, J., Leidheiser, W., Pak, R.: Effects of information visualization on older adults' decision-making performance in a medicare plan selection task: a comparative usability study. JMIR Hum. Fact. **3**(1), (2016)
6. Mahendiran, J., Kirstie Hawkey, N.Z.H.: Exploring the need for visualizations in system administration tools. In: CHI 2014 Extended Abstracts on Human Factors in Computing Systems, pp. 1429–1434. ACM (2014)
7. de Borja, F.G., Freitas, C.M.D.S.: CivisAnalysis: interactive visualization for exploring roll call data and representatives' voting behaviour. In: 28th SIBGRAPI Conference on Graphics, Patterns and Images (SIBGRAPI 2015), pp. 257–264. IEEE Computer Society (2015)
8. Heer, J., Card, S.K., Landay, J.A.: Prefuse: a toolkit for interactive information visualization. In: Proceedings of the SIGCHI Conference on Human Factors in Computing Systems, pp. 421–430. ACM (2015)
9. Sun, L., et al.: WebGIVI: a web-based gene enrichment analysis and visualization tool. BMC Bioinf. **18**(1), 237 (2017)
10. Pantazos, K., Kuhail, M., Lauesen, S., Xu, S.: uVis Studio: an integrated development environment for visualization. Vis. Data Anal. **2013**, 8654 (2013)
11. Fisher, D., Drucker, S., Fernandez, R., Ruble, S.: Visualizations everywhere: a multiplatform infrastructure for linked visualizations. IEEE Trans. Vis. Comput. Graph. **16**(6), 1157–1163 (2010)
12. Bostock, M., Ogievetsky, V., Heer, J.: D3 data-driven documents. IEEE Trans. Vis. Comput. Graph. **17**(12), 2301–2309 (2011)
13. Viégas, F.B., Wattenberg, M., van Ham, F., Kriss, J., McKeon, M.M.: ManyEyes: a site for visualization at internet scale. IEEE Trans. Vis. Comput. Graph **13**(6) (2007)
14. Teixeira, J., Barata, C., Gonçalves, D.: Metabrain: web information extraction and visualization (2012)
15. Díaz, O., Arellano, C.: The augmented web: rationales, opportunities, and challenges on browser-side transcoding. ACM Trans. Web **9**(2) (2015)
16. Firmenich, S., Bosetti, G., Rossi, G., Winckler, M., Barbieri, T.: Abstracting and structuring web contents for supporting personal web experiences. In: Bozzon, A., Cudre-Maroux, P., Pautasso, C. (eds.) ICWE 2016. LNCS, vol. 9671, pp. 77–95. Springer, Cham (2016). https://doi.org/10.1007/978-3-319-38791-8_5
17. Toomim, M., Drucker, S.M., Dontcheva, M., Rahimi, A., Thomson, B., Landay, J.A.: Attaching UI enhancements to websites with end users. In: Proceedings of the SIGCHI Conference on Human Factors in Computing Systems, pp. 1859–1868. ACM (2009)
18. Nguyen, D.Q., Schumann, H.: Visualization to support augmented web browsing. In: International Joint Conferences on Web Intelligence (WI) and Intelligent Agent Technologies (IAT), pp. 535–541. IEEE/WIC/ACM (2013)
19. Aldalur, I., Diaz, O.: Addressing web locator fragility: a case for browser extensions. In: Proceedings of the ACM SIGCHI Symposium on Engineering Interactive Computing Systems, pp. 45–50. ACM (2017)
20. Card, S.K., Mackinlay, J.D., Shneiderman, B.: Readings in Information Visualization: Using Vision to Think. Morgan Kaufmann, San Francisco (1999)

DotCHA: A 3D Text-Based Scatter-Type CAPTCHA

Suzi Kim and Sunghee Choi(✉)

School of Computing, Korea Advanced Institute of Science and Technology,
Daejeon, Republic of Korea
kimsuzi@kaist.ac.kr, sunghee@kaist.edu

Abstract. We introduce a new type of 3D text-based CAPTCHA, called DotCHA, which relies on human interaction. DotCHA asks users to rotate a 3D text model to identify the correct letters. The 3D text model is a twisted form of sequential 3D letters around a center pivot axis, and it shows different letters depending on the rotation angle. The model is not composed of a solid letter model, but a number of spheres to resist character segmentation attacks, and this is why DotCHA is classified as a scatter-type CAPTCHA. DotCHA is tolerant to machine learning attacks because each letter is only identified in each particular direction. We demonstrate that DotCHA, while maintaining usability, is resistant to existing types of attacks.

Keywords: CAPTCHA · 3D CAPTCHA · Text-based CAPTCHA ·
3D typography · Mental rotation · Security · Usability

1 Introduction

Completely Automated Public Turing tests to tell Computers and Humans Apart (CAPTCHA) [31] was developed to protect systems from denial of service (DoS) attacks by malicious automated programs. It is a Turing test to discriminate human users from malicious bots by using tasks that humans can perform easily but machines cannot. Two-dimensional (2D) CAPTCHAs are the most commonly used form of CAPTCHA to identify humans. However, the rapid enhancement of machine learning has enabled bots to overcome the 2D text-based CAPTCHAs [12,25] and 2D image-based CAPTCHAs [29] with high accuracy. In particular, with advances in Optical Character Recognition (OCR), sophisticated attacks have been introduced to break 2D text-based CAPTCHAs. These attacks have led to the development of three-dimensional (3D) CAPTCHAs that are relatively hard to be decoded by computers.

3D CAPTCHAs are categorized into two types: 3D model-based CAPTCHAs and 3D text-based CAPTCHAs. Previous 3D text-based CAPTCHAs were formed by a simple extrusion of alphabets, making them easily recognizable with a single glance. However, the simple extrusion is vulnerable to OCR attacks because it has the same visual effects as distorted 2D text. 3D model-based

© Springer Nature Switzerland AG 2019
M. Bakaev et al. (Eds.): ICWE 2019, LNCS 11496, pp. 238–252, 2019.
https://doi.org/10.1007/978-3-030-19274-7_18

CAPTCHAs have improved security by reducing usability, which is the strength of 3D text-based CAPTCHAs. They are based on the mental rotation ability [4,27], which enables users to find answers by inferring from the direction of various 3D objects [14,26,33], such as vehicles and animals. However, 3D model-based CAPTCHAs have a low correct response rate, because they require the users to not only recognize the 3D object but also judge and infer the answer by performing elaborate operations. As a result, it takes a long time to obtain the right answer for 3D model-based CAPTCHAs compared with 3D text-based CAPTCHAs. Moreover, for those who are accustomed to conventional text-based CAPTCHAs, 3D model-based CAPTCHAs cause usability issues.

This paper proposes a new type of 3D CAPTCHA, called *DotCHA*, which satisfies both security and usability. DotCHA combines the strengths of text-based CAPTCHAs and 3D model-based CAPTCHAs. It presents different alphabets that are rotated at different angles. The alphabets are composed of several small spheres instead of being shown as a single solid model so that it is resistant to segmentation attack. DotCHA provides usability to users who are familiar with text-based CAPTCHAs while preserving the security of 3D model-based CAPTCHAs. In Sect. 2, we briefly review previous works. Section 3 describes the generation of DotCHA, and Sect. 4 evaluates DotCHA using some attack scenarios. The prototype implementation is available at https://suzikim.github.io/DotCHA/.

2   Related Work

In this section, we briefly discuss three main types of CAPTCHAs, as shown in Fig. 1, which are closely related to DotCHA: 2D text-based, 3D model-based, and interactive CAPTCHAs.

2.1   2D Text-Based CAPTCHAs

2D text-based CAPTCHAs are the most widely used form, due to their ease of use and simple structure. A sequence of alphabets and numbers are presented to a user, and the user should identify the correct text to pass the test. Usually, noise and distortion appear in the letters to make the test robust to automated attacks.

Gimpy and EZ-Gimpy [2] are based on the human ability to read heavily distorted and corrupted text. Gimpy picks up 10 random words from the dictionary and arranges them to be overlapped with each other. Users have to identify at least three words to pass the test. EZ-Gimpy uses only one random word from the dictionary, but instead increases its security by deformation, blurring, noise, and distortion of letters. Mori and Malik [23] break Gimpy and EZ-Gimpy using object recognition algorithms and dictionary attacks.

Baffle text [6] minimizes the instances of dictionary attack by using pseudo-random but pronounceable words. The users are asked to infer the correct answer from words that have missing parts of letters. MSN Passport CAPTCHA [7] has eight characters, including alphabets and numbers, which are highly warped to distort the characters.

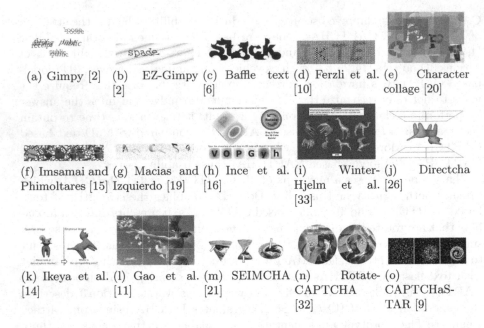

(a) Gimpy [2] (b) EZ-Gimpy [2] (c) Baffle text [6] (d) Ferzli et al. [10] (e) Character collage [20]

(f) Imsamai and Phimoltares [15] (g) Macias and Izquierdo [19] (h) Ince et al. [16] (i) Winter-Hjelm et al. [33] (j) Directcha [26]

(k) Ikeya et al. [14] (l) Gao et al. [11] (m) SEIMCHA [21] (n) Rotate-CAPTCHA [32] (o) CAPTCHaS-TAR [9]

Fig. 1. Examples of previous 2D text-based, 3D model-based, and interactive CAPTCHAs.

The prime advantages of 2D text-based CAPTCHAs are that they are easy to generate and identify. However, it is also easy to be recognized through OCR attacks [28,34]. More advanced 2D text-based CAPTCHAs have been introduced [10,20]; however, they have been easily broken by machine learning attacks [12,25].

2.2 3D Model-Based CAPTCHAs

3D CAPTCHAs are designed to defeat bots, which use machine learning to identify 2D text-based CAPTCHAs easily, by minimizing the legibility. Most of the 3D model-based CAPTCHAs are based on the rotation of 3D models [14,26,33]. They take advantage of the cognitive ability of humans, called mental rotation [4,27], which is an inherent characteristic of human nature. Mental rotation enables humans to compare two models in different orientations. However, users find it difficult to deal with an unfamiliar model, so they spend a long time to solve the problem.

3D text-based CAPTCHAs are more familiar to users because they originated from text-based CAPTCHAs that users have been accustomed to. Ince et al. [16] introduce a cubic-style 3D CAPTCHA, which contains six alphabets on each side of a cube. However, it is vulnerable to segmentation attacks because the letters are simply attached to each side of the cube without interference. There have been several CAPTCHAs using a sequence of 3D letter models created with extrusion and warping [15,19]. Ye et al. [37] demonstrate that CAPTCHAs with such a simple distorted form could easily be broken with a high degree of accuracy.

2.3   Interactive CAPTCHAs

Interactive CAPTCHAs rely on user interaction to mitigate automated attacks. They require users to solve the problem by cognitive abilities and human actions. The 3D model-based CAPTCHAs [16,33], which require rotation of the 3D model to get the answers, also belong to the interactive CAPTCHAs.

2D images are the most commonly used sources in interactive CAPTCHAs. Gossweiler et al. [13] introduce a 2D-image based interactive CAPTCHA that requires users to rotate a randomly oriented image to its upright orientation. SEIMCHA [21] applies geometric transformations to 2D images, and users are required to identify the upright orientation of the image. Gao et al. [11] introduce a CAPTCHA that asks users to solve a jigsaw puzzle of a 2D image divided into small pieces and shuffled. In rotateCAPTCHA [32], which combines the orientation and puzzle solving techniques, the users have to recreate the original image by rotating the segmented image.

CAPTCHaStar [9] requires the users to change the position of a set of randomly scattered small squares by moving the cursor to recognize the correct shape. Our DotCHA adopts the movement of small scattered objects from CAPTCHaStar to ensure resistance to random guessing attacks [18]. The main problem with interactive CAPTCHAs, which focus more on security than usability, is that it is difficult and time-consuming to solve the problem. This is due to the fact that users are not accustomed to solving visual problems. Our DotCHA combines the strengths of text-based and interactive CAPTCHAs to satisfy both security and usability.

3   Generation of DotCHA

DotCHA is designed to satisfy both security and usability by improving the security of 2D text-based CAPTCHAs and the usability of 3D model-based CAPTCHAs. All letters of the 2D text-based CAPTCHAs are visible at once, and the letters are legible because of the clear form of lettering; therefore, it is vulnerable to OCR attacks. Each letter of DotCHA is only legible at a unique rotation angle, which makes this technique robust to OCR attacks, by twisting 3D extruded models around a center axis, as shown in Fig. 3(c). In addition, we remove visual unnecessary parts of the models so that each letter is not read in any direction other than in its unique direction, as shown in Fig. 3(d).

In order to improve usability, the contents of DotCHA include just 3D letter models instead of other visual representations, such as images or object models. The rotation axis of DotCHA is fixed to a single axis, shown as a black bar in Fig. 3, in order to reduce the burden and confusion for users, who may wander around the 3D space. We replace remaining cubes with spheres to prevent direction attacks, which guess the unique orientation of each letter by aligning the edges of small cubes, and more details will be given in Sect. 3.3. Figure 2 shows the pipeline to generate a DotCHA from given target alphabets.

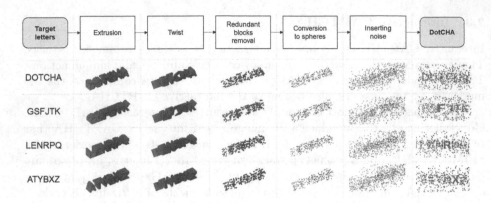

Fig. 2. System Pipeline to generate DotCHA. Target letters are extruded and twisted to 3D model, and split to small unit blocks. Redundant blocks, which do not affect the perception of letters, are removed, and the remaining blocks are converted to spheres. Finally, noise spheres are added around the model.

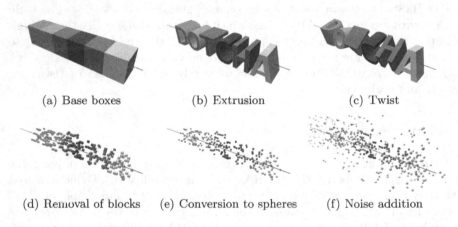

(a) Base boxes   (b) Extrusion   (c) Twist

(d) Removal of blocks   (e) Conversion to spheres   (f) Noise addition

Fig. 3. Sample result of the DotCHA generation.

3.1   Extrusion and Twist of 3D Model

We use the molecular construction method [17,22] to engrave the given letters on a solid rectangular parallelepiped model. Molecular construction [22] is a technique in which a model is divided into smaller units forming the larger model. The basic idea of generating a DotCHA involves cutting a solid cube model into small unit blocks and then deleting unnecessary blocks or adding missing blocks to represent the given letters. Figure 3(b) and (c) show the results of extrusion and twist, respectively. One letter has a size of $k \times k \times k$, and it retains the same shape as an extrusion of a 2D letter pattern.

The 3D letter models are then rotated around the center axis of the rectangular parallelepiped model at unique angles to ensure that the correct answers are not recognized from a single direction. If the number of letters used in a CAPTCHA is n, the correct answer of the DotCHA can be identified only if the machine finds all n directions.

3.2 Removal of Redundant Blocks

Although not all letters are visible at once in defense of segmentation attacks, a twisted model is still vulnerable to OCR attack. We remove a set of unit blocks from the models so that each letter is recognized only in one particular direction, not in any direction. The blocks are removed based on two conditions. Firstly, we remove unnecessary blocks that do not affect the shape of the letters. If two blocks are placed side by side along one axis, even if one block is discarded, it is still recognized as a letter in a certain direction. Secondly, the blocks are evenly removed while preserving the balance between directions, because the letters can be easily identified in an arbitrary direction if the blocks are gathered.

We use a multigraph G, which has multiple edges between a pair of vertices. Each unit block is represented as a vertex of the graph G. Two unit blocks are connected by two types of edges depending on whether the blocks are located on the same coordinates along the y or z axes. Since the rotation axis is fixed to the x axis and the overlapping in x coordinates does not affect the recognition of the letter, we ignore the x axis in G. We score all the vertices according to the scoring function S of vertex v as follows:

$$S(v) = \alpha \cdot |N_R(v)| + |N_G(v)| \tag{1}$$

where $N_G(v)$ is a set of adjacent vertices of v in graph G and $N_R(v)$ is the set of neighboring vertices. For a given vertex v, we define a neighboring vertex as the one whose Euclidean distance from vertex v is at most k. The first term is related to the dispersion of blocks in the cube. It indicates the number of blocks that exist around the block v. The second term is for calculating the number of blocks that are placed along the y and z axes. α is a constant for balancing between the two terms. We used $\alpha = 0.3$ in our experiments.

We iterate the vertices in the descending order of the scores to decide whether to remove the block or not. At each iteration, unless the block is the only block placed along the y or z axes, it is discarded from the DotCHA model. Otherwise, we leave the block and continue to the next iteration. The iterations stop when the number of iterations exceeds $\mu n k^3$, where μ represents the removal ratio and nk^3 is the volume of the bounding box. Large μ makes it take a long time for the user to find the correct answer, while small μ makes the security weaker; therefore, appropriate balance of μ is important. We used $\mu = 0.8$ in our experiments.

3.3 Prototype Implementation

Since the direction of cube blocks can be inferred from the edges of the cube, the orientation of letters can be easily identified. In order to hide the orientation of the model, we convert the unit blocks into spheres, the result of which is similar to that of the scatter-type method [3]. The post-processing involves three parameters to maximize usability and security:

- *Sphere radius (ρ)*: the radius of the sphere converted from the unit block. The edge length of a unit cube is 1, and $\rho = 1$ means that a sphere fits exactly into the cube without any cutoff or margins.
- *Sphere offset (σ)*: the location offset of the center of the sphere from the center of the unit block. $\sigma = 0$ means that the centers of the sphere and unit cube are the identical, and $\sigma = 0.5$ means that the center of the sphere exists on the surface of the unit cube.
- *Noise (δ)*: the number of noise spheres.

After the redundant blocks are removed, δ noise spheres are added to the model to prevent recognition by automated machines. The region of noise spheres is three times bigger than nk^3, and excludes the bounding box of DotCHA. This is based on the concept of motion parallax, which gives users the perception of depth from the relative motion between models [8]. The noise spheres appear to move faster or slower as compared to the alphabet spheres, and the user can distinguish them by human visual system of depth perception. We set ρ to be smaller than the half-edge of the unit block to avoid edge detection attacks. Each sphere is randomly translated within the range of $(0, \sigma)$ to avoid pixel-count attacks.

The rotation axis of DotCHA is fixed to the x axis in order to reduce the burden and confusion for users. In addition, we support both automatic and interactive rotation to improve usability. DotCHA is implemented using Three.js library, which is a lightweight 3D engine, on HTML5 Canvas, so that it is supported by a majority of the browsers. We use $k = 10$ alphabet pattern with Consolas font. In addition, to defend against segmentation attack, random clutter spheres are added to the background, which makes it difficult to separate the foreground and background to identify the letters.

4   Experiments

We analyzed the security of DotCHA by considering several different attack scenarios. The goal of all the attacks is twofold: (1) to find the correct view directions to identify the letters and (2) to read the letters in the selected view directions. For the first goal, we tested whether a particular view direction can be characterized by the attacks. We tested the second goal by applying OCR to read the sampled images. We used $n = 6$ letters of DotCHA, and a combination of random alphabet letters were used to avoid dictionary attack.

4.1   Finding the Correct View Directions

As mentioned in Sect. 3.1, an automated attack should find the $n = 6$ correct view directions to identify the correct answer. We sampled 30 different views including six ground truth views and scored them through pixel counting and edge detection.

Table 1. Result of scoring with pixel counting. Thirty views have been ranked through pixel counting, and the views of the largest and smallest pixel counts are shown in order. In addition, the pixel counting results of the correct views are shown in the right column with correct letters. The pixel counting attacks failed to find the correct view, and it shows that the correct view cannot be distinguished by pixel counting.

Pixel Counting Result		Ground Truth	
Largest	**Smallest**		
241,608	238,191 A	240,544
241,027	238,435 T	240,497
240,956	238,518 C	240,276
240,949	238,710 O	239,316
240,806	238,855 H	239,180
240,544	238,896 D	239,119

Score with Pixel Counting. Pixel counting attack is based on two assumptions: first, the wider the overlap between the spheres, the clearer the shape of letters; second, the narrower the overlap between the spheres, the more information that can be represented. We counted the number of non-background pixels and checked whether the correct views can be distinguished from incorrect views by the number of pixels. We confirmed that the correct view directions cannot be identified by pixel counting, as described in Table 1, which shows the result of the pixel counting attack when $\rho = 0.5$, $\sigma = 0.2$, and $\delta = 0.001$. It shows that the correct answers are ranked arbitrarily regardless of the pixel counts. In the process of converting the unit blocks into spheres, we added a random offset to the position of the sphere, and this makes DotCHA robust to pixel counting.

Score with Edge Detection. This criterion aims to find the correct view directions by detecting edges from the original images. We ran Canny edge detection [5] on every sampled image. A DotCHA model was projected onto a 2D text form after removing unnecessary pixel information via edge detection. We counted the number of pixels in the edge-detected images to distinguish the correct view directions from the irrelevant view directions.

There was no correlation between the correct view directions and the number of edges, as shown in Table 2. While converting the unit blocks into spheres, we made the sphere smaller than the unit block. As a result, the spheres were separated from each other, and edge detection showed the edges of spheres, which lowered the prominence of the edges of letters.

Table 2. Result of scoring with edge counting. Thirty views have been ranked through edge counting, and the views of the largest and smallest edge counts are shown in order. In addition, the edge counting results of the correct views are shown in the right column with correct letters. The edge counting attacks failed to find the correct view, and it shows that the correct view cannot be distinguished by edge counting. $\rho = 0.5$, $\sigma = 0.2$, and $\delta = 0.001$ were used for edge counting.

Edge Detection Result				Ground Truth	
Largest		Smallest			
	12,668		11,856 H		12,445
	12,564		11,788 O		12,335
	12,507		11,784 D		12,318
	12,459		11,742 C		11,981
	12,445		11,693 T		11,924
	12,404		11,685 A		11,784

4.2 Reading the Letters from the Correct View Directions

In the previous subsection, we showed that it is difficult to find the correct view direction automatically. For the experiment described in this subsection, we tested the possibility of reading letters from the given correct view directions when we assumed that the machine somehow found the correct view direction.

Pixel-Count Attack. A pixel-count attack [34,36] counts the number of pixels of each segmented letter by the vertical histogram of a CAPTCHA image. The number of pixels is then mapped to the lookup table, which contains precomputed numbers of every alphabet.

The most important part in segmentation is the removal of background or clutters. However, it is difficult to remove them from DotCHA, because clutter spheres looks similar to spheres that form the letter model. As a result, it disturbs the segmentation through vertical histogram, as shown in Fig. 4.

DotCHA requires several segmentations, as many as the number of letters, and this becomes an overhead to repeat. Moreover, segmentation can be avoided by increasing the range of the random offset of spheres. Even if the segmentation works well, DotCHA is still resistant to pixel-count attack, because the number of pixels varies depending on the view direction and clutter, as depicted in Table 3. Furthermore, even if some segmentations succeed, it is impossible to guess the entire word from only a few letters obtained through segmentation, because DotCHA does not use dictionary words.

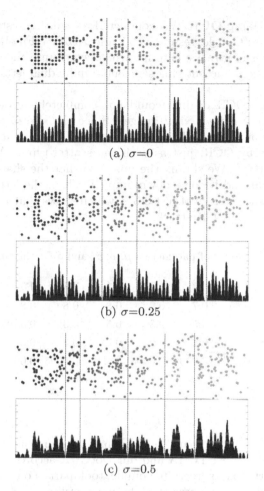

(a) σ=0

(b) σ=0.25

(c) σ=0.5

Fig. 4. Vertical histograms of DotCHA, when $\rho = 0.35$ and $\delta = 0.0015$. Noise still remains in the image and it disturbs the segmentation by affecting the histogram. As the range of random offset increases, the segmentation becomes difficult, which makes it difficult to figure out the letters.

Table 3. Pixel counts from different views of letter 'D', when $\rho = 0.4$, $\sigma = 0.3$, and $\delta = 0.001$. The pixel counts vary depending on the rotation angle, and it is resistant to pixel counting attacks.

Pixel Counts	475	451	422	416	379

Recognition by Using OCR. We conducted recognition tests using two well-known OCR engines: Google Tesseract [30] and ABBYY FineReader 14 [1]. We performed two types of attacks: entering whole words into the OCR engines for automated recognition, and entering segmented individual letters into the OCR engines.

In both attacks, OCR engines could not completely recognize any of the words, even from the correct view images. Since the size of the spheres were small, they were not connected to each other. As a result, it was difficult to identify the letters by OCR, just as with the scatter-type CAPTCHA, which is resistant to OCR [3]. We shrank the image so that the shape of the spheres seemed to disappear and become downsampled. Then, the letters are partially recognized with a success rate of just 3.3%, which shows that DotCHA provides reasonable resistance to OCR attack.

Table 4. Values of parameters μ, ρ, σ, and δ for the survey.

	T1	T2	T3	T4	T5	T6
μ	0.85	0.7	0.8	0.8	0.8	0.8
ρ	0.5	0.5	0.3	0.5	0.3	0.3
σ	0	0.2	0.2	0.3	0.3	0.3
δ	0.0005	0.0005	0.0005	0.0005	0.0005	0.001

4.3 User Study

We ran a user study to compare the response time and accuracy required to solve a 2D text-based CAPTCHA and our DotCHA according to the usability metrics [35]. 50 participants, recruited online, took part in our web-based survey, and all the participants underwent eight unsupervised tests using their own device: six DotCHA challenges (named from T1 to T6) and two 2D text-based CAPTCHA ones (T7 and T8). All the DotCHA challenges had $n = 6$ letters, and were randomly generated using the value of parameters in Table 4. T7 and T8 are generated from reCAPTCHA with single word. In order to familiarize the participants with the challenges, one practice DotCHA demo is shown to the participants at the beginning of the survey. The users were not told whether they had passed or failed each challenge.

Figure 5 plots the success response rates of the tests. 2D text-based CAPTCHAs (T7 and T8) have less response time than DotCHA, while DotCHAs achieve a higher success rates with just a few more response time. The average success rates of 2D text-based CAPTCHAs (T7 and T8) are 39.5% and 63.2%, respectively, while those of DotCHAs (T2 and T6) are 80.0% and 89.5%. When considering extra time overhead, encountered during multiple attempts to acquire the correct answer, few more response time is acceptable.

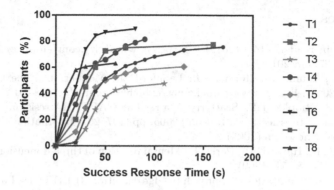

Fig. 5. Success response rates of the survey.

While T6 is the most difficult test with high μ, σ, and δ, and low ρ values, the participants acquired the correct answer than other DotCHA tests. Also, in the case of T1, which is the easiest test, it took longer time to acquired the correct answer than T2 and T4. This result shows that there is no significant effect of parameters on the user's perception, and the parameters can be adjusted by placing more emphasis on the security.

5 Conclusion

In this paper, we have proposed a new type of 3D text-based CAPTCHA, called DotCHA, which attempts to overcome the limitations of existing 2D and 3D approaches. It is a scatter-type CAPTCHA, which shows different letters according to the rotation angle, and the user should rotate the 3D model to identify the letters. We demonstrated that DotCHA is robust against several types of attacks.

There is a general consensus that it is hard to design a CAPTCHA that simultaneously combines good usability and security [24]. To improve the usability of DotCHA while preserving security, we combined the automated rotation and interactive systems. As we demonstrated, DotCHA defeats several types of attacks even when the correct view direction is given.

To improve the security, two additional strategies are possible: adding a background and using a set of a small particles instead of a single sphere. Adding a complicated background protects the CAPTCHA against machines due to the difficulties in separating the foreground from the background to identify the letters. In addition, a set of small particles increases the scatter ratio and enhances the defense against pixel-count attack or edge detection attack.

References

1. Abbyy finereader 14 (2014). https://www.abbyy.com/en-apac/finereader/. Accessed 27 Jan 2019
2. Ahn, L.v., Blum, M., Hopper, N., Langford, J., Manber, U.: The CAPTCHA project (2000). http://www.captcha.net/captchas/gimpy/. Accessed 27 Jan 2019
3. Baird, H.S., Riopka, T.P.: Scattertype: a reading CAPTCHA resistant to segmentation attack. In: Electronic Imaging 2005, pp. 197–207. International Society for Optics and Photonics (2005)
4. Bartoshuk, L., Harned, M., Parks, L.: Mental rotation of three-dimensional objects. Anim. Behav. **8**, 54 (1960)
5. Canny, J.: A computational approach to edge detection. IEEE Trans. Pattern Anal. Mach. Intell. **6**, 679–698 (1986)
6. Chew, M., Baird, H.S.: Baffletext: a human interactive proof. In: Electronic Imaging 2003, pp. 305–316. International Society for Optics and Photonics (2003)
7. Choudhary, S., Saroha, R., Dahiya, Y., Choudhary, S.: Understanding captcha: text and audio based captcha with its applications. Int. J. Adv. Res. Comput. Sci. Softw. Eng. **3**(6) (2013)
8. Chow, Y.-W., Susilo, W.: AniCAP: an animated 3D CAPTCHA scheme based on motion parallax. In: Lin, D., Tsudik, G., Wang, X. (eds.) CANS 2011. LNCS, vol. 7092, pp. 255–271. Springer, Heidelberg (2011). https://doi.org/10.1007/978-3-642-25513-7_18
9. Conti, M., Guarisco, C., Spolaor, R.: CAPTCHaStar! a novel CAPTCHA based on interactive shape discovery. In: Manulis, M., Sadeghi, A.-R., Schneider, S. (eds.) ACNS 2016. LNCS, vol. 9696, pp. 611–628. Springer, Cham (2016). https://doi.org/10.1007/978-3-319-39555-5_33
10. Ferzli, R., Bazzi, R., Karam, L.J.: A captcha based on the human visual systems masking characteristics. In: 2006 IEEE International Conference on Multimedia and Expo, pp. 517–520. IEEE (2006)
11. Gao, H., Yao, D., Liu, H., Liu, X., Wang, L.: A novel image based CAPTCHA using jigsaw puzzle. In: 2010 IEEE 13th International Conference on Computational Science and Engineering (CSE), pp. 351–356. IEEE (2010)
12. Golle, P.: Machine learning attacks against the asirra CAPTCHA. In: Proceedings of the 15th ACM Conference on Computer and Communications Security, pp. 535–542. ACM (2008)
13. Gossweiler, R., Kamvar, M., Baluja, S.: What's up CAPTCHA? a CAPTCHA based on image orientation. In: Proceedings of the 18th International Conference on World Wide Web, pp. 841–850. ACM (2009)
14. Ikeya, Y., Fujita, M., Kani, J., Yoneyama, Y., Nishigaki, M.: An image-based CAPTCHA using sophisticated mental rotation. In: Tryfonas, T., Askoxylakis, I. (eds.) HAS 2014. LNCS, vol. 8533, pp. 57–68. Springer, Cham (2014). https://doi.org/10.1007/978-3-319-07620-1_6
15. Imsamai, M., Phimoltares, S.: 3D CAPTCHA: a next generation of the CAPTCHA. In: 2010 International Conference on Information Science and Applications (ICISA), pp. 1–8. IEEE (2010)
16. Ince, I.F., Salman, Y.B., Yildirim, M.E., Yang, T.C.: Execution time prediction for 3D interactive CAPTCHA by keystroke level model. In: Fourth International Conference on Computer Sciences and Convergence Information Technology, 2009. ICCIT 2009, pp. 1057–1061. IEEE (2009)

17. Kim, S., Choi, S.: Automatic generation of 3D typography. In: ACM SIGGRAPH 2016 Posters, p. 21. ACM (2016)
18. Kumari, P., Kapoor, M.: Effect of random guessing attack on image based captchas: analysis and survey. Int. J. Innovations Adv. Comput. Sci. **4** (2015)
19. Macias, C.R., Izquierdo, E.: Visual word-based CAPTCHA using 3D characters (2009)
20. Martinović, G., Attard, A., Krpić, Z.: Proposing a new type of CAPTCHA: character collage. In: MIPRO, 2011 Proceedings of the 34th International Convention, pp. 1447–1451. IEEE (2011)
21. Mehrnejad, M., Ghaemi Bafghi, A., Harati, A., Toreini, E.: Seimcha: a new semantic image captcha using geometric transformations. ISC Int. J. Inf. Secur. **4**(1), 63–76 (2012)
22. Miller, J.A.: Dimensional Typography:: Words in Space: Kiosk Report#1, vol. 1. Princeton Architectural Press, New York (1996)
23. Mori, G., Malik, J.: Recognizing objects in adversarial clutter: Breaking a visual CAPTCHA. In: 2003 IEEE Computer Society Conference on Computer Vision and Pattern Recognition, 2003. Proceedings, vol. 1, pp. I. IEEE (2003)
24. Osadchy, M., Hernandez-Castro, J., Gibson, S., Dunkelman, O., érez Cabo, D.P.: No bot expects the DeepCAPTCHA! introducing immutable adversarial examples with applications to CAPTCHA. Cryptology ePrint Archive, Report 2016/336 (2016). http://eprint.iacr.org/2016/336
25. Ramakrushna, T.: An inventive approach for challenging AI problems in graphical passwords: captcha. IJRCCT **5**(8), 404–409 (2016)
26. Sano, A., Fujita, M., Nishigaki, M.: Directcha: a proposal of spatiometric mental rotation CAPTCHA. In: 2016 14th Annual Conference on Privacy, Security and Trust (PST), pp. 585–592. IEEE (2016)
27. Shepard, S., Metzler, D.: Mental rotation: effects of dimensionality of objects and type of task. J. Exp. Psychol. Hum. Percept. Perform. **14**(1), 3 (1988)
28. Simard, P.Y., Steinkraus, D., Platt, J.C., et al.: Best practices for convolutional neural networks applied to visual document analysis. In: ICDAR, vol. 3, pp. 958–962. Citeseer (2003)
29. Sivakorn, S., Polakis, I., Keromytis, A.D.: I am robot: (deep) learning to break semantic image CAPTCHAs. In: 2016 IEEE European Symposium on Security and Privacy (EuroS&P), pp. 388–403. IEEE (2016)
30. Smith, R.: An overview of the tesseract OCR engine. In: Ninth International Conference on Document Analysis and Recognition, 2007. ICDAR 2007, vol. 2, pp. 629–633. IEEE (2007)
31. von Ahn, L., Blum, M., Hopper, N.J., Langford, J.: CAPTCHA: Using hard AI problems for security. In: Biham, E. (ed.) EUROCRYPT 2003. LNCS, vol. 2656, pp. 294–311. Springer, Heidelberg (2003). https://doi.org/10.1007/3-540-39200-9_18
32. Wickramasingha, N., Keerawella, H., Samarasinghe, S., Ragel, R.: Rotate-CAPTCHA a novel interactive CAPTCHA design targeting mobile devices. In: 2015 IEEE 10th International Conference on Industrial and Information Systems (ICIIS), pp. 49–54. IEEE (2015)
33. Winter-Hjelm, C., Kleming, M., Bakken, R.: An interactive 3D CAPTCHA with semantic information. In: Proceedings of Norwegian Artificial Intelligence Symposium, pp. 157–160 (2009)
34. Yan, J., El Ahmad, A.S.: Breaking visual CAPTCHAs with naive pattern recognition algorithms. In: Computer Security Applications Conference, 2007. ACSAC 2007. Twenty-Third Annual, pp. 279–291. IEEE (2007)

35. Yan, J., El Ahmad, A.S.: Usability of CAPTCHAs or usability issues in CAPTCHA design. In: Proceedings of the 4th Symposium on Usable Privacy and Security, pp. 44–52. ACM (2008)
36. Yan, J., El Ahmad, A.S.: CAPTCHA security: a case study. IEEE Secur. Priv. **7**(4), 22–28 (2009)
37. Ye, Q., Chen, Y., Zhu, B.: The robustness of a new 3D captcha. In: 2014 11th IAPR International Workshop on Document Analysis Systems (DAS), pp. 319–323. IEEE (2014)

Entropy and Compression Based Analysis
of Web User Interfaces

Egor Boychuk and Maxim Bakaev[(✉)] [iD]

Novosibirsk State Technical University, Novosibirsk, Russia
bakaev@corp.nstu.ru

Abstract. In our paper we explore whether user visual perception of web interfaces (WUI) can be predicted by certain quantitative characteristics of WUI screenshots. The considered metrics are JPEG file size, PNG file size, and information entropy value calculated with frequency-based MATLAB's entropy (I) function. We ran survey with 70 subjects who provided subjective evaluations of complexity, aesthetics and orderliness for 497 website homepages. The results suggest that all the three metrics were significant, and the proposed regression models were considerably better than the respective baseline models that only used the popular JPEG-based metric. Remarkably, the entropy metric had significant positive correlations with aesthetic and orderliness evaluations, but not with the size of the image. We believe our findings might be used in development of automated WUI analysis tools to aid web engineers in their work.

Keywords: Information entropy · Web interfaces · Cognitive models

1 Introduction

As the number and diversity of web user interfaces (WUIs) increase, there is the growing demand for their qualitative analysis and prediction of users' subjective impressions. Given the shortening website update cycles and tightening IT budgets, the development of respective automated tools is deemed necessary to aid web engineers in their work [1]. Many of the tools and methods focus on evaluating usability as quality-in-use and require real or staged user interactions. However, it is also known that first but long-holding impressions of a website are formed in users after a very short visual perception, 50 ms or even less [2]. These purely visual-based subjective impressions significantly affect the subsequent user experience and usability.

Arguably, the most studied dimensions of WUI visual perception are visual complexity (VC) and aesthetics, sometimes supplemented by consistency/regularity/order. The traditional "static" analysis of WUIs that is based on code is understandably disadvantageous here, as it lacks knowledge about web pages' appearance until it's actually rendered in a browser. At the same time, the visual WUI analysis that is gaining in popularity [3] mostly works by decompounding the webpage screenshot, thus being computationally expensive and so far suffering from lower accuracy. Meanwhile, analysis of images uses some quantitative indexes (metrics) that apply to whole images, are reasonably inexpensive and accurate: byte size of files in various formats (most often, JPEG), Subband Entropy, etc. [4].

© Springer Nature Switzerland AG 2019
M. Bakaev et al. (Eds.): ICWE 2019, LNCS 11496, pp. 253–261, 2019.
https://doi.org/10.1007/978-3-030-19274-7_19

In our paper, we study applicability of metrics based on compression (JPEG and PNG algorithm) and on Shannon's information entropy as predictors of web interface users' impressions. In Sect. 2, we describe the three metrics, provide overview of related works, and describe our experimental study. In Sect. 3, we use statistical methods to analyze the data. In the final section, we discuss the results, provide conclusions and outline directions for further research.

2 Methods and Related Work

2.1 Information Entropy

Entropy reflects the degree of randomness, disorder in a system. In our study we are using Shannon's information entropy (H), which is a measure of unpredictability and uncertainty of information in an event:

$$H = -K \sum_i p_i \log_2 p_i. \tag{1}$$

K is the positive constant used to select the units of measure; p_i is the probability that the system is in a state i. The entropy filtering transforms the original image on the basis of entropy, where the local neighborhood is described by a multidimensional array of zeros and ones [5]. Figure 1 shows a screenshot of a web page before and after the entropy filtration. One can note that with this filer, interface elements like text, buttons, input fields, drawings, etc. become highlighted, whereas content of the images rather grows dim. This suggests the entropy-based image processing can be rather original with respect to WUI analysis, as it is capable of negating graphical content.

Fig. 1. Screenshot of a web page before (left) and after (right) entropy filtering.

However, the results of studies in human visual perception suggest that it is not well explained with information entropy (information-theoretic complexity), particularly since it does not consider spatial structures. Through Algorithmic Information Theory, the use of compression algorithms that can approximate Kolmogorov algorithmic complexity was justified to gauge human perception, which is mostly top-down, i.e. focused on higher-order images and structures.

2.2   Compression Algorithms-Based Metrics

JPEG Algorithm. This lossy compression algorithm (specified e.g. in ISO/IEC 10918-1:1994 standard) has gained extreme popularity, especially for photographic images. The compression ratio can be adjusted, with 100 corresponding to nearly lossless conversion. Popular implementation of the algorithm splits the image into blocks of 8*8 pixels and performs the discrete cosine transform. The subsequent quantization corresponds to particulars of human vision, which is not very sensitive to strength of high-frequency brightness variations. Finally, Huffman coding is used to further compress the image data. JPEG compression-based metrics are widely used to study complexity, aesthetics and other attributes of images perception [6], but its applicability for web UIs has not been convincingly demonstrated so far.

PNG Algorithm. This algorithm (see ISO/IEC 15948:2004 standard) supports lossless data compression for palette-based images (commonly, 24-bit RGB). Pixels in the image are represented as numbers, while palette is a separate table. The compression is performed using Deflate algorithm, which is a combination of LZ77 and Huffman coding. The format is widely used for images that contain text, line art, graphics, etc., for which it provides better compress ratio than JPEG. PNG-based metric was found to be somehow predictive of VC for both pictures [7] and abstract patterns [8], although the correlation with visual complexity was lower than for the JPEG-based metric.

2.3   The Experimental Survey

Our experimental study was performed to check the following hypotheses:

H1. Metrics based on compression algorithms (that are already know to work for images) are predictive of web UI's visual perception.
H2. The metric based on information entropy can further improve the predictive power.

Material. The material in our study was homepages of higher educational organizations (universities and colleges), since we sought to eliminate the effect of different website domains. With dedicated Python script crawling through URLs we took from various catalogues, DBPedia, etc., we collected 10639 screenshots of the homepages. Then we hand-picked 497 screenshots from the pool, using the following criteria:

- University or college corporate website with reasonably robust functionality;
- Not overly famous university (to maintain neutrality in the website evaluations);

- Website content in English and reasonably diverse (i.e. no photos-only websites);
- Reasonable diversity in website designs (colors, page layouts, etc.).

The screenshots were made for full web pages, as they were rendered, – not just of the part above the fold or of a fixed size. This was needed to test the entropy metric for images of different sizes. Also, we sought to have more novel exploration of WUI metrics, since the crop to size approach is already widely used (cf. AIM Interface Metrics).

Design. The experiment used within-subject design. The independent variables were:

- The size of the homepage screenshot file in PNG-24 format, in MB: *PNG_size*;
- File size for the same screenshot compressed in JPEG-100 format, in MB: *JPEG_size*;
- Entropy value obtained for the .png file through MATLAB's entropy(I) function [5]: *M_Entropy*.

Since we discovered the lack of standard questionnaires for assessing subjective complexity of websites (unlike for usability, aesthetics, satisfaction, etc.), the dependent variables in our study were simply represented by 3 subjective evaluation Likert scales, each ranging from 1 (lowest degree of the characteristic) to 7 (the highest degree):

- How visually complex the WUI appears: *Complex*;
- How aesthetically pleasant the WUI appears: *Aesthetic*;
- How orderly the WUI appears: *Orderly*.

Participants. In total, there were 70 participants (43 females, 27 males) in the survey, whose age ranged from 18 to 29 (mean 20.86, SD = 1.75). They were students of Novosibirsk State Technical University (NSTU) and specialists working in IT industry. The subjects took part in the experiment voluntary and no random selection was performed. All the participants had normal or corrected to normal vision and reasonable experience with websites.

There were another 10 participants, each of which provided less than 10 evaluations. Since their engagement and scrupulosity seemed doubtful, their evaluations were discarded.

Procedure. The participants were provided with a link to the online questionnaire that we specially developed for this study. While they used varying screen resolutions, the screenshots pixel dimensions were uniform for each participant. In the survey, the screenshots were randomly selected from the pool of 497 (with priority given to the ones that had lower number of evaluations at the moment of selection) and presented to participants successively. The completeness of evaluation, i.e. ranking by all the 3 scales, was mandatory and controlled by the software. The default number of screenshots to be evaluated in each session was set as 50. However, participants were allowed to run the second session (up to another 50 evaluations) if they felt like it.

3   Results

Statistical analysis was performed with SPSS software. We must warn the reader that for the sake of the analysis robustness, some methods more suitable for interval measurement scales were applied with our ordinal dependent variables.

3.1   Descriptive Statistics

In total, the valid participants provided 4235 full evaluations, per the 3 scales each. Thus, each website screenshot was evaluated by 8–10 participants (mean 8.52, SD = 0.56), the average number of full evaluations being 60.05 per participant. Due to technical issues, 4 screenshots were discarded, so 493 remained valid (99.2%). We show descriptive statistics on the image dimensions and the variables in Table 1. The websites that got the highest and lowest average *Complex* evaluations are presented in Fig. 2.

Table 1. The descriptive statistics for the variables in the study.

Variable	Range	Mean (SD)
width	1440–2862	1448 (80.89)
height	900–16571	2586 (1379.95)
JPEG_size	0.31–10.11	2.00 (1.08)
PNG_size	0.13–11.20	1.95 (1.28)
M_Entropy	1.78–7.80	5.05 (0.95)
Complex	1.75–5.78	3.58 (0.65)
Aesthetic	1.71–6.25	4.12 (0.86)
Orderly	2.11–6.13	4.44 (0.64)

Fig. 2. The website screenshots with the highest (left) and lowest (right) *Complex* values.

The Shapiro-Wilk tests suggested that the normality hypothesis had to be rejected for *Orderly* (p = 0.002), but not for *Complex* (p = 0.622) and *Aesthetic* (p = 0.085).

3.2   Correlation Analysis

The total image size (width * height) was highly correlated with *JPEG_size* (r = 0.871, p < 0.001) and *PNG_size* (r = 0.812, p < 0.001), but not with *M_Entropy* (r = 0.043, p = 0.340). In Table 2, we present Pearson's and Kendall's (tau-b, non-parametric statistic for ordinal scales) correlations for the main independent and dependent variables. The strongest correlations for each of the dependent variables are highlighted in bold.

Table 2. Correlations between the variables in the study.

	JPEG_size	PNG_size	M_Entropy	Complex	Aesthetic	Orderly
JPEG_size	1	r = 0.951 p < 0.001	r = 0.315 p < 0.001	**τ = 0.143** **p < 0.001**	τ = 0.257 p < 0.001	τ = 0.193 p < 0.001
PNG_size		1	r = 0.391 p < 0.001	τ = 0.102 p = 0.001	**τ = 0.325** **p < 0.001**	**τ = 0.233** **p < 0.001**
M_Entropy			1	τ = −0.025 p = 0.413	τ = 0.247 p < 0.001	τ = 0.186 p < 0.001
Complex				1	τ = −0.030 p = 0.329	τ = −0.078 p = 0.011
Aesthetic					1	τ = 0.574 p < 0.001
Orderly						1

We'd like to note lack of significant correlation between *Complex* and *Aesthetic*, and the expected low negative correlation between *Complex* and *Orderly*. *Aesthetic* was highly correlated with *Orderly*, which suggests the prevalence of "classic" aesthetic dimension in the target users' perception. Also as expected, *M_Entropy* had significant positive correlations with *JPEG_size* and *PNG_size*. Its correlation with *Orderly* is remarkable though, since the frequency-based entropy(I) function does not consider the spatial allocation of the image elements. Of the three independent variables, *JPEG_size* had the strongest correlation with *Complex*, which is in line with the existing works on VC. So, this factor will be used as the baseline in our regression analysis.

3.3   Regression Analysis

The baseline regression model for *Complex* with the *JPEG_size* factor had rather low $R^2 = 0.05$, but was significant ($F_{1,491} = 25.65$, p < 0.001). The baseline models for *Aesthetic* ($R^2 = 0.103$, $F_{1,491} = 56.19$, p < 0.001) and *Orderly* ($R^2 = 0.034$, $F_{1,491} = 17.38$, p < 0.001) with the same factor were also significant:

$$Complex = 3.316 + 0.133 \times JPEG\_size. \tag{2}$$

$$Aesthetic = 3.609 + 0.254 \times JPEG\_size, \tag{3}$$

$$Orderly = 4.218 + 0.109 \times JPEG\_size. \tag{4}$$

In the extended regression models (Table 3), all the 3 factors were significant at $\alpha = 0.052$:

Table 3. Summary of the regression models with the three factors.

	JPEG_size	PNG_size	M_Entropy	Model
Complex (5)	$p < 0.001$ B = 0.847	$p < 0.001$ B = −0.625	$p = 0.052$ B = −0.092	$R^2 = 0.105$, $R^2_{adj} = 0.099$, $F_{3,489} = 19.1$, $p < 0.001$
Aesthetic (6)	$p < 0.001$ B = −0.471	$p < 0.001$ B = 0.748	$p < 0.001$ B = 0.253	$R^2 = 0.248$, $R^2_{adj} = 0.243$, $F_{3,489} = 53.65$, $p < 0.001$
Orderly (7)	$p = 0.024$ B = −0.318	$p = 0.002$ B = 0.448	$p < 0.001$ B = 0.245	$R^2 = 0.127$, $R^2_{adj} = 0.122$, $F_{3,489} = 23.75$, $p < 0.001$

$$Complex = 3.504 + 0.504 \times JPEG\_size - 0.316 \times PNG\_size \\ - 0.063 \times M\_Entropy \tag{5}$$

$$Aesthetic = 2.731 - 0.373 \times JPEG\_size + 0.503 \times PNG\_size \\ + 0.229 \times M\_Entropy \tag{6}$$

$$Orderly = 3.541 - 0.188 \times JPEG\_size + 0.225 \times PNG\_size \\ + 0.166 \times M\_Entropy \tag{7}$$

To evaluate the quality of the regression models that had different number of factors (k), we used Akaike Information Criterion (AIC). The AIC values for the considered models are presented in Table 4. The minimal AIC values (highlighted in bold) were found for the models with the three factors, which suggests that the "information loss" in them is lower and therefore they should be preferred over the other models.

Table 4. AIC values for the considered regression models.

Factors in the model	Complex	Aesthetic	Orderly
JPEG_size	(2) 2602	(3) 2855	(4) 2604
JPEG_size, PNG_size	2578	2803	2582
JPEG_size, PNG_size, M_Entropy	(5) **2576**	(6) **2772**	(7) **2558**

4   Discussion and Conclusions

In our work we studied if certain compression and entropy based metrics for web page screenshots can be used as predictors of users' impressions formed on purely visual basis. Particularly, we proposed the use of straightforward Shannon information entropy metric, which was found to be not correlated with image size (in pixels), unlike most other existing metrics. Unexpectedly, we also found that higher entropy actually decreased perceived complexity (5) and increased perceived orderliness (7). The former finding is consistent with one of our previous works, where we considered a smaller sample of different websites with different evaluators [3].

In the extended regression models, we were able to considerably improve the R^2 in comparison to the baseline models: *Complex* (+110%), *Aesthetic* (+141%), *Orderly* (+274%). The adjusted R^2s and the AIC values also suggest that the three-factor models should be preferred over the others. Notably, the effects of the *JPEG_size* and of the two other factors were always the opposite, so the two latter seem to be an important supplement of the baseline factor. The *M_Entropy* factor had the lowest contributions (Beta coefficients), but still was significant and improved the models.

Contrary to many existing works (e.g. [1]), we found no correlation between *Complex* and *Aesthetic*. At the same time, *Aesthetic* was highly correlated with *Orderly*, which may suggest the prevalence of the "classical" dimension in the aesthetic perception for the target user group with the university websites. We might assume that more refined dimensions of the overall aesthetic impression would have been correlated with complexity, as it was the case in [9].

Overall, the results of our study support the conclusion that the information entropy obtained via a purely image-processing method can be a feasible metric in analyzing WUIs. So, developers of automated analysis tools for web engineering could consider inclusion of the three metrics. The limitations of our work include relatively meager R^2s in the models, as well as low fidelity of scales that described users' subjective impressions. In our future work we plan integrating more metrics in our WUI Measurement Platform [3] and combining visual and code based analyses of web user interfaces.

Acknowledgment. This work was supported by Novosibirsk State Technical University, project No. TP-EI-1_17. We also thank Sebastian Heil from TU Chemnitz (Germany) and Vladimir Khvorostov from NSTU for aiding in the data collection.

References

1. Reinecke, K., et al.: Predicting users' first impressions of website aesthetics with a quantification of perceived visual complexity and colorfulness. In: Proceedings of the SIGCHI Conference on Human Factors in Computing Systems, pp. 2049–2058 (2013)
2. Tuch, A.N., et al.: The role of visual complexity and prototypicality regarding first impression of websites: working towards understanding aesthetic judgments. Int. J. Hum Comput Stud. **70**(11), 794–811 (2012)

3. Bakaev, M., Heil, S., Khvorostov, V., Gaedke, M.: Auto-extraction and integration of metrics for web user interfaces. J. Web Eng. **17**(6&7), 561–590 (2019)
4. Rosenholtz, R., Li, Y., Nakano, L.: Measuring visual clutter. J. Vis. **7**(2), 1–22 (2007)
5. Gonzalez, R.C., Woods, R.E., Eddins, S.L.: Digital Image Processing Using MATLAB. Pearson Education, Upper Saddle River (2004)
6. Chikhman, V., et al.: Complexity of images: experimental and computational estimates compared. Perception **41**(6), 631–647 (2012)
7. Marin, M.M., Leder, H.: Examining complexity across domains: relating subjective and objective measures of affective environmental scenes, paintings and music. PLoS ONE **8**(8), e72412 (2013)
8. Gartus, A., Leder, H.: Predicting perceived visual complexity of abstract patterns using computational measures. PLoS ONE **12**(11), e0185276 (2017)
9. Michailidou, E., Harper, S., Bechhofer, S.: Visual complexity and aesthetic perception of web pages. In: Proceedings of the 26th Annual ACM International Conference on Design of Communication, pp. 215–224 (2008)

Web Security and Privacy

Domain Classifier: Compromised Machines Versus Malicious Registrations

Sophie Le Page[1], Guy-Vincent Jourdan[1(✉)], Gregor V. Bochmann[1(✉)], Iosif-Viorel Onut[2(✉)], and Jason Flood[3(✉)]

[1] Faculty of Engineering, University of Ottawa, Ottawa, Canada
{slepage2,GuyVincent.Jourdan,Bochmann}@uottawa.ca
[2] IBM Centre for Advanced Studies, Ottawa, Canada
vioonut@ca.ibm.com
[3] IBM Security Data Matrices, Dublin, Ireland
floodjas@ie.ibm.com

Abstract. In "phishing attacks", phishing websites disguised as trustworthy websites attempt to steal sensitive information. Remediation and mitigation options differ depending on whether the phishing website is hosted on a legitimate but compromised domain, in which case the domain owner is also a victim, or whether the domain itself is maliciously registered. We accordingly attempt to tackle here the important question of classifying known phishing sites as either compromised or maliciously registered. Following the recent adoption of GDPR standards now putting off-limits any personal data, few relevant literature criteria still satisfy those standards. We propose here a machine-learning based domain classifier, introducing nine novel features which exploit the internet presence and history of a domain, using only publicly available information. Evaluation of our domain classifier was performed with a corpus of phishing websites hosted on over 1,000 compromised domains and 10,000 malicious domains. In the randomized evaluation, our domain classifier achieved over 92% accuracy with under 8% false positive rate, with compromised cases as the positive class. We have also collected over 180,000 phishing website instances over the past 3 years. Using our classifier we show that 73% of the websites hosting attacks are compromised while the remaining 27% belong to the attackers.

Keywords: Phishing attacks · Machine learning · Compromised domains · Malicious domains

1 Introduction

Phishing attacks have been relentless over the recent years, with over 280,000 unique attacks in the first quarter of 2016 [2], 144,000 in 2017 [1] and 260,000 in 2018 [3]. These worrying numbers occur despite an increasing awareness of the public, and widespread availability of tools used to combat these attacks. For example, browsers such as Google Chrome, FireFox, Opera and Safari all use

© Springer Nature Switzerland AG 2019
M. Bakaev et al. (Eds.): ICWE 2019, LNCS 11496, pp. 265–279, 2019.
https://doi.org/10.1007/978-3-030-19274-7_20

Google Safe Browsing[1] to provide their users some level of built-in protection against phishing attacks. Microsoft Internet Explorer and Edge browsers also include a similar built-in defense mechanism, called *SmartScreen*[2].

Most of the literature on phishing attacks focuses on detection, *e.g.* by using machine learning to train a detection model [12,22], by using the reputation of the domains hosting the attacks [13], by performing visual comparisons between the phishing site and its target [7,14], or by using similarity measures to known attacks [9]. In this work we attempt to better understand the large ecosystem that phishing is, and determine how often known phishing websites are hosted on legitimately owned (compromised) domains *vs* maliciously registered domains.

Classifying the type of domains that host phishing sites offers insight on how attackers commit their crimes and can present different remediation and mitigation options. For example, in the case of take down strategies, the owner of a compromised domain hosting the attack is also a victim and is presumably willing to cooperate with defenders. However, this is not true with a malicious domain. Take down strategies also differ based on who needs to be contacted, such as the sysadmin or the domain name registrar for compromised or malicious domains respectively [18]. Classifying phishing domains also offers further insight into which registrars effectively prevent fraudulent registrations. For example, a 2016 study by the Anti-Phishing Work Group (APWG) [5] found registrars such as GoDaddy had a ratio of malicious to compromised domains of 25%, whereas other registrars had a ratio well over 90%. Similarly, detecting an increase in compromised domains may offer insight into new indicators of compromise [6]. Lastly, classifying phishing domains can help advance research which specialize in studying either malicious or compromised phishing attacks. For example, for some such researchers, their feed source already distinguished between the two cases [13,17], whereas for other researchers manual inspection was required [7,16]. Therefore automatically classifying phishing domains in the latter case would help save time and remove human error.

In this work we propose our domain classifier, which exploits the history and internet presence of a domain with machine learning techniques to classify known phishing attacks as being hosted on either compromised domains or maliciously registered domains, using only publicly available information. This is especially relevant due to the recent adoption of General Data Protection Regulation (GDPR), which prevents certain registration information to be made publicly available. Note that our domain classifier can also be used to detect malicious domains from normal domains, where normal domains are those which are not hosting phishing attacks. However our classifier cannot be used to detect compromised domains from normal domains: the features we use to detect compromised domains are those that lend legitimacy to a domain such as domain history, which both compromised and normal domains share.

---

[1] https://safebrowsing.google.com/.
[2] https://support.microsoft.com/en-us/help/17443/windows-internet-explorer-smartscreen-filter-faq.

The remainder of this paper is organized as follows. Section 2 presents a literature review, followed by a description of our domain classifier architecture in Sect. 3. Section 4 describes our feature set and machine learning algorithms. The experiment setup is described in Sect. 5, and the full experimental results using randomized evaluation are reported in Sect. 6. In Sect. 7, we present our analysis of the proportion of phishing websites hosted on compromised and malicious domains over time. In Sect. 8 we discuss runtime performance and limitations of our proposed approach. We conclude in Sect. 9.

All resources for this work can be found at http://ssrg.site.uottawa.ca/icwe2019/.

2 Related Work

In this section, we discuss different types of hosting for phishing websites, as well as work related to identifying various types of hosting for phishing websites.

The types of hosting for phishing websites are identified by Moore *et al.* [18] as free web-hosting services, compromised machines, rock phish and fast-flux attacks. In [18] the authors analyze the different "notice and take-down" strategies for each case.

As an example, a typical URL for a website that has been set up at a free web-hosting provider would be http://www.brand.freehostsite.com/login, where the brand name is chosen to match or closely resemble the domain name of the brand being attacked. It is usually sufficient to compile a list of known free web-hosting domains, and then use this list to determine which websites are hosted on free space. In this case, to get the phishing website removed it is necessary to contact the webspace provider and draw their attention to the fraudulent site.

For compromised machines, attackers may have restricted permissions, and are limited on where files can be placed. They add their own web pages within an existing structure, leading to URLs for their websites that have the typical form http://www.example.com/user/www.brand.com/ where the brand name lends legitimacy. The attacker may also find that the existing DNS configuration permits URLs of the form www.brand.com.example.com. In this case, in order to get a website removed from a compromised machine it is generally necessary to get in touch with the sysadmin who looks after it.

To further hide suspicion, attackers sometimes go through the effort of registering their own domain name. The domain names are usually chosen to be a variation of brand.com such as "brand-usa.com", or they will use the brand name as a subdomain of a misleading domain such as "brand.verysecuresite.com". We refer to these domains as maliciously registered. If a domain name has been registered by an attacker, the defenders will ask the domain name registrar to suspend the offending domain.

In regards to rock phish and fast-flux attacks, these attacks require the attackers to purchase a number of cheap or free domains with meaningless names such as "vbe10.info", with unique identifiers in order to evade spam filters. We also consider these domains to be maliciously registered domains.

In this way we distinguish three types of hosting for phishing websites; free web-hosting domains, compromised domains, and malicious domains. Since free web-hosting identification simply requires a list of known hosting websites, we are left with the problem of classifying between compromised and malicious domains.

In 2009, Moore *et al.* [17] worked on so-called "evil searching" of servers running known vulnerable software to compromise them and upload phishing sites. The authors mentioned that 75.8% of their database is made of compromised servers with no explanation about how they reached this number. More recently, in 2017 Corona *et al.* [7] proposed a method to detect phishing sites by evaluating the visual differences between the phishing page and the other pages hosted on the same domain. The authors suggest that 71% of the domains hosting phishing sites are compromised. However the authors used manual checking and did not provide any reusable method.

In 2016, Catakoglu *et al.* [6] use honey pots to lure attackers to compromise their server, and propose an automated technique to extract and validate indicators of compromise (IOCs) for web applications. Our work is orthogonal to this method and does not require server access to find out whether a domain has been compromised if a phishing attack is launched. In 2016, Hao *et al.* [13] detected malicious domains upon registration, for the purpose of phishing as well as spamming. Their strategy also uses machine learning in combination with designed features derived primarily from information known by registrars or registries, as well as lexical patterns of the domain name. Our approach includes most of the lexical pattern features from [13]. However most of the information known by registrars and registries is not publicly available. In 2017, Lin *et al.* [16] detected domain shadowing, which are compromised domains whose subdomains are malicious. The authors find that instead of generating subdomain names, several domain shadowing cases exploit the wildcard DNS records.

The work most closely related to ours is the 2016 [5] study done by The Anti-Phishing Work Group (APWG) which reports phishing trends on malicious and compromised domains. For phishing attacks launched only in 2016, APWG report almost 49% are malicious domains, while the rest are compromised. Their strategy is to identify malicious domains by checking (1) short timeframe from domain registration to phishing report, (2) brand name or misleading string in the domain names and (3) batch domain names registration. In our approach we include check (2) and a variation of check (1) but do not have the means to check (3) since it is not publicly available. APWG's strategy focuses on properties that indicate malicious domain cases and otherwise simply considers that the domain is compromised. In contrast, our solution balances criteria suggesting malicious domains and criteria suggesting compromised ones. In addition our solution only relies upon publicly available information, and is thus widely usable.

3   System Architecture

Figure 1 shows the overall flow of our domain classifier. The feature extractor, shared by the training and testing phases, is the core of our system, in which the values of the 15 features described below in Sect. 4.1 are automatically extracted.

Specifically, the goal of the training phase is to obtain the feature values for each instance of the training domains. Those features are then used by the machine learning engine to build classifiers. The goal of the testing phase is to label real phishing websites as either a compromised or a malicious domain.

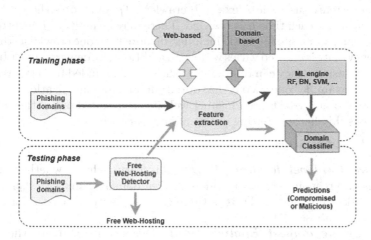

Fig. 1. System architecture of our domain classifier. Types of hosting for phishing websites include; free web-hosting providers, compromised machines, and maliciously registered domains.

In the testing phase, we first apply a free web-hosting detector using a list of known hosting websites. If the phishing website is not detected to be hosted on a free web-hosting site, we move on to extract the 15 features from the domain using domain-based features as well as other publicly available web resources. Finally we apply a pre-trained model to classify a phishing domain as compromised or malicious. In real-world scenarios, we can use a sliding window to include the most recent labeled phishing domains in the training data.

4   Feature-Based Machine Learning Framework

The present paper hinges on the set of high-level features detailed below in Sect. 4.1. Features 1 and 6 are inspired by work from APWG [5]. Features 2–5 are taken from [13]. Features 7–15 are the novel ones we propose here. Section 4.2 lists the machine learning algorithms we use.

4.1   Feature Set

Features are organized into two categories. The first category (features 1 through 6) deals with the domain name of the phishing website. We deal with domain names rather than full URLs because we want our system to be usable widely and early, at domain registration time or by looking at the DNS traffic. The second category (features 7 through 15) exploits the history and internet presence of a domain and involves crawling the web for public information.

In particular, we make use of The Wayback Machine, a digital archive of the Internet Archive[3] which allows retrieving the crawl history of a URL. Specifically, the Internet Archive uses the Alexa web crawler [11], and stores the HTML of a URL as a snapshot each time it is crawled. There may be multiple crawls ongoing at any one time, and a site might be included in more than one crawl list, therefore the frequency a site is crawled varies widely. In addition, site owners who fit Internet Archive's exclusion policy can request that the site be excluded from the Wayback Machine. For example "quora.com" has opted out due to anonymization issues [20]. However we did not detect any phishing websites that opted out of the Wayback Machine, possibly because opting out would appear suspicious.

Domain-Based Features

1. *Freenom top level domain (TLD)*: This feature checks whether the TLD belongs to Freenom[4]. Freenom provides free domain names on ".cf", ".gq", ".ml", ".tk" and ".ga" TLD. It is therefore not a surprise that a lot of these domains are abused [5].
2. *Ratio of the longest English word*: This feature matches the longest English word that a domain name contains, and normalizes it by dividing by the length of the domain name. Attackers may generate pseudo-random names to avoid conflict with existing domains, or deliberately include readable words in the domain names to attract clicks from victims.
3. *Containing digits*: This feature checks whether the domain name contains digits. Hao *et al.* [13] observe that spam and malicious phishing domains are more likely to use numerical characters than legitimate domains. Possible reasons may be that attackers add digits to generate several names from the same word or generate random names from a character set containing digits.
4. *Containing "-"*: This feature checks whether the domain name contains any hyphens. Similarly, attackers can insert hyphens to break individual words or concatenate multiple words.
5. *Name length*: This feature checks the domain name length (number of characters). Attackers may create domains using a specific template, such as random strings of a given length.
6. *Partial match of brand name*: This feature matches the largest partial match of a brand name contained in a domain. We use a curated list of the top 50 brand names from Alexa[5]. Given a brand name, we find the most similar substring in a domain name, and divide the number of similar characters by the length of the brand name. The ratio ranges from 0 to 1, where 0 indicates no match to any brand name and 1 indicates an exact match. Attackers may create domains which include the brand name or a variation to lend legitimacy and trick victims.

---

[3] http://archive.org/.
[4] https://www.freenom.com/.
[5] http://www.alexa.com/.

Web-Based Features

7. **Archived domain**: This feature checks whether the domain has been archived on The Wayback Machine, which is part of The Internet Archive. An archived domain is more likely to be legitimately owned.

8. **Timespan in years the domain has been archived**: This feature checks the time in years the domain has been archived. The longer a domain has been archived, the more likely the domain is legitimately owned.

9. **Timespan in years of the domain's last archive before 2019**: This feature checks the time in years of the domain's last archive relative to 2019. For example if the domain's last archive was in 2017, then it has been 2 years since the last archive. A recently archived domain is more likely to be legitimately owned.

10. **Number of domain archive captures**: This feature checks the number of archive captures for a domain. A frequently captured domain is an indication of legitimate ownership.

11. **Archive redirected**: This feature checks whether the latest archive capture redirects to a different domain. This implies that the archive information is no longer relevant to the original domain. This constitutes a suspicious flag adding to other features.

12. **Reachable domain**: This feature checks whether the domain returns a status code 200. Phishing sites usually last a short time: most pages do not last more than a few days because they are taken down by attackers to avoid tracking [4]. For this reason, legitimately owned domains are more likely to be reachable.

13. **Blocked domain**: This feature checks whether access to the domain returns a status code 404, or whether the title or content of the page contains keywords such as "404", "down" or "under maintenance". Legitimately owned domains are less likely to be blocked. This follows a similar reasoning to the feature above.

14. **Alexa rank**: This feature checks whether the domain appears in Alexa top 1 million, and if so records the rank. Domains in the Alexa ranking are more likely to be legitimately owned domains.

15. **Wildcard subdomain**: This feature checks whether the domain is registered to accept all subdomains, known as a "wildcard" subdomain. A wildcard DNS record will match any request for an undefined domain name, making it easy for attackers to advertise a working URL with a subdomain of their choosing despite not controlling the DNS entries of the domain itself. This may influence determination of whether a domain is compromised or malicious.

4.2   Machine Learning Algorithms

We compare five learning algorithms in training the domain classifier with the primary goal of evaluating the effectiveness of our feature set: K Neighbors (KN), Support Vector Machines (SVM), Neural Networks (NN), Random Forest (RF), and Bayesian Network (BN). All the machine learning algorithm implementations were taken from the *sklearn* package[6]. RF turned out to be the top performing algorithm in our experiments. We accordingly report here only on the performance of RF in this paper.

5 Experimental Setup

5.1 Evaluation Metrics

In our experiment, we use true positive (TP) rate, false positive (FP) rate and accuracy (Acc.) as the main evaluation metrics. In tuning the machine learning models, we used Receiver Operating Characteristics (ROC) curves [10] as well as the area under the ROC curve (AUC) [8] metric. This is an approach to evaluate binary classification performance and portray the trade-off between TP and FP. Statistically, the AUC equals the probability that given a randomly generated positive instance and negative instance, a classifier will rank the positive one higher than the negative one, and thus is a good summary statistic for model comparison.

5.2 Phishing Domain Corpus

Our phishing domain collection is summarized in Table 1 and consists of malicious cases from PhishLabs [19], and compromised cases from both PhishLabs and DeltaPhish [7].

Table 1. Compromised and malicious phishing domain collection from 2 sources.

	PhishLabs	DeltaPhish
# compromised domains (timespan)	675 (Sep 2018 to Oct 2018)	694 (Oct 2015 to Jan 2016)
# malicious domains (timespan)	9,475 (May 2018 to Oct 2018)	–

For the domain instances from PhishLabs, we received a list of 9,475 malicious domains collected from May 2018 to October 2018. The analysts reviewing phishing attacks at PhishLabs manually classify the domain as malicious if they believe it was created by the attackers for the purpose of phishing. Since this list was manually checked by the analysts at PhishLabs, we consider this list to be accurate.

We also received a list of 17,427 confirmed phishing URLs from PhishLabs, collected from September 2018 to October 2018. As instructed by PhishLabs,

---

[6] https://scikit-learn.org/.

intersecting the list of malicious domains and phishing URLs on "domain" gives the phishing URLs using malicious domains. The remaining phishing URLs are *most likely* those using compromised domains. Specifically, the 17,427 phishing URLs consist of 695 unique domains, 20 of which were in the list of malicious domains, resulting in a list of 675 likely compromised domains. However this list is less accurate, since the compromised domains were not manually inspected by the analysts at PhishLabs.

Indeed, quick examination of the list of 675 likely compromised domains exposed a number of clearly malicious domains: "my-apple-id.cf", "doocs.gq", "my-sharepointofficedrive.tk", "outlook-livesl.cf". There are two reasons why these domains are malicious: (1) The TLDs belong to Freenom, a registry that provides free domains, so a lot of these domains are abused; (2) The domain name contains suspicious keywords such as "apple", "docs", "officedrive", and "outlook" mimicking legitimate brand names.

Since the list of compromised domains from PhishLabs contain some noise, we looked for other open source lists of compromised domains, and found a list shared by the authors of DeltaPhish [7]. The authors manually checked the list of 1,012 phishing websites hosted on 694 compromised domains that were retrieved from PhishTank from October 2015 to January 2016. Since this list was manually checked by the authors and used in their research, we consider this list to be accurate.

5.3   Evaluation Method

We use randomized evaluation to inspect the overall performance on all the available data. We also adopted the train, validation and test methodology from machine learning.

For the train/test splits, we used the following strategy. For our train set we used the compromised domains from PhishLabs collected from September 2018 to October 2018, and a random selection of an equivalent number of malicious domains in the same timespan, ensuring a balanced train set, mainly due to two reasons. First, a balanced train set is more realistic since in the real-world scenario, the volumes of malicious and compromised cases are similar. For example in 2016, APWG reports that almost 49% of domains are malicious, while the rest are compromised [5]. Second, machine learning classifiers such as Random Forest have difficulty coping with imbalanced train sets as they are sensitive to the proportions of the different classes. As a consequence, these algorithms tend to favor the majority class, creating misleading accuracy.

For our test set, we used the compromised domains from DeltaPhish collected from October 2015 to January 2016, and the remainder of the malicious domains from PhishLabs collected from May 2018 to October 2018.

We train on the compromised domains from PhishLabs because we knew that these domains contained noisy labels, as discussed in Sect. 5.2. This way we take advantage of the noise in the data in order to limit model over-fitting, ensuring better model generalization [15]. Conversely, we test on the compromised domains from DeltaPhish [7] because they were manually checked by the authors and are therefore likely to be a better indication of the accuracy of our classifier. Note that since the compromised domains come from two different sources, they also have different distributions. This also allows evaluation of classifier robustness towards a distribution of data it has not trained on, anticipating real world applications when the classifier will be deployed.

In optimizing the algorithm parameters, the training set was further divided *via* stratified sampling into a training portion and a validation portion. Stratification ensures that the class distribution is preserved between the training and validation parts. In performing the final tests with the optimal model parameters, the whole training sets were used to train the classifiers. We used the average statistics over 5 runs in all our experiments in order to reduce random variation and avoid lucky train/validation splits.

6   Experimental Results

6.1   Randomized Evaluation

The main goal of randomized evaluation is to inspect the overall performance of our domain classifier on all our data via stratification and multiple run averaging. In this section, we show the performance of our classifier trained under a balanced data set, using different machine learning algorithms.

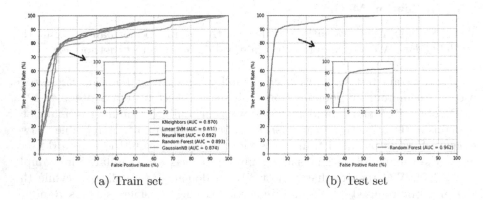

(a) Train set   (b) Test set

Fig. 2. Left: ROC curve (5-run average) and AUC of our domain classifier using five machine learning algorithms. The domain classifier was trained with a balanced data set, with compromised domains as the positive class. **Right**: ROC curve of our trained RF model on the test set.

For each machine learning algorithm, we found the optimal parameter with the best AUC via 5-run tuning. We show our final tuning results in a ROC curve in Fig. 2(a). We found through our experiments that Random Forest (RF) was the top performing algorithm. In the testing phase of randomized evaluation, we assigned RF (the top performing model) with the optimal parameters, and tested the model on a separate testing set. This way we reproduce a real deployment, where one could tune models offline and then employ the optimal setup for online scenarios. We also show the ROC curve on the test set in Fig. 2(b).

In Table 2, we show the performance of our domain classifier in this experiment. Since noisy compromised cases from PhishLabs were used in the train set and manually verified compromised cases from DeltaPhish in the test set (as discussed in Sect. 5.3), our model generalizes well to unseen data. As a result the test set performs better than the train set. As shown in Table 2, our domain classifier achieved a high TP of 91.29% with a reasonably low FP of 7.86%.

Table 2. Performance (5-run average) of our domain classifier using Random Forest (RF) network. The domain classifier was trained with a balanced data set, with compromised domains as the positive class.

	TP (%)	FP (%)	Acc. (%)
Train	78.74	10.44	84.27
Test	91.29	7.86	92.07

6.2 Learning with Individual and Grouped Features

The statistics in the previous sections were obtained by using the whole feature set (15 features in total). In this section, we evaluate the contribution of each individual feature, as well as grouped features, to the overall performance. We use the summary statistic AUC to measure the performance of each individual feature. We only report the result with Random Forest under a balanced train set in Fig. 3. Figure 3(a) shows that the archive features, which are novel features we proposed, stand out from the others with over 0.8 AUC, including *Archived*, *Years active*, *Years inactive*, *Number of captures* and *Archive redirected*. Features *Reachable* and *Blocked* also perform fairly well with over 0.75 AUC. The remaining features are ranked as inferior, with under 0.7 AUC. All features are over 0.5 AUC, although some are close to 0.5 AUC, almost amounting to random guessing. As an example, if we look at our *Alexa rank* feature, only a few domains in our data set have an *Alexa rank* in the top 1 million. This leaves the majority of domains with no rank, giving the classifier little information to distinguish between compromised and malicious domains given only *Alexa rank* as a feature. The usefulness of these lower ranked features however comes when combined with related higher ranked features, yielding better performance.

This can be seen in Fig. 3(b), where we compare top ranked features *Archived*, *Reachable* and *Contain hyphen* against related features grouped together to show better performance than individually. In this case *All reachable* refers to all web-based features which do not use the Internet Archive. In particular we find grouped *Domain-based* features improves the AUC from 0.66 to 0.75 compared to *Contain hyphen*. We can also compare grouped rankings, where *All*

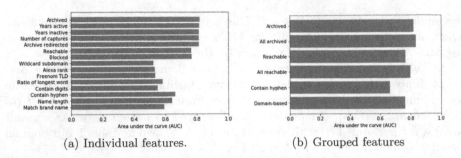

(a) Individual features.   (b) Grouped features

Fig. 3. Area under the ROC curve (AUC) of RF with individual features (**Left**) and grouped features (**Right**) under a balanced train set. Top-performing features include the archive features, as well as reachable and blocked features.

archive features perform best, followed by *All reachable*, and then by *Domain-based* features. Although the grouped *Domain-based* features rank lowest, the performance is still impressive considering the computations only involve string analysis of the domain name.

7 Analysis

In this section, using our domain classifier we present our analysis of the proportion of phishing websites hosted on compromised *vs* malicious domains over time. Specifically, we collected over 180,000 phishing website instances hosted on over 69,000 domains over the past 3 years. Our sources include PhishTank, IBM X-Force, and OpenPhish. Our analysis is shown for every quarter in Fig. 4. Note that our results from the first two quarters in 2016 may not be representative since the volume of phishing websites is much lower, due to the fact that our initial feed consisted of just PhishTank.

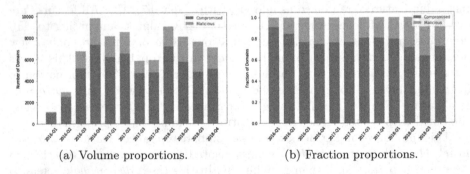

(a) Volume proportions.   (b) Fraction proportions.

Fig. 4. Classification results of unique phishing domains hosted on either compromised or malicious domains. The proportions are shown for every quarter in volume and ratio over a three year timespan from 2016 to 2018.

Over a 3 year period we find that 73% of the websites hosting attacks are compromised while the remaining 27% belong to the attackers. This ratio of compromised *vs* malicious is reasonably aligned with other findings [5,7,17]. In particular, with regards to APWG [5], our findings agree with registries such as GoDaddy that have only 25% malicious registrations. This may indicate that more registries are following GoDaddy and are actively defending against malicious registration.

However, overall APWG finds that 49% of domains are malicious. There may be a few reasons that explain this difference: first we classify hosting sites as compromised or malicious while AWPG detects domains as malicious and assumes the rest are compromised. Second, we believe that the criteria used in [5] may be too aggressive and will for example classify any site that is hacked almost immediately upon creation as malicious. Finally, APWG report that more than half of the servers flagged as malicious in their database are related to Chinese phishing attacks. In contrast, our data sources for phishing attacks are mostly made of North-American and European phishing attack reports.

That being said, we do see an increase in malicious registration in the year of 2018, in particular the 3rd quarter of 2018, as shown in Fig. 4, where the maximum malicious ratio reaches almost 40%. One reason the three latest quarters in 2018 have more malicious domains may be because we are performing this experiment "after the fact". For example a domain which may have been malicious in 2016 may now be registered as a legitimate domain. Overall we find that the proportion of compromised domains has remained relatively consistent over 2016 and 2017, with a 5% decrease of compromised domains in 2018.

8 Discussion

8.1 Runtime Performance

Our framework is composed of a training phase and a testing phase (Fig. 1). The training phase can be done periodically offline. Users then experience no time delay in this stage. When deployed, the testing phase is conducted online as each phishing domain arrives.

All our experiments were conducted on a standard computer with a 2.10 GHz processor and 14.7 GB of available RAM. The free web-hosting detector caused no apparent delay in the work flow. The module with critical time issue is the feature extractor. For example fetching archive features take the longest time since we use a crawler and wait 10 s for the page to load. The average run time of the feature extractor module is 25 s per domain. Various measures exist for improving the time performance of the feature extraction module. For example we used 5 threads in the experiments in order to process 5 domains in parallel. This way we process 5 domains on average after 25 s (or 1 every 5 s). Another essential strategy we use is caching. For example caching the query and result web-based features improves runtime performance. Once the feature values have been extracted, applying the pre-trained machine learning model consumes a trivial amount of time.

8.2   Limitations

One limitation to our approach is that The Internet Archive is unintentionally internationally biased [21] towards North-American websites. For example, our approach may not work as well for Chinese phishing websites, since archive is less likely to have captured Chinese websites.

One way around this limitation would be to include search engines results as an indicator of domain presence and reputation. For example, in the Google search engine, one can search for "inurl:example.com" which returns indexed URLs with the string "example.com". To address international bias, one could then use several international search engines. However this solution may not be scalable since search engines usually place a limit on the number of requests.

Another limitation to our approach would be if attackers intentionally register a domain with history. For example, an owner may have a domain for several years until dropping the domain, at which point an attacker may be ready to pick it up. However this also limits the attacker, since domains with history may be more expensive, and may take more time to identify and acquire. This also prevents attackers from choosing a domain name that is misleading, or from choosing a domain name resembling a brand name to lend legitimacy.

A previous way around this limitation would be to check registration history to see whether the domain has recently changed owners. However this approach has become increasingly difficult to automate, and the information may not be publicly available. Another option around this limitation would be to use the captures in archive and compare the HTML of a domain over time, to see whether there are any recent and sudden changes in the HTML. HTML that has suddenly changed and is not relevant to the previous content implies that the domain has probably passed on to a new owner.

9   Conclusion

In this paper, we presented a solution for classifying the domains of known phishing websites as either hosted on legitimately owned (compromised) domains or on maliciously registered domains. By exploiting the generalization power of machine learning techniques, our domain classifier achieves acceptable levels of TP and FP using a classification engine with a set of features of our design, which is the main originality of the present work. In particular, we achieved these acceptable levels based on the remark that the majority of compromised domains have more internet history and presence than malicious domains.

All resources for this work can be found at http://ssrg.site.uottawa.ca/icwe2019/.

References

1. APWG: Phishing Activity Trends Report 1st Half 2017. bit.ly/2KKTUzw
2. APWG: Phishing Activity Trends Report 1st Quarter in 2016. bit.ly/1qNLrk5

3. APWG: Phishing Activity Trends Report 1st Quarter in 2018. bit.ly/2HfK0Ik
4. APWG: Phishing Activity Trends Report 3rd Quarter in 2018. bit.ly/2VTVYuh
5. APWG: Trends and Domain Name Use in 2016. bit.ly/2TvHyE6
6. Catakoglu, O., Balduzzi, M., Balzarotti, D.: Automatic extraction of indicators of compromise for web applications. In: Proceedings of the 25th International Conference on World Wide Web, pp. 333–343. International World Wide Web Conferences Steering Committee (2016)
7. Corona, I., et al.: DeltaPhish: detecting phishing webpages in compromised websites. In: Foley, S.N., Gollmann, D., Snekkenes, E. (eds.) ESORICS 2017. LNCS, vol. 10492, pp. 370–388. Springer, Cham (2017). https://doi.org/10.1007/978-3-319-66402-6_22
8. Cortes, C., Mohri, M.: AUC optimization vs. error rate minimization. In: Advances in Neural Information Processing Systems, pp. 313–320 (2004)
9. Cui, Q., Jourdan, G.V., Bochmann, G.V., Couturier, R., Onut, I.V.: Tracking phishing attacks over time. In: Proceedings of the 26th International Conference on World Wide Web. pp. 667–676. International World Wide Web Conferences Steering Committee (2017)
10. Fawcett, T.: An introduction to ROC analysis. Pattern Recogn. Lett. **27**(8), 861–874 (2006)
11. Forbes: The Internet Archive Behind the Scenes (2016). bit.ly/2CjomPa
12. Gowtham, R., Krishnamurthi, I.: A comprehensive and efficacious architecture for detecting phishing webpages. Comput. Secur. **40**, 23–37 (2014)
13. Hao, S., Kantchelian, A., Miller, B., Paxson, V., Feamster, N.: Predator: proactive recognition and elimination of domain abuse at time-of-registration. In: Proceedings of the 2016 ACM SIGSAC Conference on Computer and Communications Security, pp. 1568–1579. ACM (2016)
14. Jain, A.K., Gupta, B.B.: Phishing detection: analysis of visual similarity based approaches. Secur. Commun. Netw. **2017**, 20 (2017)
15. Krogh, A., Hertz, J.A.: Generalization in a linear perceptron in the presence of noise. J. Phys. A: Math. Gen. **25**(5), 1135 (1992)
16. Liu, D., Li, Z., Du, K., Wang, H., Liu, B., Duan, H.: Don't let one rotten apple spoil the whole barrel: towards automated detection of shadowed domains. In: Proceedings of the 2017 ACM SIGSAC Conference on Computer and Communications Security, pp. 537–552. ACM (2017)
17. Moore, T., Clayton, R.: Evil searching: compromise and recompromise of internet hosts for phishing. In: Dingledine, R., Golle, P. (eds.) FC 2009. LNCS, vol. 5628, pp. 256–272. Springer, Heidelberg (2009). https://doi.org/10.1007/978-3-642-03549-4_16
18. Moore, T., Clayton, R.: The impact of incentives on notice and take-down. In: Johnson, M.E., et al. (eds.) Managing Information Risk and the Economics of Security, pp. 199–223. Springer, Boston (2009). https://doi.org/10.1007/978-0-387-09762-6_10
19. PhishLabs: Threat intelligence & mitigation solutions (2019). https://www.phishlabs.com/
20. Quora: Why Does Quora Block the Wayback Machine from Accessing It (2016). bit.ly/2XSbeKa
21. Thelwall, M., Vaughan, L.: A fair history of the web? Examining country balance in the internet archive. Libr. Inf. Sci. Res. **26**(2), 162–176 (2004)
22. Xiang, G., Hong, J., Rose, C.P., Cranor, L.: Cantina+: a feature-rich machine learning framework for detecting phishing web sites. ACM Trans. Inf. Syst. Secur. **14**(2), 21:1–21:28 (2011)

The "Game Hack" Scam

Emad Badawi[1]([⊠]), Guy-Vincent Jourdan[1], Gregor Bochmann[1],
Iosif-Viorel Onut[2], and Jason Flood[3]

[1] Faculty of Engineering, University of Ottawa, Ottawa, Canada
{ebadawi,GuyVincent.Jourdan,Bochmann}@uottawa.ca
[2] IBM Centre for Advanced Studies, Ottawa, Canada
vioonut@ca.ibm.com
[3] IBM Security Data Matrices, Dublin, Ireland
floodjas@ie.ibm.com

Abstract. Game Hack Scam (GHS) is a cyberattack in which the attacker attempts to convince the victim, often a child or a young adult, that they will be provided with free, unlimited resources or other advantages for their favorite game. To obtain these claimed advantages, the victims are asked to complete one or more tasks, called "offers". These so-called offers include, but are not limited to, subscriptions to questionable services and installation of executable files on the victim's device. Although recent research has provided important insights into different types of scam such as "Technical Support Scam", "Survey Scam", and "Romance Scam", to the best of our knowledge GHS has not been studied up to now.

In this paper, we report the first systematic study of GHS. We use a data-driven approach to investigate and gain knowledge on this type of scam: we formulated GHS-related search queries, and used multiple search engines to collect data about the websites to which GHS victims are directed when they search online for various game hacks and tricks. We analyze the collected data to provide new insight into GHS, and research the extent of this scam. We show that GHS attackers abuse social media, streaming sites, blogs, and even unrelated sites such as *change.org* or *researchgate.net* to carry out their attacks and reach a large number of victims. We estimate that these attacks have been clicked close to 60 million times since mid-2014. Our data collection spans over nine months; over the last five months, we uncovered over 3,000 GHS domains and over 100 different offer domains. Furthermore, we find that GHS instances are on the rise and so is the number of victims. Finally, in keeping with similar large-scale scam studies, we find that the current public blacklists are inadequate and suggest that our method is more effective at detecting these attacks.

Keywords: Game scam · Scam analysis · Fraud detection · Cyberattack

© Springer Nature Switzerland AG 2019
M. Bakaev et al. (Eds.): ICWE 2019, LNCS 11496, pp. 280–295, 2019.
https://doi.org/10.1007/978-3-030-19274-7_21

1   Introduction

The gaming industry is one of the biggest profitable industries in the world. Its total market value is worth 115.3 billion worldwide. This value is expected to increase and reach 131.3 billion in 2020 [28], and the number of game players is expected to increase from 2.341 billion in 2018 to be 2.725 billion by 2021 [25].

Game developers depend mostly on the purchase of in-game resources as well as in-game adds to make a profit [9,10]. To obtain these resources, some players are willing to bypass the normal route and use "cracks", game-modifying software (e.g. cheat-engines [22]), or any other means of hacking. The popularity of these games provides an opportunity for hackers to release their attacks and reach out to more victims. The most common victims for such attacks are young adults and under-aged players who do not understand the risk of publishing their personal information, their parents' credit card information and installing executable files on their devices.

In this paper, we give insight on an understudied social engineering attack targeting everyday web users, especially games players. We call this attack the Game-Hack Scam (GHS). In a nutshell, in GHS the attackers claim that they can hack a specific game and provide the victim with free, unlimited resources or other advantages for their favorite game. To obtain these claimed advantages, the victims are asked to complete one or more tasks, called "offers". These so-called offers include, but are not limited to, subscriptions to questionable services and installation of executable files on the victim's device. Figure 1 illustrates GHS and how a user is exposed to malicious advertisements or malware. Usually, the scam starts when a victim searches for cheats and hacks for their game using search engines, social media, streaming sites, blogs, or any other site. The returned search results may directly contain GHS instances (GHSi) such as https://cpbldi.com/c26a2bb in Fig. 1. In other cases, the search results link to pages that have links to GHSis. For example, the article published in *change.org*[1] shown in Fig. 1 contain such links. These GHSis are carefully designed web pages which attempt to convey to the victim the advanced technical abilities of the scammer and a large, satisfied user base for the GHSi. The GHSis tend to use a variety of similar templates that are used to create the attack instances. Some of these templates simply ask for the victim's identifier on the game and the resources that should be provided. Other templates attempt to be more convincing by asking for additional information such as the game platform, the hacking server, and the ability to use a proxy. In addition, these complex templates could display a fake chat box and a pop-up showing claimed current users and the number of resources they supposedly gained. Once the information is provided, the GHSi pretends to perform some hacking process, as seen in Fig. 1 image 2.2. Thereafter, a pop-up appears claiming that the hack was successful and the victim then invited to a "verification" step. During this verification process, some screen is shown to the user, asking to complete one or more tasks, called "offers". This type of screens is called a "content-locker" (CL) by the

---

[1] Accessible at https://bit.ly/2F4IE2I at the time of writing.

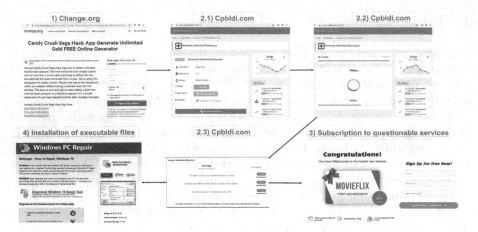

Fig. 1. An example of GHS attack

creator of these scams. The "CL" is what the scammer ultimately wants the victim to see, as they lead to the payload. An example is shown Fig. 1 image 2.3. These offers include, but are not limited to, subscriptions to questionable services (such as image 3) in Fig. 1 and installation of executable files on the victim's device (such as image 4) in Fig. 1.

Another type of GHS targeting specifically android phones and tablets does not use GHSis. Instead, the victim is asked to install new software, claimed to be either a modified version of the original game or some sort of game modifying software ("cheat-engines"). These software contain various malware which are flagged by some of the anti-viruses used by virus total online scan, and other anti-viruses did not catch them. In this study, we focus on the GHSi side of GHS and leave the malware distribution side out of the scope.

In this paper, we perform the first study of GS. We have developed a model for generating thousands of GS-related search queries. We have used these queries daily on popular search engines for five months. We look for GHSis in the pages directly returned by the search engines, and we crawl the other pages down one level to find additional GHSis. By this method, we have discovered thousands of domains associated with GS. Our main contributions are the following:

- We designed the first search-engine-based system for discovering GS, and utilize it for five months to uncover more than 3,000 GS-related domains.
- We show that scammers use systematic techniques and pre-built templates in their attacks. This helps them build many GHSis and target many games with little effort.
- We show that the existing public blacklists (PBLs) are ineffective against this type of scam.
- By analyzing the GHS URLs that use Bitly shortening services, we estimate that these attacks have been clicked close to 60 million times since mid-2014. We show that GHS attack has been on a sharp rise throughout 2018.

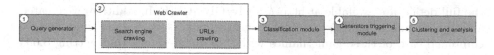

Fig. 2. Games scam detection and analysis model

All the data used in our study is available at http://bit.ly/GHSICWE.

2   Methodology

We started our research by manually searching for and exploring games scam pages. This helped us getting an initial broad understanding of the scam and provided our initial data samples, which we used to build a data-driven model similar to the one used in [33]. That allowed us to run automatic crawls on the web to find GHS pages which we then analyzed. Figure 2 describes our system. It includes five modules:

1. *Search query generator module.* This module generates keywords that are likely to be used in GHS pages.
2. *Web Crawler module.* This module uses the previous queries to search for GHS pages using popular search engines. We crawl the resulting pages and recursively crawl once all the links that they contain.
3. *Classification module.* This module categorizes the crawled pages as either "GHSi" or "clean" pages based on their text.
4. *GHSis triggering module.* This module interacts with the GHSis and provides the requested information to reach the "offers" pages.
5. *Clustering and analysis.* We conducted an analysis of the collected data to identify similarities and cluster related attacks.

2.1   Search Query Generator

Choosing good search queries that have a high likelihood to lead to the scam pages is an important task. Kharraz *et al.* [11] used Google Trends service to generate such queries. Srinivasan *et al.* [33] used a probabilistic analysis. In our work, we started from our initial corpus of pages leading to GHSis as well as the GHSi pages themselves. We extracted the bag of words from our corpus. We found 1,964 words that have a frequency greater than ten. We selected manually 39 of these words based on their direct connection to GHS and added the stop words "without" and "no". We then generated our queries using the Markov assumption to approximate n-gram probabilities [8]. We generated our n-grams for $n = 3$ to 7^2. That gave us 795 n-grams, and we manually selected 410 search queries from them. Table 1 shows some examples of the generated n-grams, and

---

^{2} Our experiments showed that 8-grams and up did not improve our results.

the full details are available at http://bit.ly/GHSICWE. In addition, we created a list of 966 game names by searching on Facebook, Google, and iTunes and we combined each of these game names with 9 of our n-grams, thus getting 8,694 new queries, for a total of 9,104 queries.

2.2   Web Crawler

Our search crawler uses the previously identified search queries as a seed to search daily for GHS pages using *Google.com*, *Bing.com*, *search.yahoo.com*, and *search.1and1.com*. For each query, we only consider the first page (that is, 10 search results) returned by each engine. The crawler is based on ChromeDriver [23] and Python Selenium [27]. Using Python beautifulsoup [21] and the CSS selectors, we extract and crawl the URLs resulting from our searches. For the crawling process, we use a lightweight scripted headless browser built using python by integrating Selenium [27], PhantonJS [26] and Beautiful-Soup [21]. We collect data about the crawled URLs including URL redirections, HTML contents, a screen-shot of the landing page and its resources (scripts, CSS files etc.).

2.3   Classification Module

The majority of the pages that our crawler collects are not directly GHSis. Instead, they are often either pages hosted on benign sites with URL links that lead to a GHSi (such as the page hosted on *change.org* in Fig. 1), or completely benign pages related to games, usually with forms that make them similar to some GHSis (such as https://server.pro/). Therefore, we need a classifier to automatically identify actual GHSis in our results.

Pages Classifier: Our classifier is trained on the text of the GHSi and non-GHSi pages. We use the "ScikitLearn" python library [2] LinearSVC classifier for our data. Our training set consists of 470 benign pages and 495 GHSi pages fetched at the beginning of our experiment. We manually annotated all of our data. The 10-cross validation results showed that our classifier achieved 96.7% TPR and a 2.1% FPR. To verify our classifier accuracy, We manually checked 200 pages chosen at random, 100 from the ones classified as GHSis and 100 from the ones that were not. We found that 2 GHSi pages were misclassified clean (2% FN) while only 1 clean page was misclassified GHSi (1% FP), which is coherent with our rates.

2.4   Interacting with GHSis

To collect information about the GHSis, we need to interact with them, provide the necessary inputs and follow each GHSis instructions in order to reach the final stage, at which point the list of "offers" is provided. Following these offers, the victim is asked to provide personal information, subscribe to fraudulent services or install malware. At this stage, we collect for analysis the set of offers that are provided by the GHSis we have found. At this stage, we did interact with these pages manually to extract the CLs URLs, this is planned to be automated in our future research.

Table 1. Summary and examples of generated n-grams related to GS.

n	#n-grams	Example English Phrase
3	233	generate unlimited coin
4	109	hack tool no survey
5	44	hack cheats unlimited free coin
6	18	hack cheats unlimited coins ios android
7	6	hack cheats unlimited free coins diamonds generator

Fig. 3. Breakdown of the number of GHSis per ID.

2.5 Clustering and Analysis

We then conduct four different analyses of the different pages and domains that our model identified as a scam. Our first analysis is done on the GHSis themselves. We use the identifiers found in the pages to detect similarities and infer common ownership of the GHSis. Our second analysis is done on the "offers", the final step in the scam life-cycle. We classify the different types of offers and show the convergences between seemingly unrelated GHSis and the much smaller set of offers. Our third analysis is done on the domain names hosting the GHSis and the offers. We also study the effectiveness of the current PBLs against GS. Our fourth and last analysis is done on these GHSis that use the URL shortener Bitly. Bitly provides publicly available statistics for its shorten URLs, which in turns gives us a unique insight into the effectiveness and the trends of the scam.

Our analyses are presented in Sects. 3 and 4.

3 Results and Analysis

We used our university's servers to deploy the aforementioned model to collect the possible GHS pages. The results reported in this paper come from data collected over a five-month period from May to September 2018.

In this section, we discuss the results obtained from the analysis of the data collected. We first present the results of our classification and the basic numbers we obtained. We then shed some light over the GHSis, their similarities, and the games they targets. We also show that scammer relies on pre-built templates which makes it very easy to create new attacks without any technical knowledge. After that, we present a study about the offers reached when interacting with the GHSis. Finally, we look at the domain names used by servers hosting the GHSis and the offers. We show that public blacklists are mostly ineffective against GS.

3.1   Classification Result

Our system identified 33,324 different GHSi URLs, mapped onto 3,319 unique domains. 58.5% of these domains have only 1 GHSi URL. However, there are many domains with a large number of GHSis URLs. The two of largest domains hosted 2,421 and 1,002 URLs respectively.

Search URLs Classification: Throughout our crawling period, we have collected 657,578 different pages resulting directly from our daily queries on search engines. We only retained pages with English text, reducing the total number of pages to 576,476. Our classifier identified 11,969 of these pages as GHSis, which represent 2.07% of the search results.

Our data contains many URLs hosted on popular sites such as *Youtube, Pinterest, Facebook*, and many more domains which belong to Alexa top 1k, representing 56.7% of our results. None of these top 1K domains contained actual GHSis, only links to GHSis which will be extracted and discovered in our second crawling. In other words, if we focus our classification process on domains that are not in Alexa top 1K (which are 43.3% of our results), our search queries yield directly an instance of the scam 4.7% of the time.

Extracted URLs Classification: We now look at the pages reached after crawling set above down one level (that is, we fetch the URLs included in each non-GHSi page returned by the search engine). In total, around 18.5M URLs were extracted. We crawled around 1.5M pages hosted on domains outside Alexa top 1K by the end of Sep-18 in which 497,986 pages were reachable. Removing non-English pages again, we ended up with 378,147 pages. Our classifier identified 21,353 new GHSis in these pages, which represent 5.6% of the pages.

An analysis of the data shows that the attackers target some domains more often to advertise their scams. Usually, the targeted domains host public blogs and domains with high traffic. For example, we found 10,877 unique links leading to GHSis in posts hosted on the site *jeuxvideo.com*. Table 2 the domains with the most links to GHSis in our database,[3]. We also found these links in popular websites and social media, such as *Google.com* (235 URLs), *pinterest.com* (143 URLs) or FaceBook, YouTube, Linkedin, or even ResearchGate!

3.2   GHS Analysis

In this section, we present our analysis of the GHSis we collected. Here we provide an insight into the relationship between the different GHSis. We first cluster GHSIs into groups based on unique identifiers that we have found in the GHSis. We then look at the set of games that are targeted by related scammers.

GHS Groups: This analysis was conducted based on the finding that many GHS pages are built using similar templates. We found at least two different

---

[3] For sure this percentage only reflect the URLs collected by our crawler. The percentage of the scam URLs on this domains is way less if we consider all the URLs published there.

Table 2. Domains with many pages that have URLs linking to GHSis.

Domain	#Links	#GHS	%GHS	Domain	#Links	#GHS	%GHS
jeuxvideo.com	12,294	10,877	88.47	runkit.com	1,178	922	78.26
change.org	2,396	2,059	85.93	loancoin.com	593	552	93.08
tapas.io	1,699	1,446	85.1	jsdo.it	319	298	93.41

online advertisement websites that either provide GHSi templates, or provide tutorials on how to copy existing templates and deploy it in the scam. These two websites are https://ogads.com/ and https://cpabuild.com/.

We manually inspected the DOM of several GHSi pages in search of identifiers that would allow us to detect when GHSis are created by the same attacker. We also created our own attacks [4]. using the sites mentioned above to confirm our findings. The attack can be reached at https://dwnlds.co/3396a94. We have identified seven identifiers that can be found in many GHSis. Some of these identifiers relate to analytics collections. For example, we found links to the site *histats.com* in 10,667 of our GHSis, about a third of them and *statcounter.com* in 1,419 of the pages. It does not mean that either *histats.com* or *statcounter.com* have any part in the scam, merely that scammers tend to use these sites for their analytic. Other identifiers commonly found in the DOM of the GHSis relate to the account of the scammer on the site that provides the offers at the end of the scam, e.g. *cpabuild.com* and *ogads.com*. Identifiers for these two websites appear in more than a third of our GHSis, with 13,393 occurrences.

Each if these 7 identifiers has unique IDs, we assumed that each ID belongs to a different scammer, as suggested by our experiments on *cpabuild.com* and *ogads.com*. Some of the IDs appear in more than one GHSi, which suggests that these attacks belong to the same attackers. Overall, we have identified 4,040 unique IDs. 3,848 of them (95.2%) were found in less than 5 GHSis thus we excluded them to reduce the skew in our analysis. The breakdown of the number of GHSis per ID for IDs found in at least 5 pages is given in Fig. 3.

Targeted Games: having identified cluster of attacks belonging to the same attackers, we then turn out attention to the targets of these related attacks. In particular, we wanted to understand why a given attacker would carry several attacks: was it to avoid detection, or was it to cast a wider net?

To answer this question, we looked at the actual games targeted by related GHSis. We have extracted around 19,000 different game titles in our database of GHSis. In this analysis, we only consider the IDs that have at least five occurrences in our database, since we are interested in trends among the scammer publishing several attacks. Some titles have a great number of occurrences. These are typically "generic" titles. We have identified 13 such titles. The top one is **"Generate Resources For Your Game!"** with 1,263 occurrences. It means

---

[4] Of course, we did not deploy these attacks, so no one was victimized by our tests.

that the scammer pretends that the GHSi will work with any game. Since no actual game is connected to these instances, we also removed them for this analysis. Overall, we have conducted this analysis on 192 different unique IDs.

Figure 4 shows our results. The x-axis represents the number of unique game title over the number of related pages, and the y-axis represents the fraction of unique IDs. We can see that around 80% of the IDs have at least 50% diversity in the game title they target, and 35% of the IDs target each game title only once. This clearly shows that scammer generates new attacks primarily in order to cover additional games and increase the spread of their scams.

3.3 Offers

In this section, we provide two different analyses of the tasks that a victim needs to complete in order to obtain the claimed game resources at the "offers" stage of the scam. We first look at the spread of offers across different GHSi. We then relate our attempts at contacting some of the "services" that are proposed by these scams.

To collect the offers, we have manually interacted with 42 randomly selected GHSis that are hosted on different domains. Of these 42 seemingly unrelated GHSis, we only got 14 different CLs, already showing convergence across attacks. This shows that many of these GHSis use the same CL, and thus will send the victim to the same offer sites. Moreover, as already noted, 41% of our GHSis contain identifiers from *cpabuild.com* and/or *ogads.com*. This indicates that these GHSis use CLs provided by these two sites.

Each CL gives a choice of several offers (see e.g. Figure 1 image 2.3). An initial crawling of the various CL links suggested that they would lead to different offers. However, we found that the CLs are actually dynamically loading the offers, and thus consecutive accesses to the same CL provides different offers to the victim. We therefore crawled continuously all of our 14 different CLs and found that overall, 115 different offers were presented across all the CLs. We saw a large overlap between the offers provided by the different CLs. Figure 5 provides some details. Almost 22% of the 115 offers were reached by all 14 CLs, and almost

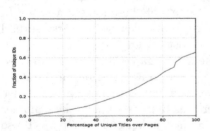

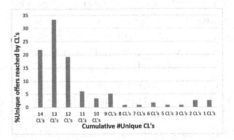

Fig. 4. Number of games each scammer spans

Fig. 5. Percentage of offers reached per number of CLs

75% of the 115 offers were reached by at least 12 of the 14 CLs. In other words, on our database, all the attacks basically lead to the same set of offers.

The identified offers are mainly subscriptions for services advertising online libraries and video/music streaming. All of these domains use very similar site templates and similar sign-up forms. The domain names tend to be created following similar patterns; the books sites contain "book" in the domain name and the streaming sites contain "music"/"play" in the domain name. In general, the site claims to have a free trial period, but a valid credit card must be provided to enroll. It is very doubtful that any of these sites would actually provide any service at all should the victim provide their credit card information. For example, such subscription scams are the sixth highest scam causing money loss in Canada with $2.9 M in 2015 [12]. Other websites ask the victim to download and install executable files as shown in Fig. 1. Unsurprisingly, these executables are flagged as malware by sites such as VirusTotal [29].

Finally, some of the offers are sites that promise free vouchers, gift cards, and free products in exchange for completing surveys. These websites are part of the survey scam which has recently been explored in prior work [5,11]. Prize scams are the third highest scam that caused money loss in Canada with $6.5M in 2015 [12].

Offers Reach-Out: We attempted to contact ten of these offers using the email and phone listed on their websites. We targeted sites that claim to provide books and streaming subscriptions, inquiring about the content of their offerings. Nine of these sites replied back with the same auto-reply message, stating that a support ticket had been created and that a representative will follow-up as soon as possible. Only one of these sites reached out to us. Its representative simply suggested to sign-up to the service to check what the site offers. Moreover, the representative stated that we should use a credit card with at least 50$ to create a free trial account.

When we called the services and managed to get through, we ended up on automated answering systems with similar options across all sites. Most of the time, the system simply loops between options and repeats the same messages. Other users report their inability to get through at all [34]. In the rare cases in which we reached a human customer support, that person was answering for several sites and couldn't provide any useful information beside advising to register for an account. Many negative reviews can be found online for these sites, all suggesting that these sites are indeed scams.

In order to not provide financial support to the attackers, we had to stop our experiments when a valid credit card with available funds was necessary to proceed. We did not pursue our inquiries past that point.

3.4   Overlap with Blacklists

In this section, we analyze if there is an overlap between the domains names of the servers hosting GHSis and offers and public blacklists (PBLs).

We checked if the domains of the final URLs of our GHSis are flagged by some of the popular PBLs, including malwaredomains [15], SANS [19], abuse.ch [20],

Malc0de database [17], malwaredomainlist [18], and hpHosts [16]. For each domain, we checked if it was blacklisted and if so, when it was first added to the list. Only 53 for the 3,319 domains hosting GHSi are blacklisted by at least one PBL (1.56% of the domains).

Moreover, we have scanned our domains against Google Safe Browsing [24] and VirusTotal [29]. We found that 108 (5.57%) of the domains are flagged by VirusTotal, and 11 (0.33%) by Google Safe Browsing. Cumulatively, we have only 225 (6.7%) domains identified as a scam. This value is much lower than the 26.8% reported for the Technical Support Scam overlap in [33]. These results indicate the ineffectiveness of the current PBLs against this type of scam.

The PBLs fare better when it comes to the offer domains. Although five of the PBLs do not flag any of the offer domains, hpHosts [16] flagged 91 (79%) of our domains. However, these domains were black-listed long after their registration date. On average, they were black-listed 506 days after the domain registration, and only one domain was black-listed within 100 days. However, we should note that we do not know when the domain started to actively host scams.

These results suggest that the current PBLs are ineffective against GHS attacks, as they are against other scams such as the Technical Support Scam [33]. A system such as our classifier is much more effective at protecting end users.

4 Bitly Links Analysis

In our corpus, many of the GHSi URLs were shortened before being published. Out of these, we have 2,215 links shortened by Bitly. As pointed out in [13], Bitly shortening services provides a public API that can be used to collect metrics related to its URLs. In this section, we utilize this Bitly API to gain some insights about how successful GHS attacks are. We look at four different metrics. We look at the lifespan of the links and at the number of clicks each link received. Then, we look at click through over time. Finally, we analyze the traffic, to find out the most common country of origin and referrer for the victims.

4.1 Click Through Analysis

Looking at the click through activity seen on the GHSi links, we see that 99.% of the URLs received at least 2 clicks and 30% of the URLs receive at least 452 clicks. On average, we see an astonishing average of 1,774 clicks per link, accumulating a total of 3,894,964 clicks in our database of links. Our click-count analysis is presented in Fig. 6. This shows that the scam attracts a large number of people[5]. If we assume that in our database, the links that go through Bitly are reasonably representative of the other links, it suggests that our 33,324 URLs have generated about 60 million clicks. What is more, our method is almost

---

[5] Of course, we cannot tell apart real victims from curious onlookers. We show that this scam does generate a lot of traffic, but what percentage of this materialize into an actual victim remains unknown, and it's less than the actual traffic for sure.

certainly not exhaustive and we are probably missing many GHSi URLs, so the number of people clicking through the scam is probably even greater still.

As for the link click duration, our analysis shows that the links have a relatively long lifespan. Around 11% of our Bitly links have been created in August of 2018 or after, which limits their possible lifetime. Indeed, 10% of the URLs have click duration of 58 days or less. On the other hand, 20% of the links register clicks over a period of a year or more. This suggests that the links remain effective for a long time. Click-through-duration analysis is presented in Fig. 6.

4.2   Monthly URL Clicks and Creation Analysis

We now look at when the scam was most active. The links creation date analysis is presented Fig. 7. As seen in the figure, the attack started in 2014, but really peaked in 2018, with a lot of activity throughout the year.

Perhaps the most telling metrics is shown Fig. 7. In this figure, we show the number of clicks received each month by our Bitly URLs since 2014. As can be clearly seen in the figure, the number of clicks is on the rise, with a very sharp increase throughout 2018, reaching its maximum at our last data-point with more than 575k clicks in September. This shows that this scam is very active and the number of victims is growing. Awareness of GHS must be increased and some good protection mechanisms are needed to stop it.

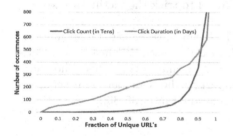

Fig. 6. GHS click through and click duration analysis

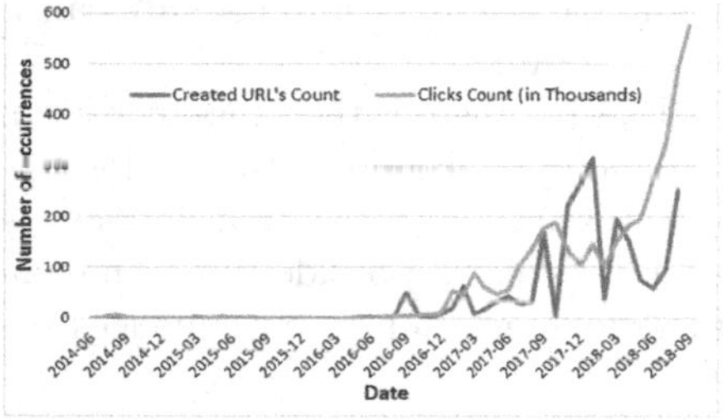

Fig. 7. GHS click and creation by date

4.3   Country and HTTP Referrer Clicks

If we look at the countries from which the links have been clicked, we find a total of 243 countries, out of 254 possible country codes [1]. It shows that GHS attracts victims from nearly everywhere on earth. In terms of volume, victims in the US and India have generated the largest number of clicks, with 22.67% and 10.37% respectively. If we look at the referrers, we find that GHS URLs were accessed from 1,211 domains. "Direct" access is the most common source with 77.17%. Direct access includes sources like email clients, instant messages, and

dedicated applications [13]. Unsurprisingly, *jeuxvideo.com* and *change.org* are in
the top referrer lists. This matches our findings reported in Sect. 3.1.

Table 3 gives the breakdown of the top 7 origin countries and referrers.

5   Related Work

Although recent researches have provided important insights into different types
of scam, to our knowledge, this paper is the first systematic study on GS. The
works most closely related to ours are studies about the so-called "Technical Support Scam" (TSS) as well as studies on online survey scams. In TSS, scammers
combine online scam and telephone fraud activities to convince their victims
that their machines are infected with malware, and offer a fake technical support service. Miramirkhani *et al.* presented the first systematic TSS study [14],
which was continued and improved by Srinivasan *et al.* [33]. TSS was also studied
in [31,32], and several reports were published about the scam [30,38].

In the case of survey scam, victims are tricked into providing sensitive information and installing malware and unwanted programs. Usually, this happens
while asking the victims to complete some surveys in exchange of some expected
award. A variety of awards are advertised, for example, free software's, gifts, as
well as gift cards for different stores such as Amazon and Costco [5,11]. Several
security companies have published reports about survey scams [7,37].

Another type of scam is the Internal Revenue Service (IRS) scam. In the IRS
scam, the scammer impersonates an IRS official to trick the victim into sending
money [3,6].

Finally, there is the "romance scam", which can cause considerable emotional
damage in addition to financial losses. In this case, a false relationship is initiated
by the scammer using chat services, social media, and dating sites. The victim
is then asked to provide some financial support to the scammer. This scam and
its serious emotional consequences has been studied in [4,35,36].

Table 3. Referrers and countries with the highest number of clicks

Rank	Top countries		Top referrals	
	Countries	% Clicks	Referrer	% Clicks
1	US	22.67	direct	77.17
2	India	10.37	jeuxvideo.com	5.18
3	Indonesia	6.7	piktochart.com	3.36
4	Philippines	5.82	kabam.com	1.51
5	UK	4.58	google.com	1.13
6	Brazil	3.78	flasygames.com	1.12
7	France	2.66	change.org	1.02

6   Limitations and Future Work

One of the main limitations of our study is that we only look for GHSis based on the ones we have already found. Our goal was not to be exhaustive, but rather to gather enough data to get an understanding of the scam, and we believe that we achieved that. However, we are now planning on a more systematic and exhaustive study of the scam, to better gauge the extent of the problem and the number of victims. It is possible that some of our current results are biased by the type of GHSis we are looking for, and a more systematic search would shed new lights to the situation (for example, other template providers might come to light).

Another limitation is our focus on GHSis. As explained, GHS either directs victims towards GHSis and offers, or tries to have them install malware. In our next study, we will be looking at the malware distribution side of the scam, in order to get a full picture of the attack.

Finally, we would like to study in more details the offer side of the scam. As explained before, the difficulty here is to be able to gain insight without contributing financially to the scam. We are in discussion with our ethics board to find the best solution to achieve this.

7   Conclusions

In this paper, we reported on the first systematic investigation of what we call the "Game scam". We used a data-driven approach to investigate and gain knowledge on this type of scam: we formulated GS-related search queries; we used multiple search engines to collect data about the websites to which GHS victims are directed when they search online for various game hacks and tricks. We looked at the pages returned directly by the search engines, as well as the pages linked from these pages.

Our research showed that GHS attackers use popular websites to publish links leading to this type of scam. A variety of sites are used to disseminate these links: social media, streaming sites, blogs, and even unrelated sites such as *change.org or* or *researchgate.net*. Our data collection spans five months, during which we uncovered over 3,000 GHS domains and over 100 different offer domains.

Analyzing our data showed that the attackers use pre-built templates to create their attacks. We also found that they tend to target different games. By analyzing the analytics of the GHSi published through Bitly, we were able to estimate that these links have been clicked through at least 60 million times. Furthermore, we found that GHS attacks are rising sharply, and so is the number of victims. Finally, we found that the current public blacklists are inadequate and suggest that our method is more effective at detecting these attacks.

All the data used in our study is available at http://bit.ly/GHSICWE.

References

1. List: the two-letter country code/country abbreviation (2018). bit.ly/2ROvg8N
2. Supervised learning: scikit-learn 0.20.0 documentation (2018). bit.ly/2RjUEi4
3. Bidgoli, M., Grossklags, J.: "Hello. this is the irs calling.": a case study on scams, extortion, impersonation, and phone spoofing. In: 2017 APWG Symposium on Electronic Crime Research (eCrime), pp. 57–69. IEEE (2017)
4. Buchanan, T., Whitty, M.T.: The online dating romance scam: causes and consequences of victimhood. Psychol. Crime Law **20**(3), 261–283 (2014)
5. Clark, J.W., McCoy, D.: There are no free ipads: an analysis of survey scams as a business. In: Presented as part of the 6th USENIX Workshop on Large-Scale Exploits and Emergent Threats. USENIX, Washington, D.C. (2013). bit.ly/2My6C6J
6. Cross, C., Richards, K., Smith, R.G.: The reporting experiences and support needs of victims of online fraud. Trends Issues Crim. Crim. Justice **518**, 1–14 (2016)
7. Doshi, N.: Survey scammers moving to pinterest (2012). symc.ly/2SwIfbZ
8. Jurafsky, D., Martin, J.H.: Markov assumption (2014). stanford.io/29zsjAy
9. Kaszor, D.: How free-to-play games make money (2012). bit.ly/2QgHpPc
10. Kershner, K.: How do free-to-play games make money? (2018). bit.ly/2yN3huU
11. Kharraz, A., Robertson, W., Kirda, E.: Surveylance: automatically detecting online survey scams. In: 2018 IEEE Symposium on Security and Privacy (SP), pp. 70–86. IEEE (2018)
12. Laanela, M.: Canada's top 10 scams earned crooks $1.2b last year, say bbb (2016). bit.ly/2P6r2IC
13. Le Page, S., Jourdan, G.V., Bochmann, G.V., Flood, J., Onut, I.V.: Using url shorteners to compare phishing and malware attacks. In: APWG Symposium on Electronic Crime Research (eCrime), pp. 1–13. IEEE (2018)
14. Miramirkhani, N., Starov, O., Nikiforakis, N.: Dial one for scam: A large-scale analysis of technical support scams. arXiv preprint arXiv:1607.06891 (2016)
15. DNS-BH malware domains (2017). http://www.malwaredomains.com/
16. hpHosts online, simple, searchable & free (2017). https://hosts-file.net/
17. Malcode database (2017). http://malc0de.com/database/
18. MDL: malware domain list (2017). https://www.malwaredomainlist.com/
19. Sans: suspicious domains (2017). bit.ly/2FNCzHv
20. The swiss security blog (2017). bit.ly/2EE7HK1
21. Beautifulsoup (2018). https://pypi.org/project/beautifulsoup4/
22. Cheat engine (2018). bit.ly/2yn5gpn
23. Chromedriver - webdriver for chrome (2018). bit.ly/2CMwVBG
24. Google safe browsing API (2018). https://goo.gl/4yAFyQ
25. Number of the video gamers worldwide (2018). bit.ly/2HE4m9Y
26. PhantomJS - scriptable headless browser (2018). http://phantomjs.org/
27. Selenium with python, selenium python bindings (2018). bit.ly/2LNldJn
28. Value of the global video game market (2018). bit.ly/2kmSvEU
29. Virustotal (2018). https://www.virustotal.com/
30. Orla: technical support phone scam (2010). symc.ly/2OdDyR3
31. Rauti, S., Leppänen, V.: "you have a potential hacker's infection": a study on technical support scams. In: 2017 IEEE International Conference on Computer and Information Technology (CIT), pp. 197–203. IEEE (2017)
32. Sahin, M., Relieu, M., Francillon, A.: Using chatbots against voice spam: analyzing lenny's effectiveness. In: Thirteenth Symposium on Usable Privacy and Security (SOUPS 2017), pp. 319–337. USENIX Association, Santa Clara (2017)

33. Srinivasan, B., et al.: Exposing search and advertisement abuse tactics and infrastructure of technical support scammers. In: In Proceedings of the 2018 World Wide Web Conference on World Wide Web, pp. 319–328. International World Wide Web Conferences Steering Committee (2018)
34. Vanessa: detailed information about 888.980.9787 or 888.980.9787 phone number in free number 888 free 8xx us (2018). bit.ly/2RMmbxv
35. Whitty, M.T.: Anatomy of the online dating romance scam. Secur. J. **28**(4), 443–455 (2015)
36. Whitty, M.T., Buchanan, T.: The online romance scam: a serious cybercrime. CyberPsychology Behav. Soc. Netw. **15**(3), 181–183 (2012)
37. Wueest, C.: Fast-flux facebook application scams (2011). symc.ly/2ADviGF
38. Zeltser, L.: Conversation with a tech support scammer (2015). bit.ly/1PXKDlN

Decentralized Service Registry and Discovery in P2P Networks Using Blockchain Technology

Peter de Lange[✉][iD], Tom Janson[iD], and Ralf Klamma[iD]

RWTH Aachen University, Lehrstuhl Informatik 5, Ahornstr. 55,
52074 Aachen, Germany
{lange,janson,klamma}@dbis.rwth-aachen.de

Abstract. Decentralized information systems radically change the power dynamics of the Web by establishing participants as equal peers, which form a self-governing community. However, decentralized infrastructures currently do not offer a way for users to easily explore available services in the network, nor the ability to securely verify their origin and history. In this contribution, we approach these challenges by exploiting the tamper-proofness of blockchain technology to build a decentralized service registry and discovery system for an existing decentralized microservice infrastructure. With this, users are able to find services in a network and are also able to verify their integrity and origin. Our first evaluations show promising results with this kind of system in the domain of decentralized service provisioning, while also raising research questions for future research in this field.

Keywords: Service discovery · Decentralization · Microservices · Blockchain

1 Introduction

When Tim Berners-Lee proposed the Web in 1989, he envisioned a decentralized system of information repositories that facilitate organizational knowledge transfer by allowing anyone to create, reference, and access content [2]. However, Web authoring and publication required both technical expertise and hardware infrastructure. With the rise of the Web 2.0 in the early 2000s, Social Networking Sites (SNS) and Content Management Systems (CMS) enabled all users to create Web content [12]. But it simultaneously put the users at the mercy of the platform operators. Services may suddenly be shut down, erasing content and disrupting communities. As well, private data is often stored insecurely, used for commercial purposes, or even revealed in data breaches. The proprietary nature of the vast majority of these platforms leaves users little bargaining power to change those terms.

Decentralized information systems radically change this dynamic by establishing participants as equal peers, which form a self-governing community.

© Springer Nature Switzerland AG 2019
M. Bakaev et al. (Eds.): ICWE 2019, LNCS 11496, pp. 296–311, 2019.
https://doi.org/10.1007/978-3-030-19274-7_22

A peer-to-peer (P2P) structure can provide scalability and distribute the utilization of computing resources. In combination with public key cryptography, it allows users to sign messages and store private data securely, providing privacy without relying on trusted infrastructure. It is clear that these properties are especially appealing to online *Communities of Practice* (CoPs) [22]. These groups of people with a shared craft or profession, but not bound by a formal context, collaborate informally via the Web. In previous work [9] we presented a P2P microservice infrastructure for CoPs. This network of nodes can be hosted by the CoP itself. Microservices [11], once uploaded into the network, can be replicated through the community members' nodes according to the current need.

However, decentralized infrastructures currently don't offer a way for users to easily explore available services in the network, nor the ability to securely verify their origin and history. In distributed systems, this task is commonly solved by using service registries, providing a publish-lookup API facilitating service discovery and interoperation. Transferring this concept into the setting of open, decentralized systems is a technical challenge, since the architecture of traditional service registries relies on trusted servers, while existing P2P approaches compromise queriability and security. Beyond this technical challenge, it also raises research questions regarding end-user service discovery in the context of online communities.

In this contribution, we approach these challenges by exploiting the tamper-proofness of blockchain technology to build a decentralized service registry and discovery system for a decentralized P2P microservice infrastructure. We first briefly recap the real-world use case from previous work to then point out the challenges and potential threats this community infrastructure faces (Sect. 2). We then introduce the background and related work done in the domain of both "traditional" service discovery and blockchain technology (Sect. 3), before we present our decentralized, blockchain-based service registry as an approach to tackle the previously mentioned challenges (Sect. 4). By securely recording the release history of services, this approach provides service authors control over their services' update process and the ability to establish a reputation for quality contributions within the community. Service users, on the other hand, are able to verify the integrity, origin, and history of service releases. On this basis, the service discovery system enables searching for services both programmatically and via a user-friendly, browser-based interface, taking into account the different requirements of developers and end-users. In Sect. 4.2, we describe the technical integration of this approach into a purely P2P based architecture. Our contribution ends with a report on our evaluation of the system as well as its implications for future research (Sect. 5), before we conclude our paper (Sect. 6).

2   Use Case

In our initial use case that lead to the development of the decentralized microservice infrastructure, we supported a CoP preparing for a training course of the European Voluntary Service (EVS) program. To cope with the diverse background of the participants, the trainers used a form of question-based dialog some days before the actual (on-premise) training course started. This application, consisting of a set of microservices and a Web frontend, enables users to participate in a sort of mind-mapping process. Our infrastructure allows members of the community to start a node and all services needed to locally run the application, or only start the node and access services of other members via the network. Another possibility is to just access the Web frontend of a community member to participate. This scenario fulfilled the need for the whole infrastructure being distributed only among the community itself without the need for any central authority. To our knowledge, this type of fully community-owned decentralized microservice infrastructure is unique. However, there are several shortcomings to it, which come to light once one takes a look at the "bigger picture". In Fig. 1 we depict this scenario. In this example, *Community A* stands for the above mentioned CoP, whilst a second *Community B* also participates in the network. Additionally, we consider a malicious actor *Eve*. This raises several problems, which we point out next.

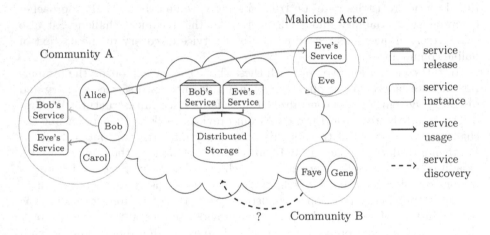

Fig. 1. Usage scenario with multiple communities

How to Explore Services Available in the Network? When *Community B* joins the network, there neither exists an overview of available service releases nor information on currently deployed service instances in the network. To new communities and community members, the network appears "empty", and information about services of interest has to come from external sources, like overview websites. Previously, our infrastructure used a "Catalog Service" for this task, that held information added by community members and displayed them on a public frontend. Since users could add any unverified service information, this approach was fundamentally insecure and also required continuous manual curation.

Where Can I Find More Information About that Service? The knowledge of services existing in the network might not always be enough to get an impression of what usage possibilities exist. Additional information, like service descriptions, source code location, available frontends, or even usage patterns by other communities may be of relevance to new members or new communities entering the network. Also, the identity of the service developer is of relevance, since trust in a service is highly dependent on its author. In the above example, members of *Community B* might for example be interested in seeing service releases by a particular developer of *Community A*, e.g., because she is a member of both communities and forms a binding link between them.

How to Verify the Integrity and Origin of a Service? Once a community has established both the knowledge of which service might be worth exploring and where a running instance can be found, P2P networks offer no way of verifying the integrity and origin of services. Specifically, that a remotely running service instance is in fact an unmodified instance of the service release it claims to be. Even when replicating a service locally and checking its integrity via its cryptographic signature, in the absence of a registration authority, the signing key cannot be linked to the (real-life or pseudonymous) identity of the service release's author. This could result in a malicious service instance being executed on the community member's node. In the above example *Bob* has published the initial "correct" service release, the actor *Eve* publishes a malicious service release that imitates this one. Since there is no way of tracing the origin of a service instance or its release in the network, both communities could accidentally call a malicious service instance. This is depicted by *Alice* and *Carol* calling *Eve's Service Instance*, instead of the "correct" one published by *Bob*.

Derived Requirements for Decentralized Service Discovery: From the above use case, a number of requirements arise regarding service discovery in decentralized systems. It should enable both end-users and developers to easily find service releases, verify their origin and either use remote instances or replicate the release to their own node. Although most of these requirements can be solved by using some kind of central service registry (see also Sect. 3), this approach has one major drawback: It redirects the power over the infrastructure from the community to the maintainer of this centralized component and thus contradicts the whole idea of decentralization. Without the knowledge of available services and also the ability to authorize service releases, the community relies on the service registry to forward their discovery requests, which raises the same issues a decentralized infrastructure tries to tackle. To be in line with the concept and preserve its advantages, a decentralized service registry has to be governed by the whole community in terms of authorizing service releases and validating service instances. The Blockchain approach fits this idea perfectly.

3 Related Work

Service Discovery and Registration Architectures. The term *service discovery* encompasses varying degrees of functionality, depending on the context: In its most basic form, it refers to the publication and lookup of the network location of a service which is already known by name in a registry (*service location discovery*). This registry may also allow the retrieval of services matching a formal description (*semantic service discovery* or *matchmaking*), and thus requires that services publish a machine-interpretable description of their capabilities. This meaning is central to the vision of the Semantic Web [3], in which data stored in potentially disparate sources (e.g., published in different formats, by different communities) can be automatically discovered, processed, and to some degree understood by machines [21]. Finally, *end-user service discovery* goes beyond programmatic discovery and aims to help users find Web services relevant to their interests, e.g., by employing recommender systems or the user's physical and logical context [8]. A great variety of architectures for service discovery has been proposed. They are often classified according to the degree of centralization of the registry [7,15]. However, the most simple scheme is to not use a registry at all, but to propagate service queries or advertisements via flooding. It is clear that the communication overhead of this approach prevents it from scaling to large networks, instead it was suggested for home networks or even in cars, where the number of participating devices was presumed to be very small [4,6]. For medium-sized networks, a single central registration server may be used. The API of such a registry consists of *service publication* and *service lookup*. The registry simply caches the service description published by the *service provider* until some time-out is met and answers the *service requesters'* queries accordingly. While this approach can work well in controlled environments, several issues arise when attempting to serve large, geographically distributed, or heterogeneous networks: First, having a single registry server is neither fault-tolerant nor scalable. Further, if services should be accessible from across the globe, latency may be an issue. Finally, the registry is under the control of and must be maintained by a single entity. Out of these considerations emerged distributed service registry architectures, which can be classified into three domains according to the way they store service descriptions and state information:

1. *Replicating*, where registries attempt to have the same, complete state [19]
2. *Distributed* or *federated*, where registries only store information about local services, but forward queries about other services to a cooperating registry
3. *Peer-to-peer*, where information is also stored decentrally, but all participating registries use a common P2P protocol, negating the need for manually configuring and setting up sharing agreements between them [7,20]

Each of these is appropriate for certain use cases. Current commercial systems such as Netflix's Eureka[1] and HashiCorp's Consul[2] fall into the first two categories (or some hybrid combining both), with local registries assigned to each data center or region. P2P service registries have to our knowledge been primarily the subject of academic inquiry rather than deployed in practice. Most of them utilize a distributed hash table (DHT), where service descriptions are

---

[1] https://github.com/Netflix/eureka.
[2] https://www.consul.io/intro/.

addressed by the hash of their contents. However, unstructured P2P registries have also been proposed [7]. In both cases queriability is a crucial issue, specifically the search capabilities of the P2P storage beyond exact match lookup and even *completeness*, i.e., the guarantee that an existing entry can be located. Much effort has been put into extending structured P2P overlays to allow attribute, wildcard-based and other advanced queries (e.g., [13, 16–18, 24]), but these limitations remain a major obstacle.

Trust and Consensus in Decentralized Systems. When we discussed distributed service registries in the previous section, we implicitly assumed that all nodes comprising the system are trustworthy, i.e., operating correctly without either accidental or malicious misbehavior. For corporate networks and many other use cases this is a reasonable assumption. But for a decentralized system that is open for anyone to participate in, as a peer among equal peers, a different approach is required. We use the term *open decentralized system* to denote exactly that: A system of autonomous peers, who may join or leave at any time, and whose goals may not align with one another. Further, there is no single centralized authority, which could coordinate or serve as a universally trusted entity in the system. A fundamental problem of such decentralized systems is how to ensure that received information is up-to-date and authentic, despite being unable to trust any particular node [10]. This is an instance of a *consensus problem*, which has been in the focus of distributed systems research since the early 1980s [14]. More recently the topic has come into the spotlight due to the apparent success of cryptocurrencies, first and foremost *Bitcoin*, which purport to solve the problem on a global scale. In essence, a functioning decentralized system needs to agree on a common state. The nodes of a distributed database need to agree on the contents and order of the applied operations, while cryptocurrencies deal with the specific case of tracking the participants' account balances. Thus a secure, scalable consensus algorithm lies at the heart of decentralized systems. We argue that consensus algorithms, with their ability to keep a shared state across network nodes, are promising candidates for the storage backend of a decentralized service registry.

Smart Contracts. *Ethereum* [23], as a so-called second generation cryptocurrency, utilizes a proof-of-work and blockchain based consensus scheme. But instead of being only used as a cryptocurrency (like for example Bitcoin), Ethereum sees itself as a general purpose platform for decentralized applications. This is reflected technically in the syntax of its transactions. These can include code in a Turing-complete, stack-based bytecode language, whereas the transactions in Bitcoin's blocks are deliberately less expressive. This allows Ethereum users to write and upload scripts to the network, whose functions can be invoked by sending special transactions. Such scripts are called *Smart Contracts*. Each deployed smart contract consists of its program code, a data store, as well as an account containing *Ether*, Ethereum's currency. When a transaction triggers a smart contract function, the miner that includes the transaction executes the code and includes the updated state in the new block. All other nodes must also execute the code in order to determine whether the new block is valid (includes the correct result of the computation). Given certain restrictions on the computing power of an attacker in comparison to the nodes behaving correctly, this approach provides an immutable history of transactions.

It is clear that this massively redundant code execution is expensive in terms of resources. Ethereum charges a dynamic fee based on the number of executed instructions, which must be paid for by the transaction's sender. If its funds are insufficient, the execution is stopped. It is thus not economically feasible to deploy computationally expensive code or to directly store large amounts of data. It should be noted that the cost of executing smart contracts limits Ethereum's scalability (in terms of throughput), and there are numerous proposals to alter the Ethereum protocol in order to improve performance, including radical changes to the consensus system [5]. Examples of smart contract applications currently in use include financial contracts, games of chance, and notary applications [1], which can largely be implemented with very simple program logic, while documents can sometimes be stored elsewhere (e.g., via IPFS[3], a peer-to-peer storage system) and securely referenced.

4 A Decentralized Service Registry

4.1 Conceptual Overview

We propose a decentralized service registry based on a private blockchain that enables the discovery of services and the secure verification of their release metadata. Combining the completeness and time-preserving properties of a blockchain with space-efficient distributed storage allows us to utilize the strengths of each technology and compensate their respective weaknesses. Specifically, the registry consists of two smart contracts for both services and users. The data written to the blockchain belongs to four types, which are shown along with their respective fields in Fig. 2. Because storing data "on-chain" is inefficient and expensive, only essential fields are stored directly on the blockchain, while supplemental fields (marked in italics) are stored "off-chain" in the distributed storage and securely referenced by their hash.

The *user contract* serves as a decentralized identity management system that ties usernames to their (online) identities via public key cryptography. In contrast to a centralized public key infrastructure, the user has direct control (i.e., ownership) of their entry, including the decision to reveal personal data. Thus some users may reveal their real life identities in order to facilitate trust, while others may choose to remain pseudonymous. Registered users can then use the *service contract* to publish *service releases*. This encompasses reserving a service name and linking specific releases to additional metadata. Just like the usernames, these entries are owned by their author by linking them to the author's public key. Finally, we allow the announcement of *service instances*, indicating that a user is running a publicly usable instance of the service on their node. Storing this data in a blockchain provides an immutable, auditable historic record of

---

[3] InterPlanetary File System, https://ipfs.io/.

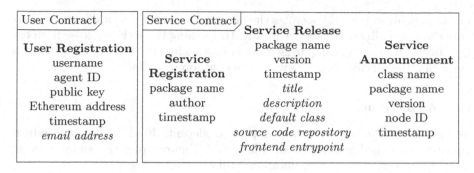

Fig. 2. The registry smart contracts' data

the registry entries and ensures that they can only be updated by their owners, while also making the data readily available and queriable to all peers.

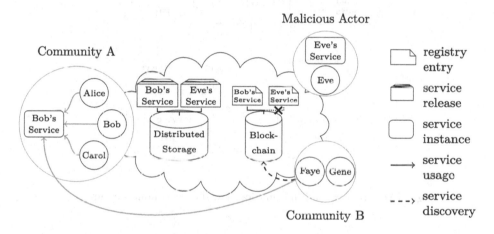

Fig. 3. Usage scenario with decentralized service registry

Returning to our example (Fig. 3), *Bob* registered both a username and the name of his service in the network's decentralized registry. The registry entry for *Bob's Service* is linked to his username and key pair, which Bob uses to sign his service releases. *Eve* can still store her malicious, modified release of Bob's Service in the distributed storage. However, she is unable to register it under the same name, nor can she attach Bob's name to it. All network participants can access the blockchain to see published services and their running instances, and can perform arbitrary queries (e.g., a keyword search over the service metadata). Thus *Faye* can easily discover Bob's Service even if they are part of disjoint communities. Just like *Alice* and the other members of *Community A*, Faye also sees the running instance of Bob's Service. If she feels she can trust the user who sent the service announcement and operates the instance, she can access it directly. Otherwise, she can replicate the service locally. By fetching the service release from the distributed storage and comparing its signature against the registry entry, she can verify that the service she starts was in fact authored by *Bob*.

4.2   Architecture

We implemented our approach on top of the decentralized microservice infrastructure introduced in Sect. 2, called *las2peer*[4]. Figure 4 provides an overview of its extended architecture and information flow.

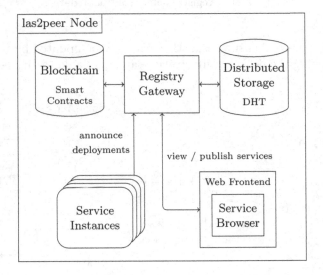

Fig. 4. Architecture and information flow during common operations

There are three main components realizing the decentralized service registry:

1. Smart Contracts: The foundation of the registry is implemented as Ethereum smart contracts that store and retrieve data from the blockchain. The contracts are written in Ethereum's high-level scripting language *Solidity*[5]. In addition to the user and service smart contracts described above, a small library contract is employed to handle the verification of signatures for delegated function calls.

2. Registry Gateway: Every node contains a registry gateway for accessing the Ethereum blockchain. It transparently stores and fetches the supplemental data fields in the distributed storage, realized as a DHT, and combines them with the

---

[4] https://las2peer.org/.
[5] https://solidity.readthedocs.io/.

data retrieved from the blockchain to utilize the benefits of both storage types. The registry gateway also caches service information to provide efficient lookup.

3. Service Browser: The node's Web frontend contains a service browser that allows viewing and uploading service releases, as well as managing local service instances and accessing their frontends. Figure 5 gives an impression of it.

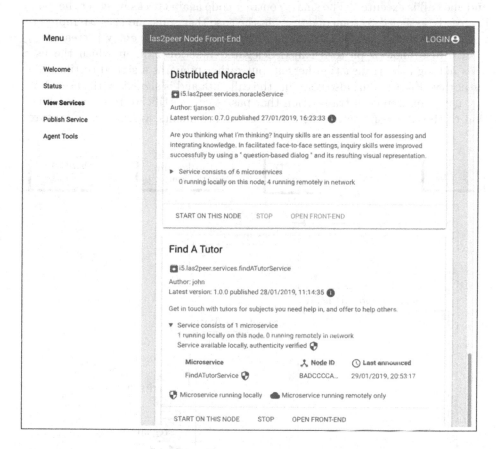

Fig. 5. The service browser

4.3   Interacting with the Registry

User Registration. The user and service smart contracts are essentially *name registries* that assign human-friendly names on a first come, first served basis. As such, the user contract provides functions to check the availability, register, and look up the data associated with a username. An important concept of smart contracts is the distinction between *state-changing* functions and those that are "read-only". The former are processed as transactions appended in a new block (and thus transmitted to and executed by all nodes), while the latter are executed locally and immediately return a value. When a user wishes to register a username, a read-only function is used to check whether the desired name is still available. If so, we call the registration function, which is state-changing: The call data, consisting of the function name and the arguments, is encoded and broadcast in the form of a transaction signed by the user. When a miner processes the transaction to include it in a block, the arguments are extracted and the call is executed. The smart contract code again checks whether the name is already assigned to someone (e.g., in the case that someone else attempted to register the name at nearly the same time). If not, the user entry is created.

We also allow a pattern called delegated function call, in which the user does not sign the transaction herself, but rather prepares a signed certificate of authority (Fig. 6). This also contains the call data and is signed by the user. Now any user can prepare a transaction that passes this certificate to a special function of the user contract, which unpacks the arguments, verifies the signature,

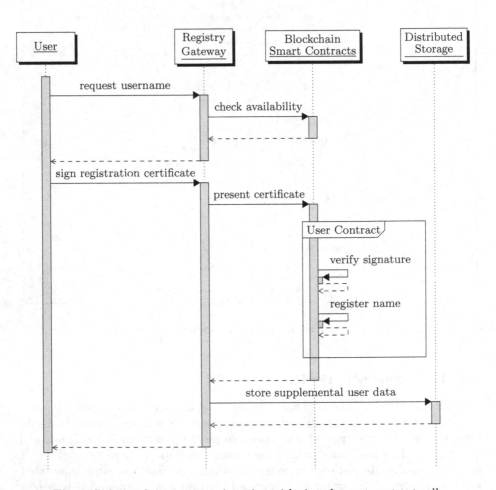

Fig. 6. Delegated username registration with signed smart contract call

and registers the username on behalf of the original user. The advantage of this pattern is that it transfers the burden of paying any transaction fees from the user wishing to register to the user who actually sends the transaction. In our use case, we expect that established community members who operate a node may offer to cover the registration fees for users who are unable to run their own node. If the registration was successful, a file containing the supplemental data fields is uploaded to the distributed storage.

Service Registration, Discovery, and Replication. The service contract operates using the same principles as the user contract. Once again we employ the delegated function call pattern to allow users to cover the transaction fees for a service author. The registration of a service name and publication of a service release is analogous to the user registration procedure. When the deployment of a service instance is requested (e.g., through a node's Web frontend), the service release is fetched from the distributed storage. Through two subsequent smart contract calls, first the username of the author of the service release is looked up in the service contract, then her public key is looked up in the user contract, enabling the system to verify the signature of the service release. Once its authenticity is established, the service is started. If the instance is intended for public use, its deployment is announced to the registry.

5   Preliminary Evaluation

Setup. In order to gather feedback from users, we carried out five evaluation sessions with two to three participants each. The network setup consisted of five permanent nodes and up to three additional nodes started during the session by the participants. Technically, the nodes were started as Docker containers on a single server in order to simulate ideal network conditions. Further, we used a modified version of the Go Ethereum client, `geth`. Since we did not focus on the technical parameters of the blockchain network in this evaluation, we started the client with a very low mining difficulty, leading to short block creation intervals (the "block time"). While many of the participants had experience with software development, the majority was unfamiliar with las2peer, our decentralized community service infrastructure. After a brief introduction to las2peer and its service registry, the participants were given written tasks that included finding existing services as well as registering a user and publishing their own service. During these tasks, the users first accessed the Web frontend of one of the permanent nodes. Later they accessed a newly started node, that joined the existing network. This hands-on experience lasted about 30 min. Afterwards, participants filled out a questionnaire.

Results. Figure 7 shows the results of our questionnaire. As one can see, most of the participants were able to understand the basic concepts of the approach and were also able to fulfill the given tasks. We received lowest scores for the question regarding node ownership. This is due to the fact that the majority

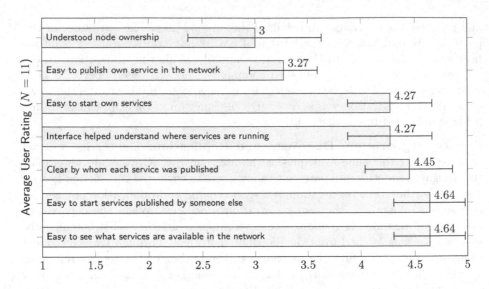

Fig. 7. Evaluation results

of participants were not very familiar with P2P infrastructures and mixed up concepts like running services and nodes. Another quite low rating was received for the question about the ease of publishing own services in the network. This was mostly colored by the fact that it was necessary to post exact class names and frontend URLs, that were not checked for correctness in our initial prototype. This will be improved in future versions of the frontend. The remaining questions received quite high scores, which confirms the usability of our developed service registry and its user interface in form of the service browser. We also asked free-text questions about the relevance of (verified) service authorship. Most of the participants stated that this depended highly on the context, and was only relevant for sensitive data. This is in line with our expectations that decentralized infrastructures are valued particularity in the context of sensitive data exchange. We also received interesting statements regarding the question of contribution to the infrastructure, e.g., in terms of computing power. The majority of responses stated that they would support "their" community if resources were sparse and highly in need. Finally, we asked the participants about the trade-off between response time and required storage space. On average, participants were willing to wait up to ten minutes (although a large minority voted for ten seconds or less) for their actions, e.g., service releases and announcements, to be visible on the blockchain.

Implications for Future Work. One aspect that received little attention in this contribution is transaction fees and incentives to participate in the mining process. Our private blockchain's currency is specific to its corresponding network and does not have any economic value. In future work we want to explore whether this currency can represent status in the community. One direction worth investigating is allowing users to provide bounties for certain actions in the network, like the development or deployment of needed services.

Another technical aspect that requires further evaluation is the trade-off between required storage space and block time, as well as between CPU usage and security, i.e., the integrity of the blockchain data. The block time used in our evaluation was set to an extremely short value (1 s with a difficulty of 1) that is not feasible for real-world settings, since it requires about 500 MB of space per day per node, regardless of the amount of information stored in the blocks. This amount scales inversely with the block time. To study this further, we started modified versions of the Ethereum client with more "realistic" difficulties of 4×10^5 and 128×10^5. These numbers are to be interpreted as the average number of hashes required before a new, valid block is found. We ran these clients over a period of a week, letting each mine with a single CPU core of an Intel® Xeon® Processor E5-4627 v4, resulting in an average block time of 9.3 s (for the lower difficulty) and 271 s (for the higher difficulty), respectively. Both of these block times are within the acceptable range for the majority of our evaluation participants. Over six days, the blockchain size on disk was 61 MB and 2.1 MB, respectively, which certainly a is is a more manageable and scalable requirement.

6   Conclusion

In this paper, we presented a service registry and discovery system for a decentralized community information system. With its foundation in blockchain technology, it keeps the advantages of decentralization, such as empowering communities to take control over their infrastructure. Simultaneously, it enables many properties "traditional", centralized services registries provide, like searching for service releases and instances, and verification of these. While in the future further evaluations will provide deeper insights into the long-time effects of this approach, we are confident that blockchain-based decentralized service registries can provide a valuable addition in the domain of P2P systems.

Acknowledgments. The authors would like to thank the German Federal Ministry of Education and Research (BMBF) for their kind support within the project "Personalisierte Kompetenzentwicklung durch skalierbare Mentoringprozesse" (tech4comp) under the project id 16DHB2110.

References

1. Bartoletti, M., Pompianu, L.: An empirical analysis of smart contracts: platforms, applications, and design patterns. In: Brenner, M., Rohloff, K., Bonneau, J., Miller, A., Ryan, P.Y.A., Teague, V., Bracciali, A., Sala, M., Pintore, F., Jakobsson, M. (eds.) FC 2017. LNCS, vol. 10323, pp. 494–509. Springer, Cham (2017). https://doi.org/10.1007/978-3-319-70278-0_31
2. Berners-Lee, T.: Information management: a proposal (1989)

3. Berners-Lee, T., Hendler, J.A., Lassila, O.: The semantic web. Sci. Am. **284**(5), 28–37 (2001)
4. Bettstetter, C., Renner, C.: A comparison of service discovery protocols and implementation of the service location protocol. In: EUNICE 2000, 6th Open European Summer School (2001)
5. Buterin, V.: A Modest Proposal for Ethereum 2.0 (2017)
6. Guttman, E.: Service location protocol: automatic discovery of IP network services. IEEE Internet Comput. **3**(4), 71–80 (1999)
7. Klusch, M.: Semantic web service coordination. In: CASCOM: Intelligent Service Coordination in the Semantic Web, pp. 59–104. Birkhäuser Basel (2008)
8. La Torre, G., Monteleone, S., Cavallo, M., D'Amico, V., Catania, V.: A context-aware solution to improve web service discovery and user-service interaction. In: 2016 International IEEE Conferences on Ubiquitous Intelligence & Computing, Advanced and Trusted Computing, Scalable Computing and Communications, Cloud and Big Data Computing, Internet of People, and Smart World Congress, pp. 180–187 (2016)
9. de Lange, P., Göschlberger, B., Farrell, T., Klamma, R.: A microservice infrastructure for distributed communities of practice. In: Lifelong Technology-Enhanced Learning, pp. 172–186 (2018)
10. Mattila, J.: The Blockchain Phenomenon - The Disruptive Potential of Distributed Consensus Architectures (2016)
11. Newman, S.: Building Microservices: Designing Fine-Grained Systems. O'Reilly, Sebastopol (2015)
12. O'Reilly, T.: What is web 20: design patterns and business models for the next generation of software. Commun. Strat. **65**, 17–37 (2007)
13. Paolucci, M., Sycara, K.P., Nishimura, T., Srinivasan, N.: Using DAML-S for P2P discovery. In: Proceedings of the International Conference on Web Services, pp. 203–207 (2003)
14. Pease, M., Shostak, R., Lamport, L.: Reaching agreement in the presence of faults. J. ACM **27**(2), 228–234 (1980)
15. Rambold, M., Kasinger, H., Lautenbacher, F., Bauer, B.: Towards autonomic service discovery a survey and comparison. In: IEEE International Conference on Services Computing, pp. 192–201 (2009)
16. Sahin, O.D., Gerede, C.E., Agrawal, D., El Abbadi, A., Ibarra, O., Su, J.: SPiDeR: P2P-based web service discovery. In: Service-Oriented Computing, pp. 157–169 (2005)
17. Schlosser, M., Sintek, M., Decker, S., Nejdl, W.: A scalable and ontology-based P2P infrastructure for semantic web services. In: Peer-to-Peer Computing, pp. 104–111 (2002)
18. Schmidt, C., Parashar, M.: A peer-to-peer approach to web service discovery. World Wide Web **7**(2), 211–229 (2004)
19. Sun, C., Lin, Y., Kemme, B.: Comparison of UDDI registry replication strategies. In: IEEE International Conference on Web Services, pp. 218–225 (2004)
20. Thaden, U., Siberski, W., Nejdl, W.: A Semantic Web based Peer-to-Peer Service Registry Network (2003)
21. W3C: W3C Data Activity: Building the Web of Data (2013). https://www.w3.org/2013/data/

22. Wenger, E.: Communities of Practice: Learning, Meaning, and Identity. Cambridge University Press, Cambridge (1998)
23. Wood, G.: Ethereum: A Secure Decentralized Transaction Ledger (2014)
24. Yan, F., Zhan, S.: A peer-to-peer approach with semantic locality to service discovery. In: Jin, H., Pan, Y., Xiao, N., Sun, J. (eds.) GCC 2004. LNCS, vol. 3251, pp. 831–834. Springer, Heidelberg (2004). https://doi.org/10.1007/978-3-540-30208-7_116

Web Programming

Amalgam: Hardware Hacking for Web Developers with Style (Sheets)

Jorge Garza$^{(\boxtimes)}$ ⓘ, Devon J. Merrill ⓘ, and Steven Swanson ⓘ

Department of Computer Science and Engineering,
University of California San Diego, San Diego, CA, USA
{jgarzagu,djmerrill,swanson}@eng.ucsd.edu

Abstract. Web programming technologies such as HTML, JavaScript, and CSS have become a popular choice for user interface design due to their capabilities: flexible interface, first-class networking, and available libraries. In parallel, driven by the standards set by the mobile companies, embedded devices manufacturers now want to replicate these capabilities. As a result, embedded devices that use web technologies for their graphical interface have started to emerge. However, the programming effort required to integrate web technologies with embedded software hinders its adaption. In this paper, we introduce Amalgam, a system that facilitates the development of embedded devices that use web programming technologies. Amalgam does this by translating the physical interface of embedded hardware components found (e.g., a push button) directly into the HTML and CSS syntax. Our system reduces the programming effort required to develop new embedded devices that use web technologies, as well as adds new interesting capabilities to the design of these. We show Amalgam's capabilities by exploring three embedded devices built using web programming technologies. Also, we demonstrate how Amalgam reduces programming effort by comparing two traditional approaches of building one of these devices against Amalgam. Results show our system reduces the lines of code required to integrate hardware elements into an embedded device application to a line of code per hardware component added to the device.

Keywords: Rapid development · Embedded devices · IoT · Web user interface · CSS · HTML

1 Introduction

With the rise of the Internet of Things (IoT) and smart, connected devices in the home, workplace, and environment, the web and its underlying technologies are pushing up against the real world in a wide range of domains. Connected sensors, web-enabled appliances, and personal electronics all require software that interacts seamlessly with the physical world (e.g., the user or the environment), cloud-based services, and local compute resources. The growing demand for these devices means they need to be easy to program.

© Springer Nature Switzerland AG 2019
M. Bakaev et al. (Eds.): ICWE 2019, LNCS 11496, pp. 315–330, 2019.
https://doi.org/10.1007/978-3-030-19274-7_23

Building these smart, connected devices requires programmers to manually bridge the gap between tangible user interfaces (e.g., buttons, knobs, and displays), sensors (e.g., temperature, light, and movement), and actuators (e.g., servos, motors, and lab equipment) and software.

On the software side, web technologies – Javascript, CSS, HTML and the universe of libraries available for them – are state-of-the-art for developing rich user interfaces, provide deep integration network services, and are the languages of choice for a large population of developers.

Web programming technologies provide a clean separation between program logic, interface structure, and appearance. They make it simple to re-style an interface for a new device or adapt an existing interface to a new form factor (such as desktop to mobile). These tools are so powerful that they have become the default user interface design tools for fixed-function mobile devices, desktop applications, and mobile applications.

For hardware, the tools of choice remain C and C++ which can easily handle controlling hardware components (e.g., interrupts, pin assignments, and device drivers). However, they make building user interfaces and networking communication more cumbersome.

Creating a seamless experience that blends on-screen, soft controls, sensors, and actuators is challenging because the elegant separation that HTML, CSS, and JavaScript have does not extend across the hardware/software boundary. In practice, the tools available for hard and soft elements differ in syntax, operation philosophy, and requirements.

This problem is ubiquitous in modern devices. The interfaces to embedded devices – from personal fitness monitors to home appliances – have sophisticated, polished, and powerful user interfaces. Even small devices (e.g., the Apple Watch) typically run full-blown operating systems that can support high-level languages for graphical user interfaces. According to an annual industry survey of embedded designers, 67% of new embedded designs utilize an operating system, and 49% use graphical interfaces [17].

Embedded devices with graphical interfaces can have a blending of *soft* and *hard* components that provide information to or from the user. Examples of soft components can be on-screen buttons, range sliders, and indicators in the form of text or graphics. Hard or physical components include tactile buttons, knobs, and sensors (such as temperature, heart rate, and so forth), actuators (such as servo motors) and hardware indicators (for example, status lights).

Previous attempts to address this problem simply translate the same complex interfaces into higher-level languages, rather than deeply integrating hard elements into the idioms and tools high-level languages provide. This does not solve the problem: Programmers must still treat physical interface components differently than their soft counterparts.

Indeed, several projects [21,23] provide JavaScript libraries for controlling robots [6] and general embedded systems [18], but they leave behind the power of CSS and HTML, preventing deeper integration with existing programming toolkits and tools.

As a result, web programmers that want to build software that deeply integrates software and hardware cannot leverage their own experience; the wealth of training, documentation, and message boards; or the myriad web programming frameworks that are available. Instead, they must develop custom solutions to bridge the gap.

We propose Amalgam, a toolkit that extends web programming technologies across the hardware/software boundary by seamlessly including hardware devices into Javascript, CSS, and HTML. Amalgam exposes the interfaces of hardware components like buttons, sensors, lights, and motor as document object model (DOM) objects with the same interface as their analogous HTML elements (e.g., `<button>`, `<input type=range>`, etc.).

Amalgam lets programmers *harden* conventional DOM objects into hardware device components using a simple CSS directive. The directive controls whether a particular component appears on-screen or as a physical component, and describes how the device connects physically to the computing platform.

As a result, moving a button from on-screen to the real world requires just editing a CSS property and physically connecting the button. Application logic does not change because the interface remains the same. More important, existing frameworks like Angular [1] and JQuery [15] work just as well with hard elements as soft.

This paper makes the following contribution: By integrating hardware component interfaces into the web user interface syntax, our system allows for rapid development and prototyping of complex embedded devices. To the best of our knowledge, this is the first work that explores the integration of hardware interfaces directly into the HTML and CSS syntax. Furthermore, with our system, extra capabilities are observed.

For instance, hardware components can inherit CSS capabilities. For example, the programmer can create complex lighting effects by using CSS to animate the color of an RGB LED. Likewise, setting the HTML content of a `<span>` that has been hardened into a display can change the contents of the display.

We have implemented Amalgam as a Javascript framework and developed a small but useful library of hardware components. We demonstrate Amalgam's capabilities by using these components to create three embedded devices with rich hardware/software interfaces. We demonstrate that Amalgam works seamlessly with existing web-programming frameworks and libraries to build complex, responsive interfaces for these devices. We also describe Amalgam's implementation and measure how Amalgam makes it easier to develop these kinds of devices.

The rest of this paper is organized as follows. Section 2 gives a overview of Amalgam, and Sect. 3 illustrates Amalgam's capabilities by describing three Amalgam devices. Section 4 evaluates the impact of Amalgam on developer effort. Finally, Sect. 5 describes related work, and Sect. 6 presents our conclusions.

2   Amalgam

Amalgam is a Web API that integrates hardware components into web programming tools in a natural and transparent way. It provides a new style attribute (`hardware`) that convert on-screen elements of web-based interfaces into a hardware device. We call this process *hardening* the on-screen element. Hardening allows, for instance, the replacement of an on-screen button with a physical button. The element's interface remains the same, so the application software does not need to change.

We have implemented Amalgam as a JavaScript library. It leverages Web Components [11] and Web Assembly [13] to build DOM elements that interface with hardware, and it provides a simple compiler that parses a web page's CSS style sheets and hardens elements according the `hardware` directives it finds.

This section describes Amalgam's programming interface, presents a simple example of Amalgam in action, describes the library of physical components we have implemented, and what is required to create a new one.

a) Web Application HTML (Soft elements)

```
<div id="display">0</div>
<input id="slider" type="range" min="0" max="9" value="0"
oninput="getElementById('display').innerHTML = this.value"/>
```

b) Amalgam-enhanced CSS

```
#display {
  hardware: physical-seven-segments ( spi-port:
                                      url('/dev/spidev0.0') );
}

#slider {
  hardware: physical-pot ( adc-channel: 1, i2c-addr: 0x48,
                           i2c-port: url('/dev/i2c-1') );
}
```

c) Software components   d) Hardware components

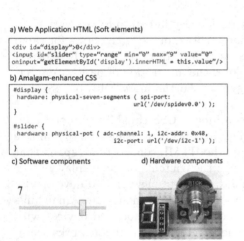

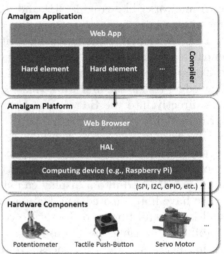

Fig. 1. Styling hardware with Amalgam (a) Describes the interface for a simple numerical display controlled by a slider. Applying an Amalgam-enhanced CSS style sheet (b), produces the same on-screen version of the interface (c) implemented in hardware (d).

Fig. 2. Amalgam Platform: An Amalgam application, a web app that includes the Amalgam Web API, can run on Amalgam Platforms which includes a web browser engine that can communicate with hardware through the HAL.

2.1   Overview

Amalgam's programming interface is simple by design. It lets programmers convert existing DOM elements, which we call *soft elements*, into hardened elements that exist in the real world.

Figure 1 shows a simple Amalgam application. In the figure, (a) shows the HTML for a range `<input>` and a `<div>` along with the event callbacks to ensure that the `<div>` displays the value of the `<input>`. (c) depicts the web page in browser running on a Raspberry Pi [9].

The CSS code in (b) hardens both elements by setting their `hardware` attribute. It converts the `<div>` into a seven-segment LED display and the `<input>` into a rotary knob potentiometer. The photo (d) shows the hardware. Turning the knob updates the display. No other changes are necessary to the code.

The value of the `hardware` attribute describes what kind of hardware to use (in this case, the knob and the display) and how the two components connect to the Raspberry Pi. In this case, the display connects via SPI and the potentiometer connects to the first channel of an analog-to-digital (ADC) integrated circuit connected via I2C

Once hardened, the components continue to behave just like the original soft components. It has the same DOM methods and emits the same events (e.g., when the knob moves, the `<input>` emits `onchange`). If the hardened component has a display capability (e.g., an RGB LED), the programmer can style or animate it with CSS.

Since hard elements have the same interface as soft elements, existing application code requires no modification. In particular, web programming frameworks function as expected without any changes. Cleanly integrating hardware components into web programming technologies offers multiple benefits.

- **Easy Hardware Emulation.** Amalgam decouples application design from hardware design. Software developers can implement the software for a soft version of a device long before the hardware is complete.
- **Faster Design Iteration.** Developers can rapidly explore different designs by hardening different parts of a user interface without needing to modify the application logic.
- **Faster Development.** Amalgam lets developers leverage the universe of available JavaScript frameworks to quickly build complex applications.
- **Automatic Web Integration.** Because they are web applications, Amalgam applications have first-class access to web services, the cloud, etc.

Amalgam makes it easy for programmers to control hardware devices, but they still need to assemble the device. Moreover, they need some familiarity with the hardware and its limitations. Amalgam can replace any HTML element with any hard component, but the programmer must be aware of potential limitations. For example, setting the `value` attribute for `<input>`, used for setting the slider position, when hardened into a normal potentiometer it will not move the potentiometer. If the programmer needs that capability, he should use a rotary encoder or a motorized potentiometer. Likewise, the designer must be aware of which pins connect the hardware components, and if those connections change, the programmer must update the CSS.

2.2   Amalgam Platforms

Amalgam applications run an Amalgam *platform*. A platform includes a computing device (e.g., a RaspberryPi), a web programming runtime that includes JavaScript, DOM, and CSS (e.g., a web browser) that the applications run in and a *hardware abstraction layer (HAL)* that provides low-level access to hardware. A web server (running on the platform or remotely) serves the application. Figure 2 shows the components of an Amalgam platform and their relationships to an Amalgam application.

The HAL exposes a standard software interface (i.e., function calls) to common hardware interfaces (i.e., electrical connections to the platform hardware). For the HAL in Amalgam we implemented a version of the Arduino Reference Language [2] for Linux, we call it Linuxduino [7]. Linuxduino accesses low-level hardware through Linux's standard drivers, so it should be portable across the many Linux-based embedded systems that are available. Since it is Arduino-compatible, it supports a huge array of hardware components. Linuxduino was implemented in C++ and compiled to web assembly, so it runs directly in the JavaScript runtime.

The main difference between different Linux-based platforms is the set of electrical interfaces they provide. For instance, Raspberry PI provides 26 digital IO pins, two I2C interfaces, and two SPI interfaces, but no analog inputs or outputs. In addition, the platforms use different naming schemes for their pins.

These differences are visible to Amalgam programmers so moving an Amalgam program between platforms requires adjustments to the CSS that hardens the components. Likewise, if the hardware designer changes which pins connect a particular device to the platform, the CSS must change as well.

2.3   The Amalgam Library

To explore Amalgam's ability to accelerate the design of complex hard/soft interfaces, we built seven hard elements that match existing soft elements HTML interfaces. Table 1 summarizes the elements Amalgam currently supports.

The range of possible hard elements is broader than the set of elements that HTML provides, because many different hardware devices can replace a single HTML element, and even similar hardware devices may connect to the system through different interfaces.

For instance, the example in Fig. 1 hardened the <input> into a potentiometer (or "pot") that connected via one ADC channel. It could have instead used a "rotary encoder" that connects via two digital IO lines or a "motorized slide pot" that requires an ADC line and three digital IO lines, two lines to control the motor direction and one to get the user slider touch feedback.

The Amalgam library has entries for each of these alternatives. Their internal software implementations are quite different despite appearing the same to the application (i.e., as a range <input>).

Adding new hard elements to Amalgam requires two steps. The first is creating a web component that will interface with the hardware device. The component encapsulates the firmware (written in JavaScript) that controls the hardware via the HAL.

For example, Listing 1.1 is a class that implements a hard button by extending HTMLElement and providing three methods: get_observedAttributes() defines the attributes this element supports. Whenever an attribute changes, including when an element is hardened, attributeChangedCallback() runs and gets updated. Finally, the runtime invokes connectedCallback() once after the attributes are updated, indicating that the web component is ready. Here initialization and configuration of hardware is carried out. In this case, a given GPIO number, set in the GPIO attribute value, is configured as input and is physically connected to a button. After that, another function sets up a call back that polls the IO pin every 200 ms, which is enough to detect a button press, and emulates a click when it detects a physical button press (lines 13–18). For this example, the GPIO number can only be initialized once but it works for our embedded device prototypes requirements.

```
1   class PHYSICAL_BUTTON extends HTMLElement {
2     constructor () { super(); this.gpio; }
3
4     // Monitor attribute changes.
5     static get observedAttributes() {
6       return ['onclick', 'gpio'];
7     }
8
9     connectedCallback() {
10       // Initialize GPIO
11       Linuxduino.pinMode(this.gpio, Linuxduino.INPUT);
12       // Start Reading GPIO
13       setInterval( () => {
14         // Call 'onclick' if physical button pressed
15         if (Linuxduino.digitalRead(this.gpio) == Linuxduino.HIGH) {
16           this.click();
17         }
18       },200);
19     }
20
21     // Respond to attribute changes.
22     attributeChangedCallback(attr, oldValue, newValue){
23       if (attr == 'gpio') {
24         this.gpio = parseFloat(newValue);
25       }
26     }
27
28   }
29   customElements.define('physical-button',PHYSICAL_BUTTON);
```

Listing 1.1. A hard element button code example which consist of a typical web component code plus calls to hardware using the Linuxduino HAL library.

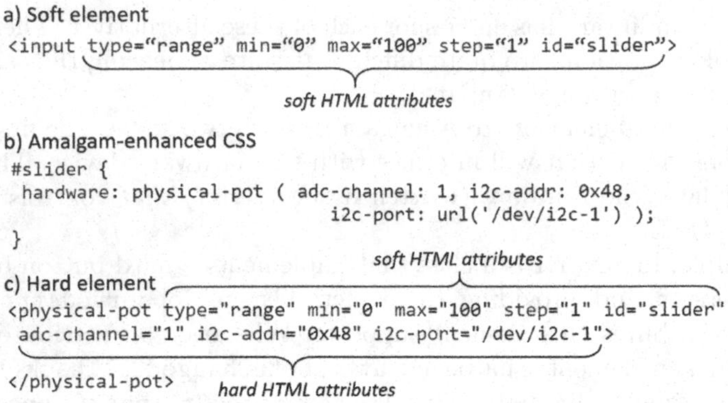

a) Soft element

```
<input type="range" min="0" max="100" step="1" id="slider">
```
soft HTML attributes

b) Amalgam-enhanced CSS

```
#slider {
  hardware: physical-pot ( adc-channel: 1, i2c-addr: 0x48,
                           i2c-port: url('/dev/i2c-1') );
}
```
soft HTML attributes

c) Hard element

```
<physical-pot type="range" min="0" max="100" step="1" id="slider"
 adc-channel="1" i2c-addr="0x48" i2c-port="/dev/i2c-1">

</physical-pot>
```
hard HTML attributes

Fig. 3. Amalgam compiler hardening of soft elements, (a) Shows a soft element selected by an Amalgam-enhanced CSS property in (b). After compilation (c) shows the hard element HTML which replaces (a).

Table 1. Amalgam's hard elements

Hard element tag	Amalgam version	Compatible soft element tag	Notes
\<physical-pot>	Rotary Potentiometer (or "pot")	\<input type="range">	Triggers 'oninput' when potentiometer input value is changed
\<physical-encoder>	Rotary encoder	\<input type="range">	Triggers 'oninput' when potentiometer input value is changed
\<physical-motorized-pot>	Linear motorized pot	\<input type="range">	Triggers 'oninput' when potentiometer input value is changed, also setting the 'value' attribute can set the slider position
\<physical-rgb-led>	RGB LED	\<div>	Color is set to the CSS background-color property
\<physical-button>	Tactile push-button	\<button>	Triggers 'onclick' event at button press
\<physical-servo-motor>	Servo motor	\<div>	Servo angle is set to angle rotation of CSS transform property
\<physical-lcd>	LCD text display	\<span>	Text is set with a hard attribute
\<physical-seven-segments>	LED numerical display	\<spa>	Numbers are set with a hard attribute
\<physical-weight-sensor>	Load cell	\<input type="range">	Measured weight is available via Angular ng-bind attribute

The final step is to register the new class with Amalgam so the programmer can use it to harden elements. The code in Listing 1.1 defines a new HTML tag called `<physical-button>` that the programmer can use directly (e.g., `<physical-button onclick="foo()" gpio="1"></physical-button>`) to create a hard button. The registration process makes the Amalgam CSS compiler aware of the class so it can replace an existing tag (e.g., a `<button>`) with a `<physical-button>`.

2.4 Amalgam-Enhanced CSS Style

The `hardware` CSS style attribute controls if and how Amalgam hardens a DOM element. The value of `hardware` describes which hard component should replace the software component and describes which electrical interfaces the corresponding hardware device will connect to.

Figure 3 exemplifies the Amalgam compiler. There (b) shows the CSS code required to harden a soft element (a). Each value for `hardware` starts with the name of the hard component that Amalgam will use to replace the soft element. The remaining arguments are of the form $attr(value)$ that Amalgam uses to set the hard HTML attributes on the hard element (c) it creates. The hard element as well will inherit soft HTML attributes from the soft element in (a) to keep the same web application functionality without any changes. Our prototype implementation uses a JavaScript CSS processor to scan a pages style sheets for `hardware` declarations, and then harden the elements appropriately.

3 Examples

To demonstrate Amalgam, we built three devices[1]: A video player, an commercial food scale, and a dancing speaker. Each device started with an on-screen, soft prototype. We hardened some of the soft components and built a physical prototype of the device. The Amalgam platform used is Raspberry Pi running Linux and Electron [3]. Electron is used to allow web applications to access the file system and hardware through Node.js [8].

3.1 Video Player

The video player appliance (Fig. 4) demonstrates Amalgam's ability to transform an existing web page into the firmware for a physical device. The left side of the figure shows the soft video player built with the Youtube Player API [14]. It provides a familiar on-screen interface for playing videos, including the slider that both displays and controls the playhead location.

---

[1] The code is available at https://github.com/NVSL/amalgam.

The right side of the figure shows the appliance we built. Videos appear on the screen, but all the rest of the interface is hard. The only difference in software the CSS directives to hardened the three buttons, the volume control, and slider (Listing 1.2). The appliance mimics all the behavior of the original, including the progress bar. We hardened it into a motorized potentiometer that both the software and the user can actuate.

3.2   Commercial Scale

The scale appliance (Fig. 5) shows Amalgam's ability to simplify and accelerated prototyping iterations. The scale has two users: the customer and the salesperson. The salesperson can select products from an illustrated list, see the price per pound, weigh the item, and adjust the scale by zeroing it or setting a tare weight (to account for the weight of a container), and show the total. The customer can see the item's name and the total price displayed on a second display on the reverse side.

Fig. 4. Video Player: At left, a demo of a video player which provides a familiar on-screen interface for playing videos. At right, Amalgam allows the same demo to drive a fully-tactile interface, the only difference being the style sheet.

The soft version (at left) implements the application logic and these interfaces and via soft elements. The developer can perfect the application logic (including varying the weight on the virtual scale) in a web browser without access to any hardware. The hardware prototype in the center provides a completely soft salesperson interface. While the one at right uses hard components for the buttons and numeric displays. Both of them have a hard customer display. The only software difference between all three versions is a few lines of CSS.

We implemented the soft version using Angular [1], a sophisticated model-view-controller library. Angular makes it trivial to "bind" the output of the load cell to the weight display. Since Amalgam's hard elements have the same interface as normal DOM elements, this works just as easily with hard elements.

```
1   <link rel="import" href="amalgam/amalgam.html">
2   ...
3   <!-- Soft elements -->
4   <body>
5   <button onclick="playPause()" id="playPause">Play/Pause</button>
6   <input type="range" min="0" max="10" step="1" value="0" id="progressBar">
7   </body>
8   <!-- Amalgam-enchanced CSS -->
9   <style>
10  #playPause {
11      hardware: physical-button(gpio:var(--gpio5));
12  }
13  #progressBar {
14      hardware: physical-motorized-pot (motora:var(--gpio23), motorb:var(
            --gpio24),
15      touch:var(--gpio25), adc-channel: 2, i2c-addr: 0x48, i2c-port:url("
            /dev/i2c-1"));
16  }
17  </style>
```

Listing 1.2. Video Player Code. At the top we show only two of the software components of the Video Player web application, the play-pause button and the progress bar. At the bottom the Amalgam-enhanced CSS required to harden the software elements, process that is carried out by the compiler at run-time.

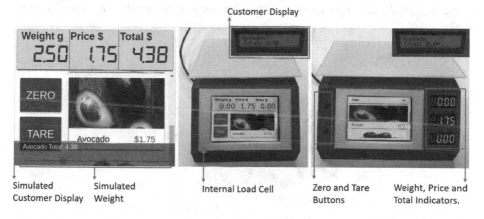

Fig. 5. Evolving Scale: Amalgam allows a spectrum of different implementations with minimal developer effort. From left to right: a software-only mock-up includes a virtual, on-screen load cell and supports software development; a "soft" interface version that uses a touch screen for the main screen and buttons and an LCD for the rear screen; and hybrid version that uses 7-segment displays and tactile buttons.

3.3 Dancing Speaker

Our dancing speaker is a simple demo that (Fig. 6) highlights the power of CSS animations to control hardware. The speaker plays and "dances" to music by waving its arms and flashing lights in time to music. It is a fanciful design that a "maker" might assemble as a hobby project.

Assembling the hardware for the dancing elements is simple, but writing the software for control (e.g., beat detection and complex coordinated transitions) is complex. Instead of writing that code from scratch, our design leverages an unmodified, third-party library called Rythm.js [10] that can make any website dance in time to the music. Rythm.js uses CSS classes (e.g. "rythm twist1") to represent background color and angle rotation changes to <div> tags. Applying those classes to the servos and LEDs makes them dance just as well. Listing 1.3 shows the HTML and CSS implementation of our dancing speaker.

4 Impact on Development Time

Amalgam's goal is to make it easier for developers to build physical devices with rich interfaces. To quantify its effectiveness, we built two other versions of the video player: One using pure JavaScript and another using JavaScript and C.

The "C+JS" version uses a simple server implemented in C that exposes hardware components via a TCP socket. The JavaScript that implements the application logic communicates with it via TCP sockets. The "Pure JS" version calls the HAL directly to control the hardware and implements the same functionality that Amalgam's hard elements implement internally. We refer to this as *glue code*.

Fig. 6. Our dancing speaker

```
1   <link rel="import" href="amalgam/amalgam.html">
2   ...
3   <body>
4   <button onclick="playPause()" id="playPause"
5     style="hardware: physical-button( gpio: var(--gpio5) )"> playPause
6   </button>  <!-- Play/Pause button -->
7   <button onclick="prevSong()" id="prev"
8     style="hardware: physical-button( gpio: var(--gpio6) )"> Prev
9   </button>  <!-- Previous Song button -->
10  <button onclick="nextSong()" id="next"
11    style="hardware: physical-button( gpio: var(--gpio12) )"> Next
12  </button> <!-- Next Song button -->
13  <input type="range" min="0" max="1" step="0.1" value="1" id="slider"
```

```
14    style="hardware: physical-pot( adc-channel: 1, i2c-port: url('/dev/i2c-1'),
15    i2c-addr: 0x48"> <!-- Volume -->
16  <div class="rythm color1"
17    style="hardware: physical-rgb-led( spi-port: url('/dev/spidev0.0') )">
18  </div> <!-- RGB LEDs -->
19  <div class="rythm twist1"
20    style="hardware: physical-servo-motor( servo-channel: 0, i2c-port: url('/dev/i2c-1
       ' ), i2c-addr: 0x48 )">
21  </div> <!-- Servo Motor 1 -->
22  <div class="rythm twist2"
23    style="hardware: physical-servo-motor( servo-channel: 3, i2c-port: url('
       /dev/i2c-1' ),  i2c-addr: 0x40 )">
24  </div> <!-- Servo Motor 2 -->
25  </body>
```

Listing 1.3. Dancing speaker code implementation using Amalgam-enhanced CSS.

Figure 7 compares the lines of code (LOC) required to integrate the hardware components into each version of the application. The measurements do not include the frameworks, libraries, or the server and communication code for C+JS. We also include the lines of code added or changed in the application code to accommodate the change from soft element to hard elements (labeled as "invasive" changes).

The figure shows that Amalgam vastly reduces the effort required to harden components: five lines of CSS in one file compared to over eighty lines of JavaScript and CSS spread throughout the application for Pure JS and C+JS. Amalgam avoids invasive changes completely.

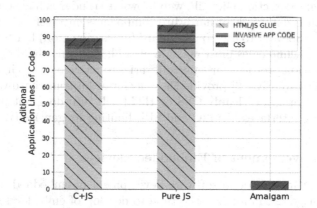

Fig. 7. Programming Effort: Deeply integration of hardware components interfaces into the web languages allows Amalgam to reduce the lines of code needed to integrate these components into web application based electronic devices, therefore reducing development time.

5   Related Work

Amalgam seamlessly integrates hardware components into HTML, CSS, and JavaScript to reduce development effort and facilitate faster prototyping. Below, we place Amalgam in context with other projects with similar goals.

5.1   Integration of Hardware to Web Technologies

Several previous projects have focused on the integration of hardware to web technologies. In particular, the Web of Things [20], and IoT protocols such as MQTT [22] and SOAP [16]. These IoT protocols use web programming technologies (e.g., HTTP, Web Sockets, XML, etc.) to interface remotely with hardware devices which have integrated sensors and actuators. As hardware devices become more powerful at a reduced cost [24] embedded developers are looking to use web programming technologies to also interface locally with hardware. Related efforts adapt JavaScript to run on constrained devices (e.g JerryScript [18]).

Web Browsers have become an extensively used platform that can run across heterogeneous hardware and software platforms, and they provide access to a limited number of hardware components like cameras and microphones [5] via standardized JavaScript APIs.

As web technologies are becoming popular on embedded, mobile devices, other standards for interfacing with hardware components have been included, such as Bluetooth low energy [12] and sensors like accelerometers, gyroscopes and ambient light detection [4]. Still, web browsers standards have not been able to keep up with the myriads of hardware components currently available.

Developers who want to use non-standard (or less common) hardware components with web technologies must do so in an ad hoc manner by developing custom communication protocols or "glue" libraries to provide access in JavaScript. Projects like Jhonny-Five [6] provide these facilities for some hardware devices, but it does not integrate cleanly CSS or HTML. It also does not provide easy access to generic interfaces like I2C and SPI, limiting its generality.

5.2   Rapid Development of Embedded Devices

Many tools exist for the rapid software development of embedded devices. The Arduino Language [2], minimizes the time to develop of embedded software on microcontroller platforms by hiding their low level complexity behind a simple library. TinyLink [19] reduces the lines of code by providing tools that generate the underlying hardware interfaces and binaries required for a target platform. Microsoft .NET Gadgeteer [25] uses a modular hardware platform that is deeply integrated into the Microsoft Visual Studio IDE. Gadgeteer provides hardware abstraction libraries for each supported module and facilitate development by using C# as its main programming language.

Amalgam is similar in some respects to both Arduino and the software support in Gadgeteer: All three projects aim to integrate hardware support into the host language (C for Arduino, C# for Gadgeteer, and Javascript/CSS/HTML for Amalgam). Amalgam, however, improves on the usability of the others by leveraging the flexibility and power of web programming technologies.

6 Conclusions

In this paper, we present Amalgam, a toolkit that deeply integrates hardware devices into web programming technologies. Amalgam enables rapid development and more flexible design iteration for embedded devices. Amalgam lets developers replace soft interface components with hardware components just by changing a CSS file. We implemented Amalgam and evaluated its capabilities by prototyping three devices in a web browser and then "hardening" them into standalone devices. Our results show that Amalgam can significantly reduce the programmer effort required to implement the software for electronic devices.

References

1. AngularJS - Superheroic JavaScript MVW Framework. https://angularjs.org/
2. Arduino Reference. https://www.arduino.cc/reference/en/
3. Electron—Build Cross Platform Desktop Apps with JavaScript, HTML, and CSS. https://electronjs.org/
4. Generic Sensor API. https://www.w3.org/TR/generic-sensor
5. HTML Media Capture. https://www.w3.org/TR/html-media-capture/
6. Johnny-Five: The JavaScript Robotics & IoT Platform. http://johnny-five.io/
7. Linuxduino - A JavScript Library for Communicating with Hardware in a Arduino Style Programming for Any Linux Platform. http://www.w3.org/TR/html5
8. Node.js. https://nodejs.org/en/
9. Raspberry Pi - Teach, Learn, and Make with Raspberry Pi. https://www.raspberrypi.org/
10. Rythm.js - GitHub Pages. https://okazari.github.io/Rythm.js/
11. Specifications - webcomponents.org. https://www.webcomponents.org/specs
12. Web Bluetooth Community Group. www.w3.org/community/web-bluetooth
13. WebAssembly. https://webassembly.org/
14. YouTube Player API Reference for iframe Embeds - Google Developers. https://developers.google.com/youtube/iframe_api_reference
15. Volder, K.: JQuery: a generic code browser with a declarative configuration language. In: Van Hentenryck, P. (ed.) PADL 2006. LNCS, vol. 3819, pp. 88–102. Springer, Heidelberg (2005). https://doi.org/10.1007/11603023_7
16. Dürkop, L., Imtiaz, J., Trsek, H., Jasperneite, J.: Service-oriented architecture for the autoconfiguration of real-time ethernet systems. In: 3rd Annual Colloquium Communication in Automation (KommA) (2012)
17. EETimes: 2017 Embedded Markets Study: Integrating IoT and Advanced Technology Designs, Application Development Processing Environments, April 2017. https://m.eet.com/media/1246048/2017-embedded-market-study.pdf

18. Gavrin, E., Lee, S.J., Ayrapetyan, R., Shitov, A.: Ultra lightweight JavaScript engine for Internet of Things. In: Companion Proceedings of the 2015 ACM SIG-PLAN International Conference on Systems, Programming, Languages and Applications: Software for Humanity, SPLASH Companion 2015, pp. 19–20. ACM, New York (2015). https://doi.org/10.1145/2814189.2816270. http://doi.acm.org/10.1145/2814189.2816270
19. Guan, G., Dong, W., Gao, Y., Fu, K., Cheng, Z.: TinyLink: a holistic system for rapid development of IoT applications. In: Proceedings of the 23rd Annual International Conference on Mobile Computing and Networking, pp. 383–395. ACM (2017)
20. Guinard, D., Trifa, V.: Towards the Web of Things: web mashups for embedded devices. In: Workshop on Mashups, Enterprise Mashups and Lightweight Composition on the Web (MEM 2009), in Proceedings of WWW (International World Wide Web Conferences), Madrid, vol. 15 (2009)
21. Kuc, R., Jackson, E.W., Kuc, A.: Teaching introductory autonomous robotics with JavaScript simulations and actual robots. IEEE Trans. Educ. **47**(1), 74–82 (2004)
22. Locke, D.: MQ Telemetry Transport (MQTT) v3. 1 Protocol Specification. IBM Developer Works Technical Library (2010)
23. Osentoski, S., Jay, G., Crick, C., Pitzer, B., DuHadway, C., Jenkins, O.C.: Robots as web services: reproducible experimentation and application development using rosjs. In: IEEE International Conference on Robotics and Automation (ICRA), pp. 6078–6083. IEEE (2011)
24. Schlett, M.: Trends in embedded-microprocessor design. Computer **31**(8), 44–49 (1998). https://doi.org/10.1109/2.707616
25. Villar, N., Scott, J., Hodges, S., Hammil, K., Miller, C.:NET gadgeteer: a platform for custom devices. In: Kay, J., Lukowicz, P., Tokuda, H., Olivier, P., Krüger, A. (eds.) Pervasive 2012. LNCS, vol. 7319, pp. 216–233. Springer, Heidelberg (2012). https://doi.org/10.1007/978-3-642-31205-2_14

Jekyll RDF: Template-Based Linked Data Publication with Minimized Effort and Maximum Scalability

Natanael Arndt[1,2]([✉]) [iD], Sebastian Zänker[2], Gezim Sejdiu[3] [iD], and Sebastian Tramp[4] [iD]

[1] AKSW, Leipzig University, Augustusplatz 10, 04109 Leipzig, Germany
`arndt@informatik.uni-leipzig.de`
[2] Institut für Angewandte Informatik e.V., Goerdelerring 9, 04109 Leipzig, Germany
`zaenker@infai.org`
[3] Smart Data Analytics, University of Bonn, Endenicher Allee 19a, 53115 Bonn, Germany
`sejdiu@cs.uni-bonn.de`
[4] eccenca GmbH, Hainstr. 8, 04109 Leipzig, Germany
`sebastian.tramp@eccenca.com`
`http://aksw.org/NatanaelArndt`,
`http://aksw.org/SebastianZaenker`, `http://sda.tech/Person/GezimSejdiu/`,
`https://sebastian.tramp.name`

Abstract. Over the last decades the Web has evolved from a human–human communication network to a network of complex human–machine interactions. An increasing amount of data is available as Linked Data which allows machines to "understand" the data, but RDF is not meant to be understood by humans. With Jekyll RDF we present a method to close the gap between structured data and human accessible exploration interfaces by publishing RDF datasets as customizable static HTML sites. It consists of an RDF resource mapping system to serve the resources under their respective IRI, a template mapping based on schema classes, and a markup language to define templates to render customized resource pages. Using the template system, it is possible to create domain specific browsing interfaces for RDF data next to the Linked Data resources. This enables content management and knowledge management systems to serve datasets in a highly customizable, low effort, and scalable way to be consumed by machines as well as humans.

Keywords: Data visualization · Data publication · Static site generation · Content Management · Semantic templating · Linked Data

1 Introduction

In 2001 Tim Berners-Lee and James Hendler stated: *The Web was designed as an information space, with the goal not only that it should be useful for human–human communication, but also that machines would be able to participate and*

© Springer Nature Switzerland AG 2019
M. Bakaev et al. (Eds.): ICWE 2019, LNCS 11496, pp. 331–346, 2019.
https://doi.org/10.1007/978-3-030-19274-7_24

help users communicate with each other [6]. Now 18 years later we are at the point that a huge amount of data is published as Linked Data as it is apparent in the *Linked Open Data Cloud*[1] with 1,234 datasets and 16,136 links between the datasets[2]. But the RDF data is not suited and meant to be read and understood by humans. On the informal *Semantic Web Layer Model*[3] the top most layer represents *User Interface & Applications*. A great variety of applications exist to visualize RDF data. Such applications are table based triple explorers, like *pubby*[4], *LOD View*[5], and *LD Viewer/DBpedia Viewer* [17,18] and visual graph explorers like *LodLive*[6], *LODmilla* [20], and *Linked Data Maps* [21]. These applications are restricted to a view that is very close to the RDF data model and are thus suited for data experts who understand the concepts of RDF and the respective vocabularies, but not suitable for end users.

Web Content Management Systems (WCMS) are software systems to support the processes to create, manage, provide, control, and customize content for websites [11]. Besides the management of the content in a Content Repository, the customizable presentation using templating systems is a key aspect of WCMS. Semantic Content Management Systems (SCMS) extend Content Management Systems with additional functionality to enrich the content with semantic metadata in a Knowledge Repository. Nowadays we are at the point that the semantic data is not "only" meta-data, but encodes the information itself. The activity to manage the semantic data as information by itself is called Semantic Data Management and gets a lot of attention [4,8]. To make this semantic data available to end users there is a need for semantic templating systems which is experiencing little research so far.

In this work, we present an approach for the generation of static Web exploration interfaces on Linked Data. The approach is based on devising a declarative DSL to create templates to render instance data. The templates are associated to RDF classes and a breath-first search algorithm determines the best-suitable template for any given data resource. To demonstrate the feasibility of the approach, we implemented it as an extension to the popular Jekyll[7] Static Site Generator and CMS[8]. In contrast to dynamic web pages, static web pages are preparatively generated and can be served without further server-side computation, thus providing highest possible scalability. This approach is complementary to the data focused approach of Linked Data Fragments[9] to reduce costly server-side request evaluation. By rendering RDF data to static HTML sites we provide a method to browse the Semantic Web seamlessly integrated with the rest of the

---

[1] http://lod-cloud.net/.

[2] As of June 2018.

[3] https://www.w3.org/2007/03/layerCake.svg.

[4] http://wifo5-03.informatik.uni-mannheim.de/pubby/.

[5] http://lodview.it, https://github.com/dvcama/LodView.

[6] http://en.lodlive.it/, https://github.com/dvcama/LodLive.

[7] https://jekyllrb.com/, https://www.staticgen.com/, https://www.netlify.com/blog/2016/05/02/top-ten-static-website-generators/.

[8] https://www.siteleaf.com/, https://www.netlifycms.org/.

[9] http://linkeddatafragments.org/.

Web and close the gap between structured data and human accessible exploration interfaces. To the best of our knowledge Jekyll RDF[10] is the first approach to apply the concept of Static Site Generators to RDF knowledge bases. In contrast to the state of the art (cf. Sect. 2) it does not require programming knowledge of its user, does not need a dynamic back-end nor it is integrated in an IDE. It is provided as a standalone tool inspired by the UNIX (and more recently micro-service) philosophy to *make each program do one thing well* [12]. Because of the separation of concerns it is integrable with existing content management and knowledge management workflows. Due to the modular conception the presented method should be transferable to further Static Site Generators like Next, Hugo, and Hyde[11] or complex frameworks like Gatsby[12].

In this paper we first give an introduction to the state of the art in Sect. 2. Then we provide an overview on the Static Site Generator architecture with detailed descriptions of the core components in Sect. 3. An important aspect of the separation of concerns approach is the ability to integrate a tool with larger systems to accomplish high-level tasks. We present the integration of the Static Site Generator in a Linked Data tool chain in Sect. 4. The Jekyll RDF system is already used in several setups from various domains which we present in Sect. 5. Finally, we draw our conclusions and outline future work in Sect. 6.

2   State of the Art

The generic data model provided by RDF allows the publication of data representing various domains and their aspects on the Web. The abstraction of the data model from its representation opens the possibility for arbitrary visualizations of the data. A great variety of systems exists that provide ways to access and visualize RDF data [13,16]. Many systems are created to serve a specific purpose such as visualizing a specific dataset or data expressed using a specific vocabulary. In the following we focus on frameworks and template based systems that provide a generic tooling to create custom exploration and visualization interfaces that are usable for any RDF dataset.

Templating systems usually provide a flexible approach for inserting data into a scaffolding of an HTML page. The *SPARQL Web Pages*[13] system defines a templating language that allows to incorporate data from an RDF graph into HTML and SVG documents. It is shipped with the commercial version of the *TopBraid Composer*. A similar approach is followed by *LESS* [5] which later was integrated with the *OntoWiki* [10]. The *OntoWiki Site Extension*[14] [9] allows to render RDF resources in HTML views using a PHP base templating language. To serve the required representation of a Linked Data resources the OntoWiki

---

[10] https://github.com/AKSW/jekyll-rdf.
[11] https://nextjs.org/, https://gohugo.io/, http://hyde.github.io/.
[12] https://gatsbyjs.org/.
[13] http://uispin.org/.
[14] https://github.com/AKSW/site.ontowiki.

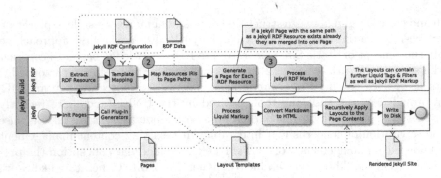

Fig. 1. The architecture of Jekyll RDF and its interplay with Jekyll.

Linked Data server uses content negotiation to dynamically serve an HTML view to web browsers and an RDF representation to Linked Data systems.

A different approach to provide customizable web interfaces to explore and even edit RDF data is presented by Khalili et al. with the *LD-R* [14]. It provides a framework to define *Linked Data-driven Web Components* in JavaScript. With this framework it is possible to reuse existing components and compose new dynamic web interfaces. A similar approach to build *Semantic Interfaces for Web Applications* is presented with the MIRA framework [7]. It defines an *abstract interface definition* that composes elements to form a hierarchy of widgets. These widgets can be used in JavaScript applications to build responsive user interfaces.

In summary, the related work of LD-R and MIRA [7,14] as well as complex frameworks like Gatsby aim at programmers and software engineers. The previous work of LESS and the OntoWiki Site Extension [5,9,10] provides a template based approach. But LESS and OntoWiki Site Extension as well as the application frameworks presented in [7,14] rely on a server side complex *dynamic* data management system. In this paper, our aim is to provide a *static* approach to maximize the scalability while minimizing the effort by following a templated based approach that can be used without programming knowledge.

3   The Static Site Generation Architecture

We conceived our system as an extension to existing Static Site Generators. A Static Site Generator usually translates a set of HTML and Markdown files (*pages*) to a collection of HTML files (*site*) by using structural *templates*. Pages and templates can be conditionally formatted and enriched with tags and filters defined by a markup language to embed data values and alter the presentation. The generated site is served either with an integrated web server or any other HTTP server. To showcase our approach we implemented Jekyll RDF[15] as a plugin for the popular Jekyll system.

The plugin system of Jekyll provides among others the possibility to add a *generator* to create new pages and to implement custom *tags* and *filters* for the

---

[15] https://github.com/AKSW/jekyll-rdf.

Listing 1. The sections of the Jekyll configuration relevant for Jekyll RDF including base url, data source, selection of resources, and template mappings.

```
1   baseurl: "/sachsen/"
2   url: "http://pfarrerbuch.aksw.org"
3   plugins: [jekyll-rdf]
4   jekyll_rdf:
5     path: "sachsen.ttl"
6     restriction: "SELECT ?resourceUri WHERE {?resourceUri ?p ?o . FILTER
      ↪ regex(str(?resourceUri),
      ↪ '^http://pfarrerbuch.aksw.org/sachsen/')}"
7     default_template: "resource"
8     class_template_mappings:
9       "http://xmlns.com/foaf/0.1/Person": "person"
10      "http://purl.org/voc/hp/Place": "place"
11      "http://purl.org/voc/hp/Position": "position"
12    instance_template_mappings:
13      "http://pfarrerbuch.aksw.org/": "home"
```

Liquid markup language[16]. Jekyll RDF uses this system to provide its main functionalities as depicted in Fig. 1: (1, 2) generate a Jekyll page for each resource from the RDF graph (cf. Sects. 3.1 and 3.2), and (3) extend the markup language by a set of filters and tags to query the RDF graph (*Jekyll RDF Markup Language*, cf. Sect. 3.3). *Jekyll* controls the main flow of the build process which is depicted in the lower row. The particular tasks which are relevant for the rendering of RDF data are depicted in the upper row. The process needs several data artifacts namely, the *pages* to be rendered by Jekyll, the *configuration* options which are specific to Jekyll RDF, the *RDF data*, and the *templates* to defined the layout of the pages and RDF resources. The process to generate a Jekyll page for each RDF resource is split into four steps, extract the RDF resource from the RDF data model as specified in the configuration (cf. Listing 1) and create program objects accordingly, map the resources to templates, map the IRIs of the RDF resources to according page paths, and generate a Jekyll page object for each RDF resource. The template mapping (no. 1 in Fig. 1) can happen directly per RDF resource or based on the RDF types of a resource, this is described in detail in Sect. 3.1. Design decisions required to represent the RDF resource's IRIs in the path system of Jekyll are explained in Sect. 3.2 (no. 2). Further, Liquid is extended to the *Jekyll RDF Markup Language* which is presented in Sect. 3.3 (no. 3).

In Listing 1 an exemplary configuration file for Jekyll is provided with the relevant sections to configure a Jekyll RDF setup. Lines 1 and 2 together represent the URL under which a Jekyll site is served. In line 3 the Jekyll RDF plugin is registered. Lines 4 to 13 are the specific parameters to configure Jekyll RDF, the path (line 5) specifies the data source for the RDF data and the restriction (line 6) specifies the list of RDF resources to be rendered. Lines 7 to 13 specify the template mapping and are further described in Sect. 3.1.

---

[16] https://shopify.github.io/liquid/,
https://shopify.github.io/liquid/basics/introduction/.

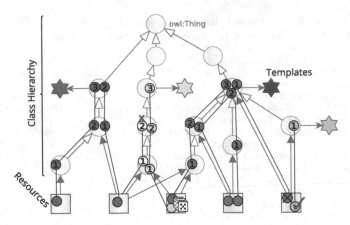

Fig. 2. The class hierarchy is used to select the template to render a resource.

3.1   Template Mapping

Jekyll provides a templating system to allow the reuse of components on multiple pages and allow similar pages to look alike. The template for a Jekyll page is specified in a header in the page. During the rendering process Jekyll applies this template to the content of the page. In contrast to a Jekyll page an RDF resources has no "content" and no header and thus we need to specify the representation of the resource. In the following we introduce three mapping mechanisms to determine which template should be applied for a resource. The template assignment configuration is shown in lines 7 to 13 in Listing 1. In the `instance_template_mappings` section each resource can be directly assigned to a template by specifying the resource IRI and the template name. Further, two indirect options to assign a template are specified. In the section `class_template_mappings` RDF classes are mapped to templates. Each resource that is an instance of a specified class or its subclasses gets this template assigned. The precedence order of the template mappings is: instance based, class based, `default_template`.

Other than for the instance based and default mapping the class template mapping introduces ambiguity as depicted in Fig. 2. If a resource has multiple classes and each has a template assigned, it can not be decided which template to use for the resource. The template selection can not be limited to the trivial evaluation of rdf:type triples as this would not take the assignment of templates to super classes into account. Inferencing along rdfs:subClassOf relations would also be no good approach as it introduces more ambiguity and hides precedence information about the most specific class for a resource.

We decided to select the template for an instance according to three rules as depicted in Fig. 2 (a *candidate* is a class that has a template assigned). (1) Select the closest candidate in the class hierarchy, (2) if more then one candidate exists with different templates but with the same shortest path distance, take the candidate with the most *specific* class, (3) if still no candidate could be

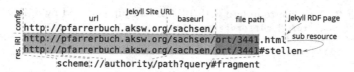

Fig. 3. Scheme of the selection of page paths based on the configured Jekyll Site URL.

selected, produce a warning and randomly select one of the candidates. A class
a is considered more *specific* than *b* if an rdfs:subClassOf property path exists
from *a* to *b* but not the other way around. To implement the template selection
we chose a breath-first-search algorithm on the class hierarchy. To avoid cycles,
visited classes are marked. Once a suitable templates is selected all classes along
the search path are annotated with their distance to the selected candidate and
a reference to the selected template. These annotations can be used to prune
the search space of subsequent iterations. To optimize the overall process for
resources with the same sets of classes we maintain a dictionary of the hashed
sorted list of class IRIs and the selected template throughout the rendering
process. Using this dictionary no resource that is subsequently rendered with
the same set of classes needs to initiate a new template selection process.

3.2   Resource Mapping and Site Creation

Jekyll RDF is meant to provide an HTML view for Linked Data resources and
thus we need to map the resource's HTTP IRIs to file system paths, which is
depicted in Fig. 3. Taking an RDF resource Jekyll RDF matches it with the
Jekyll Site URL as it is set in lines 1 and 2 of the configuration in Listing 1.
The matched part is than removed from the resource IRI and the remaining part
`ort/3441` is mapped to the file path `ort/3441.html`. A query string in an IRI
can be treated in the same way as a path. A fragment part is interpreted and
truncated by the browser during a request, thus the second resource IRI ends
up at the same IRI as the previous one. As fragment identifiers are usually used
to identify anchors in HTML pages, all IRIs with a fragment are added to a list
data structure (`page.subResources`) of the respective non fragment IRI page.
All resources that do not match the configured base IRI are rendered with a,
currently unstable, fallback solution under the directory `rdfsites`.

It is possible that a resource created by Jekyll RDF would overwrite a page
that was already generated by Jekyll or any other plugin. In this case Jekyll
RDF merges the two page object into one page and copies the content of the
previously existing page into the content variable (cf. Sect. 3.3) of the template
selected for the RDF resource. If a template is specified for the Jekyll page it
overwrites the template selected for the RDF resource.

Listing 2. A simple template with HTML markup enriched by JML filters.

```
1    <h1>{{ page.rdf | rdf_property: "rdfs:label", "en" }}</h1>
2    <div>{{ page.rdf | rdf_property: "dct:created" | date: "%Y-%m-%d"
       ↪ }}</div>
3
4    {% assign publicationlist = "ex:publicationlist" | rdf_container %}
5    <ul>
6    {% for pub in publicationlist %}
7    <li>{{ pub | rdf_property: "dc:title" }}</li>
8    <li>{{ pub | rdf_property: "dct:creator", false, true | join: ","
       ↪ }}</li>
9    {% endfor %}
10   </ul>
```

Table 1. The filters defined by Jekyll RDF and the tasks performed by them.

Filter	Parameters ([optional])	Description
`rdf_get`		Get a variable representing a resource from the RDF graph
`rdf_property`	IRI, [language, bool]	Get a value of a property of a resource (lines 1, 2, and 7 of Listing 2). If the last parameter is set to true an array is returned (line 8)
`rdf_inverse_property`	IRI, [bool]	Get the value of an inverse property
`rdf_collection` and `rdf_container`	[IRI]	Get RDF collections and RDF containers from the RDF graph as shown in line 4 of Listing 2
`sparql_query`	sparql query	Execute a SPARQL Query on the RDF graph, the passed value is bound to `?resourceUri` or to `?resourceUri_n` if an array is provided

3.3   Jekyll RDF Markup Language

The Jekyll RDF Markup Language (JML) is based on Liquid and extends it by filters to access the RDF graph from within a template. Liquid provides the concepts of *objects*, *tags*, and *filters* (See Footnote 16). *Objects* define placeholders in a template to insert values and are denoted by two curly braces `{{ ... }}`. The special object `{{content}}` in templates is a placeholder for the content of the rendered page. *Tags* are used to embed control flow into the template, they are denoted by curly braces and percent signs `{% ... %}`. The tag `{% assign = "some value" %}` is used to assign a value to a variable. *Filters* manipulate the output of objects or the value of variables, they are chained and applied from left to right and separated by a vertical bar `|`. A filter gets a *value* passed from the left and can get *parameters* passed to the right after a colon `:` and separated by commas.

On every page which is generated by Jekyll RDF the variable `page.rdf` is present to reference the RDF resource represented by that page. To provide a way to access the RDF graph from within the template Jekyll RDF defines new Liquid filters as shown in Table 1 and Listing 2. The usage of Liquid filters allows to chain existing filters and filters defined by further plugins to the output of the JML filters. The JML filters accept a resource IRI as string or a resource object to be passed as value, they are shown and described in Table 1.

4   Integration with Data Publication Workflows

With our approach we follow the single responsibility principle: *Make each program do one thing well* [12]. This principle is recently gaining attention with the increase of the importance of *micro services* to manage complex software systems. Following this principle it is possible to integrate Jekyll RDF with existing tools, workflows, management systems, and interfaces to build a full SCMS or to support data engineers to publish RDF graphs as HTML pages. A pragmatic and in software engineering already proven successful approach for coordinating collaboration and exchange of artifacts is the usage of Git repositories. The Quit Store [2,3] is a method on top of Git to version and collaboratively manage RDF knowledge repositories. In the following we show two aspects to consider when integrating Jekyll RDF with data management and content management workflows. We present two setups that adapt the continuous integration method from software engineering to build flexible data publication workflows with Jekyll RDF in Sect. 4.1. To close the gap between structured data and human accessible browsing interfaces based on Jekyll RDF it is equally important to make the underlying RDF data available. We discuss possibilities to integrate the HTML and RDF publication with each other in Sect. 4.2.

4.1   Using Jekyll RDF with a Continuous Integration

Continuous Integration (CI) is a concept used in software engineering to automatically test, build, and deploy software artifacts. This concept recently increases in usage for data engineering [19]. With Jekyll RDF it is possible to define a step in a CI system to render and deploy pages whenever the data is updated. Travis CI[17] is a hosted continues integration service used to build and test software projects at GitHub. Using a continuous integration system during the work in a team allows to produce automated builds and feedback during the development process whenever a contributor updates the templates or data in the Git repository. In Fig. 4 we show two possible setups of automatic continuous deployment pipelines to publish Jekyll RDF sites. The setup in Fig. 4a shows a completely publicly hosted setup that uses the Travis CI service to build the Jekyll RDF site and the webspace provided by GitHub pages to serve the produced Static Site. This setup allows a flexible collaboration system combined with a free of charge deployment without the need to maintain a complex

---

[17] https://travis-ci.org.

340   N. Arndt et al.

infrastructure. The setup in Fig. 4b is slightly complexer and allows the differentiation between a stable "master" version and an unstable "develop" version. In combination with Docker it is possible to build ready to deploy system images including the rendered site. Whenever an updated system image is available the deployment restarts the respective service with the updated image.

4.2 Integration with RDF Publication

Following the Linked Data principle: *When someone looks up a URI, provide useful information, using the standards (RDF*, SPARQL)*[18] one page is created for each resource in the knowledge graph. Each resource page *provides useful information* in a human accessible format. Since the web page is build based on RDF data, besides the HTML representation, it is also important to make the underlying RDF data available to Semantic Web agents. To achieve this, various methods exist to make the respective data available as needed. In the following we discuss possibilities that have an overlap with the setup of Static Sites.

A way to embed data in a document is to use RDFa properties within the HTML tags. Since RDFa interferes with the surrounding HTML-tags it is not subject to Jekyll RDF. Instead the embedding has to be performed by the template designer. To support the designer this problem could also be subject to future work for building a *Jekyll RDFa* plugin on top of Jekyll RDF. Instead of embedding the RDF data each resource can also be served in a separate file. In this case a script is employed to process the same data source as Jekyll RDF and

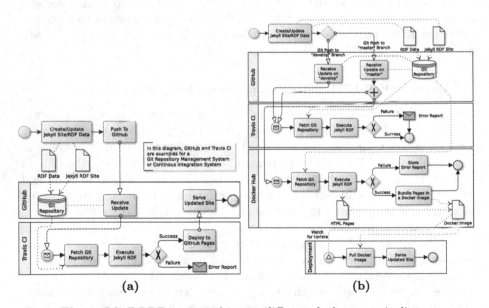

Fig. 4. Jekyll RDF integrated in two different deployment pipelines.

---

[18] http://www.w3.org/DesignIssues/LinkedData.html.

produce individual Linked Data resource pages. To provide a possibility for an agent to find the respective resource page a link can be set or the HTTP server employs content negotiation. But in many cases, where Static Sites are used, the user has no ability to interfere with the HTTP protocol of the server. In this case the only way is to add an *HTML header link tag*[19] to point to the resource page, this can be embedded directly in any Jekyll template. If the HTTP protocol of the server can be configured the same link can be set as *HTTP Link header*[20]. In this case also *content negotiation*[21] is an elegant commonly used way to serve the correct representation of the resource based on the request.

5   Application

In the following we show a selection of use cases where we have successfully applied Jekyll RDF to build customized data exploration interfaces. The use cases are from different domains and provide very individual user interfaces as shown in Figs. 5 and 6. The first two use cases are from the Digital Humanities, followed by a Current Research Information System, and finally we eat our own dogfood and present the usability of Jekyll RDF to build vocabulary description pages. In Table 2 we compare the setups according to the number of triples, defined templates and pages, resulting pages, and execution time.

Digital Humanities. The *Multilingual Morpheme Ontology* (MMoOn; [15]) is an ontology in the linguistics to create language resources of morphemic data (inventory) for inflectional languages. With the Open Hebrew Inventory we created a language specific extension of the MMoOn vocabulary for the Modern Hebrew language. The dataset currently consists of 197,374 RDF Statements describing Hebrew words, lexemes, and morphs. Using the Jekyll RDF system we could create an interface to the Open Hebrew dataset that is specifically adapted to the presentation of Hebrew language data. To define the templates we created a Git repository[22] that consists of four class templates, two overview pages, and the dataset. On each update to the Git repository the Travis CI (cf. Sect. 4.1) executes the Jekyll RDF process to create the 13,404 inventory pages, 20 vocabulary pages, and two overview pages. Figure 5a shows the exploration interface at the example of the word הִכְתַּב (hukhtav). Next to the HTML interface we created RDF resource pages in Turtle and RDF/JSON serialization. This RDF representation of the data is used to attach a system for users to contribute to the data through Structured Feedback [1]. In this way further dynamic elements can be provided in a static page based on the RDF data.

---

[19] https://www.w3.org/TR/2017/REC-html52-20171214/document-metadata.html# the-link-element.

[20] http://www.rfc-editor.org/rfc/rfc5988.txt.

[21] https://tools.ietf.org/html/rfc7231#section-5.3, https://www.w3.org/DesignIssues/ Conneg.

[22] http://mmoon-project.github.io/JekyllPage/.

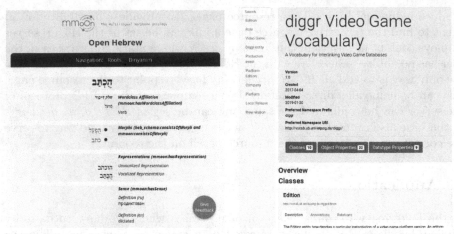

(a) MMoOn exploration interface showing the example of the resource for the Hebrew word הְכתָּב (hukhtav).

(b) The documentation page for the diggr OWL vocabulary used to model the interplay of games and publishers in global game culture research.

Fig. 5. Images of Jekyll RDF pages to depict the variety of usage scenarios.

Another Project from the Digital Humanities is the *Pfarrerbuch* project[23]. In this project we build a Research Data Management system for historians to create a database of all pastors who served in Saxony, Hungary, the Church Province of Saxony, and Thuringia since the reformation. Especially in the filed of history we see a great need for customized and easily accessible user interfaces.

Table 2. Comparison of the presented Jekyll RDF setups. The average runtime is measured at the Travis CI over the last 10 runs.

Setup	#Triples	#Templates/#Pages	#Res. Pages	Avg. Runtime
Open Hebrew Inventory	197,374	4/2	13,426	1952.4 s (32.54 min)
Pfarrerbuch (demo subset)	1,685	4/-	138	8 s
SDA Work Group	27,295	8 (Class) + 49 (Inst.)/2	253	327.3 s (5.45 min)
diggr Vocabulary	221	1/-	1	8 s

---

[23] https://github.com/AKSW/pfarrerbuch.jekyllrdf.

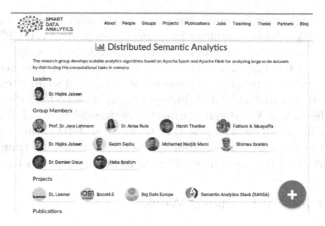

Fig. 6. A work group page showing the members and projects.

Smart Data Analytics Work Group. The Smart Data Analytics research group (SDA[24]) investigates machine learning techniques (*analytics*) using structured knowledge (*smart data*). Machine learning requires sufficient data as training datasets. SDA investigated techniques which could help also to build such a dataset to depict the organizational structure and entities representing SDA. The SDA knowledge graph contains entities about persons, groups, projects, and publications as well as their relations. It is used for question answering, faceted search, data mining, and analysis for better decision making while hiring or restructuring the group. Using Jekyll RDF and the Linked Data principles helps to reuse the existing knowledge graph to build the work group homepage. In this way it is possible to publish a Current Research Information System (CRIS) with Jekyll RDF based on the SDA knowledge graph on the Web as shown in Fig. 6.

Vocabulary Documentation. One of the major advantages of using RDF to describe resources is the universality of the model and the ability to describe the schema resources as part of the same graph as the described data. This enables consumers and producers of the data to use an exploitable, executable, and metadata rich knowledge framework. eccenca[25] is a European enterprise based in Germany with a strong vision how semantic vocabularies and Linked Data can be used to integrate project data and data management. An important aspect of semantic data integration are vocabularies which capture essential concepts from the customers domain. These vocabularies build the foundation for a semantic data landscape which interlinks all customer datasets into an exploitable graph. In order to communicate the results of an ontology specification work, it is necessary to visualize and document the vocabularies. Existing ontology documentation tools lack the ability to extensively customize the result. Using Jekyll

---

[24] http://sda.tech, https://github.com/SmartDataAnalytics/sda.tech.
[25] http://www.eccenca.com.

RDF we could build a set of templates for all major ontology classes and publish it as a theme called Jekyll Ontology Documentation project (JOD)[26]. However, fetching OWL constructs is problematic with SPARQL based graph access alone and also complex functionality such as the generation of a Manchester Syntax description is currently missing and should be integrated soon. It can easily be integrated in an existing RDF vocabulary project as shown at the example of the diggr Video Game Vocabulary project[27] performed by the Leipzig University Library. The deployment of Jekyll RDF with the JOD theme and a CI/CD pipeline in order to create the vocabulary documentation was straight forward. The user interface of the vocabulary documentation is shown in Fig. 5b.

6   Conclusion and Future Work

With the presented Jekyll RDF system we provide a methodology to close the gap between RDF data publishing and highly customizable publication and exploration interfaces. With our system it is possible to separate the management of RDF dataset from the creation of appropriate templates for the data presentation. Because we piggyback on the successful concept of Static Site Generators a low entry barrier is provided and the system requirements for the HTTP server are low. There is no need for costly dynamic server side computations which often also rely on the availability of a hard to maintain SPARQL endpoint. As shown in Sect. 5 and Table 2 the system allows the quick publication of small RDF dataset like RDF vocabulary, but also the creation of pages for huge datasets of more then $10k$ pages is possible with just a view templates. Especially, for the publication of highly interlinked datasets the usage of Jekyll RDF has assets as shown by the CRIS use case. As a Static Site Generator performs the work of creating the HTML pages in advance, the creation and the serving can be separated. The use of computing power is predictable and not affected by the amount of page visits. The separation allows a maximum flexibility in scaling the delivery of the site. It is possible to make extensive use of caching mechanisms such as *content delivery networks* to reduce the workload on the server and increase the availability of a site. In contrast to caching of dynamic pages the maintenance of static sites does not suffer from the problem of cache invalidation which lowers the effort of the publication.

In contrast to the related work of LD-R and MIRA [7,14] and Gatsby we provide a template based approach that aims at users without software developing experience. With the JML we minimize the effort of publishing Linked Data without the need to write a single line of programming code. Using JML as domain specific language allows also Web Designers to integrate knowledge from RDF graphs into their work. The template based approach is similar to our previous work with LESS and the OntoWiki Site Extension [5,9,10]. However, the previous work as well as the application frameworks presented in [7,14] relies on a complex dynamic data management back-end and SPARQL endpoint.

---

[26] https://github.com/eccenca/jod, https://rubygems.org/gems/jekyll-theme-jod.
[27] https://diggr.github.io/diggr-video-game-vocabulary/.

With Jekyll RDF we present a static approach to maximize the scalability as it is independent of the availability of dynamic components at runtime.

As we extended Jekyll for our prototype we can benefit from the big ecosystem of plugins to enrich the created site. For the future work the performance of the generation process can be improved by an incremental build process to reuse pages from previous builds. To increase the usability of the presented method as a SCMS a set of predefined themes to be used with Jekyll RDF can support users, as shown by JOD. Looking at the possibilities of this concept in combination with the successful and generic design of RDF we see a great potential for future use cases. Due to the plethora of Static Site Generators we hope to see implementations to adopt our conception and methods to further systems like Next, Hugo, and Hyde[15]. There is no need to decide whether to publish data or a customized human readable interface anymore as the can be server next to each other on a static webspace.

Acknowledgements. Thanks to the 2016 *Software Technik Praktikum* course group who did the initial implementation of Jekyll RDF: Elias Saalmann, Christian Frommert, Simon Jakobi, Arne Jonas Präger, Maxi Bornmann, Georg Hackel, Eric Füg. This work was partly supported by grants from the German Federal Ministries of Education and Research (BMBF) for the LEDS Project (03WKCG11C, 03WKCG11A), Ministry of Transport and Digital Infrastructure (BMVI) for the LIMBO project (19F2029A, 19F2029G), and the Ministry for Economic Affairs and Energy (BMWi) for the PlatonaM project (01MT19005A).

References

1. Arndt, N., et al.: Structured feedback: a distributed protocol for feedback and patches on the web of data. In: LDOW (2016)
2. Arndt, N., Naumann, P., Radtke, N., Martin, M., Marx, E.: Decentralized collaborative knowledge management using Git. J. Web Semant. (2018). https://doi.org/10.1016/j.websem.2018.08.002
3. Arndt, N., Radtke, N.: A method for distributed and collaborative curation of RDF datasets utilizing the quit stack. In: INFORMATIK 2017. LNI (2017). https://doi.org/10.18420/in2017_187
4. Auer, S., et al.: Managing the life-cycle of linked data with the LOD2 stack. In: Cudré-Mauroux, P., et al. (eds.) ISWC 2012. LNCS, vol. 7650, pp. 1–16. Springer, Heidelberg (2012). https://doi.org/10.1007/978-3-642-35173-0_1
5. Auer, S., Doehring, R., Dietzold, S.: LESS - template-based syndication and presentation of linked data. In: Aroyo, L., et al. (eds.) ESWC 2010. LNCS, vol. 6089, pp. 211–224. Springer, Heidelberg (2010). https://doi.org/10.1007/978-3-642-13489-0_15
6. Berners-Lee, T., Hendler, J.: Publishing on the semantic web. Nature **410**(6832) (2001)
7. Bertti, E., Schwabe, D.: MIRA: a model-driven framework for semantic interfaces for web applications. In: Bozzon, A., Cudre-Maroux, P., Pautasso, C. (eds.) ICWE 2016. LNCS, vol. 9671, pp. 40–58. Springer, Cham (2016). https://doi.org/10.1007/978-3-319-38791-8_3

8. Bizer, C., Heath, T., Berners-Lee, T.: Linked data - the story so far. Int. J. Semantic Web Inf. Syst. **5** (2009)
9. Frischmuth, P., Arndt, N., Martin, M.: OntoWiki 1.0: 10 years of development - what's new in OntoWiki. In: SEMANTiCS P&D Track (2016)
10. Frischmuth, P., Martin, M., Tramp, S., Riechert, T., Auer, S.: OntoWiki - an authoring, publication and visualization interface for the data web. Seman. Web J. **6**(3) (2015). https://doi.org/10.3233/SW-140145
11. Gams, E., Mitterdorfer, D.: Semantische Content Management Systeme. In: Blumauer, A., Pellegrini, T. (eds.) Social Semantic Web, pp. 207–226. X.media.press. Springer, Heidelberg (2009). https://doi.org/10.1007/978-3-540-72216-8_11
12. Gancarz, M.: Linux and the Unix Philosophy. Digital Press (2003)
13. Jacksi, K., Dimililer, N., Zeebaree, S.R.M.: State of the art exploration systems for linked data: a review. IJACS **7**(11) (2016)
14. Khalili, A., Loizou, A., van Harmelen, F.: Adaptive linked data-driven web components: Building flexible and reusable semantic web interfaces - building flexible and reusable semantic web interfaces. In: ESWC (2016)
15. Klimek, B., Arndt, N., Krause, S., Arndt, T.: Creating linked data morphological language resources with mmoon - the hebrew morpheme inventory. In: LREC (2016)
16. Klímek, J., Skoda, P., Necaský, M.: Survey of tools for linked data consumption. Semant. Web J. (2018)
17. Lukovnikov, D., Kontokostas, D., Stadler, C., Hellmann, S., Lehmann, J.: DBpedia viewer - an integrative interface for DBpedia leveraging the DBpedia service eco system. In: LDOW (2014)
18. Lukovnikov, D., Stadler, C., Lehmann, J.: LD viewer - linked data presentation framework. In: SEMANTiCS (2014)
19. Meissner, R., Junghanns, K.: Using DevOps principles to continuously monitor RDF data quality. In: SEMANTiCS (2016). https://doi.org/10.1145/2993318.2993351
20. Micsik, A., Tóth, Z., Turbucz, S.: LODmilla: shared visualization of linked open data. In: Bolikowski, L., Casarosa, V., Goodale, P., Houssos, N., Manghi, P., Schirrwagen, J. (eds.) TPDL 2013. CCIS, vol. 416, pp. 89–100. Springer, Cham (2014). https://doi.org/10.1007/978-3-319-08425-1_9
21. Valsecchi, F., Abrate, M., Bacciu, C., Tesconi, M., Marchetti, A.: Linked data maps: Providing a visual entry point for the exploration of datasets. In: IESD@ISWC (2015)

On the Web Platform Cornucopia

Tommi Mikkonen[1(✉)], Cesare Pautasso[2], Kari Systä[3], and Antero Taivalsaari[4]

[1] University of Helsinki, Helsinki, Finland
tommi.mikkonen@helsinki.fi
[2] USI, Lugano, Switzerland
cesare.pautasso@usi.ch
[3] Tampere University, Tampere, Finland
kari.systa@tuni.fi
[4] Nokia Bell Labs, Tampere, Finland
antero.taivalsaari@nokia-bell-labs.com

Abstract. The evolution of the Web browser has been organic, with new features introduced on a pragmatic basis rather than following a clear rational design. This evolution has resulted in a cornucopia of overlapping features and redundant choices for developing Web applications. These choices include multiple architecture and rendering models, different communication primitives and protocols, and a variety of local storage mechanisms. In this position paper we examine the underlying reasons for this historic evolution. We argue that without a sound engineering approach and some fundamental rethinking there will be a growing risk that the Web may no longer be a viable, open software platform in the long run.

Keywords: Web platform · Technology design space ·
Software engineering principles · Web Engineering ·
Progressive Web applications · HTML5

1 Introduction

The Web was originally designed for global document publishing. The scripting capabilities that were added later evolved into a myriad of overlapping programming capabilities. Today, after more than two decades of organic evolution, there are (too) many ways to build software for the Web platform, with developers continuously chasing after the latest and greatest frameworks and development paradigms[1]. This evolution has been driven by competition against other platforms (e.g., native mobile applications or traditional desktop applications) and by competition within the Web platform (i.e., among Web browser vendors and framework developers). The result is a cornucopia of choices providing a rich, complex and ever-growing set of features that need to be mastered by developers and maintained by browser vendors.

---

[1] https://stateofjs.com/.

© Springer Nature Switzerland AG 2019
M. Bakaev et al. (Eds.): ICWE 2019, LNCS 11496, pp. 347–355, 2019.
https://doi.org/10.1007/978-3-030-19274-7_25

In this position paper we look at the design of the Web platform from a Web Engineering standpoint to present a deeper understanding of the driving forces behind its growth and evolution; such continuous organic evolution has made us concerned of the long term sustainability of the Web as a software platform. In addition, we compare the Web to more traditional software platforms, especially in light of how they fulfill MacLennan's classic software engineering principles [1]. We focus on two key principles, *simplicity* and *consistency*: there should be a minimum number of non-overlapping concepts with simple rules for their combination; things that are similar should also look similar and different things should look different. Using the words of Brooks: "It is better to have a system reflect one set of design ideas than to have one that contains many good but independent and uncoordinated ideas" [2].

In continuation to our previous papers (e.g., [3–5]), we claim that the evolution of the Web browser has been driven by new features introduced on a pragmatic basis (often purely for commercial needs) instead of being based on a justified long-term design rationale[2]. This has resulted in redundant features, including multiple architecture and rendering models, communication primitives and protocols, local storage mechanisms and programming language constructs. In this paper, we study this cornucopia of overlapping features inside the browser, their origins, relations, and intended use cases. Sharing the concerns of many[3], we argue that without a sound engineering approach and fundamental rethinking there will be a growing risk that the Web may no longer be seen as the open, universal, stable and viable software platform it has attempted to become in the past decades [7].

2   Evolution of the Web as a Software Platform

In the early life of the Web, Web pages were truly *pages*, i.e., semi-structured textual documents that contained some primitive forms of multimedia content (e.g., images) without animation support (except for the controversial blinking tag that was eliminated later) or any interactivity beyond the basic ability to navigate back and forth between pages. Navigation was based on simple *hyperlinks*, and a new Web page was loaded from the Web server each time the user followed a link. For reading user input some pages were presented as *forms* with simple text fields, buttons and selection widgets.

The Web became increasingly interactive when Web pages started containing animated graphics and audio tracks, some of which were rendered by browser plug-in components (such as Java Applets, Flash, RealPlayer, Quicktime and Shockwave), while others were scripted using the JavaScript language [8], introduced in Netscape Navigator version 2.0B almost as an afterthought in December 1995. From technological standpoint, this phase was driven by efforts and investment into various competing browser plugins, which would provide a proprietary

---

[2] See for example the controversial decisions to provide standard support for Digital Rights Management in clear conflict with the Open Web Principle [6].

[3] https://extensiblewebmanifesto.org/.

browser-independent layer and a common runtime environment for applications that could deliver an interactive user experience beyond the limits of the underlying Web browser.

The introduction of dynamic *DHTML*, Cascading Style Sheets (CSS), and the JavaScript language, with programmatic access to the Document Object Model (DOM) and the underlying HTTP client (with the XMLHttpRequest object), enabled highly interactive Web pages with built-in support for modifying the content of Web pages without reloading them. This effectively decoupled the page navigation lifecycle from the communication exchanged with the server, while still using the original HTTP protocol. This technology mix became known as Ajax (Asynchronous JavaScript and XML) [9]. In this phase, the Web started moving in unforeseen directions, with Web sites behaving more like multimedia presentations and traditional low-latency rich client applications rather than simple static pages.

In the early 2000s, the concept of Software as a Service (SaaS) emerged. At that point, people realized that the ability to offer software applications seamlessly over the Web and then perform instant worldwide updates would require a truly universal runtime execution environment, which become familiar under the HTML5 brand [10]. Observing the benefits of this model, developers started to build Web sites that behave much like desktop applications [11], for example, by allowing Web pages to be updated partially, rather than requiring the entire page to be refreshed. This also increased the demand for a full-fledged programming language that could be used directly from inside the Web browser instead of relying on external plug-in components. Since JavaScript was readily available inside every browser [12], it became a target of significant investment, especially to improve its performance [13] and add language features to make the language more amenable to developers.

This brings us to the current Web platform, featuring a continuously evolving, evergreen Web browser, with support – at the time of writing – for two hundred and one HTML5-related specifications published by the W3C and the Web Hypertext Application Technology Working Group (WHATWG). Out of these 59 have been abandoned or are already superseded[4]. These specifications define a myriad of APIs, formats and browser features for building progressive Web applications [14] that can run in a standards-compatible Web browser.

3   Redundancy Within Web Platform APIs

The evolution of the Web differs from the evolution of many other software platforms. While many popular open source platforms have grown under the leadership of a benevolent dictator, the governance of the Web has shifted from a design-by-committee approach to multiple committees with many players pulling the evolution in different directions.

Just like classic native software platforms, the modern Web browser offers a number of APIs that provide abstractions to applications. However, taking

---

[4] http://html5-overview.net/.

graphics rendering as the first example, the browser includes multiple alternatives – DOM/DHTML, 2D Canvas, SVG, and 3D WebGL – each of which introduces a very different development paradigm, e.g., regarding whether rendering is performed declaratively or programmatically, or whether the graphics is expected to be managed by the browser or explicitly by the developers themselves [3]. In contrast, many graphical user interface toolkits used in traditional software platforms contain several layers of rendering capabilities for developing graphical user interfaces, with carefully designed abstractions and implementation layers. In such designs, one can identify distinct layers that implement intermediate abstractions, which at some point in history were intended for the programmers, but which over time were complemented with simpler and more powerful higher-level interfaces. Unlike in the Web browser, these lower-level APIs form a layered architecture wherein each layer offers a coherent set of abstractions that are open for 3rd party developers, and not only to the internal implementation of the framework itself.

Such layered designs are common in software platforms. For instance, layering is used in the Unix/Linux file system abstractions, providing uniform access to several types of storage and communication devices. Instead, Web application developers need to choose between overlapping APIs for storing data inside the browser, such as Cookies, Local/Session Storage, or IndexedDB (without counting the now deprecated WebSQL). Another example is the area of communication mechanisms. On many traditional software platforms, there is a stack of protocols, such as the TCP/IP stack, wherein each layer provides an abstraction of a particular type of service. In the browser there are different protocols (HTTP version 1, 1.1, 2.0, 3.0, WebSockets, WebRTC) exposed through several APIs and programming techniques, such as Programmatic HTTP (originally known as XMLHttpRequest; now being replaced by Fetch), Server-Sent Events, or Service Workers – again partially redundant and at the API level mostly unrelated to each other.

In the area of programming languages, JavaScript is the *lingua franca* of the Web. After making the jump to also server side with Node.js, JavaScript has become one of the most widely used programming languages in the world. This popularity has put a lot of pressure on JavaScript language evolution, e.g., to improve its performance, clean up some of its original idiosyncrasies, and generally make the language more approachable to developers familiar with other languages (such as Java). Out of many possible examples, we mention variable declaration constructs (the attempt to replace the original `var` with function scoping with `let` and `const` with block scoping), and three contrasting approaches to inheritance: prototypical, parasitic (or closure-based), and the recently added class-based (with mixins). For asynchronous event-based programming, developers can choose from callbacks, futures/promises and the recently added `async`/`await` constructs. Each addition is intended to be an improvement over the previous one(s), but the language keeps growing after improvement added on top of previously added constructs.

Things mentioned above are just few examples of the ongoing emergence of redundant options available to Web developers within what we call the Web Platform Cornucopia. Next, we place the focus on the sources of this cornucopia, and study some of the patterns in browser API formation.

4   Patterns for Browser API Formation: A Technical View

Vendor-Specific Browser APIs and Features. Looking back to the history of browser evolution, almost all the facilities we take for granted were once specific to one browser vendor. Today's core features, such as JavaScript, Cascading Style Sheets (CSS) and various HTML tags – apart from a small core of HTML1 tags originating from Tim Berners-Lee – were vendor-specific at some point during the so-called browser wars[5]. While conventions such as prefixing features with vendor-specific names helps ensure that developers are more aware of vendor-specific extensions (with the expectation that they eventually become part of standards), in some cases vendor-specific extensions spread into other browsers even before they are standardized. For instance, some `-webkit` prefixed features are supported by non-WebKit browsers. In the light of recent developments, the era of browser-specific features may not be over yet, since each browser vendor follows a different roadmap in embracing and implementing new standards.

Plugin Components. Historically, Web browser plugin components played an important role in the development of browser features. Probably the best example are video codecs inside the browser. For a long time, the Flash player[6] was the dominant technology in that role, whereas now almost all browsers include HTML5 video support, and the role of Flash is diminishing rapidly.

Versioned Recommendations Versus Living Standards. Today, there are two sets of guidelines that the browser vendors should follow. W3C[7] aims at providing versioned recommendations, whereas the WHATWG[8] community introduces living, continuously evolving standards. Both forums advance at a different pace, and their operations are uncoordinated[9]. While at present the differences are small, we expect that more and more diverging features will be proposed in the long run.

New Hardware. The introduction of new hardware capabilities can spark the need for new software platform APIs. Examples pertaining to the Web platform include the Geolocation API and the WebGL API[10], which is almost identical to OpenGL[11]. The total the number of direct-access low-level APIs in the context

---

[5] Wikipedia https://en.wikipedia.org/wiki/Browser_wars in fact lists three separate browser wars (1995–2001, 2004–2018, 2018-present).

[6] https://www.adobe.com/fi/products/flashplayer.html.

[7] https://www.w3.org/.

[8] https://whatwg.org/.

[9] https://dzone.com/articles/w3c-vs-whatwg-html5-specs.

[10] http://www.khronos.org/webgl/.

[11] https://www.opengl.org/.

of the Web browser is still low. Key reasons for this are the concerns regarding the security of the Web browser sandbox, and privacy concerns due to increased user fingerprinting exposure.

Web Frameworks. Yet another source of new browser features is the evolution of Web frameworks – especially those frameworks that reach dominant status. Dominant frameworks are used so extensively in application development that their abstractions start gradually "leaking into" standards as well. There are many examples, e.g., in the area of model-view-controller programming patterns, data binding, and reactive programming. A very concrete example are the jQuery[12] library's $ selectors, which became part of the standard DOM as *document.querySelector*.

Language Pre-compilers. JavaScript has effectively taken the role of the "assembly language of the Web" – literally in the case of the WebAssembly subset [15]. There are a growing number of languages such as CoffeeScript, TypeScript, Elm, Emscripten, RubyJS, Pyjamas, Processing.js, Scala.js, ClojureScript and PharoJS that can be compiled or translated into JavaScript. These languages take advantage of the JavaScript engine in the Web browser or in the cloud backend (Node.js) as a universal execution target platform.

A similar pattern can be observed with CSS – the declarative language for styling Web content. Preprocessors such as Less, Sass, or SCSS offer additional stylesheet features (e.g., variables, macros, mixins, nesting of selectors within formatting rules, and the parent selector) that can be compiled into plain CSS. Features of these higher-level languages have also started trickling down into the core platform. Good examples are, e.g., CSS variables and computed expressions, and JavaScript arrow functions.

5   Web Frameworks to the Rescue?

Ideally, in a software development environment there should be only one, clearly the best and most obvious way to accomplish each task. However, in Web development – even in a generic Web browser without add-on components or libraries – there are several overlapping ways to accomplish even the most basic tasks. A popular approach to bring back simplicity and consistency into the development process is to leverage Web frameworks. Applications built on top of higher-level frameworks typically use the lower-level browser APIs only indirectly, through the frameworks. For instance, the XMLHttpRequest API mentioned earlier was available in many browsers well before it became a key building block for Single-Page Web Applications and AJAX [9]. Similarly, one can view Mercure[13] as a variation of the well-established Server-Sent Events (SSE) technology, augmented with additional library support. Likewise, the controversial CSSinJS proposal[14] (using the JavaScript syntax to encode CSS rules) would remove

---

[12] https://jquery.com/.

[13] https://github.com/dunglas/mercure.

[14] https://cssinjs.org/.

the need to use one of the three core languages of the Web platform (HTML, CSS and JavaScript).

This role is where Web frameworks excel. They offer a more coordinated and coherent set of development facilities, development patterns and experiences, but in the end rely on standard browser APIs. Frameworks can be designed to follow established software engineering principles, bypassing the incoherent and rather organically evolved features underneath. Furthermore, it is possible to take specifics of the application genre and habits of the developer community into account. Furthermore, the frameworks can propose higher-level APIs that hide the diversity of the underlying APIs. Movements such as Progressive Web Apps set their goals even further by considering mobile devices, too. New rendering and visualization techniques such as WebVR[15] and WebXR Device API[16] take the Web towards virtual and augmented reality rendering with new APIs, building upon the well-established WebGL API discussed above. Obviously, facilities provided by the most successful libraries and frameworks can eventually gravitate down to be adopted as standard browser features, following the pattern presented above.

Unfortunately, instead of forming a set of compatible components that build upon each others' strengths, many of the most commonly used frameworks partly overlap, thus extending the Web cornucopia to the framework area, making it difficult for developers to pick the right one. Furthermore, probably even more so than with the core browser, the decision regarding which framework to use reflects the current trends and fashion instead of careful consideration of application needs. The oversupply of Web frameworks, as well as the risk of them being abandoned as they get replaced by yet another frameworks, unfortunately diminishes their role as drivers for Web browser API evolution.

6 Conclusion

To conclude, we are surprised how poorly the Web platform meets the consistency and simplicity advocated by software engineering principles. Given the current popularity of the Web browser as a software platform, we are even more surprised how little discussion these issues have generated in the Software Engineering and Web Engineering communities. This discussion raises many questions: Is the Web Platform Cornucopia viable for the Web ecosystem? What is the effort required to maintain a reasonably coherent Web platform in the long term? Are Web developers becoming more or less productive over the years? Is Web Engineering dominated by the frameworks or the browser features (or vendors) underneath them? Will there be a coherent, long-lasting set of key frameworks that are deliberately set to drive browser API evolution? How much time and effort is spent by the developers in rewriting their code to follow the rapid evolution of frameworks, or to port Web applications between frameworks? Will browser vendors give up, leading to a "monoculture" in which only one browser

---

[15] https://webvr.info/.

[16] https://immersive-web.github.io/webxr/.

engine remains? While such a monoculture would have a better chance to keep the feature cornucopia under control, would it really be the desirable end state for the long term sustainability of the Web? All these questions ultimately boil down to where innovation is happening: within browsers, within frameworks, in the applications above (further growing the stack), or outside or beside the Web (making it irrelevant), e.g., in areas such as mobile or pervasive computing. In the Web of Things area HTTP-like protocols have been adopted, but otherwise the adoption of the Web as a platform for running embedded software is still rare. Also, as the Web platform keeps changing, will the users be forced to upgrade their hardware (upgrading browsers may require to upgrade the OS which may make the hardware obsolete) just like it is effectively required in the mobile apps area today? Has the Web lost its way in the area of backwards and forward compatibility? While the first Web site can still be opened in a browser 30 yr later, what is the likelihood that today's Web applications can still run unmodified in future browsers in the late 2040s?

References

1. MacLennan, B.J.: Principles of Programming Languages Design, Evaluation, and Implementation, 3rd edn. Oxford University Press, Oxford (1999)
2. Brooks Jr., F.P.: The Design of Design Essays from a Computer Scientist. Pearson Education, London (2010)
3. Taivalsaari, A., Mikkonen, T., Pautasso, C., Systa, K.: Comparing the built-in application architecture models in the web browser. In: 2017 IEEE International Conference on Software Architecture (ICSA), pp. 51–54. IEEE (2017)
4. Gallidabino, A., Pautasso, C.: Maturity model for liquid web architectures. In: Cabot, J., De Virgilio, R., Torlone, R. (eds.) ICWE 2017. LNCS, vol. 10360, pp. 206–224. Springer, Cham (2017). https://doi.org/10.1007/978-3-319-60131-1_12
5. Taivalsaari, A., Mikkonen, T., Systä, K., Pautasso, C.: Web user interface implementation technologies: an underview. In: Proceedings of the 14th International Conference on Web Information Systems and Technologies, WEBIST 2018, pp. 127–136. Seville, Spain, September 18–20 (2018)
6. Daubs, M.S.: HTML5, digital rights management (DRM), and the rhetoric of openness. J. Media Critiques (JMC) 3(9), 77–94 (2017)
7. Mikkonen, T., Taivalsaari, A.: Reports of the web's death are greatly exaggerated. Computer 44(5), 30–36 (2011)
8. Flanagan, D.: JavaScript: The Definitive Guide, 6th edn. O'Reilly Media Inc., Sebastopol (2011)
9. Paulson, L.D.: Building rich web applications with Ajax. Computer 38(10), 14–17 (2005)
10. Anthes, G.: HTML5 leads a web revolution. Commun. ACM 55(7), 16–17 (2012)
11. Fraternali, P., Rossi, G., Sánchez-Figueroa, F.: Rich internet applications. IEEE Internet Comput. 14(3), 9–12 (2010)
12. Severance, C.: JavaScript: designing a language in 10 days. Computer 45(2), 7–8 (2012)

13. Richards, G., Gal, A., Eich, B., Vitek, J.: Automated construction of JavaScript benchmarks. In: Proceedings of the 2011 ACM International Conference on Object Oriented Programming Systems Languages and Applications, OOPSLA 2011, pp. 677–694. ACM, New York (2011)
14. Ater, T.: Building Progressive Web Apps: Bringing the Power of Native to the Browser. O'Reilly Media Inc., Sebastopol (2017)
15. Haas, A., et al.: Bringing the web up to speed with webassembly. In: ACM SIG-PLAN Notices, vol. 52, pp. 185–200. ACM, New York (2017)

Web Services and Computing

Linked USDL Extension for Cloud Services Description

Hajer Nabli[1]([✉]) [iD], Raoudha Ben Djemaa[1,2], and Ikram Amous Ben Amor[1,3]

[1] Higher Institute of Computer Science and Multimedia of Sfax, University of Sfax, MIRACL, 3021 Sfax, Tunisia
nabli.hajer@yahoo.fr
[2] Higher Institute of Computer Science and Communication Techniques of H. Sousse, University of Sousse, 4011 H. Sousse, Tunisia
raoudha.bendjemaa@isimsf.rnu.tn
[3] National School of Electronics and Telecommunications of Sfax, University of Sfax, 3018 Sfax, Tunisia
ikram.amous@isecs.rnu.tn

Abstract. Cloud computing has become the most influential paradigm in recent years, both in industry and academia. A Cloud provider delivers Cloud services to businesses or individuals. However, each Cloud provider uses its own techniques to describe their Cloud services. It is therefore difficult to compare Cloud offers and then provide the appropriate service to the user. Especially that the Cloud services can provide the same functionalities, but they differ by their quality of service, price, Cloud characteristics, service credibility, and so on. The variety of these techniques is due to the lack of Cloud service description standardization. To deal with such issues, we propose in this paper a Cloud service description ontology that assists the Cloud service publication, discovery and selection processes. The proposed description will be extended from the Linked USDL language to describe Cloud services thanks to its expressiveness by covering four aspects namely technical, operational, business and semantic.

Keywords: Cloud service · Cloud service description ontology · Cloud characteristics · Linked USDL

1 Introduction

Cloud computing allows users to remotely access, and use computer hardware and software over the Internet. Users can use a shared pool of computing resources provisioned with their minimal management efforts [1]. It is an open standard model, which can easily and on-demand provide a scalable environment for the benefit of end users by offering Cloud services, which can be categorized by the type of IT resource they offer: Infrastructure-as-a-Service (IaaS), Platform-as-a-Service (PaaS) and Software-as-a-Service (SaaS). IaaS services can

© Springer Nature Switzerland AG 2019
M. Bakaev et al. (Eds.): ICWE 2019, LNCS 11496, pp. 359–373, 2019.
https://doi.org/10.1007/978-3-030-19274-7_26

provide users with pre-configured hardware resources through a virtual interface, additional storage space for data backups, network bandwidth for servers, and even access to high power computing that previously only accessed with supercomputers. PaaS services deliver a platform to users from which they can develop, initialize and manage applications. PaaS offerings typically include a base operating system and a suite of applications and development tools. Finally, SaaS services deliver to users a fully functional and complete software product through a Web browser.

As the number of providers continues to grow, the number of Cloud services is growing exponentially. However, many issues emerge for users and complicate Cloud service discovery and selection tasks. It stems from the fact that providers use different descriptions, non-standardized naming conventions and diverse types and features for their Cloud services. This lack of a standard Cloud service description makes, on the one hand, the comparison between Cloud offerings a tedious task for users, and on the other hand, prevents the interoperability between Cloud services. Especially that Cloud providers typically publish their services on their websites in various formats. Thus, even if users succeed to discover the services that meet their functional needs, they find a big problem by comparing them according to their requirements in terms of quality of service, price, Cloud characteristics, service credibility, and so on.

Analysis of existing research work on Cloud services revealed some crucial limitations: the need for a unified description of Cloud services covering multiple aspects, and the proposed service descriptions depends solely on QoS parameters. Therefore, we conclude that there is a lack of a standard Cloud service representation that can specify Cloud services from different aspects, against different types of Cloud services (IaaS, PaaS, and SaaS), for different service users, and for different usage requirements.

In order to address the above problems, our purpose in this paper is to describe Cloud services in an informed way. To do this, we propose a Cloud service description ontology according to identified Cloud-specific principles and requirements. The proposed Cloud description ontology is extended from the Linked USDL language [2,3] by taking into consideration Linked USDL limitations in a Cloud environment.

The remainder of this paper is constructed as follows. In Sect. 2, we present the related works on Cloud service description. In Sect. 3, we introduce the Linked USDL language and specify its limitations in the Cloud environment. An overview of the proposed Cloud service description ontology is outlined in Sect. 4. Finally, Sect. 5 concludes our paper and gives an outlook on possible future research directions.

2   Related Works

Various researches emerged in recent years that attempt at standardizing Cloud service description. In what follows, we briefly review some works.

Zhang et al. [4] proposed a CloudRecommender system that implements a domain ontology, called CoCoOn (Cloud Computing Ontology), in a relational model. The proposed ontology represents the configuration information related to Cloud-based IaaS services including compute, storage, and network. This system uses regular expressions and SQL to match users' requests to service descriptions in order to discover and to select IaaS services based on their functionality and Quality of Service (QoS) parameters.

Zhou et al. [5] used WSDL-S to semantically describe services that will be discovered. They proposed a P2P-based unstructured method for SaaS discovery. They developed a localized search scheme by using semantic routing protocols and topology reconstruction techniques for service query routing.

Afify et al. [6] proposed a semantic-based system that facilitates the SaaS publication, discovery and selection processes. This system is based on a unified ontology that combines services domain knowledge, SaaS characteristics, QoS metrics, and real SaaS offers.

Nagireddi et al. [7] proposed a Cloud ontology that provides the description of Cloud services and their attributes to facilitate Cloud service discovery. The Cloud ontology is used to order the query, rank services as well as to store the services. They employed the SPARQL query language to extract information from the ontology and match services according to user requests.

Quinton et al. [8] proposed an approach for selecting a Cloud environment, setting the configuration of this environment, and deploying applications. This approach is based on a combination of Software Product Lines (SPLs) and a domain model, enabling the developer to automatically select a Cloud environment that fits a set of requirements, and obtain the description les and executable scripts to configure the related Cloud environment. Authors proposed an extension of feature models (FMs) with cardinalities and attributes as variability models to describe Cloud environment.

Alfazi et al. [9] developed a comprehensive ontology based on the NIST Cloud computing standard to discover and categorize Cloud services in real environments. They used the Cloud service ontology concepts to categorize the Cloud services into several clusters.

Kang et al. [10] presented a four-stage, agent-based Cloud service discovery protocol using Cloud ontology. Indeed, two Cloud ontologies (CO-1 and CO-2) are designed to semantically define the relationship between Cloud services. Whereas CO-1 contains only Cloud concepts, CO-2 contains a set of Cloud concepts, individuals of those concepts, and the relationship among those individuals. The similarity among Cloud services is determined by three kinds of reasoning methods namely concept similarity reasoning, object property similarity reasoning, and datatype property similarity reasoning.

Rekik et al. [11] proposed a comprehensive ontology for Cloud service description that covers the three layers of Cloud models (IaaS, PaaS and SaaS). The proposed ontology treats the functional and non-functional properties of services to help users to discover and select appropriate Cloud services.

Ghazouani et al. [12] proposed a Cloud service description that covers all Cloud service types with all aspects (technical, business, operational, and semantic). The proposed description is based on USDL (Unified Service Description

Language) [15] and WSMO (Web Service Modeling Onology) to describe and define semantically Cloud services.

Sun et al. [13] proposed a semantic Cloud Service Description Model called CSDM, which is extended from the basic structure of USDL [15], by defining Cloud-service-specific attributes. CSDM allows the description of different services with different delivery and deployment models. Furthermore, the authors added, in their proposed description, an additional module named transaction module, which models the rating system of Cloud services from several aspects, such as risk, trust, and reputation.

Shetty et al. [14] used XML technology for modeling the infrastructure services. The proposed data representational model helps users to discover services through a hybrid method, which combines both syntactic and semantic approaches of service discovery. The representational model consists of service name, server locations, functional properties, and non-functional properties.

Based on the findings from the comparative study and analysis of different Cloud service description approaches, we can conclude that the Cloud service description should be comprehensive and complete in order to facilitate, on the one hand, the Cloud service discovery and selection tasks to the users, and, on the other hand, the Cloud service publication task to the providers. We notice, from Table 1, that studied works provide interesting solutions for the description of three types of Cloud services (IaaS, PaaS, and SaaS) [7,9–13]. Moreover, most research works move towards a semantic Cloud service description using ontology [4,6,7,9–13]. As indicated in Table 2, certain works cover all aspects such as functional, technical, operational, business, and semantic aspects [7,12, 13]. Others give more importance to the business aspect such as QoS, pricing policy, etc. [4,6,7,11–14]. From Table 3, we notice that only [6] have considered the common characteristics of Cloud services in their SaaS description.

Table 1. Comparison of Cloud service descriptions by type, proposed representation, and approach used.

Research	Type of Cloud service	Proposed representation	Approach used
[4]	IaaS	CoCoOn ontology	OWL
[5]	SaaS	WSDL-S	WSDL-S
[6]	SaaS	Unied ontology	OWL
[7]	IaaS, PaaS, SaaS	Cloud ontology	OWL
[8]	PaaS	Feature models extended	Feature models
[9]	IaaS, PaaS, SaaS	Cloud service ontology	OWL
[10]	IaaS, PaaS, SaaS	Cloud ontology	OWL
[11]	IaaS, PaaS, SaaS	Cloud description ontology	OWL
[12]	IaaS, PaaS, SaaS	WSMO	WSMO, USDL
[13]	IaaS, PaaS, SaaS	Cloud Service Description Model	OWL, USDL
[14]	IaaS	Data representation model	XML

Table 2. Comparison of the proposed Cloud service descriptions by Functional, Technical, Operational, Business, and Semantic aspects.

Research	Functional description	Technical description	Operational description	Business description	Semantic description
[4]	✓			✓	✓
[5]		✓	✓		✓
[6]	✓			✓	✓
[7]	✓	✓	✓	✓	✓
[8]	✓				
[9]	✓				✓
[10]	✓				✓
[11]	✓			✓	✓
[12]	✓	✓	✓	✓	✓
[13]	✓	✓	✓	✓	✓
[14]	✓			✓	✓

In summary, we conclude that existing service descriptions are incomplete because they do not cover all the concepts needed to describe the three types of Cloud services (IaaS, PaaS, and SaaS). To address these issues, we propose a Cloud service description ontology that is an extension of the Linked Unified Service Description Language (Linked USDL) [2,3] for the definition of Cloud services. Our choice is particularly oriented towards Linked USDL for many reasons. First, Linked USDL is the only standardization attempt to express not only the purely technical aspects of the service but also the business and operational aspects. Second, this language goes one step forward in the adoption of Web technologies to embrace the emerging standard approach for data sharing online, namely Linked Data [16]. Moreover, it reuses existing RDF(S) vocabularies such as the Minimal Service Model, GoodRelations, FOAF and SKOS, which

Table 3. Comparison of the proposed Cloud service descriptions by Business aspect, and Cloud characteristics.

Research	Business description					Cloud characteristics	
	Actors	SLA	Pricing	Legal	Security	Common	Specific
[4]		✓					
[6]		✓	✓			✓	
[7]		✓	✓	✓	✓		
[11]	✓		✓	✓			
[12]	✓	✓	✓	✓			
[13]	✓	✓	✓	✓			
[14]			✓		✓		

simplifies its extension and adaptation. The proposed Cloud service description ontology covers all Cloud service types and merges technical, operational, business and semantic aspects with Cloud characteristics (common and specific) to obtain a complete and comprehensive Cloud service description.

3   An Overview of Linked USDL

The need for service descriptions that address business and operational levels has guided efforts to develop new languages to capture these aspects besides the technical one. The Unified Service Description Language (USDL) [15] is probably the most comprehensive attempt. It supports service description by covering three aspects: technical, operational, and business. USDL aims to offer a platform-neutral language for describing services. However, USDL does not support semantic aspect and is not designed to Cloud Computing domain.

Linked Unified Service Description Language (Linked USDL) [2,3] is a remodeled version of USDL build upon the Linked Data principles and represented with RDFS. Linked USDL aims to provide a language for an open, adaptable and scalable description of services using decentralized management. Linked USDL is segmented into five modules. Each module is a set of concepts and properties. The purpose of this division is to reduce the overall complexity of service descriptions by allowing providers to use only the necessary modules [17]. The five modules are as follows:

usdl-core. The core module covers the operational aspects of a service, such as interaction points between the provider and consumer that occur during provisioning, as well as the description of the business entities involved.

usdl-price. The pricing module covers a set of concepts that are needed to appropriately describe the price structures of a service.

usdl-agreement. The service level agreement module gathers functional and nonfunctional information on the quality of the service provided, such as availability, response time, and reliability.

usdl-sec. This module describes the main security properties of a service.

usdl-ipr. This module defines the rights and obligations under which services may be consumed.

Linked USDL offers several benefits for service description, including coverage of technical, operational, and business aspects, extensibility, reusability of existing data models, and simplicity in publishing services. However, it does not capture all the concepts necessary to effectively describe Cloud services, such as Cloud characteristics. To address these issues, we extend Linked USDL to describe Cloud services in all respects, including Cloud characteristics. Our contribution aims to develop a standardized description of Cloud service to favor the publication, discovery, and selection of Cloud services. Consequently, we propose a Cloud service description ontology to provide a complete and comprehensive description of Cloud services.

4   Cloud Service Description Ontology

In this section, we focus on defining the new concepts of the extended Linked USDL. Therefore, our proposed Cloud service description ontology defines the domain knowledge of the three types of Cloud services (IaaS, PaaS, and SaaS). IaaS is defined as on-demand infrastructure resources delivered as services such as compute, network and storage services. PaaS is essentially defined as on-demand development environments delivered as services such as services for developing, testing, and deploying applications. SaaS is simply defined as on-demand ready-to-use applications delivered as services such as communications, security, accounting and invoicing services [18,19]. Cloud service description ontology facilitates the publication, discovery, and selection of Cloud services based on their functionality, Quality of Service (QoS), and Cloud characteristics parameters. The ontology is defined in the Web Ontology Language (OWL)[1]. This ontology is designed using the Protégé v4.3 ontology editor[2].

Therefore, we expand the Linked USDL language by introducing new concepts that describes the Cloud characteristics. Our extension, as shown in Figs. 1 and 2, is defined by the relationship between the *Service* concept and the *Cloud*

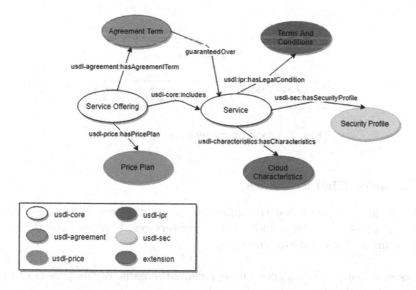

Fig. 1. Linked USDL extension to represent the Cloud characteristics concept.

[1] https://www.w3.org/TR/owl2-overview/.
[2] https://protege.stanford.edu/.

```
1  <owl:Class rdf:about="http://www.linked-usdl.org/ns/usdl-characteristics#Cloud_Characteristics">
2      <rdfs:label>Cloud Characteristics</rdfs:label>
3  </owl:Class>
4
5  <owl:ObjectProperty rdf:about="http://www.linked-usdl.org/ns/usdl-characteristics#hasCharacteristics">
6      <rdfs:domain rdf:resource="http://www.linked-usdl.org/ns/usdl-core#Service"/>
7      <rdfs:range rdf:resource="http://www.linked-usdl.org/ns/usdl-characteristics#Cloud_Characteristics"/>
8  </owl:ObjectProperty>
```

Fig. 2. Extension code.

Characteristics concept. This relationship is represented using the Object Property *hasCharacteristics*. Each instance of *Cloud Characteristics* is used to represent the characteristics of Cloud services.

In Cloud service description ontology, the characteristics of Cloud services, represented by the *Cloud Characteristics* concept, provide the necessary information to describe and discover the services searched by the user. These Cloud characteristics are classified into two main concepts: *Common_Characteristics* and *Specific_Characteristics* (as shown in Fig. 3). Each of these major concepts is composed of different minor sub-concepts. The required Cloud characteristics are collected from multiple resources such as Cloud taxonomy [20,21], Cloud ontology [22], and the National Institute of Standards and Technology (NIST) [23]. Common characteristics are shared by IaaS, PaaS, and SaaS Cloud services such as Owner, Creator, License Type, Formal Agreement, and Auto scaling. While, for each category (such as Storage, Compute, CRM, Database, and so on), more specific characteristics are considered.

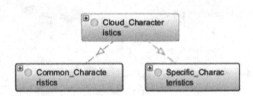

Fig. 3. Cloud characteristics concepts.

4.1 Common Characteristics

In this section, we introduce the different concepts representing the common characteristics of Iaas, Paas, and SaaS Cloud services. Figure 4 depicts the different common characteristics concepts.

The Creator Concept. This concept represents the name of the person or organization responsible for creating the service.

The Contributor Concept. The person or organization responsible for making contributions to the service.

The Owner Concept A person or organization which the service belongs to.

The Initial_Release Concept. The date of the initial release of the service of which is involved its seniority.

The Language Concept. It represents the list of languages supported by the service.

The License_Type Concept. Few Cloud providers prefer to create their services using *open-source* software and platforms, while most opt for the *proprietary* software and licenses. Amazon EC2 and other public Cloud services are largely built with open-source components such as MySQL, JBoss, Tomcat, Xen, and Linux. Nevertheless, their basic Cloud computing service and their additional services are kept closed-source.

The Formal_Agreement Concept. The Service Level Agreement, or SLA, is the formal contract most commonly used in the Cloud. It is a document that defines the specific objectives and the quality of service that a customer is entitled to expect from the provider.

The Auto_Scaling Concept. Auto-scaling services have the ability to increase or decrease resources (scale-up, scale-out) based on fluctuations in demand.

The Intended_User_Group Concept. Some Cloud services make the difference between *Individual* and *Corporate* use. Most IaaS and PaaS offerings are for business, while SaaS offerings exist for businesses, individuals, or both. However, this does not imply that business services can not be purchased by individuals.

The Deployment_Model Concept. Cloud computing defines four types of Cloud deployment models: *Public* Cloud, *Private* Cloud, *Community* Cloud, and *Hybrid* Cloud.

The Payment_System Concept. The most commonly used payment system in the Cloud is *pay-per-use*. Some services use a *dynamic* (or variable) payment model. Some Cloud services are *free*.

The Standardization Concept. In Cloud computing, standardization usually refers to the use of APIs (Application Programming Interface), as well as to technical standards approved and maintained by standardization organizations.

The External_Security Concept. In order to secure access to the Cloud, strong authentication and access control with encrypted transmission must be used on all Cloud services.

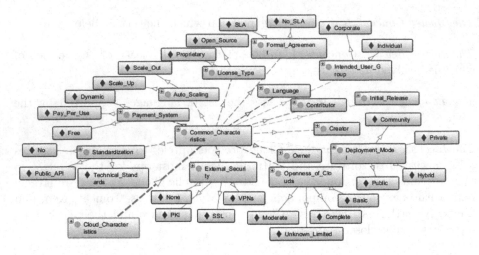

Fig. 4. Common characteristics concepts.

The Openness_of_Clouds Concept. Four levels of information are considered: The *Unknown / Limited* level, limited information is provided by the provider on the Cloud service. The *Basic* level, basic information is available. The *Moderate* level is similar to the Basic level, however, more details are provided. The most open level is the *Complete* level, detailed information is available.

4.2   Specific Characteristics

The common Cloud characteristics explained above are not the only type of Cloud characteristics, but there is another type named specific characteristics. Indeed, Cloud services include several Cloud service categories such as data storage, virtual networks, application hosting and more, grouped into three main service models namely IaaS, PaaS, and SaaS. Each category of Cloud services is characterized by a set of specific characteristics. The *Specific_Characteristics* concept contains all elements needed for describing specific characteristics of Cloud service categories. We distinguish the following three sub-concepts.

The IaaS_Specific_Characteristics concept. This concept describes the specific characteristics for each of the following Cloud service categories: Compute (Server resources for running cloud-based systems that can be dynamically provisioned and configured as needed), Storage (Massively scalable storage capacity that can be used for applications, backups, archival, and file storage), CDN (Content Delivery Networks store content and files to improve the performance and cost of delivering content for web-based systems), Platform_Hosting (It provides the hosting of platforms on virtual servers), Service_Management (Services that manage Cloud infrastructure platforms). These sub-concepts are described in Fig. 5.

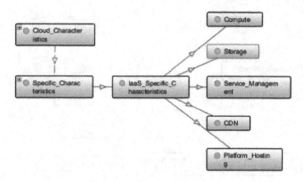

Fig. 5. IaaS service categories.

The PaaS_Specific_Characteristics concept. We define, as shown in Fig. 6, the following categories: Integration (Development platforms for building integration applications in the Cloud and within the enterprise), Development (Platforms for the development of applications), Database (Services offering scalable relational database solutions or scalable no-SQL datastores), Business_Intelligence (Platforms for the creation of applications such as dashboards, reporting systems, and data analysis), and Application_Deployment (Platforms suited for general purpose application development. These services provide databases, web application runtime environments, etc.).

The SaaS_Specific_Characteristics Concept. We define the following sub-concepts as shown in Fig. 7: Document_Management (Applications for managing documents, enforcing document production workflows, and providing workspaces for groups or enterprises to find and access documents), Collaboration (Tools that allows the managing, sharing, and processing of files, documents and other types of data among multiple users within and across enterprises), Content_Management (Services for managing the production of and access to content

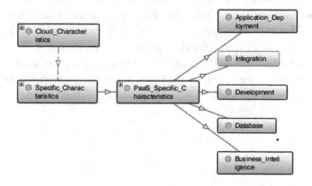

Fig. 6. PaaS service categories.

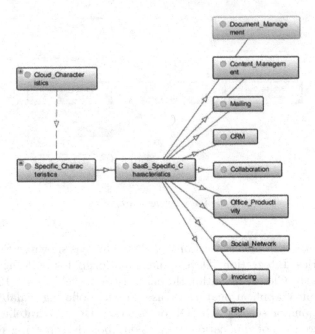

Fig. 7. SaaS service categories.

for web-based applications), CRM (Customer Relationship Management applications for managing the relationships and interactions of a company with its
customers or potential customers), ERP (Enterprise Resource Planning, it is a
modular software designed to integrate the main functional areas of business
processes of a company in a unified system), Invoicing (Application services for
managing customer billing based on usage and subscriptions to products and services.), Mailing (Applications for email), Office_Productivity (Applications for
word processing, spreadsheets, presentations, etc.), and Social_Network (Social
software that establishes and maintains a connection between users to bring
people together to discuss, share ideas and interests, or make new friends).

In this paper, we define the specific characteristics of the *Compute* category
as IaaS service. The proposed ontology serves as a semantic-based registry across
the publication, discovery and selection processes. As shown in Fig. 8, a group of
specific characteristics (e.g. CPU number, memory size, network performance,
operating system, instance storage) that are potentially provided by several service providers facilitate the process of selection of *Compute* services at the IaaS
layer.

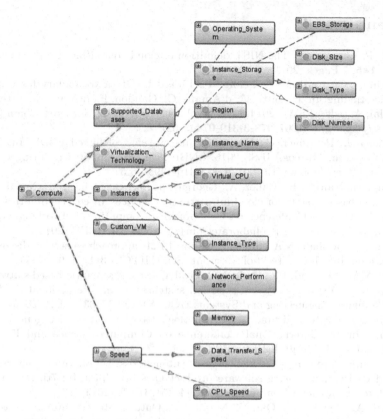

Fig. 8 Specific characteristics concepts of compute services.

5 Conclusion

In this work, we proposed a Cloud service description ontology that covers the three layers of Cloud models, namely IaaS, PaaS and SaaS. The proposed Cloud service description ontology that is extended from Linked USDL, merges technical, operational, business and semantic aspects with Cloud characteristics (common and specific) to obtain a complete and comprehensive Cloud service description. In addition, it ensures high interoperability between multiples Cloud infrastructures, platforms, and software providers. Furthermore, it helps users to discover and select the appropriate Cloud services, as well as providers to publish their services. The proposed ontology is based on standards, a literature review, Cloud providers catalogs, analysis and comparisons of existing ontologies and taxonomies of Cloud services.

As a future work, we intend to complete the ontology with the specific characteristics of PaaS and SaaS categories. Moreover, we aim to use the proposed ontology as a standardized Cloud service description in order to discover and select Cloud services according to user requirements.

References

1. Mell, P., Grance, T.: The NIST definition of cloud computing. NIST Spec. Publ. **800–145**, 7 Pages (2011)
2. Pedrinaci, C., Cardoso, J., Leidig, T.: Linked USDL: a vocabulary for web-scale service trading. In: Presutti, V., d'Amato, C., Gandon, F., d'Aquin, M., Staab, S., Tordai, A. (eds.) ESWC 2014. LNCS, vol. 8465, pp. 68–82. Springer, Cham (2014). https://doi.org/10.1007/978-3-319-07443-6_6
3. Cardoso, J., Pedrinaci, C.: Evolution and overview of linked USDL. In: Nóvoa, H., Drăgoicea, M. (eds.) IESS 2015. LNBIP, vol. 201, pp. 50–64. Springer, Cham (2015). https://doi.org/10.1007/978-3-319-14980-6_5
4. Zhang, M., Ranjan, R., Haller, A., Georgakopoulos, D., Menzel, M., Nepal, S.: An ontology-based system for cloud infrastructure services' discovery. In: 8th International Conference Conference on Collaborative Computing: Networking, Applications and Worksharing (CollaborateCom), pp. 524–530. IEEE (2012)
5. Zhou, J., Abdullah, N.A., Shi, Z.: A hybrid P2P approach to service discovery in the Cloud. Int. J. Inf. Technol. Comput. Sci. (IJITCS) **3**(1), 1–9 (2011)
6. Afify, Y.M., Moawad, I.F., Badr, N.L., Tolba, M.F.: A semantic-based software-as-a-service (SaaS) discovery and selection system. In: 8th International Conference on Computer Engineering and Systems (ICCES), pp. 57–63. IEEE (2013)
7. Nagireddi, V.S.K., Mishra, S.: An ontology based cloud service generic search engine. In: 8th International Conference on Computer Science and Education (ICCSE), pp. 335–340. IEEE (2013)
8. Quinton, C., Romero, D., Duchien, L.: Automated selection and configuration of cloud environments using software product lines principles. In: 7th International Conference on Cloud Computing, pp. 144–151. IEEE (2014)
9. Alfazi, A., Sheng, Q.Z., Qin, Y., Noor, T.H.: Ontology-based automatic cloud service categorization for enhancing cloud service discovery. In: 19th International Enterprise Distributed Object Computing Conference (EDOC), pp. 151–158. IEEE (2015)
10. Kang, J., Sim, K.M.: Ontology-enhanced agent-based cloud service discovery. Int. J. Cloud Comput. **5**(1–2), 144–171 (2016)
11. Rekik, M., Boukadi, K., Abdallah, H.B.: Cloud description ontology for service discovery and selection. In: 10th International Joint Conference on Software Technologies (ICSOFT), pp. 1–11. IEEE (2015)
12. Ghazouani, S., Slimani, Y.: Towards a standardized cloud service description based on USDL. J. Syst. Softw. **132**, 1–20 (2017)
13. Sun, L., Ma, J., Wang, H., Zhang, Y., Yong, J.: Cloud service description model: an extension of USDL for cloud services. IEEE Trans. Serv. Comput. **11**(2), 354–368 (2015)
14. Shetty, J., D'Mello, D. A.: An XML based data representation model to discover infrastructure services. In: International Conference on Smart Technologies and Management for Computing, Communication, Controls, Energy and Materials (ICSTM), pp. 119–125. IEEE (2015)
15. Cardoso, J., Barros, A., May, N., Kylau, U.: Towards a unified service description language for the internet of services: requirements and first developments. In: IEEE International Conference on Services Computing (SCC), pp. 602–609. IEEE (2010)
16. Bizer, C., Heath, T., Berners-Lee, T.: Linked data: the story so far. Int. J. Semant. Web Inf. Syst. **5**(3), 1–22 (2009)

17. Stadtmüller, S., Cardoso, J., Junghans, M.: Service semantics. In: Cardoso, J., Fromm, H., Nickel, S., Satzger, G., Studer, R., Weinhardt, C. (eds.) Fundamentals of Service Systems. SSRISE, pp. 137–178. Springer, Cham (2015). https://doi.org/10.1007/978-3-319-23195-2_5

18. Ben Djemaa, R., Nabli, H., Amous Ben Amor, I.: Enhanced semantic similarity measure based on two-level retrieval model. Concurrency and Computation: Practice and Experience, e5135 (2019)

19. Nabli, H., Ben Djemaa, R., Amous Ben Amor, I.: Efficient cloud service discovery approach based on LDA topic modeling. J. Syst. Softw. **146**, 233–248 (2018)

20. Höfer, C.N., Karagiannis, G.: Cloud computing services: taxonomy and comparison. J. Internet Serv. Appl. **2**(2), 81–94 (2011)

21. Arianyan, E., Ahmadi, M.R., Maleki, D.: A novel taxonomy and comparison method for ranking cloud computing software products. Int. J. Grid Distrib. Comput. **9**(3), 173–190 (2016)

22. Fortis, T. F., Munteanu, V. I., Negru, V.: Towards an ontology for cloud services. In: Sixth International Conference on Complex, Intelligent, and Software Intensive Systems, pp. 787–792. IEEE (2012)

23. Liu, F., Tong, J., Mao, J., Bohn, R., Messina, J., Badger, L., Leaf, D.: NIST cloud computing reference architecture. NIST Spec. Publ. **500–292**, 1–28 (2011)

An Automatic Data Service Generation Approach for Cross-origin Datasets

Yuanming Zhang$^{(\boxtimes)}$, Langyou Huang, Jiawei Lu, and Gang Xiao

Zhejiang University of Technology, Hangzhou, China
{zym,2111612010,viivan,xg}@zjut.edu.cn

Abstract. As a unified data access model, data service has become a promising technique to integrate and share heterogeneous datasets. In order to publish overwhelming data on the web, it is a key to automatically extract and encapsulate data services from various datasets in cloud environment. In this paper, a novel data service generation approach for cross-origin datasets is proposed. An attribute dependency graph (ADG) is constructed by using inherent data dependency. Based on the ADG, an automatic data service extraction algorithm is implemented. The extracted atomic data services are further organized into another representation named data service dependency graph (DSDG). Then, a data service encapsulation framework, which includes an entity layer, a data access object layer and a service layer, is designed. Via a flexible RESTful service template, this framework can automatically encapsulate the extracted data services into the RESTful services which can be accessed by the exposed interfaces. In addition, a data service generation system has been developed. Experimental results show that the system has high efficiency and good quality for data service generation.

Keywords: Data service · Service extraction · Service encapsulation ·
Service dependency graph · Cross-origin datasets

1 Introduction

Large numbers of datasets are increasingly being published by organizations, such as national data[1], which allow the public to access on the web. Generally, data from different organizations tends to be in different formats and organized differently. To enable better utilization of existing data resources and to reduce duplication of data collection, it is necessary to integrate data from distributed and autonomous datasets while maintaining data integrity and consistency. Then, a unified data access interface for upper-layer applications is required.

The data integration methods based on database federation have good scalability but low query efficiency. Data reproduction methods have a short processing time when the datasets are widely distributed and the network delay is large, but at a high cost,

---

[1] http://data.stats.gov.cn.

© Springer Nature Switzerland AG 2019
M. Bakaev et al. (Eds.): ICWE 2019, LNCS 11496, pp. 374–390, 2019.
https://doi.org/10.1007/978-3-030-19274-7_27

such as data warehouse [8]. Furthermore, the overwhelming data in big data era [6] become too large and complex to be effectively processed by these traditional approaches.

With the rapid development of service computing, the content and scope of services are expanded dramatically. Not only are various functions of software encapsulated into the services, named web service (WS) [1], but diverse data produced from software are also encapsulated into services, called data service (DS) [5]. Data service, deployed on the web, shields heterogeneous datasets through a set of access interfaces and provides a unified model for cross-origin data access, data sharing and data analysis. The service-based integration approach is based on XML and HTTP, which is widely adopted by the industry as standard protocols, and can overcome the defects of traditional data integration. Many companies offer the data service interfaces that are exposed to get easier data access, such as the Google, Twitter and Facebook APIs. However, these conventional data service interfaces fail to support responsive and comprehensive data retrieval [18].

It would be beneficial for the service-based integration to automatically generate the data services and satisfy complex data requirements. Several key issues should be handled. First, automatic data service extraction is the initial step. The current existing data services are designed to answer the specific data requirements, which is grounded on the underlying database schema and pre-assembled index [7]. The service granularity should also be considered to improve the reusability and flexibility for decoupling the data services from the clients, and data services can be further composed. Second, automatic data service encapsulation is necessary. There is no standard mechanism to achieve implementation details of data services. The existing approach [17] requires developers to manually implement data services, which is labor-intensive and repetitive and may results in inconsistent style and non standard service internal implementation. Furthermore, with the enormous explosion of datasets, it is practically impossible to manually encapsulate a large number of data services. Third, an appropriate data service modeling technique is required. Some work [10] has been done to integrate multiple datasets by using data formal semantics and ontology-based concepts based on data service. The inherent data dependencies can be mapped onto the dependencies among services, and the data services are further organized into a service dependency graph for automatic service composition.

In this paper, we present an automatic data service generation approach. Our main contributions include:

1. We propose an automatic data service extraction approach and organize the data services into a dependency graph according to their inherent dependencies.
2. We design a data service encapsulation framework that can automatically generate RESTful services with a flexible template.
3. We develop a system which has functions of data service extraction, encapsulation and management. This system has high efficiency and good quality with the actual datasets.

The remainder of this paper is structured as follows. Section 2 reviews the related work on data services. Section 3 introduces an atomic data service extraction approach.

Section 4 presents the data service encapsulation framework. Section 5 describes the data service generation system, then evaluates key algorithms and generated data services in detail. Finally, Sect. 6 concludes the paper.

2 Related Work

In 2008, the BEA proposed encapsulating the data into the data service [4], which is similar to the general web service. The data service can be accessed by the interface and output a desired dataset, is one of the hot spots in the current service computing field.

The data service can not only directly access the data source but can also integrate into the SOA through a standard interface [3], which makes up shortcomings of traditional SOA in the data access and provides a new effective approach to integrate multiple datasets on the web [12]. Data services can be extracted from heterogeneous data for easy data management and rapid data manage and sharing in the enterprise systems [17]. The data service also offers an important way to implement the delivery and usage model for various Cloud-based resources and abilities. Wang [16] discusses the issue of streaming data integration and services based on Cloud computing, then summarizes the challenges and future trends. Zhang [19] proposes a method for encapsulating stream sensor data which processes sensor stream data with service modeling operations and distributes data on-demand based on Pub/Sub mechanism.

Besides limitation for the data sharing, traditional approaches in data technologies do not achieve to fully separate software services from data and thus impose limitations in inter-operability. Terzo [14] takes advantage of data service to proposes an approach for sharing and processing of large data collections which abstracts the data location to fully decouple the data and its processing. Liu [10] provides uniform semantic for heterogeneous datasets that different data source database schema mapping a unified global ontology, and then composites data services through the model mapping for solving the interoperability of heterogeneous data. Hong [9] shows a cloud data service architecture for sharing and exchanging multiple data between the server and client in a distributed system which adopts three levels of data security to protect sensitive data. Existing data service platforms, like AquaLogic [2], support data service modeling and help developers to do data queries, which require the users to have certain expertise and relevant rules before they can operate the data services. To make better use of the data service, Vu [15] proposes a description model for data service (DEMODS) which covers all the basic service information for automatic service lookup. Zorrilla [21] describes a data mining service addressed to non-expert data miners which can be delivered as SaaS. Zhang [18] designs a data service API for data analysts to retrieve data that the REST properties and its related hypermedia-driven features are used to generate resource APIs and navigate each other automatically based on analytical needs.

The general trend has been toward low-code and no-code tools that do not require specialized knowledge for data service generation. However, some approaches fall short of the automaticity and increase the learning cost for those who lack of development experience [17]. Moreover, the data service APIs generation driven by user's specific requirements tends to produce tight coupling, which will impact the reusability and scalability of data service [18]. In order to automatically obtain data service from cross-origin datasets, we present a feasible data service generation approach with the aim of supporting multiple application systems for data sharing. Our approach does not require data providers to do additional programming work, and allow data end-users to directly access the data services without any additional constraints.

3 Atomic Data Service Extraction

3.1 Attribute Dependency Graph

Most datasets include a small section known as metadata that contains the contents for understanding the data and its profiling information. The data owner, who wants to publish data services, needs to provide the necessary data connection information. With existing data connectivity APIs, we can obtain the tables, attributes and dependencies from the metadata, which are the basis for data service extraction. For example, Java DatabaseMetaData interfaces[2] provide methods to get metadata of the databases.

Table 1 gives the metadata of two actual datasets which are extracted from an elevator design dataset and an elevator maintenance dataset, and shows their tables and corresponding attributes. Generally, an attribute is the abstract characteristic description of an object, and data are the specific values of an attribute. The data dependencies are the inherent constraint among the attributes.

Table 1. Datasets extracted from two elevator enterprises

Dataset	Table name		Attributes
Design dataset	elevator_info		a; b; c; d;
	client_info		e; f; g; h;
	order_info		i; a'; e'; j;
Maintenance dataset	elevator_info		k; l; m; n;
	record_info		o; p; q; r;
	component_info		k'; o'; s; t.
(1) a: Elevator no	b: Elevator model	c: Elevator specifications	d: Elevator interior
(2) e: Client no	f: Client name	g: Client address	h: Client contact
(3) **i: Registration no**	a': Elevator no	e': Client no	j: Elevator price
(4) **k: Registration no**	l: Floor number	m: Building name	n: Elevator address
(5) o: Maintenance id	p: Elevator fault	q: Repair time	r: Maintenance time
(6) k': Registration no	o': Maintenance id	s: Maintenance parts	t: Maintenance price

Definition 1 (Functional dependency). *Given a relation R, there exists a functional dependency between two set of attributes X and Y, if, and only if, the X value precisely determines the Y value. It is represented as $X \rightarrow Y$.*

---

[2] docs.oracle.com/javase/9/docs/api/java/sql/DatabaseMetaData.html.

According to the definition of functional dependency, we can derive the full dependency, partial dependency and inter dependency.

Inference 1: *In a relation, there exists a Full Dependency between two set of attributes X and Y, when Y is dependent on X and is not dependent on any proper subset of X. It is represented as $X \xrightarrow{f} Y$. Otherwise, it is a Partial Dependency between X and Y, represented as $X \xrightarrow{p} Y$.*

Inference 2: *In a relation, there exists an Inter Dependency between two set of attributes X and Y, when X and Y are dependent one another. It is represented as $X \leftrightarrow Y$.*

Definition 2 (Join dependency). *A set of attributes X is the common attributes of relation $R_1(U_1)$ and relation $R_2(U_2)$. If $X \rightarrow U_2$, then U_2 is join dependent on X.*

We consider the join dependency as a special functional dependency. Then, the functional dependency defines all the inner and outer data dependencies between relations. A dependency graph can be established through functional dependency among attributes, called attribute dependency graph.

Definition 3 (Attribute dependency graph, ADG). *The attribute dependency graph is an extended directed graph that describes the dependencies among attributes. It can be defined as a tuple.*

ADG = (U, E), where U = {a_1, a_2, ..., a_n}, in which a_i is an attribute; E = {e_1, e_2, ..., e_m}, in which $e_i = X \rightarrow a_j$ represents the a_j is dependent on the X ($X \subseteq U$).

Figure 1 shows the ADG constructed according to the functional dependency of attributes in Table 1. Each node of the graph represents an attribute, and each arrow of the graph represents a dependency between two nodes. For example, the attributes **b, c,** and **d** are dependent on the attribute **a**. The attribute **a** is inter-dependent on the attribute **a'** and the attributes **o'** and **k'** are partial dependent on the attribute **t**. The attributes **i** and **k** represent the elevator registration number. The semantic equivalence of the two attributes **i** and **k** provide a bridge for data integration and data sharing.

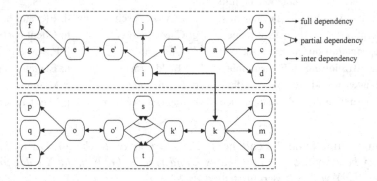

Fig. 1. Attribute dependency graph.

3.2   Atomic Data Service Extraction Algorithm

The data services are extracted from the ADG by encapsulating a set of attributes. The service granularity directly affects the reusability, flexibility and efficiency. If the encapsulated attributes cannot be further subdivided, the corresponding data service is an atomic data service (ADS). We give the formal definition as follows.

Definition 4 (Atomic data service, ADS). *A semantically non-dividable data service is called an atomic data service. Formally, it is a tuple.*

ADS = (ID, Name, Fields, Description, Inputs, Outputs, Operations, Publisher), where ID represents the identification of the ADS; Name represents the name of the ADS; Fields represent the encapsulated attributes of the ADS; Description represents the semantic information of the ADS; Inputs show the multiple input parameters of the ADS; Outputs show the execution result of the ADS; Operations give the possible operations to the ADS; Publisher shows the source of the ADS.

The atomic data service extraction algorithm is shown in Algorithm 1. The input is the metadata of dataset, and the output is the set of ADSs. The attribute set ($U = \{a_1, a_2, ..., a_n\}$) and dependency set ($E = \{e_1, e_2, ..., e_m\}$) are obtained from the metadata. Based on the ADG, the algorithm selects each dependency ($e_i = X \rightarrow a_j$, $X \subseteq U$) in turn and extracts the ADSs with the following rules: (1) Each attribute in X will be extracted as an ADS, whose input and output are the specified attribute; (2) All the attributes in X and the attribute a_j will be extracted as an ADS, whose input is one attribute of X or the attribute a_j, and outputs are all the attributes in X and a_j.

Algorithm 1. Data service extraction algorithm

Input: Metadata of dataset
Output: ADSs
  1: U: The attribute set $\{a_1, a_2, ..., a_n\}$, a_i is an attribute
  2: E: The dependency set $\{e_1, e_2, ..., e_m\}$, $e_i = X \rightarrow a_j$ $(X \subseteq U)$
  3: **for Each** table in Metadata **do**
  4:     Add the attributes of table into U
  5:     Add the dependencies into E
  6:     X ← the primary key of table
  7:     **for Each** attribute in X **do**
  8:         ADS_1 ← attribute
  9:         Add ADS_1 into ADSs
 10:     **end for**
 11: **end for**
 12: **for Each** e in E **do**
 13:     ADS_2 ← e.X + e.a
 14:     Add ADS_2 into ADSs
 15: **end for**
 16: **return** ADSs

Table 2 lists the ADSs extracted from the ADG of Fig. 1. For example, given the dependency $\{k', o'\} \rightarrow s$, the attribute k' and o' are extracted as two ADSs individually, i.e. the ADS_{21} and ADS_{22}. In addition, the attributes $\{k', o', s\}$ are extracted as one ADS, whose input can be any attribute of $\{k', o', s\}$ and outputs are the attributes of $\{k', o', s\}$, i.e. the ADS_{23}. According to the above extraction rules, the total extracted ADS number is equal to the total attribute number. The ADS_9 and ADS_{13} encapsulate the attribute i and k respectively which express the same semantics and mainly used for connection. The ADS_2 encapsulates the attributes a and b, and used to query the elevator number or the elevator model.

Table 2. Atomic data services extracted from the attribute dependency graph.

ID	Name	Fields	Description	Input	Output	Operation	Publisher
01	ADS_1	{a}	Query elevator no	Elevator no	Elevator no	Get	Design Depart.
02	ADS_2	{a, b}	Query elevator no, elevator model	Elevator no **or** elevator model	Elevator no **and** elevator model	Get	Design Depart.
03	ADS_3	{a, c}	Query elevator no, elevator specifications	Elevator no **or** elevator specifications	Elevator no **and** elevator specifications	Get	Design Depart.
...	...	...	...	...	...	...	...
09	ADS_9	{i}	Query registration no	Registration no	Registration no	Get	Design Depart.
...	...	...	...	...	...	...	...
13	ADS_{13}	{k}	Query registration no	Registration no	Registration no	Get	Maintenance Depart.
...	...	...	...	...	...	...	...
21	ADS_{21}	{k'}	Query registration no	Registration no	Registration no	Get	Maintenance Depart.
22	ADS_{22}	{o'}	Query maintenance id	Maintenance id	Maintenance id	Get	Maintenance Depart.
23	ADS_{23}	{k', o', s}	Query registration no, maintenance id, maintenance parts	Registration no, maintenance id **or** maintenance parts	Registration no, maintenance id **and** maintenance parts	Get	Maintenance Depart.
24	ADS_{24}	{k', o', t}	Query registration no, maintenance id, maintenance price	Registration no, maintenance id **or** maintenance price	Registration no, maintenance id **and** maintenance price	Get	Maintenance Depart.

Since the ADSs are obtained by encapsulating attributes, the inherent data dependencies among attributes can be directly mapped onto the dependencies among data services. We define the data service dependency graph as follows.

Definition 5 (Data service dependency graph, DSDG). *The data service dependency graph is an extended directed graph that describes the dependencies between atomic data services. It can be defined as a tuple.*

$DSDG = (DS, E)$, where $DS = \{ADS_1, ADS_2, ..., ADS_n\}$, in which ADS_i is an atomic data service; $E = \{e_1, e_2, ..., e_m\}$, in which $e_i = A \rightarrow ADS_j$ represents that ADS_j is dependent on the A ($A \subseteq DS$).

The DSDG of the data services in Table 2 is given in Fig. 2. In essence, the DSDG shows the logical structure of the ADSs and provides a foundation for further data service composition. Based on the service dependency graph, data services can be composed into composite data services to satisfy users' complex data requirements in the future.

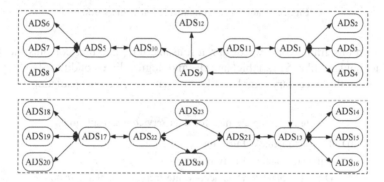

Fig. 2. Data service dependency graph.

4 Data Service Encapsulation

4.1 Data Service Encapsulation Framework

We encapsulate the extracted ADSs into RESTful services, which is based on the representational state transfer (REST) technology. This kind of service defines a set of constraints and properties, and uses HTTP requests to GET, PUT, POST and DELETE resources [13].

We take advantage of the Spring Boot[3] framework to build the RESTful services. Figure 3 shows the data service encapsulation framework. It includes three layers. The entity layer is a mapping of the dataset. An entity object provides a representation of data from a table or other types of data sources. The data access object (DAO) layer provides specific data access operations to the dataset or other persistence mechanism.

---

[3] http://spring.io/projects/spring-boot/.

The service layer defines the RESTful services that uses the GET operation to retrieve the resource, PUT operation to change or update the resource, the POST operation to create the resource, and the DELETE operation to remove the resource.

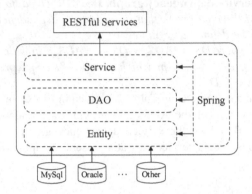

Fig. 3. Data service encapsulation framework.

Based on this framework, we design a reusable template that contains the desired code, placeholders like ${variableName}, and logics like conditionals, loops, etc. Table 3 shows the necessary template files for data service encapsulation.

Table 3. Template files for data service encapsulation.

ID	Template name	Function
1	Entity template	Entity object
2	DAO template	Data access interface and implementation
3	Service template	Data service interface and implementation

The entity template contains the entity object template file. Its fields are all attributes of tables or other data sources, and its methods are the field access methods, such as GET and SET methods. The data type of attributes is unified into String.

The DAO template contains data access interface and implementation details. This template provides abstract interfaces of data operations and the implementation of the interfaces.

The service template contains data service interface and implementation details. The data service interface defines the name, inputs, outputs, operations and URI of the RESTful services. We create RESTful services with CXF[4] that implements the JAX-RS specification and can be easily integrated with the Spring framework.

Figure 4 shows the data service encapsulation procedure. We first extract the meta-data according to the requirements of data service template and generate the data-model

---

[4] http://cxf.apache.org/.

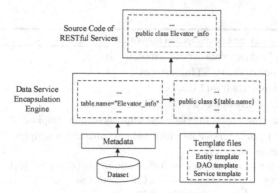

Fig. 4. Data service encapsulation procedure.

that represents the totality of data for template. Then, we utilize a mature template engine, named FreeMarker[5], to parse the data service template files. The engine takes the data-model and data service template files as inputs, then generates the source code of RESTful services by inserting desired code in the template files according to the data-model.

4.2 Data Service Encapsulation Algorithm

The data service encapsulation algorithm is given in Algorithm 2. The input is the metadata of dataset and data service template files, and the output is the source code of RESTful services. The metadata contains all the profiling information of the dataset, such as the tables and the attributes. The table is packed into the data-model of entity template. Combined with the dependencies among attributes, the data-model of DAO template is obtained. According the extracted ADSs, the data-model of service template is organized. Then FreeMarker supplies the data-model for template files in turn and generates the source code of RESTful services. Finally, the source code is compiled to complete the encapsulation.

Taking ADS_2 as an example. This data service has two methods of the GET operation. One is the *getElevatorInfoElevatorModel*. Its input is the elevator no, and its outputs are the list of elevator no and elevator model. The other is the *getElevatorInfoByElevatorModel*. Its input is the elevator model, and its outputs are the list of elevator no and elevator model. The interface source code of the ADS_2 is shown as follow.

---

[5] https://freemarker.apache.org/.

Algorithm 2. Data service encapsulation algorithm

Input: Metadata of dataset, data service template files

Output: Source code of the RESTful services

1: Objects: Entity objects from Metadata

2: Entity template: entity object template file

3: DAO template: data access interface and implementation template files

4: Service template: data service interface and implementation template files

5: **for** Each object in Objects **do**

6:      Get all attributes and the dependencies among attributes of object

7:      entity_data ← get the data-model of Entity template

8:      Source code ← Entity template + entity_data

9:      dao_data ← get the data-model of DAO template

10:     Source code ← DAO template + dao_data

11:     service_data ← get the data-model of Service template

12:     Source code ← Service template + service_data

13: **end for**

14: **return** Source code

```
@Path("/ElevatorInfo") @Produces({MediaType.APPLICATION_JSON+"; charset=UTF-8"})
public interface ElevatorInfoService {
    @GET @Path("/ElevatorModel/{elevatorNo}")
    List<ElevatorInfo> getElevatorInfoElevatorModel (@PathParam(value="elevatorNo") String ele-
vatorNo);
    @GET @Path("/ElevatorNo/ElevatorModel/{elevatorModel}")
    List<ElevatorInfo>    getElevatorInfoByElevatorModel    (@PathParam(value="elevatorModel")
String elevatorModel);
    …}
```

Corresponding to the interface of the ADS_2, the implementation source code of the ADS_2 is shown as follow.

```
@Component ("elevatorInfoService")
public class ElevatorInfoServiceImpl implements ElevatorInfoService {
    @Resource
    private ElevatorInfoDao elevatorInfoDao;
    public List<ElevatorInfo> getElevatorInfoElevatorModel (String elevatorNo) {
        return elevatorInfoDao.getElevatorInfoElevatorModel (elevatorNo);}
    public List<ElevatorInfo> getElevatorInfoByElevatorModel (String elevatorModel) {
        return elevatorInfoDao.getElevatorInfoByElevatorModel (elevatorModel);}
    …}
```

5   Experimental Results

5.1   Prototype System Development

We have developed a data service generation system. Currently, the main functions of the system include dataset management, data service extraction, data service encapsulation, and data service management. Cross-origin datasets from the elevator enterprises which are medium-sized and poor sharing ability of data resources, have been utilized as test data in current system. The datasets include a design dataset, a sales dataset, a customer dataset, a manufacturing dataset, and a maintenance dataset.

Take the elevator design dataset stored in MySQL as an example, Fig. 5 shows the main interfaces of data service extraction. Figure 5(a) shows the interface of obtaining the necessary data connection information provided by the data owner, such as the URL (jdbc:mysql://<host>:<port>/<database_name>), the data driver (com.mysql.jdbc. Driver), username and password, to access a specific dataset. With the methods in Java DatabaseMetaData interfaces, like getTables(), getColumns() and getPrimaryKeys(), the system can obtain all tables, attributes and dependencies among attributes. The description of attributes can be further added to make end-user better understand in Fig. 5(b). Then, the attribute dependency graph (ADG) shown in Fig. 5(c) is built. According to the Algorithm 1, the system will extract the atomic data services (ADSs) based on the ADG. The extracted ADSs are listed in Fig. 5(d). The default description of ADSs is encapsulated attributes and can be edited by end-user. Figure 5(e) shows the relationships among ADSs, where a data service dependency graph (DSDG) is built. After that, the data service extraction is completed. The extracted datasets are shown in the Fig. 5(f).

Figure 6 shows the main interfaces of data service encapsulation. According to Algorithm 2, the system will encapsulate the extracted ADSs into RESTful services using the encapsulation framework. Then, the data services can be deployed on any server node specified by the data owner to ensure service availability, as shown in Fig. 6(a). The data owner can temporarily shutdown or permanently remove the ADSs which involve sensitive date for data security. End-user can access the data services with the provided URL, and get the desired dataset, as shown in Fig. 6(b). These encapsulated ADSs can be directly accessed, and can also be further composed into composite data services to acquire more complex data.

5.2   System Evaluation

In this subsection, we evaluate the two key algorithms adopted in the system: the data service extraction algorithm, and the data service encapsulation algorithm. The experimental hardware is a 2.50 GHz 8-core CPU, 16 G RAM, and 290 GB disk storage. The operation system is a 64-bit Ubuntu 16.04. All algorithms are implemented with the Java programming language.

We select five different experimental datasets [20] for the evaluation. Table 4 shows the information of the datasets including the total number of tables and attributes, the total number of ADSs extracted by Algorithm 1 and total number of source files generated by Algorithm 2.

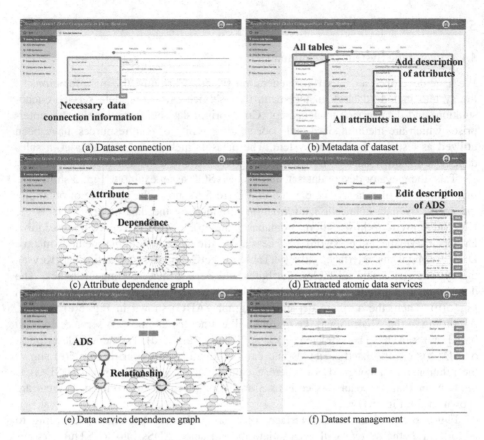

(a) Dataset connection

(b) Metadata of dataset

(c) Attribute dependence graph

(d) Extracted atomic data services

(e) Data service dependence graph

(f) Dataset management

Fig. 5. Main interfaces of data service extraction.

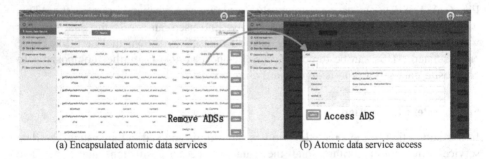

(a) Encapsulated atomic data services

(b) Atomic data service access

Fig. 6. Main interfaces of data service encapsulation.

We first evaluate the system performance of the metadata extraction. Figure 7 shows the overall time consumed to complete the extraction by varying the number of tables and attributes, where the X axis represents the total number of tables, Y axis represents the total number of attributes and the Z axis represents the execution time.

Table 4. Experimental datasets for data service extraction and encapsulation algorithm.

Datasets	Total table number	Total field number	Total ADS number	Total source file number
Customer dataset	14	120	120	74
Sales dataset	27	231	231	139
Made dataset	37	317	317	189
Maintenance dataset	47	400	400	239
Design dataset	62	473	473	314

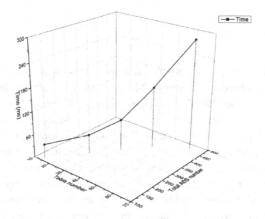

Fig. 7. Performance of the metadata extraction.

It shows that metadata can be obtained in a short time and more attributes in the tables require more time to deal with dependencies among attributes.

Then, we evaluate the system performance that aims to show the overall time consumed by the ADS extraction and encapsulation algorithm. Figure 8(a) shows the overall time consumed to complete the extraction by varying the ADS number, where the X axis represents the total number of ADSs and the Y axis represents the execution time. It can be seen that the execution time rises slightly with the increasing number of the ADSs. Figure 8(b) shows the overall time required to complete the service encapsulation with different number of source files, where the X axis represents the total number of source files and the Y axis represents the execution time. The encapsulation algorithm consumes obviously more time than the extraction algorithm. The reason is that the service encapsulation involves I/O time due to file reading and writing. Totally, the system has high efficiency for both service extraction and service encapsulation.

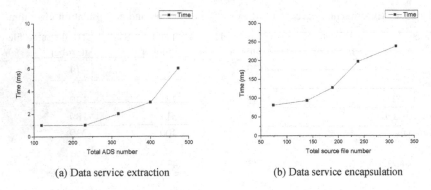

(a) Data service extraction   (b) Data service encapsulation

Fig. 8. Performance of the data service extraction and encapsulation algorithm.

5.3   Analysis

Maturity. We use a model of restful maturity that was developed by Leonard Richardson, called Richardson Maturity Model [11], to evaluate the RESTfulness of our data service APIs. The RESTful services are classified into four levels of maturity according to the design constraints of the REST architectural style: (1) Level 0: Tunneling messages through an open HTTP port leads only to the basic ability to communicate and exchange data. (2) Level 1: Making use of multiple identifiers to distinguish different resources. (3) Level 2: Making proper use of the REST uniform interface in general and of the HTTP verbs in particular. (4) Level 3: In addition to exposing multiple addressable resources which share the same uniform interface also make use of hypermedia to model relationship between resources. Compared with the service APIs of Microsoft's OData (Open Data Protocol)[6] which are not up to the highest level of REST for the reason that there is no navigation for services to include links or self-documentation in response [18], our approach has the capacity to return a response body with a set of resources which associated with the user's request based on the data service dependency graph model. Therefore, our data services reach the maturity level 3.

Discoverability. Discoverability means that the desired data services can be accessed when user requests a resource, which facilitates the composition of data services. Compared with the conventional service interfaces that the process of service discovery is fallible and time-consuming, such as Twitter APIs, our approach can automatically obtain the user-desired data services by searching the data service dependency graph which enables achieving the discoverability.

Reusability. Reusability means that the data services can be reused multiple times without configuration or minor changes. Compared with [18] that there is a one-to-one correspondence between data services and user's data needs, our approach provides a finer granularity and a higher degree of flexibility, which can be composed according to

---

[6] https://www.odata.org/.

various kinds of requirements without replaceability of bindings or binding configuration. The flexible and extensible data services allow users to customize the composite data services for specific requirements which benefits to improve the reusability.

6 Conclusion

To automatically obtain data services from cross-origin datasets, we presented an automatic data service generation approach. The attribute dependency graph (ADG) was built according to inherent data dependencies among dataset. Based on the ADG, data services could be automatically extracted. Then, we designed a data service encapsulation framework. It could automatically encapsulate the extracted ADSs into RESTful services with a specific implementation template. We have developed a data service generation system, and actual cross-origin datasets have been carried out in the system to generate data services. We also evaluated the performance of the extraction and encapsulation algorithms, then demonstrated our data services in maturity, discoverability and reusability. In the future, we will focus on the research of automatic data service generation for unstructured data to improve the availability.

Acknowledgments. The authors gratefully acknowledge the support from the Zhejiang Natural Science Foundation, China (No. LY19F020034).

References

1. Abiteboul, S., Benjelloun, O., Milo, T.: Web services and data integration. In: International Conference on Web Information Systems Engineering, pp. 3–6 (2002)
2. Borkar, V., et al.: Graphical XQuery in the aqualogic data services platform. In: ACM SIGMOD International Conference on Management of Data, pp. 1069–1080 (2010)
3. Carey, M.: Declarative data services: this is your data on SOA. In: IEEE International Conference on Service-Oriented Computing and Applications, p. 4 (2007)
4. Carey, M., Reveliotis, P., Thatte, S., Westmann, T.: Data service modeling in the aqualogic data services platform. In: Services, pp. 78–80 (2008)
5. Carey, M.J., Onose, N., Petropoulos, M.: Data services. Commun. ACM **55**(6), 86–97 (2012)
6. Chen, C.L.P., Zhang, C.Y.: Data-intensive applications, challenges, techniques and technologies: a survey on big data. Inf. Sci. **275**(11), 314–347 (2014)
7. Dillon, S., Stahl, F., Vossen, G.: Towards the web in your pocket: curated data as a service. In: International Conference on Computational Collective Intelligence Technologies and Applications, pp. 25–34 (2012)
8. Halevy, A.Y., Rajaraman, A., Ordille, J.J.: Data integration: the teenage years. In: International Conference on Very Large Data Bases (2006)
9. Hong, X., Rong, C.M.: Multiple data integration service. In: International Conference on Advanced Information NETWORKING and Applications Workshops, pp. 860–865 (2014)
10. Liu, X., Hu, C., Li, Y., Jia, L.: The advanced data service architecture for modern enterprise information system. In: International Conference on Information Science and Applications, pp. 1–4 (2014)

11. Pautasso, C.: RESTful web services: principles, patterns, emerging technologies. In: Bouguettaya, A., Sheng, Q., Daniel, F. (eds.) Web Services Foundations, pp. 31–51. Springer, New York (2014). https://doi.org/10.1007/978-1-4614-7518-7_2
12. Rajesh, S., Swapna, S., Reddy, P.: Data as a service (DaaS) in cloud computing. Glob. J. Comput. Sci. Technol. **12**(11), 25–29 (2012)
13. Richardson, L., Ruby, S.: Restful Web Services, pp. 199–204. O'Reilly Media Inc., Sebastopol (2007)
14. Terzo, O., Ruiu, P., Bucci, E., Xhafa, F.: Data as a service (DaaS) for sharing and processing of large data collections in the cloud. In: Seventh International Conference on Complex, Intelligent, and Software Intensive Systems, pp. 475–480 (2013)
15. Vu, Q.H., Pham, T.V., Truong, H.L., Dustdar, S., Asal, R.: Demods: a description model for data-as-a-service. In: IEEE International Conference on Advanced Information Networking and Applications, pp. 605–612 (2012)
16. Wang, G.L., Han, Y.B., Zhang, Z.M., Zhu, M.L.: Cloud-based integration and service of streaming data. Chin. J. Comput. 107–125 (2017)
17. Yu, H., Cai, H., Zhou, J., Jiang, L.: Data service generation framework from heterogeneous printed forms using semantic link discovery. Future Gener. Comput. Syst. **79**, 514–527 (2017)
18. Zhang, Y., Zhu, L., Xu, X., Chen, S., Tran, A.B.: Data service API design for data analytics. In: Ferreira, J.E., Spanoudakis, G., Ma, Y., Zhang, L.-J. (eds.) SCC 2018. LNCS, vol. 10969, pp. 87–102. Springer, Cham (2018). https://doi.org/10.1007/978-3-319-94376-3_6
19. Zhang, Z.M., Liu, C., Su, S., Zhang, S.L., Han, Y.B.: SDaaS: a method for encapsulating sensor stream data as services. Chin. J. Comput. **40**(2), 445–463 (2017)
20. Zhang, Z.J., Zhang, Y.M., Lu, J.W., Xu, X.S., Gao, F., Xiao, G.: CMfgIA: a cloud manufacturing application mode for industry alliance. Int. J. Adv. Manuf. Technol. **98**(9–12), 2967–2985 (2018)
21. Zorrilla, M., Garca-Saiz, D.: A service oriented architecture to provide data mining services for non-expert data miners. Decis. Support Syst. **55**(1), 399–411 (2013)

Merging Intelligent API Responses Using a Proportional Representation Approach

Tomohiro Ohtake[1]([✉]) [iD], Alex Cummaudo[2] [iD], Mohamed Abdelrazek[1] [iD], Rajesh Vasa[1] [iD], and John Grundy[3] [iD]

[1] Faculty of Science, Engineering and Built Environment,
Deakin University, Geelong, Australia
{tomohiro.otake,mohamed.abdelrazek,rajesh.vasa}@deakin.edu.au
[2] Applied Artificial Intelligence Institute, Deakin University, Geelong, Australia
ca@deakin.edu.au
[3] Faculty of Information Technology, Monash University, Caulfield, Australia
John.Grundy@monash.edu

Abstract. Intelligent APIs, such as Google Cloud Vision or Amazon Rekognition, are becoming evermore pervasive and easily accessible to developers to build applications. Because of the stochastic nature that machine learning entails and disparate datasets used in their training, the output from different APIs varies over time, with low reliability in some cases when compared against each other. Merging multiple unreliable API responses from multiple vendors may increase the reliability of the overall response, and thus the reliability of the intelligent end-product. We introduce a novel methodology – inspired by the proportional representation used in electoral systems – to merge outputs of different intelligent computer vision APIs provided by multiple vendors. Experiments show that our method outperforms both naive merge methods and traditional proportional representation methods by 0.015 F-measure.

Keywords: Application programming interfaces · Web services · Data integration · Artificial intelligence · Supervised learning

1 Introduction

With the introduction of intelligent web services that make machine learning (ML) more accessible to developers [8,20], we have seen a large growth of intelligent applications built using such APIs [5,14]. For example, consider the advances made in computer vision, where objects are localised within an image and labelled with associated categories. Cloud-based computer vision APIs (e.g., [1–3,6,10,11,15,23]) utilise machine-learning techniques to achieve image recognition via a remote black-box approach, thereby reducing the overhead for application developers to understand how to implement intelligent systems from scratch. Furthermore, as the processing and training of the machine-learnt

© Springer Nature Switzerland AG 2019
M. Bakaev et al. (Eds.): ICWE 2019, LNCS 11496, pp. 391–406, 2019.
https://doi.org/10.1007/978-3-030-19274-7_28

algorithms is offloaded to the cloud, developers send simply send RESTful API requests to do the recognition, making it more accessible to them. There are, however, inherit differences and drawbacks between traditional APIs and intelligent APIs, which we describe with the motivating scenario below.

1.1 Motivating Scenario: Intelligent APIs vs Traditional APIs

An application developer, Tom, wishes to develop a social media Android and iOS app that catalogues photos of him and his friends, common objects in the photo, and generates brief descriptions in the photo (e.g., all photos with his husky dog, all photos on a sunny day etc.). Tom comes from a typical software engineering background with little knowledge of computer vision and its underlying concepts. He knows that intelligent computer vision web APIs are far more accessible than building a computer vision engine from scratch, and opts for building his app using these cloud services instead.

Based on his experiences using similar cloud services, Tom would expect consistency of the results from the same API and different APIs that provide the same (or similar) functionality. As an analogy, when Tom writes the Java substring method `"doggy".substring(0, 2)`, he expects it to be the same result as the Swift equivalent `"doggy".prefix(3)`. Each and every time he interacts with the substring method using either API, he gets `"dog"` as the response. This is because Tom is used to deterministic, rule-driven APIs that drive the implementation behind the substring method.

Tom's deterministic mindset results in three key differentials between a traditional API and intelligent API:

(1) **Given similar input, results differ between similar intelligent APIs.** When Tom interacts with intelligent APIs, he is not aware that each API provider trains their own, unique ML model, both with disparate methods and datasets. These intelligent APIs are, therefore, nondeterministic and data-driven; input images—even if they contain the same conceptual objects—often output different results. Contrast this to the substring method of traditional APIs; regardless of what programming language or string library is used, the same response is expected by developers.

(2) **Intelligent responses are not certain.** When Tom interprets the response object of an intelligent API, he finds that there is a 'confidence' value or 'score'. This is because the ML models that power intelligent APIs are inherently probabilistic and stochastic; any insight they produce is purely statistical and associational [18]. Unlike the substring example, where the rule-driven implementation provides certainty to the results, this is not guaranteed for intelligent APIs. For example, a picture of a husky breed of dog is misclassified as a wolf. This could be due to adversarial examples [22] that 'trick' the model into misclassifying images when they are fully decipherable to humans. It is well-studied that such adversarial examples exist in the real world unintentionally [4,12,19].

(3) **Intelligent APIs evolve over time.** Tom may find that responses to processing an image may change over time; the labels he processes in testing may evolve and therefore differ to when in production. In traditional APIs, evolution in responses is slower, generally well-communicated, and usually rare (Tom would always expect "dog" to be returned in the substring example). This has many implications on software systems that depend on these APIs, such as confidence in the output and portability of the solution. Currently, if Tom switches from one API provider to another, or if he doesn't regularly test his app in production, he may begin to see a very different set of labels and confidence levels.

1.2 Research Motivation

These drawbacks bring difficulties to the intended API users like Tom. We identify a gap in the software engineering literature regarding such drawbacks, including: lack of best practices in using intelligent APIs; assessing and improving the reliability of APIs for their use in end-products; evaluating which API is suitable for different developer and application needs; and how to mitigate risk associated with these APIs. We focus on improving reliability of intelligent APIs for use in end-products. The key research questions in this paper are:

RQ1: Is it possible to improve reliability by merging multiple intelligent API results?

RQ2: Are there better algorithms for merging these results than currently in use?

Previous attempts at overcoming low reliability include triple-modular redundancy [13]. This method uses three modules and decides output using majority rule. However, in intelligent APIs, it is difficult to apply majority rule: these APIs respond with a list of labels and corresponding scores. Moreover, disparate APIs ordinarily output different results. These differences makes it hard to apply majority rule because type of outputs are complex and disparate APIs output different result for the same input. Merging search results is another technique to improve reliability [21]. It normalises scores of different databases using a centralised sample database. Normalising scores makes it possible to merge search results into a single ranked list. However, search responses are disjoint, whereas they are not in the context of most intelligent APIs.

In this paper, we introduce a novel method to merge responses of intelligent APIs, using image recognition APIs as our motivating example. Section 2 describes naive merging methods and requirements. Section 3 gives insights into the structure of labels. Section 4 introduces our method of merging computer vision labels. Section 5 compares precision and recall for each method. Section 6 presents conclusions and future work.

2 Merging API Responses

Image recognition APIs have similar interfaces: they receive a single input (image) and respond with a list of labels and associated confidence scores.

Similarly, other supervised-AI-based APIs do the same (e.g. detecting emotions from text and natural language processing [9,24]. It is difficult to apply majority rule on such disparate, complex outputs. While the outputs by *multiple* AI-based API endpoints is different and complex, the general format of the output is the same: it follows a list of labels and associated scores.

2.1 API Façade Pattern

To merge responses from multiple APIs, we introduce the notion of an API façade. It is similar to a metasearch engine, but differs in their external endpoints. The façade accepts the input from one API endpoint (the façade endpoint), propagates that input to all user registered concrete (external) API endpoints simultaneously, then 'merges' outputs from these concrete endpoints before sending this merged response to the API user. We demonstrate this process in Fig. 1.

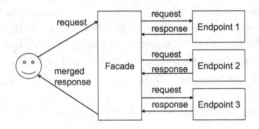

Fig. 1. The user sends a request to the façade; this request is propagated to the relevant APIs. Responses are merged by the façade and returned back to the user.

Although the model introduces more time and cost overhead, both can be mitigated by caching results. On the other hand, the façade pattern provides the following benefits:

- **Easy to modify:** It requires only small modifications to applications, e.g. changing each concrete endpoint URL.
- **Easy to customise:** It merges results from disparate concrete APIs according to user's preference.
- **Improves reliability:** It enhances reliability of the overall returned result by merging results from different endpoints.

2.2 Merge Operations

The API façade is applicable to many use cases. However, this paper focuses on APIs that output a list of labels and scores, as is the case for many image recognition APIs. Merge operations involve the mapping of multiple lists and associated scores, produced by multiple APIs, to just one list. For instance, an image recognition API receives a bowl of fruit as the input image and outputs [[apple, 0.9], [banana, 0.8]], where the first item is the label and the second item is the score. Similarly, another computer vision API outputs [[apple, 0.7], [cherry, 0.8]] for the same image. Merge operations, therefore, merges these two lists into just one.

Naive ways of merging results could make use of max, min, and average operations on the confidence scores. For example: (i) *max* merges results to [[apple, 0.9], [banana, 0.8], [cherry, 0.8]]; (ii) *min* merges results to [[apple, 0.7]; (iii) *average* merges results to [[apple, 0.8], [banana, 0.4], [cherry, 0.4]]. However, object labels in the results are natural language words in many cases; thus, max, min, and average operations do not exploit label semantics – the conceptual meanings of these labels – when conducting label merging. To improve the quality of the merged results, we consider the meaning of these labels, as we describe below.

2.3 Merging Operators for Labels

Merge operations on labels are n-ary operations that map R^n to R, where $R_i = \{(l_{ij}, s_{ij})\}$ is a response from endpoint i, and contains pairs of labels (l_{ij}) and scores (s_{ij}). Merge operations on labels have the following properties:

- *Identity* defines that merging single response should output same response. That is $R = \mathrm{merge}(R)$ is always true.
- *Commutativity* defines that the order of operands should not change the result. That is $\mathrm{merge}(R_1, R_2) = \mathrm{merge}(R_2, R_1)$ is always true.
- *Reflexivity* defines that merging multiple same responses should output same response. That is $R = \mathrm{merge}(R, R)$ is always true.
- *Additivity* defines that, for a specific label, the merged response should have higher or equal score for the label if a concrete endpoint has a higher score. Let $R = \mathrm{merge}(R_1, R_2)$ and $R' = \mathrm{merge}(R'_1, R_2)$ be merged responses. R_1 and R'_1 are same, except R'_1 has a higher score for label l_x than R_1. The additive score property requires that R' score for l_x should be greater than or equal to R score for l_x.

Max, min, and average operations in Sect. 2.2 follow each of these rules as all operations calculate the score by applying these operations on each score.

3 Graph of Labels

Image recognition APIs typically return a lists of labels (in most cases, an English word or words) and associated scores. Lexical databases, such as WordNet [16], can therefore be used to describe the ontology behind these labels' meanings. Figure 2 is an example of graph of labels and synsets. A synset is a grouped set of synonyms for the input word. We label red nodes as labels from Endpoint 1, yellow nodes as labels from Endpoint 2, and blue nodes as synsets. As actual graphs are usually more complex, Fig. 2 is a simplified graph to illustrate the usage of associating labels from two concrete sources to synsets.

3.1 Labels and Synsets

The number of labels depends on input images and concrete API endpoints used. Table 1 and Fig. 3 show how many labels are returned from Google Cloud Vision [6], Amazon Rekogition [1] and Microsoft Azure Computer Vision [15] image recognition APIs, using 1,000 images from Open Images Dataset V4 [7] Image-Level Labels set.

Table 1. Number of labels

Endpoint	Average number of labels	Has synset	No synset
Amazon	11.42 ± 7.52	10.74 ± 7.10 (94.0%)	0.66 ± 0.87
Google	8.77 ± 2.15	6.36 ± 2.22 (72.5%)	2.41 ± 1.93
Microsoft	5.39 ± 3.29	5.26 ± 3.32 (97.6%)	0.14 ± 0.37

Labels from Amazon and Microsoft tend to have corresponding synsets. That means these endpoints return common words that are found in WordNet. On the other hand, Google's labels have less corresponding synsets. Examples of labels without corresponding synsets are car models and dog breeds. Google tries to identify objects in greater detail.

3.2 Connected Components

A connected component (CC) is a subgraph in which there are paths between any two nodes. In graphs of labels and synsets, CCs are clusters of labels and synsets with similar meanings. For instance, there are two CCs in Fig. 2. CC 1 in Fig. 2 has *beverage, dessert, chocolate, hot chocolate, drink,* and *food* labels from the red first endpoint and *coffee, hot chocolate, drink, caffeine,* and *tea* labels from the yellow second endpoint. Therefore, these labels are related to *drinks*. On the other hand, CC 2 in Fig. 2 has *cup* and *coffee cup* labels from the first red endpoint and *cup, coffee cup,* and *tableware* labels from the yellow second endpoint. These labels are, therefore, related to *cups*.

Figure 4 shows a distribution of number of CCs for 1,000-image label detections on Amazon, Google, and Microsoft APIs. The average number of CCs is 9.36 ± 3.49. The smaller number of CCs means that most of labels have similar meanings, while the larger number means that the labels are more disparate.

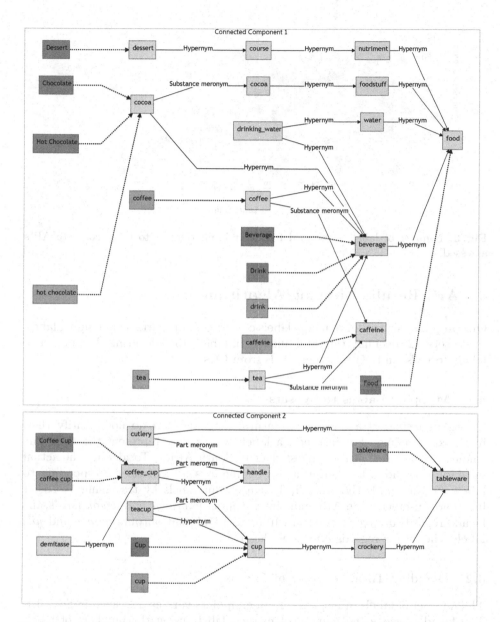

Fig. 2. Graph of labels from two concrete endpoints (red and yellow) and their associated synsets to related both words. (Color figure online)

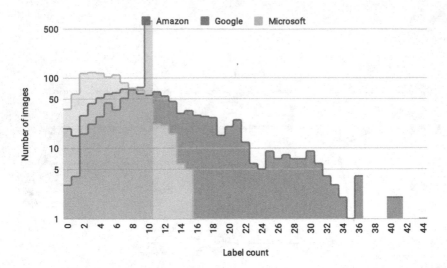

Fig. 3. Number of labels responded from our input dataset to three concrete APIs assessed.

4   API Results Merging Algorithm

Our proposed algorithm to merge labels consists of four parts: (1) mapping labels to synsets, (2) deciding the total number of labels, (3) allocating the number of labels to CCs, and (4) selecting labels from CCs.

4.1   Mapping Labels to Synsets

Labels in responses are words in natural language and do not identify their intended meanings. For instance, a label *orange* may represent the fruit, the colour, or the name of the longest river in South Africa. To identify the actual meanings behind a label, the façade enumerates all synsets corresponding to labels. It then finds the most likely synsets for labels by traversing WordNet links. For instance, if an API endpoint outputs the *orange* and *lemon* labels, the façade regards *orange* as the fruit. If an API endpoint outputs *orange* and *nile* labels, the façade regards *orange* as the river.

4.2   Deciding Total Number of Labels

The number of labels in responses from endpoints vary as described in Sect. 3.1. The façade decides the number of merged labels using the numbers of labels from endpoints. A simple equation about number of labels is established.

$$\min_i(|R_i|) \leq \frac{\Sigma_i |R_i|}{n} \leq \max_i(|R_i|) \leq \Sigma_i |R_i|$$

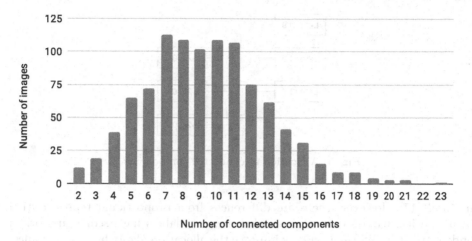

Fig. 4. Number of connected components

Where $|R|$ is number of labels and scores in response, and n is number of endpoints.

In case of naive operations in Sect. 2.2, equations following are true.

$$|\text{merge}_{\text{max}}(R_1,\ldots,R_n)| \le \min_i(|R_i|)$$

$$\max_i(|R_i|) \le|\text{merge}_{\text{min}}(R_1,\ldots,R_n)| \le \Sigma_i|R_i|$$

$$\max_i(|R_i|) \le|\text{merge}_{\text{average}}(R_1,\ldots,R_n)| \le \Sigma_i|R_i|$$

The proposal uses $\lfloor \Sigma_i|R_i|/n \rfloor$ to conform the necessary condition in Sect. 4.3.

4.3 Allocating Number of Labels to Connected Components

The graph of labels and synsets is then divided into several CCs. The façade decides how many labels are allocated for each CC. In Fig. 5, there are three CCs. Square-shaped nodes are labels in responses from endpoints. Text within these label nodes describe which endpoint outputs the label and score, for instance, "L-1a, 0.9" is label *a* from endpoint *1* with a score *0.9*. Circle-shaped nodes represent synsets, where the edges between the label and synset nodes are the relationships between them. Edges between synsets are links in WordNet.

Allegorically, allocating the number of labels to CCs is similar to proportional representation in a political voting system, where CCs are the political parties and labels are the votes to a party. Several allocation algorithms are introduced in proportional representation, for instance, D'Hondt method and Hare-Niemeyer

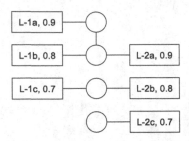

Fig. 5. Allocation to connected components.

method [17]. However, there are differences from proportional representation in a political parties context. For label merging, labels have scores and origin endpoints. This information may improve the allocation algorithm. For instance, CCs supported with more endpoints should have a higher allocation than CCs with fewer endpoints, and CCs with higher scores should have a higher allocation than CCs with lower scores. We introduce an algorithm to allocate number of labels to CCs. This allocates more to a CC with more supporting endpoints and higher scores. The steps of the algorithm are:

1. Sort scores separately for each endpoint.
2. If all CCs have an empty score array or more, remove one, and go to step 2.
3. Select highest score for each endpoint. Calculate product of highest scores.
4. A CC with the highest product score receives an allocation. This CC removes every first element from score array.
5. If requested number of allocation has been done, quit allocation. Otherwise, go to step 2.

Tables 2, 3, 4 and 5 are examples of allocation iterations. In *Table* 2, the façade sorts scores separately for each endpoint. For instance, the first CC in Fig. 5 has scores of 0.9 and 0.8 from endpoint 1 and 0.9 from endpoint 2. All CCs have a non-empty score array or more, so the façade skips step 2. The façade then picks the highest scores for each endpoint and CC. CC 1 has the largest product of highest scores and receives an allocation. In *Table* 3, the first CC removes every first score in its array as it received an allocation in Table 2. In this iteration, the second CC has largest product of scores and receives an allocation. In *Table* 4, the second CC removes every first score in its array. At step 2, all the three CCs have an empty array. The façade removes one empty array from each CC. In *Table* 5, the first CC receives an allocation. The algorithm is applicable if total number of allocation is less than or equal to $\max_i(|R_i|)$ as scores are removed in step 2. The condition is a necessary condition.

Table 2. Allocation iteration 1

Scores	Highest	Product	Allocated
[0.9, 0.8], [0.9]	[0.9, 0.9]	0.81	0+1
[0.7], [0.8]	[0.7, 0.8]	0.56	0
[], [0.7]	[NA, 0.7]	NA	0

Table 3. Allocation iteration 2

Scores	Highest	Product	Allocated
[0.8], []	[0.8, NA]	NA	1
[0.7], [0.8]	[0.7, 0.8]	0.56	0+1
[], [0.7]	[NA, 0.7]	NA	0

Table 4. Allocation iteration 3

Scores	Highest	Product	Allocated
[0.8], []			1
[], []			1
[], [0.7]			0

Table 5. Allocation iteration 4

Scores	Highest	Product	Allocated
[0.8]	[0.8]	0.8	1+1
[]	[NA]	NA	1
[0.7]	[0.7]	0.7	0

4.4 Selecting Labels from CCs

For each CC, the façade applies average operator in Sect. 2.2, and takes labels with n-highest scores up to allocation in Sect. 4.3.

4.5 Conformance to Properties

Section 2.3 defines four properties: identity, commutativity, reflexivity, and additivity. Our proposed method conforms to these properties: **identity:** the method outputs same result if there is one response; **commutativity:** the method does not care about ordering of operands; **reflexivity:** the allocations to CCs are same to number of labels in CCs; and **additivity:** increases in score increases or does not change the allocation to the corresponding CC.

5 Evaluation

5.1 Evaluation Method

To evaluate the merge methods, we merged image label detection results from three representative image analysis API endpoints and compared these merged results against human-verified labels. Images and human-verified labels are sourced from 1,000 randomly-sampled images from Open Images Dataset V4 [7] Image-Level Labels test set.

The first three rows in Table 7 are the evaluation of original responses from each API endpoint. Precision, recall, and F-measure in Table 7 do not reflect actual values: for instance, it appears that Google performs best at first glance, but this is mainly because of Google's label is similar to that of the Open Images Dataset label set.

The Open Images Dataset V4 uses 19,995 classes for labelling and human-verified labels for the 1,000 images of the test set contain 8,878 of these classes. Table 6 shows the correspondence between each APIs' labels and the Open Images Dataset classes. For instance, Amazon outputs 11,416 labels in total for 1,000 images. There are 1,409 unique labels in 11,416 labels. 1,111 labels out of 1,409 can be found in Open Images Dataset classes. Amazon's labels matches to Open Images Dataset classes at 78.9% ratio, while Google has an outstanding matched percentage of 94.1%. This high match is likely due to the Open Images Dataset also being provided by Google. An endpoint with higher matched percentage has a more similar label set to the Open Images Dataset classes. However, a higher matched percentage does not mean imply better quality of an API endpoint; it will increase apparent precision, recall, and F-measure only.

The true and false positive (TP/FP) label averages as well as the TP/FP ratio is shown in Table 7. Where the TP/FP ratio is larger, the scores are more reliable. It is possible to increase the TP/FP ratio intentionally by adding more false labels with low scores. On the other hand, it is impossible to increase F-measure intentionally, because increasing precision will decrease recall, and vice versa. Hence, the importance of the F-measure statistic is critical here.

Let R_A, R_G, and R_M be responses from Amazon, Google, and Microsoft, respectively. There are four sets of operands, i.e., (R_A, R_G), (R_G, R_M), (R_M, R_A), and (R_A, R_G, R_M). Table 7 shows evaluation of each operands set. Table 8 shows averages of four operands sets. Figure 6 shows comparison of F-measure of methods.

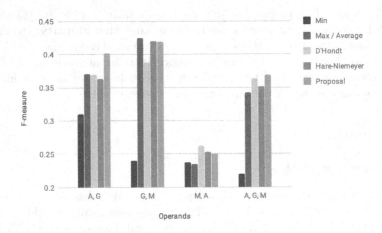

Fig. 6. F-measure comparison

5.2 Naive Operators

Results of *min*, *max*, and *average* operators are shown in Tables 7 and 8 and Fig. 6. The *min* operator is similar to *union* operator of set operations, and outputs all labels of operands. The precision of the *min* operator is always greater

Table 6. Matching to human-verified labels

Endpoint	Total	Unique	Matched	Matched %
Amazon	11,416	1,409	1,111	78.9
Google	8,766	2,644	2,487	94.1
Microsoft	5,392	746	470	63.0

Table 7. Evaluation result

Operands	Operator	Precision	Recall	F-measure	TP average	FP average	TP/FP ratio
A		0.217	0.282	0.246	0.848 ± 0.165	0.695 ± 0.185	1.220
G		0.474	0.465	0.469	0.834 ± 0.121	0.741 ± 0.132	1.126
M		0.263	0.164	0.202	0.858 ± 0.217	0.716 ± 0.306	1.198
A, G	Min	0.771	0.194	0.310	0.805 ± 0.142	0.673 ± 0.141	1.197
A, G	Max	0.280	0.572	0.376	0.850 ± 0.136	0.712 ± 0.171	1.193
A, G	Average	0.280	0.572	0.376	0.546 ± 0.225	0.368 ± 0.114	1.485
A, G	D'Hondt	0.350	0.389	0.369	0.713 ± 0.249	0.518 ± 0.202	1.377
A, G	Hare-Niemeyer	0.344	0.384	0.363	0.723 ± 0.242	0.527 ± 0.199	1.371
A, G	Proposal	0.380	0.423	0.401	0.706 ± 0.239	0.559 ± 0.190	1.262
G, M	Min	0.789	0.142	0.240	0.794 ± 0.209	0.726 ± 0.210	1.093
G, M	Max	0.357	0.521	0.424	0.749 ± 0.135	0.729 ± 0.231	1.165
G, M	Average	0.357	0.521	0.424	0.504 ± 0.201	0.375 ± 0.141	1.342
G, M	D'Hondt	0.444	0.344	0.388	0.696 ± 0.250	0.551 ± 0.254	1.262
G, M	Hare-Niemeyer	0.477	0.375	0.420	0.696 ± 0.242	0.591 ± 0.226	1.179
G, M	Proposal	0.414	0.424	0.419	0.682 ± 0.238	0.507 ± 0.209	1.143
M, A	Min	0.693	0.143	0.237	0.822 ± 0.201	0.664 ± 0.242	1.239
M, A	Max	0.185	0.318	0.234	0.863 ± 0.178	0.703 ± 0.229	1.228
M, A	Average	0.185	0.318	0.234	0.589 ± 0.262	0.364 ± 0.144	1.616
M, A	D'Hondt	0.271	0.254	0.262	0.737 ± 0.261	0.527 ± 0.223	1.397
M, A	Hare-Niemeyer	0.260	0.245	0.253	0.755 ± 0.251	0.538 ± 0.218	1.402
M, A	Proposal	0.257	0.242	0.250	0.769 ± 0.244	0.571 ± 0.205	1.337
A, G, M	Min	0.866	0.126	0.220	0.774 ± 0.196	0.644 ± 0.219	1.202
A, G, M	Max	0.241	0.587	0.342	0.857 ± 0.142	0.714 ± 0.210	1.201
A, G, M	Average	0.241	0.587	0.342	0.432 ± 0.233	0.253 ± 0.106	1.712
A, G, M	D'Hondt	0.375	0.352	0.363	0.678 ± 0.266	0.455 ± 0.208	1.492
A, G, M	Hare-Niemeyer	0.362	0.340	0.351	0.693 ± 0.260	0.444 ± 0.216	1.559
A, G, M	Proposal	0.380	0.357	0.368	0.684 ± 0.259	0.484 ± 0.200	1.414

than any precision of operands, and the recall is always lesser than any precision of operands. *Max* and *average* operators are similar to *intersection* operator of set operations. Both operators output intersection of labels of operands. There is no clear relation to precision and recall of operands. Since both operators have same precision, recall, and F-measure, Fig. 6 groups them into one. The *average* operator performs well on TP/FP ratio. Most of same labels from multiple

Table 8. Average of evaluation result

Operator	Precision	Recall	F-measure	TP/FP ratio
Min	0.780	0.151	0.252	1.183
Max	0.266	0.500	0.344	1.197
Average	0.266	0.500	0.344	1.539
D'Hondt	0.361	0.335	0.346	1.382
Hare-Niemeyer	0.361	0.336	0.347	1.378
Proposal	0.257	0.242	0.360	1.289

endpoints are true positives. In any cases of four operand sets, all naive operators' F-measures are between F-measures of operands. None of naive operators improve results by merging responses from multiple endpoints.

5.3 Traditional Proportional Representation Operators

There are many existing allocation algorithms [17] in proportional representation, e.g., D'Hondt and Hare-Niemeyer methods. These methods may be replacements of those in Sect. 4.3. Other steps, i.e. Sects. 4.1, 4.2 and 4.4, are same as for our proposed technique. Tables 7 and 8 and Fig. 6 show result of these traditional proportional representation algorithms. Averages of F-measures by traditional proportional representation operators are almost equal to that of *max* and *average* operators. It is worth noting that merging M and A results in a better F-measure than each F-measure of M and A individually. Because endpoints M and A are not biased to human-verified labels, situations in the real world should, therefore, be similar to the case of M and A. So, RQ1 is true.

5.4 New Proposed Label Merge Technique

As shown in Table 8, our proposed new method performs best in F-measure. Instead, TP/FP ratio is less than average, D'Hondt, and Hare-Niemeyer. As described in Sect. 5.1, we argue that F-measure as more important than TP/FP ratio in this case. Therefore, RQ2 is true. Shown in Table 7, our proposed new method improves the results when merging M and A non-biased endpoints. It is similar to traditional proportional representation operators, but performs less well than them. However, it performs better on other operand sets, and performs best on overall as shown in Fig. 6.

5.5 Performance

We used AWS EC2 m5.large instance (2 vCPUs, 2.5 GHz Intel Xeon, 8 GiB RAM); Amazon Linux 2 AMI (HVM), SSD Volume Type; Node.js 8.12.0. It takes 0.370 s to merge responses from three endpoints. Computational complexity of the algorithm in Sect. 4.3 is $O(n^2)$, where n is total number of labels in responses.

The estimation assumes that the number of endpoints is a constant. Complexity of step 1 in Sect. 4.3 is $O(n \log n)$, because the worst case is that all n labels are from one single endpoint and all n labels are in one CC. Complexity of step 2 to 5 is $O(n^2)$ because number of CCs is less than or equal to n and number of iterations are less than or equal to n. As Table 1 shows, the averaged total number of three endpoints is 25.58. Most of time for merging is consumed by looking up WordNet synsets (Sect. 4.1). The API façade calls APIs on actual endpoints in parallel. It takes about 5 s, which is much longer than 0.370 s taken for the merging of responses.

6   Conclusions and Future Work

In this paper, we propose a method to merge responses from intelligent APIs. Our method merges API responses better than naive operators and other proportional representation methods (i.e., D'Hondt and Hare-Niemeyer). The average of F-measure of our method marks 0.360; the next best method, Hare-Niemeyer, marks 0.347. Our method and other proportional representation methods are able to improve the F-measure from original responses in some cases. Merging non-biased responses results in 0.250 of F-measure, while original responses have an F-measure between 0.246 and 0.242. Users can improve their applications' precision by small modification, e.g. changing endpoint URL from API endpoints to façades. Performance impact by applying façades is small, because overhead in façades is much smaller than API invocation. The proposal method conforms identity, commutativity, reflexivity, and additivity properties. These properties are advisable for integrating multiple responses.

Our idea of a proportional representation approach can be applied to other intelligent APIs. If response type is a list of entity and score, and if there is a way to group entities, a proposal algorithm can be applied. The opposite approach is to improve results by inferring labels. Our current approach picks some of the labels returned by endpoints. intelligent APIs are not only based on supervised machine learning. Thus to cover a wide range of intelligent APIs, it is necessary to classify and analyse APIs, and establish a method to improve results by merging. Currently graph structures of labels and synsets (Fig. 2) are not considered when merging results. Propagating scores from labels could be used, losing the additivity property but improving results for users. There are many ways to propagate scores. For instance, setting propagation factors for each link type would improve merging and could be customised for users' preferences. It would be possible to generate an API façade automatically. APIs with same functionality have same or similar signatures. Machine-readable API documentation, for instance, OpenAPI Specification, will help a generator to build an API façade.

References

1. AWS: Amazon rekognition. https://aws.amazon.com/rekognition/
2. Clarifai, Inc.: Clarifai. https://www.clarifai.com
3. Deep AI, Inc.: Image Recognition API. https://deepai.org/ai-image-processing
4. Eykholt, K., et al.: Robust physical-world attacks on deep learning visual classification. In: Proceedings of the IEEE Conference on Computer Vision and Pattern Recognition, pp. 1625–1634 (2018)
5. FileShadow: Fileshadow delivers machine learning to end users with google vision API. https://www.businesswire.com/news/home/20180723005503/en/FileShadow-Delivers-Machine-Learning-Users-Google-Vision
6. Google: Google cloud vision API. https://cloud.google.com/vision/
7. Google: Open images dataset v4. https://storage.googleapis.com/openimages/web/index.html
8. Hwang, K.: Cloud Computing for Machine Learning and Cognitive Applications: A Machine Learning Approach. MIT Press, Cambridge (2017)
9. IBM: Tone analyzer. https://www.ibm.com/watson/services/tone-analyzer/
10. IBM: Watson Visual Recognition. https://www.ibm.com/watson/services/visual-recognition/
11. Imagga: Imagga's API. https://imagga.com
12. Kurakin, A., Goodfellow, I., Bengio, S.: Adversarial examples in the physical world, July 2016. arXiv.org
13. Lyons, R.E., Vanderkulk, W.: The use of triple-modular redundancy to improve computer reliability. IBM J. Res. Dev. 6(2), 200–209 (1962). https://doi.org/10.1147/rd.62.0200
14. Geospatial Media and Communications: Mapillary and Amazon Rekognition collaborate to build a parking solution for US cities through computer vision. https://www.geospatialworld.net/news/mapillary-and-amazon-rekognition-collaborate/
15. Microsoft: Microsoft azure computer vision API. https://azure.microsoft.com/en-us/services/cognitive-services/computer-vision/
16. Miller, G.A.: WordNet: a lexical database for English. Commun. ACM 38(11), 39–41 (1995). https://doi.org/10.1145/219717.219748
17. Niemeyer, H.F., Niemeyer, A.C.: Apportionment methods. Math. Soc. Sci. 56(2), 240–253 (2008). https://doi.org/10.1016/j.mathsocsci.2008.03.003
18. Pearl, J.: The seven tools of causal inference with reflections on machine learning (2018)
19. Pezzementi, Z., et al.: Putting image manipulations in context: robustness testing for safe perception. In: IEEE International Symposium on Safety, Security, and Rescue Robotics, SSRR, pp. 1–8, April 2018
20. Ribeiro, M., Grolinger, K., Capretz, M.A.M.: MLaaS: machine learning as a service. In: 2015 IEEE 14th International Conference on Machine Learning and Applications (ICMLA), pp. 896–902. IEEE, December 2015
21. Si, L., Callan, J.: A semisupervised learning method to merge search engine results. ACM Trans. Inf. Syst. 21(4), 457–491 (2003). https://doi.org/10.1145/944012.944017
22. Szegedy, C., et al.: Intriguing properties of neural networks (2013). arXiv:1312.6199
23. Talkwalker: Image Recognition for Visual Social Listening. https://www.talkwalker.com/image-recognition
24. TheySay: Sentiment analysis API. http://www.theysay.io/sentiment-analysis-api/

Semantic Web and Linked Open Data Applications

Analyzing the Evolution of Linked Vocabularies

Mohammad Abdel-Qader[1,2]([✉]) [iD], Iacopo Vagliano[2] [iD], and Ansgar Scherp[3] [iD]

[1] Christian-Albrechts University, Kiel, Germany
`stu120798@mail.uni-kiel.de`
[2] ZBW – Leibniz Information Centre for Economics, Kiel, Germany
`{m.abdel-qader,i.vagliano}@zbw.eu`
[3] University of Essex, Colchester, UK
`ansgar.scherp@essex.ac.uk`

Abstract. Reusing terms results in a Network of Linked vOcabularies (NeLO), where the nodes are the vocabularies that use at least one term from some other vocabulary and thus depend on each other. These dependencies become a problem when vocabularies in the network change, e.g., when terms are deprecated or deleted. In these cases, all dependent vocabularies in the network need to be updated. So far, there has been no study that analyzes vocabulary changes in NeLO over time. To address this shortcoming, we compute the state of NeLO from the available versions of the vocabularies over 17 years. We analyze static parameters of NeLO such as its size, density, average degree, and the most important vocabularies at certain points in time. We further investigate how NeLO changes over time. Specifically, we measure the impact of a change in one vocabulary to others, how the reuse of terms changes, and the importance of vocabularies changes. Our analyses provide for the first time in-depth insights into the structure and evolution of NeLO. This study helps ontology engineers to identify shortcomings of the data modeling and to assess the dependencies implied with reusing a specific vocabulary.

1 Introduction

For modeling and publishing data on the web, we use properties and types defined in one or multiple vocabularies. It is common practice to reuse existing terms, i.e., properties and types, from other vocabularies for modeling one's own data. The goal is to prevent the proliferation of terms and to reduce the range of choices when modeling data. This reuse of terms leads to a Network of Linked vOcabularies (NeLO). In essence, NeLO is a directed graph of connected vocabularies that have at least one reuse from some other vocabulary. By connected vocabularies, we mean that a vocabulary v is reusing at least one term from another vocabulary w.

The connections between the vocabularies become a problem when one or more of the vocabularies in the network change. For instance, the vocabulary w could declare a term t as deprecated or even delete it while the dependent

© Springer Nature Switzerland AG 2019
M. Bakaev et al. (Eds.): ICWE 2019, LNCS 11496, pp. 409–424, 2019.
https://doi.org/10.1007/978-3-030-19274-7_29

vocabulary v is reusing this term t. The changes of vocabularies have a direct impact on all dependent vocabularies, i.e., those that reuse any of the changed terms. Furthermore, all the data that are modeled with these outdated vocabularies have also to be updated. The outdated terms are those that were deleted or deprecated when updating a vocabulary.

Previous research focused on analyzing the interlink at an instance level. In contrast, with analyzing NeLO, we focus on the evolution of the web of data at the schema level. In a previous work [1], we showed that some deleted and deprecated terms are still reused by data publishers to represent their data. In this paper, we consider the reuse of vocabulary terms in other vocabularies. Specifically, we analyze NeLO by addressing the following research questions:

RQ1. What is the state of the Network of Linked Vocabularies? This includes several subquestions: What is its size in terms of the number of nodes and edges? What is its density, and average degree? Which are the important vocabularies, i.e., central nodes?

RQ2. How are vocabulary terms reused by other vocabularies? More specific subquestions are: How many vocabularies do reuse terms from others? How many terms are reused? Are the reused terms the most recent ones? How does the change (addition or deletion) of terms in one vocabulary impact the other vocabularies on the network?

RQ3. How do ranking metrics, such as *PageRank*, *Hypertext Induced Topic Selection* (HITS), and *Centrality*, change during the evolution of the Network of Linked Vocabularies? We are specifically interested in understanding how the important nodes, i.e., the central vocabularies, as well as the reuse of terms changes over time.

To address these questions, we analyzed 994 vocabularies and their changes in a time span of over 17 years. We considered vocabularies as part of the network if they import or export at least one term from some other vocabularies. We employed a broad range of network-analysis metrics on the extracted network and applied them during the evolution of NeLO to find out how the important nodes change over time. We investigated how the change of one vocabulary impacts the others that reuse its terms.

Our analysis shows that at the beginning the growth of the Network of Linked Vocabularies was large, but recently the increase has been lower. Moreover, the percentage of reused terms by other vocabularies has decreased over time. This study also summarizes how the reused vocabularies changed over time. Overall, we believe that our study can help ontology engineers by raising awareness on the changes occurred in NeLO. This may lead to an increase of the reuse of terms among vocabularies, and to avoid or decrease terms' redundancy.

The remainder is structured as follows. We introduce a motivating example for analyzing NeLO in Sect. 2. We review related work in Sect. 3. In Sect. 4, we describe our experimental apparatus to analyze the evolution of NeLO. We present our results in Sect. 5 and discuss them in Sect. 6, before we conclude.

2   Motivating Example

Figure 1 shows a selected part of NeLO, with some of the dependencies of the vocabularies depicted. The arrows represent the relation between exporters and importers. An arrow from a vocabulary w to another vocabulary v indicates that v imports terms from w, or, in other words, that w exports terms to v. The size of the nodes represents the number of exports, i.e., more exports imply a bigger node. The width of the edges represents the total number of types and properties that the target vocabulary imports from the source vocabulary. For example, the *adms* vocabulary exports terms to *food*, *gn*, *search*, and *void*, while *schema*, and *voaf* export terms to *adms*.

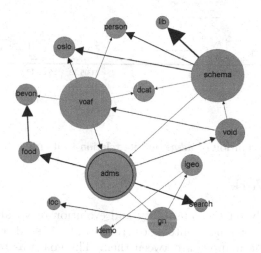

Fig. 1. Vocabularies that import terms from *adms* and other vocabularies.

Regarding the evolution of NeLO, we consider the example of the *adms* vocabulary. *adms* deals with describing highly reusable metadata and reference data, which are called Semantic Assets[1]. Figure 2 shows the evolution of the *adms* vocabulary within six versions over five years (bottom). Furthermore, the *food* vocabulary (top) reuses some terms of *adms* and also has different versions over its lifespan. The *adms* vocabulary published six versions between May 2012 and July 2015, and introduced the adms:SemanticAsset type and adms:accessURL property in its version published in June 2012 (V2). The *food* vocabulary reuses those two terms in its first version, which were published in November 2012. Afterwards, a new version of the *adms* vocabulary has been released in May 2013, which deleted the adms:SemanticAsset and adms:accessURL terms. In September 2013, the *food* vocabulary was updated, but the updated version of the *food* ontology kept using the two terms that were deleted from *adms*.

---

[1] https://www.w3.org/TR/vocab-adms/.

Such a scenario may mean that *food* still needs the deleted terms and its ontology engineers have found no alternatives. However, it could also denote that the ontology engineers of the *food* vocabulary are not aware of the changes in *adms*. This study analyzes the problem of evolution in NeLO and the possible effects that changes in vocabularies have on the dependent vocabularies.

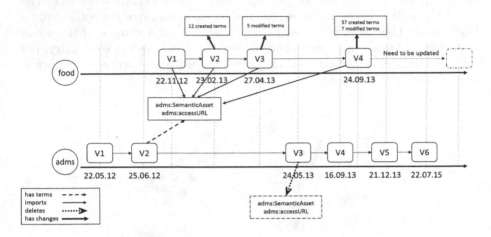

Fig. 2. Evolution of *adms* and its relation to its importer *food*.

3   Related Work

Several works analyzed the reusability and evolution of vocabularies. Some of these focused on biomedical ontologies. Reis et al. [4] studied how changes of ontologies affect the mappings between them. The goal was to understand the evolution of biomedical ontologies to propose an automatic mechanism for mapping. Hartung et al. [7] selected 16 life science ontologies since 2004 to measure the impact of ontology evolution on semantic annotations. They proposed a framework to analyze the life science ontologies and their instances. Cardoso et al. [2] analyzed the impact of ontology evolution on existing annotations. They considered over 66 million annotations from 5,000 biomedical articles and ontologies to support semi-automatic annotation maintenance mechanisms. Ghazvinian et al. [5] studied the overlap between the biomedical ontologies. They found more than 4 million mappings between concepts. Using those mappings, they analyzed the ontologies, their repositories, and how they can help in ontology design and evaluation. Kamdar et al. [11] published a study regarding terms reuse on ontologies in the BioPortal repository. The authors found reuse between 25–31%, and the percentage of reused terms was less than 9%. However, none of these studies applied network analysis metrics to the evolved ontologies. Furthermore, they studied the mappings and overlap between ontologies in the biomedical domain, while we analyze the vocabularies from various domains.

Vandenbussche et al. [18] described Linked Open Vocabularies (LOV) and provided some related statistics. They also provided a system that shows the dependencies between vocabularies, but it does not give information about which terms are reused by other vocabularies. In contrast, we provide information about the reusability of terms in NeLO, such as the most reused terms and whether terms, which have been deleted, are still reused or not. Most of the analyses of Linked Open Data focused on the instance level. Vassilis et al. [16] discussed the state-of-the-art systems that manage the evolving RDF data by proposing a benchmark generator that evaluate the ability of the current versioning strategies to manage LOD datasets. Käfer et al. [10] collected 29 weekly snapshots of a seed list with 86,696 RDF documents and analyzed the changes between pairs of two consecutive snapshots. The results showed that RDF documents change frequently. Gottron and Gottron [6] compared the accuracy of various RDF indices over the weekly snapshots from Käfer et al. [10]. Dividino et al. [3] analyzed the dynamics of the data by Käfer et al. [10] and proposed a monotone, non-negative function to represent the dynamics of RDF statements as a single numerical value. Nishioka and Scherp [13] computed periodicities of temporal changes in the dataset by Käfer et al. [10].

Palma et al. [15] proposed guidelines to execute the ontology evolution activity. Their approach covered two aspects: the description of the ontology evolution process and the tasks involved, and the facilitation of the process using semi-automatic techniques. While their methodology is to undertake the evolution process, we analyze the evolution in NeLO. Meusel et al. [12] analyzed the evolution of *schema.org* over four years. Thus, they focused on analyzing only a single but widely used data schema. They studied the top-down adoption and bottom-up evolution approaches and found that some of the deprecated terms are still used. Noura et al. [14] identified the most popular ontologies on the Internet of Things to identify the most used terms in this domain. They selected 14 ontologies. They found out that 71% of the ontologies reuse less than 18% of the terms defined, and 20% of ontologies are not reused at all. Jiménez-Ruiz et al. [9] described a logic-based approach to reuse terms between ontologies. Their approach specified that the reuse should be safe, i. e., the reused terms are valid (have not been changed/deleted in the source). Furthermore, the reuse should be economic, i. e., only the relevant parts of an ontology are imported. Previously, we presented a qualitative assessment of vocabulary changes [1], but we focused on their impact on instances. In this paper, we complement our prior work and consider the schema-level, i. e., the reuse of vocabulary terms in other vocabularies and the impact of their changes on each other.

4 Network Analysis Method

To answer our research questions, we conducted the following steps. First, we extracted all types and properties from all the available versions of vocabularies (from June 2001 to June 2018), which are listed in the Linked Open Vocabularies (LOV) dataset[2]. The terms extracted are classified into two categories: the *own terms* are the terms created by the ontology engineers of the considered

---

[2] http://lov.okfn.org/dataset/lov/, last accessed: June 2018.

vocabulary, while the *reused terms* are the terms that are reused from other vocabularies. Second, we employed different network-analysis metrics to study the Network of Linked Vocabularies, such as degree, PageRank, and HITS. We checked if the *reused terms* are the most recent ones, i.e., whether the terms that appear in the latest published version of the source vocabulary are actually those that are reused in the target vocabulary. This procedure was repeated on the evolving NeLO in a yearly basis to analyze the change of the Network of Linked Vocabulary over time.

For the first step, we examined 636 vocabularies listed in LOV. We employed the OWL API[3] version 5.1.6 to extract all the *own terms* and *reused terms* from the latest version of all the 636 vocabularies. While extracting the reused terms, some additional vocabularies that are not contained in LOV, were found. Thus, we considered a total of 994 ontologies. For the second step of the methodology, we used the Open Graph Viz Platform (Gephi)[4] version 0.9.2 to visualize and analyze the Network of Linked Vocabularies. Subsequently, we identified the deleted and deprecated terms of the vocabularies by parsing and comparing all versions of a vocabulary. Finally, we checked if the vocabularies on NeLO are still reusing the deleted or deprecated terms.

5   Results

We present the results of our analysis in Sects. 5.1, 5.2 and 5.3 along the research questions RQ1, RQ2, and RQ3. We only present the main results. The complete results can be found online.[5]

5.1   State of NeLO in 2018

Figure 3 shows the current state of NeLO after extracting all import relations between the latest versions of the vocabularies until June 2018. One can see three main circles in the network. Those circles are formed depending on the number of exports to the other vocabularies. The inner circle contains the vocabularies that have the most exports (more than 100 edges), which are represented by the larger node sizes. The middle circle (the denser area of smaller nodes) includes the vocabularies which have between 5 and 100 edges. The outer circle (the sparser external area) contains all the vocabularies that have been imported by less than five vocabularies. A fully scalable version of the figure is available at our website (see Footnote 5).

In June 2018, NeLO consists of 994 vocabularies and 7,046 edges between those vocabularies, with a density of 0.007. Thus, the actual number of edges in the graph is far away from the maximal number of possible edges (when each node has an edge to all other nodes) and the maximal density (equal to 1 with the maximal number of possible edges). The average degree for NeLO 2018 is 7.09, with a standard deviation of 7.46.

---

[3] https://github.com/owlcs/owlapi, last accessed: June 2018.

[4] https://gephi.org/, last accessed: June 2018.

[5] https://sites.google.com/view/nelo-evolution.

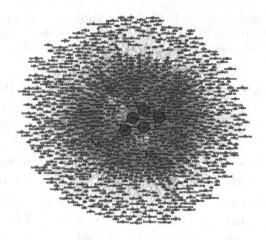

Fig. 3. The Network of Linked Ontologies (NeLO) as it appears in June 2018.

Tables 1, 2 and 3 list the top-10 vocabularies that have the highest scores for degree, HITS, and PageRank, respectively.[6] PageRank and HITS can help to identify nodes which can be problematic because they have many dependencies, or their changes may affect many other nodes because they are widely reused. We exploit these measures in addition to the degree since they take into account indirect dependencies (indirect links in NeLO). Most of the vocabularies are the same for all these metrics, with some differences in their order. Furthermore, *dcterms*, *dce*, *foaf*, *skos*, and *vann* appear in the top of the three tables.

Please note, we remove meta-vocabularies since it is quite natural that they are mostly used. Since we could not find a clear definition of meta-vocabularies, we excluded *owl*, *rdf*, *rdfs*, *xml*, and *xsd*, which clearly belong to this category. Some other vocabularies may be considered meta-vocabularies, too. For example, *cc* and *vann* are normally used to annotate metadata of the ontology itself. Our data are publicly available (see Footnote 5), and we welcome researchers to recompute the results excluding these or other ontologies.

5.2   Reuse of Vocabularies and Adoption of Their Changes

Reusing existing terms is one of the main principles of Linked Data. Table 4 lists the top-10 terms reused by other vocabularies. Those terms are extracted from the latest NeLO snapshot (June 2018). After excluding the meta-vocabularies, the most reused term is `dcterms:modified`, which represents the date on which a resource was changed. The term `dcterms:modified` has 281 vocabularies that reuse it.

Figure 4 shows a histogram of the vocabularies that reuse outdated terms from other vocabularies in the 2018 snapshot. We can notice that 16 vocabularies reuse one outdated term. On the other hand, we found six vocabularies that reuse more than six outdated terms.

---

[6] We refer to Zaki et al. [19] for a description of degree, HITS, and PageRank.

Table 1. Top-10 vocabularies for Degree, In-degree, and Out-degree in 2018, sorted by Degree. The scores are calculated over both types and properties.

Vocabulary	Degree	In-degree	Out-degree
dcterms	435	425	10
dce	347	339	8
foaf	330	317	13
vann	255	244	11
skos	235	229	6
cc	153	146	7
voaf	121	103	18
vs	116	108	8
dctype	82	74	8
schema.org	73	61	12

Table 2. Top-10 vocabularies for HITS (Hub and Authority) scores in 2018, sorted by Authority.

Vocabulary	Authority	Hub
dcterms	0.305421	0.037978
dce	0.242374	0.037727
foaf	0.234664	0.044112
vann	0.184754	0.045030
skos	0.171827	0.034529
cc	0.113386	0.034723
vs	0.081972	0.040256
voaf	0.080739	0.045920
dctype	0.058152	0.037727
schema.org	0.046659	0.040364

Table 3. Top-10 vocabularies for PageRank in 2018.

Vocabulary	PageRank
dce	0.045954
dcterms	0.027649
skos	0.017678
foaf	0.013986
dcam	0.009152
vann	0.009117
grddl	0.008740
dctype	0.005744
cc	0.005446
vs	0.005005

Table 4. Top-10 terms that are reused by other vocabularies in 2018.

Term	Importing vocab.
dcterms:modified	281
dcterms:title	276
dce:title	266
dce:creator	263
vann:preferredNamespacePrefix	257
dcterms:description	249
vann:preferredNamespaceUri	241
foaf:Person	175
foaf:name	164
cc:license	122

There are three vocabularies that removed the reused terms after they were deleted from their original vocabularies, which are listed in Table 5. The *Updated version* column represents the version of the vocabulary where the update occurred. Notably, the *oslo* vocabulary removed five outdated terms, but it still reuses two outdated terms in its latest version.

5.3   Evolution of NeLO

Figure 5 shows the total number of available types and properties, and the total number of reused terms in NeLO. The reuse percentage was at its top with 10% and 11% in 2010 and 2011, respectively, while for all other years it remains in the range between 5% and 7%.

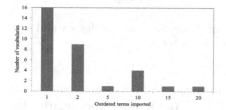

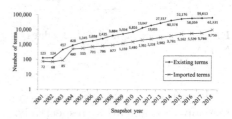

Fig. 4. The number of vocabularies that reuse outdated terms by the number of outdated terms reused.

Fig. 5. The total number of existing types and properties and the terms reused from other vocabularies.

Table 5. Vocabularies that removed outdated terms.

Vocabulary	Removed terms	Updated version	Prior version
qudt	12	9-Oct-2016	1-Jun-2011
oslo	5	30-May-2014	30-Sep-2013
dcat	1	28-Nov-2013	20-Sep-2013

Figure 6 depicts the total number of nodes and edges for each NeLO snapshot. It is worth noting that the number of nodes (vocabularies) and edges almost doubled from the 2003 to the 2004 snapshots compared to 2002 and 2003, respectively. Then they continued to roughly double every two years until 2013. After that year, the growing-rate decreased, and, since 2016 until June 2018, the number of new vocabularies that entered the network becomes small (around 70 new vocabularies per year), while the number of new links is still slightly higher (about 600 per year).

Figure 7 presents the density, network diameter [19], and average degree measures over time. The network average degree has a slow but steady increase. The density of the network is slightly decreasing over time. More specifically, in 2001, the network density was 0.273, and in 2018 it was 0.007. The network diameter sharply grew over the period considered, although its increase is not steady. First, it quadrupled from 2002 to 2003, then there is another small peak from 2004 to 2005. From 2010 to 2015 we can see the highest growth. The diameter of 2015 also represents the maximum value in the whole period. Finally, in the last three years, it is almost constant.

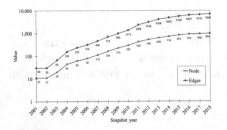

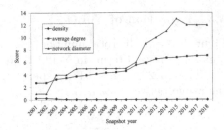

Fig. 6. Number of nodes and edges in NeLO.

Fig. 7. Density, average degree, and network diameter.

Figure 8 illustrates the evolution of the in-degree and out-degree metrics for the top-5 vocabularies, respectively. We selected the top-five vocabularies for these measures in the latest snapshots of NeLO (from 2015 to 2018), excluding the meta-vocabularies. Subsequently, we calculated the scores for those top-five vocabularies for each NeLO snapshot. This selection process holds also for the following analyses that consider PageRank and HITS (Figs. 9 and 10).

Figure 8a depicts the number of imported vocabularies. While the out-degree for the vocabularies selected tends to steadily grow, the in-degree is mostly constant and abruptly increased in 2011 for *mo*, in 2015 for *interval*, and in 2018 for *semio*, with some exceptions. We can notice that *qudt* decreases the number of imported vocabularies. This number was 39 in 2011, then increased to 44 in 2012. Subsequently, it has continuously decreased to 25 imported vocabularies. Furthermore, the *oa* vocabulary decreases the number of imported vocabularies from 23 in 2013 to only 9 in 2016. Later, this number has increased again to reach 27 imported vocabularies. The *mo* vocabulary shows a constant number of imports from 2011 until 2018. While *mo* was introduced in 2007, it did not reuse any term from the other vocabularies until 2011.

Figure 8b presents the out-degrees for the top-5 vocabularies. The out-degree corresponds to the total number of other ontologies that reuse at least one term from those vocabularies, i. e. the number of exports to different ontologies. From 2003 to 2007, all the vocabularies shown have a similar out-degree. From 2009, *skos* started to increase more than the others, and the same holds for *vann* starting from 2012. We can notice that *vann* and *skos* have become widely more popular than the other vocabularies. Additionally, from 2015, *vann* exceeded *skos*, while earlier *skos* had the highest out-degree overall. However, the gap between their out-degrees is rather small. In 2014, *cc* achieved about the same out-degree of *vs*, and later on *cc* has a higher value than *vs*. The *voaf* vocabulary is introduced in 2011 and in 2018 accounts for almost the same in-degree as *vs*.

Figures 9 and 10 show the PageRank and HITS scores, respectively, for the same top-five vocabularies selected as for the degree analysis. In Fig. 9, we can notice that all vocabularies have decreasing PageRank scores except *skos* and *vann*. The *skos* vocabulary started to increase its score from 2009, although from 2013 to 2018 it is again steady. However, this is almost half than the original

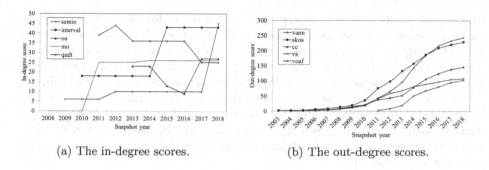

(a) The in-degree scores.   (b) The out-degree scores.

Fig. 8. The in- and out-degree for the top-5 vocabularies on each NeLO snapshot.

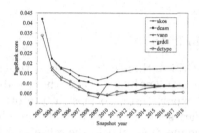

Fig. 9. The PageRank scores for the top-five vocabularies for each year.

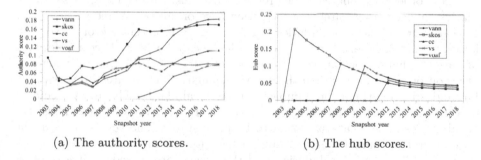

(a) The authority scores.   (b) The hub scores.

Fig. 10. The HITS scores for the top-five vocabularies on each NeLO snapshot.

skos's PageRank score in 2003. Instead, *vann* had its lowest point in 2010, and started to slowly grow again from 2011. The *grddl* vocabulary appeared in 2008, with the lowest PageRank score, although it was close to *dctype* and *vann*. It slightly decreased in 2009. In 2010, it increased and remained almost constant in the following years, with roughly the same value as *dcam*.

Regarding the HITS scores, Fig. 10a shows that there is a general trend of increasing authority scores for all the vocabularies, although with some fluctuations. Specifically, *vann* started to grow from 2007, after an initial slight decrease. In 2018, it achieved the highest authority score. The *skos* vocabulary has a similar trend, with a more pronounced initial decrease from 2003 to 2004 and a peak in 2011. Subsequently, there is almost no further growth. Notably, *vs* has a score decrease starting from 2013, and then the score becomes stable. The *voaf* vocabulary appeared in 2011 and has steadily grown until 2018, where it achieved the same value as *vs*. The latter has the lowest scores among the vocabularies presented. Regarding the hub scores depicted in Fig. 10b, the vocabularies show a similar pattern of a continuously decreasing score after an initial peak. The difference is in their peak value and in the year. Note that the early versions of vocabularies had no terms imported by other ontologies. Afterward, they started to be reused. In 2018, all the vocabularies achieved similar hub scores, around 0.05.

6   Discussion

6.1   State of NeLO in 2018

The vocabularies in NeLO form three categories (the three circles in Fig. 3 introduced in Sect. 5.1). The first one corresponds the vocabularies, including the meta-vocabularies, that export terms to most of the other vocabularies in the network. These vocabularies in the central circle are the most important in NeLO 2018. They are the most popular in the sense that their terms are highly reused, but updating their terms is critical because of their potential impact on many other vocabularies which reuse their terms. Nevertheless, these vocabularies change rather rarely. In fact, they have on average three versions over 17 years. Overall, the vocabularies in this category represent 2% of all vocabularies, export their terms to 71% of the other vocabularies, and account for 66% of outgoing links. Vocabularies in the second category still have many edges to other ontologies, but less than the meta-vocabularies. These are also very popular, and updating them could impact various vocabularies. The average number of versions of the second category of vocabularies is around three. Thus, the vocabularies in this category seem to be more stable. The vocabularies in the middle circle account for around 20% of the outgoing links. These vocabularies represent 13% of the vocabularies, and their terms are reused by 56% of other vocabularies in NeLO 2018. The third category contains rarely-reused vocabularies, such as the newcomers, or the ones that cover a very specific domain.

6.2   Reuse of Vocabularies and Adoption of Their Changes

Overall, 16% of the terms in NeLO are reused in June 2018. This number is still low and there is a need to increase the reuse of the existing types and properties, in order to avoid overlap and redundancy in the data representation [8]. Tools to suggest existing terms like TermPicker [17] could play a major role in increasing the number of terms reused by helping ontology engineers to select and discover terms to reuse.

Many vocabularies are up-to-date in NeLO 2018. There are 35 vocabularies that are affected by term updates in other vocabularies. 33 vocabularies are still using outdated types or properties. Although this number may seem low, it can have a strong impact on the published data, as shown in our previous study [1]. The number of outdated terms reused by those vocabularies ranges between 1 and 20. We think that the process of checking for changes in order to update the ontologies is done manually. The SemWeb Vocabulary Status ontology (*vs*)[7] provides information about the status of a term, but it is not widely used. This vocabulary (or similar ones) can help ontology engineers to check the recent status of terms before reusing them, e. g. to avoid reusing terms which are not stable and are likely to be removed in the future.

From the 35 vocabularies affected by changes in 2018, three have been updated by removing some of the outdated terms. For instance, the *oslo* vocabulary removed five terms, one from *adms* and four from *rov*. However, *oslo* still reuses two terms from *vcard*, although they have been deleted in *vcard*. This could either mean that the deleted terms are still needed and no alternatives have been found, or that some updates have been missed because the process for looking for changes in the other vocabularies is done manually. Reusing terms from older vocabulary versions, which can still be accessed by the IRI of the version, is possible, but we recommend checking the reason and update such terms.

There is a lack of tools to notify ontology engineers about changes in the vocabularies. Such tools may help ontology engineers to keep track of the changes and reduce the update effort. Tool support becomes especially important when a vocabulary has many dependencies: the more terms the ontology reuses, the higher is the effort to update the vocabulary when a change occurs. With many dependencies, it is challenging to keep an ontology up-to-date as any change in one of the imported vocabularies could require an update of the importer. Some vocabularies have edges from more than 40 others. Overall, 12% of the vocabularies imported from 59% of others, accounting for 22% of incoming links.

6.3   Evolution of NeLO

The number of new vocabularies and relations between them has decreased over time. While in 2003, 55% of the vocabularies were new, this percentage decreased to 4% in 2018. Regarding the edges, 57% of them were introduced in 2003. This percentage decreased to 27% in 2009, increased to 43% in 2010, and dropped to 4% in 2018. We can observe fluctuations in the number of new vocabularies and edges. Ontology engineers keep adding terms to their existing vocabularies, rather than introducing new ontologies, in order to fulfill their domain requirements. Therefore, over time we expect that the number of new vocabularies will continue to decrease or perhaps there will be a slower growth rate. Given that less new vocabularies have been introduced over time, it is not surprising that also less import/export links have been created.

Considering the reuse of terms from 2004 to 2010, the percentage of reused terms with respect to the available ones ranges between 58% and 22%.

---

[7] https://www.w3.org/2003/06/sw-vocab-status/note.

This percentage decreased to 10% in June 2017, although slightly increased in 2018, accounting for 16% of the available terms. This suggests that reusing terms was initially more common. One reason could be that initially much fewer vocabularies were available, it was easier to be aware of them and reuse their terms. Nevertheless, more specific vocabularies, which are less suitable to be reused, may have been created over time.

Some vocabularies have become more popular (their out-degree has increased). When excluding the meta-vocabularies, *vann*, *skos*, *cc*, *vs*, and *voaf* are the most popular vocabularies. By taking into account the out-degree and centrality measures on all NeLO snapshots for the vocabularies with the highest scores in the last three years, we found that *vann*, *skos*, *cc*, *vs*, and *voaf* have increased their scores. Notably, *vann* and *skos* have a more rapid increase than the other three vocabularies, i. e., they have become more popular over time. Overall, the meta-vocabularies, which are suitable for most domains, are the most popular ones. Interestingly, our findings show a decline in the growth of out-degree scores, i. e., the average number of exports per vocabulary decreases over time. This could be due to the fact that less new vocabularies have been introduced over time. Consequently, fewer terms are exported to those new vocabularies. Nevertheless, the reuse of terms could still be increased among existing vocabularies, according to the needs of the particular application scenario considered. Regarding the in-degrees, we observed that they vary among the nodes in the network over time. Some of the vocabularies with the highest in-degree over time, such as *mo*, *interval*, and *semio*, have a sudden and large growth of imports at a specific point in time. This corresponds to a new version with a considerable extension of the previous vocabulary which reuses many terms from other ontologies. Thus, more effort is needed to keep track of the changes in the reused terms.

Similarly, the changes in the vocabularies with high PageRank and HITS scores affects many other vocabularies. The difference between those with high PageRank and HITS scores with a high out-degree is that their changes can significantly impact also ontologies that are indirectly related to it. Therefore, these changes can be even more critical. We recommend that ontology engineers of vocabularies that reuse terms from vocabularies with high PageRank and HITS scores periodically check them for changes.

7   Conclusion

By this study, we aim to raise ontology engineers' awareness about the changes in NeLO. As our analysis of the evolution of NeLO shows, the dynamics of changes has slowed down after some fast evolution between 2001 and 2010. As of today, 33 of the considered 994 vocabularies do reuse outdated terms. We recommend ontology engineers to check the evolution in NeLO and assess why a term is deleted or deprecated. Furthermore, we like to further stimulate an increase in reusing terms to prevent redundancy. As future work, we will consider the other types of updates, such as adding/removing constraints to terms or their subclasses, and different types of reuse of terms between vocabularies, e. g., introducing sub-classes or sub-properties, or using terms for annotation.

Acknowledgment. This work was supported by the DFG (German Research Foundation) with the LOC-DB project (Grants No. GZ:SCHE 1687/5-1) and the EU's Horizon 2020 programme under grant agreement H2020-693092 MOVING.

References

1. Abdel-Qader, M., Scherp, A., Vagliano, I.: Analyzing the evolution of vocabulary terms and their impact on the LOD cloud. In: Gangemi, A., et al. (eds.) ESWC 2018. LNCS, vol. 10843, pp. 1–16. Springer, Cham (2018). https://doi.org/10.1007/978-3-319-93417-4_1
2. Cardoso, S.D., et al.: Leveraging the impact of ontology evolution on semantic annotations. In: Blomqvist, E., Ciancarini, P., Poggi, F., Vitali, F. (eds.) EKAW 2016. LNCS (LNAI), vol. 10024, pp. 68–82. Springer, Cham (2016). https://doi.org/10.1007/978-3-319-49004-5_5
3. Dividino, R., Gottron, T., Scherp, A.: Strategies for efficiently keeping local linked open data caches up-to-date. In: Arenas, M., et al. (eds.) ISWC 2015, Part II. LNCS, vol. 9367, pp. 356–373. Springer, Cham (2015). https://doi.org/10.1007/978-3-319-25010-6_24
4. Dos Reis, J.C., Pruski, C., Da Silveira, M., Reynaud-Delaître, C.: Understanding semantic mapping evolution by observing changes in biomedical ontologies. J. Biomed. Inform. **47**, 71–82 (2014)
5. Ghazvinian, A., Noy, N.F., Jonquet, C., Shah, N., Musen, M.A.: What four million mappings can tell you about two hundred ontologies. In: Bernstein, A., et al. (eds.) ISWC 2009. LNCS, vol. 5823, pp. 229–242. Springer, Heidelberg (2009). https://doi.org/10.1007/978 3 642 04930 9_15
6. Gottron, T., Gottron, C.: Perplexity of index models over evolving linked data. In: Presutti, V., et al. (eds.) ESWC 2014. LNCS, vol. 8465, pp. 161–175. Springer, Cham (2014). https://doi.org/10.1007/978-3-319-07443-6_12
7. Hartung, M., Kirsten, T., Rahm, E.: Analyzing the evolution of life science ontologies and mappings. In: Bairoch, A., Cohen-Boulakia, S., Froidevaux, C. (eds.) DILS 2008. LNCS, vol. 5109, pp. 11–27. Springer, Heidelberg (2008). https://doi.org/10.1007/978-3-540-69828-9_4
8. Janik, M., Scherp, A., Staab, S.: The semantic web: collective intelligence on the web. Inform. Spektrum **34**(5), 469 (2011)
9. Jiménez-Ruiz, E., Grau, B.C., Sattler, U., Schneider, T., Berlanga, R.: Safe and economic re-use of ontologies: a logic-based methodology and tool support. In: Bechhofer, S., Hauswirth, M., Hoffmann, J., Koubarakis, M. (eds.) ESWC 2008. LNCS, vol. 5021, pp. 185–199. Springer, Heidelberg (2008). https://doi.org/10.1007/978-3-540-68234-9_16
10. Käfer, T., Abdelrahman, A., Umbrich, J., O'Byrne, P., Hogan, A.: Observing linked data dynamics. In: Cimiano, P., Corcho, O., Presutti, V., Hollink, L., Rudolph, S. (eds.) ESWC 2013. LNCS, vol. 7882, pp. 213–227. Springer, Heidelberg (2013). https://doi.org/10.1007/978-3-642-38288-8_15
11. Kamdar, M.R., Tudorache, T., Musen, M.A.: A systematic analysis of term reuse and term overlap across biomedical ontologies. Semantic web **8**(6), 853–871 (2017)

12. Meusel, R., Bizer, C., Paulheim, H.: A web-scale study of the adoption and evolution of the schema.org vocabulary over time. In: International Conference on Web Intelligence, Mining and Semantics, p. 15. ACM (2015)
13. Nishioka, C., Scherp, A.: Temporal patterns and periodicity of entity dynamics in the Linked Open Data Cloud. In: K-CAP, p. 22. ACM (2015)
14. Noura, M., Gyrard, A., Heil, S., Gaedke, M.: Concept extraction from the web of things knowledge bases. In: The International Conference WWW/Internet (2018)
15. Palma, R., Zablith, F., Haase, P., Corcho, O.: Ontology evolution. In: Suárez-Figueroa, M.C., Gómez-Pérez, A., Motta, E., Gangemi, A. (eds.) Ontology Engineering in a Networked World, pp. 235–255. Springer, Heidelberg (2012). https://doi.org/10.1007/978-3-642-24794-1_11
16. Papakonstantinou, V., Fundulaki, I., Flouris, G.: Assessing linked data versioning systems: the semantic publishing versioning benchmark. In: International Workshop on Scalable Semantic Web Knowledge Base Systems@ISWC, pp. 219–234 (2018)
17. Schaible, J., Gottron, T., Scherp, A.: *TermPicker*: enabling the reuse of vocabulary terms by exploiting data from the Linked Open Data Cloud. In: Sack, H., Blomqvist, E., d'Aquin, M., Ghidini, C., Ponzetto, S.P., Lange, C. (eds.) ESWC 2016. LNCS, vol. 9678, pp. 101–117. Springer, Cham (2016). https://doi.org/10.1007/978-3-319-34129-3_7
18. Vandenbussche, P.Y., Atemezing, G.A., Poveda-Villalón, M., Vatant, B.: Linked Open Vocabularies (LOV): a gateway to reusable semantic vocabularies on the web. Semantic Web 8(3), 437–452 (2017)
19. Zaki, M.J., Meira Jr., W., Meira, W.: Data Mining and Analysis: Fundamental Concepts and Algorithms. Cambridge University Press, Cambridge (2014)

Comparison Matrices of Semantic RESTful APIs Technologies

Antoine Cheron[1]([envelope])(iD), Johann Bourcier[2]([envelope])(iD), Olivier Barais[2]([envelope])(iD),
and Antoine Michel[1]([envelope])

[1] FABERNOVEL, 46 rue Saint-Lazare, 75009 Paris, France
{antoine.cheron,antoine.michel}@fabernovel.com
[2] Univ Rennes, Inria, CNRS, IRISA, 263 Avenue General Leclerc, 35000 Rennes,
France
{johann.bourcier,olivier.barais}@irisa.fr

Abstract. Semantic RESTful APIs combine the power of the REST
architectural style, the Semantic Web and Linked Data. They picture a
world in which Web APIs are easier to browse and more meaningful for
humans while also being machine-interpretable, turning them into platforms that developers and companies can build on. We counted 36 technologies that target building such APIs. As there is no one-size-fits-all
technology, they have to be combined. This makes selecting the appropriate set of technologies to a specific context a difficult task for architects
and developers. So, how the selection of such a set of technologies can be
eased? In this paper we propose three comparison matrices of Semantic
RESTful APIs enabling technologies. It is based on the analysis of the
differences and commonalities between existing technologies. It intends
to help developers and architects in making an informed decision on the
technologies to use. It also highlights the limitations of state-of-the-art
technologies from which open challenges are derived.

Keywords: Hateoas · Semantic REST · Comparison · Linked Data ·
Web

1 Introduction

Today, RESTful APIs [18] have become the de-facto standard for building web
applications. The main reason behind this popularity lies in the appropriate
trade-off between the facility to build such applications and the benefits provided
by this approach in such an opened large-scale distributed system: evolutivity,
scalability and loose-coupling. However, 95% of APIs are not RESTful [12] as
they claim.

Until today, no single standard has emerged to design truly RESTful APIs.
Consequently, software architects are facing the challenge of selecting the right
technologies for the design and implementation of these systems. Typically, a
software architect has to select the right interface description language (IDL),
interchange format and framework to ease the development of such APIs.

© Springer Nature Switzerland AG 2019
M. Bakaev et al. (Eds.): ICWE 2019, LNCS 11496, pp. 425–440, 2019.
https://doi.org/10.1007/978-3-030-19274-7_30

In addition, a new trend has recently emerged to create RESTful APIs that carry their own semantics, they are called Semantic RESTful APIs [14]. It is a vision that proposes to make fully REST-compliant APIs compatible with the Semantic Web [3] and Linked Data [4]. From our experience at FABERNOVEL, we found that building such APIs does not require much more effort than truly RESTful systems, whereas it offers great benefits, such as loose-coupling, automated API mash-ups [2], machine-interpretability and very powerful querying.

However, the design of semantic RESTful APIs considerably increases the complexity for the architect to choose the appropriate technology. Indeed, the specific criteria and properties to be taken into account are not explicit when choosing an IDL, an interchange format and a framework. The industrial needs are growing for proper tools to support trade-off decisions of the architect; a tool that would help him/her to understand the consequences of a design decision, i.e. the characteristics and limitations of each approach.

In this paper, we propose to fill this gap by providing three decision matrices that help architects to choose the technologies that will best fit their needs. The main contributions of this paper are:

- three comparison matrices of interchange formats, interface description languages and frameworks that help choosing the appropriate set of technologies to build Semantic RESTful APIs;
- key features that are missing from state-of-the-art technologies to assist and make the creation of Semantic RESTful APIs more beneficial.

Using these comparison matrices, we illustrate their usage on an industrial case and draw the outline of a research road-map to ease the adoption of Semantic RESTful APIs in the industry.

The remainder of this paper is organized as follows. Section 2 provides the required background on Semantic REST APIs and the reference maturity model to choose the functionality level of an API along, with its limitation. The two following sections describe our comparison matrices and an illustration that highlights the benefits of our proposition. Finally, Sect. 5 discusses the role of the existing frameworks to build Semantic REST APIs.

2   Background

This section describes the main concepts related to the design and implementation of Semantic RESTful APIs and the process of selecting an API functionality.

Semantic RESTful Services. Combining REST with Semantic Web and Linked Data is a promising path since it enables the description of APIs that can change without breaking client applications. These APIs advertise their available state transitions, therefore enabling automatic composition to create high level services [1]. Smart software agents can then automatically discover the suite of operations to realize complex workflows and even make APIs compatible with voice assistants. This is achieved by semantically enriching the data and operations of REST systems with Semantic Web ontology technologies and by linking resources to other resources.

2.1   Selecting an API Functionality Level

Today, Web systems offer a wide range of functionalities. For example, they may offer multiple media types or a single one, comply with the HTTP protocol or use it as a transfer protocol, or even semantically describe their resources. This diversity can make the process of comparing and selecting the minimum set of features to be implemented very time-consuming. Maturity models have been proposed as a solution to this problem [11,14].

In companies, architects use them to decide features which must be supported by their APIs. In general, a maturity model is a scale that represents the compliance of a technology with a given architecture. To reach a level, a technology must meet each constraint of the targeted level and the previous levels. Currently, the de-facto standard in the industry is the Richardson Maturity Model [6], which targets building REST APIs. However, we recommend using the WS3 maturity model [14] as it combines the models proposed by Richardson, and SoHA [17], and extends them with semantic and documentation constraints.

The WS3 Maturity Model. In [14], authors describe the WS3 maturity model for classifying Semantic REST Web APIs. It classifies APIs along three independent dimensions: *design, profile* and *semantic*, as shown in Fig. 1.

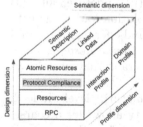

Fig. 1. WS3 maturity model (from [14])

The **design dimension** represents the different modeling strategies adopted for designing the technical access to a Web API through four levels: (i) RPC, (ii) resources have dedicated URI and the API is stateless, (iii) operations on a resource are mapped to HTTP verbs in compliance with the protocol and (iv) the smallest data unit that can be handled by operations is the resource.

The **profile dimension** reflects the quality of documentation that can be interpreted by software agents through two levels. The first level: *interaction profile*, requires the description of all available HTTP operations and how to trigger them. The second level: the *domain profile*, requires the description of domain specific details such as the order of operation execution, pre- and postconditions, business constraints, etc.

The **semantic dimension** represents the use of semantic technologies through two levels. To reach the *Semantic Description level*, an API must semantically describe properties and operations of resources. The next level: *Linked Data*, is reached when the API semantically describes relationships between resources.

Usage. In their paper [14], Salvadori *et al.* propose to rate systems along each dimension independently, with a score going from 0 to the number of levels in the dimension. For example, a non-documented API with no semantic support that reaches level 3 of the Richardson Maturity Model will be rated D3-S0-P0[1]. As another example, a system that supports HATEOAS and provides a swagger-like documentation along with the data is rated D3-S0-P2[2].

2.2 Discussion on the WS3 Maturity Level

At FABERNOVEL, we experienced two limitations to the applicability of the maturity model to a wider audience. These limitations are related to the *Atomic Resources level* and the granularity of the WS3 levels.

According to WS3, the *Atomic Resources* constraint requires that the resource is the smallest data unit handled by operations. Respecting this constraint may introduce negative properties in the API. Let us consider an API handling insurance contracts which offers read and update operations on the postal address, email address and insurance manager. Two solutions can be considered to respect the *Atomic Resources* constraint. The first solution is to create one resource, where every properties can be modified at once, which increases the risk of concurrent modification. With this solution, the API would have two operations. The second solution is to create one resource for each concept: contract, email address, postal address and the manager. The API would have eight operations. This solution increases dramatically the number of operations which complexifies the documentation and maintainability. Another solution would be to create one resource with four operations: (i) read, (ii) update email, (iii) update postal address and (iv) update manager. This solution lowers the concurrency risk while maintaining a reasonable complexity and offering meaningful operation names. Unfortunately this solution breaks the *Atomic Resources constraint*. We therefore argue that respecting this last constraint may not always lead to better API quality.

The second limitation relates to the granularity of the maturity levels. Indeed, each level implies more than one feature. This granularity allows for a coarse-grained categorization of systems. However, to precisely differentiate systems based on the features they implement, a deeper study is needed. Given two systems that reach P1, which means they describe all available HTTP operations and how to trigger them, one might also describe its authentication process and errors while not the other one. And yet they reach the same maturity level. We therefore argue for a finer grain categorization of APIs.

3   Comparison Matrices

We propose three detailed matrices which address the limits of WS3 identified in the previous section. The proposed matrices enable the comparison of technologies along a set of precise criteria to highlight their differences. These matrices

---

[1] D3-S0-P0: Atomic Resources Design, no Semantic Description, no Profile description.

[2] D3-S0-P2: Atomic Resources Design, no Semantic Description, Domain Profile.

extend the WS3 levels by adding new criteria which are used in practice (see
Sect. 3.1) and not linked to any WS3 levels.

3.1   Insights from Developers and Architects

We interviewed 14 developers and architects from FABERNOVEL and clients on
their experience with Semantic REST technologies. Raw results and the analysis
are available online[3]. Our key findings are:

- *Selecting the technology:* 10 respondents have already built Semantic REST
  APIs: **30%** spent more than two weeks selecting the technologies; **80%**
  reported that the most difficult task was to understand the feature provided
  by each technology.
- *Interchange Formats:* **6 out of 7** did not find a technology providing all
  required features (most often the missing features were the description of
  HTTP operations with their data model (3/8) and the Linked Data (2/8)).
- *Interface description languages:* All respondents said that none of them provide all required features (60% said they lack the ability to describe links
  to other resources and business constraints; and 20% of them would like to
  model the resources as finite state machines (FSM)).
- *Frameworks:* 6 out of 7 reported that no framework offered the required feature. The missing features are related to the auto-documentation of the API,
  the automatic generation of link and a mechanism to model resources as FSM.
- *Technology score:* The median value of the score is 2/5.

These results emphasize the difficulties in selecting technologies associated
to Semantic REST APIs. They also highlight that these technologies are not yet
mature and give a rough idea of the missing features.

3.2   Comparison Matrices Design Method

The design of our comparison matrices follows a 5-step sequential process: *(i)*
search for candidate technologies, *(ii)* **select** candidate technologies, *(iii)* **read**
carefully each candidate technology, *(iv)* **elaborate fine grain criteria** to characterize and differentiate technologies, *(v)* **verify** that the elaborated criteria
highlighted the differences between technologies. We looped on step *(iv)* and *(v)*
to avoid duplicating criteria or hiding important details.

The research of candidate technologies (step i) was done by:

1. Searching Google and Google Scholar for Semantic REST Technologies using combinations of keywords from the set: ["web", "semantic", "restful", "rest", "service", "API", "interface", "description", "documentation","language", "modeling", "hypermedia", "document", "format",
   "RDF", "data-interchange", "linked data", "hateoas", "rest api", "framework"];

---

[3] https://github.com/AntoineCheron/comparison-matrices-semantic-rest-api-
   techno.

2. Searching Google Scholar for tools automating tasks from services description, using keywords: "matchmakers", "service composition", "service discovery", "rest service analysis", "automated mashups", we then selected papers and technologies from their references and the papers that cite those we selected;
3. Searching the proceedings of ICWE and WS-REST.

We selected 81 papers, standards, articles and web pages (step ii) based on abstract or introduction. We selected documents that were specifications of interface description languages or models, frameworks supporting HATEOAS features, interchange formats that support RDF or HATEOAS features, comparisons between these technologies or tools leveraging them. We considered frameworks available as programming libraries that helps implementing HTTP APIs in any programming language. We opened our research to technologies from the 1990s to today and retained those that are still available today.

Then, we read the specification of each chosen technology (step iii) and elaborated classification criteria (step iv). We included those of the H Factor [4] which *is a measurement of the level of hypermedia support and sophistication of a media-type*. Others were carefully designed to highlight differences between technologies, based on the core design of the technologies, the features they provide and the details of the WS3 maturity model. All the material is available online[5].

As a final step (step v), we read the specifications again to verify results and validate that the selected criteria highlighted differences and commonalities well.

Popularity Criteria. We defined a popularity criteria to provide a rough idea of the community support and the likelihood of the technology to last in time. It respects the following rules: **0** - Not enough to reach 1; **1** - More than 100 questions on Stack Overflow AND (2500+ NPM weekly downloads OR 100+ maven usages); **2** - More than 400 questions on Stack Overflow AND (500.000+ total downloads OR 15.000+ NPM weekly downloads OR 500+ maven usages).

3.3   Interface Description Languages

Interface Description Languages (IDLs) provide a vocabulary to document domain, functional and non-functional aspects of an API. We identified 16 candidates that are classified according to 31 criteria in Fig. 2. Among them, 4 are meta-models from conference papers [7,8,15,21]. The 11 others are open-source projects or W3C recommendations.

In [8] authors present a tool to sketch CRUD or Hypermedia APIs. On the latter mode, users sketch the application using state-machines and then obtain a description in the HAL or Collection+JSON format. [15] models each resource type as a finite-state-machine with deterministic transitions and conditions to inform about the availability of transitions. However, they are not modeled in more details, which make them not machine-interpretable. In [21], authors propose to model systems as non-deterministic state machines. This method thus

---

[4] http://amundsen.com/hypermedia/hfactor/.
[5] https://github.com/AntoineCheron/comparison-matrices-semantic-rest-api-techno.

makes software agents unable to discover the set of messages to exchange in order to make an operation available. Haupt et al. [7] propose a multi-layered model that separates the domain model from the URI model. However, resources have a fixed model, which prevent them from having one data model per state.

It is important to note than when **IDLs and interchange formats** are both **compatible with RDF**, they can be combined to form a file format usable as data-interchange format and IDL. This has great benefits to lower the overall complexity and increase the evolvability of the system.

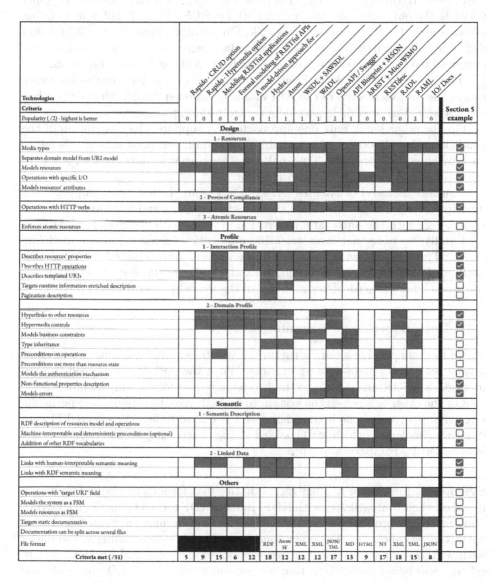

Fig. 2. Interface description languages comparison matrix

Synthesis. First, the matrix highlights the fact that most technologies help with building mature systems on the *design* dimension and *interaction profile* level of the *profile* dimension, D3-P1 following the WS3 categories. On the other hand on the *semantic* dimension, we notice that 5/16 technologies support the use of RDF vocabulary, which allows to build Linked Data APIs. As a reminder, this is required to reach full Semantic REST compliance. Moreover, by supporting the use of RDF vocabulary, IDLs can be enriched to reach a higher level of maturity.

Among the technologies, four can be distinguished by the number of criteria they meet: Hydra (18), RADL (18), OpenAPI (17) and RESTdesc (17). OpenAPI is the only one that has no support for RDF. Thus, it helps in building systems up to D3-P2-S0 on the WS3 scale. On the other hand, Hydra, RADL and RESTdesc support the use of RDF vocabulary, which makes these technologies better suited to build systems that are mature on the semantic dimension.

Towards HATEOAS APIs. From the matrix, we notice that most technologies target the documentation of the API in a single, non-splittable file. Hence, they are not suited to provide hypermedia controls at runtime.

On the other hand, only one approach, [15], supports the description of the conditions that determine the availability of a link, and none makes this meta-data machine-interpretable. This makes software agents unable to find a way to make an operation available when it is not.

Towards Better-Documented APIs. Only four technologies support the description of business constraints which lowers coupling and improves user experience, e.g., with the automatic generation of forms with client-side validation.

Finally, we note that most scientific publications recommend the modeling of RESTful systems with state-machines whereas open-sourced or W3C IDL authors don't consider this design method. And yet, the use of deterministic state-machines eases the determination of the available operations of a resource.

3.4   Data-Interchange Formats

These formats provide a data-structure, a vocabulary and a layout to represent a resource and its meta-data at runtime. When the API does not need to send meta-data, JSON and XML are the two widely used formats in the industry.

On the other side, when the system to be built have to support a hypermedia interchange format, none is considered as a standard today. We selected 11 candidate technologies, which are classified in Fig. 3 according to 24 criteria. JSON is included for comparison purposes.

Synthesis. First, from this matrix, we notice that formats can be differentiated based on their compatibility with RDF. Indeed, RDF formats (Turtle, RDF XML and JSON-LD) propose very few features by default because they can be enriched with RDF vocabularies. To depict what is achievable by combining vocabularies with a RDF format, we selected two vocabularies: Hydra and SHACL, a RDF schema validation vocabulary, that we combined with JSON-LD and evaluated them. As a result, they match 12 more criteria than JSON-LD alone. From this, we infer that combining RDF formats with vocabularies allow building mature Semantic REST systems. However, this requires additional effort to find relevant vocabularies. On the other hand, non-RDF formats help building systems that can be mature on the *profile* dimension but not on the *semantic* dimension.

Furthermore, the matrix shows that no format supports the description of constraints despite the fact that it can be leveraged to reduce coupling and improve the user-experience.

Finally, it highlights that no format advertise the state of the resource even though most scientific approaches we found describe REST APIs as state-machines.

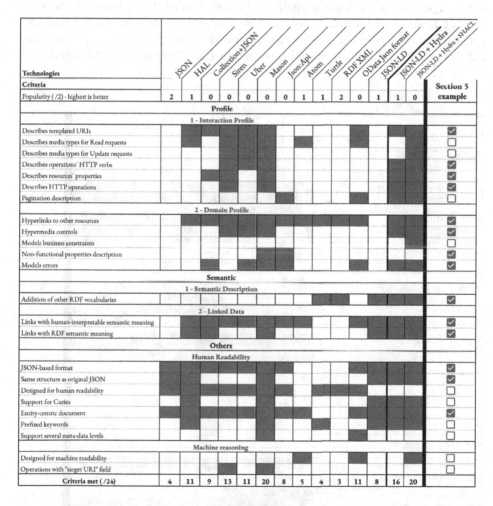

Fig. 3. Data-interchange formats comparison matrix

3.5 Implementation Frameworks

Implementation frameworks are software libraries that guide developers through the implementation of Web APIs. We limit the comparison to frameworks that claim to support HATEOAS. We identified six frameworks that do so. Frameworks to build Semantic Web Services are excluded because their triple-centric approach differs too much from REST.

Among the selected papers, in [13] authors propose *Hypermedia Web API Support*, a Java framework based on JAX-RS 2.0 that offers annotations to semantically describe REST APIs. The end result is the description of the whole API in a JSON-LD document enriched with the Hydra vocabulary. Unfortunately, the framework is not available in Maven Central. In [9] Parastatidis et al. present *Restfulie*, a framework that uses resources, state transitions and content-negotiation as its core building blocks. We found 4 other frameworks that support HATEOAS features. They are all classified in Fig. 4 according to 23 criteria.

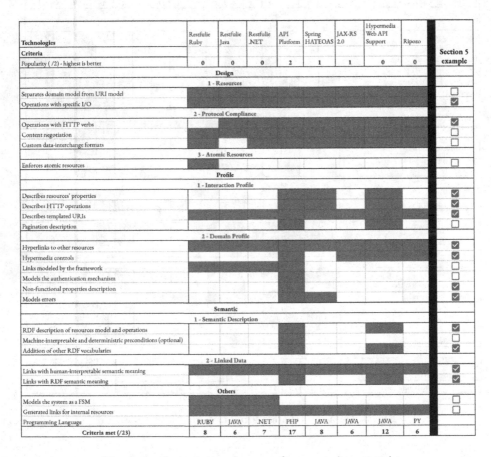

Technologies	Restfulie Ruby	Restfulie Java	Restfulie .NET	API Platform	Spring HATEOAS	JAX-RS 2.0	Hypermedia Web API Support	Ripozo	Section 5 example
Criteria									
Popularity (/2) - highest is better	0	0	0	2	1	1	0	0	
Design									
1 - Resources									
Separates domain model from URI model									☐
Operations with specific I/O									☑
2 - Protocol Compliance									
Operations with HTTP verbs									☑
Content negotiation									☐
Custom data-interchange formats									☐
3 - Atomic Resources									
Enforces atomic resources									☐
Profile									
1 - Interaction Profile									
Describes resources' properties									☑
Describes HTTP operations									☑
Describes templated URIs									☑
Pagination description									☐
2 - Domain Profile									
Hyperlinks to other resources									☑
Hypermedia controls									☐
Links modeled by the framework									☐
Models the authentication mechanism									☐
Non-functional properties description									☑
Models errors									☑
Semantic									
1 - Semantic Description									
RDF description of resources model and operations									☑
Machine-interpretable and deterministic preconditions (optional)									☐
Addition of other RDF vocabularies									☑
2 - Linked Data									
Links with human-interpretable semantic meaning									☑
Links with RDF semantic meaning									☑
Others									
Models the system as a FSM									☐
Generated links for internal resources									☐
Programming Language	RUBY	JAVA	.NET	PHP	JAVA	JAVA	JAVA	PY	
Criteria met (/23)	8	6	7	17	8	6	12	6	

Fig. 4. Implementation frameworks comparison matrix

Synthesis. Despite the fact that only one framework enforces the *Atomic Resources* constraint, all frameworks allow to reach the highest level of maturity on the *design* dimension easily. This is because supporting the *Atomic Resources* constraint only requires developers to use the data model of the resource as the input of write operations and as the output of read operations.

We notice that only *API Platform* and *Restfulie* offer a mechanism to model relations between resources from which links are generated, instead of adding them programmatically in the response, thus increasing maintainability. Otherwise, most frameworks do not ease the semantic and domain description of APIs. To us, this is the biggest challenge framework designers should tackle.

Last, as for IDLs, most frameworks creators do not provide mechanisms to describe resources as state machines, thus not taking advantage of its benefits.

4   Matrices Usage Example

In this section, we present the service of an insurance company that manages insurance contracts to illustrate how the presented comparison matrices can be used in a real world scenario. This example is a light version of projects we have carried out at FABERNOVEL for large French insurance companies.

4.1   Domain Description

To manage insurance contracts, the service holds five kinds of resources: (i) third-parties, (ii) contracts, (iii) warranties, (iv) cases and (v) services. Third-parties, for example customers or contractors, enter into contracts with the company. These contracts include warranties from the closed list that the company offers. For example a Person A has the following warranties: (i) damage coverage with a deductible of $500 and a maximum repair amount of $30.000 and (ii) premium vehicle loan in the event of immobilization of the damaged vehicle. A contract can have several cases. When an customer of the insurance has a claim the company creates a case that holds its details and the services provided to the insured. For example, Person A has a car accident, he opens the insurance's web application and reports a claim, which leads to the company opening a case. His car has been destroyed and he is expected to attend a diner. Thus, on the app, he asks for the loan of a car that he will immediately recover.

4.2   Technological Constraints

The service has to communicate with both internal and external components. Internal components are front-end applications, such as mobile or web applications, and other kernel services, such as payments. External components are contractors APIs, for example taxi or mechanics companies.

In the insurance domain, there is a huge amount of business rules that determine (i) the warranties an insured can include in a contract and (ii) the available services for a case, based on the specificity of the given case and the warranties of the contract. Writing and maintaining these rules both on the server and its clients is very costly and error prone. Thus, we decided to keep these business rules on the server-side only. This constraint leads to the use of HATEOAS.

The project constitutes the core of the company's business, it should then be built with state-of-the-art technologies such as Linked Data. This enables the automatic creation of mash-ups and the use of a HyperGraphQL[6] middleware to easily query the whole IS [19]. Moreover, considering that the contractors providing services are very diverse and numerous, the interactions with their APIs should leverage the automatic discovery and composition offered by the use of RDF semantics.

There is also a high probability that new client systems will be built in the future, the API must document its resources, resource attributes, operations, URI templates, HTTP verbs, hypermedia controls and errors in a machine-interpretable way. Moreover, because the service applies the CQRS pattern[7] we needed the IDL to enable associating an operation to its own input and output data model.

Last, to minimize the disruption for software developers, we have chosen to keep the interchange formats as close as possible to what developers already know. It has therefore to be entity-centric, based on JSON and its structure had to be as close as possible to a JSON document without meta-data.

4.3   Selection of the Technologies

From these constraints, we selected the set of criteria and features that the technologies should provide. These criteria are checked in the last column of Fig. 2, 3, and 4. We then count the number of criteria that were provided by each existing technology. Results are presented in Figs. 5, 6 and 7. For each matrix, the three technologies matching the highest amount of selected criteria are highlighted in green. It is important to note that the technologies do not have to match every criteria to be selected. Most of the time, missing features can be implemented afterwards, or proposed to the maintainers of the technologies.

Interface Description Languages. Hydra, OpenAPI and RADL are the technologies matching the highest number of selected criteria. However, none matches all criteria. Hydra lacks the ability to describe non-functional properties and media-types, which can be done with other RDF vocabularies. RADL lacks the ability to semantically describe resources models, operations, errors and non-functional properties, which can also be done with other vocabularies. On the other hand, OpenAPI does not support the usage of RDF vocabulary. In this project, we have chosen to setup both Hydra and OpenAPI. OpenAPI because it has most features and it is a must-have today because of its tooling and popularity. Hydra because it can be easily completed with other vocabularies and used with JSON-LD.

---

[6] https://www.hypergraphql.org/.
[7] https://martinfowler.com/bliki/CQRS.html.

Technologies	Rapido - CRUD option	Rapido - Hypermedia option	Modeling RESTful applications	Formal modeling of RESTful APIs	A model-driven approach for...	Hydra	Atom	WSDL + SAWSDL	WADL	OpenAPI / Swagger	API Blueprint + MSON	hREST + MicroWSMO	RESTdesc	RADL	RAML	IO/Docs
Popularity (/2) - highest is better	0	0	0	0	0	1	1	1	1	2	1	0	0	0	2	0
File format						RDF	Atom SF	XML	XML	JSON/ YML	MD	HTML	N3	XML	YML	JSON
Selected criteria met (/15)	3	6	10	4	9	13	8	9	9	12	8	6	10	12	9	5
Other criteria met	2	3	5	2	3	5	4	3	3	5	5	3	7	6	6	3
Criteria met (/31)	5	9	15	6	12	18	12	12	12	17	13	9	17	18	15	8

Fig. 5. Results for interface description languages

Technologies	JSON	HAL	Collection+JSON	Siren	Uber	Mason	Json:Api	Atom	Turtle	RDF XML	OData Json format	JSON-LD	JSON-LD + Hydra	JSON-LD + Hydra + SHACL
Popularity (/2) - highest is better	2	1	0	0	0	0	0	1	1	2	0	1	1	0
Selected criteria met (/14)	3	7	8	9	8	13	6	3	2	2	6	6	13	13
Other criteria met	1	4	1	4	3	7	2	2	2	1	5	2	3	7
Criteria met (/24)	4	11	9	13	11	20	8	5	4	3	11	8	16	20

Fig. 6. Results for data interchange formats

Technologies	Restfulie Ruby	Restfulie Java	Restfulie .NET	API Platform	Spring HATEOAS	JAX-RS 2.0	Hypermedia Web API Support	Ripozo
Popularity (/2) - highest is better	0	0	0	2	1	1	0	0
Programming Language	RUBY	JAVA	.NET	PHP	JAVA	JAVA	JAVA	PY
Selected criteria met (/15)	7	6	7	15	10	8	13	8
Other criteria met	4	4	4	6	2	2	3	2
Criteria met (/23)	11	10	11	21	12	10	16	10

Fig. 7. Results for implementation frameworks

Interchange Formats. Mason, JSON-LD + Hydra are the two technologies matching the highest number of selected criteria. JSON-LD + Hydra + SHACL is ignored as it does not match more selected criteria than without SHACL. While JSON-LD + Hydra lacks the ability to describe non-functional properties, Mason does not allow to use RDF vocabularies. Being incompatible with RDF requires a lot more effort to compensate than finding another vocabulary. This explains why JSON-LD + Hydra was preferred over Mason in this context.

Implementation Frameworks. API Platform, Spring HATEOAS and Hypermedia Web API Support [13] are the three technologies matching the highest number of criteria. The latter is immediately removed from the candidates because no public library is available. In this example, API Platform should be preferred over Spring HATEOAS because it matches five more criteria than Spring. However, developers of the companies we worked with know Java and not PHP. Moreover the Spring framework is very popular with them, which compensates the need to develop some features by hand. This is why we decided to go with Spring.

Easing the Selection of the Technologies. We have developed an open-source, two-step, web recommender system[8] to ease the selection of the technologies.

5 Discussion

This section provides our perspective on why no standard solution exists to meet all our criteria, and highlights the possibility of new research initiatives.

First, there is no de-facto neither IETF or W3C standard Interchange Format for building Semantic REST APIs. In addition, none of the existing interchange formats support all the criteria described above, making it likely that new formats will emerge. For this reason, frameworks supporting Semantic REST APIs will rely on formats that are likely to evolve, which will require additional effort and costs. This reduces the likelihood of framework editors to invest time in developing such features.

To us, the second and also the most important reason is that the well-known and widely used tools do not rely on Semantic REST APIs to provide additional and useful features. Among the possible functionalities, we envision various tools to automate API testing, REST client generation, API gateways, middleware and smarter desktop REST clients. We believe that this limits the adoption of Semantic REST APIs because the cost of building these APIs is not perceived as offering a sufficient short-term return on investment.

6 Related Work

In [20], and [14], authors justify the need to provide a semantic description of REST APIs to avoid that programmers who develop client applications have to understand in depth several APIs from several providers. Based on this motivation, they survey academic approaches to add semantic to such APIs description and technique to automatically compose restful services.

In [16] authors present a framework for automatic REST-service integration based on Linked Data models. API providers semantically describe their REST services. API consumers then use a middleware developed by the authors that automatically compose API calls to respond to data queries they expressed with SPARQL.

In [19], Tuchinda *et al.* describe a programming-by-demonstration approach to build mashups by example. Their approach addresses the problems of extracting data from web sources, cleaning and modeling the extracted data, and integrating the data across sources. It illustrates the benefits of getting meta-data on top of services to improve the definition of mashups and decrease the technical coupling between systems and the complexity of developing mature Semantic REST APIs. In [5], Duke *et al.* propose an approach to reduce the complexity for describing, finding, composing and invoking semantic rest services. They mainly provide an approach where they show how they can combine services when they get semantic information.

---

[8] https://antoinecheron.github.io/morice/.

Other research efforts were done to lower the entry barrier for developing mature Semantic REST APIs. Among them is the semi-automatic annotation of web services as done by Patil *et al.* in [10].

7 Findings Summary

In this paper, we have presented three comparison matrices that assist architects in choosing Semantic REST APIs enabling technologies that meet their needs. Through a real example, we have illustrated how the use of these matrices simplifies the choice of these technologies. As stated in the paper, technologies should be chosen not only according to the number of criteria they meet, but also according to the specific needs of the project. To facilitate this selection, we have developed an assistant available online.

We also pointed out some interesting features missing in current technologies. The description of constraints and conditions indicating the availability of state transitions is ignored by IDLs, vocabularies, interchange formats and frameworks. On the other hand, resource modeling as FSM is not available in most frameworks. More importantly, well-known tools do not take advantage of the power of Semantic REST APIs to provide additional and useful features.

Based on these findings, we identify areas for improvement in the tools around Semantic REST APIs that we believe can increase its adoption. By leveraging the semantic description of state transitions and non-functional properties, automated testing tools can become smarter, REST client libraries can lower the coupling with the server and automate tasks such as login, and middleware can automatically create responses from the composition of several APIs.

References

1. Alarcon, R., Saffie, R., Bravo, N., Cabello, J.: REST web service description for graph-based service discovery. In: Cimiano, P., Frasincar, F., Houben, G.-J., Schwabe, D. (eds.) ICWE 2015. LNCS, vol. 9114, pp. 461–478. Springer, Cham (2015). https://doi.org/10.1007/978-3-319-19890-3_30
2. Benslimane, D., Dustdar, S., Sheth, A.: Services mashups: the new generation of web applications. IEEE Internet Comput. **12**(5), 13–15 (2008)
3. Berners-Lee, T.: The semantic web. Sci. Am. **284**(5), 28–37 (2001)
4. Berners-Lee, T.: Linked data principles, 07 2006. https://www.w3.org/DesignIssues/LinkedData.html. Accessed 15 Jan 2019
5. Duke, A., et al.: Telecommunication mashups using RESTful services. In: Di Nitto, E., Yahyapour, R. (eds.) ServiceWave 2010. LNCS, vol. 6481, pp. 124–135. Springer, Heidelberg (2010). https://doi.org/10.1007/978-3-642-17694-4_11
6. Fowler, M.: Richardson maturity model. https://martinfowler.com/articles/richardsonMaturityModel.html. Accessed 15 Jan 2019
7. Haupt, F., Karastoyanova, D., Leymann, F., Schroth, B.: A model-driven approach for rest compliant service. In: Proceedings of the IEEE International Conference on Web Services (ICWS 2014), pp. 129–136. IEEE (2014)
8. Mitra, R.: Rapido: a sketching tool for web API designers. In: World Wide Web Conference (2015)

9. Parastatidis, S., Webber, J., Silveira, G., Robinson, I.S.: The role of hypermedia in distributed system development. In: Proceedings of the First International
   Workshop on RESTful Design, pp. 16–22. ACM (2010)
10. Patil, A.A., Oundhakar, S.A., Sheth, A.P., Verma, K.: Meteor-s web service anno-
    tation framework. In: Proceedings of the 13th International Conference on World
    Wide Web, pp. 553–562. ACM (2004)
11. Paulk, M.C.E.A.: Capability maturity model, version 1.1. IEEE Softw. **10**(4), 18–
    27 (1993)
12. Rodríguez, C., et al.: REST APIs: a large-scale analysis of compliance with prin-
    ciples and best practices. In: Bozzon, A., Cudre-Maroux, P., Pautasso, C. (eds.)
    ICWE 2016. LNCS, vol. 9671, pp. 21–39. Springer, Cham (2016). https://doi.org/
    10.1007/978-3-319-38791-8_2
13. Salvadori, I.E.A.: A framework for semantic description of restful web APIs. In:
    2014 IEEE International Conference on Web Services (ICWS). IEEE (2014)
14. Salvadori, I., Siqueira, F.: A maturity model for semantic restful web APIs. In:
    2015 IEEE International Conference on Web Services, pp. 703–710, June 2015
15. Schreier, S.: Modeling restful applications. In: Proceedings of the Second Interna-
    tional Workshop on RESTful Design. WS-REST 2011, pp. 15–21. ACM, New York
    (2011). https://doi.org/10.1145/1967428.1967434
16. Serrano, D., Stroulia, E., Lau, D., Ng, T.: Linked rest APIs: a middleware for
    semantic rest API integration. In: 2017 IEEE International Conference on Web
    Services (ICWS), pp. 138–145. IEEE (2017)
17. Soha, 02 2010. https://tinyurl.com/ya43vefk. Accessed 16 Jan 2019
18. Fielding, R.T.: Architectural Styles and the Design of Network-based Software
    Architectures. Ph.D. thesis, University of California, Irvine (2000)
19. Tuchinda, R., Knoblock, C.A., Szekely, P.: Building mashups by demonstration.
    ACM Trans. Web **5**(3), 1–45 (2011). https://doi.org/10.1145/1993053.1993058
20. Verborgh, R., et al.: Survey of semantic description of REST APIs. In: Pautasso,
    C., Wilde, E., Alarcon, R. (eds.) REST: Advanced Research Topics and Practical
    Applications, pp. 69–89. Springer, New York (2014). https://doi.org/10.1007/978-
    1-4614-9299-3_5
21. Zuzak, I., Budiselic, I., Delac, G.: Formal modeling of RESTful systems using
    finite-state machines. In: Auer, S., Díaz, O., Papadopoulos, G.A. (eds.) ICWE
    2011. LNCS, vol. 6757, pp. 346–360. Springer, Heidelberg (2011). https://doi.org/
    10.1007/978-3-642-22233-7_24

DRAGON: Decision Tree Learning for Link Discovery

Daniel Obraczka[1]([📧]) [iD] and Axel-Cyrille Ngonga Ngomo[2]([📧])

[1] University of Leipzig, 04109 Leipzig, Germany
`obraczka@informatik.uni-leipzig.de`
[2] University of Paderborn, 33098 Paderborn, Germany
`axel.ngonga@upb.de`

Abstract. The provision of links across RDF knowledge bases is regarded as fundamental to ensure that knowledge bases can be used joined to address real-world needs of applications. The growth of knowledge bases both with respect to their number and size demands the development of time-efficient and accurate approaches for the computation of such links. This is generally done with the aid of machine learning approaches, such as e.g. Decision Trees. While Decision Trees are known to be fast, they are generally outperformed in the link discovery task by the state-of-the-art in terms of quality, i.e. F-measure. In this work, we present DRAGON, a fast decision-tree-based approach that is both efficient and accurate. Our approach was evaluated by comparing it with state-of-the-art link discovery approaches as well as the common decision-tree-learning approach J48. Our results suggest that our approach achieves state-of-the-art performance with respect to its F-measure while being 18 times faster on average than existing algorithms for link discovery on RDF knowledge bases. Furthermore, we investigate why DRAGON significantly outperforms J48 in terms of link accuracy. We provide an open-source implementation of our algorithm in the LIMES framework.

Keywords: Link discovery · Decision trees · Machine learning · Entity resolution · Semantic web

1 Introduction

RDF is now ubiquitous on the Web. For example, more than 1 billion URLs embed RDF data in different serialization formats. A representative fragment of the RDF data available on the planet, the Linked Open Data Cloud, has grown from merely 12 to almost 10,000 knowledge bases [9] over the last decade. The growth in the number of knowledge bases is accompanied by a growth in size. For example, DBpedia–one of the most popular bases–has grown from $\approx 10^8$ triples (DBpedia 2.0) in 2007 to $\approx 10^{10}$ triples in 2016 (DBpedia 2016-04). This growth in the number and size of knowledge bases has led to an increase of the necessity for efficient and accurate link discovery (i.e., the computation of links between knowledge bases) approaches.

© Springer Nature Switzerland AG 2019
M. Bakaev et al. (Eds.): ICWE 2019, LNCS 11496, pp. 441–456, 2019.
https://doi.org/10.1007/978-3-030-19274-7_31

In this paper, we consider the *declarative link discovery setting* [15], in which the set of conditions under which two resources are to be linked is to be devised explicitly and subsequently executed to compute links across two (not necessarily distinct) sets of RDF resources S and T. The declarative link discovery problem has been shown to be challenging even for domain experts, since this set of conditions, which we call a *link specification*, can be very complex [11]. This complexity is due to

1. the plethora of similarity measures (e.g., edit distance, cosine similarity, Jaccard similarity) that are used to compare the property values of entities to find links and
2. the manifold means through which these similarities can be combined (e.g., min, max, linear combinations).

A large number of dedicated machine learning algorithms ranging from genetic programming [11] to refinement operators [25] has hence been devised to simplify the declarative link discovery process (see [15] for a survey). While the F-measure of these machine learning approaches has increased steadily, little attention has been paid to their time efficiency. Most commonly, the approaches are declared scalable by virtue of the bound similarity computation algorithms they rely upon, e.g., AllPairs [1], PPJoin+ [30], EdJoin [29]. First pruning approaches are developed in works such as [25] but solely for particularly slow versions of the algorithm. Given that the time efficiency of learning approaches for link discovery is critical for their usefulness in practical applications (e.g., in learning scenarios with humans in the loop), the primary aim of this work is hence *to improve the time efficiency of link discovery algorithms, while maintaining their classification performance* (i.e. maintaining the same F-measure). We achieve this goal with our novel approach DRAGON, a decision-tree-based approach for link discovery. The contributions of this work are as follows:

1. We devise an efficient and effective algorithm for learning link specifications within the decision tree paradigm.
2. We evaluate our algorithm on nine benchmark data sets against state-of-the-art link discovery and decision-tree-learning approaches. Our results show that DRAGON outperforms existing link discovery solutions significantly w.r.t. runtime, while achieving equally good performance w.r.t. the F-measure. Moreover, our approach outperforms generic solutions to learning decision trees significantly.
3. We investigate why our approach produces better link specifications than common decision-tree algorithms.

An open-source implementation of DRAGON is provided in the LIMES [18] framework[1].

This paper is structured as follows: We start by giving a formal definition of the key concepts underlying this work. Thereafter, we give a brief overview of the state of the art. We subsequently present our approach to link discovery, which we finally evaluate on synthetic and real-world datasets.

---

[1] https://github.com/dice-group/LIMES/.

2 Preliminaries

Definition 1 (Link Discovery). *Given two sets S (source) and T (target) of RDF resources and a relation R, compute the set M of pairs of instances $(s, t) \in S \times T$ such that $R(s, t)$.*

We call M a mapping. Commonly, the set S is a subset of the instances contained in the knowledge base $\mathcal{K}_S$. The same applies to the set T and a knowledge base $\mathcal{K}_T$. Note that neither S and T nor $\mathcal{K}_S$ and $\mathcal{K}_T$ are necessarily disjoint. Since computing M is a non-trivial task, most frameworks compute an approximation $M' = \{(s, t) \in S \times T : \sigma(s, t) \geq \theta\}$, where σ is a similarity function and θ is a similarity threshold. The relation $R(s, t)$ is then considered to hold if $\sigma(s, t) \geq \theta$. The similarity function σ and the threshold θ are expressed in a *link specification* (LS). Different grammars have been proposed to describe LSs [12,14,19]. We adopt the following formal setting, which is akin to that of [25]. This grammar is equivalent to that used in a large body of work [15].

We begin by defining the syntax of link specifications. To this end, we define a similarity measure m to be a function $m : S \times T \to [0, 1]$. These functions commonly compare attributes (or sets of attributes) of pairs of resources to compute a similarity value. Mappings $M \subseteq S \times T$ are used to store the results of the application of a similarity function to $S \times T$. We define a *filter* as a function $f(m, \theta)$ over the set of all mappings (i.e., the powerset of $S \times T$). A link specification is called *atomic* iff it comprises exactly a single filtering function. A complex specification L can be obtained by combining two link specifications L_1 and L_2 with the operators $\sqcap, \sqcup$ and $\setminus$.

We define the semantics $[[L]]_M$ of a LS L w.r.t a mapping M as follows:

- $[[f(m, \theta)]]_M = \{(s, t) | (s, t) \in M \wedge m(s, t) \geq \theta\}$
- $[[L_1 \sqcap L_2]]_M = \{(s, t) | (s, t) \in [[L_1]]_M \wedge (s, t) \in [[L_2]]_M\}$
- $[[L_1 \sqcup L_2]]_M = \{(s, t) | (s, t) \in [[L_1]]_M \vee (s, t) \in [[L_2]]_M\}$
- $[[L_1 \setminus L_2]]_M = \{(s, t) | (s, t) \in [[L_1]]_M \wedge (s, t) \notin [[L_2]]_M\}$

Moreover, we write $[[L]]$ as a shorthand for $[[L]]_{S \times T}$.

Definition 2 (Link Discovery as Classification). *The goal of link discovery can be translated to finding a classifier $\mathcal{C} : S \times T \to \{-1, +1\}$ which maps non-matches (i.e. $(s, t) \in S \times T : \neg R(s, t))$ to the class -1 and matches to $+1$.*

The classifier returns $+1$ for a pair (s, t) iff $\sigma(s, t) \geq \theta$ for the corresponding link specification. In all other cases, the classifier returns -1. In this work, we use decision trees for link discovery. The attributes we use are similarity measures. Because these measures have numeric values, we compute decision trees with binary splits. An example tree is shown in Fig. 1.

3 The DRAGON Algorithm

In the following, we present how we use decision trees to learn accurate LSs efficiently. We begin by giving a brief overview of our approach. Thereafter, we show how we tailor the construction of decision trees to the LS learning problem. Finally, we show how to prune trees to avoid overfitting.

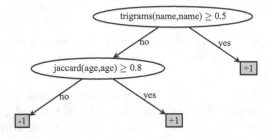

Fig. 1. A decision tree learned by DRAGON for the dataset of which a part is shown in Table 1. The classification decisions are shown in the gray nodes.

Table 1. Example datasets containing persons and link candidates with appropriate labeling showing corresponding similarity values using cosine similarity on name attributes. We represent the data as tables and omit namespaces for the sake of legibility.

URI	name	age
:S1	"Hans-Peter"	26
:S2	"Heiko Kurt"	13
:S3	"Amata"	52
:S4	"Ariane"	25
:S5	"Sib"	56

URI	name	age
:T1	"Hans Peter"	26
:T2	"Heiko"	13
:T3	"Amata K."	52
:T4	"Ariane"	25
:T5	"Ffion"	12

Pair	Label	sim
(S2, T2)	+1	0.707
(S2, T3)	-1	0.0
(S3, T3)	+1	0.816
(S4, T4)	+1	1.0
(S5, T5)	-1	0.0

(a) Source Dataset   (b) Target Dataset   (c) Link candidates

3.1 Overview

Algorithms 1 and 2 give an overview of our approach depending on the measure we use. We assume that we are given a maximum height for the tree. To determine the root of the tree we detect the best split attribute. We considered two measures for this purpose: the **global F-measure** aims to maximize the total F-measure achieved by the decision tree while the **Gini** measure acts locally and aims to ensure that the split attribute is optimal. We elaborate on how we use these fitness functions to find good split attributes in the section "Determining Split Attributes". DRAGON continues recursively by constructing the left and right child of the tree if it found a split attribute and has not yet reached the maximum height. For **Gini**, it updates the training data depending on the split attribute by removing any link pairs that are not accepted by the split attribute. For example, for the decision tree shown in Fig. 1, the training data for the right child of the root node would not include the pair (S5, T5) from Table 1(c), because the similarity value of the qgrams measure on the name attribute is lower than 0.4. The training data for the left child (ergo, the "no" child, see Fig. 1) is the global training data used to initialize our approach minus the training data for the right child of the root node. For example, the pair (S4, T4) would not be contained in the training data for the left child, since the similarity value of the qgrams measure on the name attribute is 1.0, and it therefore belongs to the training data of the right child. For **global F-measure**, the training data does not need to be changed, since we try to optimize globally.

In the following, we take a closer look at how the split attributes are computed.

Algorithm 1. Overview of DRAGON using Gini Index

---

1 constructTree(*int maxHeight, int currentHeight, boolean rightNode, data trainingData*)
2 splitAttribute = getBestSplitAttribute(trainingData)
3 **if** *splitAttribute ≠ null AND currentHeight < maxHeight* **then**
4 | currentHeight++
5 | rightData = updateTrainingData(splitAttribute,trainingData)
6 | leftData = trainingData \ rightData
7 | rightChild = *constructTree(maxHeight, currentHeight,*
8 | **TRUE**, *rightData*)
9 | leftChild = *constructTree(maxHeight, currentHeight,*
10 | **FALSE**, *leftData*)
11 **return** this;

Algorithm 2. Overview using global F-measure

---

1 constructTree(*int maxHeight, int currentHeight, data trainingData*)
2 splitAttribute = getBestSplitAttribute(trainingData)
3 **if** *splitAttribute ≠ null AND currentHeight < maxHeight* **then**
4 | currentHeight++
5 | rightChild = *constructTree(maxHeight, currentHeight,*
6 | *trainingData*)
7 | leftChild = *constructTree(maxHeight, currentHeight,*
8 | *trainingData*)
9 **return** this;

3.2   Initialization

The goal of the initialization is to determine the set of mappings that will be used during the construction of the decision tree. We assume that we are given a training data set TS with $TS \subseteq S \times T \times \{+1, -1\}$ (see Table 1 for an example). Every triple $(s, t, +1) \in TS$ is a positive example, while every triple $(s, t, -1) \in TS$ is a negative example. We begin by calculating the subsets $S' \subseteq S$ and $T' \subseteq T$ that can be found in our training dataset as follows:

$$S' = \{s \in S : \exists t \in T \text{ with } (s,t,+1) \in TS \vee (s,t,-1) \in TS\},$$

$$T' = \{t \in T : \exists s \in S \text{ with } (s,t,+1) \in TS \vee (s,t,-1) \in TS\}.$$

We use the sets S' and T' as test sets for our algorithm.

If we use the **global F-measure** as fitness function, we adopt the approach used by [25] by computing the mapping $M_i = \{(s, t) \in S' \times T' : m_i(s,t) \geq \theta_i\}$

which achieves the highest F-measure on the training dataset TS for each of the similarity measures m_i available to our approach. We determine the threshold θ_i by lowering the value of the said threshold from 1 to a lower bound λ by a given rate $\tau \in [0,1)$.

For the **Gini Index**, we begin by calculating the similarity of each entity pair $(s,t) \in S' \times T'$ using all the measures m_i available to our learner. Any similarity values below the lower bound λ are disregarded i.e., set to 0. For each measure $m \in m_i$ we now have a list of similarity values $[sim_{i1}, ..., sim_{in}]$ ordered from lowest to highest, with the corresponding entity pair $(s,t) \in S' \times T'$.

3.3   Determining Split Attributes

We build our decision tree using top-down induction [24]. We implement two measures to decide on the attribute to use for the splits: *Global F-measure* and *Gini Index*. With the global F-measure, we target the improvement of the overall performance of the decision tree we learn. In contrast, the Gini Index aims to improve the local performance of a given leaf. The performance of the two strategies is compared in the evaluation section.

Learning with the Global F-Measure. The trees we learn with the global F-measure are a combination of the atomic LS computed during the initialization step. Let k be the number of these atomic LSs. We set the atomic link specification which leads to the mapping with the highest F-measure over all measures m_i as our first split attribute. After this initialization of the tree, our tree consists of a root and 2 leaves. In the example shown in Fig. 1, the root would be the node $jaccard(name, name) \geq 0.4$. We first remove the root from the set of LSs that can be added to the tree, leading to $k-1$ LSs still being contained in the set of candidate LSs. We sequentially position every of the remaining $k-1$ LSs at every of the 2 leaf nodes, hence generating $2(k-1)$ trees. We then compute the resulting mapping and select the tree with the best F-measure. After removing the LS used from the set of candidate LSs, we iterate the addition approach until we cannot improve the F-measure achieved by the tree or until we have used all atomic LS we computed during the initialization step.

Formally, at iteration $i \in \{1, \ldots, k\}$, we have $(k-i+1)$ trees to try out and i nodes in the decision tree where an atomic LS can be added. Hence, the maximal number of trees we need to generate is given by the following:

$$\sum_{i=1}^{k} i(k-i+1) = \frac{k(k+1)(k-2)}{6} \in O(k^3). \tag{1}$$

Our algorithm is hence clearly polynomial in the number of trees computed. In contrast, generating all possible decision trees which can be created using k atomic link specifications is exponential in complexity.

Learning with the Gini Index. We use the similarity values we determined in the initialization in combination with the Gini Index as follows: We determine which measure will be our splitting attribute by calculating the average Gini Index of all measures still available as follows:

$$\overline{G}(\mathcal{N}, sim_{ij}) = \frac{|\mathcal{N}_l|}{|\mathcal{N}|} \times G(\mathcal{N}_l) + \frac{|\mathcal{N}_r|}{|\mathcal{N}|} \times G(\mathcal{N}_r), \qquad (2)$$

where $|\mathcal{N}|$ is the number of pairs accepted by the node $\mathcal{N}$ of the decision tree. In the first iteration, $\mathcal{N}$ contains the training data. $\mathcal{N}_l$ accepts the pairs with similarity values below sim_{ij}, $\mathcal{N}_r$ permits the pairs with values above or equal to sim_{ij}. For each m_i we calculate the average Gini Index for all sim_{ij}, with $j \in \{1, \cdots, n\}$, to determine the best split point for each measure.

The Gini Index is

$$G(\mathcal{N}) = 1 - \left(\left(\frac{|\mathcal{N}^+|}{|\mathcal{N}|} \right)^2 + \left(\frac{|\mathcal{N}^-|}{|\mathcal{N}|} \right)^2 \right), \qquad (3)$$

where $|\mathcal{N}^+|$ is the number of positive examples and $|\mathcal{N}^-|$ the number of negative examples accepted by $\mathcal{N}$. The splitting attribute will be the measure m with the corresponding threshold $\theta = sim_{ij}$. Common decision tree algorithms will set the threshold in the splitting attribute to be $\theta = (sim_{ij} + sim_{i(j-1)})/2$, whereas we set it to the higher value (i.e. sim_{ij}). In the evaluation section we will see that this choice improves the quality of our decision tree considerably.

After finding the root node the training data is provided as seen in Algorithm 1, we stop when we either have reached the maximum tree height or measure with an average Gini Index below 1 can be found.

For example, imagine we were to use the example in Table 1 to learn a tree using Gini Index. $S' \times T'$ are the link pairs from the training data, therefore the first step will be to determine the similarity value for these pairs using all available measures on all attributes. We provided the cosine similarity on the name attributes in Table 1(c). To test how well the cosine similarity performs we have to find the ideal split point. We start with the lowest similarity value, that is bigger than 0, which in our case is 0.707. $|\mathcal{N}_l| = 2$, since only two links have a similarity value below 0.707. $|\mathcal{N}_r| = 3$ containing the remaining links. To calculate the average Gini Index we need to determine the Gini Indices for the left and right node. Both are 0 since the left node only contains negative and the right only positive examples. Since our split attribute perfectly divides the examples to the appropriate classes we have a pure leaf with the average Gini Index of 0 and our tree induction is finished. Bear in mind that we choose $\theta = 0.707$ in our link specification in contrast to common decision tree algorithms that would take $\theta = (0.707 + 0.0)/2 = 0.3535$.

3.4   Pruning

Previous works (e.g., [24]) have shown that pruning decision trees can improve their performance significantly. Given our approach to decision tree generation,

Table 2. Characteristics of the used datasets.

Label	#Attributes	$|S| \times |T|$	|reference dataset|
Person1	11	250,000	500
Person2	11	240,000	400
Restaurants	5	72,433	112
DBLP-ACM	4	6,000,000	2,224
DBLP-Scholar	4	168,100,000	5,347
Amazon-GP	4	4,400,000	1,300
Abt-Buy	4	1,200,000	1,097
Drugs	1	1,090,000	1,047
Movies	2	1,090,000	1,047

we devised a *Global F-measure pruning* and implemented the *error estimate pruning* used by [24] for the sake of comparison. Given a tree $\mathcal{N}$ with height h, we start our pruning process by iterating over the nodes $\mathcal{N}_i$ at height $h-2$, with $i \in \{1, \ldots, n\}$, where n is the number of nodes at height $h-2$. We compute the F-measure of $\mathcal{N}$, after we pruned the left, right and both leaves of $\mathcal{N}_i$ respectively. The tree with the best F-measure is kept, i.e. $\mathcal{N}$ will be overwritten by it. After repeating this process for all nodes at height $h-2$, we continue at height $h-3$ and so on until we reach the root node and terminate.

If we were to prune the tree from Fig. 1, we would subsequently compute the F-measure of the whole tree and after we removed the node $jaccard(age, age) \geq 0.8$.

4   Evaluation

The aim of our evaluation was to evaluate the effectiveness (i.e., the F-measure) and the efficiency (i.e., the runtime) achieved by DRAGON. We were especially interested in the performance of DRAGON on real datasets. Hence, we evaluated DRAGONon the four real-world datasets from [14]. These datasets were obtained by manually curating data harvested from the Web and determining links between these datasets manually. In addition, we aimed to compute the performance of DRAGON on synthetic datasets. We selected three datasets from OAEI 2010 benchmark[2] and the two datasets *Drugs* and *Movies*, used in [19]. Table 2 presents some details pertaining to these datasets. We ran two series of experiments. In the first series on experiments, we tested whether our approach to setting thresholds in decision trees is superior to that followed by other decision-tree learning approaches. To this end, we compared different ways of setting thresholds in our algorithm. We also used this experiment to determine the default settings for subsequent experiments. In our second series of experiments, we compared DRAGON with state-of-the-art link discovery algorithms.

---

[2] http://oaei.ontologymatching.org/2010/im/.

In all experiments we used a ten-fold cross validation setting were the training folds consist of 50% positive and 50% negative examples. We present the average results achieved by all algorithms over the ten runs of the crossvalidation setting. To make a comparison between algorithms over all datasets easier we also calculated the average rank of the approaches given the performance measure (time or f-measure). To achieve this the approaches are ranked by their performance per dataset, for ties the mean of the ranks are assigned, and the ranks are averaged columnwise to get the final value. This average rank is added as last row in the tables we present. All experiments were carried out on a 64-core 2.3 GHz Server running Oracle Java 1.8.0_77 on Ubuntu 14.04.4 LTS, with each experiment assigned 20 GB of RAM.

4.1 Parameter Discovery

To check whether our approach to discovering settings is better than that followed by other decision-tree-based approaches, we ran our Gini approach combined with the Global F-measure pruning (G) and the error estimate pruning (E). We set λ between 0.05 and 0.8. Our results are displayed in Table 3. In our experiments, $\lambda = 0.4$ achieves the best rank and is therefore an appropriate setting for our algorithm. We hence selected this value as default.

Table 3. F-measure for 10-fold cross validation averaged over 10 results. UP indicates choosing the upper value as split point while MP uses the middle between two similarity values as split point in the node. The best, second- and third-best value in a row are highlighted using colored cells of decreasing strength.

Data	UP,λ = .05		UP, λ = .2		UP, λ = .4		UP, λ = .8		MP, λ = .05		MP, λ = .4	
	G	E	G	E	G	E	G	E	G	E	G	E
Movies	0.969	0.969	0.975	0.975	0.969	0.969	0.994	0.832	0.967	0.967	0.734	0.905
Person1	0.978	0.970	0.966	0.965	0.980	0.983	0.985	0.986	0.945	0.931	0.940	0.947
Person2	1.000	1.000	0.999	0.999	1.000	1.000	0.999	0.999	0.980	0.980	0.980	0.980
Drugs	1.000	1.000	1.000	1.000	1.000	1.000	1.000	1.000	0.978	0.978	0.938	0.938
Restaurants	0.976	0.976	0.986	0.986	0.976	0.976	1.000	1.000	0.961	0.944	1.000	1.000
DBLP-ACM	0.881	0.918	0.872	0.912	0.895	0.961	0.974	0.966	0.858	0.894	0.388	0.939
Abtbuy	0.441	0.496	0.573	0.545	0.644	0.617	0.209	0.208	0.442	0.498	0.661	0.661
DBLP-GS	0.928	0.694	0.938	0.695	0.972	0.970	0.871	0.905	0.906	0.830	0.185	0.711
AMAZON-GP	0.429	0.641	0.467	0.711	0.761	0.704	0.351	0.343	0.429	0.581	0.682	0.717
Avg Rank	6.625	6.438	6.188	6.188	3.938	3.938	5.688	5.813	9.438	9.250	8.250	6.250

We then compared our approach to setting thresholds in split points with that implemented by classical decision-tree-learning approaches such as J48 (see two right-most columns of Table 3). Note that we used $\lambda = 0.05$ to test if a higher threshold to calculate the initial similarity values improves the quality of the constructed decision tree. While choosing the middle between similarity values as split point seems to be beneficial on some datasets (e.g., Abtbuy), it is clear that choosing the upper value bears better results overall. A comparison of the difference in F-measure achieved by the settings $\lambda = 0.05$ (first column in

Table 3) and $\lambda = 0.4$ (third column in Table 3) further reveals that preventing a decision tree from learning measures with a low threshold value can improve the quality up to 43% (Amazon-GP).

4.2 Comparison with Other Approaches

Our choice of state-of-the-art link discovery algorithm to compare with DRAGON was governed by the need to provide a fair evaluation. Firstly, the algorithms we were to test against needed to learn link specifications explicitly, since our approach tackles the task of *declarative link discovery*. Secondly, we needed approaches able to perform supervised learning, since our approach would have an unfair advantage over unsupervised classifiers. We hence chose WOMBAT since it fits these requirements and to perform as well as [13] w.r.t. the F-measure it achieves. In addition, WOMBAT was shown to be robust w.r.t. the number of examples used for learning. We also ran our experiments with EAGLE [19] and EUCLID [20]. We selected EAGLE [19] because it was shown to outperform MARLIN [2] and FEBRL [4] significantly in terms of runtime, while achieving comparable F-measure [19]. EUCLID's major advantage over EAGLE is the fact that it is deterministic and reaches similar F-measure to EAGLE. In our evaluation we use the supervised linear version of EUCLID. All the chosen approaches and especially DRAGON are contained in the open-source LIMES link discovery framework and are free to use. We decided not to compare DRAGON with classifiers from e.g. SILK [28], since LIMES has been shown [18] to be significantly faster than SILK and therefore runtime comparisons would not be fair. We also compare our approaches with J48, an often used implementation of the C4.5 algorithm [10].

To test our hypothesis that common decision tree approaches choose threshold values that are too low, we also implemented *J48opt*. In this approach, we took the decision tree we get from *J48*, parsed it into a LS, raised all its thresholds by δ and calculated the F-measure it achieved. We repeated this process until all thresholds equal 1. We took the LS with the threshold setting that resulted in the highest F-measure. In our experiments, we set δ to 0.05. For DRAGON, we tested *Global F-measure* (in the following referred to as DRAGON$_{GL}$) and *Gini Index* (DRAGON$_{GI}$), as well as the two pruning algorithms *Global F-measure pruning* and *error estimate pruning*. We will also indicate the pruning method in subscript as well. Hence, DRAGON$_{GL \cdot E}$ is a configuration of DRAGON which was achieved by the use of *Global F-measure* for finding split attributes and *error estimate pruning*. In contrast, DRAGON$_{GL \cdot G}$ is DRAGON with global F-measure and global F-measure pruning. We set the maximum tree height to 3. For the Gini configurations, we set λ to 0.4. For the global F-measure configurations, we set λ to 0.6. We discovered that each approach performs best with these parameters through empirical tests. The termination criteria for WOMBAT was either finding a link specification with F-measure of 1 or a refinement depth of 10. The coverage threshold was set to 0.6 and the similarity measures used were

Table 4. Averaged results for 10-fold cross validation. We highlight the best, second- and third-best value in a row using colored cells of decreasing strength.

Data	DRAGON				WOMBAT	EUCLID	EAGLE	J48	J48opt
	$GI \cdot G$	$GI \cdot E$	$GL \cdot G$	$GL \cdot E$					
Movies	0.971	0.971	0.994	0.994	0.993	0.984	0.989	0.835	0.989
Person1	0.984	0.985	0.980	0.978	1.000	0.983	0.993	0.855	0.957
Person2	1.000	1.000	0.998	1.000	0.991	0.823	0.952	0.924	1.000
Drugs	0.998	0.998	0.998	0.998	0.998	0.996	0.996	0.938	0.998
Restaurants	1.000	1.000	0.980	1.000	0.994	0.953	0.952	0.905	0.962
DBLP-ACM	0.934	0.932	0.970	0.983	0.983	0.978	0.980	0.768	0.860
Abtbuy	0.679	0.642	0.529	0.555	0.647	0.003	0.555	0.429	0.582
DBLP-GS	0.973	0.973	0.906	0.934	0.963	0.899	0.945	0.880	0.955
Amazon-GP	0.741	0.711	0.620	0.354	0.761	0.712	0.731	0.408	0.450
Avg Rank	3.333	3.889	5.111	4.278	2.778	6.611	5.056	8.667	5.278

(a) F-measure

Data	DRAGON				WOMBAT	EUCLID	EAGLE	J48	J48opt
	$GI \cdot G$	$GI \cdot E$	$GL \cdot G$	$GL \cdot E$					
Movies	152	134	1652	1652	1623	4414	122539	170	204
Person1	473	488	21433	21783	12527	210140	1343	272	991
Person2	114	119	3144	3050	2350	39109	1080	148	337
Drugs	48	41	307	297	246	215	1047	60	88
Restaurants	19	20	487	478	631	9721	1013	27	51
DBLP-ACM	2626	2618	40614	40562	46002	308044	94873	680	23109
Abtbuy	1619	1574	6419	6310	19002	31065	1243	510	34762
DBLP-GS	5623	5517	28454	28541	143973	496948	110168	948	45036
Amazon-GP	3126	3102	21593	21741	56651	325759	26638	1331	134693
Avg Rank	2.3	2	6.2	5.9	6.6	8.3	6.6	1.9	5.2

(b) Time in ms

the same as in DRAGON: *jaccard, trigrams, cosine* and *qgrams*. EAGLE was configured to run 100 generations. The mutation and crossover rates were set to 0.6 as in [19]. EUCLID was set to the default parameters. For *J48*, we discovered, that using reduced error pruning with 5 folds delivered the best results overall. Otherwise we used the default parameters found in the Weka framework [10].

To determine the significant differences between classifier performances usually a pair-wise Wilcoxon signed-ranks test is performed. However, this would lead to a multiple testing problem in our case, since we compare more than two classifiers. We therefore follow the recommendations given in [7] to use a Friedman test to determine if the average ranks of the algorithms are significantly different and, if this is true, perform a Nemenyi test to compare all classifiers. In Table 4 the results are presented. Concerning F-measure we have significant differences between the algorithms (Friedman p-value = 0.009).

We can see that WOMBAT and DRAGON$_{GI.G}$ produce the best results regarding F-measure and there is no significant difference in performance (Nemenyi p-value = 0.999). WOMBAT achieves a higher F-measure than DRAGON$_{GI.G}$ on four datasets (Movies, Person1, DBLP-ACM, AMAZON-GP) and is tied with DRAGON on the Drugs dataset. DRAGON outperforms WOMBAT on the remaining four datasets. The only significant difference in F-measure is between WOMBAT and j48 (Nemenyi p-value = 0.007) and between DRAGON and j48 (Nemenyi p-value = 0.023). We can also see that *J48opt* performs better than *J48*, albeit not significantly better (Nemenyi p-value = 0.326).

In Table 4b, we present the average runtimes of the approaches. We can determine, that there is a significant difference in runtime-efficiency between the algorithms (Friedman p-value = 1.127×10^{-8}). It is evident, that DRAGON(specifically DRAGON$_{GI}$) and *J48* are the fastest approaches. We determined no significant difference between them (Nemenyi p-value = 0.999). The DRAGON$_{GI}$ configurations of our approach are on average 18 times faster than WOMBAT[3] , while DRAGON$_{GL}$ is roughly as efficient as WOMBAT. The performance advantage of DRAGON$_{GI}$ is due to the fact that, after calculating the initial similarity values of the entity pairs, it does not need the costly calculations of mappings.[4] Overall, our results suggest that DRAGON performs as well as the state of the art w.r.t. the quality of the LSs it generates, but clearly outperforms the state of the art w.r.t. its runtime[5], making it more conducive to practical application.

4.3   Efficiency of Pruning

Since pruning is an important factor in decision tree learning, we recorded the effect pruning had in the second experiment. The results are displayed in Fig. 2.

First note that the configuration DRAGON$_{GL.GL}$ was omitted in the figures since the unpruned and pruned trees were identical. This is not surprising because the measure for building the tree is the same as for pruning it. Therefore, any leaves that would be pruned simply do not appear in the tree in the first place. For the other configurations, we can observe, that pruning has on average a positive impact on F-measure. The exceptions are datasets for which LS of the size 1 are learned in the first place (such as Movies and Person2 for DRAGON$_{GI}$) and Amazon-GP, where pruning has a negative effect.

---

[3] This difference is significant with a p-value = 0.0297 for the Nemenyi test.

[4] Note that in DRAGON$_{GL}$ these costs are linear for each mapping computation, since we only need to use set-operations on the mappings from the initial atomic specifications.

[5] DRAGON$_{GI}$ is also significantly faster than EUCLID (Nemenyi p-value = 0.0001) and EAGLE (Nemenyi p-value = 0.0297).

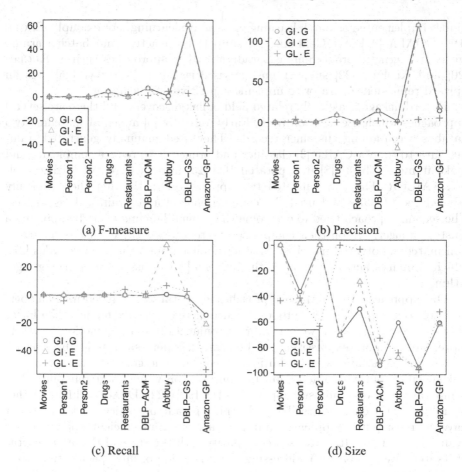

(a) F-measure

(b) Precision

(c) Recall

(d) Size

Fig. 2. Percentage change between unpruned and pruned trees in the averaged results of the ten-fold crossvalidation

5 Related Work

A plethora of approaches for link discovery has been developed recently. We give a brief overview of existing approaches and refer the reader to the corresponding surveys and comparisons [6,15,26] for further details. A popular link discovery framework is SILK [28], which uses multi-dimensional blocking to achieve lossless link discovery. Another lossless framework is LIMES [17], which combines similarity measures using a set-theoretical approach. An overview and a comparison of further link discovery frameworks can be found in [15].

As we have seen in definition 2, link discovery is a binary classification problem and therefore can be tackled with classical machine learning approaches such as *support vector machines* [2], *artificial neural networks* [16] and *genetic programming* [11]. [26] give an overview of these approaches and compare them. Most dedicated approaches to learning link specifications are supervised techniques implemented as batch learning or as active learning. For example, EAGLE [19], COALA [21] and GenLink [11] support both active and batch learning within the genetic programming paradigm. Other approaches such as EUCLID [20] and KnoFuss [22] support unsupervised learning. WOMBAT [25] uses an upward refinement operator to implement positive-only learning.

Record linkage is a closely related field of link discovery and there are several approaches which use decision trees. Early works by [5] aimed at matching two databases containing customer records. They used manually generated training data to train a CART [3] classifier and pruned it to reduce complexity and make it more robust. [8] incorporated ID3 [23] into their record linkage toolbox TAILOR. They implemented two approaches: In the first they manually labeled record pairs and used the comparison vector to train a decision tree. The second approach tried to overcome the manual labeling effort by applying a clustering algorithm on their comparison vectors to get three clusters: matches, non-matches, potential matches. Another notable approach is Active Atlas [27], which combines active learning with the C4.5 [24] decision tree learning algorithm.

Our approach extends these approaches in several ways. By learning an operator tree our approach is able to learn much more expressive models than linear classifiers (e.g. [2]), since we can express conjunction and disjunction. Furthermore, we are more expressive than boolean classifiers such as [4,16], because we can model negations. We additionally combine the generation of expressive link specifications with a deterministic approach, providing more reliability than comparable non-deterministic approaches [11,19,21,22]. DRAGON differs further by relying on a decision-tree-based learning paradigm, which allows it to not have to recompute mappings, leading to a more time-efficient approach (see evaluation section). It shares some similarity with the state of the art by virtue of its iterative approach to addressing the generation of link specifications (see, e.g., [25]).

6   Conclusion and Future Work

In this work, we presented DRAGON, a decision tree learning approach for link discovery. We evaluated our approach on nine benchmark datasets against three state-of-the-art approaches WOMBAT, EUCLID and EAGLE. Our approach delivers state-of-the-art performance w.r.t. the F-measure it achieves while on average being more than 18 times faster than the state of the art. We investigated why our approach outperforms other decision tree approaches by optimizing the choice of thresholds in similarity measures. Interestingly, our Global F-measure approach is biased towards precision while using Gini leads to a bias towards recall. In future work, we will investigate how we can use these biases for ensemble learning. We will also look into the possibility to perform active learning with DRAGON, in particular with the use of incremental decision trees.

Acknowledgements. This work has been supported by the BMVI projects LIMBO (project no. 19F2029C) and OPAL (project no. 19F20284).

References

1. Bayardo, R.J., Ma, Y., Srikant, R.: Scaling up all pairs similarity search. In: 16th International Conference on World Wide Web. WWW 2007, pp. 131–140. ACM, New York (2007). https://doi.org/10.1145/1242572.1242591
2. Bilenko, M., Mooney, R.J.: Adaptive duplicate detection using learnable string similarity measures. In: International Conference on Knowledge Discovery and Data Mining. KDD 2003, pp. 39–48. ACM, New York (2003). https://doi.org/10.1145/956750.956759
3. Breiman, L., Friedman, J., Olshen, R., Stone, C.: Classification and Regression Trees. Chapman & Hall, New York (1984)
4. Christen, P.: Febrl: an open source data cleaning, deduplication and record linkage system with a graphical user interface. In: International Conference on Knowledge Discovery and Data Mining. KDD 2008, pp. 1065–1068. ACM, New York (2008). https://doi.org/10.1145/1401890.1402020
5. Cochinwala, M., Kurien, V., Lalk, G., Shasha, D.E.: Efficient data reconciliation. Inf. Sci. **137**(1–4), 1–15 (2001). https://doi.org/10.1016/S0020-0255(00)00070-0
6. Daskalaki, E., Flouris, G., Fundulaki, I., Saveta, T.: Instance matching benchmarks in the era of linked data. J. Web Sem. **39**, 1–14 (2016). https://doi.org/10.1016/j.websem.2016.06.002
7. Demsar, J.: Statistical comparisons of classifiers over multiple data sets. J. Mach. Learn. Res. **7**, 1–30 (2006). http://www.jmlr.org/papers/v7/demsar06a.html
8. Elfeky, M.G., Elmagarmid, A.K., Verykios, V.S.: Tailor: a record linkage tool box. In: International Conference on Data Engineering, pp. 17–28 (2002). http://iccexplore.ieee.org/xpls/abs_all.jsp?arnumber=994694
9. Ermilov, I., Lehmann, J., Martin, M., Auer, S.: LODStats: the data web census dataset. In: Groth, P., et al. (eds.) ISWC 2016. LNCS, vol. 9982, pp. 38–46. Springer, Cham (2016). https://doi.org/10.1007/978-3-319-46547-0_5
10. Holmes, G., Donkin, A., Witten, I.: Weka: a machine learning workbench. In: Proceedings of the Second Australia and New Zealand Conference on Intelligent Information Systems, pp. 357–361. Brisbane, Australia (1994). http://www.cs.waikato.ac.nz/~ml/publications/1994/Holmes-ANZIIS-WEKA.pdf
11. Isele, R., Bizer, C.: Learning expressive linkage rules using genetic programming. Proc. VLDB Endow. **5**(11), 1638–1649 (2012). https://doi.org/10.14778/2350229.2350276
12. Isele, R., Jentzsch, A., Bizer, C.: Efficient multidimensional blocking for link discovery without losing recall. In: 14th International Workshop on the Web and Databases (2011). http://wifo5-03.informatik.uni-mannheim.de/bizer/pub/IseleJentzschBizer-WebDB2011.pdf
13. Kejriwal, M., Miranker, D.P.: Semi-supervised instance matching using boosted classifiers. In: Gandon, F., Sabou, M., Sack, H., d'Amato, C., Cudré-Mauroux, P., Zimmermann, A. (eds.) ESWC 2015. LNCS, vol. 9088, pp. 388–402. Springer, Cham (2015). https://doi.org/10.1007/978-3-319-18818-8_24
14. Köpcke, H., Thor, A., Rahm, E.: Evaluation of entity resolution approaches on real-world match problems. Proc. VLDB Endow. **3**(1), 484–493 (2010). https://doi.org/10.14778/1920841.1920904
15. Nentwig, M., Hartung, M., Ngomo, A.N., Rahm, E.: A survey of current link discovery frameworks. Semant. Web **8**(3), 419–436 (2017). https://doi.org/10.3233/SW-150210

16. Ngomo, A.N., Lehmann, J., Auer, S., Höffner, K.: RAVEN - active learning of link specifications. In: Ontology Matching Workshop, pp. 25–36 (2011). http://ceur-ws.org/Vol-814/om2011_Tpaper3.pdf

17. Ngonga Ngomo, A.C.: On link discovery using a hybrid approach. J. Data Semant. **1**, 203–217 (2012). https://doi.org/10.1007/s13740-012-0012-y

18. Ngonga Ngomo, A.C., Auer, S.: Limes: a time-efficient approach for large-scale link discovery on the web of data. In: ICJAI. IJCAI 2011, pp. 2312–2317. AAAI Press (2011). https://doi.org/10.5591/978-1-57735-516-8/IJCAI11-385

19. Ngonga Ngomo, A.-C., Lyko, K.: EAGLE: efficient active learning of link specifications using genetic programming. In: Simperl, E., Cimiano, P., Polleres, A., Corcho, O., Presutti, V. (eds.) ESWC 2012. LNCS, vol. 7295, pp. 149–163. Springer, Heidelberg (2012). https://doi.org/10.1007/978-3-642-30284-8_17

20. Ngonga Ngomo, A.C., Lyko, K.: Unsupervised learning of link specifications: deterministic vs. non-deterministic. In: Ontology Matching Workshop, pp. 25–36 (2013). http://ceur-ws.org/Vol-1111/om2013_Tpaper3.pdf

21. Ngomo, A.-C.N., Lyko, K., Christen, V.: COALA – correlation-aware active learning of link specifications. In: Cimiano, P., Corcho, O., Presutti, V., Hollink, L., Rudolph, S. (eds.) ESWC 2013. LNCS, vol. 7882, pp. 442–456. Springer, Heidelberg (2013). https://doi.org/10.1007/978-3-642-38288-8_30

22. Nikolov, A., d'Aquin, M., Motta, E.: Unsupervised learning of link discovery configuration. In: Simperl, E., Cimiano, P., Polleres, A., Corcho, O., Presutti, V. (eds.) ESWC 2012. LNCS, vol. 7295, pp. 119–133. Springer, Heidelberg (2012). https://doi.org/10.1007/978-3-642-30284-8_15

23. Quinlan, J.R.: Induction of decision trees. Mach. Learn. **1**(1), 81–106 (1986). https://doi.org/10.1023/A:1022643204877

24. Quinlan, J.R.: C4.5: Programs for Machine Learning. Morgan Kaufmann Publishers Inc., San Francisco (1993)

25. Sherif, M.A., Ngonga Ngomo, A.C., Lehmann, J.: WOMBAT – a generalization approach for automatic link discovery. In: Blomqvist, E., Maynard, D., Gangemi, A., Hoekstra, R., Hitzler, P., Hartig, O. (eds.) ESWC 2017. LNCS, vol. 10249, pp. 103–119. Springer, Cham (2017). https://doi.org/10.1007/978-3-319-58068-5_7

26. Soru, T., Ngonga Ngomo, A.C.: A comparison of supervised learning classifiers for link discovery. In: 10th International Conference on Semantic Systems, pp. 41–44. ACM (2014). https://doi.org/10.1145/2660517.2660532

27. Tejada, S., Knoblock, C.A., Minton, S.: Learning object identification rules for information integration. Inf. Syst. **26** (2001). https://doi.org/10.1016/S0306-4379(01)00042-4

28. Volz, J., Bizer, C., Gaedke, M., Kobilarov, G.: Silk - a link discovery framework for the web of data. In: Workshop on Linked Data on the Web, LDOW (2009). http://ceur-ws.org/Vol-538/ldow2009_paper13.pdf

29. Xiao, C., Wang, W., Lin, X.: Ed-join: an efficient algorithm for similarity joins with edit distance constraints. Proc. VLDB Endow. **1**(1), 933–944 (2008). https://doi.org/10.14778/1453856.1453957

30. Xiao, C., Wang, W., Lin, X., Yu, J.X., Wang, G.: Efficient similarity joins for near-duplicate detection. ACM Trans. Database Syst. **36**(3), 15 (2011). https://doi.org/10.1145/2000824.2000825

Web Application Modeling and Engineering

Catch & Release: An Approach to Debugging Distributed Full-Stack JavaScript Applications

Kijin An[(⊠)] and Eli Tilevich

Software Innovations Lab, Virginia Tech, Blacksburg, USA
{ankijin,tilevich}@cs.vt.edu

Abstract. Localizing bugs in distributed applications is complicated by the potential presence of server/middleware misconfigurations and intermittent network connectivity. In this paper, we present a novel approach to localizing bugs in distributed web applications, targeting the important domain of full-stack JavaScript applications. The debugged application is first automatically refactored to create its semantically equivalent centralized version by gluing together the application's client and server parts, thus separating the programmer-written code from configuration/environmental issues as suspected bug causes. The centralized version is then debugged to fix various bugs. Finally, based on the bug fixing changes of the centralized version, a patch is automatically generated to fix the original application source files. We show how our approach can be used to catch bugs that include performance bottlenecks and memory leaks. These results indicate that our debugging approach can facilitate the challenges of localizing and fixing bugs in web applications.

Keywords: Full-stack JavaScript applications ·
Distributed computing · Debugging

1 Introduction

Most programmers abhor debugging, due to its arduous, wasteful, and tedious nature. It can be much harder to debug distributed applications than centralized ones. Distributed systems suffer from partial failure, in which each constituent distributed component can fail independently. In addition, non-trivial bugs, including performance bottlenecks and memory leaks, can be caused by server/middleware misconfigurations or intermittent network connectivity rather than by any problems in the programmer-written code. Programmers need novel debugging approaches that can pinpoint whether the cause of a non-trivial bug in a distributed application is indeed in the programmer-written code.

To alleviate the challenges of debugging distributed applications, we present a novel debugging approach that takes advantage of automated refactoring to

© Springer Nature Switzerland AG 2019
M. Bakaev et al. (Eds.): ICWE 2019, LNCS 11496, pp. 459–473, 2019.
https://doi.org/10.1007/978-3-030-19274-7_32

remove much of the uncertainty of distributed execution from the debugged programs. Our approach first transforms a distributed application into its semantically equivalent centralized version by applying our domain-specific refactoring, *Client Insourcing*, which automatically moves a server-based remote functionality to the client, replacing middleware communication with local function calls. *Client Insourcing* is a refactoring, as the resulting centralized application retains its execution semantics. Then standard debugging techniques are applied to debug this centralized application. After the bug is localized and fixed, our approach generates a patch that is applied to the faulty part of the distributed application. We call our approach *Catch & Release* or CANDOR for short, as it *catches* bugs in the centralized version of a distributed application, and after fixing the bugs, *releases* the application for its continued distributed execution.

We implement CANDOR for the important domain of full-stack JavaScript applications, in which both the client and server parts are written and maintained in JavaScript, and evaluate its effectiveness in fixing two important types of bugs known to be prevalent in this domain: memory leaks and performance bottlenecks. Our evaluation applies our approach to localize and fix bugs that were previously found in third-party applications. We verify the correctness and value of our approach by applying our bug-fixing patches to the faulty versions of these applications and then confirming that the patched versions pass the provided test suites. We argue that CANDOR reduces the complexity of the debugging process required to fix these bugs by reporting on our experiences.

This paper makes the following contributions:

1. We present a novel debugging approach for distributed applications that uses automated refactoring to produce a semantically equivalent, centralized versions of the debugged subjects. Any of the existing state-of-the-art debugging techniques become applicable to track and localize bugs in such centralized versions. (CATCH)
2. We develop automated bug patching, which given the bug-fixing changes of the debugged application's centralized version, replays thcsc changes on the application's client or server parts. (RELEASE)
3. We empirically evaluate the correctness and value of our approach by applying it to track and localize known bugs in real-world third-party full-stack JavaScript applications.

The rest of this paper is structured as follows. Section 2 discusses the state of the art in software debugging. Section 3 introduces our approach for debugging full-stack JavaScript applications. Section 4 presents the design and implementation details of CANDOR. Section 5 reports on the evaluation results of applying CANDOR to debug real-world subject applications. Section 6 presents future work directions and concluding remarks.

2 Background and Related Work

Numerous prior approaches have pursued the goal of improving the effectiveness and lowering the cognitive burden of software debugging. It would be unrealistic to discuss all of them here. Hence, we outline only some major prior efforts, particularly those that had introduced some of the techniques we used to implement our approach. An important part of the debugging process is exercising the runtime behaviour of the debugged subject. When it comes to testing web applications, client-side scripting and UI interfacing have been introduced to automatically exercise UI elements and to conduct state-based testing [8, 10, 12, 13]. These approaches approximate server-side application logic as simple states. In contrast, CANDOR first transforms a distributed application into its equivalent centralized version, in which the original server-side logic is encapsulated in regular functions that can be debugged by applying any of these prior approaches.

To debug distributed applications that execute over middleware, Record and Replay (R&R) is an execution framework that efficiently captures distributed execution traces [1, 14]. One of the weaknesses of R&R is its heavy performance overhead due to the need to execute instrumented code over middleware. To reduce this overhead, Parikshan [2] replicates network inputs to remove the need for heavyweight instrumentation by using lightweight containers, thus triggering buggy executions in production with low overhead. By eliminating distribution altogether, CANDOR enables localizing bugs in the centralized equivalent of the debugging subjects, thereby providing a low-overhead debugging approach.

Since JavaScript defeats static analysis approaches, dynamic analyses have been applied to help understand various properties of JavaScript programs, including performance and memory consumption. MemInsight [7], a profiling framework, can analyze complex JavaScript programming constructs, the memory behavior of DOM objects, and the exact object lifetimes. Dynamic analysis has also been used to identify promising refactoring opportunities in JavaScript code, such as detecting Just-In-Time (JIT)-unfriendly code sections that can be restructured to improve performance. To understand how prevalent JIT-unfriendly code is, JITProf [5] applies dynamic analysis to help developers detect such code regions. To help identify harmful JavaScript coding practices, DLint [6] features a dynamic checker based on formal descriptions. To detect performance bottlenecks, JSweeter [21] analyzes the code patterns related to the type mutation of the V8 engine.

To detect memory leaks in web applications, BLeak [20], an automated debugging system, identifies memory leaks by checking for a sustained memory growth between consecutive executions. Currently, all these approaches need to be applied separately to the server or client parts of full-stack JavaScript applications. With CANDOR, these approaches becomes immediately applicable for debugging these applications in their insourced versions that execute within a single JavaScript engine.

3   Debugging Full-Stack JavaScript Applications with CANDOR

In this section, we explain our approach to debugging distributed full-stack JavaScript applications by discussing how it facilitates the process of locating bugs in two real-world examples.

462   K. An and E. Tilevich

```
//server part in theBrownNode
var express = require('express'), app =
    express.createServer(..);
var users=[]; ...
app.post('/users/search', function(req,
    res) {
 var data = req.body; //client-input
 var result=getUsers(data);//serv-output
 res.send(result);});
function getUsers(searchUser) {
    return getObjsInArray(searchUser,
        users);}


//inefficient for-in loop in server part
, lines are from 5 to 18
function getObjsInArray(obj, array) {
 var foundObjs = [];
  for (var i=0; i < array.length; i++){
   for(var prop in obj) {
    if(obj.hasOwnProperty(prop)) {
     if (obj[prop] === array[i][prop]) {
      foundObjs.push(array[i]);
      break;
 }}}}
  return foundObjs;
}
```

```
//client part in the BrownNode
$.ajax({
url: '/users/search',
data: {fName: $('#fName').val(),
    ...},//client-input
type: 'POST',
success: function(data) {//serv-output
$('#results').text(JSON.stringify(data)
    );}});
```

```
//patch for server part

5,18c1,16
<(original code for getObjsInArray)
---
> function getObjsInArray(obj, array) {
>  var foundObjs = [];
>  var keys = Object.keys(obj);
>  for (var i=0; i < array.length; i++)
    {
>   for (var j = 0, l = keys.length; j <
    l; j++) {
>    var key = keys[j];
>    if (obj[key] === array[i][key]) {
>     foundObjs.push(array[i]);
>     break;
>  }}}
>  return foundObjs;
> }
```

Fig. 1. Distributed App theBrownNode (left:server part, upper right:client part) and patch for inefficient iteration. (shaded)

3.1 Motivating Example I: *Removing Performance Bottlenecks*

Consider the code snippet in Fig. 1, in which the remote service /users/search of the distributed app **theBrownNode** calls function getUsers, which contains nested for loops. The client portion invokes the server-side script /users/search, passing various query parameter data to obtain the search query results. The code of the inner loop is quite inefficient, as it performs two conditional checks. Being on a hot execution path, this inefficiency causes a noticeable performance degradation. One can remove this bottleneck by eliminating the need to check whether the property prop is indeed defined in the object searchUser and not inherited from searchUser prototype: to exclude the inherited properties, the code can be optimized to use Object.keys() [17].

Notice that in the original distributed version of this application, it would be non-trivial to locate the actual source of this performance bottleneck. The performance of a distributed application can be affected by myriad factors, many of which have nothing to do with the application's implementation. To meet the expected performance requirements, servers must be properly configured for the actual usage scenarios, and so is the middleware infrastructure that encapsulates the communication functionality between the client and server components. In addition, network connectivity and utilization can affect the overall performance. Intermittent network connectivity and bandwidth saturation can lead to uncertain periods of poor network performance.

Even if the programmer were to become certain that the cause of the observed performance bottleneck lies in the implementation, localizing the source location of the bug in a distributed application can be a complex undertaking that requires generating a large volume of synthetic HTTP traffic against a specially instrumented version of the server. Then the client parameters would have to be matched against the resulting server execution profiles. This debugging procedure is complicated, as it requires a customized server deployment and the examining of the remotely generated performance profiles.

With CANDOR, the programmer first replaces the remote invocation of /users /search with an equivalent local function call, thus eliminating all middleware functionality and server-side execution. Once the remote code is insourced, the resulting centralized program can be easily debugged by using any existing tools for JavaScript programs. Rather than transferring log files from the server to the client and trying to correlate different remote executions with their parameters, the programmer can debug the execution of local function users_search. Once the programmer changes the insourced version to fix the bug, CANDOR automatically generates a fix patch (the shaded code snippet in Fig. 1) to be executed against the original server or client part of the distributed application (i.e., the "release" phase).

3.2 Motivating Example II: *Detecting Memory Leak*

Some of the most common bugs afflicting remote services are memory leaks. Consider function leakingService in Fig. 2 that represents a simplified server-side service invoked by various remote clients. These clients invoke the service by means of distribution middleware that hides all the low-level details on the client-server communication. Notice that every time this function completes its execution, it leaks some memory, as random String is appended to the globally declared Array leak, which is never garbage-collected. Although this example is simplified for ease of exposition, it is representative of numerous anti-patterns that can quickly exhaust the server's memory upon heavy utilization.

This bug is also quite challenging to detect and fix. One first has to be certain that the memory leak in question is not due to server/middleware configuration problems. In addition, the very presence of middleware functionality makes it hard to locate memory bugs in the programmer-written code. Much of the client/server distributed execution flows through middleware libraries, whose memory consumption and footprint can conceal the actual locations in the programmer-written code that contain memory-related bugs.

To help developers test the remote functionality, the Node.js framework provides testing libraries, using which one can script HTTP requests against a given server. These libraries help verify whether the input and output values of a service being tested are as expected. These functional testing utilities cannot help identify whether the server code is leaky, however.

In the absence of fully automated techniques for debugging *Full-Stack JavaScript Applications*, developers have no choice but to manually instrument

```
// every time this service is invoked,      // invoking leakingService in client
// it "leaks" a bit of memory, as           let data = '';
// var leak is never garbage-collected       http.get(S_URL, (res) => {
var leak = [];                                  res.on('data', (chunk) => {
function leakingService() {                       data = JSON.parse(chunk);
 leak.push(Math.random()+" on a stick,          });...);
     short!");
}
http.createServer(function (req, res) {     //patch for server part
    leakingService();                       16,18c1,19
    res.end("success");                     <(original code for leakingService)
}).listen(1337);                            ---
                                            >(definition of delegating writeToFile)
                                            > function leakingService() {
                                            >  writeToFile(Math.random()+" on a
                                                   stick, short!");
                                            > } //leakage detected in var leak
```

Fig. 2. Memory leak examples for server and client parts

both the client and the server parts of the debugged applications. More specifically, the current state of the art in detecting memory leaks in JavaScript programs involves taking and comparing with each other multiple heap snapshots in the suspect regions of the server-side functionality. A commonly used technique for finding memory leaks in web applications is *three snapshots* [20]. Even detecting a sufficient degradation in performance of the server-side functionality requires some client to execute multiple consecutive HTTP requests. As a result, to reproduce a memory leak bug, programmers are expected to follow a complex and tedious debugging process.

In contrast, CANDOR takes a drastically different approach to debugging full-stack JavaScript applications. It performs all bug localization tasks on the distributed application's centralized version, in which both the client and server parts execute within the same JavaScript interpreter. This centralized version is generated automatically via a new refactoring that we call *Client Insourcing*. This refactoring moves the server-side functionality to the client, so it can be invoked by calling local functions rather than through the layers of distribution middleware such as HTTP Client[1]. In essence, Client Insourcing integrates the remote, potentially buggy functionalities with the client code, so all the debugging techniques for centralized JavaScript applications can be applied to the insourced application. For example, state-of-the-art modern JavaScript execution environments provide built-in profiling infrastructures that can be applied to any running application. A centralized application can be re-executed at will without having to coordinate the execution of multiple remote execution nodes. Because Client Insourcing replaces all distributed functionality with direct local function calls, the identified memory leaks would indeed stem from the programmer-written code rather than any server/middleware misconfiguration.

---

[1] Angular HTTPClient (https://angular.io/guide/http),
  JQuery AJAX (http://api.jquery.com/jquery.ajax/),
  Node.js HTTP module (https://nodejs.org/api/http.html).

4 CANDOR: Design and Reference Implementation

CANDOR works in three phases. First, the server part is automatically insourced, producing a centralized application whose semantics is equivalent to the original distributed full-stack JavaScript application. The resulting centralized application is then debugged by means of any of the existing techniques for locating and fixing bugs in JavaScript programs. Finally, based on the before (i.e., buggy) and after (i.e., fixed) versions of the centralized application, CANDOR generates a patch to be executed against the application's original client or server parts, thereby applying the fix to the correct portion of the distributed application.

4.1 The Client Insourcing Automated Refactoring

Full-stack JavaScript applications comprise client-side and server-side JavaScript code. The *Client Insourcing* automated refactoring first identifies the remotely invoked functionalities of the server code by statically analyzing the corresponding marshaling points of the parameters passed by the client to the server and the server's output to the client (i.e., marked as //client-input and //serv-output parts respectively in Fig. 1). The process requires no manual steering from the programmer, whose role is limited to running the application's test suites under standard input and transferring the generated log file of the marshaling points to the server. Parameterized with this file, dynamic symbolic execution then computes a transitive closure of the server-side statements executed by the remote invocations. Client Insourcing analyzes JavaScript programs by using the z3 SMT solver [4], similarly to other declarative program analysis frameworks [9,18].

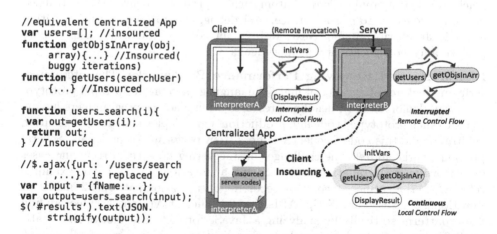

Fig. 3. Continuous control flow of distributed codes (theBrownNode in Fig. 1) constructed by Client Insourcing (left: generated code for centralized applications)

The computed relevant server statements are then insourced into the application's client part. The insourced statements are placed in automatically generated client-side functions. These functions are invoked directly without any middleware. So the refactoring process completes by replacing all middleware-based invocations with direct calls to these functions (see the equivalent centralized version of theBrownNode in Fig. 3). This refactoring preserves the application's business logic, while significantly simplifying its control flow. Rather than spanning across two JavaScript engines (client and server), the resulting centralized applications require only one engine. Since JavaScript engines often differ in terms of their debugging facilities (e.g., logging support, information messages, etc.), interacting with only one engine reduces the cognitive load of debugging tasks. In addition, one of the key hindrances that stand on the way of debugging distributed applications is the necessity to keep track when the control flow changes execution sites. The control flow of a full-stack JavaScript application can go through any of the constituent application parts: client, server, and middleware. Ascertaining when the flow crosses the boundaries between these parts can be challenging, particularly if the maintenance programmer, in charge of a debugging task, is not the same programmer who wrote the original buggy code. By transforming the original application into its centralized counterpart, Client Insourcing creates a debugging subject with a regular local control flow that is easy to follow with standard debugging tools (Fig. 3).

4.2   Catching and Fixing Bugs in Insourced Apps

Insourcing produces centralized applications that can be debugged by means of any of the existing or future JavaScript debugging techniques. CANDOR makes all these state-of-the-art debugging techniques immediately applicable to full-stack JavaScript applications. Automatically produced equivalent centralized versions are easier to execute, trace, and debug, due to their execution within a single JavaScript engine. Next, we explain how CANDOR can help remove performance bottlenecks and memory leaks.

Identifying and Removing Performance Bottlenecks. The interpreted, scripting features of JavaScript make the language a great fit for rapid prototyping tasks. Unfortunately, deadline pressures often leads to programmers having to move such prototyped code into production. Once deployed in actual execution environments, this code frequently suffers from performance problems. Several previous works address the challenges of uncovering non-trivial recurring cases of performance degradation in JavaScript applications [5,7,17]. For example, reference [17] identifies 10 common recurring optimization patterns: 2 inefficient iterations, 6 misused JavaScript APIs, and 2 inefficient type checks. One can find these patterns statically by analyzing a JavaScript codebase. Notice that static analysis can be applied separately to the client and server parts of a full-stack JavaScript application. However, applying the *Pareto Principle* [22] to program optimization, one can expect a typical program to spend 90% of its execution time in only 10% of its code. Hence, to verify whether the found inefficiencies are indeed the sources of performance bottlenecks requires dynamic analysis, which is much easier to perform on the centralized version of a debugged distributed application. Specifically, the centralized version is instrumented and its runtime performance profile is generated. Then each candidate inefficiency is removed in turn and another profile is generated. By comparing the original profile and that of a modified version, one can verify whether the latest fix was indeed for a performance bottleneck-causing bug. Without a centralized version, the number of performance profiles would need to at least double, and the server part would require a separate execution driver to generate its profiles.

Fixing Memory Leaks. When fixing memory leaks, programmers typically store the execution traces of leaky code persistently for a subsequent examination. When debugging real-world web applications, programmers often can delegate the logging task to a third-party service. However, to fix a memory leak in a distributed version, both the client and server parts need to be logged. In contrast, with CANDOR, programmers can localize memory leaks by applying a memory profiler such as MEMWATCH [11] to the debugged application's centralized version. As shown in the Fig. 2, MEMWATCH detects the leaking global array leak in the centralized version, with the fix replacing leak.push with writeToFile[2]. CANDOR then generates a patch to be applied to the application's server part.

4.3   Releasing the Bug Fixes

Once the programmer fixes the bug in the application's centralized version, the resulting fixes have to be applied to the actual client and server parts of the original application, thus completing the final *release* phase of the CANDOR debugging process. To that end, CANDOR automatically generates input scripts for GNU Diffutils[3], which executes these scripts against the source files of the original full-stack JavaScript application by using GNU patch[4].

To correctly generate a diff script that modifies the affected lines of the original applications, CANDOR keeps track of the correspondences between the application's original and insourced versions. This process is complicated by the multi-step nature of Client Insourcing transformations. Because the basic insourcing unit is a function, all free-standing server statements are first placed into individual functions, through a process that synthesizes new function names and applies the *extract function* refactoring on the free-standing statements. We call this process *normalization*. The actual insourcing transformation is applied at the function level of granularity.

CANDOR keeps track of how the lines map between the original client and server source files and their centralized version. This mapping is used to automatically generate a patch that replays the bug fixing changes of the centralized version on the original source code's client or server portions (Fig. 4).

---

[2] For additional implementation details, see https://bit.ly/2B9a3wf.

[3] https://www.gnu.org/software/diffutils.

[4] http://savannah.gnu.org/projects/patch.

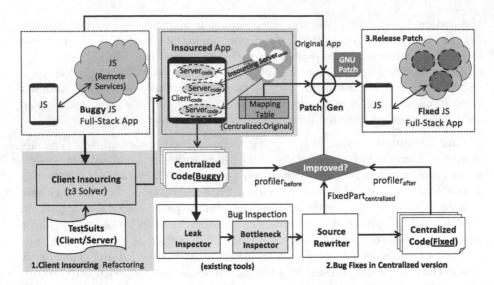

Fig. 4. Debugging full-stack JavaScipt applications with CANDOR

5   Evaluation

- **RQ1—Correctness:** Does Client Insourcing preserve the execution semantics of full-stack JavaScript applications? Are existing test-suits still applicable to the centralized variants of the debugged applications? (Sect. 5.1)
- **RQ2—Value:** By how much does CANDOR reduce the debugging complexity
  in terms of the number of steps and tools required to localize and fix bugs?
  (Sect. 5.2) How much programmer effort can CANDOR save? (Sect. 5.3)

5.1   Evaluating the Correctness of Client Insourcing

Table 1 shows subject full-stack applications and their remote services. The size
of each subject application is shown in terms of the number of uncommented
lines of JavaScript code (ULOC) for the server (S_{ULOC}) and the client (C_{ULOC})
parts. Client Insourcing changes the architecture of full-stack JavaScript applications from distributed to centralized by combining their server and client parts.
CI_{ULOC} indicates ULOC for the centralized version of each subject.

The applicability of CANDOR hinges on whether Client Insourcing preserves
the execution semantics (i.e., business logic) of the refactored applications, a
property we refer to as *correctness*. In modern software development practices,
applications are maintained alongside their test suites, a collection of test cases
that verify each important unit of application functionality. In our correctness
evaluation, we leverage the ready availability of such test suites for our subject
applications. In other words, the original and refactored versions of a subject
application is expected to successfully pass the same set of test cases.

Some tests in the available test suits are also distributed, in that they invoke remote services by means of HTTP client middleware, which marshals input parameters and unmarshals returned values. It is the returned values that are used as test invariants. We had to manually transform such distribution-specific tests to work against the centralized (insourced) versions of their test subjects.

Table 1. Subject distributed apps and Client Insourcing results

Subject Apps	S_{ULOC}	C_{ULOC}	Remote services	CI_{ULOC}
theBrownNode [19]	147	43	/users/search	37
			/users/search/id	36
Bookworm [3]	371	1814	/api/ladywithpet	394
			/api/thedea	394
			/api/theredroom	394
			/api/thegift	394
search_leak [16]	34	13	/search_leak	17
ionic2_realty_rest [15]	453	387	/properties/favorites	24

Table 1 shows the total number of tests in each evaluated test suite, including the number of tests manually transformed to work against the centralized versions of subject applications; the table shows whether tests successfully passed in the original and refactored version of each subject. Based on these results, we can conclude that Client Insourcing shows a high degree of correctness ($\frac{8}{8} \cdot 100 = 100(\%)$), as the same of number of successful tests is passed by the refactored applications, making them suitable for debugging.

5.2 Case Study: Traditional vs. CANDOR-Enabled Debugging

In this case study, we compare and contrast a traditional approach to localizing a bug in a full-stack JavaScript application and the CANDOR debugging approach. In this case study, we assume that a programmer needs to debug a distributed application with n remote functionalities[5] $ftn_{remote}^{1...n}$ to produce i corrective patches $P^{1...i}$; applying the patches fixes the found bugs. We assume that standard profiling is used to stamp the start and the end of executing each remote service, so as to obtain the total execution time and memory footprint. To the best of our knowledge, no automated tools can identify the entry/exit points of a server-side remote functionality invoked by clients. Hence, the programmer is expected to manually examine the server-side code to locate and instrument these entry and exit points for every remote functionality in question. In some cases, in order to instrument some business logic functionality, it must first be

---
[5] Each remote functionality is exposed as a remote service invoked via some middleware API.

disentangled from any middleware-specific functionality. However, for ease of exposition, we disregard this additional required debugging-related task. Once the instrumentation is in place, a typical debugging procedure involves continuously invoking client-side HTTP requests against the instrumented remote functionalities. After a certain number of requests, the server-side logs then can be collected, transferred to the client, and examined for the obtained execution time and memory footprint numbers profiles (Fig. 5a).

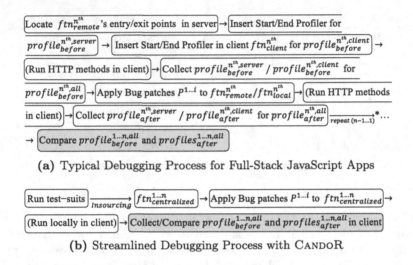

(a) Typical Debugging Process for Full-Stack JavaScript Apps

(b) Streamlined Debugging Process with CANDOR

Fig. 5. Comparing the debugging processes

In essence, our approach reduces the accidental complexity of debugging; the essential complexity cannot be reduced, so localizing and fixing bugs will always remain a delicate and complex task. Nevertheless, our approach allows programmers to focus on the actual debugging activities, unencumbered by the complexity of having to trace the execution of a buggy application across distributed sites. CANDOR simplifies the process by automatically identifying n remote functionalities and transforming them into equivalent n centralized local functions $ftn_{centralized}^{1...n}$, integrated with the client code. Afterwards, all the relevant debugging procedures can be applied to the resulting centralized application. Since these procedures are strictly local, they can be repeated at will, with their output examined in place. As a result, the number of debugging procedures decreases as compared to the traditional process, as shown in Fig. 5b.

5.3   Quantifying the Debugging Effort Saved by CANDOR

We see the main draw of CANDOR in that it reduces the amount of effort required to debug distributed applications to approximately that required to debug centralized ones. Although any debugging task can be cognitively taxing, tedious, and laborious, removing the complexity of distributed communication is expected to reduce these burdens. However, to be able to perform all debugging-related changes on the centralized version of a distributed application, these changes must affect the performance and memory consumption of both the distributed and centralized versions in comparable ways. In other words, if a change to the centralized version improves its performance or memory consumption, a similar improvement should be expected in the distributed version.

To check this hypothesis, we fixed different types of bugs in the centralized versions of 8 subjects, measuring their before and after execution time and memory consumption numbers. We then obtained the same measurements for their original and fixed distributed versions. Table 2 presents the performance and memory consumption improvements for these debugging subjects. To measure performance, we use the V8 profiler. To reduce noise, we repeated each use case 2000 times and compared the average observed time elapsed: P_{before} and P_{after}, with the performance improvement calculated as $P_{improved} = \frac{P_{before} - P_{after}}{P_{before}} \cdot 100(\%)$. For the memory leakage bugs, we compared how much memory was used before and after the bug fixes by repeatedly executing the subjects 2000 times. The table's last column ($P_{improved}^{D}$ and $P_{improved}^{CI}$) shows the resulting percentage improvements for the distributed and centralized versions. As one can see, the improvement percentages are very close to each other, confirming that the centralized version can serve as a viable debugging proxy for its distributed application.

We also approximate the debugging effort saved by counting the number of uncommented lines of code (ULOC) that need to be examined by hand to successfully perform a debugging task. A successfully executed debugging task involves two phases: (1) localize the source line of the bug, (2) fix the bug by modifying the source code (i.e., generate a fix patch). In traditional debugging, phase 1 requires that all the executed client and server statements be examined, while with CANDOR, Client Insourcing puts all the server statements executed by remote services into regular local functions (CI_{ULOC} in Table 1), thus eliminating the need to examine any remotely executed code to localize bugs. In phase 2, the bugs are fixed by applying automatically generated patches (F_{ULOC}).

5.4   Threats to Validity

When implementing the patch generation module of CANDOR, we made several design choices that may affect our evaluation results. For example, we measured the performance improvement of subjects running on a specific V8 Engine (v 6.11.2) and instrumenting machine (DELL-OPTIPLEX5050). However, the actual amount of improvement can change based on the specific choice of running environments. Also, the ULOC for the patches automatically generated by CANDOR can differ in size from those generated by humans. Because CANDOR generates patches at statement granularity, no additional lines can be added for readability or commenting. Human programmers are free to format the patches in an arbitrary fashion, thus affecting the total number of lines taken by their bug fixing patches.

Table 2. Quantifying debugged results by CANDOR

Remote services	Bug types [17]	F_{ULOC}	P^D_{before} (P^{CI}_{before})	P^D_{after} (P^{CI}_{after})	$P^D_{improved}$ $(P^{CI}_{improved})$
/users/search	Inefficient iteration	31	0.36 ms (0.19 ms)	0.26 ms (0.13 ms)	27.8% (31.58%)
/users/search/id	Inefficient iteration	31	1.7 ns (2.5 ns)	1.19 ns (1.63 ns)	29.53% (34.8%)
/api/ladywithpet	Misused APIs	18	5.89 ms (2.74 ms)	4.99 ms (2.24 ms)	15.28% (18.13%)
/api/thedea	Misused APIs	18	5.63 ms (2.71 ms)	4.82 ms (2.25 ms)	14.39% (16.97%)
/api/theredroom	Misused APIs	18	0.65 ms (1.87 ms)	0.53 ms (1.56 ms)	18.06% (16.58%)
/api/thegift	Misused APIs	18	1.17 ms (0.36 ms)	1.04 ms (0.31 ms)	11.11% (13.89%)
/search_leak	Memory leak	24	619.10 kb (476.16 kb)	519.13 kb (409.10 kb)	16.15% (14.08%)
/properties/favorites	Memory leak	42	824.62 kb (1431.28 kb)	511.37 kb (922.51 kb)	37.99% (35.54%)

6   Conclusions and Future Work

We have presented a new debugging approach—CANDOR—that facilitates the debugging of full-stack JavaScript applications. As a future work direction, we plan to conduct a systematic user study of JavaScript programmers to assess the effectiveness and usability of the CANDOR debugging approach.

Acknowlegements. The authors would like to thank Yin Liu and the anonymous reviewers, whose insightful comments helped improve the technical content of this paper. This research is supported by the NSF through the grants # 1650540 and 1717065.

References

1. Altekar, G., Stoica, I., Altekar, G., Stoica, I.: Odr: output-deterministic replay for multicore debugging. In: SOSP (2009)
2. Arora, N., Bell, J., Ivančić, F., Kaiser, G., Ray, B.: Replay without recording of production bugs for service oriented applications. In: Proceedings of the 33rd ACM/IEEE International Conference on Automated Software Engineering, pp. 452–463. ACM (2018)
3. Bookworm. https://github.com/davidwoodsandersen/Bookworm
4. de Moura, L., Bjørner, N.: Z3: an efficient SMT solver. In: Ramakrishnan, C.R., Rehof, J. (eds.) TACAS 2008. LNCS, vol. 4963, pp. 337–340. Springer, Heidelberg (2008). https://doi.org/10.1007/978-3-540-78800-3_24

5. Gong, L., Pradel, M., Sen, K.: JITprof: Pinpointing JIT-unfriendly JavaScript code. In: Proceedings of the 2015 10th Joint Meeting on Foundations of Software Engineering, pp. 357–368. ESEC/FSE 2015 (2015)
6. Gong, L., Pradel, M., Sridharan, M., Sen, K.: Dlint: dynamically checking bad coding practices in JavaScript. In: Proceedings of the 2015 International Symposium on Software Testing and Analysis, pp. 94–105. ISSTA 2015 (2015)
7. Jensen, S.H., Sridharan, M., Sen, K., Chandra, S.: MemInsight: platform-independent memory debugging for JavaScript. In: Proceedings of the 2015 10th Joint Meeting on Foundations of Software Engineering, pp. 345–356. ACM (2015)
8. Kiciman, E., Livshits, B.: AjaxScope: a platform for remotely monitoring the client-side behavior of web 2.0 applications. In: ACM SIGOPS Operating Systems Review, pp. 17–30. ACM (2007)
9. Livshits, B., Lam, M.S.: Finding security vulnerabilities in Java applications with static analysis. In: Proceedings of the 14th Conference on USENIX Security Symposium, vol. 14 (2005)
10. Marchetto, A., Tonella, P., Ricca, F.: State-based testing of AJAX web applications. In: 2008 1st International Conference on Software Testing, Verification, and Validation, pp. 121–130, April 2008
11. Memwatch. https://github.com/eduardbcom/node-memwatch
12. Mesbah, A., Bozdag, E., Van Deursen, A.: Crawling AJAX by inferring user interface state changes. In: Eighth International Conference on Web Engineering. ICWE 2008, pp. 122–134. IEEE (2008)
13. Mesbah, A., Van Deursen, A.: A component-and push-based architectural style for AJAX applications. J. Syst. Softw. **81**(12), 2194–2209 (2008)
14. Patil, H., Pereira, C., Stallcup, M., Lueck, G., Cownie, J.: Pinplay: a framework for deterministic replay and reproducible analysis of parallel programs. In: Proceedings of the 8th Annual IEEE/ACM International Symposium on Code Generation and Optimization, pp. 2–11. ACM (2010)
15. Realty_rest. https://github.com/ccoenraets/ionic2-realty-rest
16. Search_leak. https://github.com/newarmy/test
17. Selakovic, M., Pradel, M.: Performance issues and optimizations in JavaScript: an empirical study. In: 2016 IEEE/ACM 38th International Conference on Software Engineering (ICSE), pp. 61–72 (2016)
18. Sung, C., Kusano, M., Sinha, N., Wang, C.: Static DOM event dependency analysis for testing web applications. In: Proceedings of the 2016 24th ACM SIGSOFT International Symposium on Foundations of Software Engineering, pp. 447–459. FSE 2016 (2016)
19. theBrownNode. https://github.com/clintcparker/theBrownNode
20. Vilk, J., Berger, E.D.: Bleak: automatically debugging memory leaks in web applications. In: Proceedings of the 39th ACM SIGPLAN Conference on Programming Language Design and Implementation, pp. 15–29. ACM (2018)
21. Xiao, X., Han, S., Zhang, C., Zhang, D.: Uncovering JavaScript performance code smells relevant to type mutations. In: Feng, X., Park, S. (eds.) APLAS 2015. LNCS, vol. 9458, pp. 335–355. Springer, Cham (2015). https://doi.org/10.1007/978-3-319-26529-2_18
22. Zhang, H.: On the distribution of software faults. IEEE Trans. Softw. Eng. **34**(2), 301–302 (2008)

Multi-device Adaptation with Liquid Media Queries

Andrea Gallidabino[(✉)] and Cesare Pautasso[(✉)]

Software Institute, Faculty of Informatics, Università della Svizzera italiana (USI),
Lugano, Switzerland
andrea.gallidabino@usi.ch, c.pautasso@ieee.org
https://liquid.inf.usi.ch

Abstract. The design of responsive Web applications is traditionally based on the assumption that they run on a single client at a time. Thanks to CSS3 media queries, developers can declaratively specify how the Web application UI adapts to the capabilities of specific devices. As users own more and more devices and they attempt to use them to run Web applications in parallel, we propose to extend CSS media queries so that they can be used to adapt the UI of liquid Web applications while they are dynamically deployed across multiple devices. In this paper we present our extension of CSS media queries with liquid-related types and features, allowing to detect the number of devices connected, the number of users running the application, or the role played by each device. The liquid media query types and features defined in this paper are designed and suitable for liquid component-based Web architectures, and they enable developers to control the deployment of individual Web components across multiple browsers. Furthermore we show the design of liquid media queries in the Liquid.js for Polymer framework and propose different adaptation algorithms. Finally we showcase the expressiveness of the liquid media queries to support real-world examples and evaluate the algorithmic complexity of our approach.

Keywords: Liquid software · Media queries ·
Multi-device adaptation · Responsive user interface ·
Complementary view adaptation

1 Introduction

Liquid software [14] stands for a metaphor [20] that associates the shape of liquids with software: as a liquid is able to flow into and adapt its shape to any container, liquid software is able to flow across and adapt itself to fit on all the devices it is deployed on. Liquid software allows to seamlessly migrate at runtime parts of an application (e.g. individual components of the user interface) or the whole application from a device to another. Liquid applications are responsive (e.g. they are able to adapt to any device running it), but more importantly they are

© Springer Nature Switzerland AG 2019
M. Bakaev et al. (Eds.): ICWE 2019, LNCS 11496, pp. 474–489, 2019.
https://doi.org/10.1007/978-3-030-19274-7_33

also able to adapt to the *set* of devices simultaneously running the application. Finally liquid applications can share their state across multiple devices while keeping it synchronized [18].

Nowadays, due to the improvement of Web technologies with the release of new Web standards (e.g. supporting full-duplex, direct communication between clients), we are witnessing the shift towards more complex and decentralized Web architectures [3], which in turn enable developers to create Web applications featuring support for the liquid user experience.

In our previous works we showed how we designed liquid abstractions for the data and logic layers in liquid Web architectures [5]. In this paper we focus on the user interface layer as we introduce *liquid media queries*, an upgrade to standard CSS3 media queries [2] that allows the developers to create their own CSS style sheets that get activated when their Web applications are deployed across multiple devices. While as part of the liquid user experience, end users can control which user interface components are deployed on each device (e.g., by swiping or drag and drop), developers can use liquid media queries to declarative describe how their applications can automatically react to changes in their deployment environment.

The developers of liquid applications should be able to offer to the users an automatic rule-based deployment mechanism for populating all of the users' devices with pieces of the application they are running, because a misuse of the manual liquid user experience may lead to non-intuitive deployments which contradict with the developer expectations and intent. For example, in case of a picture sharing application, it should be possible to provide constraints for placing the components for taking and selecting pictures on the phones, while the picture viewer component gets deployed on a larger display. This way, users can select which picture to display from their personal smartphone photo library and take advantage of a public device to have a shared slideshow.

The rest of this paper is structured as follows. After reviewing related work in Sect. 2, we present the design of liquid media queries in Sect. 3 and show how they are encoded within the Liquid.js for Polymer [4] framework (Sect. 4). The queries drive the algorithms outlined in Sect. 5, which are used to automatically adapt a distributed user interface across multiple devices [13] – as shown in the example scenarios of Sect. 6 – making it possible to shift from the traditional *responsive* UI adaptation [12], to a *complementary* one [15] able to automatically migrate Web components across the set of heterogeneous devices running a liquid Web application simultaneously.

2   Related Work

In the literature we can find several research topics concerning adaptive multi-device user interfaces [19] such as Distributed User Interfaces (DUI) [11] or Cross-Device Interfaces [17]. All deal with distributed component-based user interfaces deployed across multiple devices [1]. User interface elements can be distributed across the devices either synchronously or asynchronously: when we talk about asynchronous distribution the devices do not need to be connected in parallel when the UI elements are moved, while for synchronous distribution the devices need to be simultaneously connected [1].

In this paper we deal only with synchronous distribution, and design the *automatic complementary view adaptation* for the components of liquid web applications. In our scenario multiple devices are used together to accomplish a common task, however each device may play a different role and thus display different and complementary visual components. If the set of connected devices changes, then the distributed user interface should flow and adapt accordingly to the new configuration of the environment [10].

In the literature there are several attempts to use rules to describe cross-device user interfaces. Most of them rely on centralised architectures for computing the configuration and then the distribution of the components across multiple device. Zorrilla *et al.* [21] discuss a centralized custom rule-based approach that allows to assigns properties both to components and devices, it scores the best targets for distribution, and then shows and hides the corresponding components depending on the devices they are deployed on. Liquid media queries are also rule-based as they extend the CSS3 media query standard. However, the implementation of our algorithm is meant to be decentralized and involve every device on which the application is running.

Husmann *et al.* [7] implement cross-device user interfaces in a decentralized environment and define a similar rule-based approach. They do not associate the rules to CSS media queries, nor they support multiple CSS style sheets that need to be enabled or disabled on the target devices. Their approach instead deploys the whole application on all the connected devices and then hides the components that should not be displayed. Our approach is more fine-grained as it moves across the devices only the components that need to be deployed, migrating them directly from the device they are currently running on, instead of deploying the whole application from a centralized server.

3   Liquid Media Types and Features

CSS3 media types and features can be used to adapt the user interface of an application to multiple devices by associating a CSS style sheet with some expected device characteristics. Standard media features consider qualities of the Web browser and its environment (e.g., the screen size and resolution, the output media, the device orientation). If the media query matches what the device supports, the corresponding style is activated.

Standard CSS3 media queries are at the foundation for responsive user interfaces that adapt the Web application user interface layout to a single device at the time. However, they lack sufficient expressive power to describe the user interface adaptation in a multi-device environment. For this reason in this Section we introduce and describe new media types and features for liquid web applications (Table 1). Together they enable developers to perform cross-device user interface adaptation by declaratively constraining on which devices a component should be deployed on and by controlling which style sheets should be applied depending on properties of the set of devices connected to their application.

Table 1. Proposed media types and features for liquid media queries.

Name	Description
Features	
liquid	Shortcut for `min-liquid-devices: 2`
liquid-devices	The number of connected devices
liquid-users	The number of connected users
liquid-device-ownership	Whether the device is private, shared or public
liquid-device-role	The application-specific role of a device
Types	
liquid-device-type	The type of device(s) running the application

liquid and liquid-devices - Liquid software is strongly tied to multi-device environments, especially when *parallel screening* scenarios are considered [5]. In these scenarios liquid applications must be deployed on multiple devices in parallel. Understanding when the liquid application is running on multiple devices is required for the adaptation. The *liquid* feature refers to any environment with at least two connected devices, while the *liquid-devices* feature allows to tune this value for specific uses cases. Similarly to CSS3 media queries, it is also possible to define the minimum and maximum values for the *liquid-devices* feature by setting the values for *min-liquid-devices* and *max-liquid-devices* (e.g. it is possible to dynamically change the view of the liquid application when there are at least three connected devices instead of two, or create different views for specific number of connected devices).

liquid-users - In *multi-user parallel scenarios* [5] the liquid application is deployed across multiple devices and multiple users can interact with it at the same time. The *liquid-users* media feature allows to adapt a user interface depending on the number of users connected to the application. The features *min-liquid-users* and *max-liquid-users* can also be used for creating styles for single user applications (e.g. `max-liquid-users: 1`) and multi-user application (e.g. `min-liquid-users: 2`).

liquid-device-ownership - The types of access granted to devices can be either *private, shared,* or *public*. A *private* device is owned and used exclusively by one user. *Shared* devices are owned by one user, but they can be used by another. *Public* devices (e.g. public displays [16]) can be used by both registered and authenticated users or anonymous guests.

liquid-device-role - The *device role* is an application-specific feature. In Liquid.js for Polymer is possible to configure the connected devices and assign *roles* to them (e.g. *controller, console, multimedia display*). When the role of a device in a liquid application is not tightly bound to the type of device, the

Listing 1.1. Liquid-style element

```
1   <liquid-style
2     liquid          // Default: "true"
3     devices="" min-devices="" max-devices=""  // Default:  ""
4     users="" min-users=""  max-users=""        // Default:  ""
5     device-ownership="" device-role=""         // Default:  ""
6     device-type=""                             // Default:  ""
7     priority=""   // Default:  "1"
8     clone=""      // Default:  ""
9     css-media=""  // Default:  ""
10  > <!-- CSS Stylesheet --> </liquid-style>
```

device-role can be used by the developers to assign specific styles to the user
interface. When using the *liquid-device-role* feature, any device connected to
the application must be configured with the chosen role. The role meta data
associated with the device can change at any time, thus activating or deactivating
the corresponding media query.

liquid-device-type - The latest standard media types only distinguish
between *screen*, *print*, or *speech* devices. Depending on the context of the application, it can be useful to distinguish the types of screen devices connected so that
they can be assigned to perform certain kind of tasks (e.g. desktop computers are
used more for working in an office) [9], while other devices are more convenient
in certain social situations (e.g., smartphones as opposed to laptops are more
convenient during meals) [8]. In our current implementation *liquid-device-type*
can be set to *Desktop, Laptop, Tablet, Phone*.

4   Liquid Style Element

CSS3 media queries do not allow us to define new query types or features, nor
they support customizing existing ones[1]. The solution we designed for extending
the standard media queries is to create a new Web component labeled as *liquid-
style* inside the Liquid.js for Polymer framework [4].

The *liquid-style* element shown in Listing 1.1 allows developers to write their
own liquid media queries and encapsulate a standard CSS style sheet that is automatically activated when the media query expression is accepted by the device.
The *liquid-style* component allow developers to assign values to their attributes
(e.g., `device-role`) that are mapped to the previously defined liquid media types
and features by adding the `liquid-` prefix (e.g., `liquid-device-role`). Developers define new liquid media queries by assigning values to the corresponding
attributes, as shown in Listings 1.2 and 1.3.

---

[1] https://drafts.csswg.org/mediaqueries-4.

Listing 1.2. Liquid media query expression mapped to liquid-style component attributes

```
1  @media liquid and (liquid-device-type:phone) {
2      body { flex-direction: row; }
3  }
4  <!-- Maps to --->
5  <liquid-style device-type="phone">
6      body { flex-direction: row; }
7  </liquid-style>
```

Listing 1.3. Liquid media query expression including standard CSS media features mapped to liquid-style component attributes

```
1  @media liquid and
2    (liquid-device-role:controller) and
3    (min-liquid-users:3) and
4    (min-height:900px) {
5      :root { background-color: red; }
6  }
7  <!-- Maps to --->
8  <liquid-style device-role="controller" min-users="3"
       css-media="min-height:900px">
9      :root { background-color: red; }
10 </liquid-style>
```

In the first example, the liquid media query expression contains both the *liquid* feature and the *liquid-device-type* type. Inside the *liquid-style* component is not necessary to explicitly set the *liquid* feature to *true*, since it is the default value for the element, while *liquid-device-type* maps to the attribute *device-type*.

The second media query expression contains the liquid media features *liquid-device-role* and *min-liquid-users*, which map directly to the attributes *device-role* and *min-users*. Furthermore the expression also contains the standard media feature *min-height*, which is set into the *css-media* attribute as any non-liquid part of the query expression.

4.1   Automatic Component Migration and Cloning

Automatic complementary view adaptation is achieved through the liquid media query expressions that both define when styles should be enabled on a device and constrain where the components should be migrated if any device with the appropriate features connects to the application. The *liquid-style* component is designed to be attached directly to a Liquid.js *liquid-component* [4] and bundled with a standard Polymer component. The framework extracts the liquid media query expressions from within every instantiated component and shares them with all other connected devices so that they can check whether they would satisfy the liquid media queries. Whenever a query is accepted on a device, that device becomes a possible target for the migration of the corresponding component. Since it is possible to define multiple *liquid-style* elements inside a component, each can have a different *priority* (see Listing 1.1). The *priority* attribute helps the developers to define multiple styles for different environments, while still being able to influence the migration process, as described in Sect. 5.

In addition to the migration, the *liquid-style* component provides another liquid user experience primitive for deploying components across multiple devices [5] called cloning, in which components are copied and kept synchronized across two or more devices. Migration enables to redistribute pre-existing user interface components across multiple devices, however it does not allow developers to create adaptive user interfaces with rules for instantiating new components like "*component X needs to be instantiated in all public displays*" or "*component Y needs to be instantiated on phones devices, but only once per user*". While the migration of a component is obtained by simply adding a *liquid-style* element, cloning components requires additional configuration.

The attribute labeled *clone* in Listing 1.1 is used to enable multiple instances of the same source component to be cloned across multiple devices instead of just migrating it on one of them. The *clone* attribute accepts values in the form of $N-feature$, where N is a positive non-zero integer or the symbol $*$, and $feature \in \{user, device, phone, tablet, desktop, laptop, shared, public, private, role = X\}$.

The value N specifies the maximum number of instances of the source component which should be cloned across the set of available devices which match the liquid media query constraints in relation to the chosen $feature$. Their combination allows to write cloning rules such as:

1-user, clone the component once per user, picking one of their available devices;

1-device, the component is cloned at most once per device type;

2-tablet, up to two component instances are cloned among all available tablets;

*-public, the component is cloned on all available *public* devices.

*-role=dashboard, the component is cloned on all devices playing the dashboard role;

The *clone* attribute works in conjunction with the other attributes of the *liquid-style* component, so that the liquid media query expression mapped from the attributes must be accepted on the device so that it is considered a valid cloning target.

5   Liquid UI Adaptation Algorithm

The UI adaptation algorithm operates on three distinct phases: constraint-checking and priority computation, migration and cloning, and local component adaptation. First it decides which devices are suitable for displaying a component encapsulating the liquid media query, then it migrates or clones the component on the highest priority device and activates the corresponding style sheet as soon as the component is loaded on the target device.

5.1   Phase 1: Constraint-Checking and Priority Computation

The constraint-checking phase decides if there is a suitable device in the pool of connected devices that satisfies the liquid media query expressions encapsulated inside the components.

Algorithm 1. Incremental Constraint-checking and Priority Computation

Data: Input: $priorityMatrix$, $cloneMatrix$
Data: Shared global state: $components, devices, users, deviceConfigurations$
Data: Event

1 **if** $Event ==$ component c created **then**
2   Add a new row in the $priorityMatrix$;
3   **forall** $d \in devices$ **do**
4   **forall** $liquid\text{-}style$ in the created component **do**
5   Check if the $device$ accepts the liquid-style and save the highest priority in $priorityMatrix[c][d]$ and in $cloneMatrix[c][d]$;
6 **else if** $Event ==$ component deleted **then**
7   Remove the corresponding $component$ row from the $priorityMatrix$;
8 **else if** $Event ==$ device d configuration changed **then**
9   **forall** $c \in components$ **do**
10   **forall** $liquid\text{-}style$ in the component **do**
11   Check if the $device$ accepts the liquid-style and save the highest priority in $priorityMatrix[c][d]$ and in $cloneMatrix[c][d]$;
12 **else if** $Event ==$ device connected $\parallel$ $Event ==$ device disconnected $\parallel$ $Event ==$ user connected $\parallel$ $Event ==$ user disconnected **then**
13   **forall** $c \in components$ **do**
14   **forall** $d \in devices$ **do**
15   **forall** $liquid\text{-}style$ in the component **do**
16   Check if the $device$ accepts the liquid-style and save the highest priority in $priorityMatrix[c][d]$ and in $cloneMatrix[c][d]$;

Result: updated $priorityMatrix$ and $cloneMatrix$

Algorithm 1 computes the matrix of valid target devices in which at least one liquid media expression is accepted. The matrix has size $\#components \times \#devices$. Each element represents with a positive integer the highest $priority$ value of all the accepted liquid media queries encapsulated in the component, or $zero$ if there are no accepted queries.

The matrix shown in (1) is the $priorityMatrix$ produced by Algorithm 1 during the example scenario shown in Fig. 2, when both $UserA$ and $UserB$ are connected. There are four instantiated components and seven devices connected to the application. c_{video}'s liquid media queries (see Sect. 6) are accepted by device d_{laptop}, d_{tv}. At least one query of priority 2 was accepted by device d_{laptop} and at least one query of priority 4 was accepted by devices d_{tv}. d_{phone1} accepts at least one query encapsulated in components $c_{videoController}$, $c_{suggestedVideo}$, the first one with priority 2 and the latter with priority 1.

$$priorityMatrix = \begin{array}{c} \\ c_{video} \\ c_{videoController} \\ c_{suggestedVideo} \\ c_{comments} \end{array} \begin{array}{ccccccc} d_{phone1} & d_{phone2} & d_{phone3} & d_{tablet} & d_{laptop1} & d_{laptop2} & d_{tv} \\ \left(\begin{array}{ccccccc} 0 & 0 & 0 & 0 & 2 & 2 & 4 \\ 2 & 2 & 2 & 0 & 0 & 0 & 0 \\ 1 & 1 & 1 & 3 & 0 & 0 & 0 \\ 0 & 0 & 0 & 0 & 1 & 1 & 0 \end{array}\right) \end{array} \quad (1)$$

$$\text{cloneMatrix} = c_{videoController} \overset{d_{phone1}\ d_{phone2}\ d_{phone3}\ d_{tablet}\ d_{laptop1}\ d_{laptop2}\ d_{tv}}{\left(\begin{array}{ccccccc} 2 & 2 & 2 & 0 & 0 & 0 & 0 \end{array}\right)} \quad (2)$$

Algorithm 1 also computes the *cloneMatrix* shown in (2), which has a similar structure to the *priorityMatrix*, but stores only the information about the components that define at least one clone rule in the attributes of the *liquid-style* elements they encapsulate. The matrix has size $\#components_{clone} \times \#devices$ where $\#components_{clone} \leq \#components$.

Liquid.js runs the Algorithm 1 whenever one of the following *events* occurs:

- **A component is created or deleted from a device.** Creating or deleting a components does not affect the acceptance of the liquid media queries of any other components. When a new component is created (or removed), a row is added (or removed) to the *priorityMatrix* and the algorithm recomputes the highest priority score. If the component defines a liquid media query with the clone attribute, then the highest priority value between the clone styles is also stored in the *cloneMatrix*.
- **The meta-configuration of a device is changed.** When the device *type*, *ownership*, and *role* change, the priority values of the corresponding column are updated for both matrices.
- **A device joins or leaves the current session.** These events affect the *devices*, *min-devices*, and *max-devices* features of the liquid media queries, which triggers the recomputation of the whole *priorityMatrix* and *cloneMatrix*.
- **A user connects or disconnects from the application.** Changes to the *users*, *min-users*, and *max-users* features also require a complete recomputation of the *priorityMatrix* and *cloneMatrix*.

5.2   Phase 2: Migration and Cloning

The migration and cloning phase uses the previously computed *priorityMatrix* and *cloneMatrix* to determine on which device each component should be migrated or cloned on. The algorithm prepares a migration plan where each component is assigned a given target device. The choice follows a best fit algorithm so that the number of components running on each device is minimized, thus spreading the liquid Web application across as many devices as possible. If the component instances outnumber the available devices, some of the components will be co-located on the same device still according to their priority. Equation (3) shows the resulting *migrationPlan* computed by the algorithm. c_{video} is migrated to d_{tv} with the highest priority, $c_{comments}$ is migrated to d_{laptop} with the lowest. Once it is ready, Liquid.js uses the migration plan to redeploy the components across the set of devices.

$$\text{migrationPlan} = [\{c_{video}, d_{tv}\}, \{c_{suggestedVideo}, d_{phone1}\}, \\ \{c_{videoController}, d_{tablet}\}, \{c_{comments}, d_{laptop2}\}] \quad (3)$$

$$\text{clonePlan} = [\{c_{videoController}, d_{phone3}\}] \quad (4)$$

After the migration step is complete, the cloning routine can start. This process exploits the *cloneMatrix* computed in phase 1 and the clone rules associated to the components that need to be cloned. All the devices that were not used in the previous migration step are flagged as candidates for running a cloned component. The candidates are grouped and prioritized following the clone rules, the device that contains the source component that needs be cloned is never considered as a possible target of the cloning, and every component which can be cloned is associated with a list of target devices on which it can be copied. Similarly to the previous step, the algorithm prepares a clone plan that is used by Liquid.js for cloning components. Equation (4) shows the output *clonePlan* computed with the matrix shown in Eq. (2) under the constraints of the liquid media queries of the scenario depicted in Fig. 2 (see Sect. 6 for the constraints).

The algorithm that computes the migration plan attempts to minimize the number of component instances running on each device. Also, it resolves ties by selecting components based on the order of instantiation. This could be improved by prioritising components with higher score values that have the least number of possible targets devices. This approach works with an initial configuration where all components are initially running on one devices, so the outcome does consider the overall migration cost, seen in terms of the number of migration operations to be performed and the time required to migrate a given component instance. Minimizing such cost would become important when the algorithm is applied to an input configuration of components already instantiated across multiple devices.

5.3   Phase 3: Component Adaptation

The *component adaptation* phase happens once the migration and cloning is complete. Each device checks for each instantiated component which liquid media queries are accepted and activates the associated style sheet. The standard CSS mechanisms for dealing with overlapping selectors take over.

5.4   Run-Time Complexity

The complexity of the algorithm we discussed in Sect. 5 depends on three factors: the number of devices (D), the number of the components (C), and the number *liquid-style* elements (S). In the worst case, the run-time complexity of Algorithm 1 is $\mathcal{O}(D * C * S)$. However, the actual run-time complexity depends on the event that triggered the incremental version of the algorithm: $- \mathcal{O}(D * S)$ for newly created components; $- \mathcal{O}(C)$ for deleted components; $- \mathcal{O}(C * S)$ for changed device configurations; $- \mathcal{O}(D * C * S)$ for all other events. The run-time complexity of the migration and cloning phase is $\mathcal{O}(C * D^2)$, and the adaptation algorithm explained in Subsect. 5.3 has complexity $\mathcal{O}(S)$.

The execution for Algorithm 1 can be parallelized as the responsibility for computing the priority Matrix columns can be offloaded on each device, assuming that they all have access to the component liquid style definitions. Each device takes care of updating their columns whenever an event occurs and stores the result in the application shared state, which is automatically synchronized among all devices.

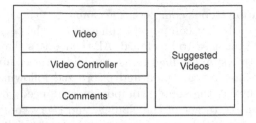

Fig. 1. Liquid video player user interface split into four components: *video, video controller, suggested videos, comments*

6   Liquid UI Adaptation Example

We show the expressiveness of liquid media queries by designing the *liquid-style* components on a realistic multi-device video player application.

The video player is built with four components (see Fig. 1): – the **video** component which displays and plays the video; – the **video controller** component which allows the user to play/pause and seek to a specific time in the selected video; – the **suggested videos** component that displays a list of recommended videos, which can be selected to be played; – the **comments** component where the user can read or post comments about the video.

These components can be deployed across different devices (phones, tablets, laptops, and televisions) owned by one or multiple users.

Listing 1.4. The *liquid-style* elements defined for the **video** component.

```
1  <liquid-style device-ownership="shared" min-users="2"
       priority="4">
2  <!-- CSS Style Sheet --></liquid-style>
3  <liquid-style device-role="display" priority="3">
4  <!-- CSS Style Sheet --></liquid-style>
5  <liquid-style device-type="laptop" priority="2">
6  <!-- CSS Style Sheet --></liquid-style>
```

Listing 1.5. The *liquid-style* element defined for the **comments** component.

```
1  <liquid-style device-type="laptop">
2  <!-- CSS Style Sheet --></liquid-style>
```

Listing 1.6. The *liquid-style* element defined for the **video controller** component.

```
1  <liquid-style device-type="phone" priority="2"
2       clone="1-user">
3  <!-- CSS Style Sheet --></liquid-style>
```

Listing 1.7. The *liquid-style* elements defined for the **suggested videos** component.

```
1  <liquid-style device-type="phone">
2  <!-- CSS Style Sheet --></liquid-style>
3  <liquid-style device-type="tablet" priority="3">
4  <!-- CSS Style Sheet --></liquid-style>
```

It is best to display the video component (see Listing 1.4) on the devices with big screens, for this reason we define three liquid media query expressions including the attributes `device-type: laptop`, `device-role: display`, and `device-ownership: shared` with different priorities. The rule for `device-type: laptop` has an higher priority over the rule defined for the *comments* component (see Listing 1.5) so that whenever a laptop device is available, the video component is migrated to the laptop. If the user configures the role of any device and assigns the role *display* to it, then this device will have priority over the laptop. Finally, if there are multiple users connected to the application (attribute *min-users:2*), the priority for deploying the *video* component is given to *shared* devices (e.g., a television).

Component		Video	Video Controller	Comments	Suggested Videos
Initial	*Priority*	2	2	1	3
Configuration	*Migration Target*	laptop 1	phone 1	laptop 2	tablet
User B	*Priority*	4	2	1	3
connects	*Migration Target*	television	(phone 1)	(laptop 2)	(tablet)
phone	*Cloning Target*		**phone 2**		

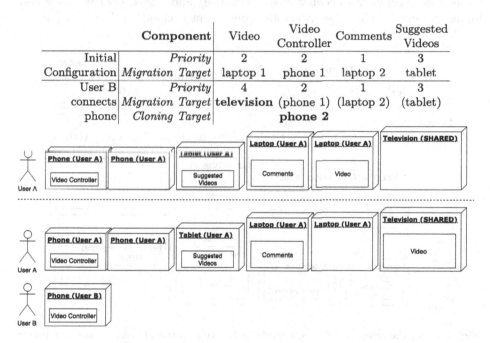

Fig. 2. When a second user connects to the application the video component is migrated to the shared device and a new instance of the video controller is deployed on the new user's phone.

The video controller component (see Listing 1.6) defines a liquid media query expression with the attribute *clone:1-user*. The clone rule migrates the component to a phone owned by a user, then it clones the component for every other user, if they connect at least another phone to the application.

The suggested video component (see Listing 1.7) defines two styles: one for tablets and the other for phones. The tablet style has an higher priority with respect to the phone style.

Scenario 1: Second User Connects a Phone. In Fig. 2 we show the component redistribution for a set of devices before and after a second user connects to the application. The initial configuration with only devices owned by *User A* is obtained following the priorities associated with the liquid-style elements of each component. Starting from the suggested video component, which migrates to the tablet, then the video component migrates to a laptop device, because the higher priority rules it holds are not accepted by any other device. The video controller migrates to a phone device, but it is not cloned on both available phones because of the clone rule set to 1-user. Finally, the comments component migrates to the second laptop device.

After *User B* logs in the application and connects an additional phone device, the user interface is redistributed as follows. The video component is migrated to the television device because of the *ownership* and *min-users* rules have now higher priority 4. The video controller component is cloned to *User B*'s phone.

Component	Video	Video Controller	Comments	Suggested Videos
Initial — *Priority*	2	0	1 (0)	3
Configuration — *Migration Target*	laptop	tablet	television	tablet
Television role — *Priority*	4	0	1	3
set to display — *Migration Target*	**television**	(tablet)	**laptop**	(tablet)

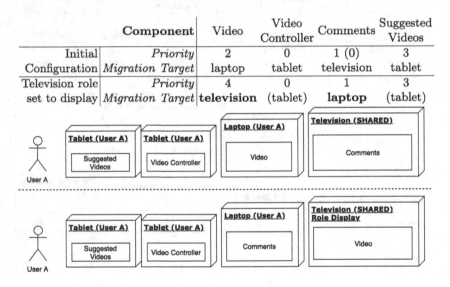

Fig. 3. After the television device changes role configuration, the video and comments components are swapped following different priorities.

Scenario 2: Dynamic Device Role Change. In Fig. 3 we show an example of dynamic change in the metadata configuration of the connected devices. The initial device configuration is not accepted by at least one liquid media query defined in the video controller component, and the target device for the video and comments components points the same laptop. Starting from the highest priority, the suggested video component is deployed on the tablet and the video component is deployed on the laptop. Since the laptop component is already the target of the video component, the comments component migrates to the television, which was ranked as the next possible target for migration. The video controller component is deployed on the tablet device with the lowest priority.

When *UserA* assigns the role *display* to the television, the device metadata changes. The user interface is redistributed and the video component migrates to the television, because the *liquid-style* that defines the property *device-role* is now accepted by the device with an higher priority. The comment component migrates to the now available laptop device.

7   Conclusion and Future Work

This paper describes a rule-based approach that can be used by developers to declaratively specify how the components within a liquid web application can dynamically and automatically be deployed across multiple devices. The liquid media query concept allows developers to define CSS style sheets for Web components in relation to the dynamic multi-device environment they are expected to be deployed on. We identify the main features defining the liquid environment properties (e.g., the number of connected devices, their types, the number of users, various kinds of device ownership, and the application-specific role played by a device). The *liquid-style* element we designed takes care of encoding the liquid media queries so that the Liquid.js for Polymer framework can automatically choose where to deploy a component by evaluating which devices accept the corresponding liquid media query constraints.

The algorithms in this paper are designed under the assumption that the number of devices running a liquid Web application is limited and small. While this is true for single user environments, in which the number of devices owned by one user is small (3 on average [6]), further work is needed to assess the scalability of the approach to deal with a large number of devices in a multi-user collaborative scenario where it may become impractical to declare liquid media queries matching all possible device combinations.

Another direction for future work concerns the use of logical operators such as *not* and *only* found in standard CSS media queries but which are not supported by the proposed encoding using attributes of the *liquid-style* element.

Acknowledgements. This work is supported by the SNF with the "Fundamentals of Parallel Programming for PaaS Clouds" project (Nr. 153560).

References

1. Elmqvist, N.: Distributed user interfaces: state of the art. In: Gallud, J., Tesoriero, R., Penichet, V. (eds.) Distributed User Interfaces. HCIS, pp. 1–12. Springer, London (2011). https://doi.org/10.1007/978-1-4471-2271-5_1
2. Frain, B.: Responsive Web Design with HTML5 and CSS3. Packt Publishing (2012)
3. Gallidabino, A., Pautasso, C.: Maturity model for liquid web architectures. In: Cabot, J., De Virgilio, R., Torlone, R. (eds.) ICWE 2017. LNCS, vol. 10360, pp. 206–224. Springer, Cham (2017). https://doi.org/10.1007/978-3-319-60131-1_12
4. Gallidabino, A., Pautasso, C.: The liquid user experience API. In: Companion of the The Web Conference 2018, Developers Track (TheWebConf2018), pp. 767–774 (2018)
5. Gallidabino, A., Pautasso, C., Mikkonen, T., Systa, K., Voutilainen, J.P., Taivalsaari, A.: Architecting liquid software. J. Web Eng. **16**(5&6), 433–470 (2017)
6. Google: The connected consumer (2015). http://www.google.com.sg/publicdata/explore?ds=dg8d1eetcqsb1_
7. Husmann, M., Spiegel, M., Murolo, A., Norrie, M.C.: UI testing cross-device applications. In: Proceedings of the 2016 ACM on Interactive Surfaces and Spaces (ISS2016), pp. 179–188. ACM (2016)
8. Jokela, T., Ojala, J., Olsson, T.: A diary study on combining multiple information devices in everyday activities and tasks. In: Proceedings of the 33rd Annual ACM Conference on Human Factors in Computing Systems (CHI2015), pp. 3903–3912. ACM (2015)
9. Kawsar, F., Brush, A.: Home computing unplugged: why, where and when people use different connected devices at home. In: Proceedings of the 2013 ACM International Joint Conference on Pervasive and Ubiquitous Computing (UbiComp2013), pp. 627–636. ACM (2013)
10. Levin, M.: Designing Multi-device Experiences: An Ecosystem Approach to User Experiences Across Devices. O'Reilly, Sebastopol (2014)
11. Luyten, K., Coninx, K.: Distributed user interface elements to support smart interaction spaces. In: Seventh IEEE International Symposium on Multimedia. IEEE (2005)
12. Marcotte, E.: Responsive Web Design. Editions Eyrolles (2011)
13. Melchior, J., Grolaux, D., Vanderdonckt, J., Van Roy, P.: A toolkit for peer-to-peer distributed user interfaces: concepts, implementation, and applications. In: Proceedings of the 1st ACM SIGCHI Symposium on Engineering Interactive Computing Systems, pp. 69–78. ACM (2009)
14. Mikkonen, T., Systä, K., Pautasso, C.: Towards liquid web applications. In: Cimiano, P., Frasincar, F., Houben, G.-J., Schwabe, D. (eds.) ICWE 2015. LNCS, vol. 9114, pp. 134–143. Springer, Cham (2015). https://doi.org/10.1007/978-3-319-19890-3_10
15. Mori, G., Paterno, F., Santoro, C.: Design and development of multidevice user interfaces through multiple logical descriptions. IEEE Trans. Softw. Eng. **30**(8), 507–520 (2004)
16. Müller, J., Alt, F., Michelis, D., Schmidt, A.: Requirements and design space for interactive public displays. In: Proceedings of the 18th ACM International Conference on Multimedia, pp. 1285–1294. ACM (2010)
17. Nebeling, M., Mintsi, T., Husmann, M., Norrie, M.: Interactive development of cross-device user interfaces. In: Proceedings of the 32nd Annual ACM Conference on Human Factors in Computing Systems, pp. 2793–2802. ACM (2014)

18. Nicolaescu, P., Jahns, K., Derntl, M., Klamma, R.: Yjs: a framework for near real-time P2P shared editing on arbitrary data types. In: Cimiano, P., Frasincar, F., Houben, G.-J., Schwabe, D. (eds.) ICWE 2015. LNCS, vol. 9114, pp. 675–678. Springer, Cham (2015). https://doi.org/10.1007/978-3-319-19890-3_55
19. Paternò, F., Santoro, C.: A logical framework for multi-device user interfaces. In: Proceedings of the 4th ACM SIGCHI Symposium on Engineering Interactive Computing Systems, pp. 45–50. ACM (2012)
20. Taivalsaari, A., Mikkonen, T., Systa, K.: Liquid software manifesto: the era of multiple device ownership and its implications for software architecture. In: 38th Computer Software and Applications Conference (COMPSAC 2014), pp. 338–343 (2014)
21. Zorrilla, M., Borch, N., Daoust, F., Erk, A., Flórez, J., Lafuente, A.: A web-based distributed architecture for multi-device adaptation in media applications. Pers. Ubiquit. Comput. **19**(5–6), 803–820 (2015)

Conversational Data Exploration

Nicola Castaldo, Florian Daniel[iD], Maristella Matera[✉][iD],
and Vittorio Zaccaria[iD]

Dipartimento di Elettronica Informazione e Bioingegneria, Politecnico di Milano,
Piazza Leonardo da Vinci, 32, 20133 Milan, Italy
nicola.castaldo@mail.polimi.it,
{florian.daniel,maristella.matera,vittorio.zaccaria}@polimi.it

Abstract. This paper presents a framework for the design of *chatbots for data exploration*. With respect to conversational virtual assistants (such as Amazon Alexa or Apple Siri), this class of chatbots exploits structured input to retrieve data from known data sources. The approach is based on a conceptual representation of the available data sources, and on a set of modeling abstractions that allow designers to characterize the role that key data elements play in the user requests to be handled. Starting from the resulting specifications, the framework then generates a conversation for exploring the content exposed by the considered data sources.

Keywords: Chatbots for data exploration · Chatbot design · Conversational UIs

1 Introduction

Chatbots are growing fast in number and pervade in a broad range of activities. Their natural language paradigm simplifies the interaction with applications to the point that experts consider chatbots one of the most promising technologies to transform instant messaging systems into software delivery platforms [2,3]. The major messaging platforms have thus opened their APIs to third-party developers, to expose high-level services (e.g., messaging, payments, bot directory) and User Interface (UI) elements (e.g., buttons and icons), to facilitate and promote the development of innovative services based on conversational UIs [4].

Despite the huge emphasis on these new applications, it is still not clear what implications their rapid uptake will have on the design of interactive systems for data access and exploration. The applications proposed so far mainly support the retrieval of very specific data from online services. It is still unclear how this paradigm can be applied for the interaction with large bodies of information and machine agents. A critical challenge lies in understanding how to make the development of bots for data exploration scalable and sustainable, in terms of both software infrastructures and design models and methodologies [1,5].

In this paper, we present a *data-driven design paradigm* for building conversational interfaces for data exploration. In line with traditional Web Engineering

© Springer Nature Switzerland AG 2019
M. Bakaev et al. (Eds.): ICWE 2019, LNCS 11496, pp. 490–497, 2019.
https://doi.org/10.1007/978-3-030-19274-7_34

methodologies, we exploit properties of data models and propose schema annotations to enable the generation of conversation paths for the exploration of a database content. After clarifying the main requirements characterizing chatbots for data exploration, we introduce *(i)* a set of *conversational annotations* that characterize the role that data elements play in the exploration of a database content, and *(ii)* a design process and an enabling architecture that exploit the conversational annotations to generate a dialogue for exploring the database. We then conclude the paper and outline our future work.

2   Chatbots for Data Exploration

With respect to conversational virtual assistants (e.g., Amazon Alexa or Apple Siri), *chatbots for data exploration* use conversations to let the users move across different data items within a body of organized content. In order to exemplify the main characteristics of this class of chatbots, let us consider a simple yet expressive conversation for exploring an example database storing data on orders and customers (see Fig. 1). The respective database schema is reported in Fig. 2.

Current approaches would already support the development of such a chatbot. However, some of them would require using conventional programming languages to write rule-based scripts for handling the dialog. For example, Microsoft's Bot Framework[1] requires using the .NET family of languages, while IBM's Watson Conversation Service comes with SDKs for Node, Java, Python, .NET. In order to simplify the development, some *dedicated platforms* (e.g., Dialogflow[2] and Motion AI[3]) offer visual, flowchart-based development paradigms also equipped with advanced AI and NLP support that only needs to be properly configured.

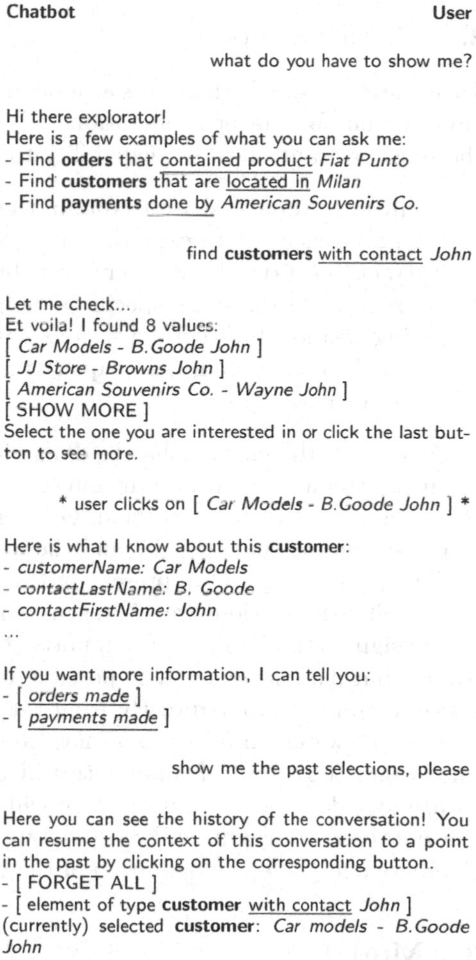

Chatbot   **User**

what do you have to show me?

Hi there explorator!
Here is a few examples of what you can ask me:
- Find **orders** that contained product *Fiat Punto*
- Find **customers** that are located In *Milan*
- Find **payments** done by *American Souvenirs Co.*

find **customers** with contact *John*

Let me check...
Et voila! I found 8 values:
[*Car Models - B.Goode John*]
[*JJ Store - Browns John*]
[*American Souvenirs Co. - Wayne John*]
[SHOW MORE]
Select the one you are interested in or click the last button to see more.

* user clicks on [*Car Models - B.Goode John*] *

Here is what I know about this **customer**:
- *customerName: Car Models*
- *contactLastName: B. Goode*
- *contactFirstName: John*
...

If you want more information, I can tell you:
- [*orders made*]
- [*payments made*]

show me the past selections, please

Here you can see the history of the conversation! You can resume the context of this conversation to a point in the past by clicking on the corresponding button.
- [FORGET ALL]
- [element of type **customer** with contact *John*]
(currently) selected **customer**: *Car models - B.Goode John*

Fig. 1.   Exemplary conversational data exploration by a user assisted by the envisioned data exploration bot.

[1] https://docs.botframework.com/en-us/.

[2] https://dialogflow.com/.

[3] https://www.motion.ai/.

Other frameworks propose proprietary, textual languages for the design of conversation paths. For example, PandoraBots[4] proposes AIML (Artificial Intelligent MarkUp Language), an XML-based language for tagging conversation elements, such as parameters in the user requests, query patterns and answer templates. However, all these approaches still require the explicit configuration of predetermined utterances, intent interpretation and actionable answers to be assembled in the conversation. In contrast, our work has the ultimate goal of generating conversational paths for data exploration starting from the schema of the data source and taking advantages of data properties that can be derived from the schema itself.

2.1 Requirements

To achieve our goal, there are a number of requirements to be fulfilled by the environment for chatbot generation and execution, for example, just to mention the most relevant ones, the capability to:

1. Connect to the database to obtain the schema;
2. Support generic data exploration vocabulary and actions;
3. Extract/learn database-specific vocabulary from schema and instances;
4. Extract/learn database-specific actions from the schema, for example navigating relationships can be seen as data access actions;
5. Allow the user to manipulate query results, e.g., further filtering results based on some attributes.

Moreover, the chatbot has to dynamically identify intents and entities from the user utterance, translate the interpreted elements into queries and connect to the database for query execution. Other important aspects then refer to proper visualizations of query results and the management of context memory.

The approach that we present in this paper goes exactly into this direction. In the following sections we will discuss some preliminary results in the definition of a design methodology that supports the generation of a conversation starting from a database schema. It is possible to think of scenarios where the conversation could come out directly from the analysis of properties of the database schema. However, in order to achieve conversations that can be effective for the final users (e.g., free of ambiguities in the possible suggested paths and able to use an adequate vocabulary), we will show how a *designer*, who knows how the database is organized, can annotate the schema to model how some data elements can guide the definition of the conversation.

3   Model

To translate an input phrase into a specific query on the database, we propose the definition of a mapping between what can be understood by the chatbot (intents and entities) and the elements of the database (relations, attributes,

---

[4] https://www.pandorabots.com/.

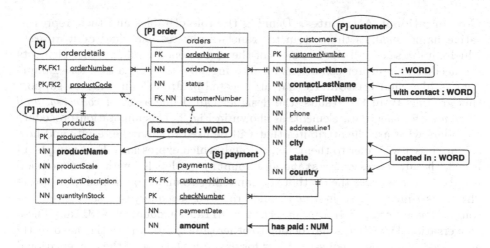

Fig. 2. Database schema and annotations for *table types* and *conversational attributes*.

relationships). This mapping is defined by a *designer*, who knows the structure of the database and is in charge of modeling the dialogue flow for the interaction with the database by the final user. In the following we will illustrate the main ingredients of our conceptual modeling approach; to make the description easier to follow, we will refer to an example database shown in Fig. 2.

Conversational Entities Based on Table Types. The first step is to characterize the database tables as *Primary* (tag [P]), *Secondary* (tag [S]), or *Crossable Relationship* (tag [X]), to express the role that data entities play in the exploration of data. The distinction between the first two types is that while values belonging to a Primary table may represent useful information without the need of a context, Secondary tables contain data strongly related to other entities, which become clear only when that specific relationship is considered. For example, tagging as Secondary the table **payments** means that the access to its values depends on another table, **customers**. In other words, with this characterization the designer defines that instances of **payment** can be retrieved only by passing first through instances of **customers** – for example because payments data would not be meaningful otherwise. Labeling tables as Primary, in contrast, relaxes this dependence constraint and enables direct queries on tables. Finally, Crossable Relationship characterization is dedicated to bridge tables, i.e., the ones that represent many-to-many relationships between entities. Their rows may have a meaning only when a join operation across them is executed; thus no direct or deferred search is allowed on them.

Some tables might have names not suitable in the context of a conversation. Thus, as reported in Fig. 2, each primary and secondary table has to be labeled with a keyword, i.e., the name that will represent it during the conversation. For example, in the request "find **customer** <u>with contact</u> *John*", the chatbot understands that **customer** is the placeholder for the table **customers**. Multiple words can be associated to a table.

Conversational Attributes. Defining the role of tables and their representative names enables the system to translate phrases like "find **customers**", which aim to select all the instances of the corresponding table. Other elements are needed to interpret conditions for filtering subsets of instances, for example queries like "find **customers** that are <u>located in</u> *Milan*". In order to support this granularity in the results, the designer can define a set of *conversational attributes* for each data element, as shown in Fig. 2. This annotation procedure considers what are the attributes that will be used to filter the results and how the final user will refer to them, i.e., through which expressions. For example, in Fig. 2, the attributes `city`, `state` and `country` are labeled with the expression **located in**: this gives the chatbot the capability to understand the input phrase "find **customer** <u>located in</u> *Milan*", and process it as a query that selects the customers having `city = Milan`, or `state = Milan`, or `country = Milan`. These conversational attributes may belong to other tables, rather than the one directly addressed by the user request. This is for example the case of the conversational attribute `has ordered`: even if it is defined for the field `productName` of table `products`, it can be used also in queries like "find **customer** that <u>has ordered</u> *Fiat Punto*". The table `customers` is indeed reachable through the tables `orders` and `orderdetails`. This is graphically represented in Fig. 2 by means of dotted arrows.

In some cases the user may also ask: "find **customer** *Car Models*", without specifying in the utterance any conversational attribute, e.g., without specifying that `Car Models` in the previous query is a value for the customer name. The system will anyway search for related instances in the table `customer` by the attribute `customerName` that, as represented in Fig. 2, is tagged as a conversational attribute for the table. However, as indicated by the graphic symbol "_", the user does not need to specify any additional expression.

In order to help the chatbot process and interpret correctly the utterance, for each conversational attribute it is important to specify its *conversational type*:

- `WORD`: any information without a particular structure or syntax;
- `NUM`: numerical values;
- `DATE`: datetime/date values;
- `Custom ENUM`: entities that can assume enumerable values.

The last one can be useful when an attribute can assume only a fixed set of values. An example could be the attribute `businessName` for the table `customers` with values `Public Administration` and `Private Company`.

Conversational Relationships. In the conversation example in Fig. 1, after the user has successfully selected a customer, its data and a few buttons are displayed. These last represent the relationships that can be navigated starting from the instance being examined. These relationships have to be specified in the annotated database schema (see labeled arcs in Fig. 3) so that user utterances can also imply navigation in the database through join operations. The arcs in Fig. 3 are not bidirectional, since during conversation the user may refer differently to

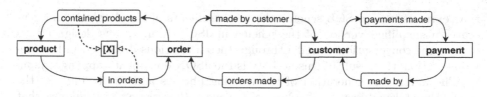

Fig. 3. Annotations to specify conversational relationships.

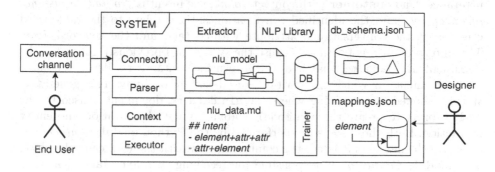

Fig. 4. Functional architecture for conversation generation and execution.

relationships depending on the direction in which they are traversed. Note that the relation between `product` and `order` needs to be supported by a crossable relationship table, being it a many-to-many relationship.

4   Design Process and System Architecture

The chatbot design process consists of both automatic and manual phases:

1. *Parsing of the database schema* (automatic): this is needed to interpret the database schema and generate a simplified version enabling the annotation activity;
2. *Schema annotation* (manual): the designer produces a new schema with all the annotations needed to generate the conversation;
3. *Generation of the training phrases* (automatic): this consists of the training of the Natural Language Understanding (NLU) model.

Figure 4 shows the organization of the current system prototype that supports the previous phases. In this version the system works with relational databases and SQL schemas; we are however working to generalize the approach to other data models.

The first artifact is the JSON document, `db_schema.json`, that the system generates automatically by means of the *Parser* module. This is a Python script that extracts from a SQL schema the main elements of the database and generates a simplified version of the schema in JSON format. The designer thus defines the conversational model through the annotations described in the previous section; the result of this activity is the JSON document `mappings.json`.

The automatic generation of the training phrases and the training of the model then take advantage of a *Natural Language Processing (NLP) library*, that in the current prototype is RASA NLU[5]. This component interprets sentences by performing intent classification and entity extraction. For example, in the utterance "find **customer** <u>with contact</u> *John*", the intent is *"to find an instance of an entity"*, and the identified conversation entities relate to the table word **customer**, the conversational attribute <u>with contact</u>, and the keyword *John*. This interpretation is possible because the system has previously generated the document `nlu_data.md`, that is a MarkDown file containing a list of sentences for each intent, in which the entities are labeled accordingly. This generation step is followed by a training where the `nlu_data.md` document is used by the NLP Library to create the `nlu_model` enabling intent classification and entity extraction. Both these steps are performed by the Python module *Trainer*.

Once the model is defined, the communication with the user can take place. The module *Connector* is responsible for receiving utterances and delivering answers through different channels[6]. At runtime, the *Extractor* module uses the NLP Library and the model previously created to classify the correct intents and extract the entities. The *Executor* module then executes the resulting queries on the database content. This last component represents the core of the chatbot, since it manages the communication with the database and with the *Context* module and, based on the results of a query or on the current status of the conversation, identifies what and how to answer to the user.

To track the status of the conversation, the *Context* module registers every action performed during conversation, as well as the instances retrieved from the database to compose the answers. For sake of brevity, and because the focus of this paper is on modeling primitives for conversational elements, we will not describe here the logics underlying this module. It is however worth mentioning that managing the context is not just maintaining the list of the previous utterances. Other aspects need to be considered, for example whether the entity of the current utterance has been already shown in previous requests and answers and so these old messages can be now discarded.

5 Conclusion

This paper has illustrated some preliminary results in the definition of a framework for the development of chatbots for data exploration. As observed in [5], conversation-based interaction may simplistically lead to believe that chatbot development mainly implies writing rule-based scripts governing the dialogue. At the other extreme, NLP- and AI-sophisticated techniques may appear as the

---

[5] https://rasa.com/docs/nlu/.
[6] The current prototype implementation exploits Telegram.

only viable solutions. While these approaches may be valid in several scenarios, our position is that model-based methodologies, which are typical of Web Engineering, could offer several advantages to the chatbot world, especially when conversational interfaces are meant to support the access to extensive collections of data. With this paper we aim to give a first contribution in this direction. In particular, we highlight that chatbot development may require focusing on data modeling concerns that can guide the generation of conversations for data exploration. Some aspects, however, still remain open and our future work will focus on them.

A challenge is understanding how the conversational paradigm can integrate – or even replace – the traditional, visual paradigm for data exploration. This is not only a problem of data presentation, but also of adequate data analysis techniques, such as summarization, interactive drill-down and roll-up data exploration capabilities or the automatic generation of graphical charts. Our future work will study how these aspects impact the different layers (data, application logic, presentation). It will also try to understand whether the current approach can be adapted on top of different models (e.g., graph data models), also covering the integration of distributed data sources. Since we expect that the effort needed to manually define annotations would grow with very complex databased schemas, we will devise mechanisms to automatically identify notable elements in a database schema, and recommend their annotation within a usable visual environment.

Assessing the validity of the approach with respect to the experience of the final users is another challenge. We already planned some user studies with the aim of evaluating to what extent the generated conversations support user needs in data exploration. Gathering data about the user performance and satisfaction will help us verify the expressiveness of the modeling approach with respect to the elements to be provided for the conversations to be effective. Thus the user studies will have a double value: to improve the user experience of the generated applications as well as to validate the effectiveness of the modeling method.

References

1. Akcora, D.E., et al.: Conversational support for education. In: Penstein Rosé, C., et al. (eds.) AIED 2018, Part II. LNCS (LNAI), vol. 10948, pp. 14–19. Springer, Cham (2018). https://doi.org/10.1007/978-3-319-93846-2_3
2. Grech, M.: The current state of chatbots in 2017. GetVoIP.com, April 2017. https://getvoip.com/blog/2017/04/21/the-current-state-of-chatbots-in-2017/
3. Inbenta Technologies Inc.: The ultimate guide to chatbots for businesses. Technical report (2016). www.inbenta.com
4. Klopfenstein, L.C., Delpriori, S., Malatini, S., Bogliolo, A.: The rise of bots: a survey of conversational interfaces, patterns, and paradigms. In: Proceedings of the 2017 Conference on Designing Interactive Systems, DIS 2017, Edinburgh, 10–14 June 2017, pp. 555–565. ACM (2017)
5. Pereira, J., Díaz, Ó.: Chatbot dimensions that matter: lessons from the trenches. In: Mikkonen, T., Klamma, R., Hernández, J. (eds.) ICWE 2018. LNCS, vol. 10845, pp. 129–135. Springer, Cham (2018). https://doi.org/10.1007/978-3-319-91662-0_9

Distributed Intelligent Client-Centric Personalisation

Rebekah Storan Clarke$^{(\boxtimes)}$ and Vincent Wade

Trinity College Dublin, Dublin, Ireland
clarker7@tcd.ie

Abstract. Personalisation is used extensively to improve user engagement, to optimise user experience and to enhance marketing and advertising online. While privacy has always been an issue in personalised websites, only recently have we seen a noticeable change in consumer's behaviour's. User's are seeing breaches of the personal information harvested, stored and shared by content providers and increasingly adjusting privacy controls, thus negatively impacting the effectiveness of personalisation services. Client-Side personalisation (CSP) approaches offer a privacy-conscious solution, keeping the user data and user model on the client's own device, allowing users to enjoy personalised content without compromising the privacy of their personal data. However, these solutions have significant problems with scalability and performance due to client-device resource limitations. With an ever-increasing demand for rich multimedia, particularly on more lightweight mobile devices, performance is critical to provide a seamless user experience. This research proposes a hybrid approach which we term Intelligent Client-Centric Personalisation (ICCP), this minimises the leakage of user data while enhancing performance through predictive webpage prefetching. This paper performs a comparative framework evaluation, comparing the ICCP framework performance with a typical client-server personalisation approach. It uses a large dataset of user interactions across three contrasting consumer websites, following case study based methodology. Evaluation shows that such a framework can realise the performance benefits of a client-server approach but with enhanced privacy and reduced personal data leakage.

Keywords: Client side personalisation · Privacy · Prefetching · Click prediction · Interaction modelling

1 Introduction

Personalisation is becoming ever more important in the delivery of timely, contextually aware information, with websites capable of recomposing and adapting content on-the-fly for the user. However, there is growing concern by both user's and legislators over privacy on the web. This concern is particularly seen in

© Springer Nature Switzerland AG 2019
M. Bakaev et al. (Eds.): ICWE 2019, LNCS 11496, pp. 498–505, 2019.
https://doi.org/10.1007/978-3-030-19274-7_35

the personalisation domain, which inherently requires collection of user's personal information [3]. The EU recently adopted the General Data Protection Regulation, aiming to give control to individuals over their personal data, a similar act, California's Consumer Privacy Act (CCPA), will go into effect in 2020 [4] and there are numerous other regulations under consideration in the US, China, Brazil and many other countries [9]. Regardless, companies continue to employ personalisation techniques as these have consistently shown to increase user engagement and increase economic returns [14]. For users, personalising webpages to their individual needs makes browsing more convenient, efficient and relevant. Thus there is a conflict between privacy and personalisation; The more information there is about a user, the better the system can adapt to the user's needs but the less the privacy of the user's personal data is protected. This situation has been referred to as the *personalisation-privacy paradox* [10]. While privacy has always been an issue in personalised websites, only recently have we seen a notable change in consumer's behaviour. The personal information harvested, stored and shared by content providers [14] has become more apparent through regulations and users are seeing frequent consumer data breaches. As users realise how exposed they are to personal information leakage, they are increasingly adjusting privacy controls, thus negatively impacting the effectiveness of personalisation services. As personalised content is essential to the success of online providers, securing customer privacy and therefore trust is necessary for the future of personalisation.

Privacy-conscious frameworks such as *Client-Side Personalisation* (CSP), attempt to shift the data storage approach, storing user data with trusted third parties or on the client's own device [5,18]. This keeps the user data and user model under the control of the client, allowing users to enjoy personalised content without compromising the privacy of their personal data. Each approach successfully reduces the leakage of the user's personal information, gaining some privacy on their behalf. Pure client-side solutions not only store user data on the client but also perform the personalisation of webpages at the client-side. This creates intellectual property issues, as content providers are unwilling to deliver personalisation or user modelling algorithms to the client device. Distributed architectures propose tackling this by utilising trusted external services to perform operations, while maintaining control and storage of the data on the client. However, both solutions have significant problems with scalability and performance. As client-devices are resource limited, they struggle to handle the client-side processing requirements for coordinating personalisation or service interaction. With an ever-increasing demand for rich multimedia, particularly on more lightweight mobile devices, improving performance is critical to provide a seamless user experience.

This study explores a responsive, lightweight, privacy-conscious personalisation approach, termed **Intelligent Client-Centric Personalisation (ICCP)**. This aims to enhance the performance of current distributed approaches through **predictive precaching**. The framework is microservice based, employing trusted third-party services for personalisation and user modelling while maintaining data storage on the client only. Maintaining user privacy in an ICCP framework requires a series of principles to be followed; user data must be stored

on the client-side, it can only be shared explicitly with trusted service providers
and no external service may store any user data. This enables privacy while also
allowing for service scalability and protection of content provider's intellectual
property. To combat the increased network activity and overhead on the client
in interacting with these services precaching techniques are used to preload webpages on the client device before they are requested.

This paper presents the design of an ICCP framework, along with an initial evaluation aiming to examine it's performance compared to a traditional
server-side approach. It is established that performance can be improved through
predictive prefetching.

2 Related Work

2.1 Privacy Focused Frameworks

A range of techniques have been researched aiming to provide personalisation
without unduly compromising user's privacy. These can be grouped into three
broad categories; Architectural, Algorithmic and User-centric [12]. Architectural
approaches look at Software architectures, platforms, and standards designed to
minimize personal data leakage [7,13]. Architectural solutions to user privacy
vary in three broad aspects; where the user data is stored, where the data analysis is performed and where the personalisation occurs. Client-side personalization
(CSP) originally proposed that all of these process occurred on the user's own
device i.e. the client [13]. This results in very little, if any, personal data stored
on the content server. However, this approach puts the processing burden on
the client which, particularly on mobile phones, may significantly impact performance [11]. It also raises proprietary concerns as the personalisation logic must
be delivered to the client device in order to perform the personalisation on the
client. This code often includes confidential algorithms and is at risk of exposure
through reverse engineering. As these concerns have grown a second branch of
CSP has emerged in which trusted third party software is used to create a distributed approach [18]. The user's data must still be stored on the client device,
however, the data analysis and personalisation may occur remotely. This distributed approach requires user information to be transmitted to a remote service
as such, additional measures must be in place to maintain privacy. Employing
an associated security model has been explored with the PersonisJ architecture
[11]. This proposes an access mechanism which mediates interactions and trans-
mits only necessary data; for example, allowing a playlist application access to
a persons favourite genre but not the full catalogue of favourite songs. Another
branch of research looks at the use of trusted software [12]. This is software that
can make guarantees about data storage policies, linkability, and disclosure. It
is proposed that these systems would undergo technical audits and obtain cer-
tification by a trusted third party in order to be incorporated into such an
architecture [12]. Distributed Client-Side personalisation techniques enable the
privacy benefits of the traditional pure-client side approach. However, by using
trusted third party microservices, they tackle the issues relating to scalability

and Intellectual Property. Given the increased network activity and overhead on the client these Distributed approaches while inherently more efficient than CSP frameworks, still suffer performance issues when compared with the traditional server side model. The research into Distributed CSP to date, has been focused on the development and regulation of these trusted micro-services [5,11,18]. Few frameworks have been proposed which tackle the orchestration of these services and a full framework has not been evaluated.

2.2   Prefetching

Web caching and prefetching play an important role in improving web performance. Resources that are likely to be visited in the near future are kept closer to the client. This ranges from storage on the server, storage in a proxy to storage on the user's own device i.e. Client-Side Caching [6]. Traditionally, caching strategies simply chose frequently used or recently used resources to cache. However, even with a cache of infinite size, it has been shown that the hit ratio i.e. the number of requested resources that are cached lies between 40–50% regardless of the caching scheme employed [15,16]. This is due to the fact that most users frequently request webpages they have not yet visited. To address this fact and improve the hit ratio, content providers are attempting to predict in advance what a user might be interested in visiting i.e. web prefetching. Many studies have shown that the combination of caching and prefetching doubles the performance compared to single caching [2]. According to [1] a combination of web caching and prefetching can potentially improve latency up to 60%, whereas web caching alone improves the latency up to 26%. However, if a prefetching scheme is deployed and the user ends up requesting very few of these prefetched resources, the scheme can actually slow down performance. Thus, a prefetching approach must be carefully designed to ensure a net benefit effect. In the literature, prefetching strategies are generally separated into two types; content- based and history-based. Content-based prefetching analyses the layout and content on a webpage to predict the likely links the user might click [19] whereas history-based prefetching observes the user's previous access behaviour. Content-based prefetching is not well suited to a server side implementation as the overhead for parsing every single page served is too great [8]. In recent years, the data mining techniques have been shown to be the most effective for prefetching [17]. In this research, Clickstream data and other fine-grained navigational patterns are analysed to predict the future behaviour of the user.

3   ICCP Framework

Figure 1 shows the architecture of an ICCP framework, involving a client coordinator along with external personalisation and prediction services. The client coordinator is embedded in the user's browser and is responsible for gathering, storing and managing both user information and web caches as well as orchestrating microservice interactions. The logic for prefetching is contained within the

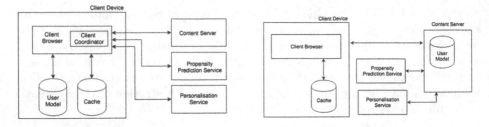

Fig. 1. ICCP architecture   **Fig. 2.** Comparative architecture

client coordinator, deciding which resources to fetch and when. Once prefetched the contents of a page are stored in the client-side cache.

Prediction Service: For this research, the user modelling is achieved through a prediction service. This predicts the behaviour of a user, more specifically their propensity to click on certain links on a webpage. The output from this Propensity Prediction Service (PPS) is used both to inform the cache prefetching strategy and the page's personalisation. The client coordinator passes the user model to the PPS for prediction which then returns an updated model without storing any user information.

Personalisation Service: The personalisation microservice uses propensity as an influencing factor in its personalisation decisions. Thus, the context of the real-time page interactions must impact the result of the personalisation service. e.g. The user's interaction behaviour, like moving the mouse, must be one of the factors determining how the next page will be personalised. Content layout is therefore personalised, this involves rearranging the layout of the page to meet the user's preferences. For example, If a user always scrolls past the wall of text in an article to get to the video at the end the video might be moved up to the top on future pages.

In order to implement a privacy conscious distributed service no user data or profiles can be stored. Therefore the following requirements must be applied to the server-based prediction and personalisation services: User data must be processed as a stream; User profiles must be updated incrementally; and User data and profiles must be discarded immediately after use.

Privacy is maintained by ensuring no user data persists on the server-side. Instead the client coordinator passes the relevant parts of the user model to the services which is then returned for storage on the client device. As the control of user data lies with the client, access controls could also be utilised to restrict the information available to the distributed services.

The content server provides both a template and context for each webpage; the template outlines the barebones structure of the page with placeholders for personalised content and the context then provides the array of options available to fill out those placeholders. The context objects used are then selected through the subsequent external personalisation step.

4   Evaluation

The evaluation aims to investigate the performance of the ICCP, comparing it's system latency to a traditional server-side approach.

The users for this experiment were gathered through Prolific[1], a crowd-sourcing platform for research participants. A reverse proxying method was used to allow users to interact with live sites while their interaction data such as mouse movements and scrolling was tracked. Three website case studies were used to reflect diversity in interaction behaviour, these were an e-commerce website, an informational website and a commercial website. A simulation based, comparative evaluation was performed against a typical server-side approach.

In the server-side approach shown in Fig. 2, the personalisation and prediction occur on the content server along with the prefetching logic. While regular resource caching occurs on the client-side, the caching of prefetched and pre-personalised pages remains on the server. For the evaluation the Content Server, PPS and Personalisation Service were deployed on an external server to the client.

4.1   Simulation Evaluation

The simulation consisted of replaying the webpage interactions captured during user trials to mimic the same behaviour on the two architectures. This put each architecture under considerably more strain due to the large quantity of background processes which may trigger prefetching and personalisation refreshes.

Unseen Page: Initially, the response time of a page which the user had not previously seen and which the system had not prefetched was examined. This meant that page fetching and personalisation was performed at request time. The average user latency response times for an ICCP and comparative framework were 93.5 ms and 90.52 ms respectively. As expected the ICCP framework performs slightly more slowly due to the increased network requests. However, the response time falls within a reasonable margin, providing no noticeable difference to the user. The variation in these response times over the 100 requests is illustrated in Fig. 3.

Prefetched Page: The response time of a page which has been predicted and prefetched by the framework was then examined. The results from repeating this process 100 times are shown in Fig. 4. Here the average response times for the ICCP and comparative framework are 21.15 ms and 75.19 ms. When a page has been prefetched we would expect the speed of the ICCP framework to be better than that of the server-side as prefetched pages are cached on the client and server side respectively. The results align with this expectation, the ICCP performs considerably faster under these conditions.

---

[1] https://prolific.ac/.

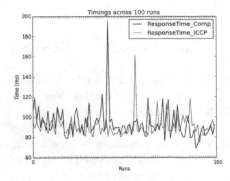

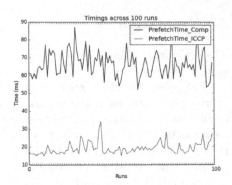

Fig. 3. Unseen page response time   **Fig. 4.** Prefetched page response time

5 Conclusion

This study proposed Intelligent Client-Centric Personalisation (ICCP) which minimises the leakage of user data while using server-based personalisation and prediction. It was proposed that through the addition of prefetching to a Client-Side Personalisation framework, performance and user latency could be improved. The ICCP could then provide a more privacy-conscious framework than a traditional server-side approach while offering reasonable performance.

The evaluation aimed to investigate the system latency of the ICCP, comparing this to a traditional server-side approach. It was shown that for an unseen page the ICCP framework performs, on average, more slowly; though the response time falls within reasonable bounds. However, for a prefetched page the ICCP framework performs considerably faster than the traditional approach.

Thus, performance benefits can be achieved in Client-Side Personalisation through the incorporation of prefetching techniques. In use cases where the prefetching strategy has high predictive accuracy the average user latency over a session should be lower than the traditional approach. Further research is required to investigate and quantify when the ICCP offers a better solution than the traditional server-side approach.

References

1. Acharjee, U.: Personalized and artificial intelligence web caching and prefetching (2006)
2. Ali, W., Shamsuddin, S.M., Ismail, A.S.: A survey of web caching and prefetching. Int. J. Adv. Soft Comput. Appl. **3**(1), 1–27 (2011)
3. Andrade, E.B., Kaltcheva, V., Weitz, B.: Self-disclosure on the web: the impact of privacy policy, reward, and company reputation. Adv. Consum. Res. **29**(1), 350–353 (2002)
4. California Act: California Consumer Privacy Act (2018)
5. Cassel, L., Wolz, U.: Client side personalization. DELOS-NSF workshop on personalization and recommender systems in digital libraries, p. 57 (2001). http://portal.acm.org/citation.cfm?doid=1370888.1370904

6. Chen, T.: Obtaining the optimal cache document replacement policy for the caching system of an EC website. Eur. J. Oper. Res. **181**(2), 828–841 (2007). https://doi.org/10.1016/j.ejor.2006.05.034

7. Cissée, R., Albayrak, S.: An agent-based approach for privacy-preserving recommender systems. In: Proceedings of the 6th International Joint Conference on Autonomous Agents and Multiagent Systems - AAMAS 2007, vol. 5, p. 1 (2007). https://doi.org/10.1145/1329125.1329345

8. Domenech, J., Gil, J.A., Sahuquillo, J., Pont, A.: Using current web page structure to improve prefetching performance. Comput. Netw. **54**(9), 1404–1417 (2010). https://doi.org/10.1016/j.comnet.2009.11.016

9. Emily Leach, CIPP/E, CIPP/US: 2019 Global Legislative Predictions. International Association of Privacy Professionals iapp.org (2018)

10. Farag Awad, N., Krishnan, M.: The personalization privacy paradox: an empirical evaluation of information transparency and the willingness to be profiled online for personalization. MIS Q. **30**, 13–28 (2006)

11. Gerber, S., Fry, M., Kay, J., Kummerfeld, B., Pink, G., Wasinger, R.: PersonisJ: mobile, client-side user modelling. In: De Bra, P., Kobsa, A., Chin, D. (eds.) UMAP 2010. LNCS, vol. 6075, pp. 111–122. Springer, Heidelberg (2010). https://doi.org/10.1007/978-3-642-13470-8_12

12. Knijnenburg, B.P., Berkovsky, S.: Privacy for recommender systems. In: Proceedings of the Eleventh ACM Conference on Recommender Systems - RecSys 2017, pp. 394–395 (2017). https://doi.org/10.1145/3109859.3109935

13. Kobsa, A., Knijnenburg, B.P., Livshits, B.: Let's do it at my place instead? In: Proceedings of the 32nd Annual ACM Conference on Human Factors in Computing Systems - CHI 2014, pp. 81–90 (2014). https://doi.org/10.1145/2556288.2557102

14. Lee, C.H., Cranage, D.A.: Personalisation-privacy paradox: the effects of personalisation and privacy assurance on customer responses to travel web sites. Tour. Manage. **32**(5), 987–994 (2011). https://doi.org/10.1016/j.tourman.2010.08.011

15. Lee, H.K., An, B.S., Kim, E.J.: Adaptive prefetching scheme using web log mining in Cluster-based web systems. In: IEEE International Conference on Web Services, ICWS 2009, pp. 903–910 (2009). https://doi.org/10.1109/ICWS.2009.127

16. Lin, J., Huang, T., Yang, C.: Research on WEB cache prediction recommend mechanism based on usage pattern. In: Proceedings of the 1st International Workshop on Knowledge Discovery and Data Mining, WKDD, pp. 473–476 (2008). https://doi.org/10.1109/WKDD.2008.9

17. Liu, Q.: Web latency reduction with prefetching, Ph.D. thesis, Ontario, Canada (2009)

18. Toch, E., Wang, Y., Cranor, L.F.: Personalization and privacy: a survey of privacy risks and remedies in personalization-based systems. User Model. User-Adap. Inter. **22**(1–2), 203–220 (2012). https://doi.org/10.1007/s11257-011-9110-z

19. Xu, C.Z., Ibrahim, T.I.: A keyword-based semantic prefetching approach in internet news services. IEEE Trans. Knowl. Data Eng. **16**(5), 601–611 (2004). https://doi.org/10.1109/TKDE.2004.1277820

Demonstrations

Webifying Heterogenous Internet of Things Devices

Mahda Noura[(⊠)], Sebastian Heil, and Martin Gaedke

Technische Universität Chemnitz, Chemnitz, Germany
{mahda.noura,sebastian.heil,martin.gaedke}
@informatik.tu-chemnitz.de

Abstract. Internet of Things (IoT) applications incorporate heterogenous smart devices that support different communication protocols (Zigbee, RFID, Bluetooth, custom protocols). Enabling application development employing different protocols require interoperability between the different types of heterogenous devices that co-exist in the IoT ecosystem. In this paper we propose WoTDL2API tool, that automatically generates a running RESTful API based on the popular OpenAPI specification and integrating with the existing OpenAPI code generation toolchain. This solution provides interoperability between the devices by wrapping IoT devices with a Web-based interface enabling easier integration with other platforms. We showcase our approach using a smart home scenario available online.

Keywords: Internet of Things · Web of Things · Semantic web · OpenAPI · Interoperability

1 Introduction

Internet of Things (IoT) devices such as smart shutters, lamps, thermostats etc., allow developers to build innovative smart applications. These devices are implemented by leading companies using their proprietary protocols and interfaces. This results in the deployment of highly heterogenous devices in terms of both hardware and software resources which complicates the development of applications. The integration of IoT and the Web, called the Web of Things (WoT) [1] simplifies access to smart devices and properties for users by making them controllable via a unified HTTP-based interface, and by exposing the functionality of physical devices as services on the Web. This enables communications among physical world objects and control and data access to create IoT applications on top of RESTful Web APIs.

Service description languages such as WSDL provide interface descriptions in terms of operations, messages and protocols used by traditional Web Services. WoT development is like service-based engineering with regard to its composition-based basic model. However, service description languages are not sufficient to represent all required characteristic of concrete WoT scenarios. IoT related concepts such as device (*sensors* and *actuators*), device capabilities in terms of *precondition* and *effects*, WoT operations (*sensing* and *actuation*), and the current/desired state of the environment are missing. These concepts are represented by various WoT ontologies [2] to allow

© Springer Nature Switzerland AG 2019
M. Bakaev et al. (Eds.): ICWE 2019, LNCS 11496, pp. 509–513, 2019.
https://doi.org/10.1007/978-3-030-19274-7_36

automatic composition of WoT applications [3]. However, to achieve automatic composition, a set of IoT devices should not only be described using an ontology like WoTDL[1], but the device interfaces have to be webified, i.e. provided with an HTTP interface.

We propose **WoTDL2API (Web of Things Description Language to API)** which is a model-driven method to automatically generate and deploy RESTful APIs for controlling and accessing IoT devices from WoTDL instances. It fosters re-use through separation of the generated interface from device implementations. This research contributes to *Device* and *Platform* interoperability [4, 5] by wrapping IoT devices with a web interface, thus turning them into WoT devices. The WoTDL2API is an important component in the context of GrOWTH [3].

Regarding related work, the current interoperability solutions are based on (1) a gateway i.e., Ponte[2], IFTTT[3] to bridge different communication protocols and specifications and (2) providing a single API abstractions or protocol [6] which requires all developers to follow. Our approach is most similar to category 2 in that it provides a uniform RESTful interface for an IoT scenario. However, WOTDL2API does not require device providers to agree on a common API standard. Instead we provide a pragmatic wrapper-based interoperability solution.

In the remainder of this paper we introduce WoTDL2API approach and demonstrate the approach on a smart home testbed.

2   The WoTDL2API Approach

The WoTDL ontology derived from analysis of existing IoT/WoT ontologies [2] represents the *device description* component of the GrOWTH *knowledge repository* [3], modeling *devices* as *actuators* and *sensors* which have *actuations* and *measurements* along with information required for automatic composition such as *preconditions*, *effects* and *timings*. These are linked to their interface realizations as *HTTP requests*.

We propose a Model Driven Engineering (MDE) approach to automate the process of generating runnable RESTful APIs from WoTDL ontology instances. To develop the REST API the OpenAPI[4] specification is used. Figure 1 illustrates an overview of WoTDL2API. As can be seen, the process starts from the *developer* who is responsible for identifying the IoT devices that are appropriate for the scenario (step 1) as well as describing the device capabilities using the WoTDL ontology (step 2). The API generation toolchain then automatically constructs a running API for the IoT devices described according to the WoTDL ontology in 5 main steps (see steps 3–7). Step 3 performs the first phase of model-to-model transformation to generate a model

---

[1] cf. LOV4IoT catalog http://lov4iot.appspot.com/?p=ontologies#wot.

[2] https://www.eclipse.org/proposals/technology.ponte/.

[3] https://ifttt.com/.

[4] https://swagger.io/docs/specification/about/.

conforming to the OpenAPI specification from the WoTDL model. This transformation queries the WoTDL graph to identify the available device capabilities. Then, in step 4 each device capability (*actuation* or *measurement*) is queried to extract its intended HTTP interface realization (*HTTP method, query parameters, URL,* and *Body*). Step 5 finalizes the model-to-model transformation into a corresponding valid instance of the OpenAPI specification by iterating over the HTTP realizations to create a single path for every *actuation* and *measurement*. The model-to-text transformation is performed in Step 6 which generates source code from the OpenAPI description. The OpenAPI Generator[5] is employed to generate the REST API code for the python Flask target platform. In Step 7, the generated REST API is then deployed, and the API is run. During runtime, every HTTP request to the generated API is sent to the central *WoTDL Hub* which has the role to identify, deploy and execute the device specific implementations on the physical IoT devices at runtime. In the last step of the process (step 8) the WoT developer can now simply create WoT applications based on the set of HTTP endpoints provided for the WoT devices regardless of the hardware type and its communication technology.

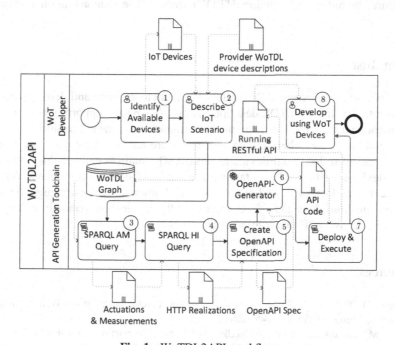

Fig. 1. WoTDL2API workflow

---

[5] https://openapi-generator.tech/.

3   Demonstration

We demonstrate WoTDL2API within a *smart home testbed* consisting of three sensors (temperature, humidity, light) and three actuators (lamp, fan, shade). These IoT devices are connected to a Raspberry Pi and each device is accessed through different, non-web interfaces. We model the existing testbed using WoTDL. Then WoTDL2API is executed on the ontology instance to compose the OpenAPI specification and deployed using the methodology described in Sect. 2. WoTDL2API is developed in Python and is accessible online[6] as open source project. For each actuation and measurement an HTTP callback method is created according to the parameterized URL, with the corresponding fields specifications of HTTP method, parameters and HTTP Body. For the implementation of WoTDL2API, reflection is used to provide extensibility.

During the demonstration session, we invite the audience to test WoTDL2API by creating WoTDL models of their choice or changing provided WoTDL models, automatically generate the WoT interface layer. Once the WoT interface (API) is generated, the developer can interact with it to (1) control the physical devices (i.e., turn lamp off/on) and (2) monitor the current state of the testbed (i.e., current value of temperature, humidity) by sending HTTP requests. The demonstration is available online[7].

4   Conclusion

In this paper we have presented WoTDL2API, a tool to generate and deploy web-based RESTful interface from WoTDL descriptions for IoT devices supporting heterogeneous communication interfaces. This is particularly important for the realization of i.e., smart factory, smart city, etc. where the smart devices are not web-based, and the communication protocol differs from device to device. The main benefit of this approach is reuse of device specific implementations through WoT device components. As future work, we would like to extend the GrOWTH framework by extracting the device *actuations*, *preconditions* and *effects* automatically, rather than manually adding these instances in the WoTDL ontology Graph.

References

1. Guinard, D., Trifa, V., Wilde, E.: A resource oriented architecture for the Web of Things. In: Internet of Things (IOT), pp. 1–8 (2010)
2. Noura, M., Gyrard, A., Heil, S., Gaedke, M.: Concept extraction from the Web of Things knowledge bases. In: Proceedings of the International Conference WWW/Internet (2018)
3. Noura, M., Heil, S., Gaedke, M.: GrOWTH: goal-oriented end user development for Web of Things devices. In: Mikkonen, T., Klamma, R., Hernández, J. (eds.) ICWE 2018. LNCS, vol. 10845, pp. 358–365. Springer, Cham (2018). https://doi.org/10.1007/978-3-319-91662-0_29

---

[6] https://github.com/heseba/wotdl2api.

[7] https://vsr.informatik.tu-chemnitz.de/projects/2019/growth.

4. Noura, M., Atiquzzaman, M., Gaedke, M.: Interoperability in Internet of Things infrastructure: classification, challenges, and future work. In: Lin, Y.-B., Deng, D.-J., You, I., Lin, C.-C. (eds.) IoTaaS 2017. LNICST, vol. 246, pp. 11–18. Springer, Cham (2018). https://doi.org/10.1007/978-3-030-00410-1_2
5. Noura, M., Atiquzzaman, M., Gaedke, M.: Interoperability in Internet of Things: taxonomies and open challenges. Mob. Netw. Appl., 1–14 (2018)
6. Cherrier, S., Ghamri-Doudane, Y.M., Lohier, S., Roussel, G.: D-lite: building Internet of Things choreographies. arXiv Preprint arXiv:1612.05975 (2016)

VR-Powered Scenario-Based Testing for Visual and Acoustic Web of Things Services

KyeongDeok Baek[✉], HyeongCheol Moon, and In-Young Ko

School of Computing, Korea Advanced Institute of Science and Technology, Daejeon,
Republic of Korea
{kyeongdeok.baek,hc.moon,iko}@kaist.ac.kr

Abstract. Web of Things (WoT) services are Web services that interact
with physical things in the environment. Testing of WoT services should
be performed considering the physical and human factors that affect their
quality. Scenario-based testing is known to be one of the most effective
testing techniques by which we can test software while considering various real-world scenarios. However, applying scenario-based testing to
real-world WoT testbed environments is not practical in terms of cost
and reconfigurability. In this work, we utilize Virtual Reality (VR) technology to mimic real-world WoT environments for cost-effective testing
over various scenarios.

Keywords: Scenario-based testing · Virtual reality-powered testing ·
Web of things services

1 Introduction

Recent advances in networking systems have expanded the boundaries of the
traditional Web to Web of Things (WoT). WoT enables services on the Web,
called WoT services, to actively interact with physical things in the environment.
In particular, visual and acoustic WoT services, which produce lights and sounds
respectively via physical devices, are the most common types of WoT services.
To test the actuating or sensing functions of such WoT services, scenario-based
testing can be performed by building real-world testbeds that are composed of
various physical devices. Scenario-based testing is usually regarded as an effective
technique to test software while considering various human factors that cannot be
tested using a limited set of test suites. However, building real-world testbeds has
a high cost of installing numerous physical devices or changing configurations.

In a recent work, Virtual Reality (VR) techniques have been used to mimic
psychological experiments [4]. Utilizing Head Mount Displays (HMD), users
experienced virtual environments visually and acoustically, and also interacted
with services in the environment by using controllers. Further, another recent
work suggested utilizing VR for user studies to experience the perspectives of
elderly people who have poor eyesight [3].

© Springer Nature Switzerland AG 2019
M. Bakaev et al. (Eds.): ICWE 2019, LNCS 11496, pp. 514–518, 2019.
https://doi.org/10.1007/978-3-030-19274-7_37

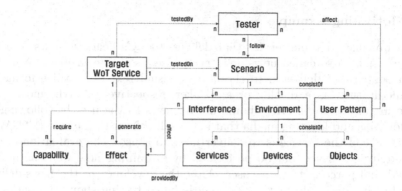

Fig. 1. VR-powered Scenario-based Testing Framework for WoT Services

In this paper, we first propose our scenario-based testing framework for WoT services to enable the systematic development of test environments for various test scenarios. Next we describe the VR-powered implementation of our framework, i.e. virtual WoT environments for scenario-based testing to reduce the cost of testing various scenarios. Obviously, developing a physical environment virtually requires a lower cost than building real-world testbeds, and it is also relatively easier to change its configurations. In the demo, we show our implementations of the framework and let users experience how scenario-based testing of WoT services can be performed based on our framework.

2   Scenario-Based Testing of WoT Services

2.1   Framework

Figure 1 shows the preliminary model of our scenario-based testing framework for WoT services. A target WoT service $s = \{\mathbb{E}, \mathbb{R}\}$ for testing consists of the effects generated by the service, $\mathbb{E}$, and the required capabilities, $\mathbb{R}$. A service can be tested on a set of scenarios $\mathbb{C}_s$, by a set of testers $\mathbb{T}$. A scenario $c = \{\mathbb{U}, env, \mathbb{I}\}$, consists of the user pattern, $\mathbb{U}$, the environment configuration, env, and the service interference, $\mathbb{I}$. In our framework, patterns for some dynamics of users such as mobility can be inserted, so the tester may follow a pre-determined mobility pattern or by simply move freely. An environment env consists of services, $\mathbb{S}$, devices, $\mathbb{D}$, and physical objects, $\mathbb{O}$, where a service may be a Web or a WoT service. According to a service's required capability, an appropriate device is discovered and gets acquired by the service. An environment may contain other services that cause interference within the target service in terms of physical effects, and models of such interference should be included in the scenario definition.

2.2   Motivating Example

We can imagine a simple service that delivers today's headline news to a user in the morning, a so-called news-delivery service, as shown in Fig. 2. News can be represented and delivered to the user as visual text or in voice format by using media such as a display or a speaker, respectively. Furthermore, users may be mobile, so the service should deliver news to the user by following the user's location and locating media that is spatially closer to the user [1,2]. While the objective of the service is to deliver news to a user, the evaluation of such a news-delivery service can be performed by examining how well the news is delivered and perceived by the user. After the developer of the news-delivery service finishes its implementation, scenario-based testing should be performed in various environments to evaluate whether or not the functions of the news-delivery service work in general.

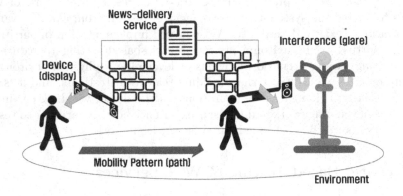

Fig. 2. Example News-delivery Service

Following our framework, the news-delivery service can be defined as follows: $s_{news} = \{\{light, sound\}, \{display, speaker\}\}$. To test the news-delivery service, a basic scenario is designed as $c = \{\emptyset, env_c, \emptyset\}$, where env_c contains configurations for every entity of the scenario. An empty set of user patterns and interference means that there are no pre-determined user patterns or interfering services. Extended scenarios can be designed based on the basic scenario, as follows. A specific travel path would be included in a scenario: $c_{mobility} = \{\{mobility_u\}, env_c, \emptyset\}$. To test whether news is delivered to a user even when other services are also generating lights or sounds, we can extend the basic scenario by inserting the interference model: $c_i = \{\{mobility_u\}, env_c, \{noise, glare\}\}$. To test the news-delivery service in a different environment, the environment of a scenario can simply be replaced by another environment, env'_c: $c_{env} = \{\{mobility_u\}, env'_c, \{noise, glare\}\}$.

3   VR-Based Simulation of WoT Services

As shown in Fig. 3a, we implemented virtual environments in a 3-dimensional space by using Unreal Engine[1], which is the most commonly used game engine for developing VR-based simulations. Testers wore HTC Vive Pro[2] as shown in Fig. 3b, which is one of the most common HMD for VR, for immersion inside the virtual environment and interaction through HMD and controllers.

(a) Environment   (b) User

Fig. 3. VR-powered Scenario-based Testing

4   Conclusion

In this paper, we proposed a physical environment aware scenario-based testing framework for visual and acoustic WoT services, and described a VR-powered implementation of the framework. By using VR, multiple testing scenarios can be efficiently developed, and testers may test the target service to reflect as many real-world cases as possible.

Acknowledgements. This work was supported by the National Research Foundation of Korea (NRF) grant funded by the Korea government (MSIT) (No. 2016R1A2B4007585).

References

1. Baek, K.-D., Ko, I.-Y.: Spatially cohesive service discovery and dynamic service handover for distributed IoT environments. In: Cabot, J., De Virgilio, R., Torlone, R. (eds.) ICWE 2017. LNCS, vol. 10360, pp. 60–78. Springer, Cham (2017). https://doi.org/10.1007/978-3-319-60131-1_4

---

[1] https://www.unrealengine.com.
[2] https://www.vive.com/us/product/vive-pro/.

2. Baek, K.D., Ko, I.-Y.: Spatio-cohesive service selection using machine learning in dynamic IoT environments. In: Mikkonen, T., Klamma, R., Hernández, J. (eds.) ICWE 2018. LNCS, vol. 10845, pp. 366–374. Springer, Cham (2018). https://doi.org/10.1007/978-3-319-91662-0_30

3. Krösl, K., Bauer, D., Schwärzler, M., Fuchs, H., Suter, G., Wimmer, M.: A VR-based user study on the effects of vision impairments on recognition distances of escape-route signs in buildings. Vis. Comput. **34**, 911–923 (2018)

4. Ma, X., Cackett, M., Park, L., Chien, E., Naaman, M.: Web-based VR experiments powered by the crowd. In: Proceedings of the 2018 World Wide Web Conference on World Wide Web, pp. 33–43. International World Wide Web Conferences Steering Committee (2018)

Posters

User's Emotional eXperience Analysis of Wizard Form Pattern Using Objective and Subjective Measures

Muhammad Zaki Ansaar, Jamil Hussain, Asim Abass,
Musarrat Hussain, and Sungyoung Lee[✉]

Department of Computer Science and Engineering, Kyung Hee University,
Seoul, South Korea
{zakiansaar, jamil, asimabbasturi, musarrat.hussain,
sylee}@oslab.khu.ac.kr

Abstract. Forms are the ordinary medium to collect data from prospective users and indirectly build a cordial relationship with them. This communication bridge can affect the user emotional reaction, whenever a user finds an unexpected error during or submitting the form. This paper presents an empirical user emotional eXperience study on wizard form pattern (Multi Step Form). The study mainly uses both objective measures through brain wave activity (EEG) with eye tracking data and subjective measures through a self-reported metrics. Fifteen participants (N = 15) joined the experiment by filling the wizard form pattern. We manipulated the experiment by generating a sudden error at one step and grouped these experiments by their step number. We observe that the error affects the motivational emotion of group1 (got an error on the first step), the excitement emotion of group2 (got an error on the second step), the frustration emotion of group3 (got an error on the third step) and group4 (got no error). We thus argue that an error while filling or submitting a form is more emotional than technical.

Keywords: User experience · Multi-steps form · Emotional experience

1 Introduction

Forms are the most commonly used method for data collection [1]. Various formats of interactive forms have been designed to streamline user's interaction in order to collect data from the end user with minimal effort. In most cases, designers use wizard form pattern when a large amount of data entry is required. Wizards divides the complex task into simpler and understandable steps [2]. Users appreciate forms that indicate the clear process through the steps. Conversely, they got frustrated when they had to repeatedly got an unavoidable error in wizard form. Error becomes a pain-point for a user which leads to the negative User eXperience (UX). UX includes users emotional, cognitive, perceptions, preferences, beliefs and behaviors aspects that occur before, during, or after the use of product, system, or services. In literature, different UX assessment methods have mentioned to measures the different aspects of UX related to usability, user perception, and human emotional reaction [3–5]. Emotion is one of the major

M. Bakaev et al. (Eds.): ICWE 2019, LNCS 11496, pp. 521–524, 2019.
https://doi.org/10.1007/978-3-030-19274-7_38

aspect/dimension of the UX. Therefore, understanding the user's emotions have always been the goal of UX moderators. Emotional UX helps the UX moderators to know about the attractive elements of the product, system, or service.

Emotions are the complicated psycho-physiological processes that are related to many internal and external activities of the user. Emotional reaction can be measured by subjective measures through questionnaire and objective measure through physiological sensors (EEG, EMG, HR, EDA, Respiration rate, and others) and ocular devices (camera, Kinect, eye tracker, and webcam). Different modalities characterize particular aspects of emotions through containing related information extracted from those modalities. Integrating modalities information can improve emotion recognition performance as compared with the unimodal approach.

In order to evaluate the emotional UX on wizard form pattern (multi-step form), we proposed three hypotheses. (a) Error on the first step affects the feeling of motivation (b) Error on the second step affects the feeling of excitement (c) Error on the last step affects the feeling of frustration. To analyze our hypotheses, we employed a multimodal user emotion recognition methodology, which collects both subjective and objective data on the multi-step form. First, we analyzed the utilized information from the physiological sensor such as EEG combined with eye tracker for the cognitive state, then we collect subjective measures by self-assessment information through the questionnaire for validating the mentioned hypotheses.

2 Experimental Setup and Procedure

2.1 Subjects and Apparatus

A total number of fifteen subjects (N = 15) including Ten males and Five females participated in the experiment on a voluntary basis. All Subjects were healthy with normal vision and adequate sleep. We used Tobii Pro X2-30 screen-based eye tracker to track, collect eye tracking metrics such as Fixations and gaze data, area of Interest, heatmap, and fixation sequences. Gaze data provides pupil diameter to identify the user emotions, pupil diameter was chosen as a feature in our experiment because it is correlated with different emotional states and provides a measure of emotional response. At the same time, An EMOTIV EPOC+ 14-channel EEG was used for the assessment of the inner state of the user. EEG collects brain activity in the central nervous system. The sampling rate was 40 Hz (±2 Hz) with 40–90 cm operation distance. Furthermore, brain activity data recorded at 2048 Hz sample rate.

2.2 Design and Procedure of the Experiment

This study used a wizard form pattern (Multi Step Form) based on single subject simulation. The form consists of three small steps and an average takes five minutes to fill the form. Every participant's filled the form randomly and completed one particular task. In order to change the subject experience, the experiment was manipulated by generating a sudden error. After completing the task, the participant was asked to report their experience by using the self-assessment (AttrakDiff) questionnaire.

2.3   Validation of Experimental Results

In order to extract quantitative values of fixation eye movement, first Area of interest (AOI) was defined on the presented stimuli as the location of the triggered error. We extracted the total duration of dwell time from our defined AOI which shows the required cognitive load by the participant to find the AOI.

To extract the real-time changes in the objective emotions of the user, Emotiv Xavier was used during the experiment with the help of EEG. The emotion that have taken into account in the experiments includes stress level, relaxation, focus level, sadness, and happiness. We grouped the participants on the basis of their errors. The participants who got an error on the first step, second step, third step, and no error in wizard form pattern (Multi Step Form) was named as G1, G2, G3, and G4 respectively. The results achieved for each group is shown in Fig. 1.

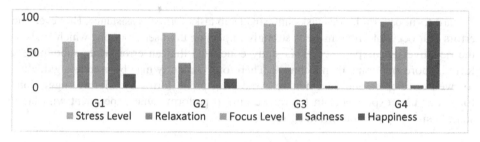

Fig. 1. The average emotional experience result achieved for each group.

The experimental result shows that the stress level of G4 is very low (10.4) because of no error. The stress level of G1 was less (65.3) as compared to G2 (78.58). While G3 participants noted as high (92.3) stress level. Similarly, G4 participants seem more relax as compare to other groups. While G3 was the most tensed compare to others. The focus level of G4 was the least compare to other groups. While G3 where the most focused group. There was no error for G4 participants. Therefore, the sadness level was minimum while the G3 where the sadness due the effort they required to fill the form again. The happiness level of G4 was the most and least for G3 due to the error generation. From the Fig. 1 we can conclude that the G3 participants has worst experience with the application and G4 has the best compared to other groups.

The AttrakDiff questionnaire's self-reporting results given by the participant is shown in Fig. 2. Graph (a) shows the comparison between G1, graph (b) represents G2 compare to G3. While graph (c) represents the evaluation result of error (G1, G2, G3) compare to no-error (G4). As we can see in Fig. 2(a), the pragmatic quality, hedonic quality and attractiveness of G1 is higher than G2. Similarly, all three qualities of G2 is greater than G3. The primary reason is the step at which error occurs and the task user needs to complete again. It is easy to refill the form at step one compare to refilling all three step like in case G3. The comparison of error vs no-error shown in Fig. 2(c) represents the user fell satisfied and happy while there is no error in the system and they complete the task smoothly.

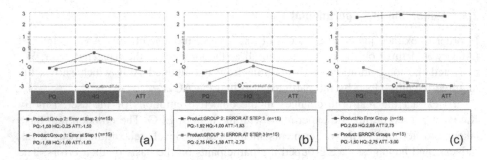

Fig. 2. Group wise value of user experience dimensions.

3 Conclusion

Wizard form pattern divides tasks into small sub tasks for user assistance. However, the errors that occur at different steps strongly impact on the user emotions which leads to the negative user experience. This study concluded that an error while submitting a form is more emotional than technical. Therefore, our study may be used as a guideline for web developers and designers to avoid error-prone forms by offering suggestions for better user experience. In future, we aim to perform same experiment with large sample size to get more informed results.

Acknowledgment. This research was supported by the MSIT (Ministry of Science and ICT), Korea, under the ITRC (Information Technology Research Center) support program (IITP-2017-0-01629) supervised by the IITP (Institute for Information & communications Technology Promotion) and This work was supported by Institute for Information & communications Technology Promotion (IITP) grant funded by the Korea government (MSIT) (No. 2017-0-00655).

References

1. Bargas-Avila, J.A., Brenzikofer, O., Roth, S.P., Tuch, A.N., Orsini, S., Opwis, K.: Simple but crucial user interfaces in the world wide web: introducing 20 guidelines for usable web form design. In: User Interfaces. InTech (2010)
2. Bargas-Avila, J.A., Orsini, S., Piosczyk, H., Urwyler, D., Opwis, K.: Enhancing online forms: use format specifications for fields with format restrictions to help respondents. Interact. Comput. **23**, 33–39 (2010)
3. Väänänen-Vainio-Mattila, K., Roto, V., Hassenzahl, M.: Towards practical user experience evaluation methods. In: Meaningful Measures: Valid Useful User Experience Measurement (VUUM), pp. 19–22 (2008)
4. Zheng, W.-L., Dong, B.-N., Lu, B.-L.: Multimodal emotion recognition using EEG and eye tracking data. In: 2014 36th Annual International Conference of the IEEE Engineering in Medicine and Biology Society (EMBC), pp. 5040–5043. IEEE (2014)
5. Phelps, E.A.: Human emotion and memory: interactions of the amygdala and hippocampal complex. Curr. Opin. Neurobiol. **14**, 198–202 (2004)

Integration Platform for Metric-Based Analysis of Web User Interfaces

Maxim Bakaev[1](✉) ⓘ, Sebastian Heil[2] ⓘ, Nikita Perminov[1],
and Martin Gaedke[2] ⓘ

[1] Novosibirsk State Technical University, Novosibirsk, Russia
bakaev@corp.nstu.ru,
nikfroly@gmail.com
[2] Technische Universität Chemnitz, Chemnitz, Germany
{sebastian.heil,
martin.gaedke}@informatik.tu-chemnitz.de

Abstract. We present a software tool for collecting web UI metrics from different providers and integrating them in a single database for further analysis. The platform's architecture supports both code- and image-based UI assessment, thus allowing to combine advantages of the two approaches. The data structures are based on a web UI measurement domain ontology (OWL) that organizes the currently disperse set of metrics and services. Our platform can be of use to interface designers, researchers, and UI analysis tools developers.

Keywords: User interaction quality · Design mining · HCI vision ·
User behavior modeling

1 Introduction

Automated assessment of web user interfaces (WUI) quality can be grouped into three major approaches: based on actual interactions, UI metrics, and models [1]. The more advanced hybrid approach implies obtaining the considered UI's quantitative characteristics (metrics) and then using them as input for user behavior models [2]. The output is predicted values for attributes that characterize user interaction quality, which can be used e.g. in automated UI design based on optimization.

The more conventional method for obtaining the metrics is "static" analysis of UI code or model representation. It boasts high performance and accuracy and is particularly suitable for web UIs whose HTML/CSS code is easily available. Code-based analysis is widely used to check compliance with accessibility guidelines and other standards and recommendations. However, the increasing popularity of Web Components leads to an abundance of code with many custom elements that cannot be easily recognized in the DOM. Also, "static" code analysis lacks in considering UI's context of use, so most usability-related quality attributes cannot be assessed with it.

On the other hand, the increasingly popular UI visual analysis [3], which is based on image recognition techniques, assesses the WUI as the target user witnesses it. This "dynamic" method deals with UI's visual representation (e.g. screenshot of a webpage rendered in a browser) and is naturally good at considering layouts, spatial properties of

M. Bakaev et al. (Eds.): ICWE 2019, LNCS 11496, pp. 525–529, 2019.
https://doi.org/10.1007/978-3-030-19274-7_39

web UI elements, graphical content, etc. The main challenge of image-based analysis, besides computational expensiveness, is the accuracy of the recognition. Visual variability in WUI elements nowadays is extremely high, which rules out simple pattern matching. The Machine Learning approach has been shown to be somehow effective [4, 5], but for supervised learning of the classifiers, an annotated training data of appropriate size is needed.

Another challenge in the rapidly developing domain of UI analysis is the abundance and diversity of metrics proposed by various researchers. The names for the metrics are still evolving, different algorithms (not always fully disclosed) can be used to calculate metrics of the same name, one metric can characterize different quality attributes in different models. Thus, we feel there is a need for a conceptual organization of UI metrics and a meta-tool for integrating diverse metrics from different sources and services. So, in our work, we present an OWL-based ontology and a *WUI measurement integration platform* capable of collecting different sets of WUI metrics for further analysis and usage in user behavior models.

2 WUI Measurement Integration Platform

In order to structure the WUI metrics domain, we built an ontology in OWL (Protégé 5.5.0-beta-4 editor was used). Since no existing ontologies in the field came to our attention, we mostly extracted concepts from published research works and available software. For instance, W3C cataloged more than 100 tools/services for assessing web accessibility[1] and proposed a set of attributes to organize them, including:

- Guidelines (WCAG of different versions, German BITV, French RGGA, Japanese JIS, Korean MAAG, US Section 508, etc.);
- Type of tool (API, Browser plugin, Command line, Desktop, Mobile, Online, etc.);
- Technology (WAI-ARIA, CSS, (X)HTML, ODF, PDF, SVG, SMIL, etc.);
- Output/assistance type (report, evaluation guidance, webpage modification, etc.);
- License type (Commercial, Free, Open Source, Trial or Demo).

The top-level concepts in the ontology include Interface, Attribute, Metric, and Service. The current version has more than 100 classes and about 200 individuals. An extract of the ontology structure visualized with OntoGraph is presented in Fig. 1.

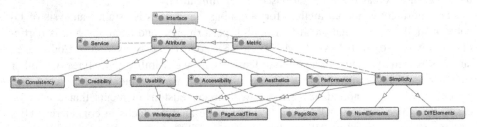

Fig. 1. Selected classes from the WUI measurement ontology.

---

[1] https://www.w3.org/WAI/ER/tools/.

The ontology served as the basis for the meta-tool that we developed for assessing WUIs using metrics from different providers (cf. Fig. 2). A WUI screenshot or website URI is sent to a remote service using its supported protocol, the metrics and other output are received and saved in the platform's database. The architecture also allows the use of remote services that use code analysis to supply WUI metrics. The platform can be accessed at our "knowledge portal" (http://va.wuikb.online, database dumps with the metrics can be provided upon request).

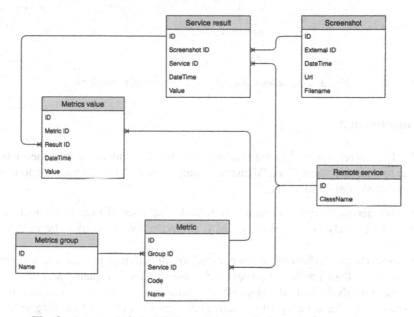

Fig. 2. An extract from WUI measurement platform database structure.

The scheme for the platform is shown in Fig. 3. The remote services currently used are:

1. WUI visual analyzer that we previously developed [4], hosted by TU Chemnitz[2];
2. AIM Interface Metrics [5] launched in 2018 by the team from Aalto University[3].

---
[2] http://webmining.wuikb.online/ratio/screenshot.php.
[3] http://userinterfaces.aalto.fi/.

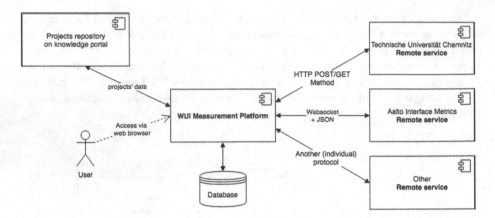

Fig. 3. The scheme for the WUI measurement platform

3   Conclusions

The WUI measurement integration platform that we developed and launched has the potential to combine "static" and "dynamic" analysis of web UIs. We see the following practical advantages in its usage:

- for **interface designers:** obtaining an extended number of metrics for more complete WUI analysis or selecting only project-relevant metrics from different services;
- for **researchers:** performing cross-comparison of different metrics and algorithms and studying their predictive powers w.r.t. user interaction quality assessment;
- for **visual analysis tools developers:** loosening requirements towards amounts of annotated data for training UI element classifiers in supervised learning mode (as element's type can often be easily extracted from the code).

Further prospects include implementation of "batch mode" so that the platform could collect metrics for a specified list of web pages under analysis. Since our tool is open to everyone's use, we welcome collaborators and hope to gradually increase the number of involved services. A more detailed description of the platform, together with an example of its application for researching WUI visual complexity can be found in [6].

Acknowledgment. This work was supported by Novosibirsk State Technical University, project No. TP-EI-1_17.

References

1. Speicher, M.: Search interaction optimization: a human-centered design approach. Ph.D. Dissertation, TU Chemnitz, Germany (2016)
2. Zen, M., Vanderdonckt, J.: Towards an evaluation of graphical user interfaces aesthetics based on metrics. In: IEEE International Conference on Research Challenges in Information Science, pp. 1–12 (2014)

3. Pu, J., Liu, J., Wang, J.: A vision-based approach for deep web form extraction. In: (Jong Hyuk) Park, J.J., Chen, S.-C., Raymond Choo, K.-K. (eds.) Advanced Multimedia and Ubiquitous Engineering. LNEE, vol. 448, pp. 696–702. Springer, Singapore (2017). https://doi.org/10.1007/978-981-10-5041-1_111
4. Bakaev, M., Heil, S., Khvorostov, V., Gaedke, M.: HCI vision for automated analysis and mining of web user interfaces. In: Mikkonen, T., Klamma, R., Hernández, J. (eds.) ICWE 2018. LNCS, vol. 10845, pp. 136–144. Springer, Cham (2018). https://doi.org/10.1007/978-3-319-91662-0_10
5. Oulasvirta, A., et al.: Aalto Interface Metrics (AIM): a service and codebase for computational GUI evaluation. In: 31st Annual ACM Symposium on User Interface Software and Technology Adjunct Proceedings, pp. 16–19. ACM (2018)
6. Bakaev, M., Heil, S., Khvorostov, V., Gaedke, M.: Auto-extraction and integration of metrics for web user interfaces. J. Web Eng. 17(6&7), 561–590 (2019)

Personal Information Controller Service (PICS)

Marco Winckler[1](✉), Laurent Goncalves[2], Olivier Nicolas[2],
Frédérique Biennier[3], Hind Benfenatki[3], Thierry Despeyroux[4],
Nourhène Alaya[4], Alex Deslée[5], Mbaye Fall Diallo[5],
Isabelle Collin-Lachaud[5], Gautier Ubersfeld[6],
and Christophe Cianchi[7]

[1] Université Nice Sophia Antipolis, Nice, France
winckler@unice.fr
[2] Softeam, Toulouse, France
{lgoncalves, onicolas}@e-citiz.com
[3] LIRIS, INSA Lyon, Lyon, France
[4] Inria, Le Chesnay, France
[5] Université de Lille, Lille, France
[6] Anyware Service, Labège, France
[7] Business Card Associates, Paris, France

Abstract. This paper presents a view at glance of the project PICS (which stands for Personal Information Controller Service) that is concerned by personal data protection. More specifically we present a software platform that allows users to control the exchanges between Web-based Personal Information Management Systems (the so-called PIMS that store users' personal data) and SaaS services (such as e-commerce applications) using a reinforced authentication. The ultimate goal of this platform is to empower users by allowing them to have full control on personal data exchange. Moreover, the platform includes specific components to help users to solve cognitive demanding tasks related to the data protection such as how to properly interpret Terms of Service (ToS) imposed by the SaaS, recall previous users interactions with the SaaS (ex. personal data exchanged with the SaaS and the corresponding term of services), and detect unauthorized use of personal data. The technical solution proposed by PICS is a suitable implementation of the General Data Protection Regulation (GDPR). We present the motivations, challenges and research questions that lead to the technical solution proposed by PICS.

Keywords: Personal data protection · Personal information systems · GDPR

1 Towards User-Centric Data Protection

It is a terribly thing to think that personal data is being collected without user's consent for that a simple answer to privacy problems would be to maximally inform the users about how much data was being kept and sold about them. Personal data protection has been a long concern in many countries like France but only more recently it has been regulated by the means of the European General Data Protection Regulation (GDPR) [3] forcing many companies to adjust their data handling processes, consent forms, and

M. Bakaev et al. (Eds.): ICWE 2019, LNCS 11496, pp. 530–533, 2019.
https://doi.org/10.1007/978-3-030-19274-7_40

privacy policies to comply with the GDPR's transparency requirements. The basic premise for the GDPR is that users must be informed about the use made of their personal data [1]. Notifying users about a system's data practices is supposed to enable users to make informed privacy decisions and yet, current notice and choice mechanisms, such as public policies and Terms of Service (ToS), are often ineffective because they are neither usable nor useful, and are therefore ignored by users [2]. Whilst the GDPR tries to regulate the use of personal data, it also creates two cognitive demanding tasks to the users: (i) how to analyze ToS, and (ii) how to remember huge amount of personal data that the SaaS is authorized to store.

Nowadays, users store many personal data in Web applications (such as Dropbox, Google drive, Linkedin, Facebook, etc.) that act as Personal Information Data Management Systems (PIMS) [4]. Connecting PIMS and SaaS offer two advantages: on one hand it is a suitable solution for delivering personal data to the SaaS; on the other hand, the PIMS can store ToS and recall users of whom possess his personal data. The interoperability between PIMS and SaaS (such as e-commerce Web sites) is not a technical problem per se but a security failure on one service might increase the risk of data disclosure of other services [5].

It important to recall that according to the GDPR, data protection relies on a promise of use of personal data for a specific purpose, defined by a ToS. However, if users suspect that a SaaS violates the agreement, the number of complaints can quickly increase given that the rest of the procedure has to be done by service providers who might have juridical and IT divisions overbooked of request of clarification.

In order to solve these problems, we have created a consortium of researchers and industrialists that came up with a software platform called PICS (Personal Information Controller Service), which is eponym of the project. The rest of this paper present the overall architecture of this platform and illustrate the prototype. The last section summarizes the underlying research questions and the future work.

2   Overall Architecture of PICS

The overall architecture of the PICS platform is illustrated by Fig. 1. As we shall see, PICS mediates all the user interaction with third-party services that might contain (or require) personal data from the users, this includes both the SaaS and the PIMS. This mediation is meant to promote data protection and prevent that a security failure of a SaaS would affect the PIMS (and vice-versa). The security of PICS is enhanced by strong authentication mechanisms featuring a combination of user login plus physical authentication via a wearable device (such as an electronic bracelet). PICS is made of three core modules, as follows:

- The *personal data controller* is the central piece that connects all the other components. It includes a user interface allowing users to connect to third-party services (PIMS or Saas) and mediate the transfer of personal data between them. It is important to say that the PICS itself does not store any personal data. For that, users should identify a data storage (such as Google drive, Dropbox, Linkedin, etc.) that will act as a PIMS for recording all personal data, ToS and transactions made between the PIMS and SaaS.

- The *ToS analyzer* is a specialized tool that is able to process a ToS provided by a SaaS and codify the terms of ToS according to a specialized Ontology that covers all the dimensions of personal data protection referred by the GRDP [6]. The results of *ToS analyzer* are accessible to the users via the *personal data controller* by the means of a visual language as illustrated by Fig. 2.
- The *data mining traces of use* is a very specialized tool which is able to perform advanced search over the Web to discover traces of uses of personal data. This tool allow users to check where their personal data is available to SaaS. The results are shown at the *personal data controller*.

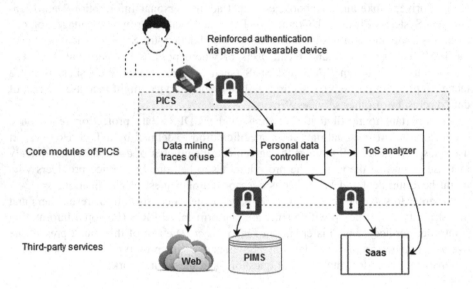

Fig. 1. Overall architecture of PICS

Fig. 2. A view at glance of PICS featuring the analysis of Terms of Service of SaaS. (Color figure online)

3   Tool Support

The PICS architecture was implemented featuring a Web plugin as illustrated by Fig. 2. Once installed in the browser, the PICS menu appears in the tool bar allowing the user to access to all features supported by the PICS core modules. When the users connect to the PICS for the first time, he must register a login plus a physical wearable device that will be asked to identify the user in the future. Every time the user connects to the PICS it must provide the login plus the wearable device which communicate with PICS via a FIDO interface [7]. Figure 2 illustrates a scenario where after visiting a SaaS Web site, the user use the PICS menu to triggers the analysis of ToS. The results of such as an analysis is shown as a floating window featuring a list of GRDP dimensions. The icons, the keywords and color coding (green/red/gray/yellow) are meant to provide the users with a quick synthesis of the ToS.

4   Research Questions and Future Work

The project PICS raise many research questions. First, how to formalize the dimensions (such as duration of storage, location of the storage, data ownership...) recognized by the GDPR? That led us to the development of an Ontology [6] for processing ToS. The second question was how to secure the access to the data so that sensible personal data is not easily stolen by cracking a password? For that, we have investigated the use of wearable devices to reinforce the authentication. Another question is which architecture would prevent accidental personal data disclosure? We have proposed two complementary solutions: first, an independent module that does not store any data but mediate the data transfer between the PIMS and SaaS; second, a specialized data-mining tool for discovery of the use of personal data over the Web. Currently we have a proof of concept that demonstrates the feasibility of our ideas and an advanced prototype for demonstrations. Our on-going work includes the testing of the prototype with end-users to identify the potential adoption of the solution.

References

1. Lazar, J., Stein, M.A.: Disability, Human Rights, and Information Technology, 1st edn. University of Pennsylvania Press, Philadelphia (2017)
2. Terms of Service - didn't read. https://tosdr.org/. Accessed 25 Mar 2019
3. GDPR. https://eur-lex.europa.eu/eli/reg/2016/679/oj. Accessed 25 Mar 2019
4. Firmenich, S., Gaits, V., Gordillo, S., Rossi, G., Winckler, M.: Supporting users tasks with personal information management and web forms augmentation. In: Brambilla, M., Tokuda, T., Tolksdorf, R. (eds.) ICWE 2012. LNCS, vol. 7387, pp. 268–282. Springer, Heidelberg (2012). https://doi.org/10.1007/978-3-642-31753-8_20
5. Schaub, F., Balebako, R., Durity, A., Cranor, L.: A design space for effective privacy notices. In: SOUPS 2015, pp. 1–17. USENIX Association, Berkeley (2015)
6. Benfenatki, H., Biennier, F., Winckler, M., Goncalves, L., Nicolas, O., Saoud, Z.: Towards a User Centric Personal Data Protection Framework. http://chi-gdpr.webflow.io/. Accessed 25 Mar 2019
7. FIDO Alliance. https://fidoalliance.org/. Accessed 25 Mar 2019

Enabling the Interconnection of Smart Devices Through Semantic Web Techniques

Daniel Flores-Martin[1]([✉])[iD], Javier Berrocal[1][iD], José García-Alonso[1][iD], Carlos Canal[2][iD], and Juan M. Murillo[1][iD]

[1] Universidad de Extremadura, Badajoz, Spain
{dfloresm,jberolm,jgaralo,juanmamu}@unex.es
[2] Universidad de Málaga, Málaga, Spain
canal@lcc.uma.es

Abstract. Nowadays, there are millions of devices connected to the Internet. This is what we know as called Internet of Things. The integration of these smart devices with the web protocols makes them more accessible and understandable by people. The purpose of these devices is to make people's lives easier. Thanks to the collaboration between devices, the possibilities that the Web of Things offers can be even more exploited. However, many manufacturers develop their own devices and protocols in order to protect their market share, limiting in many ways the collaboration between devices of different manufacturers. This paper presents a solution based on semantic web techniques with the purpose of achieving collaboration between devices regardless of the technologies and protocols developed by their manufacturers.

Keywords: Web of Things · Semantic web · Collaboration

1 Introduction and Motivations

Internet of Things (IoT) and Web of Things (WoT) main aim is making people's lives simpler. While IoT allows us to remotely monitor and control smart devices, WoT integrates Things with the Web even more intimately; hence, making those devices more accessible for applications and humans [3]. These paradigms are used in many different domains as smart home, automotive, smart cities, healthcare, agriculture, wearable, etc. [2]. The great evolution of these technologies allows us to develop increasingly smart devices and truly useful services that a few years ago were unthinkable.

But the real potential of WoT comes from the collaboration among smart devices to perform complex tasks. For this to be possible, the next evolution of WoT is to ensure that smart devices can proactively collaborate among themselves [1,5,6].

Unfortunately, the possibility of collaboration among smart devices is still far from being realized. Indeed, manufacturers develop their own protocols so

M. Bakaev et al. (Eds.): ICWE 2019, LNCS 11496, pp. 534–537, 2019.
https://doi.org/10.1007/978-3-030-19274-7_41

that their devices can be seamlessly integrated with each other but not with other brands' devices. This allows manufacturers to save their market share. This also inevitably leads to the well-known *vendor lock-in* problem [4]. This phenomenon implies that if one want to obtain the maximum benefit from the WoT, (s)he must purchase devices from the same manufacturer to ensure maximum compatibility. Consequently, the interaction between devices from different manufacturers is made more difficult, or they will have to give up certain activities to be assisted by these devices.

In this paper we propose a tool that relies on web semantic techniques to achieve the collaboration among smart devices regardless of the manufacturer. We achieve this collaboration by providing smart devices with *goals* (desired states of the environment) and *skills* (abilities to influence or change the environment). These goals and skills are defined in semantic web terms and related by semantic reasoners and query languages. Therefore, the possibility of collaboration between devices is fostered while maintaining the independence of the manufacturer, without forcing any device or manufacturer to use any specific technology, in a simple way, at low cost and effectively.

The rest of the document is structured as follows. Section 2 details our proposal to interconnect different smart devices regardless of the manufacturers. Finally, in Sect. 3 some conclusions are detailed.

2 Proposal

Manufacturers usually develop devices based on their own protocols, making it difficult to integrate with devices from other manufacturers. When a manufacturer develops a device, it is develop specific applications getting associated with an API that is often distributed to developers so they can get the most out of the device and provide services. Each device has its own features that are the functionalities that are able to change the state of the context, such as varying the temperature or brightness of a room, and that are described by the manufacturers themselves. In this work we reuse these APIs to generate the different skills giving them a semantic connotation so that they can be easily interpreted and related to other skills or goals. Thus, skills can be generated regardless of the technology used by the manufacturer and offered as services to other devices in the environment that need to use them. Below the architecture that models the process of converting features into skills and offering them services between WoT devices is shown, as well as a prototype.

2.1 Proposed Architecture

The architecture has a main component, the controller, composed by several modules, the *API Consume, Skills and Goals Generator* and the *Skill Service*. Figure 1 shows the complete process to convert devices features into skills: first (1) APIs are consumed to discover the features of the entities, second (2) once

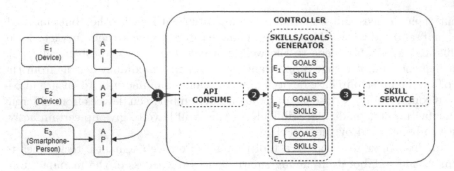

Fig. 1. Architecture for skills and goals conversion

the API has been explored, the skills are generated from the detected features, and finally (3) the skills are offered as services to be used by the rest of devices.

At this point, the controller knows all information about the entities, so it builds its ontology with this data. The purpose of this ontology is to relate the discovered entities through their skills and goals. The resolution of the goals of a given entity is to find a skill that is capable of solving it adequately. In order to obtain additional information about the entities and search for skills and goals more accurately, we use reasoners to detect what types of entities we can find within the context. After that, the entities mapping is done through SPARQL queries. Regarding the goals, these are currently defined manually to show the viability of the architecture. This will be done automatically in the future.

2.2 Use Case

To evaluate the feasibility of the proposed architecture, a prototype focused on a smart office environment is being developing. This use case has been chosen because it is being carried out in our laboratory.

The smart office has a variety of smart devices from different manufacturers, such as a smart air conditioning and a smart illumination. Both smart devices are connected to the office router. In order to integrate the devices with the defined architecture we have installed a Raspberry Pi. This device is able to manage the entities connected to the same network, both devices and people. The Raspberry Pi will be in charge of managing them, so it takes the role of the controller module in the previous defined architecture. In order to validate the viability of the proposal, the devices present in the network must be specified in this controller. In addition, when employees arrive to the office they must also be incorporated to the knowledge base of the controller so that it has evidence of them. The goals of the entities are specified manually through the controller's web interface, while the skills are built from the information in their APIs and incorporating extra information from external ontologies. In Table 1 we show an example of the SPARQL query to obtain all goals related to temperature. In this case, the air conditioner is discovered as well as all its goals and skills.

Table 1. SPARQL query for "temp" solution

All present skills that cover the "temp" goal

```
1  SELECT * WHERE {
2  ?Goal a :Goal .
3  ?Goal :requiresSkill ?skill .
4  ?Goal rdfs:comment ?comment .
5  FILTER (CONTAINS(lcase(str(?Goal)),
       lcase("temp"))) .
6  ?Entity a :Entity .
7  ?Entity :hasSkill ?skill . }
```

Result

Goal	g_setTemp
Skill	sk_setTemp
comment	Change temp
Entity	airconditioner

To validate the proposed architecture the definition of the skills and goals has been carried out manually. As future work this will be done automatically.

3   Conclusions

In this paper we addressed the interconnection problems to favor the collaboration of smart devices of the WoT. The proposed architecture uses the semantic web for the interconnection of devices and is validated through a prototype. The prototype is a proof of concept that allows us to understand the interconnection limitations and possibilities in a smart scenario. This work is a another step towards achieving a higher level of interconnection in WoT.

Acknowledgments. This work was supported by the Spanish Ministry of Science and Innovation through projects TIN2015-69957-R, TIN2014-53986-REDT, and TIN2015-67083-R (MINECO/FEDER, UE), by the Department of Economy and Infrastructure of the Government of Extremadura (GR15098, IB18030), by the European Regional Development Fund (ERDF) and by 4IE project (0045-4IE-4-P) funded by the Interreg V-A España-Portugal (POCTEP) 2014-2020 program.

References

1. Al-Fuqaha, A., Guizani, M., Mohammadi, M., Aledhari, M., Ayyash, M.: Internet of Things: a survey on enabling technologies, protocols, and applications. IEEE Commun. Surv. Tutor. **17**(4), 2347–2376 (2015)
2. Gubbi, J., Buyya, R., Marusic, S., Palaniswami, M.: Internet of Things (IoT): a vision, architectural elements, and future directions. Future Gener. Comp. Sy. **29**(7), 1645–1660 (2013)
3. Guinard, D., Trifa, V.: Building the Web of Things: With Examples in Node.js and Raspberry Pi. Manning Publications Co., Greenwich (2016)
4. Roman, R., Zhou, J., Lopez, J.: On the features and challenges of security and privacy in distributed Internet of Things. Comput. Netw. **57**(10), 2266–2279 (2013)
5. Taivalsaari, A., Mikkonen, T.: A roadmap to the programmable world: software challenges in the IoT era. IEEE Softw. **34**(1), 72–80 (2017)
6. Yafei, D., Guanyu, L., Hui, Z.: Semantic space-based semantic collaboration method in semantic Web of Things. Comput. Appl. Softw. **2**, 002 (2016)

PhD Symposium

Content- and Context-Related Trust in Open Multi-agent Systems Using Linked Data

Valentin Siegert

Technische Universität Chemnitz, Chemnitz, Germany
valentin.siegert@informatik.tu-chemnitz.de

Abstract. In open multi-agent systems, linked data enables agents to communicate with each other and to gather knowledge for autonomous decision. Until now, trust is a factor for starting communications and ignores doubts about the content or context of ongoing communications. Several approaches are used to identify whom to trust and how human trust can be computationally modeled. Yet, they do not consider a change of context or of other agents' behavior at runtime. The proposed doctoral work aims to support content- and context-related trust in open multi-agent systems using linked data. Existing trust models need to be surveyed with respect to content- and context-related trust. A framework based on a fitting trust model and working with linked data must be developed to establish and dynamically refine trust relationships on the autonomous agents' point of view. This would enhance the applicability of decentralized systems without introducing central units as the history of the web demonstrates. Web engineers are hereby supported to work on a new level of abstraction using the decentralization, but not scrutinizing specific communication sequences.

Keywords: Solid · Trust · Content trust · Multi-agent systems · Linked data

1 Introduction

The web is leveraging the decentralized internet architecture but is today centralized [1, 2]. The *walled gardens* [3] of social web applications can be gardens with freedom and user dynamism [4] but are also limiting access to the data for the creator/data subject. Different initiatives like EU's Next Generation Internet initiative (NGI)[^1] or projects like Solid [1] are advocating a decentralized vision of the web. Decentralizing the web facilitates inter- and exchangeability of system parts, partners and providers. Yet, decentralization introduces trust challenges due to many potentially unknown parties.

Building applications in a decentralized web are challenging web engineers in a new way, especially according to trust questions. As the decentralization is bringing in more privacy and freedom for data [1], web engineers will have to work with a different view on data. Data can come from anywhere and thus it is highly questionable if this data is correct and harmless or wrong, misleading and even harmful [5]. Due to the big amount of data in the web, these trust decisions cannot be made by human experts but by autonomous agents.

[^1]: cf. https://ec.europa.eu/digital-single-market/en/policies/next-generation-internet.

© Springer Nature Switzerland AG 2019
M. Bakaev et al. (Eds.): ICWE 2019, LNCS 11496, pp. 541–547, 2019.
https://doi.org/10.1007/978-3-030-19274-7_42

These trust decisions should not be evaluated on a static trust relationship, nor only on a relationship certified by any external authority. As the agents should be autonomous to proceed with the decentral concept of the web, an external authority would bring back the pilloried centralization. The dynamic evaluation of trust will give certain advantages about the fast-changing unknown parties, which can even change their behavior in specific contexts after being trusted in the first place. Thus, the autonomous agents should be able to work with dynamic trust relationships, which are content-and/or context-related and not dictated by another entity.

In the following three use cases with different complexity are presented, and their similarities are analyzed. The paper goes on with a description of the research objectives in Sect. 3, and a related work in Sect. 4. It concludes in Sect. 5 with the research agenda.

2   Use Cases

Use Case: Solid. Solid is a well-known project which tries to give back control over the data to the creator/data subject by decentralizing online data storages [1] called *pods*. As everyone should be free to bring his pod to any application, Solid is separating the data from the application. Therewith Solid enables two novel business models for web applications: (1) the data management layer with pod hosting/providing, and (2) the application business itself avoiding data silos. Yet, there is no clear mechanism how to decide if certain data should be trusted by any application nor if the pod should accept new data from a specific application in/with a specific context or content.

Use Case: Smart Cities. The digitalization of cities also includes trustworthy systems in domains like energy distribution and public/personal traffic management. As such systems should ensure a trustworthy behavior and a respective comfortable usage, several autonomous decisions must be made at runtime. The autonomous agents making these decisions must be able to react to unpredictable events in their environment. It is required to observe how trustworthy each input data is and if it should be considered for the decision. Thus, they must ensure the overall trustworthy behavior at each intermediate decision. Otherwise, the system declaration as behaving trustworthy can be jeopardized by decisions, which were made on non-trusted or distrusted data.

Use Case: Goods Transportation. Within the goods transport sector, delivery logistics is a complex process with manual planning beforehand. It lacks an optimized dynamic, autonomous, secure and trustable way of conceptual linking one delivery to a carriage within a transportation system. The dynamic interchanging of goods in between carriages, the dynamic separation of one delivery in parts, the inferring remerging of one delivery and the dynamic separation of each carriage are also closely connected aspects at the goods transport. All these aspects need a special consideration upon trust mechanisms when it comes to an AI controlled logistics planning and execution. Regulating everything in detail without individual autonomous decisions will not support autonomous and dynamic transportation of goods.

Analysis of Use Cases. All three use cases have in common that they are separating two layers by introducing decentralization with autonomous decisions at runtime These two layers were considered as one, but the decentralization is acquiring the need to separate them. These two layers subsequently cause new trust challenges. Solid is e.g. separating the data layer from the application layer. In the context of smart cities, the autonomous agents' decision is separated from the outer view of the system. And at the goods transportation, the routing and delivering of goods and its actual transportation methods are separated. Without consideration of trust, the decentralization would decrease the trustworthy behavior of all use cases and respectively the security.

If the trust is evaluated only once for each participating party, all use cases would lack the possibility that context and content can change, and that the party could change its behavior after some time passed. Thus, all use cases benefit to evaluate the trust for each changed content and context. As the content and context can change between two communication parties without the participation of any authority, authority for specific trust mechanism would cause not only an undermining of the decentralization but also a shift in the point of view about trust. The trust would respectively not fit to a specific agent, but to the authority. Thus, all use cases require a framework which is useable for all agents and based on a respective trust model.

To share information and knowledge between all participating parties, services, and sensors, it is for all use case suitable to use linked data. Hereby, participating entities do not have to stare the complete set but can leverage on the distributed and decentral description of data. While the use case of Solid is even conceptual based on linked data, the other use cases also benefit from the usage of linked data.

3   Research Objectives

The goal of this doctoral work[2] is to support content- and context-related trust in open multi-agent systems using linked data. Open multi-agent systems use many independent agents, which collaborate to achieve a common purpose, e.g. to prevent traffic jams in a city while ensuring the fastest route for all individuals. The aspect of openness describes that all agents can join and leave the system without restrictions or influence by/on other agents, e.g. any application provider using Solid can enter or leave the Solid ecosystem.

To support web engineers in building trustworthy applications in a decentralized web, the uncertainty about the inclusion of foreign content has to be abolished, i.e. *content-related trust* is required. Agents can change their behavior in a decentralized system without perception by other agents, thus incoming content must be checked for each individual communication. Subsequently, such checks could change the trust in another agent, which infers a trust check when commencing a communication and not only once per sensing a new agent.

---

[2] Supervised by Prof. Dr.-Ing. Martin Gaedke, martin.gaedke@informatik.tu-chemnitz.de.

Trustworthiness depends on the communication context, i.e. *context-related trust* is required. The context comprises agent context, situation context, system context, and temporal context. The agent context is describing the agent's preferences and capabilities. The situation context is describing the goals, the availability, and the communication sequence of an agent and its involved peers, while the system context comprises the entire system. The temporal context intersects the context types since context properties of all other context types are related to the time dimension. As context is emergent and can therefore not be predicted nor predefined. Thus, the understanding of the context is an important aspect for solving the trust uncertainty.

To reach this objective, a respective framework has to be developed. As notifiable in Fig. 1, trust models should be used as a basis to dismantle the uncertainty in the introduced use cases but are having gaps. These gaps are demonstrated by the use cases as mentioned in the Analysis of Use Cases. A framework for the respective trust model in linked data is required to be developed, such that the agents in the use cases can use it. Thus, it will base on the trust model(s) and will be applied to the use cases for evaluation purposes. To utilize trust establishment in the correct way, the framework must solve the demonstrated gaps with a correct trust model underneath but also the requirements specified by the gaps. It is envisaged to find or create the perfect trust model, but the framework could also exchange the underlying model from scenario to scenario.

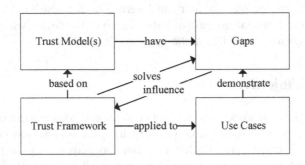

Fig. 1. Solution concepts

4   Related Work

Policy- and Reputation-Based Trust. Trust inferences based on policies or strict security mechanism can be grouped as *policy-based trust* [6]. Trust is here compounded "by obtaining a sufficient amount of credentials pertaining to a specific party, and applying the policies to grant that party certain access rights" [6, p. 59]. Another type of trust establishing is called *reputation-based trust* [6], where the reputation of others is used to infer trust. Thereby a *web of trust* [6] is established without any authority.

Trust Models. To further compare trust values a computational trust model is required. Recent work shows that a lot of different models exist for specific scenarios [7, 8]. Cao et al. [9] introduce a model, which is very close to the mentioned use case in smart cities, where the sharing of data in such a city is modeled with regards to transparency, accountability, and privacy. Falcone and Castelfranchi [10] are "dealing with the dynamic nature of trust, and making the realization that an agent that knows he's trusted may act differently from one who does not know his level of trust" [6, p. 65]. Besides the computational models of trust, the meaning of trust is leveraging out of social sciences, and their respective modeling of trust [11].

Content Trust. Since the mentioned problem of this doctoral work requires to generate dynamic trust relationships within linked data the approach of *content trust* [12] is very important for this work. It changes the stasis of once evaluated trust relations to dynamic ones with regard to the mentioned content. But this approach is establishing a trust to another agent's content, while it lacks aspects like forgiveness, regret, distrust, mistrust and a cooperation threshold like specified by Marsh and Briggs [8].

Trust in Multi-agent Systems. As all three named use cases in Sect. 2 consider many agents in one system the interactivity between those agents also influence trust. Such multi-agent systems have respectively also to talk about the interference of others and the knowledge that others are trusting an agent in regard to the agent's behavior [13]. Huynh et al. [14] are already mentioning the uncertainty in open multi-agent systems and presenting an integrated trust and reputation model. Yet, they have issues regarding lies and do not consider a change of trust after first trust establishment.

5 Research Agenda

Trust Models Selection. At first, the correct computational trust model(s) must be found. Respective survey research about available trust models with regards to identify, analyze and evaluate them is the intended start as in Fig. 2. This survey may show the need to create a new trust model to fit in the content and context relations, which benefits from the survey to not develop a new one from scratch. But as the purpose of this doctoral work is not the creation of a new trust model, the intention is to combine available trust models. As already mentioned in 0, this survey could also come to the result that several models are important and have to exchanged from use case to use case.

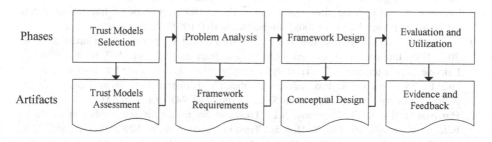

Fig. 2. Research agenda

Problem Analysis. The framework design needs to fit the actual problem. The requirements can be found with a problem analysis with respect to the observed trust models' gaps. Some requirements are already written down within the problem statement. Yet, there could be more as the framework should be integrated into the use cases and their specific multi-agent systems.

Framework Design. With the problem analysis finished, the conceptual design of the framework can be started. A corresponding first prototype will be implemented for the utilization of the framework and its further evaluation.

Evaluation and Utilization. After the framework has a clear conceptual design with respect to its requirements, the framework is required to fit into the use cases. Therefore, the framework will be implemented and reworked by including it in each use case. The framework will hereby be included in one use case after another. Every use case utilization is thus improving the framework itself with a small evaluation in a specific scenario. After three successful use case integrations, the framework will be further evaluated with a focus on all requirements of the problem analysis.

References

1. Sambra, A.V., Mansour, E., Hawke, S., et al.: Solid: a platform for decentralized social applications based on linked data (2016)
2. Ibáñez, L.-D., Simperl, E., Gandon, F., et al.: Redecentralizing the web with distributed ledgers. IEEE Intell. Syst. **32**, 92–95 (2017)
3. Appelquist, D., Brickley, D., Carvahlo, M., et al.: Social Web XG Wiki (2010)
4. Mehra, S.K.: Paradise is a walled garden? In: Trust, Antitrust and User Dynamism, pp. 889–952 (2011)
5. Langer, A., Siegert, V., Göpfert, C., Gaedke, M.: SemQuire - assessing the data quality of linked open data sources based on DQV. In: Pautasso, C., Sánchez-Figueroa, F., Systä, K., Murillo Rodríguez, J.M. (eds.) ICWE 2018. LNCS, vol. 11153, pp. 163–175. Springer, Cham (2018). https://doi.org/10.1007/978-3-030-03056-8_14
6. Artz, D., Gil, Y.: A survey of trust in computer science and the semantic web. J. Web Semant. **5**, 58–71 (2007)
7. Golbeck, J.: computing with trust: definition, properties, and algorithms. In: 2006 Securecomm and Workshops, pp. 1–7 (2006)
8. Marsh, S., Briggs, P.: Examining trust, forgiveness and regret as computational concepts. In: Golbeck, J. (ed.) Computing with Social Trust. Human–Computer Interaction Series, pp. 9–43. Springer, London (2009). https://doi.org/10.1007/978-1-84800-356-9_2
9. Cao, Q.H., Khan, I., Farahbakhsh, R., et al.: A trust model for data sharing in smart cities. In: 2016 IEEE International Conference on Communications (ICC), pp. 1–7. IEEE (2016)
10. Falcone, R., Castelfranchi, C.: Trust dynamics: how trust is influenced by direct experiences and by trust itself. In: Proceedings of the Third International Joint Conference on Autonomous Agents and Multiagent Systems, pp. 740–747. IEEE (2004)
11. Harrison McKnight, D., Chervany, N.L.: Trust and distrust definitions: one bite at a time. In: Falcone, R., Singh, M., Tan, Y.-H. (eds.) Trust in Cyber-societies. LNCS (LNAI), vol. 2246, pp. 27–54. Springer, Heidelberg (2001). https://doi.org/10.1007/3-540-45547-7_3

12. Gil, Y., Artz, D.: Towards content trust of web resources. Web Semant. Sci. Serv. Agents World Wide Web **5**, 227–239 (2007)
13. Drawel, N., Qu, H., Bentahar, J., et al.: Specification and automatic verification of trust-based multi-agent systems. Future Gener. Comput. Syst. (2018). https://doi.org/10.1016/j.future.2018.01.040
14. Huynh, T.D., Jennings, N.R., Shadbolt, N.R.: FIRE: an integrated trust and reputation model for open multi-agent systems. In: Proceedings of ECAI 2004: 16th European Conference on Artificial Intelligence, pp. 18–22 (2004)

Facilitating the Evolutionary Modifications in Distributed Apps via Automated Refactoring

Kijin An[(⊠)]

Software Innovations Lab, Virginia Tech, Blacksburg, USA
ankijin@vt.edu

Abstract. Actively used software applications must be changed continuously to ensure their utility, correctness, and performance. To perform these changes, programmers spend a considerable amount of time and effort pinpointing the exact locations in the code to modify, a particularly hard task for distributed applications. In distributed applications, server/middleware misconfigurations and network volatility often cause performance and correctness problems. My dissertation research puts forward a novel approach to facilitating the evolutionary modifications of distributed applications that introduces a novel automated refactoring—Client Insourcing. This refactoring transforms a distributed application into its semantically equivalent centralized variant, in which the remote parts are glued together and communicate with each other by means of regular function calls, eliminating any middleware, server, and network-related problems from the list of potential problem causes. Programmers then can use the resulting centralized variant to facilitate debugging, security enhancements, and fault-tolerance adaptations (Some of the preliminary work of this dissertation is described in a paper accepted for presentation in the main technical program of ICWE 2019 [4]).

Keywords: Distributed applications · Evolutionary modifications ·
Automated refactoring

1 Problem Statement

Distributed computing has become a de-facto standard execution model for the majority of application domains. Web-based applications, mobile applications, IoT setups, embedded systems—all make use of remote execution. It is well known that the majority of software engineering effort and costs is spent on software maintenance and evolution [5,6]. In distributed applications—adaptive, corrective, and perfective modifications are particularly hard, due to the potential presence of server/middleware misconfigurations and network volatility. These mainstay conditions of distributed execution hinder the most important phase of the maintenance process: determining the exact causes of problems to solve and the locations in the code that implement them.

Advisor: Eli Tilevich.

In my dissertation, I explore a new approach that facilitates a large class of evolutionary modifications in distributed applications. This approach puts forward a novel, domain-specific automated refactoring—*Client Insourcing*—that moves remotely executed functionalities to be executed locally, thereby creating a semantically equivalent centralized version of the distributed application. This centralized version is then used to perform evolutionary modifications.

The cognitive load required to understand, trace, and modify the source code is much lower for centralized applications than for distributed ones. Distributed applications have a complex control flow and suffer from partial failure, being affected by their middleware frameworks, distributed infrastructure configurations, and network environments. The novelty of my research is in reducing the problem of evolving a distributed application by enabling programmers to operate on its equivalent centralized version. Of course, not all software evolution tasks are amenable to this approach. Hence, one of the objectives of my dissertation is to determine this approach's exact range of applicability.

2   Related Work

The research community has extended a considerable amount of effort to facilitate the comprehension and evolution of distributed applications. In modern enterprise software development, the remote parts of a distributed application are written to interact with each other by means of some middleware framework, based on synchronous or asynchronous communication paradigms. Since the presence of middleware is known to hinder maintenance tasks, several prior approaches have focused on facilitating these tasks. A dynamic analysis platform analyzes full-stack JavaScript applications by abstracting away middleware communication, so it can be emulated in dynamic profiling scenarios [7]. [2] studies implicit relations between asynchronous and event-driven entities, spread over the client and server sides of a distributed execution. Static analysis based on formal reasoning calculus has been applied to understand how asynchronous communication constructs (i.e., *callback*, *promises*) are used in distributed event-based JavaScript programs [12,13]. These prior approaches conquer the complexity introduced by middleware functionality through abstraction and modeling techniques. However, modern middleware frameworks do not lend themselves easily to being abstracted away or modelled faithfully, due to a high variability in their execution behavior as a result of dissimilar configuration options and network volatility. My approach can effectively address many of these scenarios, in which it is advantageous to completely take middleware out of the picture, so the performed maintenance tasks can focus solely on the programmer-written code, adapting and perfecting it for the ever changing requirements.

3   Research Objectives and Progress

My dissertation research explores a radical notion: a centralized equivalent of a distributed application can serve as a faithful surrogate for various maintenance and evolutionary tasks. By taking all distribution and middleware harness out of the picture, my approach makes it possible for maintenance programmers to focus exclusively on the programmer-written code, adapting and perfecting it as required by ever changing requirements. In particular, my approach can be applied to various debugging tasks, security sandboxing [1], and fault-handling adaptations as shown in the Fig. 1.

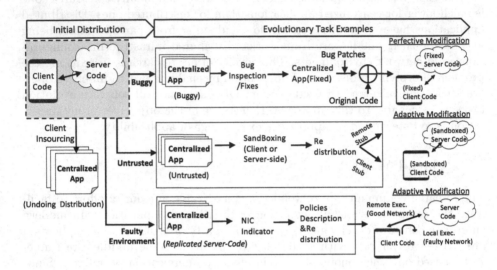

Fig. 1. Facilitated evolutionary tasks by using insourced surrogates

3.1 Progress So Far

The heterogeneity of the web architecture allows for flexible mixing of dissimilar languages and frameworks, used at the client and server ends of web applications. Nonetheless, using the same programming language for both the client and server parts is increasingly gaining prominence. Cross-platform web applications are written in JavaScript by using various application frameworks. These applications can run their client functionality in a web browser on any platform. The server functionality is typically implemented by means of the Node.js framework. Distributed applications, in which both the client and server parts are implemented in JavaScript are referred to as *full-stack JavaScript applications.*

Thus far, the focus of my dissertation research has been on the domain of full-stack JavaScript applications. The ability of operate in such a monolingual environment allows for making certain simplifying assumptions, required to create a working proof of concept. However, my long-term vision is to extend my approach to multilingual distributed applications, implemented and maintained in different languages. To that end, I plan to investigate how automatic language translation technologies can be applied to my code analysis and transformation infrastructure (See Fig. 2).

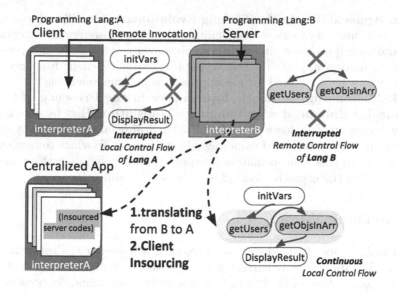

Fig. 2. Client Insourcing for multilingual distributed applications

To gain a deeper insight into the issues of automatic language translation, I explored how Java-to-Swift translations rules can be inferred from a set of cross-platform mobile applications, maintained in both languages to support both Android and iOS mobile users [3]. This experience has prepared me to be able to tackle the challenges of multilingual Client Insourcing and all the evolutionary modifications enabled by this refactoring.

Multilingual Virtual Machine (MVM) executes programs written in multiple programming languages within the same interpreter [8–10]. For multilingual distributed applications, this approach can be a viable alternative to translating the insourced code segments from the server language to the client one. With MVM, the insourced functionality can be integrated into the client code in the intermediate language-agnostic representation, thus bypassing the need for source-to-source translation.

4   Research Questions

My dissertation research is driven by the following general questions.

- **RQ1.** *Client Insourcing* **Value, Correctness, and Applicability**: How much programmer effort does Client Insourcing save? What are the preconditions for this refactoring's successful application? Can one identify those distributed functionalities to which Client Insourcing can be applied to create their centralized equivalent?

552 K. An

- **RQ2. Applicability to Facilitating Evolutionary Modifications**: What kind of evolutionary tasks can be facilitated by Client Insourcing? What architectural principles must distributed applications possess to be amenable to our modification approach? If an application cannot benefit from my approach, can it be refactored for my approach to become amenable?
- **RQ3. Maintaining Semantic Equivalence in the Presence of Client Insourcing Enhanced with Language Translation**: How feasible is it to maintain the business logic of a distributed multilingual application by transforming it into a centralized monolingual application? To which source/target languages can this transformation be applied? How much does this transformation affect the cognitive load of evolutionary modifications?

5 Remaining Work

The remaining work of this dissertation research will answer the research questions 2 and 3 above. I am currently investigating the applicability of Client Insourcing as a means of facilitating various evolutionary modifications of full-stack JavaScript applications. Centralized applications can be used as input for various automated distribution approaches, a research area that has received a lot of attention from the research community. For example, in our own research, we introduce compiler-based techniques that enable real-time systems to take advantage of trusted execution environments by automatically placing the functionality needing protection into a separate secure partition [11]. Finally, the automatically generated code of Client Insourcing can be used to put in place certain fault-handling strategies that handle various network communication problems. After this research is carried out and published, I then plan to apply my approach to multilingual distributed execution environments, with an initial target JavaScript client & Java server; due to the maturity of Java to JavaScript automatic translation tools, I am confident that it should be feasible to create a working proof of concept in a timely fashion.

6 Conclusions

In this manuscript, I have described my dissertation research, concerned with the challenges of evolving distributed applications to meet the continuously changing functional and non-functional requirements. My research puts forward a radical notion that a centralized equivalent can serve as a faithful proxy of a distributed application for many software maintenance and evolution tasks. We have successfully applied my approach to reduce the complexity of tracing and removing certain types of bugs in full-stack JavaScript applications. The remaining work will apply this approach to security sandboxing and fault-tolerance adaptations as well as extend the approach to distributed multilingual applications.

Acknowlegements. This research is supported by the NSF through the grants # 1650540 and 1717065.

References

1. Agten, P., Van Acker, S., Brondsema, Y., Phung, P.H., Desmet, L., Piessens, F.: JSand: complete client-side sandboxing of third-party JavaScript without browser modifications. In: Proceedings of the 28th Annual Computer Security Applications Conference, ACSAC 2012, pp. 1–10. ACM, New York (2012)
2. Alimadadi, S., Mesbah, A., Pattabiraman, K.: Understanding asynchronous interactions in full-stack JavaScript. In: Proceedings of the 38th International Conference on Software Engineering, ICSE 2016, pp. 1169–1180. ACM (2016)
3. An, K., Meng, N., Tilevich, E.: Automatic inference of Java-to-Swift translation rules for porting mobile applications. In: 2018 IEEE/ACM 5th International Conference on Mobile Software Engineering and Systems (MOBILESoft 2018), pp. 180–190, May 2018
4. An, K., Tilevich, E.: Catch & release: an approach to debugging distributed full-stack JavaScript applications. In: In: Bakaev, M., Frasincar, F., Ko, I.-Y. (eds.) ICWE 2019. LNCS, vol. 11496, pp. 459–473. Springer, Cham (2019)
5. Bennett, K.H., Rajlich, V.T.: Software maintenance and evolution: a roadmap. In: Proceedings of the Conference on the Future of Software Engineering, pp. 73–87. ACM (2000)
6. Chapin, N., Hale, J.E., Khan, K.M., Ramil, J.F., Tan, W.G.: Types of software evolution and software maintenance. J. Softw. Maint. Evol. Res. Pract. 13(1), 3–30 (2001)
7. Christophe, L., De Roover, C., Boix, E.G., De Meuter, W.: Orchestrating dynamic analyses of distributed processes for full-stack JavaScript programs. In: Proceedings of the 17th ACM SIGPLAN International Conference on Generative Programming: Concepts and Experiences, GPCE 2018, pp. 107–118. ACM (2018)
8. Grimmer, M., Schatz, R., Seaton, C., Würthinger, T., Luján, M.: Cross-language interoperability in a multi-language runtime. ACM Trans. Program. Lang. Syst. (TOPLAS) 40(2), 8 (2018)
9. Hirzel, M., Grimm, R.: Jeannie: granting Java native interface developers their wishes. In: ACM SIGPLAN Notices, vol. 42, pp. 19–38. ACM (2007)
10. Kell, S., Irwin, C.: Virtual machines should be invisible. In: Proceedings of the Compilation of the Co-located Workshops on DSM 2011, TMC 2011, AGERE! 2011, AOOPES 2011, NEAT 2011, & VMIL 2011, pp. 289–296. ACM (2011)
11. Liu, Y., An, K., Tilevich, E.: RT-trust: automated refactoring for trusted execution under real-time constraints. In: Proceedings of the 17th ACM SIGPLAN International Conference on Generative Programming: Concepts and Experiences, GPCE 2018, pp. 175–187. ACM (2018)
12. Madsen, M., Lhoták, O., Tip, F.: A model for reasoning about JavaScript promises. In: Proceedings of the ACM on Programming Languages (OOPSLA) (2017)
13. Madsen, M., Tip, F., Lhoták, O.: Static analysis of event-driven Node.js JavaScript applications. In: Proceedings of the 2015 ACM SIGPLAN International Conference on Object-Oriented Programming, Systems, Languages, and Applications, OOPSLA 2015, pp. 505–519. ACM (2015)

Effect-Driven Selection of Web of Things Services in Cyber-Physical Systems Using Reinforcement Learning

KyeongDeok Baek[✉] and In-Young Ko

School of Computing, Korea Advanced Institute of Science and Technology,
Daejeon, Republic of Korea
{kyeongdeok.baek,iko}@kaist.ac.kr

Abstract. Recently, Web of Things (WoT) expands its boundary to Cyber-physical Systems (CPS) that actuate or sense physical environments. However, there is no quantitative metric to measure the quality of physical effects generated by WoT services. Furthermore, there is no dynamic service selection algorithm that can be used to replace services with alternative ones to manage the quality of service provisioning. In this work, we study how to measure the effectiveness of delivering various types of WoT service effects to users, and develop a dynamic service handover algorithm using reinforcement learning to ensure the consistent provision of WoT services under dynamically changing conditions due to user mobility and changing availability of WoT media to deliver service effects. The preliminary results show that the simple distance-based metric is insufficient to select appropriate WoT services in terms of the effectiveness of delivering service effects to users, and the reinforcement-learning-based algorithm performs well with learning the optimal selection policy from simulated experiences in WoT environments.

Keywords: Service effectiveness ·
Effect-driven WoT service selection · Reinforcement learning ·
Cyber-physical System

1 Introduction

Cyber-physical systems (CPS) are the systems in which computational resources lie on abstract cyberspace and physical devices lie on physical spaces are connected and coordinated with each other to provide complex services that are necessary to accomplish users' goals [5]. Already there are many types of CPS that have been deployed in our urban environments such as smart homes, vehicle-to-everything (V2X), and smart factories. In particular, CPS has become an important part of Web of Things (WoT) because their key components are connected with each other via the Web, and it is essential to effectively find, access and utilize physical WoT resources that are necessary to accomplish users' goals.

I.-Y. Ko—Ph.D. Supervisor.

© Springer Nature Switzerland AG 2019
M. Bakaev et al. (Eds.): ICWE 2019, LNCS 11496, pp. 554–559, 2019.
https://doi.org/10.1007/978-3-030-19274-7_44

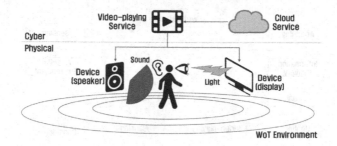

Fig. 1. WoT environments based on Cyber-physical Systems

Figure 1 shows an example of CPS-based WoT environment, that is divided in two layers, namely, cyber and physical layer, where traditional Web and WoT services are lied on the cyber layer, and physical devices and users are lied on the physical layer. Via actuating devices such as displays and speakers, a video-playing service in the cyber layer can deliver video contents to users by generating light and sound effects to the physical layer. Obviously, it is necessary to define the metrics to measure the quality of delivering service effects by WoT services to support users accomplishing their goals by providing services in required quality. Moreover, service selection problem, which is to select the most appropriate services among available candidates, becomes more challenging in WoT environments because of its physical-aware and highly dynamic nature.

In this work, we identify the essential characteristic of CPS that need to be considered to make WoT services to effectively interact with physical environments and human users while generating or sensing physical effects such as lights and sounds via physical media that are deployed over the physical environments. Especially, there are effect-generating services that produce and deliver physical effects to users, such as news-delivery and music-playing services as shown in Fig. 1. The quality of such effect-generating services affects users' satisfaction, so the selection of services should be done in a user-centric manner by evaluating how well the generated effects are delivered to the user. However, existing works on Web service selection only considers network-level quality of services (QoS) attributes, such as latency that affect the general quality perceived by users, but cannot reflect the quality of physical effects of the effect-generating services.

2 Research Issues

2.1 Service Effectiveness

Figure 2 shows an example categorization of WoT services, where solid boxes indicate categories and dashed boxes indicate an example service for each category. Most of the WoT services that interact with physical environments can be categorized as actuating or sensing services. In this work, we mainly focus on actuating services because actuating services can contribute directly to the accomplishment of users' goals by generating effects in physical environments,

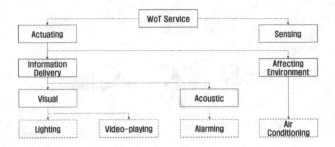

Fig. 2. Example categorization of WoT services

while the role of sensing services is simply about collecting information. Obviously, the effectiveness of such actuating services need to be evaluated differently according to their physical effects. However, to the best of our knowledge, there is no quantitative measure proposed to evaluate the quality of physical effects generated by WoT services, which we call *service effectiveness*. Therefore, it is necessary to model a specific effectiveness metric for each type of physical effects.

In addition, the physical effects generated by the actuating services may cause constructive or destructive interference when there are more than one effect generated in the same space. Moreover, in users' perspective, there can be service-level interference. For instance, the effectiveness of a movie-playing service increases if the associated display and speaker devices are located cohesively to each other in a space [1]. Another example is that if there is a service that generates bright illumination, it may cause glare and degrades the user's satisfaction on watching movies. Although there are some work done on analyzing the correlations among QoS attributes [4], there have been no efforts on modeling and measuring service-level interference in terms of delivering physical effects.

2.2 Predictive Service Selection and Dynamic Handover

Service provisioning in CPS environments needs to be done usually for a long time, and therefore, it is essential to ensure the required quality of services for a user task for a long period of time in a continuous and consistent manner. However, most of the existing dynamic service selection algorithms consider the quality of the candidate services at the time when they choose the services rather than considering the future quality of the services [11]. Especially in dynamic CPS environments, we cannot assume that the quality of a service that is monitored at a time when the service is selected will be remained the same throughout the service provisioning period. For instance, while a graphical content is shown to a user by using a nearby display device, if the user moves far from the device or the display suddenly blacked out, the content cannot be perceived by the user effectively anymore.

To deal with the above problem, we have identified two research directions. First, to maintain a certain level of service quality during a service provisioning period, dynamic service selection needs to be done in an iterative manner to replace some of the services that show degradation of their quality with alternative ones. We call this process as *dynamic service handover* [1,2]. Second, service selection should be done in a predictive manner, so that not only considering the current quality of services but also we can predict the future quality of services and make the service provisioning more stable. By performing predictive service selection, the number of handovers, which may cause service-migration overheads and service interruptions, can be minimized.

3   Previous Works

3.1   Service Effectiveness

In our previous works, we considered physical locations of mobile users and devices, and selected services that are located in a spatially cohesive manner centered by the user [1,2]. We defined a metric named *spatio-cohesiveness* to measure how the user and the selected services are located cohesively in terms of the devices associated with the services. However, one limitation of this method is that the services that are located cohesively cannot guarantee the effectiveness of delivering physical effects to users and improve the perceived service quality. As a counterexample, if we consider only spatio-cohesiveness, the service selection algorithm selects services based on the Euclidean distance between available candidates and the user, so the WoT devices that are associated with the selected services may be located behind a wall, and the user cannot perceive the effects that are generated by the devices.

In our on-going work, we define a rule-based model of visual service effectiveness, which evaluates whether the generated content can be perceived successfully by a user or not. The model was designed based on domain knowledge of the human vision system and simple physics of light, and contains three constraints. First, if the device is to far from the user, then the effectiveness is zero because the user cannot recognize the content correctly. Second, if the device is not in the Field of View (FoV) of the user, then effectiveness is zero because the user cannot perceive the light from the device at all. Third, if the device is not facing the user, then effectiveness is zero because the user would only see the back of the device. Finally, service effectiveness is 1 if all constraints are passed.

3.2   Predictive Service Selection and Dynamic Handover

In our previous works, we adopted a reinforcement learning algorithm to effectively select and dynamically handover services in a predictive manner [2]. Specifically, we developed a service selection agent that makes decisions of selecting services and trained the agent by using a reinforcement learning algorithm in a simulated WoT environments. We found that the agent could learn the optimal policy of selecting services in terms of spatio-cohesiveness. Our service selection agent is designed based on the Actor-Critic algorithm [7], Deep-Q Network (DQN) [10], and Deep Reinforcement Relevance Network (DRRN) [6].

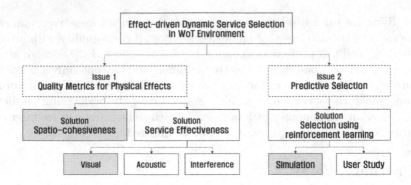

Fig. 3. Research road map

4   Research Plans

Figure 3 shows the research road map of this work, and the shaded boxes indicate the research issues that have been dealt in our previous works.

4.1   Service Effectiveness

Type-Specific Service Effectiveness Model. We have studied only the visual service effects, and we plan to investigate the ways of measuring the effectiveness of delivering acoustic effects. Furthermore, our current model of visual service effectiveness is a simple rule-based model, so we plan to evaluate and improve the practicality of the model by performing user-studies.

Service Interference. We plan to analyze service-level interference among the services that generate similar or different types of physical effects, and develop a service selection algorithm to choose cooperating services that have constructive interference and avoid destructive interference.

4.2   Predictive Service Selection and Dynamic Handover

Ideally, the training of our service selection agent should be done in real-world WoT environments, but we performed the training in simulated WoT environments. Training in real-world environments is known to be a challenging problem for reinforcement learning researchers because collecting real-world samples costs too much and difficult to make the agent experience the world in an iterative manner. We have two research directions regarding to this issue.

Virtual Reality-Powered User Study. First, we will perform user-studies in virtual WoT environments using Virtual Reality (VR) technologies. In some recent works, VR technologies are used to mimic psychological experiments through Web-based crowd sourcing platforms [9], and to let users experience elderly peoples' sight by reducing visual acuity virtually [8]. Currently, we are implementing virtual WoT environments using VR technologies to evaluate and improve our visual service effectiveness model.

Learn from Human Preferences. Second, in a recent work, the researchers studied how reinforcement learning agents can learn policies from guidance based on human preferences rather than from reward signals [3]. We plan to adopt this technique and conduct user studies to train our service selection agent following human preferences data examined by real users.

Acknowledgements. This work was supported by the National Research Foundation of Korea (NRF) grant funded by the Korea government (MSIT) (No. 2016R1A2B 4007585).

References

1. Baek, K.-D., Ko, I.-Y.: Spatially cohesive service discovery and dynamic service handover for distributed IoT environments. In: Cabot, J., De Virgilio, R., Torlone, R. (eds.) ICWE 2017. LNCS, vol. 10360, pp. 60–78. Springer, Cham (2017). https://doi.org/10.1007/978-3-319-60131-1_4
2. Baek, K.D., Ko, I.-Y.: Spatio-cohesive service selection using machine learning in dynamic IoT environments. In: Mikkonen, T., Klamma, R., Hernández, J. (eds.) ICWE 2018. LNCS, vol. 10845, pp. 366–374. Springer, Cham (2018). https://doi.org/10.1007/978-3-319-91662-0_30
3. Christiano, P.F., Leike, J., Brown, T., Martic, M., Legg, S., Amodei, D.: Deep reinforcement learning from human preferences. In: Advances in Neural Information Processing Systems, pp. 4299–4307 (2017)
4. Deng, S., Wu, H., Hu, D., Zhao, J.L.: Service selection for composition with QoS correlations. IEEE Trans. Serv. Comput. **9**(2), 291–303 (2016)
5. Gill, H., Midkiff, S.F.: Cyber-physical systems program solicitation (2009). https://www.nsf.gov/pubs/2008/nsf08611/nsf08611.htm
6. He, J., et al.: Deep reinforcement learning with an action space defined by natural language. In: Proceedings of the 2016 Workshop Tracks of International Conference for Learning Representations (ICLR) (2016)
7. Konda, V.R., Tsitsiklis, J.N.: Actor-critic algorithms. In: Advances in Neural Information Processing Systems, pp. 1008–1014 (2000)
8. Krösl, K., Bauer, D., Schwärzler, M., Fuchs, H., Suter, G., Wimmer, M.: A VR-based user study on the effects of vision impairments on recognition distances of escape-route signs in buildings. Vis. Comput. **34**, 911–923 (2018)
9. Ma, X., Cackett, M., Park, L., Chien, E., Naaman, M.: Web-based VR experiments powered by the crowd. In: Proceedings of the 2018 World Wide Web Conference on World Wide Web, pp. 33–43. International World Wide Web Conferences Steering Committee (2018)
10. Mnih, V., et al.: Human-level control through deep reinforcement learning. Nature **518**(7540), 529 (2015)
11. Moghaddam, M., Davis, J.G.: Service selection in web service composition: a comparative review of existing approaches. In: Bouguettaya, A., Sheng, Q., Daniel, F. (eds.) Web Services Foundations, pp. 321–346. Springer, New York (2014). https://doi.org/10.1007/978-1-4614-7518-7_13

Liquid Web Architectures

Andrea Gallidabino$^{(\boxtimes)}$ (iD)

Software Institute, Faculty of Informatics,
Università della Svizzera italiana (USI), Lugano, Switzerland
andrea.gallidabino@usi.ch
https://liquid.inf.usi.ch

Abstract. Nowadays users access the Web differently from what they used to in the past, the devices we use to fetch applications from the Web are not the same as the slow desktop computers that we owned twenty years ago. The Web can be accessed by devices with different sizes and capabilities, ranging from desktop to laptop computers, or even from tablets to phones. More recently, also smart and embedded devices, such as smart televisions, smart watches or parts of smart cars, are able to communicate with remote Web servers through the Web. The average number of Web-enabled devices owned by a single user has also increased and the connected user usually access the Web with multiple devices concurrently.

Web applications are traditionally designed having in mind a server-centric architecture, whereby the whole persistent data, dynamic state and logic of the application are stored and executed on the Web server. The endpoint client device running the Web browser traditionally only renders pre-computed views fetched from the server. As more data, state and computations are shifted to the client, it becomes more challenging to run Web applications across multiple devices while ensuring they can synchronize their state and react in real-time to changes of the set of available devices.

In this symposium we define how we apply the liquid software paradigm to the design of liquid Web applications and we identify and address the challenges of creating multi-device liquid user experiences. We discuss about how much is important to research on liquid software running on the Web. We also present our prototype framework called Liquid.js for Polymer, whose goal is to simplify the creation of liquid Web applications.

Keywords: Liquid software · Multi-device adaptation · Web design

1 Introduction

In the era of multiple device ownership [1], software applications are no longer ran strictly on a single device [6]. The liquid software [23] metaphor [25] associates the behavior of a fluid, which can adapt to the shape of its own container, to

© Springer Nature Switzerland AG 2019
M. Bakaev et al. (Eds.): ICWE 2019, LNCS 11496, pp. 560–565, 2019.
https://doi.org/10.1007/978-3-030-19274-7_45

software that can be deployed and can operate seamlessly across multiple devices owned by one or multiple users. Liquid software needs to adapt to the capabilities of a single device (e.g. responsive) and it must be able to adapt to the *set* of devices running the application.

The metaphor focuses on the expected liquid user experience when the users interact with applications deployed on multiple devices, in particular liquid software can: 1. adapt the user interface to the *set of* devices being concurrently used to run the application; 2. seamlessly migrate [21] the running application, or some part of it (e.g. individual components of the whole application), across multiple devices; 3. synchronize the state of the application distributed across all paired devices; 4. offload computations to neighbour paired devices in order to increase the overall performance of the application.

Web applications were traditionally developed following a thin client architecture whereby most of the logic and the entire persistent state of the application would be executed and stored on a central Web server [4]. Because of the different drivers in the design choices, traditional Web software architectures would offer only partial support for the liquid user experience [11]. However as the Web evolves, and as the Web technology standards increase in number and variety, we can evolve from traditional to new architectures suited for liquid software. For example, thanks to new communication protocols defined in the WebRTC standard, we can revisit the architectural design decision of traditional Web architectures and systematically study and design architectures driven by different software quality drivers.

2   Motivation

The development of liquid applications with high deployability, that can correctly operate and adapt their behavior in accordance to their deployment context on multiple devices, requires to address these issues at the design time. Liquid software deals with the following use cases scenarios [17]:

- **Sequential Use**: a single user runs an application on different devices at different times. The users can stop working on a device and resume their work on a new one. The application needs to be responsive and adapt to both devices and it needs to be able to resume the work accomplished by the user on the first device and display it in the new one.
- **Simultaneous Use**: a single user can access the application from several devices concurrently. The application needs to adapt to the set of devices, which can dynamically change over time, i.e. the users can connect to the application with new devices or can disconnect some of the devices. The devices can display a distributed view of the application user interface instead of just copying and adapting the user interface to each device. In the case of a distributed user interface, each device has a distinct role in the application [20].
- **Collaborative Use**: several users run the same application on their devices. The collaborative use case scenario can be either sequential or simultaneous.

All the scenarios share the same challenges in adapting the user interface to different devices and in synchronizing the data and state of the execution between them. The data and state synchronization is fundamental in the implementation of liquid software [23] because the devices and users need to be aware of the results of their actions previously or simultaneously done in other devices.

The liquid software ecosystem should allow the connection of heterogeneous devices and overcome the native software ecosystem boundaries. In this way, the developers need to implement the application once, which could then adapt itself and run on all kind of connected devices [7]. We realize the liquid software ecosystem by leveraging on the Web ecosystem, where applications are deployed on demand and through Responsive Web Design [22] are adapted to fit on the local device displays. Properties such as openness and freedom from proprietary features make the Web a natural choice over native applications that are bound to a particular operating system, manufacturer, or vendor-specific ecosystem [24].

Different solutions have been developed and researched during the past years on how liquid applications could be built, starting from server-centric approaches like the platform Joust developed in 1999 [19]. However, as the number of connected devices grows, a centralized approach is not enough and we need to switch to decentralized solutions and techniques, such as the Fluid computing middleware [5]. In the past years HTML5 standards led the Web to what Anthes called the *Web Revolution* [2]. The Web now is more developer-friendly and any device able to run a Web browser can run the same application on top of it even if the devices are completely different from one another. Thanks to the Web, liquid applications can automatically run across heterogeneous device environments by using frameworks like the Cross-Device [20] or Liquid.js for Polymer [9]. Even though most current Web applications have a strongly centralized architecture, we are quickly heading back towards the decentralized Web [3]. Shifting to a decentralized or distributed paradigm changes the way we are using the Web [18].

3   Research Questions

The objective of this research is to propose a way for developers to efficiently upgrade *solid* Web applications allowing them to become liquid. For this reason we are building a prototype framework that allows the creation of new liquid applications and the upgrading of already existing applications. By building such framework we aim to: – Show that it is possible to upgrade solid applications with all liquid features without the need to completely redesign and build the whole software again. Since the solid behavior of the software should be unaffected, we aim to add the liquid behavior of the software *around* the application itself, successfully decoupling the liquid functionalities from the solid behavior of the software. – Evaluate the overhead of the added liquid behavior on top of the solid application. From the developer's point of view, the added liquid behavior of the software should not affect the non-functional quality attributes of the solid application (such as performance, scalability, ...). However, since it is not possible to upgrade a software without affecting any of its qualities, we aim to study the trade-offs so that the execution of the application remains unaffected. From the user's perspective the Liquid User Experience should be as performant as the environment allows. The liquid software should minimize latency in the synchronization between devices, while also trying to minimize bandwidth and memory usage.

The goal of research is to answer the following research questions: – **RQ. 1**: *How can we allow Web developers to design liquid software and liquid User Experiences?* Liquid Web applications are complex software solutions able to interact with multiple devices simultaneously. The complexity of these interactions is transparently hidden behind the liquid User Experience and requires real-time message passing and data synchronization among all the connected devices in order to seamlessly move applications among them. Liquid Web software can be designed following different quality attribute drivers and the design can be reflected into a multitude of different software architectures depending on the design alternatives that are selected during the design phase. What are the design alternatives related to liquid Web applications? What are the implication of such choices? – **RQ. 2**: *Can we abstract liquid Web applications away from the current strongly centralized deployment approaches?* The vast majority of Web applications implementing a liquid User Experience rely on centralized architectures and deployment, however interactions between the devices do not necessarily need to relay on a Web server and can happen directly between them. From the user perspective, this approach can preserve privacy, since the user data and all user interactions can be modeled to be synchronized independently from a centralized Web server deployed in the Cloud outside the user's control. What are the trade-off of this choice? – **RQ. 3**: *How can we make the liquid User Experience of a Web application automatically adapt to the set of connected devices?* Developers of liquid software should provide to the user a mechanism for populating all of their devices with pieces of the application they are running. For this reasons we must provide to the developers the tools for developing automatic complementary views. This allows the developers to have a certain degree of control on how the application is migrated across the devices, instead of exclusively let the user decide how the application deployment configuration will evolve over time. A misuse of the manual liquid User Experience may lead to non-intuitive deployment configurations which contradict with the developer expectations and intent. – **RQ. 4**: *How can we take advantage of all resources provided by the connected devices?* Any connected device has access to at least a screen, a data storage and a CPU. While the Liquid User Experience takes advantage of all the screens and the decentralized synchronization can take advantage of all the provided data storages, we need to further develop a mechanism for efficiently exploit the CPUs of all connected devices in the liquid software environment. Without such a mechanism all the devices computes the same operation multiple times, even if it would be better to compute the operation in a single device and then broadcast the result.

4   Contributions

So far we have published and presented papers relative both to the design of liquid architectures and to Liquid.js for Polymer: – we modeled the *design space* of liquid software [15,16] where we discussed the implications and the relative design decisions of liquid software; – we studied the architectures of liquid applications and derived the *maturity model* for liquid architectures [11]. In the maturity model we describe the evolution of liquid applications in the Web and abstract their design from the technologies employed in the system, moreover we describe the driver quality attributes associated to each level of the maturity model. – We have several contributions related to Liquid.js for Polymer. In [10] we show how we design the migration of Web components between devices, in [9] we discuss the design of the distributed state in the framework, and in [8] we discuss how to handle child liquid components instantiated inside parent liquid components. We presented the Liquid.js API in [13], the decentralized view adaptation in [12] and the complementary view adaptation in [14].

References

1. Anderson, M.: Technology device ownership: 2015 (2015). http://www.pewinternet.org/2015/10/29/technology-device-ownership-2015/
2. Anthes, G.: HTML5 leads a web revolution. Commun. ACM **55**(7), 16–17 (2012)
3. Berners-Lee, T.: Re-Decentralizing the Web - Some Strategic Questions. Keynote Address at Decentralized Web Summit (2016)
4. Berners-Lee, T., Fischetti, M., Foreword By-Dertouzos, M.L.: Weaving the Web: The Original Design and Ultimate Destiny of the World Wide Web by its Inventor. HarperInformation (2000)
5. Bourges-Waldegg, D., Duponchel, Y., Graf, M., Moser, M.: The fluid computing middleware: bringing application fluidity to the mobile internet. In: Proceedings of the IEEE International Symposium on Applications and the Internet (SAINT 2005), pp. 54–63 (2005)
6. Di Geronimo, L., Husmann, M., Norrie, M.C.: Surveying personal device ecosystems with cross-device applications in mind. In: Proceedings of the 5th ACM International Symposium on Pervasive Displays, pp. 220–227. ACM (2016)
7. Feiner, S., Shamash, A.: Hybrid user interfaces: breeding virtually bigger interfaces for physically smaller computers. In: Proceedings of the 4th Annual ACM Symposium on User Interface Software and Technology, pp. 9–17. ACM (1991)
8. Gallidabino, A.: Migrating and pairing recursive stateful components between multiple devices with Liquid.js for polymer. In: Bozzon, A., Cudre-Maroux, P., Pautasso, C. (eds.) ICWE 2016. LNCS, vol. 9671, pp. 555–558. Springer, Cham (2016). https://doi.org/10.1007/978-3-319-38791-8_47
9. Gallidabino, A., Pautasso, C.: Deploying stateful web components on multiple devices with Liquid.js for polymer. In: Proceedings of Component-Based Software Engineering (CBSE2016), pp. 85–90. IEEE (2016)
10. Gallidabino, A., Pautasso, C.: The Liquid.js framework for migrating and cloning stateful web components across multiple devices. In: Proceedings of the 25th International Conference on the World Wide Web (WWW 2016), Demonstrations, pp. 183–186 (2016)

11. Gallidabino, A., Pautasso, C.: Maturity model for liquid web architectures. In: Cabot, J., De Virgilio, R., Torlone, R. (eds.) ICWE 2017. LNCS, vol. 10360, pp. 206–224. Springer, Cham (2017). https://doi.org/10.1007/978-3-319-60131-1_12
12. Gallidabino, A., Pautasso, C.: Decentralized computation offloading on the edge with liquid WebWorkers. In: Mikkonen, T., Klamma, R., Hernández, J. (eds.) ICWE 2018. LNCS, vol. 10845, pp. 145–161. Springer, Cham (2018). https://doi.org/10.1007/978-3-319-91662-0_11
13. Gallidabino, A., Pautasso, C.: The liquid user experience API. In: Companion of the The Web Conference 2018 on The Web Conference 2018 (TheWebConf2018), pp. 767–774 (2018)
14. Gallidabino, A., Pautasso, C.: Multi-device adaptation with liquid media queries. In: Bakaev, M. (ed.) 18th International Conference On Web Engineering (ICWE 2019). LNCS, vol. 11946, pp. 474–489. Springer (2019)
15. Gallidabino, A., et al.: On the architecture of liquid software: technology alternatives and design space. In: Proceedings of WICSA, pp. 122–127. IEEE (2016)
16. Gallidabino, A., Pautasso, C., Mikkonen, T., Systa, K., Voutilainen, J.P., Taivalsaari, A.: Architecting liquid software. J. Web Eng. **16**(5&6), 433–470 (2017)
17. Google: The new multi-screen world: Understanding cross-platform consumer behavior (2012). http://services.google.com/fh/files/misc/multiscreenworld_final.pdf
18. Grundy, J., Wang, X., Hosking, J.: Building multi-device, component-based, thin-client groupware: issues and experiences. In: Australian Computer Science Communications, vol. 24, pp. 71–80. Australian Computer Society, Inc. (2002)
19. Hartman, J.J., Bigot, P., Bridges, P., Montz, B., Piltz, R., Spatscheck, O., Proebsting, T., Peterson, L.L., Bavier, A., et al.: Joust: a platform for liquid software. Computer **32**(4), 50–56 (1999)
20. Husmann, M., Marcacci Rossi, N., Norrie, M.C.: Usage analysis of cross-device web applications. In: Proceedings 5th ACM International Symposium on Pervasive Displays, pp. 212–219. ACM (2016)
21. Luff, P., Heath, C.: Mobility in collaboration. In: Proceedings of the 1998 ACM Conference on Computer Supported Cooperative Work, pp. 305–314. ACM (1998)
22. Marcotte, E.: Responsive Web Design. Editions Eyrolles (2011)
23. Mikkonen, T., Systä, K., Pautasso, C.: Towards liquid web applications. In: Cimiano, P., Frasincar, F., Houben, G.-J., Schwabe, D. (eds.) ICWE 2015. LNCS, vol. 9114, pp. 134–143. Springer, Cham (2015). https://doi.org/10.1007/978-3-319-19890-3_10
24. Mikkonen, T., Taivalsaari, A.: Cloud computing and its impact on mobile software development: two roads diverged. J. Syst. Softw. **86**(9), 2318–2320 (2013)
25. Taivalsaari, A., Mikkonen, T., Systa, K.: Liquid software manifesto: the era of multiple device ownership and its implications for software architecture. In: 38th Computer Software and Applications Conference (COMPSAC2014), pp. 338–343 (2014)

Tutorials

Exploiting Side Information
for Recommendation

Qing Guo[1]([✉]), Zhu Sun[2], and Yin-Leng Theng[1]

[1] Nanyang Technological University, 50 Nanyang Ave, Singapore 639798, Singapore
{qguo006,tyltheng}@ntu.edu.sg
[2] Shopee, 2 Science Park Drive, Singapore 118222, Singapore
zhu.sun@shopee.com

Abstract. Recommender systems have become extremely essential tools to help resolve the *information overload* problem for users. However, traditional recommendation techniques suffer from critical issues such as *data sparsity* and *cold start* problems. To address these issues, a great number of recommendation algorithms have been proposed by exploiting the side information. This tutorial aims to provide a comprehensive analysis of how to exploit various kinds of side information for improving recommendation performance. Specifically, we present the usage of side information from two perspectives: the representation and methodology. By this tutorial, researchers of recommender system would gain an in-depth understanding of how side information can be utilized for better recommendation performance.

1 Introduction

Recommender systems are indispensable tools to help tackle with the *information overload* problem [2]. However, with merely relying on user-item interaction data, traditional recommender systems inherently suffer from the *data sparsity* (i.e., most users only rate a small portion of items) and *cold start* (i.e., new users merely rate few items) issues [12]. To address such issues, a number of recommendation algorithms have been designed by leveraging the valuable side information of users, items and their interactions to compensate for the insufficiency of rating information [4,5,7,13,17].

This tutorial provides a comprehensive analysis of state-of-the-art recommendation approaches with side information in a principle way from two perspectives: representation and methodology. By the end of this tutorial, the audiences would know how the recommendation approaches evolve with more complicated representations and methodologies for using various kinds of side information.

Various Representations. This section introduces two common ways of organizing side information (or features) in both flat and hierarchical representations.

- Flat features (FF) are mainly explored by early studies, where the features are organized independently in the same layer [7,10,16]. Such kind of side

© Springer Nature Switzerland AG 2019
M. Bakaev et al. (Eds.): ICWE 2019, LNCS 11496, pp. 569–573, 2019.
https://doi.org/10.1007/978-3-030-19274-7_46

information can be utilized for better modeling the characteristics of users or items. Many content-based recommender systems have been developed by extensively using FF.

- Feature hierarchy (FH) is a natural yet powerful structure to human knowledge, providing a machine- and human-readable description of features and the *affiliatedTo* relations among them. FH has been proven to be more effective to achieve high-quality recommendation than FF [5,6,13].
- Knowledge graph (KG) connects various types of features in a unified global representation space. KG helps with the inference of subtler user or item relations from different angles, which are difficult to uncover with the homogeneous information [11,17,18].

Various Methodologies. Early approaches with side information are mainly memory-based, which are ineffective due to the time-consuming search in the user or item space [8,10]. Thus, many prevalent recommendation algorithms with side information are devised based on more advanced models, including association rule, clustering, topic model, regression, factorization, representation learning and deep neural network. Factorization, representation learning and deep learning based models have been widely investigated in recent research:

- Factorization model (FM) can incorporate different kinds of side information [12], such as matrix factorization (MF), tensor factorization (TF) and SVD++, etc. They model users' behavior patterns by employing global statistical information of user-item interaction data. The basic idea is that both users and items can be characterized by a few latent vectors.
- Representation learning (RL) based recommendation methods have proven to be effective in capturing local item relations by modeling item co-occurrence in individual user's interaction record [1]. Some researchers attempt to integrate side information into RL models that help learn better user and item embeddings, thus achieving further performance enhancements for recommendation [3,16].
- Deep neural network (DNN) has recently attracted major research interests from the recommendation community. In contrast to factorization and RL based methods, DNN based recommendation models can learn nonlinear latent representations. Both structural (e.g., social networks, knowledge graph) and non-structural side information (visual, textual content) can be exploited by DNN models [9,15].

2   Tutorial Outlines

As this tutorial covers a variety of research topics about employing side information for recommendation, it should be organized in a structural way as below:

- Introduction (10 min).
    - A brief introduction to the history of recommender systems.
    - What are the traditional recommendation algorithms?

- What are the limitations of traditional recommendation algorithms?
  - What is side information and why does it can help create more effective recommender system?
- Various representations (60 min).
  - How are flat features utilized?
  - How are feature hierarchy utilized?
  - An introduction to our works [4,14].
  - An introduction to other representation methods for side information.
- Break (30 min).
- Various methodologies (75 min).
  - An introduction to memory-based models and their limitations.
  - How does factorization model use side information?
  - How does representation learning use side information?
  - How does deep neural network use side information.
  - An introduction to our works [13,15].
- Conclusion and future directions (5 min).

3   Biographies and Expertise of Tutors

Qing Guo is a part-time Ph.D. student in Wee Kim Wee School of Communication and Information at Nanyang Technological University. He focuses on Point-of-Interest (POI) recommendation by exploiting the heterogeneous information in location-based social networks. He obtained his M.Sc. in The University of Hong Kong in 2014 and B.E. from University of Electronic Science and Technology of China in 2013. While doing Ph.D. study, he was also a research associate in SAP Innovation Center network from 2015 to 2018, where he participated in machine learning products development in SAP products. Now, he is a data scientist in Shopee and continue to work on recommendation research and applications.

Zhu Sun is a data scientist in Shopee, Singapore. She obtained her Ph.D. degree from Nanyang Technological Univeristy in 2018. She received M.E. in 2016 and B.E. in 2013 from Yanshan University, China. Her research is highly related to artificial intelligence. Specifically, she mainly focus on applying data mining and machine learning techniques to design effective recommender systems. She is interested in leveraging side information to address data sparsity and cold start problems of recommender systems.

Yin-Leng Theng is Professor and Director of the Centre of Healthy and Sustainable Cities (CHESS) at Wee Kim Wee School of Communication and Information, and Research Director at the Research Strategy and Coordination Unit (President's Office) at Nanyang Technological University. Her research interests are mainly in user-centred design, interaction design and usability engineering. She has participated in varying capacities as principal investigator, co-investigator and collaborator in numerous research projects in the United Kingdom and Singapore since 1998.

References

1. Barkan, O., Koenigstein, N.: Item2vec: neural item embedding for collaborative filtering. In: IEEE 26th International Workshop on MLSP, pp. 1–6. IEEE (2016)
2. Desrosiers, C., Karypis, G.: A comprehensive survey of neighborhood-based recommendation methods. In: Ricci, F., Rokach, L., Shapira, B., Kantor, P.B. (eds.) Recommender Systems Handbook, pp. 107–144. Springer, Boston, MA (2011). https://doi.org/10.1007/978-0-387-85820-3_4
3. Grbovic, M., et al.: E-commerce in your inbox: product recommendations at scale. In: KDD, pp. 1809–1818. ACM (2015)
4. Guo, Q., Sun, Z., Zhang, J., Chen, Q., Theng, Y.L.: Aspect-aware point-of-interest recommendation with geo-social influence. In: UMAP, pp. 17–22. ACM (2017)
5. He, R., Lin, C., Wang, J., McAuley, J.: Sherlock: sparse hierarchical embeddings for visually-aware one-class collaborative filtering. arXiv preprint arXiv:1604.05813 (2016)
6. Kanagal, B., Ahmed, A., Pandey, S., Josifovski, V., Yuan, J., Garcia-Pueyo, L.: Supercharging recommender systems using taxonomies for learning user purchase behavior. Proc. VLDB Endowment (VLDB) 5(10), 956–967 (2012)
7. Lippert, C., Weber, S.H., Huang, Y., Tresp, V., Schubert, M., Kriegel, H.P.: Relation prediction in multi-relational domains using matrix factorization. In: NIPS Workshop, Citeseer (2008)
8. Liu, X., Liu, Y., Aberer, K., Miao, C.: Personalized point-of-interest recommendation by mining users' preference transition. In: CIKM, pp. 733–738. ACM (2013)
9. Niu, W., Caverlee, J., Lu, H.: Neural personalized ranking for image recommendation. In: WSDM, pp. 423–431. ACM (2018)
10. Sharma, M., Reddy, P.K., Kiran, R.U., Ragunathan, T.: Improving the performance of recommender system by exploiting the categories of products. In: Kikuchi, S., Madaan, A., Sachdeva, S., Bhalla, S. (eds.) DNIS 2011. LNCS, vol. 7108, pp. 137–146. Springer, Heidelberg (2011). https://doi.org/10.1007/978-3-642-25731-5_12
11. Shi, C., Liu, J., Zhuang, F., Philip, S.Y., Wu, B.: Integrating heterogeneous information via flexible regularization framework for recommendation. Knowl. Inf. Syst. 49(3), 835–859 (2016)
12. Shi, Y., Larson, M., Hanjalic, A.: Collaborative filtering beyond the user-item matrix: a survey of the state of the art and future challenges. CSUR 47(1), 3 (2014)
13. Sun, Z., Yang, J., Zhang, J., Bozzon, A.: Exploiting both vertical and horizontal dimensions of feature hierarchy for effective recommendation. In: AAAI, pp. 189–195 (2017)
14. Sun, Z., Yang, J., Zhang, J., Bozzon, A., Chen, Y., Xu, C.: MRLR: multi-level representation learning for personalized ranking in recommendation. In: IJCAI, pp. 2807–2813 (2017)
15. Sun, Z., Yang, J., Zhang, J., Bozzon, A., Huang, L.K., Xu, C.: Recurrent knowledge graph embedding for effective recommendation. In: RecSys, pp. 297–305 (2018)
16. Vasile, F., Smirnova, E., Conneau, A.: Meta-prod2vec: Product embeddings using side-information for recommendation. In: RecSys, pp. 225–232. ACM (2016)

17. Wang, X., Wang, D., Xu, C., He, X., Cao, Y., Chua, T.S.: Explainable reasoning over knowledge graphs for recommendation. arXiv preprint arXiv:1811.04540 (2018)
18. Wang, Y., Xia, Y., Tang, S., Wu, F., Zhuang, Y.: Flickr group recommendation with auxiliary information in heterogeneous information networks. Multimedia Syst. **23**(6), 703–712 (2017)

Deep Learning-Based Sequential Recommender Systems: Concepts, Algorithms, and Evaluations

Hui Fang[1(✉)], Guibing Guo[2], Danning Zhang[1], and Yiheng Shu[2]

[1] Shanghai University of Finance and Economics, Shanghai, China
fang.hui@mail.shufe.edu.cn, zhangdanning5@gmail.com
[2] Northeastern University, Shenyang, China
guogb@swc.neu.edu.cn, shuyiheng29@gmail.com
http://riis.shufe.edu.cn/index.php/people/faculty/hui-fang
https://www.librec.net/luckymoon.me/

Abstract. What is sequential recommendation? What challenges are traditional sequential recommendation models facing? How to address these challenges in sequential recommendation using advanced deep learning (DL) techniques? What factors do affect the performance of a DL-based sequential recommendation system? And how to utilize these factors to improve DL models? In this tutorial, we will carefully answer these questions by combining DL techniques with sequential recommendation, and provide a comprehensive overview of DL-based sequential recommender system. Specifically, we propose a novel classification framework for sequential recommendation tasks, with which we systematically introduce representative DL-based algorithms for different sequential recommendation scenarios. We further summarize the potentially influential factors of DL-based sequential recommendation, and thoroughly demonstrate their effects via a carefully designed experimental framework, which will be of great help to future research.

Keywords: Sequential recommendation · Deep learning techniques

1 Motivation and Overview

Similar to a typical recommendation task, the focus of sequential recommendation is to model user's preferences on items. The difference is that items are listed in a ordered sequence, for example in e-commerce, sequence is commonly called as a session [5]. Specifically, sequential recommendation focuses more on sequential information such as behavioral patterns and sequential dependencies among items [3]. It takes the user's past behaviors as input, detects behavior patterns, models sequential dependencies, and uses them to develop recommendations that match the preference of individual users. Thus, traditional sequential recommender systems are particularly interested in employing appropriate

© Springer Nature Switzerland AG 2019
M. Bakaev et al. (Eds.): ICWE 2019, LNCS 11496, pp. 574–577, 2019.
https://doi.org/10.1007/978-3-030-19274-7_47

and effective machine learning approaches to model sequential information, such as Markov Chain [2] and session-based KNN [1].

In recent years, deep learning (DL) techniques obtain tremendous achievements in nature language processing [4], demonstrating their effectiveness in processing sequence data. Thus, they have attracted an increasing interest in sequential recommender systems, and many DL-based models achieved state-of-the-art performance [6].

In this tutorial, we focus on the DL-based recommender systems. The main highlights of this tutorial are as follows:

- We will give a comprehensive overview of sequential recommender systems based on DL techniques.
- We will show an original classification framework for sequential recommendation, corresponding to three different recommendation scenarios, and then introduce the representative algorithms under each scenario.
- We will summarize the influential factors for typical DL-based sequential recommendation and demonstrate their effects by empirical studies, which can serve as a guidance for sequential recommendation research and practices.

2 Target Audience and Learning Objectives

This tutorial will cover topics related to DL and sequential recommendation. The target audience of this tutorial are researchers and practitioners who are interested in sequential recommendation or deep learning. Through this tutorial, the participants will get a comprehensive overview of deep learning based sequential recommender systems and understand how different DL techniques model deal with different types of behavioral sequences, what are the main influential factors of DL-based sequential recommenders and how to take advantage of these factors to improve model performances.

3 Outline of the Tutorial

3.1 Introduction

1. How to define a sequential recommendation problem? How do they distinguish from other recommendation tasks such as rating prediction or top-k item recommendation models?
2. What are the major types of sequential recommender systems in terms of the different input data (e.g., behavior trajectories) and what are the prediction goals for each type?
3. What are the typical DL techniques applied to sequential recommendation? What are their strengths?
4. What are the advantages of DL-based algorithms in contrast with traditional sequential recommendation algorithms? What are the suitable scenarios for both the traditional recommendation approaches and DL techniques?

3.2   Categorization of the Sequential Recommendation Systems

We design a categorization of the sequential recommendation algorithms in the literature from two perspectives: action objects (i.e., different sequential information) and user representation (i.e., whether to distinguish different users).

1. **Categorization based on action objects.** What forms of action object exist in the sequence data? How does the model handle different types of action objects? We analyze the next-item recommendation and the next-basket recommendation.
2. **Categorization based on user representation.** Does the model include user modeling modules? How does the model represent the relationship between users and sequences? Does it model user representation based on behavior sequence or other ancillary information such as user identification? We analyze the implicit and explicit user representations.

3.3   DL-Based Algorithms

In terms of the aforementioned categorization, we specifically present the definition and representative DL algorithms for each recommendation scenario:

1. **Experience**-based sequential recommendation. The input is user's behavior trajectory with the same item. The goal is to predict next item under a target action type.
2. **Transaction**-based sequential recommendation. The input is user's behavior trajectory with same action type but different action objects. The goal is to predict next action object.
3. **Interaction**-based sequential recommendation. The input is user's behavior trajectory with multiple action types and different action objects. The goal is to predict both the action type and the action object.

3.4   Empirical Evaluations

In this section, we summarize the influential factors for typical DL-based sequential recommendation, and show how we validate them through experiments.

1. **Influential Factors.** What are the major factors that possibly influence the performance of DL-based recommender systems? How and to what extent do they improve the performance?
2. **Empirical Experiment.** Through a specially designed experimental framework, we strive to answer: how does the performance change with the change of these factors? How should we utilize each factor to improve DL models?

3.5   Challenges and Future Directions

In this section, we conclude our tutorial by summarizing challenges and research directions based on our categorization and evaluation.

4 Similar Tutorials

Sequence-aware Recommender Systems (https://www.um.org/umap2018/tutorial/index.html, UMAP 2018, Singapore) - This tutorial focuses on sequence-aware recommender systems [3], which contains a large number of non-deep-learning methods. The main difference is that our tutorial will specifically focus on DL methods, and demonstrate their advantages and disadvantages.

5 Presenters

Dr. Hui Fang is an Assistant Professor in Research Institute for Interdisciplinary Sciences. She received her Ph.D. from the School of Computer Engineering, Nanyang Technological University, Singapore. Her main research interests include trust prediction in online communities, personalized product/social recommendation, link prediction and data-driven decision making. Her research has been published in top conferences like IJCAI, AAA and AAMAS. Presently she is the Associate Editor of the ECRA journal, and invited referees of other journals like TKDE, Cybernetics, and DSS. She also serves as a Program Committee Member for international conferences, including UMAP and IJCAI, etc.

Dr. Guibing Guo is an Associate Professor in the Software College, Northeastern University, Shenyang, China. He received a Ph.D degree in computer science at Nanyang Technological University, and did a post-doc at Singapore Management University. His research interests include recommender systems, deep learning, social network analysis and data mining. The main research focus is to resolve the challenges of recommender systems, including data sparsity, cold start, diversity and so on. He is the original author (and now the team leader) of the open-source library for recommender systems, LibRec, which implements a large number (over 90) of recommender algorithms.

References

1. Davidson, J., et al.: The YouTube video recommendation system. In: Proceedings of the Fourth ACM Conference on Recommender Systems, pp. 293–296. ACM (2010)
2. He, R., McAuley, J.: Fusing similarity models with Markov chains for sparse sequential recommendation. In: 2016 IEEE 16th International Conference on Data Mining (ICDM), pp. 191–200. IEEE (2016)
3. Quadrana, M., Cremonesi, P., Jannach, D.: Sequence-aware recommender systems. ACM Comput. Surv. (2018)
4. Samanta, S., Mehta, S.: Towards crafting text adversarial samples. arXiv preprint arXiv:1707.02812 (2017)
5. Wang, S., Cao, L., Wang, Y.: A survey on session-based recommender systems. arXiv preprint arXiv:1902.04864 (2019)
6. Zhang, S., Yao, L., Sun, A., Tay, Y.: Deep learning based recommender system: a survey and new perspectives. ACM Comput. Surv. (CSUR) (2019)

Architectures Server-Centric vs Mobile-Centric for Developing WoT Applications

Javier Berrocal$^{(\boxtimes)}$ (iD), Jose Garcia-Alonso (iD), and Juan Manuel Murillo (iD)

Escuela Politécnica, Quercus Software Engineering Group,
University of Extremadura, Avda. de la Universidad s/n, 10003 Cáceres, Spain
{jberolm,jgaralo,juanmamu}@unex.es

Abstract. The massive adoption of smart devices has fostered the development of Web of Things (WoT) applications. Due to the limited capabilities of these devices (some of them are battery powered, or the data exchange is limited), these applications have very stringent requirements. The success or failure of these applications largely depends on how they address these requirements, being the resource consumption a crucial one. Our experience has shown us that with different architectural styles we can obtain a similar behaviour, but the selected style directly impacts on the resource consumption. During the last few years, different frameworks, tools and activities have been proposed to estimate this consumption in early development phases in order to guide the decision making process. However, they are still not incorporated by the industry and researchers. This tutorial delves into different architectural styles that can be applied and what tools can be used to early estimate their consumption.

Keywords: Web of Things · Web application development ·
Mobile-centric · Server-centric

1 Introduction

End devices capabilities have increased tremendously. During the last few years, their storage and computational capabilities have increased in order to sense more information from the environment and execute more complex tasks. For instance, virtual assistants can identify what people are saying and interact with surrounding devices depending on their commands. This increase in the devices capacities has favoured the deployment of paradigms such as WoT (Web of Things), where they are integrated to the Web. This integration allows different devices to coordinate and their services to be consumed by any application; hence making them more accessible for applications and humans [7].

A constrained factor of these devices is the resource consumption (battery, data traffic, etc.). Many of these devices, such as mobile phones, smart speakers,

© Springer Nature Switzerland AG 2019
M. Bakaev et al. (Eds.): ICWE 2019, LNCS 11496, pp. 578–581, 2019.
https://doi.org/10.1007/978-3-030-19274-7_48

humidity and temperature sensors, etc. are battery powered. Likewise, some of them have to interact using the mobile network, either because they are mobile or because of their specific situation, which entails a consumption of the data tariff. In the development of WoT applications integrating these devices, the correct management of these resources is crucial for user satisfaction. It is well known that resource consumption, is a factor determining the success of WoT applications [8].

The consumption of a WoT application is substantially determined by the architectural style applied. The most widely extended architecture used by these applications and devices is server-centric, in which end devices act as simple clients sending the sensed information to the cloud and getting the actions to execute from it. This architectural style makes sense for those devices that do not have enough capabilities for storing and computing the sensed information. Nevertheless, there are other emerging mobile-centric architectures [6] that exploit the capabilities of end devices to improve the user experience. For instance, reducing the response time by using data closer to, or even inside, the targeted device. Resource consumption is also a concern for these architectures [2]. Server and mobile-centric architectures could be similar to centralized and distributed architectures. Initially, one might think that the behaviors implemented with one, can not be achieved with the other. Our experience has shown us that similar behaviors can be obtained with both, but that their main difference lies in the resource consumption [4]. Thus, for a greater likelihood of success, the development life cycle of WoT applications should include an early analysis of the resource consumption of different architectural styles.

During the last few years, researchers have been working on defining methods for measuring in real-time the consumption of an application, conceptual frameworks guiding developers on an early estimation of the consumption or including activities in the development process for that specific purpose. Now, all these techniques should be incorporated by researchers and the WoT application development industry.

In this tutorial we will detail different architectural styles that can be used for the development of WoT applications, when and how the consumption of a mobile application should be estimated, which software tools could assist in this process and which tools could be used for the deployment of this application on both Cloud environments and end devices.

2   Tutorial Structure

This tutorial has a duration of half-day (three hours) including both lectures and practical activities. It is divided into three parts:

- First, lectures will be focused on highlighting the importance of selecting a correct architectural style for improving the user experience. Different architectural styles will be detailed and a running example developed with the different styles will be shown to open a small debate about which style would be the most appropriate one.

- Secondly, we will introduce the resource consumption of WoT applications as another dimensions that has to be taken into account during the architectural decision making process. To estimate this consumption, a new developed tool will be explained [3]. This tool allows developers to estimate and compare in early phases the resource consumption of an application. This tool is based on previous works of the presenters [4]. To use this tool, developers should have a basic knowledge of JSON [5], since it is the language used to provide information about the functionalities of the application and to obtain consumption estimates.
- The last part of the tutorial will be focused on the deployment of WoT applications on smart devices (such as smart phones). To that end, we will explain how an application detailed using the OpenAPI standard [1] could be deployed on both a Cloud environment or an end device.

This tutorial and the related tools have not been previously presented in other conferences.

3   Learning Objectives

At the end of the tutorial, attendees will get knowledge on:

- Architectural styles that can be applied to develop WoT applications.
- Awareness about the resource consumption as an important dimension to take into account in this process.
- Tools for estimating in an early phase the resource consumption.
- Tools for deploying an initial design of a WoT application.

4   Intended Audience

The tutorial is designed for both industrial and academic attendees with an interest on developing WoT applications taking into account the resources they consume. The technical background desirable to follow the workshops is: being able to read JSON and YAML files. It will not be a requirement to know the OpenAPI specification, since the most important objects will be explained during the tutorial.

In order to participate in the hands-on part of the tutorial, a laptop with a text editor and a Web browser will be required.

5   Biographies of Presenters

During the last few years, the presenters have worked on measuring the resource consumption of mobile applications, proposing a conceptual framework that can be used by developers to get some early estimations [4]. In addition, the presenters also work in new mobile computational models for storing, computing and sharing the information gathered by an end device. Below, a brief biography of the presenters can be found.

Javier Berrocal is an associate professor in the Department of Informatics and Telematics System Engineering at the University of Extremadura (Spain) and co-founder of the company Gloin. He received a PhD degree (with European Mention) in 2014. His main research interests are Mobile Computing, Context-Awareness, Pervasive Systems, Internet of Things and Web of Things.

José García-Alonso is an associate professor in the Department of Informatics and Telematics System Engineering at the University of Extremadura (Spain) and co-founder of the Startups Gloin and Viable. He received a PhD degree (with European Mention) in 2014. His main research interests are eHealth-Care, eldercare, Mobile Computing, Context-Awareness and Pervasive Systems.

Juan Manuel Murillo is a full professor of software engineering at the University of Extremadura and co-founder of the Startups Gloin and Viable. His research interests include software architectures, mobile computing and cloud computing.

Acknowledgments. This work was supported by the Spanish Ministry of Science and Innovation through projects TIN2015-69957-R), by the Department of Economy and Infrastructure of the Government of Extremadura (GR18112, IB18030), and by the European Regional Development Fund and by 4IE project (0045-4IE-4-P) funded by the Interreg V-A España-Portugal (POCTEP) 2014-2020 program.

References

1. The OpenAPI Specification Repository. Contribute to OAI/OpenAPI-Specification development by creating an account on GitHub. https://github.com/OAI/OpenAPI-Specification
2. Hirsch, M., Rodriguez, J.M., Zunino, A., Mateos, C.: Battery-aware centralized schedulers for CPU-bound jobs in mobile grids. Pervasive Mob. Comput. **29**(C), 73–94 (2016). https://doi.org/10.1016/j.pmcj.2015.08.003
3. Berrocal, J., Garcia-Alonso, J., Murillo, J.M.: Tool - early analysis of resource consumption patterns. https://api-consumptions.herokuapp.com
4. Berrocal, J., et al.: Early analysis of resource consumption patterns in mobile applications. Pervasive Mob. Comput. **35**, 32–50 (2017)
5. Crockford, D.: The application/JSON media type for Javascript object notation (JSON). Technical report (2006)
6. Guillén, J., Miranda, J., Berrocal, J., Garcia-Alonso, J., Murillo, J.M., Canal, C.: People as a service: a mobile-centric model for providing collective sociological profiles. IEEE Softw. **31**(2), 48–53 (2014)
7. Guinard, D., Trifa, V.: Building the Web of Things: With Examples in Node.Js and Raspberry Pi, 1st edn. Manning Publications Co., Greenwich (2016)
8. Qian, H., Andresen, D.: Extending mobile device's battery life by offloading computation to cloud. In: Abadi, A., Dig, D., Dubinsky, Y. (eds.) 2015 2nd ACM International Conference on Mobile Software Engineering and Systems, MOBILESoft 2015, Florence, Italy, May 16–17, 2015, pp. 150–151. IEEE (2015)

Powerful Data Analysis and Composition with the UNIX-Shell

Andreas Schmidt[1,2]([envelope]) [ORCID] and Steffen Scholz[2] [ORCID]

[1] University of Applied Sciences, Karlsruhe, Germany
[2] Karlsruhe Institute of Technology, Karlsruhe, Germany
{andreas.schmidt,steffen.scholz}@kit.edu

Abstract. In addition to a wide range of commercially available data processing tools for data analysis and knowledge discovery, there are a bundle of Unix-shell scripting and text processing tools practically available on every computer. This paper reports on some of these data processing tools and presents how they can be used together to manipulate and transform data and also to perform some sort of analysis like aggregation, etc. Beside the free availability, these tools have the advantage that they can be used immediately, without prior transformation and loading the data into the target system. Another important point is, that they are typically stream-based and thus, huge amounts of data can be processed without running out of main-memory.

Keywords: Unix-Shell · Filter and Pipes · Transformation of data

1 Introduction

The aim of this paper, and the corresponding tutorial presented at ICWE 2019 in Daejeon/Korea, is to present the most useful tools, e.g. *cat*, *grep*, *tr*, *sed*, *awk*, *comm*, *uniq*, *join*, *split*, etc., and to give an introduction on how they can be used together. So, for example, a wide number of queries which typically will be formulated with SQL, can also be performed using the aforementioned tools, as it will be shown in the tutorial. Also, selective data extraction from different webpages and the recombination of this information (mashups) can easily be performed.

2 Filters and Pipes

The underlying architectural pattern of the stream-based data processing is called filters and pipes [1], originally suggested by McIllroy et al. [2]. The general idea is to utilize a bunch of useful programs (filters) that can be stick together using pipes (loose coupling). The programs themselves are called filters, but beside filtering, all sort of operations (e.g. sorting, aggregation, substitution, merging, etc.) can be implemented. A typical filter takes the input from standard input (STDIN) and/or one or multiple files, performs some operation on this input and generates some result on standard output (STDOUT) or one or more files. By connecting multiple programs via pipes,

© Springer Nature Switzerland AG 2019
M. Bakaev et al. (Eds.): ICWE 2019, LNCS 11496, pp. 582–585, 2019.
https://doi.org/10.1007/978-3-030-19274-7_49

the output of one filter acts as the input of the next filter (see Fig. 1). Data transferred through the filters is often in ASCII format (but don't have to be).

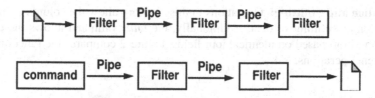

Fig. 1. Composing programs with filters and pipes.

Technically, the pipe symbol is represented by the vertical bar character (|). Additionally, it is possible to redirect data from a file to the standard input channel of a filter, as well as redirecting the standard output to a file. This redirection is typically done with the '>' and '<' symbols. Besides the STDIN and STDOUT, there is also the standard error output channel (STDERR). The STDERR is particularly used for error messages and debug outputs, respectively. The idea of composing complex programs from small well defined components allows rapid prototyping, incremental iterations and easy experimentation [3].

3 Classification of Commands

A bunch of tools have been developed, which can be used for the purpose of analyzing, composing, and transforming data-streams and files. These can be classified as follows:

File Inspection: This includes programs such as *less*, *head* and *tail*, which allow users to view and inspect files of any size. While *head* and *tail* can only show the beginning or the end of a file, *less* allows the users to browse and search the file interactively. The *less* command is also an exception in that it is the only program, among the presented ones herein, that accepts user input.

Filtering: There exist tools for line or column-wise filtering of data. If the input is comma or tab separated data, the tool *cut* can be used to extract single or multiple columns (projection) and output them to the standard output (also *awk*, which will be described later, has this ability). The *grep*, *sed* and *awk* command-line utilities allow a line by line filtering of the input data. In addition to the typical comparison operators, regular expressions can also be used, which makes the tools very powerful. *grep* can also be used for unstructured data (text), where arbitrary patterns can be specified and only the data specified by the pattern is returned.

Sorting: The *sort* command allows the specification of one or more complex sort keys on which an input file is sorted line-by-line. Internally, the sort is implemented using file based merge-sort, which allows also huge files to be sorted without the need of a big main memory. Some other programs like *comm*, *join*, and *uniq* require sorted input, and thus *sort* is needed quite often.

584   A. Schmidt and S. Scholz

Substitution Commands: *sed* and *tr* support the transformation of the input data. Whereas *tr* acts on the character level, *sed* allows the specification of complex substitution rules using regular expressions.

Composition and Splitting: Operations in this category allow the column or row-wise composition or splitting of data. Additionally, the *join* command allows the column-wise composition based on identical join-fields. Figure 2 compares the functionality of the different operations.

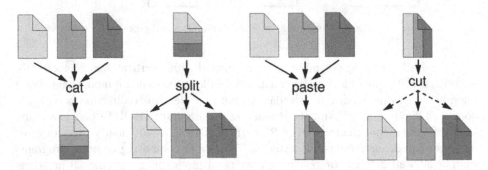

Fig. 2. Composition of input streams/files using cat, split, cut, and paste.

Aggregation: *uniq* and *wc* fall into this category. While *wc* counts the number of input lines or words, *uniq* is to handle duplicates in a file or stream. Concrete, *uniq* reports or omits repeated lines in a file or stream. So most frequently, *uniq* is used in conjunction with a preceding *sort* command.

Comparison: *diff* and *comm* are representative of this category. Both programs compare two files line by line. While *diff* reports the differences found, *comm* requires that the two input files are sorted and works on a set-semantic. As result it reports entries that only appear in the first, or the second, or in both files. Using this command, set-based intersection and minus operations can be implemented.

4 Programs sed and awk

sed stands for Stream Editor. In contrast to a "normal" editor, *sed* has no interaction with a user. However, insert, update, substitute, and delete commands must be formulated in a command file or on the command line. This allows the automation of recurring (also complex) editing tasks. As a very powerful feature, *sed* allows the specification of addresses (ranges of lines) on which the operations to be performed are restricted. Addresses can be specified as line numbers, strings, regular expressions, or a combination of them. So, for example the following command, removes all javascript-sections (from <script to </script>) from a html-file:

```
sed '/<script/,/<\/script>/d' jaccard.html
```

awk in contrast is a complete programming language, supporting loops, conditions, arrays, and dictionaries. It is mainly used on structured input data and to generate reports. Both, *sed* as well as *awk* support regular expressions.

5 Examples

As a more complex example of processing structured data, the re-implementation of a complex SQL-select statement using pipe and filters will be shown. Consider as input a relational table (Table city), resp. csv-file (file city.csv), consisting of city datasets, is shown in Table 1. The statements return all countries which have more than 100 cities in the database, together with the number of related cities. The output is sorted by the decreasing number of cities in a country.

Table 1. Comparison between SQL and piped UNIX commands

| ```
select country, count(*)
   from city
   group by country
having count(*) > 100
   order by count(*) desc
``` | ```
cut -f2 city.csv|sort -t,| \
uniq -c|sort -nr| \
awk -F' ' '$1>100 {print}'
``` |
|---|---|
| SQL-Statement | UNIX-Toolchain with Pipes |

Another example of analyzing unstructured data is the following, where a stopword-list, containing the most frequent 20 words (case-insensitive) is created from all text documents in the current directory and stored in a file stopwords.lst.

```
cat *.txt | tr -cs 'A-Za-z' '\n' | tr 'A-Z' 'a-z'| \
   sort | uniq -c | sort -nr | head -n20 > stopwords.lst
```

More examples will be presented and discussed in the corresponding tutorial [4].

References

1. Raymond, E.: The Art of Unix Programming. Addison-Wesley Professional, Reading (2003)
2. McIlroy, M.D., Pinson, E.N., Tague, B.A.: UNIX time-sharing system: foreword. Bell Syst. Tech. J. **57**(6), 1899–1904 (1978)
3. Kleppmann, M.: Designing Data-Intensive Applications. O'Reilly, Sebastopol (2017)
4. Tutorial Homepage. https://www.smiffy.de/icwe-2019. Accessed 25 Mar 2019

Non-monotonic Reasoning on the Web

Matteo Cristani[✉]

Dipartimento di Informatica, Università di Verona, Verona, Italy
matteo.cristani@univr.it

Abstract. In this tutorial we describe the approaches to non monotonic reasoning as a means for inference on the web. In particular we are focusing on the ways in which reasoning technologies have adapted to five different issues of the modern era world wide web: (a) epistemic aspects, bound by the new models of the social web, (b) changes over time, (c) language variants, including different languages of deployment of a web site, (d) agent-based knowledge deployment, due to social networks and blogs, (e) dialogue aspects, introduced again in blogs and social networks. The presentation covers these aspects by a technical viewpoint, including the introduction of specific knowledge-driven methods. The technical issues will be provided within a general logical framework known as defeasible logic.

1 Title of the Tutorial

The idea underlying the tutorial is to provide a general picture with some hints on the specific techniques of defeasible logic as applied to web engineering. Defeasible Logic is one of the most common methods of non-monotonic reasoning.

2 Contact Information of the Presenters (Name, Affiliation, Email, Mailing Address, Phone)

Matteo Cristani
Department of Computer Science, University of Verona
Strada Le Grazie 15, 37134 VERONA
matteo.cristani@univr.it
+39 045 8027983

3 Abstract Outlining the Goals and Content of the Tutorial (Max 250 Words)

The development of the communities of *Semantic Web* and *Web Engineering* have been interlacing frequently in the past twenty years. Many interesting approaches to practical issues of web engineering involving reasoning techniques

© Springer Nature Switzerland AG 2019
M. Bakaev et al. (Eds.): ICWE 2019, LNCS 11496, pp. 586–589, 2019.
https://doi.org/10.1007/978-3-030-19274-7_50

have been successful, as happened, for instance, in the linked data recent investigations [5,12]. A specific attention has also been posed on the basic issues of porting the web onto the semantic era as related to the development of XML-embedded languages, in particular OWL, as recently approached in many different applicative contexts [3,6,8,10,11,16–18,20,21].

Another community of research has deeply investigated the domain of web as related to reasoning, in a much more general way, and it is generally recognized as the *reasoning web* community. In this specific case, many studies have been dealing with problems related to change of knowledge, trustability and preference [1,2,4,7,9,13–15,19,22,23]. In many senses, a unifying semantics of the borders among the three communities (OWL-related studies, semantic web engineering, reasoning with web data) can be given by *rule-based reasoning systems* also known as nonmonotonic reasoning.

4 Definition of Intended Audience and Assumed Background and Knowledge

Although the basic knowledge on the above mentioned issues is common in practitioners and researchers of the various areas of web engineering, it is also true that a significant number of scholars and professionals, especially in the early stage of their careers can have a valuable advantage from a neater and wider survey on the nonmonotonic methods as applied to the web.

5 Overview of the Tutorial Structure, List of Topics Covered, and Short Description of Learning Objectives/Outcomes

The tutorial will be articulated in three parts:

1. A general introduction to non monotonic reasoning systems, with special care for the defeasible reasoning framework. This is introduced in a formal way, by specifying syntax of rules, priorities and defeaters, and the derivation methods based on proof tags, associated with specific derivation and conclusion inferential methods, with the corresponding associated equivalent of proof conditions.
2. A survey on the applications of the above to four typical issues of web reasoning:
   (a) Solving conflicts in definitions given within reliable sources of knowledge. The example reported is *Wikipedia*, we show how to determine and possibly solve existing conflicts in definitions;
   (b) Constructing debunking methods based on external reliable knowledge. The example reported is *The skeptical inquirer*, a scientific-oriented dissemination periodical;

    (c) Providing decisions about trust on a given individual based on external sources. We show how the theoretical framework named *Public announcement logic* works;

    (d) Ontology alignment with external sources of knowledge. The discovery of conflicts and their resolution using *Roget's thesaurus*.

3. Rule-based reasoning on the semantic web. An introduction to translation techniques and the solution of opinions, generalization, typicalization and other mitigative expressions into lambda-expressions for the translation of natural language onto rule-based semantic systems.

6 Biographies of Presenter(s), Including Information Regarding Their Expertise Relevant to the Tutorial

Matteo Cristani is Senior Researcher in the Department of Computer Science of the University of Verona. His expertise is the semantic web, and in particular, web applications with natural language processing and nonmonotonic reasoning. He has got numerous journal and conference papers in the mentioned communities. He has been the co-organised of the KDWeb (Knowledge Discovery on the WEB) workshop since 2017. The workshop has been a ICWE workshop in 2018.

7 Statement About Any Previous Related Tutorial Presentations, Including Information Regarding How the ICWE 2019 Tutorial Would Differ

It seems that no tutorial has been yet presented in the conference that covers techniques of Rule-Based web reasoning. I have no slides to include at the moment.

References

1. Antoniou, G., Bikakis, A.: Dr-Prolog: a system for defeasible reasoning with rules and ontologies on the semantic web. IEEE Trans. Knowl. Data Eng. **19**(2), 233–245 (2007)
2. Batsakis, S., Stravoskoufos, K., Petrakis, E.G.M.: Temporal reasoning for supporting temporal queries in OWL 2.0. In: König, A., Dengel, A., Hinkelmann, K., Kise, K., Howlett, R.J., Jain, L.C. (eds.) KES 2011, Part I. LNCS (LNAI), vol. 6881, pp. 558–567. Springer, Heidelberg (2011). https://doi.org/10.1007/978-3-642-23851-2_57
3. Cartwright, M., Pardo, B.: Vocalsketch: vocally imitating audio concepts. vol. 2015, pp. 43–46, April 2015
4. Cimino, M., Lazzerini, B., Marcelloni, F., Ciaramella, A.: An adaptive rule-based approach for managing situation-awareness. Expert Syst. Appl. **39**(12), 10796–10811 (2012)
5. Colomo-Palacios, R., Sánchez-Cervantes, J., Alor-Hernandez, G., Rodríguez-González, A.: Linked data: perspectives for IT professionals. Int. J. Hum. Capital Inf. Technol. Professionals **3**(3), 1–12 (2012)

6. Feng, X., Lian, J., Zhao, H.: Metabolic engineering of saccharomyces cerevisiae to improve 1-hexadecanol production. Metab. Eng. **27**, 10–19 (2015)
7. Fensel, D., et al.: Towards larkc: A platform for web-scale reasoning. pp. 524–529 (2008)
8. Gangemi, A., Alam, M., Asprino, L., Presutti, V., Recupero, D.R.: Framester: a wide coverage linguistic linked data hub. In: Blomqvist, E., Ciancarini, P., Poggi, F., Vitali, F. (eds.) EKAW 2016. LNCS (LNAI), vol. 10024, pp. 239–254. Springer, Cham (2016). https://doi.org/10.1007/978-3-319-49004-5_16
9. Golbeck, J., Rothstein, M.: Linking social networks on the web with FOAF: a semantic web case study, vol. 2, pp. 1138–1143 (2008)
10. Grangel-Gonzalez, I., Halilaj, L., Coskun, G., Auer, S., Collarana, D., Hoffmeister, M.: Towards a semantic administrative shell for industry 4.0 components, pp. 230–237 (2016)
11. Hastings, J., et al.: eNanoMapper: harnessing ontologies to enable data integration for nanomaterial risk assessment. J. Biomed. Semant. **6**(1), 10 (2015). https://doi.org/10.1186/s13326-015-0005-5
12. Heath, T., Bizer, C.: Linked data: evolving the web into a global data space. Synth. Lect. Semant. Web Theor. Technol. **1**(1), 1–121 (2011)
13. Hitzler, P., Van Harmelen, F.: A reasonable semantic web. Semant. Web **1**(1–2), 39–44 (2010)
14. Huang, Z., van Harmelen, F.: Using semantic distances for reasoning with inconsistent ontologies. In: Sheth, A., et al. (eds.) ISWC 2008. LNCS, vol. 5318, pp. 178–194. Springer, Heidelberg (2008). https://doi.org/10.1007/978-3-540-88564-1_12
15. Janowicz, K.: The role of space and time for knowledge organization on the semantic web. Semant. Web **1**(1–2), 25–32 (2010)
16. Livingston, K., Bada, M., Baumgartner, W., Hunter, L.: Kabob: ontology-based semantic integration of biomedical databases. BMC Bioinformatics **16**(1), 126 (2015)
17. Lohmann, S., Link, V., Marbach, E., Negru, S.: WebVOWL: web-based visualization of ontologies. In: Lambrix, P., et al. (eds.) EKAW 2014. LNCS (LNAI), vol. 8982, pp. 154–158. Springer, Cham (2015). https://doi.org/10.1007/978-3-319-17966-7_21
18. Lu, Y., Li, Q., Zhou, Z., Deng, Y.: Ontology-based knowledge modeling for automated construction safety checking. Saf. Sci. **79**, 11–18 (2015)
19. Margara, A., Urbani, J., Van Harmelen, F., Bal, H.: Streaming the web: reasoning over dynamic data. J. Web Semant. **25**, 24–44 (2014)
20. Nunez, D., Borsato, M.: An ontology-based model for prognostics and health management of machines. J. Ind. Inf. Integr. **6**, 33–46 (2017)
21. Pauwels, P., Zhang, S., Lee, Y.C.: Semantic web technologies in AEC industry: a literature overview. Automat. Constr. **73**, 145–165 (2017)
22. Tresp, V., Bundschus, M., Rettinger, A., Huang, Y.: Towards machine learning on the semantic web. In: da Costa, P.C.G., et al. (eds.) URSW 2005–2007. LNCS (LNAI), vol. 5327, pp. 282–314. Springer, Heidelberg (2008). https://doi.org/10.1007/978-3-540-89765-1_17
23. Van Hage, W., Malaisé, V., De Vries, G., Schreiber, G., Van Someren, M.: Combining ship trajectories and semantics with the simple event model (SEM), pp. 73–80 (2009)

Author Index

Printed in the United States
By Bookmasters